CRIMINOLOGY

CRIMINOLOGY

THIRD EDITION

EDITED BY

Chris Hale
Professor of Criminology
University of Kent

Keith Hayward
Professor of Criminology
University of Kent

Azrini Wahidin
Professor of Criminology and Criminal Justice
Nottingham Trent University

Emma Wincup
Director of Student Education, School of Law
University of Leeds

OXFORD
UNIVERSITY PRESS

UNIVERSITY PRESS

Great Clarendon Street, Oxford, OX2 6DP,
United Kingdom

Oxford University Press is a department of the University of Oxford.
It furthers the University's objective of excellence in research, scholarship,
and education by publishing worldwide. Oxford is a registered trade mark of
Oxford University Press in the UK and in certain other countries

British Library Cataloguing in Publication Data
Data available

ISBN 978-0-19-969129-6

Printed in Italy by
L.E.G.O. S.p.A.—Lavis TN

As we put the finishing touches to the third edition of this popular and encyclopaedic criminology textbook at the end of 2012, the UK media are celebrating a year of unparalleled British victories in the Olympic Games, a year topped off by the spectacular public celebrations of the Golden Jubilee of Queen Elizabeth II. Yet it has also been a year of unparalleled disgrace for those national newspapers involved in systematic hacking into private phone lines together with harassment of any celebrity or private person deemed (even potentially) newsworthy; a year of gloom and doom for the British economy; a year of mounting public cynicism about the probity of public officials (for instance, the MPs' expenses crimes and scandals; and, for another instance, bankers: to what extent were they criminally responsible for successive banking failures?); a year of soul-searching about the causes of the serious urban riots of 2011 and recurring fundamental questions about the nature of crime and social harm, and the relationships between social justice and criminal justice. In such a context, where more and more people in all ranks of life are increasingly saying that maybe there is some truth in the old adage that there is one law for the rich and another for the poor, the questions for criminology become more urgent than they ever were before, and even more explicitly central to the concerns of everyday life. At the same time, they become more complex, touching, as they do, on the disciplines of sociology, economics, history, law, psychology, philosophy, geography and ethics as well as on people's personal fears, moralities, aspirations and politics. And all within a new economic, cultural and militaristic globalism whose cultural diversity calls for a theoretical and comparative criminology reaching across national boundaries and beyond local concerns.

In his Foreword to the Second Edition (reprinted here) world famous criminologist Jock Young rightly states that the task of criminology 'must be to untangle stereotype from reality, fact from fiction'. That is truly the over-riding, intellectually exciting and socially important task of this book. And indeed, the demand for a third edition of *Criminology* suggests that the first two editions have already admirably succeeded in the job of providing sufficient research data and theoretical and methodological guidance to enable students and other interested readers to become informed and competent criminologists themselves. Nonetheless, although students of crime necessarily have to study the persisting historical and changing contemporary cultural conditions for the maintenance and displacement of social order, they also have to recognize that the conditions for social change are constantly evolving. As societies develop, moreover, what can be known and what is already known about crime changes too, begging new questions, involving new crimes, and stimulating both innovative methods of social control and new types of criminological study. Hence the need for this new and third edition of *Criminology*.

With the help of six new authors, all the chapters in the third edition of *Criminology* have been updated and two completely new chapters have been added. One new chapter is on the emergence, scope and regulation of cybercrime; and also provides an overview of the various theoretical perspectives which have been employed to explain this relatively new crime. The other addition is a seminal chapter from Jeff Ferrell and Jonathan Ilan of Kent University whose criminologists have long been leaders in the development of cultural criminology in the UK. Entitled 'Crime, Culture and Everyday Life', the chapter appositely demonstrates the relevance of cultural criminology to an understanding of the contemporary social scene.

An easily handled and pleasantly presented compendium of recent research reports, criminological arguments, sources and theoretical perspectives, this is also the most up-to-date, comprehensive and accessible volume currently available for those wishing to buy one good value-for-money text. Writing as a sociologist who has a passion for the excitement of criminological investigation, discovery and knowledge together with a passionate desire for increased social justice and a deep compassion for all those whose lives have been ruined by crime or any other form of social injustice, I wholeheartedly and most enthusiastically recommend this book to you.

Pat Carlen

Eight miles from Manhattan is the largest penal colony in the world, a place most New Yorkers could not point to on the map and many do not know exists. Home to 15,000 inmates, Riker's Island is just over the waterway 100 yards from La Guardia International airport. It is a place of invisibility from where, paradoxically, the inmates have an extraordinary view of one of the most famous skylines in the world: a tantalizing sight which no doubt only serves to increase their misery. Such a world of secret punishment sets us a whole series of puzzles for the criminologist—for the sociologist as sleuth! Why, first of all, is punishment hidden when in the past, as the French philosopher Michael Foucault pointed out in *Discipline and Punish*, it was out front and ostentatious: witness the public gallows, the whipping post, the village stocks. And why do so many people need to be punished in a rich, developed country that, supposedly, is the homeland of liberal democracy? In the United States there are 2.1 million people behind bars at any one time, and prison building, management, and maintenance has become a giant industry, vigorously competed for by state and local authorities because of its promise of employment and a pollution-free environment.

But let us look a little closer at Riker's Island: it is the size of a small town of 20,000 inhabitants (including staff) with its own schools, bakers, tailor shop, recreation, medical centre, nursery, and religious facilities. Yet it is scarcely economically sufficient: Riker's costs the US taxpayer over $800 million a year to run. Indeed the average cost of keeping an inmate is $60,000 a year—compare that to the average US wage of $37,000. And as for efficiency, about 75% of inmates will return to Riker's within a year of release. Let us say at this stage that such a paradox is repeated across the developed world—it is not an idiosyncrasy of the United States, however much the scale of imprisonment is exceptional. So a further and seemingly perennial problem occurs for the criminologist: how is such an irrational process possible and why does it persist? But the puzzles do not end here. Let us look at the inmates themselves: what strikes one immediately is that the demographic profile of Riker's is scarcely representative of the wider society. First of all they are over 90% Black and Latino, secondly they are nearly all men, thirdly one quarter have been treated for mental illness and 80% have a history of substance abuse. Lastly and perhaps most definitively, they are poor: 30% are homeless and 90% lack a high school diploma. And such a profile of race, gender, mental instability, and desperate poverty could be repeated in prisons around the globe. Why, then, is the criminal justice system skewed in such a way? Is this the shape of criminality? Each of these dimensions of the inmate population throws up its own series of questions. Is the racial disproportionality of the prison due to racism inherent in the criminal justice system or does it truly reflect the differences in levels of crime between ethnic groups? Is there some genetic characteristic of men compared to women that makes them more aggressive and liable to crime?

To what extent can the mentally disturbed be held responsible for their crimes? And are the poor incarcerated the world over because it is the deviance of the poor that we call crimes? Or is all this just another example of the golden rule: it is the people with gold who make the rules?

The study of criminology begs all these questions. It encompasses questions of sociology and psychology, of legal theory and social philosophy, of biology and the social sciences. It is at the crossroads of all these disciplines and more—it is never a marginal concern but one that takes us immediately into the relations of normality and deviance, of order and disorder, of crime and punishment, and indeed of good and evil. Because of this, crime has always been a major staple of the mass media: it is on the news every night. It is the core theme of detective fiction and of 'cops and robbers' drama on television. It alarms us and makes us fearful, but it also entertains and thrills us. We are attracted and beguiled by these images yet so many of them are patently false. The serial killer is an extreme rarity, yet it becomes a major genre of thriller fiction, its depiction a caricature of reality, a 'pornocopia' of sex and violence. Crime in the real world is frequently not detected—the criminal usually gets away. In fiction the intuitive skills and resourcefulness of the detective inevitably lead to the apprehension of the crook yet reality has no such denouement. The depiction of the violent attack from Hollywood blockbusters to video games revolves around 'stranger danger'—the threat of the unknown, of the malicious 'Other'. In most parts of the world this is the very inverse of truth. If you want to know your most likely murderer, look in the mirror. You are most likely to kill yourself, to commit suicide, than be killed by others; of those around you, your best friends and your nearest and dearest, then casual acquaintances are more likely to be your killer than those unknown to you. The stranger will only rarely look back at you, and when it does, the face looking out will be the same age, the same class, the same colour of skin as you. The only exception to this is if you are a woman: a man's face will look back at you (you are most likely to be killed by your husband or boyfriend) and, tragically, if you are a child, it is your mum or dad who will look back at you—only rarely will it be a stranger.

Criminology is intrigued by crime and the images of crime: each 'fact' which seems obvious becomes problematic on examination; each stereotype that we take for granted appears dubious or even prejudiced when we inspect it at close quarters. Our task, then, must be to untangle stereotype from reality, fact from fiction. And the search for the answers to all these questions that we have posed—and many more besides—is an endeavour of great practical importance, for it is only by their solution that we can help ameliorate both the impact of crime and the pains of imprisonment.

It is with such thoughts in mind that I recommend this book to students, practitioners and interested members of the public alike. The editors are to be congratulated for having brought together a group of contributors that pose these and many other related questions surrounding criminology and its uses in an accessible and thought-provoking way. I am certain that this book will be a cornerstone of criminology and criminal justice programs for many years to come.

Jock Young, New York City, NY

OUTLINE CONTENTS

DETAILED CONTENTS

LIST OF FIGURES

LIST OF TABLES

LIST OF CONTRIBUTORS

Rob Canton *Professor in Community and Criminal Justice, De Montfort University*

Pamela Davies *Principal Lecturer in Criminology, Northumbria University*

Jeff Ferrell *Professor of Sociology, Texas Christian University, USA*

Marian FitzGerald *Visiting Professor of Criminology, University of Kent*

Frank Furedi *Emeritus Professor of Sociology, University of Kent*

Chris Greer *Reader in Sociology and Criminology, at City University London*

Chris Hale *Professor of Criminology, University of Kent*

Keith Hayward *Professor of Criminology, University of Kent*

Tim Hope *Professor of Criminology, University of Salford*

Jonathan Ilan *Lecturer in Criminology, University of Kent*

Richard Jones *Lecturer in Criminology, Edinburgh University*

Trevor Jones *Reader in Criminology, Cardiff University*

Derek Kirton *Reader in Social Policy and Social Work, University of Kent*

Anne Logan *Senior Lecturer in Social History, University of Kent*

Roger Matthews *Professor of Criminology, University of Kent*

Wayne Morrison *Professor of Law, Queen Mary, University of London*

Larry Ray *Professor of Sociology, University of Kent*

Terry Thomas *Professor in Criminal Justice Studies, Leeds Metropolitan University*

Steve Tombs *Professor of Criminology, Open University*

Peter Traynor *Doctoral Student, University of Leeds*

Steve Uglow *Professor of Criminal Justice, University of Kent*

Azrini Wahidin *Reader in Criminology and Criminal Justice, Queen's University, Belfast*

David Wall *Professor of Criminology, Durham University*

Craig Webber *Senior Lecturer in Criminology, University of Southampton*

Matthew Williams *Senior Lecturer in Criminology, Cardiff University*

Emma Wincup *Director of Student Education, School of Law, University of Leeds*

Anne Worrall *Professor of Criminology, Keele University*

Guide to the book

Chris Hale, Keith Hayward, Azrini Wahidin, and Emma Wincup

Criminology's phenomenal expansion has shown no sign of abating since we remarked upon it in the Guide to the First Edition of this book published in 2005. Once taught exclusively as a postgraduate subject, criminology is now offered at all levels across the university system. One could also point to a large increase in the number of 'applied criminology' courses, such as community justice and police studies aimed at professionals already working within the criminal justice system or those who hope to pursue a career in criminal justice.

Inevitably such rapid expansion has precipitated the arrival of a whole host of textbooks, dictionaries, and handbooks that have sought to introduce developments in criminology and criminal justice to this new generation of students. For all their various merits, few of these works have been able to provide undergraduate criminologists with a single comprehensive and authoritative source that serves as an accessible overview of the most pertinent issues currently facing the discipline. *Criminology* is specifically intended to meet this requirement. It has been produced as a complete package both for students new to criminology and their lecturers. We also hope that *Criminology* will serve as a useful resource for criminal justice practitioners and interested members of the general public.

For students, *Criminology* offers 25 chapters on core criminological issues that can be used to help them prepare for a seminar discussion, or as the foundation stone for a presentation or undergraduate essay. Each chapter is self-contained, although links are made to relevant discussions in other chapters. Students are also encouraged to use the index to research the topic further. In addition to the substantive discussion, a number of pedagogical features are included. Chapters are accompanied by review questions, suggestions for further reading, and relevant websites. Where appropriate, students are guided to additional resources such as sources of data. Key concepts are collated in a glossary at the end of the text. All of this, we hope, adds up to a book that is pitched at an appropriate level for students with no prior knowledge of criminology, yet at the same time is challenging enough to equip them with the skills and knowledge needed for future study.

For lecturers, *Criminology* proffers sufficient material for a module spanning the whole academic year, and allows lecturers responsible for one term/semester modules to dip into the book and select an appropriate mix of topics. Each chapter is complemented by questions that can be used to structure discussions within seminars.

Accompanying this textbook is an extensive website carefully designed both to assist students with little background understanding of criminology, and to provide module leaders with a range of pedagogic tools aimed at enhancing the student learning experience. The most important resources are links to relevant websites, which allow students to access additional information at the click of a button in order to update and augment the chapter discussions. This is particularly vital given the ever-changing nature of criminal justice policy and shifting patterns of offending and victimization. For lecturers, the website offers brief lecture notes and Powerpoint® slides for each topic included in the book. The website also contains a 'Testbank' of approximately 300 multiple-choice questions. These can be used by students to test their understanding of the material covered in each chapter and employed by lecturers to assess students on a formal and informal basis. Each question is accompanied by feedback to enable students to further their understanding of criminological issues.

This book is arranged around four themes. As its name suggests Part I, 'Introducing Crime and Criminology', introduces students to the core concepts and issues needed for the study of criminology today. To begin with, Wayne Morrison tackles what is perhaps the discipline's most fundamental question: What is crime? Whilst for the uninitiated this may appear a straightforward topic, he moves quickly beyond simple definitions to consider questions of power and legitimacy, each reviewed within a historically and culturally informed discussion of how criminologists define their object of study. In her chapter, 'The History of Crime', Anne Logan provides an overview of the history of crime in Britain by exploring the changing construction of criminality and the historical development of the criminal justice system. Bringing the story up to date and using material from recent government and independent reviews of crime statistics, Tim Hope provides a comprehensive discussion of the changing and sometimes conflicting uses to which they are put. In particular he problematizes such important questions as: How do we know the level of crime? What information is available and how reliable is it? Going far beyond the standard discussions, he presents a provocative and informed account of the problems of measuring crime either from police figures or by using surveys. Shifting gear, the next chapter provides the student with a comprehensive introduction to how criminological theory has developed and is used. While all the chapters in this book are theoretically informed, Keith Hayward and Wayne Morrison offer the reader a series of theoretical vignettes, each one of which provides both an accessible introduction to a particular theory and informed signposts to more detailed readings. The following chapter by Emma Wincup focuses on the production of criminological knowledge and encourages students to adopt a critical stance when interpreting it. She charts the development of the empirical research tradition in criminology, outlines the range of research designs and methods available to criminological researchers, draws attention to the particular challenges criminologists face when conducting research, and identifies new methodological developments currently influencing criminology.

Whilst the main thrust of this text is sociological we freely acknowledge the substantial influence psychology has exerted on criminology. In Chapter 6 Keith Hayward and Craig Webber cast a sympathetic but critical eye on the interface between these two disciplines, presenting and assessing some of the major psychological theories of crime and their impact on the study of crime and criminal justice. The interconnections between crime and the media are addressed in the next chapter by Chris Greer. In a world in which crime is often packaged as entertainment and refracted in so-called 'reality television', Greer asks us to reflect upon and unpick these increasingly pervasive relationships. After critically discussing the dominant theoretical, conceptual, and methodological approaches, he considers the evidence for the 'effects' of media representations, both on criminal behaviour and importantly, on fear of crime, exploring the implications of living in a media-saturated era for crime and its control.

Part II, 'Forms of Crime' moves beyond introduction to look at some of the various types of crimes prevalent in late-modern society. Emma Wincup and Peter Traynor's chapter focuses on the problematic use of drugs and alcohol, behaviours which are often linked with acquisitive *and* violent crime, although the relationship between drug and alcohol use and crime is more complex than is typically portrayed in media and political discussions.

While violence inevitably features in other chapters, Larry Ray takes discussion to another level providing a systematic overview of some of the main sociological and criminological debates in the area. But more than this, he explores changing socio-cultural responses to crimes involving high levels of aggression and violence. He provides figures on the prevalence of different types of violence within England and Wales and discusses the impact of hate and racist crimes. In Chapter 10, Terry Thomas tackles the subject and nature of sexual offending. He examines the forms it takes as well as social and criminal justice responses made to sex offending over the last ten years.

A very different type of crime, and one that has been the focus of much media interest since the second edition of this book, is the vitally important area of corporate crime. Steve Tombs examines the emergence of this concept, discussing its meaning and reviewing the extent to which it represents a crime problem. He then considers various dimensions of corporate crime, its visibility, causation, and control, questioning society's will to censure and punish company directors and other 'rogue' capitalists. In Chapter 12 Matthew Williams and David Wall discuss the increasingly important area of cybercrime. They explore the very nature of cybercrime, its exponential growth and unravel the problems in regulating and managing new forms of deviance—some still to be rationalized in legal discourse. Another area that was historically marginalized from the criminological gaze is terrorism. While other disciplines have begun to engage with this subject in the wake of 9/11, criminology has been slow to regard the dynamics of international terrorism as one of its primary concerns. Addressing this lacuna, Frank Furedi provides a general introduction to the subject and poses a series of important questions about how one actually defines terrorism against a backdrop of contemporary fears in a risk-averse society.

In Part III, 'Social Dimensions of Crime' the authors examine how offending, victimization, and experiences of the criminal justice system (CJS) may be affected by people's class, gender, and ethnicity. Beginning with the complex relationships between crime, economic marginalization, and social exclusion, Chris Hale provides a clear introduction to the key issues and debates. Again, moving beyond the standard textbook approach of focussing on crime and unemployment, he provides a more rounded critical analysis of the impact of economic factors on offending and victimization. Next, Azrini Wahidin explores the connections between gender and crime and charts the emergence of feminist perspectives within criminology. She examines the different kinds of crimes in which men and women are involved, and considers the complex and changing relationship between masculinity(ies), femininity(ies), and crime. She then deconstructs how these relations have been typically understood in criminological theory and looks at the different ways in which men and women are dealt with by the CJS.

The treatment minority ethnic groups receive, both as victims and suspects, has rightly had an increasingly high profile in the last three decades. In her chapter on race and ethnicity, Marian FitzGerald begins by exploring the meaning of both terms in the context of discussions of crime. She critically examines the debates surrounding this vexed (and always controversial) issue and argues for the need for renewed rigour and clarity to avoid repeating past mistakes and confusions.

Anti-social behaviour, binge drinking, knife crime, and street gangs are some of the latest manifestations of society's perennial concerns about young people and their problem behaviour. Dealing with such matters is the focus of Derek Kirton's chapter. He outlines the key principles around which youth justice has evolved and how the balance between welfare and punishment has shifted over time in line with broader social and political changes. He provides, too, a profile of youth crime, making links between age and other social divisions. Young people are not the only age group to experience special problems within the CJS. In the final chapter in this section, the book's interdisciplinary approach is further evidenced in Jeff Ferrell and Jonathan Ilan's chapter on the cultural significance of crime. Their central aim is to examine the way in which crime and culture intertwine within the lived experiences of everyday life. They assert that a whole host of urban crimes are perpetuated by actors for whom transgression serves a number of purposes. Ferrell and Ilan chart a world of underground graffiti artists, gang members, street muggers, and other 'outsider' criminals, whose subcultures are increasingly the subject of media, corporate, and political interest.

In Part IV, 'Responses to Crime', the focus shifts to consider how society responds to crime through its treatment of both offenders and victims. Here we see crime's inherently political nature. The process and delivery of criminal justice, the practices of the agencies involved in 'crime control', and the treatment of victimized communities and individuals are all framed by public and political debate. In their chapter Marian FitzGerald and Chris Hale examine the rise in punitive and retributive discourses against broader economic and social changes. Echoing earlier chapters on youth crime, street crime, and public disorder, Hale and FitzGerald document how these have led to an unseemly competition between the political parties to be the 'toughest team in town'.

Picking up this theme, Steve Uglow outlines and critiques the role of the CJS in England and Wales. He provides a comprehensive and accessible account of the different parts of the criminal justice system (including recent significant changes such as the creation of the Ministry of Justice), and highlights the linkages and tensions between them.

Exploring further the themes of intensified social control discussed by Hale and FitzGerald, Richard Jones looks at how social control now operates in a different register. Over the last two decades, a range of new electronic and digital technologies have come to be employed as tools of formal control, security, exclusion, and punishment, bringing with them 'new' social practices which many commentators, rightly or wrongly, have argued are likely to have profound consequences for established civil liberties. Jones's chapter offers the reader a general introduction to theoretical debates surrounding surveillance. It then proceeds with an overview of these new technologies of social control, including the forms they currently take, how they function, and their usage. These uses include both the private sector as a form of surveillance and physical exclusion, and in the public domain as an instrument of criminal justice—for example, the electronic tagging and monitoring of offenders.

In another newly-commissioned piece, Pamela Davies's chapter on victimology examines how, from its early stereotyping of victims as blameworthy (contributing in some way to their own problems), victimology—the study of victims—has developed a more critical edge. The chapter introduces the reader to the study of victims of crime, victimological perspectives, and to the political and social changes which have brought victims to the centre of debates about crime.

Trevor Jones's discussion of policing draws out the important distinction between 'policing' and the public organizational structure 'the police'. He achieves this task by exploring the workings of a number of agencies, in both the public and private sector, engaged in governance and regulation. After outlining the historical development of the police in Britain and exploring the multitude of roles performed by the police, he considers the different models of policing in operation today and their perceived effectiveness. The key role of discretion, and how this can lead to the exercise of police powers in a discriminatory manner, is also critically assessed. This opens up an analysis of 'cop culture' and attempts by the police to overcome allegations of racial discrimination and poor relations with minority ethnic and other 'hard to reach' communities.

The final two chapters look at the treatment of convicted offenders. Anne Worrall and Rob Canton begin by exploring the development of punishment in the community from the nineteenth century onwards and the emergence of the new discourse of offender management in the twenty-first century. Focussing mainly, but not exclusively, on England and Wales, it deals largely with the punishment of adult offenders. They highlight the range of community penalties available to sentencers, and their evolution over the past 100 years, and summarize the debates about their effectiveness as a means of reducing re-offending and diverting offenders from custody. Then, in a thought-provoking chapter, Roger Matthews provides a critical discussion on the history of prisons, the role and impact of imprisonment, changes in its scale and purpose, and why imprisonment has become the dominant form of punishment in Western societies for the last 200 years.

The production of this book has been a mammoth undertaking involving 27 contributors from 16 different institutions. Whilst this has inevitably thrown up a number of editorial headaches, once again, we think the end result has been worth the struggle. Building upon the tremendous success of the first two editions, we believe we have once again produced an invaluable and comprehensive undergraduate text for criminology students and anyone else interested in the study of crime, deviance, and criminal justice. Thus, we would like to take a moment here to thank all the contributors for their patience and good grace in the face of our editorial diktats! Likewise we once again would like to thank our editorial team at Oxford University Press for their enthusiasm for the project, most especially for this edition Helen Swann and Joanna Williams.

Above all we would like to dedicate this book to the interested criminological reader. We hope you find it a useful resource and aid to study. Welcome to the wonderful and exciting world of criminological research.

Chris Hale, Keith Hayward, Azrini Wahidin and, Emma Wincup
Canterbury, Belfast, and Leeds
January 2013

Guide to the
Online Resource Centre

Criminology is accompanied by an interactive Online Resource Centre, which you can access at www.oxfordtextbooks.co.uk/orc/hale3e/. The Online Resource Centre is closely integrated with the book, and provides students and lecturers with ready-to-use teaching and learning resources. The resources are available free-of-charge, designed to complement the textbook, and offer additional materials which are suited to electronic delivery. All these resources can be downloaded and are fully customizable, allowing them to be incorporated into an institution's existing virtual learning environment (VLE).

Lecturer resources

These resources are password-protected to ensure that only lecturers can gain access. Lecturers may use these free resources to complement their own teaching materials or as a platform to update and restructure their courses. Registering is easy: go to 'Lecturer

Resources' on the Online Resource Centre, complete a simple registration form, and access will granted within three working days (subject to verification). Each registration is personally checked to ensure the security of the site.

Test bank

The test bank is a fully customizable resource containing ready-made assessments with which to test students. It offers versatile testing tailored to the contents of each particular chapter and there are questions in several different formats: multiple choice; multiple response; matching; fill in the blanks; true/false; and short answer. The test bank is available in Respondus and QTI XML formats and is downloadable into Blackboard, WebCT, and most other virtual learning environments (VLEs). The test bank questions are also downloadable in formats suitable for printing directly by the lecturer.

PowerPoint slides and lecturer notes

These complement each chapter of the book and are a useful resource for preparing lectures and handouts. They allow lecturers to guide their students through the key concepts, ideas, and theories and can be fully customized to meet the needs of the course, enabling lecturers to focus on the areas most relevant to their students.

Student resources

These are accessible to all students, with no registration or password access required, enabling students to get the most out of the textbook.

Chapter synopses

Succinct overviews of each chapter help you to locate relevant material easily and quickly.

Web links

A selection of annotated web links, chosen by the chapter authors, allows you to research easily those topics that are of particular interest.

Glossary

A useful one-stop reference point for all the keywords used within the textbook. In addition to a standard, alphabetical glossary, you will also find key term flashcards and interactive crosswords, both of which allow you to test your knowledge of important criminology vocabulary.

Further reading

Sources recommended by the chapter authors for additional reading, to assist you in understanding important issues and in developing a broader knowledge of the subject.

Part I
INTRODUCING CRIME AND CRIMINOLOGY

1

What is crime? Contrasting definitions and perspectives

Wayne Morrison

INTRODUCTION

Crime today appears as an integral part of the risks we face in everyday life. Crime is associated with harm and violence; harm to individuals, destruction of property, and the denial of respect to people and institutions. It is clear that we face pressing problems of a practical and scholarly nature in understanding crime. But we lack agreement on the most basic question: 'What is crime?'. In a bid to make sense of the diversity of opinions, definitions, and perspectives surrounding this question, this chapter will introduce some of the complex interrelationships surrounding the various ways that crime is constructed and objectified, before setting out some of the different perspectives that people actually take towards defining crime in practice. Many of the issues outlined in this chapter will be picked up in the substantive chapters that follow in this text.

BACKGROUND

Crime operates as a core concept in modern society. It seems like a common-sense category, but this is only a superficial appearance. Its widespread use, moreover, makes it necessary to ask what boundaries can be placed around the use of the term 'crime'. What does its use mean for us, individually, as speakers of the word, and collectively, as social groups that use the concept? Who has the power to make their claims as to what is a crime, and by what processes do these claims stick? These questions raise issues of social power and of popular acceptance, of objectivity and relativism; is there a settled or 'objective' way of calling things crime that is accepted across social groups and different territorial institutions, or must any use of the term crime be subjective, perhaps accepted within a particular locality or group, but leading to relativism when other perspectives are taken into account? What is the role, function, and consequences of our reliance upon 'crime' (and its related concepts, such as 'punishment') as an organizing concept in social life? These are difficult issues and lead analysis onto the acts of power of the agencies responsible for acts of public speech, for example, within the nation state, the legislature, and the courts, and the bodies responsible for enforcing the terms of that speech, notably the police and the agencies of punishment, the prisons and other instruments of coercive social control (see Chapters 19, 20, 24, and 25). This section will concentrate upon the first part of the question, while the frameworks within which different approaches make sense will be discussed in the following sections.

It is clear that there has been a great deal of variation in history and across different jurisdictions as to what has been defined as a crime. Some of the major figures in history have been termed criminals by a State process that was considered legally valid at the time. In ancient Greece, Socrates (d. 399 BC)—who we remember through Plato's dialogues as one the greatest philosophers of all time—was condemned by a court for the crime of corrupting the youth of Athens with his teachings. He died by taking hemlock after refusing the aid of his supporters to free him. In Roman-occupied Palestine, Jesus Christ was condemned and crucified along with 'two common thieves'; Martin Luther King was imprisoned for his role in the 1960s US civil rights movement. While in prison he wrote his *Letter From Birmingham Jail*, an essay that stands as one of the classic writings on civil disobedience (in which he argues that one has a duty to disobey unjust laws, but also to abide by the lawful processes of the State, including any punishment so ordered). Likewise, Nelson Mandela was convicted for activities against the apartheid State of South Africa and served 26 years in prison before his release. He subsequently became the first democratically elected President of South Africa. Are we to call individuals like these 'criminals'? Or do we say that it was a mistake to have ever called them that?

Writing in the late nineteenth century, the French sociologist Emile Durkheim—often referred to as the 'father figure of sociology'—pointed out that a great deal of social change has occurred as the result of people going against the settled rules and opposing the interests of those in power (see Chapter 4). According to Durkheim, a society that had no crime would be 'pathologically over-controlled':

> According to Athenian law, Socrates was a criminal, and his condemnation was no more than just. However, his crime, namely, the independence of his thought, rendered a service not only to humanity but to his country. It served to prepare a new morality and faith which the Athenians needed, since the traditions by which they had lived until then were no longer in harmony with the current conditions of life. (Durkheim, 1966: 71)

Following Durkheim, 'crime' is a complex interaction of many processes: from the creation of a concept of 'crime', to people identifying some event as a crime; from the responses to the event so called, to the behaviour and formal activities of State agencies (or in the emerging global arena supra-national bodies such as the International Criminal Court or the International Criminal Tribunal for Yugoslavia) that may or may not process the persons responsible as 'criminals' and punish them. These interactions all take place against the backdrop of the cultural world inhabited at that time. In understanding these interactions it is also important to notice what was not done, what was avoided, as much as cataloguing what was done. This is the subject of the next section.

Defining crime: confronting events and understanding processes

Archbishop Tutu (past recipient of the Nobel peace prize) calls for ex-UK Prime Minister Tony Blair and ex-US President George W. Bush to be indicted before the International Criminal Court as 'war criminals' for going to war with Iraq (BBC News online, 2 September 2012). Relatives of the dead in a factory fire in Karachi Pakistan, where nearly 300 workers producing cheap clothes for European store chains died in conditions where the windows were barred and fire exits locked, call for 'criminal prosecutions' and 'justice' and ask how the factory received a glowing report from an 'independent' inspection team (BBC News online, 12 September 2012). Police investigating claims that the late media celebrity Jimmy Savile sexually abused vulnerable people state that over 31 rapes and 199 sexual assaults probably occurred, and also arrest eight other people on suspicion of sexual abuse (*The Guardian*, 13 December, 2012). The UK Prime Minister David Cameron announces that a report into the killing of Belfast lawyer Pat Finucane by the Ulster Defence Association (a loyalist para-military organization) in 1989 has revealed 'shocking levels of collusion' between the UDA and British Security Forces; Secret Service agents had 'deliberately helped loyalist gunmen select their targets' (*The Guardian*, 13 December 2012).

The range of actions, omissions and events that can and are called 'crime' by someone or by formal State process is huge; reflecting on the processes offers routes into analysing the sets of beliefs, understandings, and reactions to others that constitutes our social, political and economic 'reality'. Consider the following examples: are they crimes?

- In 1781, the *Zong* was a slave ship owned by a large Liverpool slaving company employed on the well-tried route from Liverpool to West Africa and thence with a cargo of slaves to the Caribbean. On 6 September it sailed from West Africa with a cargo of 470 slaves bound for Jamaica. Twelve weeks later, closing on its destination, the *Zong* had already lost more than 60 Africans and seven of the 17-man crew because of dysentery brought on by severe overcrowding. The *Zong*'s captain ordered that sick slaves should be thrown overboard, both to preserve dwindling supplies of water and to allow the shipping company to claim their loss against insurance. One hundred and thirty-one slaves were thrown overboard and drowned, even though it had rained and there was plenty of water. None of the sick sailors were thrown overboard.

- On 5 July 1884, the yacht the *Mignonette*, crewed by three men and a cabin boy, sank in a storm 1,600 miles off the Cape of Good Hope. The crew escaped in a small open boat with no supply of food or water except a can of turnips. By 24 July, all four were in a terrible condition and one of the men, Dudley, killed the cabin boy, who was delirious, with a knife, and all three drank his blood and fed on his body. Four days later a passing boat picked them up. It is accepted that the boy would not have lived and the men probably would have died if they had not eaten him.

- On 6 August 1945, US forces dropped an atomic bomb called 'Little Boy' on the Japanese city of Hiroshima. Three days later they dropped another called 'Fat Man' on Nagasaki. By the end of 1945, less than six months later, the Hiroshima bomb had caused 140,000 deaths, and the Nagaski bomb 70,000. Five years later the totals were 200,000 and 140,000. At the time the reason put forward was that the use of atomic devices was necessary to shorten the war and save allied lives. Was this a crime? Does it matter in your opinion that at the Tokyo International Military Tribunal set up to judge Japanese war criminals, the only judge with any previous experience of 'international law', the Indian judge Pal, issued a full dissenting judgment? He refused to accept the prosecution of the Japanese defendants, as he considered that the Allies, too, should be tried and punished for crimes committed during the war, in particular for the dropping of the atomic bomb.

- In 1994, after the plane carrying the President of Rwanda was shot down, government military forces, along with perhaps as many as 50,000 civilians armed with knives and machetes, systematically killed more than 800,000 out of the 1,000,000 minority Tutsi population and at least 20,000 moderate Hutu in a three-month killing spree. This received very little international attention and the United Nations withdrew its small peacekeeping force due to an absence of Security Council pressure to protect anyone. Most commentators believe that if international action had been taken the majority of the 800,000-plus people killed would have been saved.

- In 1999, the government of a major European country facing legitimacy problems had their secret service agents stage a 'terrorist attack' on their own citizens, killing 200.

They then blamed the attack upon separatist 'terrorist' movements in one of the other provinces of the country. As a result they engaged in a military crackdown in which a reputed 100,000 civilians lost their lives. Four years later militant separatists, several of whom had lost their families in the military action, seized a school and took hostages. Government forces tried to free the children, but in the ensuing action 400 child hostages lost their lives.

- On 11 September 2001, the Twin Towers in New York, once the tallest buildings in the world, were struck by planes hijacked by members of the 'terrorist' group Al-Qaeda (literally 'a base'; the origins of Al-Qaeda can be traced to the Muslim Brotherhood in Egypt, as they developed they were aided and financed by the US CIA and factions within Saudi Arabia as part of the Afghanistan Mojahaden waging Jihad against the Soviet occupation of Afghanistan). The crashed planes started intense fires which collapsed the towers with the loss of nearly 3,000 lives. Some commentators, including the US Secretary of State, called this a massive crime but quickly the actions were redefined as 'acts of war'. The US President in a State of the Nation speech divided the world up into a civilized group that were with the US and others that stood against them. The US Congress and Senate authorized the President to 'use all necessary and appropriate force against those nations, organizations, or persons *he determines* planned, authorized, committed, or aided the terrorist attacks ... or harbored such organizations or persons' (emphasis added) (115 Stat 224, 18 September 2001: Authorizations for Use of United Stated Armed Forces).

- Inmates in a government prison learn that another inmate sentenced for a relatively minor crime has admitted to a cellmate that he has sexually abused children in the past. The inmates convene their own court, try the inmate, and find him guilty. As a sentence they beat him up, breaking both his legs and kneecaps, and leave him permanently crippled. Are their actions a crime, or are they justly punishing him?

- The owner of a factory operates in breach of health and safety regulations and keeps the fire escape exits locked. As a result of a fire on the premises many of the factory staff burn to death. Is this a crime, or an industrial accident?

- In 2003 many thousands of abortions were carried out in the US in accordance with the valid law. Members of the pro-life movement claim that the doctors carrying out the operations are guilty of murder—are they? One pro-life member shoots and kills a well-known abortion-performing doctor, because he says the doctor was breaking God's will and he needed to be punished.

Certainly all 'crimes' are unique events; however, are there common characteristics to some of these events that mark them off for special recognition and thus mean they are crimes? Is there a coherent way of distinguishing key factors and ensuring that 'we', that is the representatives of a community, come to an agreement as to what makes up a crime, or, indeed, what should then follow from agreeing that a crime has taken place? Or does the issue of agreeing on what is crime actually show how divided 'we' are? If we answer each event with a yes, that those events should be accepted as a crime, are we merely being emotive? (Emotivism is defined as a use of language that asserts something which cannot logically be backed up in such a way that it convinces the majority of others to agree.) Can we separate what *is* legally a crime (that is, it is contrary to the valid law) from what we feel ought to be a crime? Or is this way of distinguishing things a mistake? Is it a lazy way out of the dilemma of our responsibility towards the world? What, then, can we learn from following through the examples given earlier?

- The *Zong* actually went to trial as an insurance case. The boat owners had claimed insurance on the dead slaves as they said they were simply 'property' that had been thrown overboard out of necessity. The original jury agreed and ordered the underwriters to pay insurance on them, but the underwriters appealed and we do not know if any insurance money was ever paid out. Meanwhile, a group of people around a prominent individual called Glanvill Sharp tried to get the authorities to prosecute the crew for murder, but they were unsuccessful. The system did not want this to be called a crime (see Gearey, Morrison, and Jago, 2009: chapter 2). As Walvin (1992) argues, if this event had been called 'murder', it would have unpicked the legality of the whole slave system and the international trade in it. As a result, people around Glanvill Sharp got together and formed an anti-slavery and abolitionist movement that ultimately changed the system.

- In the case of the cabin boy who was killed and eaten, the men were prosecuted and the case of *Dudley and Stephens* (1884) became a leading case for the proposition that necessity cannot be a defence against the charge of murder in English law. The judge who heard the case made a wonderful statement that it was always the duty of the captain of a ship to look after his passengers and crew before himself. (Of course the *Zong* was not mentioned in argument!) The men were sentenced to death, but this was reduced to six months' imprisonment. In fact, it was a custom of the sea for men in similar conditions to cast lots and the person with the shortest lot to be killed and eaten (Simpson, 1984). In this example the men had agreed to do this, but the cabin boy was so weak that they decided to kill him without casting lots. The Admiralty opposed the trial as they did not want the customs of the sea upset, but another government department insisted on charges.

- No one has ever faced charges in respect of the atomic bomb, although Sellars (2002: 66), relying upon a biography of the US President Harry Truman (written by his daughter, Margaret) relates a stag dinner hosted by Truman in early 1953. At this dinner, the famous wartime British leader, Winston Churchill, had the bad manners to ask Truman if he had his response ready for when they both were to stand before St Peter and told to justify using the atomic bombs. This caused considerable shock, which was alleviated when the party organized a mock trial of Churchill with Truman as judge and a jury consisting of the US Secretary of State and other close US colleagues and Generals. Acquittal resulted, though Sellars could not find in Margaret Truman's account the reason; perhaps, Sellars surmised, 'they sensed that their own hands were dipped in blood. Or perhaps, they reasoned that it did not matter anyway. After all, even in real life tribunals, no one ever punishes a victor.'

Let us pause for reflection. What are the consequences if we accept the definition of crime that is presented in most criminal law textbooks, namely, a crime is some conduct (an act or omission) which, when it leads to a certain state of affairs, is treated in that jurisdiction as being capable of leading to prosecution and punishment? Glanville Williams (1955: 107), for example, defined crime as 'an act that is capable of being followed by criminal proceedings, having one of the types of outcome (punishment etc) known to follow these proceedings'. This in practice is the definition of crime most commonly accepted, as was brought out by Tappan's famous injunction that criminology accepts as its object of study crime, defined as 'an intentional act or omission in violation of criminal law (statutory and case law), committed without defence or justification, and sanctioned by the State as a felony or misdemeanor' (1947: 100). But this means that there is no common element to a crime other than the fact of the prior legal procedure defining such and such act or omission as a crime. It also means that so far in the events considered only the act of killing the cabin boy was a crime, and that was a near thing. In the great age of sail it is probable that many cases occurred where crews ended up in open boats or stranded on desolate shores and one of their company was killed and eaten. But they drew lots, thus when they were picked up everyone could be satisfied that the custom of the sea had been followed and no crime occurred and the authorities were never involved.

- In the case of Rwanda we face a situation, which most commentators now say was the most easily preventable mass crime of the twentieth century. The attention of the world's media was on events in South Africa where Nelson Mandela was elected President and apartheid ended peacefully. When the first killings began ten Belgian UN soldiers were killed, with the result that the UN withdrew the mission and all attempts to get intervention failed, in particular because of US reluctance caused in part by the previous killing of 18 US servicemen in Somalia. The subsequent official US line was that they did not have proper information; they did not appreciate the full picture. We now know that they knew fully what was going on and that President Clinton had ordered that the term 'genocide' not be used, as that might trigger calls for the US to intervene, not to mention the quasi-legal obligation to take action as a country that had ratified the Genocide Convention (see, for example, 'US chose to ignore Rwandan genocide', *The Guardian*, 31 March 2004). Thus, deliberate US inactivity was one of the crucial factors that condemned to death the equivalent of the US domestic homicide total for 1950–2000. It would be literally unthinkable for President Clinton to face penal sanctions in connection with these deaths; for his deliberate inactivity to be called a 'crime'. He was, however, pursued by extremely expensive legal proceedings (costing more than a UN force that would have deterred, or at least stopped the main killings of the genocide) for most of his second term in office. The question to be ascertained in those particular proceedings, which included impeachment hearings, was did he commit a crime or misdemeanour when he stated that an activity with a certain female intern at the White House, later found to be an oral sexual act, did not constitute 'sexual relations'? He was acquitted (his defence was that he used the term in a precise legal sense, that is, that it defined penetrative sexual intercourse which he had not engaged in).

- The situation with the 'major European country' and terrorism equates to what many have claimed the situation was between Russia and Chechnya. In the context of the current 'war on terror', most governments say that Chechnya is an internal matter for Russia, in effect closing their eyes to massive human rights violations, death, and destruction.

- The action of the prison inmates constitutes 'self-help'. It is deemed a crime and not justified 'punishment' in part because one of the principles that modern society is founded on is that the State claims a monopoly upon legitimate violence. There are many examples of groups that organize themselves in such a way that they almost constitute a State within a State—such as the Mafia or transnational drug dealing organizations—taking on State-like roles and procedures. In doing so they pose a threat to the State's existence, and since the sixteenth century the dominant mode of large-scale social organization has been the 'nation state'. It is the nation state that has the authority to define what sort of activities can be deemed crimes within its boundaries and only officials of the nation state are authorized to carry out punishments. (When the first edition of this chapter was written, in October 2004, American and Iraqi forces were waiting until after the US election to attack the Iraqi city of Falluja to establish government control. A key point has been that 'in Falluja, the insurgents are free to carry out their own brand of justice, like the public lashings of people suspected of theft and rape, and the videotaped beheading of … one of the city's National Guard commanders' (Filkins, 2004)). The English for capital punishment comes in part from the Latin word *capitalis* which means 'of the head', and was originally by decapitation, literally 'a capital offence'. The symbolism of the beheading is the denial of the legitimacy and the ability of the State to function and its replacement by a counter-state group.

- The consequences of the response to the events of 11 September 2001 are many; they include the invasion of Iraq and Afghanistan with great division in world opinion as to the legality of those actions and the bloody insurgencies that opposed the foreign presence. If the choice had been made to call 11 September 2001 a 'crime', then the response might have been an international policing action determined to bring the perpetrators to the justice of an international court; the choice of war seems to many to have weakened the movement for international or global justice.

- The final two examples are simplified examples based on real cases. They allow us, in the words of the Norwegian criminologist, Nils Christie, to hold up the processes in which crime is identified and reacted to as a mirror revealing a picture of social relations not otherwise seen. Take the example of the factory owners. Since the early 1990s similar fires have caused the deaths of hundreds of workers in the US, Thailand, India, Bangladesh, Pakistan, and China; these illustrate the downside of globalization.

Such events are not confined to the developing world: in the North Carolina Chicken Processing Plant fire of 1991, 25 workers died and 49 were injured when a fire broke out and all but one of the nine fire escapes was locked. The owners had locked the doors and boarded up the windows to prevent the staff stealing food; however, no security fence had been constructed or any security guard hired. Nineteen of the 25 dead were single mothers, predominantly black—blacks had only been allowed to work in the factories of the south since the 1970s, and even then they were non-unionized and unable to bargain for reasonable conditions. Blame for the fire was attributed to various local, federal, and State agencies. It had not been visited by health and safety officers for over 11 years and had already experienced several minor fires that year. There was no trial, the owner pleaded guilty to 25 counts of manslaughter, while his son and another manager went free as part of the plea bargain arrangement. To the extent that it was reported and picked up in the media, the fire revealed the conditions of work for many in the semi-rural areas of the US and demonstrated the divided nature of social life in the US. But if one thought that defining something as a crime invokes sympathy for the victims and that political measures would be likely to be taken to reduce victimhood or harm, this case is sobering; for less than two years later, insurance companies and the business lobby in North Carolina got together and introduced legislation to reduce compensation for injured workers. Moreover, crime in Anglo-American jurisprudence is an individualist responsibility; in other words, crime usually can only be proven when specific individuals are implicated and responsibility can be fixed upon them. Thus, it is individuals who are blamed and not the system. This can be seen even more clearly from another case where, on 10 May 1993, fire broke out at the Kader toy factory outside Bangkok, Thailand. Managers had locked exit doors to make sure the workers could not steal the toys. Hundreds of workers, mostly young women, were trapped inside. Officially 188 were killed, with 469 injured, many seriously, after they were forced to leap from second, third, and fourth floors of the buildings to avoid being burnt to death. Blame was fixed on the managers. But did the fault lie only with the managers? The fire occurred at the height of the 'Simpsons' craze and the factory was producing Simpsons toys: a melted Bart became the symbol of the tragedy and the consequences of the new global capitalist/consumer economy. The following quote is from a Malaysian labour activist, Tian Chua, who writes from prison where he had been detained from April 2001, without being charged, for attempting to organize Malaysian workers without government permission (you may note the politics here, for if she was actually charged with a 'crime' most jurisdictions require a court appearance where at least a minimal level of proof is brought forward in order that the person remains in custody!).

> The bodies of Bart Simpson scattered all over the ground—some half burned, some without heads or limbs, some half completed ... Kader was one of the largest toy manufactures in Asia. It was also a typical multinational company which moved around for cheap labour. Kader was jointly owned by Thai and Hong Kong capitalists. It mainly produced toys for European & American markets ... The toy industry is a sector which produces fun and joy. Toys bring laughter to children and parents. However, the tragedy of Kader fire revealed the sorrows and suffering behind toy manufacturing. Kader made us aware that workers use their sweat, tears and blood to exchange happiness for children around the world. (quoted from http://www.2Bangkok.com, accessed 19/10/04)

In 1993, fire broke out in the Zhili Toy factory in Shenzhen, China, with 87 deaths. Here we come to the difference between a sociological/critical criminological reading of these events as crimes and a more legalist or narrowly focused criminological interpretation of the event. From the sociological or critical criminological perspective, the international connections between market-driven consumption, demands for cheap but well-produced products, and the avoidance of operating according to full health and safety measures are apparent and have considerable bearing on the fire. From a more narrowly focused understanding of crime, those factors are all 'externalities'; what is of concern in ascertaining whether the events were a crime is then only the immediate actions and mental states of those who locked the doors and those who should have ordered them to be open. Moreover, what of the issue of responding to the victims and preventing future similar incidents? Whereas earlier, well-published industrial fires, such as the Triangle Shirtwaist Factory fire of 1911 in New York (where nearly 150 people died because of locked fire exits), led to labour agitation and improved regulations of working conditions, the conditions for workers in the so-called developing world are at the mercy of multinational corporations that can quickly relocate to cheaper, less regulated locations. The international press gave Kader some attention, but later writers said very little had improved:

> Thailand's limited building and safety codes, minimal wage levels and factory regulations are not enforced. Indeed, the government in Thailand attracts foreign capital to its shores by openly advertising the lack of restrictions on the exploitation of workers. The Kader factory was no aberration. All the horrors of nineteenth century European capitalism—child labor, dirty and unsafe working conditions, shanty housing—are on display everywhere in Bangkok. (Symonds, 1997: 58–9)

So, even if we were to agree to call this a crime, the consequence may be that a small group of individuals are blamed and punished, but the wider social conditions that caused social harm are pushed to one side and overlooked. This leads several criminologists to say we should not concentrate upon 'crime' as an organizing concept, but replace it instead with 'social harm' or protection of 'human rights' (see, for example, Hillyard *et al.*, 2004).

To summarize this section: we are therefore talking about complicated and changing interactions of governmental and discursive power, public concerns, and the different roles of officials who control key decision-making processes (see Chapter 19) as well as the media that highlights certain issues and downplays others (see Chapters 7 and 18). There are complex factors at work that influence how the edifice of public administration—including what the literature refers to as 'the criminal justice system'—relates to and processes events that may or may not be termed crimes.

REVIEW QUESTIONS

1 Many claim for criminology the status of a science; but if criminology accepts the definition of 'crime' as that which is formally labelled as such by the domestic criminal law of the State or international agreements, then criminology is attempting to study something which is controlled by another discipline, namely Law. Does that mean that criminology cannot have any independence but is reliant upon the politics of the State or international legal agreements? Should criminology then replace 'crime' with another concept that it controls?

2 Using Internet sources and the library, research the Bhopal disaster in India 1984. Who was at fault and has justice been achieved in response to that event? What role if any does racism or corruption play?

Frameworks of choice and logic: the politics of criminology and the definition of crime

So far we have explored matters with respect to practical examples. We have seen how in practice and in the literature there is much disagreement over defining exactly what a crime is. McCabe (1983: 49) says 'there is no word in the whole lexicon of legal and criminological terms which is so elusive of definition as the word "crime"'! How, then, can a discipline that has as its common focus the study of crime ever have a settled focus? The history of criminology can be read as revolving around this question. It has been said that most definitions of crime involve a drastic circularity and that criminological explanations relying upon them become tautologies. Perhaps it is the effect of this, but criminology as a scholarly discipline has moved in circles over many of its central issues. One problem is that the definition of crime adopted by an individual reflects the whole world perspective of that individual and the social groups they reside within. We are faced with various distinctions, controversies and frameworks of logic that are related to our view of the world and mankind's place in it. These include choices between the following assertions or claims:

- Crime is some action or omission that causes harm in a situation that the person or group responsible 'ought' to be held accountable and punished, irrespective of what the law books of a State say.

- Crime is an action against the law of God, whether as revealed in the holy books, such as the Bible, Koran, or Torah, or that we instinctively recognize as against God's will, irrespective of what the law books of a State say. If the State law books allow something that we know to be against God's will this does not change its status—it is still a crime.

- Crime is an act or omission that is defined by the validly passed laws of the nation state in which it occurred so that punishment should follow from the behaviour. Only such acts or omissions are crimes.

- If there is no public authority capable or ready to police social activity and punish offenders, then there is no crime. Crimes and criminals only exist when a public body has judged them such according to accepted procedures. Without the State and the criminal law there is no crime. Without criminal justice systems there are no criminals.

- Crime is an irrelevant concept as it is tied to the formal social control mechanism of the State; deviance is a concept that is owned by sociology, thus our study should be the sociology of deviance, rather than criminology.

We can identify at least four frameworks in which to make sense of how crime is defined:

(a) crime as a social construction;

(b) crime as a product of religious authority/doctrine;

(c) crime as a reflection of nation-state legality;

(d) more recent concepts beyond the nation state derived from social and political theory.

Criminology and, indeed, our present position more generally contain the legacy of these earlier positions. Let us look briefly at each in turn.

Social construction

Social construction is a highly influential and controversial current perspective. In summary it argues that our concepts and the practical consequences that flow from using them are the products (constructions) of social interaction and only make sense within the communities in which that interaction takes place. In other words, 'crime' is a label created in social interaction, but once created it has both a symbolic and practical reality. We endow the world with symbols and respond to the meanings contained in them. Language and other symbolic systems codify these meanings and by using language we impose a grid on reality; the law is a particularly strong grid system. In this case we create terms of crime and punishment that enable us to identify and distinguish different events. But these terms also impose certain consequences, as in the following statement from a very influential book on criminal justice: 'When a crime is committed, justice must be done ... a failure to punish crime is wrong and a community that does not punish its criminals is derelict in its moral duty' (Gross, 1979: xv and 18). In many accounts crime and punishment are linked as if they were unproblematic concepts reflecting a reality in which crimes are committed as a matter of identifiable facts and once the person responsible is identified certain processes must logically follow. However, those who accept social construction argue that since language and other symbolic systems are social products, this is a socially constructed grid. It is a social choice to recognize such and such an event as a crime, or such and such a person as a 'criminal'. Some other term and therefore some other course of action could be used. Two consequences follow. In one we have a research project of following through the creation of the use of the concept crime and its actual allocation to particular events or situations (the process of criminalization). A second consequence is that we can argue that there is no particular natural level of use of the concept crime, that it can imprison us in particular techniques of social ordering, and it may be better to abolish its use. This was stated clearly by the Dutch abolitionist lawyer, Louk Hulsman:

> [C]ategories of 'crime' are given by the criminal justice system rather than by victims of society in general. This makes it necessary to abandon the notion of 'crime' as a tool in the conceptual framework of criminology. Crime has no ontological reality. Crime is not the object but the product of criminal policy. Criminalization is one of the many ways of constructing social reality. (Hulsman, 1986: 34–5)

Drawing upon anthropological evidence of how different social groups identified troublesome situations and individuals, the American criminologist Howard Becker (1963) and others developed an influential school of thought in sociology known as labelling theory (see Chapter 4). This holds that the terms crime, deviance, or punishment are labels, variously applied by acts of power and not some natural reflection of events. The full potential of labelling theory was not realized. When Becker wrote, for example, he only mentioned in passing the gender divide in which men made the rules in society for other men and women. Today, in the hands not only of feminists but deconstructionists, labelling theory leads into a more radical social constructionist theory in which a multi-sided account of criminalization is given (see Chapter 4). In its abolitionist forms, such as with the Norwegian criminologist Nils Christie (2004), the major challenge for criminology is to understand the social processes of the application of these basic labels and, by implication, if we follow through the process we might come to an understanding that may lead to a lowering of the rate of 'crime' by abandoning the entire processes of criminalization. His central assertion undercuts the common-sense views of crime and disorder:

> Crime does not exist. Only acts exist, acts often given different meanings within various social frameworks. Acts and the meanings given to them are our data. Our challenge is to follow the destiny of acts through the universe of meanings. Particularly, what are the social conditions that encourage or prevent giving the acts the meaning of being crime? (Christie, 2004: 3)

Crime does not exist. Only acts exist, acts often given different meanings within various social frameworks. Acts, and the meanings attached to them … but is this actually so and even if this was the case, could humans really accept such a radical view?

Crime in 'the city of God'

The phrase 'city of God' comes from the Christian writer St Augustine (354–410), but could with only slight modification be used to describe Islamic or Judaic systems; it refers to the world view where we humans live in a universe created by God and his commands. Social construction theory is denied by many people who see in it the consequences of human ambition to position ourselves as the masters of the world and our destiny. Instead, very significant numbers of people believe that God created the universe and allocated a place for humans within his creation. To enable us to know something of his intentions God also sent messages to humanity through prophets and other forms of revelation; these messages were collected in books of authority of which the Koran, the Bible, and the Torah are best known. Each lays out various rules in terms of imperatives and warnings of the consequences if these are not followed. Let us fear God, says the Koran, 'verily, God is witness over all'. God will prepare shameful woe for those who disobey his rules. To the followers, the laws of God lay out the path to heaven and redemption. There is no problem of the legitimacy of these rules and the definition of what should be crime since God's will is the ultimate driving force of creation—even if humans have been endowed with free will and the capacity not to see the truth. There are numerous problems for social order in a complex grouping: a crucial one is who can agree on the exact message from God, what happens to constrain conflicting interpretations? As Blaise Pascal put it, 'men never do evil so openly and contentedly as when they do it from religious conviction'. Take as examples two crime-related words that have found their way into our English dictionary: thuggery and assassination. The derivation of thuggery is from the Sanskrit *sthag*, to conceal. For centuries a religious sect existed in India to rob and murder. A conservative estimate is that they killed well over a million people between 1740 and 1840 until suppressed by British colonial authorities. Thugs were devotees of the goddess Bhowani or Kali, the 'Black Mother', the Hindu goddess of death and destruction. Gangs of men operated to murder and rob, strangling their victims as sacrifices to Kali. When caught Thugs looked forward to their execution as a quick route to paradise. The English word assassination comes from the Muslim world, where after the death of the prophet Muhammad, three of his early successors were killed with daggers. A group, 'assassins', was founded by Hasan Ibn al-Sabbsh, whose followers killed rival Sunni Muslims, and many Muslim caliphs (ultimate leaders) have been killed over the subsequent centuries. The Assassins killed as acts of piety and sought to replace an allegedly corrupt Sunni regime with a supposedly ideal Shiite one; when caught they accepted their death.

Throughout the Western world the horrors of the massive religious conflicts of the late Middle Ages resulted in the separation of Church and State. The city of God became replaced by the city of man, and religious belief was deemed in practice to be a personal matter. For much of its history criminology has been a secular discipline, an applied science of the nation state; but there are now serious arguments that it has been badly compromised by neglecting to engage with the religious belief systems that many people live by (Knepper, 2001).

Nation-state legality

From the seventeenth century, slowly and with many oppositions, a secular view of crime arose where crime is understood as an act or omission as defined by the sovereign authority in factual charge of a specific territory—the nation state. It is important to note the full implications of this view. First, the substance of what is made criminal is a matter of the 'will' of the sovereign body, the Parliament, the courts, and the Senate. Second, as liberal jurisprudential writers, such as H.L.A. Hart (1961) emphasize, the fact that something is made a crime does not necessarily mean it is immoral. While in practice many crimes will be based on the shared perceptions of the people, arising from customs, religious beliefs, and common-sense conceptions of what is acceptable and unacceptable; crimes are simply posited by the rule-making power centres of the State. Third, it follows that to be called a criminal is a status conferred by the legal and political process of the State, there is no such thing as a natural criminal or a born criminal (cf Chapter 4). As Korn and McCorkle express it, this was forgotten by much individualist focused criminology, which took a naturalist view of the terms 'crime' and 'criminality'.

> The use of the term criminal to identify persons occupying a potential and removable status is in sharp contrast to the view that criminality is a sickness, a biological condition, or a type. The failure to distinguish between the ideas of status and type has led to costly errors and lost directions in criminology. It has led many to mistake the fact of a fairly clear legal category for the existence of an equally identifiable category of persons with similar characteristics. It has led brilliant investigators into life-long searches for common biological, social, or psychological traits. Despite the failure of these investigations to isolate within the offender a single characteristic not found in the law-abiding, the search for common factors continues to preoccupy those who are still unaware that the object of their quest is the product of a semantic confusion. (Korn and McCorkle, 1959: 48)

Those authors were also 'realists', saying that 'irrespective of laws, an act is not a crime until the offender is caught, tried and punished'. The consequences for criminology were clear since the knowledge base requires first the achievement of political control by a State over territory, secondly institutional processes of recognition and interpretation of activity as criminal, and lastly the scholarly reflection upon that ascription and processes of dealing with those defined. By implication, where the State has not instituted a situation of 'continuous political control' there can be no criminological reflection; criminology (at least in its conventional or mainstream forms) was the applied science of the nation state and where the nation state did not define crime, there was no criminological knowledge (see Hogg, 2002, and Morrison, 2005, for arguments for a contemporary criminology beyond the nation state).

Beyond nation-state definitions of crime

Modern Western societies have largely defined crime in the terms laid down by the nation state. A crime is an act or omission that leads to penal sanction in accordance with the constitutionally valid procedures of that nation state. Thus nation state A will prohibit the smoking of cannabis, while nation state B may say that within specified areas (for example, the coffee shops of Amsterdam) it is allowed. The examples can be multiplied; thus relativism—and, say some, the holocaust. It does not take a great leap of the imagination to see the policy of the extermination of European Jews (and all others if the State could have power over them) written into the manifesto of Hitler and adopted when the legitimate sovereign of the German people. Hitler's aggressive expansionist policies brought about World War II and after it several of the surviving Nazis were tried for the crime of waging aggressive war and associated crimes against humanity. While we now see the Holocaust as the icon of crime in the twentieth century, at the time and today, many commentators say that logically it would not have been a crime if the extermination of the Jews had remained an internal state policy. Perhaps no writer has expressed this better than George Steiner:

> I wonder what would have happened if Hitler had played the game after Munich, if he had simply said, 'I will make no move outside the Reich so long as I am allowed a free hand inside my borders'. [The death camps of] Dachau, Buchenwald, and Therasienstadt would have operated in the middle of twentieth-century civilisation until the last Jew had been made soap. There would have been brave words on Trafalgar Square and in Carnegie Hall, to audiences diminishing and bored. Society might, on occasion, have boycotted German wines. But no foreign power would have taken action. Tourists would have crowded the Autobahn and spars of the Reich, passing near but not too near to the death-camps. (Steiner, 1967: 150)

Even if we were to agree with Steiner as a tragic matter of fact, this would clearly be an affront to notions of our common humanity. Hence it is essential that we engage in a movement to construct a framework for defining crime that is neither tied to any one particular view of religion, nor to the confines of the nation state.

Within criminology a well-known attempt was made by the Schwendigers, who asked if criminologists were 'defenders of order or guardians of human rights'? They suggested that our individualist focused conceptions of crime needed to be broadened so that we could define whole 'social systems as criminal'. They argued that an expanded definition of 'crime as a label for social systems' becomes a 'warrant not for controlling atomistic individuals, or preventing an atomistic act, but rather for the regulation or elimination of social relationships, properties of social systems, or social systems as a whole' (Schwendiger and Schwendiger, 1975: 136). Post-World War II, a number of international conventions have tried to create a system for the recognition and processing of international crime under such titles as 'crimes against humanity' or 'genocide'. This is an expanding framework, though at present it is characterized more by words than actual deeds, and instances of international intervention are controversial (see Morrison, 2004, 2005).

One other attempt may be noted, perhaps the most common within the sociological imagination, namely, to replace crime by the concept of 'deviance'. Many of the works published within the criminological enterprise from the 1960s focused on the 'sociology of deviance' in order that criminality might escape from legality and create its own frame of reference. The problem was that deviance was, and remained, a sociological construct. In the public consciousness crime was the dominant and seemingly the most useful category.

This failure of sociological criminology to create a discourse that could engage successfully with the public and the political power centres is reflected in *The Culture of Control* by David Garland (2001), one of the most respected writers in criminology and the sociology of punishment. Garland highlighted the current dilemma surrounding the question of 'what is crime?' by pointing out the practical ways in which crime is approached and perceived in contemporary society. Garland did not refer to crime merely as an increasing factual reality (which is in itself a contestable proposition), nor indeed did he refer to the more complex category of the social fear of crime and ask how we can distinguish the reality of crime from the public and media image of crime; his theme was that *crime was now a core category of governing.* In his narrative, the perception that crime had increased had given rise to a new culture particularly in the US and UK, which he termed the 'culture of control'. His text was published shortly before the terrorist attacks of 11 September 2001, but those events—and the huge changes to notions of security throughout the Western and Muslim worlds—have demonstrated the interdependence of the actions of defining events as crimes and modes of social governance. Some called the events of 11 September a great crime. Others called it an act of war, while still others, alternatively, said that the terms used were unimportant, for the real task was to inquire as to why certain people were motivated to carry them out. How one reacted to those events, however, was in considerable part a result of controlling how one defined their nature. Or put it another way: the consequences that the acts invoked were not predetermined, there was a range of possible reactions; once those events were defined in such or such a way, then the range of social reactions was constrained. Thus we end where we began, by re-emphasizing the diversity of opinions, definitions, perspectives and complex interrelationships that surround what at first sight may seem a simple question: what is crime?

Given that the traditional frame of reference for doing criminology, including locating the processes whereby 'crime' was defined, has been the nation state, current scholarship that attempts to come to grips with globalization should revolutionize criminology (its impact so far has been minor). We are told that state sovereignty, the legitimate definer of crime in a territory, is being undercut. At its strongest the argument is that the State can no longer produce sovereignty—if so, this impacts on all aspects of the State's performance. In the field of crime control this results in ambivalent tactics. State sovereignty asserts itself even when it lacks control over the economy by a wave of populism in the arena of security seeking public support of its power displays in war on crime, or war on drugs, or war on terror. Consider the effect of defining the events of 11 September 2001 as war and not a crime. The choice of 'crime' would have allowed for an international policing action, working through (and building) international moves towards international criminal courts, and a broad coalition. The struggle to bring the 'terrorists' to justice would have been a global justice and not the 'justice of this nation' as George W. Bush had stated. Declaring a war on terror led to the invasion of Afghanistan and Iraq, the destabilization of a number of countries, dramatically divided world opinion, and to the clear double standards concerning the treatment of civilian deaths in the US and those of the invaded countries. The events at the 'Abu Ghraib' prison in Iraq became shorthand for the abuse of power and the 'crimes' committed in several dozen detention centres in Iraq, Afghanistan and at Guantanamo Bay. The Pentagon admitted that no less than 27 detainee deaths were criminal homicides. The CIA admitted to using 'water boarding' (near-drowning), unmistakably a form of torture, and documents released in 2005 under the Freedom of Information Act confirmed some of the more outrageous accounts of detainee abuse. In commenting on images of US soldiers killing a wounded insurgent, the war correspondent Max Hastings sums up the moral distaste the hypocrisy of this 'war for civilization' engenders:

This is a scene straight out of Platoon or Full Metal Jacket. A soldier gazing down on a prostrate enemy sees him move and shouts: 'He's f***ing faking he's dead.' Another soldier fires a single contemptuous shot into the wounded man's head, and says laconically: 'Well, he's dead now.'

On Saturday in Fallujah, that shocking melodrama was played out for real. US marines shot a wounded and helpless Iraqi—in a mosque, of all places—while an NBC television news camera recorded every detail. The images have flashed across the world, into the homes of thousands of millions of people, many of whom already hate what America is doing in Iraq.

… Here are the crusaders for democracy, as George Bush and Tony Blair portray themselves and their soldiers, acting like animals. Even before this atrocity, the world recoiled from the spectacle of Fallujah shattered in the name of freedom…

… Two months ago in Basra, a British officer said to me: 'We were appalled by those pictures from Abu Ghraib. They seemed to cut the legs off the whole moral basis for our presence here.' So they did. So, likewise, does the film footage from Fallujah.

Americans pursue a doctrine of firepower which causes Nato allies to think them unfit for any role in which 'hearts and minds' must be won. The fact is that the American way leaves few hearts and minds alive to parley with. American soldiers possess a contempt for people of alien races, which cost them defeat in Vietnam and could well cost them failure in Iraq.

… It is not enough for George Bush to declare from the distant citadels of Washington that the Coalition's forces are pursuing an honourable cause. On the battlefield, they must also be seen to be fighting in an honourable way.

… Not only have they abused Iraqis, they have been shown before the world to abuse Iraqis. The damning visual evidence is there.

… whatever happens afterwards to the Iraqi people, the way Bush has waged his war in Iraq has inflicted lasting injury on the cause of democracy. Who can again take seriously this

President's claim to be fighting for freedom and virtue, when metaphorically he delivers such proclamations from the wreckage of Fallujah?

... I would suggest that what happened in Fallujah this weekend is arguably more the handi-work of Bush, Rumsfeld and Cheney than of the wretched marine who fired the shot.

... only a fool in the White House would suppose that he can win the War Against Terror through so much blood recklessly shed, such mountains of rubble so carelessly created.

Every frame of film of Saturday's murder in Fallujah is worth another legion of recruits to al-Qaeda.

... Why shouldn't people hate George Bush? (Max Hastings, 'Marine atrocities mock US cause', *The Daily Mail*, 17 November 2004)

Different States play the sovereignty games differently and what is crime in one area may not be crime in another, additionally the efforts of one State to fight crime or drugs may actively cause crime in another. In this negative argument the decline of the State as the body that laid out the conditions of territorial security means that the State is increasingly part of the 'crime problem' and not the solution; the need, then, is to go beyond the State in the process of locating the foundations for defining what is crime and what are proper and legitimate responses to it.

REVIEW QUESTIONS

1 'The criminal law is the source of crime; without the law we would not have crime'. Discuss.

2 What value is there in advocating an 'abolitionist' approach, such as that espoused by Nils Christie or Louk Hulsman?

CONCLUSION

Defining crime is not a matter of common sense or simply following an accepted procedure. In the examples given in this chapter we can see some of the complex political and economic forces that shape how what is a crime is defined in practice—such as US domestic political pressure to downplay knowledge of the events in Rwanda, and to ensure that the specific term that would have described them as a great crime, genocide, was not used, while other domestic political pressures were behind the desperate attempts to define Clinton's explanation of his 'personal' life as a crime. What can we learn? The case of the *Zong*, for example, may seem a long time ago, but:

> On Boxing Day 1996, the crew of an old rusting freighter the *Yiohan* forced over 300 passengers off the ship and on to a small craft designed for a third of that number. Over 280 were drowned when the boat went down. Four years later, fishermen in Sicily were still hauling in corpses and body parts with their catches (*Observer*, 10 June 2001). The tragedy received very little press coverage: only the *Observer* ran the story, as an exposé of the ship's captain. (Webber, 2004: 133)

Webber's point is that of course this was not seen as a modern crime created out of the economic imbalances of the global system; rather, the problem was that of the illegal immigrants and those individuals that preyed upon them (who were not apprehended or punished). In the case of the *Zong*, the demand for cheap labour fed the eighteenth-century slave system of enforced migration. Today we enforce barriers and impose the label criminal on those who seek voluntarily to migrate outside the strict 'legal' conditions governing official migration. In August 2008 the then Italian Prime Minister Silvio Berlusconi, who also owned much of the Italian media outlets and had constantly used his political position to frustrate judicial investigations into his operations and tangled ownership relations, launched a crackdown on crime, which many Italians and his media associate with illegal immigration. A number of new 'crimes' were legislated, including making it an offence punishable by up to four years' imprisonment to enter the country illegally. Expulsions increased, but the Italian authorities often find the countries of origin of illegal arrivals reluctant to accept them back if they are deported. In a highly symbolic measure troops were deployed in joint anti-crime patrols with police in some of Italy's major cities. In 2009 some 20,000 people out of the 55,000 prisoners then serving sentences or awaiting trial in Italian jails were foreigners. This sense of national emergency was part of his political agenda, creating targets whereby he could show the citizens his ability to tackle the sources of their feelings of insecurity and unease. Yet in so doing the task of facing up to the global interconnections was downplayed.

We have a lot to learn from history in this area. Even if we can only conclude that in defining crime there is no easy answer, only controversy and struggle.

QUESTIONS FOR DISCUSSION

1 Why is it so difficult to agree upon a definition of crime?

2 'The crimes that the public are most concerned about are not the real risks that we face.' Discuss.

3 'The solution to the problems of defining crime will be found only by escaping from the confines of the nation state. We need some universal standards to use as our reference to define crime.' Discuss.

4 Take an area, such as drug prohibition, and follow through how and when this was prohibited. Ask, whose interests are served by this criminalization policy? Is criminalization a cause of social harm?

GUIDE TO FURTHER READING

Most textbooks have either a chapter or a section on defining crime. These vary drastically in quality and can be repetitive.

The classic discussion is Keith Bottomley (1979) *Criminology in Focus*, Chapter 1 'What is Crime?'. Oxford: Martin Robertson.

One of the better recent discussions is John Tierney (1996) *Criminology: Theory and Context*, Chapter 1 'Criminology, Crime and Deviance: some Preliminaries', and Chapter 2 'Measuring Crime and Criminality'. London: Prentice Hall.

Perhaps the best recent single chapter is Stuart Henry and Dragan Milovanovic (1996) *Constitutive Criminology: Beyond Postmodernism*, Chapter 5 'Definitions of Crime and Constructions of the Victim'. London: Sage.

See also Jeffrey Reiman (1996) *And the Poor Get Prison: Economic Bias in American Criminal Justice*, Chapter 2 'A Crime by Any Other Name… '. Needham Heights: Allyn & Bacon for examples of industrial accidents and other events that cause great harm not being called crimes.

On the rise and fall of the sociology of deviance Colin Sumner (1994) *The Sociology of Deviance: an Obituary*. Buckingham: Open University Press is wonderful reading.

For an instructive and relevant essay on the contrast between mainstream criminology and more realist conceptions of harm, see Phil Scraton, 'Defining "power" and challenging "knowledge": critical analysis as resistance in the UK' in Kerry Carrington and Russell Hogg (eds), (2002) *Critical Criminology: Issues, Debates, Challenges*. Devon: Willan.

Nils Christie (2004) *A Suitable Amount of Crime*. London: Routledge is an excellent consistent analysis of the proposition that 'crimes are in endless supply. Acts with the potentiality of being seen as crimes are like an unlimited natural resource. We can take out a little in the form of crime—or a lot' (p. 10).

The best argument that crime needs to be replaced by concepts of social harm is Paddy Hillyard, Christina Pantazis, Steve Tombs and Dave Gordon (eds), (2004) *Beyond Criminology: Taking Harm Seriously*. London: Pluto.

For a counter argument which analyses why Western societies appear to be treating every imaginable source of harm as a crime, see Richard Ericson (2006) *Crime in an Insecure World*. Oxford: Polity.

For the need for criminology to move beyond the nation state, see Wayne Morrison (2006) *Criminology, Civilisation and the New World Order*. London: Routledge-Cavendish.

For an alternative criminology textbook that stresses the importance of meaning and power in the construction of crime and law, see Jeff Ferrell, Keith Hayward, and Jock Young (2008) *Cultural Criminology: An Invitation*. London: Sage.

WEB LINKS

Lexis ONE
http://www.lexisone.com

A free legal research site providing searchable case law and a whole host of other useful research aids.

The Emile Durkheim Archive
http://durkheim.itgo.com/anomie.html

A detailed website dedicated to the French sociologist.

Amnesty International
http://www.amnesty.org

Find out more about the campaign for international human rights legislation and human rights abuses.

REFERENCES

Becker, H. (1964) *Outsiders*. New York: Free Press.

Brown, D. and Hogg, R. (1992) 'Law and order politics—left realism and radical criminology: a view from "down under" ', in R. Mathews and J. Young (eds), *Issues in Realist Criminology*. London: Sage.

Christie, N. (2004) *A Suitable Amount of Crime*. London: Routledge.

Durkheim, E. (1966) *The Rules of Sociological Method* (trans S.A. Solovay and J.H. Mueller, (ed) G.E.G. Catlin). New York: Free Press.

Filkins, D. (2004) 'List of Iraqi cities where US troops won't go is growing longer'. *International Herald Tribune*, 6 September.

Garland, D. (2001) *The Culture of Control*. Oxford: Oxford University Press.

Gearey, A., Morrison, W., and Jago, R. (2009) *The Politics of the Common Law: Perspectives, Rights, Processes, Institutions*. London: Routledge-Cavendish.

Gross, H. (1979) *A Theory of Criminal Justice*. New York: Oxford University Press.

Hart, H.L.A. (1961) *A Concept of Law*. Oxford: Clarendon Press.

Hogg, R. (2002) 'Criminology beyond the nation state: global conflicts, human rights and the "new world disorder"', in K. Carrington and R. Hogg, *Critical Criminology*. Cullompton: Willan.

Knepper, P. (2001) *Explaining Criminal Conduct*. Durham, North Carolina: Carolina Academic Press.

Korn, R. and McCorkle, L. (1959) *Criminology and Penology*. New York: Henry Holt & Co.

McCabe, S. (1983) 'Crime', in D. Walsh and A. Poole (eds), *A Dictionary of Criminology*. London: Routledge and Kegan Paul, pp. 49–52.

Morrison, W. (2004) 'Criminology, genocide, and modernity: remarks on the companion that criminology ignored', in C. Sumner (ed), *The Blackwell Companion to Criminology*. Oxford: Blackwell.

Morrison, W. (2005) 'Rethinking narratives of penal change in global context' in J. Pratt *et al.* (eds), *The New Punitiveness*. Cullompton: Willan.

Morrison, W. (2006) *Criminology, Civilisation and the New World Order*. London: Routledge-Cavendish.

Schwendiger, H. and Schwendiger, J. (1975) 'Defenders of Order or Guardians of Human Rights?' in Ian Taylor *et al.* (eds), *Critical Criminology*. London: Routledge & Kegan Paul.

Sellars, K. (2002) *The Rise and Rise of Human Rights*. Phoenix Mill: Sutton.

Simpson, A.W.B. (1984) *Cannibalism and the Comman Law*. Chicago and London: University of Chicago Press.

Symonds, P. (1997) *Industrial Inferno: The Story of the Thai Toy Factory Fire*. London: Labour Press Books.

Tappan, P. (1947) 'Who is the Criminal?', *American Sociological Review* 12: 96–102.

Walvin, J. (1992) *Black Ivory: A History of British Slavery*. London: HarperCollins.

Webber, F. (2004) 'The war on migration', in Paddy Hillyard *et al.* (eds), *Beyond Criminology: Taking Harm Seriously*. London: Pluto Press.

Williams, G. (1955) 'The Definition of Crime', *Current Legal Problems* 8.

Website accessed: http://www.2bangkok.com/2bangkok, posted articles 'melted Bart', 4 May 2003; 'Bart Simpson and the Kader fine commemoration' 21 May 2005.

2

History of crime and punishment

Anne Logan

INTRODUCTION

Today's legal and criminal justice systems in England are the product of centuries of evolution. Therefore some knowledge of the past is essential to students of criminology. The purpose of this chapter is to provide an overview of the major themes in the history of crime and punishment in England and Wales over the last two and a half centuries. First, the chapter briefly discusses the usefulness of historical research in this field and the research methods employed by historians. The chapter then examines some salient features of the history of crime, criminal justice and punishment: debates around crime and class; changes in the criminal justice system; and methods of punishment. The chapter also aims to identify aspects of criminal justice history which can assist in our understanding of contemporary issues and debates, and demonstrate that the nature of crime and criminal justice at any given time can only be understood within the period's specific political context. For this reason, and in view of the vastness of the topic, the chapter is almost entirely concerned with developments in England and Wales, although there are resonances for the history of crime and punishment elsewhere.

BACKGROUND

The history of crime and punishment has received increasing attention from scholars during the last 40 or so years. As a sub-specialism of history it is closely related not only to social history but also to legal and political history, but it has particularly flourished since the development of 'history from below' by predominantly Marxist scholars in the years after World War II. 'History from below' foregrounded the experiences of the poor, disadvantaged and marginalized sections of society as opposed to the conventional historical narrative of 'princes and politicians'.

Scholars employ historical methodology to describe and analyse trends in crime over time. Historical methodology consists primarily of the critical analysis of historical sources, the traces of the past that have survived into the present. Historians are especially interested in the competing currents of change and continuity between past and present, both in crime and criminal justice policy. A thorough understanding of these developments is vital for criminologists for several reasons. Central features of the modern criminal justice system (such as the prison) have evolved over time and are historically contingent, so it is important to understand the reasons for their emergence and for any changes they have undergone. Moreover, criminologists have been able to apply historical methodology to undertake longitudinal studies, for example on 'criminal careers', a topic which necessarily has to be studied over a period of time. An understanding of history can also provide different perspectives on topics of current interest, by posing the question whether there have been historical precedents for current problems. Geoffrey Pearson's classic work *Hooligan* is a case in point: amid constant media discussion of youth crime in the early 1980s, Pearson was able to demonstrate through historical investigation that press and public panic over young people was nothing new.

There is of course never one single interpretation of history, and scholars often disagree profoundly over the meaning of events and developments. Early histories of crime and punishment in Britain tended to concentrate on legal and political developments, arguing, at least implicitly, that the criminal law and modes of punishment gradually became fairer and more civilized. This view of progress over time was denounced by its detractors as a 'Whig' interpretation of history. Under the influence of 'history from below' (or 'the new social history'), a new generation of scholars in the 1970s developed a critical approach to the subject, sometimes referred to as 'revisionism'. Rejecting the premise that change was synonymous with progress revisionists posed the question: in whose interests were the various changes in the criminal law and in punishment methods during the eighteenth and nineteenth centuries made? Since the answer appeared to be the ruling classes, it was argued that these changes could hardly be seen as progress from the perspective of the poor. However, detailed archive research undertaken more recently in England suggests that there was no simple class dimension to the law, as Marxists appeared to suggest. Courts in the late eighteenth and early nineteenth centuries were utilized by a surprising range of individuals from varied social backgrounds, predominantly neither rich nor poor but the 'middling sort'. Moreover, by incorporating the insights of the 'new social history' it is possible to argue that ordinary people as well as elites were part of the political dimension.

In the final decades of the twentieth century the theories of the French scholar, Michel Foucault (1977) became highly influential among historians of crime and punishment. Foucault's thesis was that the new punishments introduced in the wake of the Enlightenment of the eighteenth century—principally the penitentiary—were not more civilized, but more controlling through the psychological discipline they attempted to impose. Importantly, he highlighted the powerful role of specialist knowledge and discourse in the development of policy. Recent scholarly work on the changes which took place in punishment in the early twentieth century has also been strongly influenced by criminologist David Garland (1985), who argued that the relatively simple and undifferentiated punishment regime of the Victorian era was replaced by a 'modern penal complex' as a result of a 'new penality' (see later in this chapter). As with all theoretical ideas, Garland's work has provided a basis for further research, reaction and critique.

As a final introductory point, it is worth noting that 'crime' is an imprecise term and a slippery concept, one which has undergone a great many changes over time, albeit there are aspects of it which have remained constant. In the early part of the period under consideration in this chapter (the eighteenth and early nineteenth century) the concept of crime had moral, religious, social and political connotations as well as legal ones (see Chapter 1). The concept was (and is) neither fixed nor uncontested, and crowds of people could—and did—express their opinions and add their voices to those of legal experts. Those who wished to bring their problems for formal, legal consideration had a variety of courts and procedures to choose from. Additionally there were many alternative methods for dealing with disputes and 'crimes', often involving a great deal of discretion on the part of both individuals and authorities. Moreover, the same authorities (local justices of the peace) were responsible for the welfare of the poor as well as for dealing with criminal matters, and these two forms of administration often overlapped to the point of being indistinguishable. For the purposes of this chapter 'crime' will be defined as actions in breach of the criminal law during the specific period in time under discussion. It is worth noting that while some actions (theft or murder for example), have been in breach of the criminal law throughout the last three centuries and longer, other actions have been criminalized, decriminalized (or even both of these) over the same period. An appreciation of this fact helps us understand just how variable and historically contingent the concept of 'crime' can be.

REVIEW QUESTION

1 Why is it important to research and understand the past in relation to crime and criminal justice?

Researching criminal justice history

It is worth considering briefly the techniques used to research criminal justice history and the way in which these methods differ from other social sciences. Historical research begins with a research question, which is often arrived at by perceiving a gap in existing literature on the given subject or by wishing to offer a challenge to the latter through an alternative approach. But in order for a historical research project to be successful, the researcher needs to identify the existence of accessible records or historical sources on the chosen topic. Historical sources—even for subjects like crime and criminal justice—can take surprisingly varied forms. Official records are undoubtedly important and include those of the various courts which dealt with offenders as well as police and prison records, government-collated statistics, policy documents and the records of Parliament including Hansard (the verbatim record of proceedings in the Houses of Parliament), and select committee and Royal Commission reports. Many of these sources are now available through the Internet. However, they might not be accessible for various reasons, or fail to elicit the information required. Older court records are prone to be missing altogether or fragmentary, while police and prison records have sometimes been lost or destroyed. Researchers working on recent periods in criminal justice history face further difficulties in the form of data protection legislation, and while the Freedom of Information Act 2000 has improved access to official documents, these are likely to be 'redacted' (have sections removed) before being made available if they are deemed to contain personal data on living persons.

In addition to official records, historians of crime and criminal justice often turn to a range of other historical sources, ranging from ballads about notorious offenders, to personal items such as diaries and letters, and a variety of artefacts from newspapers to works of art, or even buildings. For example, a good understanding of Victorian penal regimes can be obtained from a study of the prison architecture of the period, preserved in such places as the jail within Lincoln Castle, combined with study of Mayhew and Binny's illustrated book, *The Criminal Prisons of London*, published in 1862. Diaries can yield surprising evidence on questions such as victimization. Peter King (2000: 18) quotes the example of a gentleman's diary in which the wealthy author revealed his frequent experience of victimization at the hands of his employees. However, as King points out, the diary's author made very few attempts to bring the offenders to formal justice. Thus we obtain a rare insight into one man's (non)utilization of the criminal justice system of his day.

Once the historical sources have been identified, the researcher needs to apply methods of historical analysis. These include establishing the authenticity of the source, which is often achieved through attention to its provenance: where did it come from and by what route did it get to where it is now? Then the source is analysed for its reliability, a process which includes, but is not limited to, the identification of any potential bias within it. The researcher needs to consider the creator of the source—be it a government agency or an individual, the purpose behind its creation, and its intended audience. Above all, the researcher needs to be critical. As a leading historian of the French Annales school argued, historical documents are like witnesses in a court, they need to be cross-examined (Bloch, 1954). But historical sources can be used imaginatively by researchers: often they tell us about things that their creators did not intend to tell us about. The records of London's Central Criminal Court (the Old Bailey) are a case in point. Now available online as 'The Proceedings of the Old Bailey, 1674–1913' these records are 'the largest body of texts detailing the lives of non-elite people ever published, containing 197,745 criminal trials' (Old Bailey Online), which can be used to research a great many questions of interest to social historians, not just crime and criminal justice.

Crime historians and historical criminologists are naturally interested in statistics, but these provide researchers with quite specific problems, one of which is the difficulty in using them to track trends in crime over time. Over the years the methods of statistical compilation changed frequently in response to developments within the criminal justice system. In England and Wales the publication of criminal statistics commenced in 1810 (in the form of the number of indictable criminal cases committed to trial) as a result of increasing political concern about a 'rise' in crime and of a developing interest in social research. In 1837 a new statistical category of 'offences known to the police' was introduced as a result of government attempts to ensure the efficiency of publicly-funded police forces. Comparisons over time are further complicated by changes in the way that certain categories of offences were dealt with. For example, in 1850 larcenies committed by offenders under the age of 16 could be dealt with in the lower magistrates' courts or 'petty sessions', and thus were removed from the statistics of the higher courts.

More fundamentally, crime historians differ over the reliability of crime statistics, given the inevitable 'dark figure' of unreported crime as well as the variability of counting methodology. Official crime statistics are not only fragmentary and open to multiple interpretations but are also products of specific political and policy contexts (see Chapter 3). The latter point has been graphically illustrated in the work of Howard Taylor (1999), who emphasizes the 'supply side' pressures behind criminal statistics. Addressing the question as to why minor criminal offences apparently fell in the years after World War I (1914–18), Taylor rejects conventional interpretations that this trend was due to changing attitudes (for example towards drunkenness and alcoholism) and an improved system of social welfare. Instead he argues that the fall in convictions in minor offences were due to the changing priorities of police and politicians at a time when central government was increasingly taking responsibility for more of police service funding and when reductions in public expenditure were being sought. Thenceforward the priorities were reconfigured to 'serious' crime and motoring offences as police services battled to keep their service relevant—and adequately funded—in challenging financial times. Barry Godfrey (2008) interprets the long-term fall in the number of criminal prosecutions somewhat differently, while also recognizing the role that the police played as gatekeepers of the criminal justice system. Similarly, Stephan Slater (2012) has pointed to statistical variations in the prosecution of minor crime both temporally and geographically in early twentieth-century London. He concludes that there were substantial variations in local police attitudes towards certain types of offences, for example those related to prostitution.

Debates over statistics are not merely of academic interest. Regardless of their accuracy, crime statistics continually frame and influence debates about criminal justice policy.

REVIEW QUESTIONS

1 Why should historians of crime and criminal justice treat statistical sources with extreme caution?

2 'There will always come a moment when the historian will need to start counting'. Discuss Le Roy Ladurie's assertion with regard to the history of crime.

Crime and social class

Aside from arguments over long-term trends as demonstrated by statistics, academic debates on the history of crime have been dominated by arguments over the relationship between crime and class, particularly in relation to 'social crime', a concept developed by the 'historians from below' (referred to in the Background section of this chapter). A consideration of questions relating to crime and class highlights the way in which communities can exert influence both over ideologies and practices of crime and punishment.

In the latter part of the eighteenth and early decades of the nineteenth centuries the offences brought to court were overwhelmingly examples of 'property crime', often petty theft or pilfering committed by the poor. For example, according to King, in the petty sessions of rural Essex between 1785 and 1801, 'wood and vegetable theft predominated'. Moreover, the decades between *c*.1780 and 1850 were marked by rapid economic, industrial and social change as the market economy in Britain became more advanced and pervasive. While towns grew rapidly, the poor in rural areas were increasingly prone to under-employment and unrest. Sharp fluctuations in the market economy affected town and country alike: Clive Emsley (2005: 34–6) argues that the statistical data does show some inexact correlation between economic downturns and trends in crime, such as the peaks in crime statistics during the sharp recessions of the 1840s. This type of offence has therefore been related to poverty—the hard times caused by agrarian and industrial change—and its occurrence has been termed 'survival crime'.

During the 1970s historians developed a fuller concept of 'social crime' in relation to the many instances of political and protest-linked crime within this period. First coined by the leading Marxist historian Eric Hobsbawm (1917–2012), the term 'social crime' was applied to the collective law-breaking activities of poor people, including instances of rebellion and resistance (Lea, 1999). These ranged from urban food riots in the second half of the eighteenth century, to instances of politically-motivated criminal damage such as the Luddite machine-breaking in northern England during the 1810s and the Swing riots in rural areas in 1831–32. Thus acts which in a different context might be interpreted as wanton criminality are cast in a different light as examples of political protest. For theorists of 'social crime', political protest and survival crime are connected in that they were likely to receive some support within the community, especially in any one to which offenders belonged. This idea in turn is connected to the theory of the 'moral economy', developed by another of the English Marxist historians, E.P. Thompson. In his classic analysis of food riots, Thompson argued that the crowd (or 'mob' as they were known in the eighteenth century) acted rationally in pursuit of a moral—as opposed to a market—economy, acting in accordance with a political discourse of rights (those of the 'freeborn Englishman') which was held widely across society (Thompson, 1991). For example, food rioters would target for destruction the premises of specific traders whose business practices were deemed to be unethical or exploitative, while leaving others unaffected. Thompson interpreted the actions of the rioting crowd as motivated by anti-capitalist—or even pre-capitalist ideology—when they singled out profiteering merchants or cheating millers for attack: effectively the latter were the deviants who had broken the unwritten rules of society while the crowd embodied resistance to the marketization of the economy. As Thompson noted, rioting crowds would ensure fair distribution of the food seized from profiteers, and often the authorities (in the form of local magistrates) were loath to intervene, arguably because they shared the crowd's opinion of the morality of sharp business practices.

The theme of community support for criminal acts also surfaces in the debate about the criminalization of traditional practices. Due to population pressure in the late eighteenth and early nineteenth century agriculture became much more commercialized as more land was brought into cultivation. Commentators influenced by Karl Marx (1842) have interpreted enclosure of common land for commercial farming as 'class robbery' (Thomson, 1968: 237), while the poor were deprived of their rights to graze animals on commons, hunt birds and rabbits and collect wood from forests. Although agricultural historians have debated at length the precise impact of enclosure on the various social classes of agrarian England, there is wide agreement that the poorest people lost out. However, King's study of gleaning (1989) suggests that the practice was not widely criminalized as a result of enclosure. The poor of a parish were still permitted to pick up (or 'glean') the scraps of wheat left after a harvest. The fate of alleged rights to hunt for food is more debatable. The game laws, which ensured that landowners could claim ownership over game birds and animals on their land, have been frequently singled out as instances of class-based legislation in the interests of the rich rather than the poor. Yet King (2000) found few prosecutions under the game laws in late eighteenth-century Essex. Moreover, studies of poaching cases suggest that the forces of the law targeted commercial gangs intent on supplying urban meat markets rather than individuals seeking to feed their families (Archer, 1999), so these incidents do not fit the paradigm of 'survival crime', and the extent to which organized gangs had community support is also debatable. Similar discussions surround the interpretation of smuggling, a crime which was encouraged by high excise duties in the eighteenth and early nineteenth centuries, but which was often highly organized, by commercially-motivated individuals and gangs who were not afraid to use violence against the authorities if confronted. Such examples present some proponents of the 'social crime' thesis with a problem: not all instances of community-backed law breaking can be interpreted as the actions of the dispossessed poor struggling against the over-mighty power of the propertied classes. Smugglers may have had more in common with the profiteering corn merchants than the fact that they were on opposing sides of the law might suggest.

Nevertheless, as John Lea (1999) points out, the 'social crime' thesis is not merely an item of historical interest. Lea argues that 'survival' crimes continue to be tolerated in communities with a high degree of social exclusion. As was the case 200 years ago, the poor may combine several strategies in their quest for survival, including recourse to scarce public welfare resources and charity as well as theft. Meanwhile levels of tobacco and alcohol smuggling remain significant and the illegal drugs market strongly matches the paradigm of capitalist enterprise. While outbreaks of rioting and looting in August 2011 were immediately condemned by the prime minister, David Cameron, as 'sheer criminality' (and were treated as such by the police and courts) a debate remains as to whether there are still classes within society that lack alternative forms of political expression (Treadwell et al., 2013). In the twenty-first century we can also point to the existence of protest movements such as the Occupy movement who pursue their aims through direct action. The debate about 'social crime', protest and law-breaking therefore continues today.

REVIEW QUESTIONS

1 Was the criminal law an 'instrument of class oppression' in the period 1770–1850?

2 Does the concept of 'social crime' have any relevance in the twenty-first century?

Changes in the criminal justice system

The changing shape of the criminal justice system has profound effects upon the history of crime. For example, the introduction of the so-called 'new' police services in the nineteenth century brought fundamental changes to the ways in which crime was reported and dealt with (Emsley, 1996). While any notion of there having been a coherent 'system' for criminal justice at any period in the past is fundamentally unhistorical, the term is employed here as a shorthand for the forces of law and order, specifically courts of law and related police forces. The practices of these institutions have significant repercussions for the ways in which the 'problem' of crime is articulated within society.

Among the most significant changes in the system has been the development of a public system of prosecution. Peter King states that in the eighteenth century 'formal prosecution was the exception' in the country as a whole (King, 2000: 22). Since prosecutions were brought by individuals, the decision on whether the accused should be brought to court was entirely in the hands of the victims. King argues that the motivation to bring a prosecution was higher in cases involving violence. Of course, where certain crimes were concerned, the 'victim' was the government or a public authority. Hence 'coining' (the manufacture of counterfeit currency) offences were brought to court by the Royal Mint, and certain serious offences were prosecuted by the public authorities on the grounds that they attacked the good order of society as a whole. A major deterrent to prosecution was the time and expense involved. Not only did the victim have to finance the prosecution, he or she might also have to offer a reward or in some other way provide resources to apprehend the offender. By the late eighteenth century concern about rising levels of theft from business premises led merchants, shopkeepers and other business people to form prosecution associations in localities across the country. These associations provided members with a form of insurance cover to provide mutual aid if a member was the victim of crime, and support him or her through the process of bringing the offender to justice.

In cases where formal prosecutions of alleged law-breakers did take place, the vast majority—then as now—were likely to be dealt with by the local magistrates (also known as justices of the peace, or JPs). King argues that local justices in the late eighteenth century had a preference for mediation and their courts were a lot less formal than might be assumed: according to King (2000: 85) 'legal technicalities did not take pride of place in these courts'. Of course, then as now, outside the major cities magistrates were unpaid laymen and—before the mid-twentieth century when training was introduced—did not necessarily have much legal knowledge. Magistrates might try to get offenders to offer some compensation to the victim or act as an arbitrator in minor disputes. Where more serious offences were concerned, magistrates could refer the case to the higher courts such as the Quarter Sessions (quarterly meetings of county justices) or the Assizes, which were the courts held usually biannually in county towns, presided over by monarch-appointed judges. From this eighteenth-century patchwork of a system, marked by quite a large degree of discretion on the part of justices and judges at all levels, the modern courts system gradually emerged.

The American legal scholar John Langbein has described how the trial procedures in higher courts evolved from the traditional, direct confrontation between prosecutor and defendant towards the modern adversarial system. What Langbein (2003) terms as the 'lawyerisation' of the criminal trial stemmed from judges' concerns in the early eighteenth century that monetary incentives offered for successful prosecutions encouraged the involvement of professional thief takers with an incentive to perjure. As a result, judges in the Old Bailey began to permit the appearance of defence counsel, albeit with very limited power: simply to examine and cross-examine witnesses. The involvement of prosecution counsel began even earlier, initially when governmental or other official bodies such as the Royal Mint, the Treasury or the Bank of England employed solicitors to prepare a case on their behalf. Since solicitors had no right of audience in the Court, they had to brief barristers to appear on their clients' behalf. By the late eighteenth century privately-run prosecution associations were following State departments in employing lawyers. However, it is important to note that poor people, who made up the majority of defendants in courts such as the Old Bailey, would not have been able to afford the services of counsel. It is also likely that lawyers were utilized less in provincial courts than they were in London. Langbein concludes that the period between the 1730s and the 1780s witnessed the replacement of the traditional altercation trial with an early version of the modern adversarial trial. From that point counsel and judges were able to develop the law of criminal evidence, for example rules regarding the need for corroboration, the inadmissibility of hearsay evidence, and the exclusion of any confessions other than voluntary ones.

Further important changes took place in the nineteenth century with the growth of a bureaucratic State-run police service. There is not space in this chapter to recount the history of police services in detail, but the introduction of the so-called 'new police' (starting with the Metropolitan Police founded in London in 1829, and rolled out across the country in enactments such as the County and Borough Police Act 1856) is especially significant in this respect. While undoubtedly the introduction of 'new' police forces was extremely controversial (Storch, 1981) in the short term (and political arguments surround the issue of policing to this day), it is notable that once police forces were organized in a district, local residents began to turn to the police and utilize them for the purpose of reporting crime. Indeed, a locality's police force was judged to be efficient by central government if it successfully gathered and maintained crime statistics. Moreover, as policemen pounded their urban beats and arrested petty offenders such as drunkards and prostitutes under the Vagrancy Act 1824, so the police themselves became prosecutors. At the same time, responsibility for trying more minor offences, especially when committed by children, was passed down from higher courts to the magistrates' petty sessions. These developments led not only to a further marginalization of victims in the criminal courts, but also to some serious consideration of the creation of some public system of prosecution. Following prolonged discussion of the deficiencies of the system, an Act of 1879 allowed for the appointment of a Director of Public Prosecutions (DPP). In the event this was a limited reform, because while supporters of a public prosecution system regarded arrangements in other countries as superior, there was a strong current of opposition which feared that the State would become over-mighty if public prosecutors took over in all cases, that the costs of a public system would prove prohibitive, and that bribery and/or biased decisions would result (Rock, 2004). As a result, after this watered-down reform, the police continued to bring most prosecutions to court and thus had a lot of influence over which reported offences were brought to trial and which were not. Private prosecutions remained a possibility, and as Rock (2004) points out, the instigation of a public prosecution service, while begun by the 1879 Act, was not completed until the 1980s.

The role of the magistracy is often neglected in histories of criminal justice, yet local magistrates continue to handle the majority of criminal cases brought before the courts. Their role is therefore of fundamental importance in the criminal justice system. Drew Gray's (2007) research on the regulation of violence in the City of London in the late eighteenth and early nineteenth centuries shows that the City's summary courts dealt with a large quantity of assault cases. Gray argues that complainants brought charges largely in the hope of receiving an apology or possibly compensation. As the nineteenth century progressed JPs gradually lost many of their administrative functions to do with matters such as roads and poor relief when authorities especially elected or appointed for these purposes took them over. Hence the role of magistrate became more firmly associated with the JP's remaining judicial functions, and as already mentioned, minor criminal cases were increasingly delegated to their courts. In London and some other populous places where crime rates were high, stipendiary magistrates—trained lawyers—were appointed, but in most of the country the JP remained a voluntary role, as it still is today. Nevertheless, magistrates' courts have undergone some important changes over the years. At the start of the twentieth century the magistracy was democratized with the removal of property qualifications and the opening of the magisterial bench to women in 1919. Shortly after the appointment of the first women justices, the Magistrates Association was formed at the suggestion of penal modernizers to represent the country's JPs and to provide them with a forum for discussion. While no official training was required for lay magistrates until the 1960s, for the previous 40 years the Magistrates Association provided conferencing and unofficial training opportunities to its members, thus raising the level of professionalism in this vitally important part of the criminal justice system (Logan, 2006). Magistrates have continued to play an important part in the treatment of young offenders ever since legislation in 1847 and 1850 which gave JPs the power to try petty larcenies committed by children. In 1908, after experiments with a juvenile court in the city of Birmingham, the Children Act provided that all magistrates' courts should hold separate sittings to try offenders under the age of 16.

This section has taken a very broad approach towards changes in the system for the administration of justice over the years and attempted merely to mention some of the most significant ones. A detailed study of records enables historians of criminal justice to appreciate the great variations in practice over time and between different places and to adopt a sceptical approach to any grand narratives concerning change.

REVIEW QUESTIONS

1 How important was the victim to the operation of criminal justice in the late eighteenth and early nineteenth centuries?

2 How has the role of the magistrate changed over the last two centuries?

Punishment *c.*1750–1870—community action, prisons and transportation

Over the last two centuries there have been at least two major shifts in punishment practice. The first, the subject of much academic comment, was the transformation which saw a reduction in the applicability of the death penalty to criminal offences and the diminution and eventual abolition of transportation as a judicial penalty, accompanied by the rise of the prison as the principal form of punishment. The second—called the rise of the 'modern penal complex'—was a further transformation in which a relatively simple, undifferentiated prison system was complicated by increasingly complex penal regimes and complemented by a range of non-custodial penalties, such as the use of probation. Neither of these changes happened over a short or even a single timescale, or was unambiguous in its effects, or unidirectional. Arguably, elements of older punishment systems, such as the shaming of offenders, live on or are subject to revival in so-called 'new' methods of treatment, for example in the insistence today that offenders on Community Payback Orders wear fluorescent tabards while at work.

Punishment methods in the eighteenth century may appear to have been simple, but they were highly complex in application and motivation (Langbein, 1983). The general characteristics of penal methods such as whipping, branding, the stocks, the pillory and hanging have been summarized as punishments of the body rather than of the mind, but the motivations behind punishments were not exactly what we might assume. Whereas vengeance, deterrence and incapacitation were undoubtedly significant motivations, specific punishments were chosen to convey particular, precise messages about certain crimes. For example, according to McGowen (1999) a highly significant forgery statute of 1729, which made the offence a capital crime, was prompted not only by general financial insecurity following the South Sea Bubble but also by precise fears concerning confidence in private credit following a sensational fraud trial in 1728. Before that time fraudsters (other than those who targeted public finance) were customarily punished on the pillory, which served the prime purpose of making them notorious, effectively pariahs within the community. But in the specific circumstances of the 1720s the pillory came to be seen as too light a punishment for a crime which uniquely revealed high levels of deviousness in apparently respectable businessmen. Thus notoriety as a motivation for punishment was replaced by deterrence.

As was the case with crime, crowds had a vital role to play in punishment, and not merely as spectators. In addition to his work on the 'moral economy', E.P. Thompson (1991) drew attention to practices variously termed 'rough music', 'charivari', 'riding skimmington', or in Wales, 'ceffyl pren'. These titles were applied to outbreaks of community action, where an individual or individuals might be targeted for a form of shaming punishment (perhaps by being paraded on horseback, accompanied by loud noise), seemingly in retaliation for some alleged bad behaviour or breach of the community's normative standards. As with the stocks and the pillory, the motivation was not so much the infliction of physical pain—although that might be a by-product—as of humiliation. Ingram (1984: 93) argues that it was assumed that 'the populace had the right to supplement the legal system', but the dividing line between community action which upheld the law and that which broke it was exceedingly thin. As a result the authorities discouraged this kind of action as far as possible, preferring to restrict community involvement to officially approved occasions such as public executions. Nevertheless, examples of 'rough music' continued to be recorded well into the nineteenth century, by which time targets might include wife beaters, sex offenders or even strike breakers. As recent debates over 'penal populism' and vigilantes indicate, the role of community attitudes towards offenders and punishment continues to be an issue with which political and judicial authorities need to grapple.

Early punishment methods were not exclusively restricted to the public realm. Although England's network of county-town prisons, which dated back at least to the thirteenth century, are usually categorized as places for detention rather than for punishment, they were sometimes used for the latter purpose. Conditions were so poor in some jails that a prison sentence could sometimes turn into a death sentence. Generally, however, the function of prisons in the eighteenth century was to keep people secure and prevent them from absconding prior to their trial, and (if found guilty) between the trial and the execution of their sentence, be it a public whipping, the pillory, transportation or death. For similar reasons—the need to prevent absconders—debtors were held captive, often in the same jails as offenders. However, there were in addition other, usually small, prisons known as 'Bridewells' or houses of correction. These institutions occupy a highly significant place in the historiography of prisons as they are often regarded as precursors of the modern prison (Melossi and Pavarini, 1981), and an inspiration to Bentham's 'Panopticon'. Developed from the late sixteenth century onwards, houses of correction, as their name implies, were designed to adjust the way of living of petty offenders, giving them a chance to (often literally) sober up and learn some industrious habits. These institutions were naturally found only in urban areas, where they might offer magistrates a further option to dealing with petty, often young offenders. However, their role was not purely punitive, and houses of correction have a part to play in the history of welfare as well as the history of punishment, since they emerged in the context of attempts by poor law legislators to distinguish between different categories of poor, and isolate the 'vicious', malingering element from the 'deserving' poor. Magistrates were anyway not short of options for dealing with minor offenders, since they could enforce some restitution or recompense, or dispatch the wrongdoer to the army or navy, but the existence of houses of correction suggests a long-standing blurring of boundaries between penury, anti-social behaviour and crime.

A punishment of increasing importance during the eighteenth century and of continuing significance for much of the nineteenth was transportation. Far more effectively than any prison, transportation placed offenders out of sight and out of reach, simply by placing them on another continent. A sentence of transportation in itself could be handed down, or it could be applied when a death penalty was commuted. The official term of a transportation sentence could vary from seven years to life, but the expectation was that transportees would never return, they would be cut out of the nation as effectively as if they had been executed. There has been much scholarly debate over what the 'real' motives behind this policy were. Transportation undoubtedly helped to build the British Crown's overseas empire, mainly in North America and in parts of Australia (especially New South Wales) from the late 1780s until the punishment's final abolition in the 1860s. Some commentators have therefore speculated that it was unlikely to have been motivated simply by the need for a punishment short of death for those who had broken the criminal law, especially in view of the high costs of removing offenders to somewhere like Australia. But detailed calculations by Frank Lewis (1988), who compared the cost of transportation with that of the prison hulks moored in English ports during the period 1796–1810, suggest that although transportation was superficially more expensive, it represented a good bargain for the British State once the likely costs of recidivism were taken into account, let alone the cost of building new prisons. Transportation therefore made economic sense even from the point of view of the costs of punishment, let alone when growth in the colonies was taken into account. A penal colony proved in the long run to be an excellent method of empire building.

Transportation probably looked very different from the point of view of the individuals involved. Those sentenced to transportation were disproportionately young, relatively petty and/or first time offenders, so the penalty could be seen as reformative, offering a fresh start on a new continent to those unable to make themselves an honest living in their home country. From that perspective it might appear a benevolent institution, and it is possible that transportation was an attractive proposition to some offenders, especially in the later stages of the policy when it had become a less hazardous enterprise than at first. As a result, opponents of transportation such as Jeremy Bentham denied that it had any deterrent value. But for many people sent so far from home on a dangerous sea passage, unlikely ever to see their loved ones again and facing an uncertain future in an unpredictable place, transportation must have had a very different meaning. It is, of course, impossible to generalize about a phenomenon which lasted for nearly two centuries and had so many variations: it is not possible in the space available in this chapter to give a really nuanced picture of it. Approximately 160,000 convicts were sent to penal colonies in New South Wales and Van Diemen's Land (Tasmania) and according to one authoritative account, 'most served a few years of their sentences in assignment to a free settler or in government labor, never wore chains, got their tickets-of-leave and … were absorbed into colonial society as free citizens' (Hughes, 2003: xiii).

As was mentioned earlier, the gradual changes in punishment practices from the mid-eighteenth to the mid-nineteenth centuries happened according to different time-scales. While the 'bloody code' (a term applied collectively to the large number of statutes which applied the death penalty to a wide variety of crimes) was changed relatively rapidly (see later), transportation remained for a lot longer than is often appreciated, although admittedly it was in substantial decline from 1840. The relatively slow speed of its decline seems to have been primarily a result of the unpalatable nature of the alternatives, at least from the point of view of the political classes who made the decisions. While there were at times vociferous—if small—pressure groups touting various alternative penal strategies, principally the penitentiary, legislators were reluctant to take this path for a remarkably long period of time. However, as mentioned earlier, the sentencing picture is complicated by the fact that prison was sometimes used as a punishment, so prison and transportation systems existed alongside each other for a considerable period of time. Prison reform was therefore a periodic feature of the political agenda from the 1770s onwards. That decade saw not only the complete cessation of transportation to the North American colonies but also the publication of John Howard's celebrated account of *The State of the Prisons*, a record of his observations in county jails and Bridewells across England and Wales. Howard found much to criticize on his journeys, from inadequate feeding and supervision arrangements, to poor hygiene, lack of clean water and air, to moral matters such as the absence of any separation between types of prisoner (men/women, debtor/felon), the lack of work for many inmates, and their gambling habits. Effectively Howard set the prison reform agenda for decades to come, by arguing in favour of hygienic facilities, the classification of inmates, and prison labour. Yet many of the features he found in the jails of the 1770s were still the hallmark of small, unreformed prisons 60 years later, and more than a full century had passed before all of the smaller jails were closed in the aftermath of the creation of the Prison Commission in 1877.

For much of the nineteenth century until 1877, England and Wales effectively had two prison systems. Alongside the locally run institutions, new types of prison for convicted felons (convicts) were developed as an alternative to transportation. Progress however was slow, due to the high cost of building new facilities and the continued attractiveness of transportation. The penitentiary idea, pioneered in the Quaker-influenced American state of Pennsylvania, was slow to get off the ground in Britain. An early attempt to build a penitentiary under an Act of 1779 was abandoned and Bentham's plan for the Panopticon (a privately-run prison in which inmates would undertake productive labour under the gaze of supervisory staff and members of the public) likewise was not adopted.

Instead the supposedly temporary expedient of prison hulks was adopted as policy (Devereaux, 1999). Initiated in 1775, hulks (former warships with guns removed, usually moored near dockyards or naval bases where the convicts performed hard labour) were to be used for almost nine decades. When, eventually, a national penitentiary was constructed at Millbank in London in 1816, it proved both controversial and unsuccessful. It is a testament to the power of transportation that Millbank soon became merely a holding place for convicts awaiting departure to Australia. Only when a Whig government took power in the 1830s was there any decisive move towards developing a land-based convict prison system within Britain itself. What eventually emerged was a scheme which combined elements of the penitentiary and the so-called 'separate system' with the hard labour ethos of the hulks. Thus men's sentences would typically start with a period in solitary confinement followed by transfer to a public works prison such as the one built in Chatham in the1850s, where inmates toiled to extend the Royal Dockyard. For the small percentage of convicts who were women there were different arrangements, with a final stage spent in an institution which was designated as a 'refuge'.

REVIEW QUESTIONS

1 Why, despite its temporary cessation at the outbreak of the American War of Independence in 1776, did 'transportation remained the preferred secondary punishment for the worst classes of capital offenders' (Simon Devereaux) for many decades to come?

2 Discuss the reasons for changes in the role of prisons between the 1770s and the 1860s.

Capital punishment c.1750–1870

Public executions and the so-called 'bloody code' have attracted a good deal of attention both from contemporary observers and from historians, but it is important not to exaggerate the ferocity of the penal code in the eighteenth and early nineteenth centuries. Although there were over 200 capital statutes in existence by the early nineteenth century the number of executions was relatively small, especially outside London and adjoining counties. Many of the statutes were barely used, if at all, in prosecutions. They were repetitive and overlapping as the result of poor draftsmanship on the part of their creators. Whereas some historians have interpreted the 'bloody code' as an attack on the poor by the ruling class, others have argued that the victims who brought prosecutions could hardly be described as 'ruling class', that juries had 'a strong presumption against capital verdicts' and that judges made full use of the discretion available to them in sentencing (Langbein, 1983). However, there is evidence that there was a rise in the number of executions at the start of the nineteenth century, although not as a proportion of those convicted: in other words, the number of crimes brought to trial was increasing. It was at this point—and probably for this reason—that the 'bloody code' became a political issue. It is no coincidence that the same individuals who supported the introduction of penitentiaries and who frowned upon the continuation of transportation were the most vociferous critics of the 'bloody code'. By giving it this appellation, reformers were able to characterize the criminal law as a 'monolithic mass of draconian statutes inherited from a former, less civilised age' (Handler, 2005: 683).

Although the first reforms of the code, introduced by reform enthusiast parliamentarian Sir Samuel Romilly in the early years of the nineteenth century, merely picked away at it piece by piece, the country did not have to wait long for more radical reform and by the late 1830s few offences remained capital crimes, and in practice the death penalty was only applied in cases of murder, while even for these it was not mandatory. This was relatively swift progress, especially in contrast to the dilatory adoption of the penitentiary system. However, Handler (2005) argues that it was not the reasoned, intellectual arguments of the rational proponents of radical, utilitarian reform (such as Jeremy Bentham) that won the day with regard to the 'bloody code'. Rather, reform was hastened in the 1820s and 1830s by a perceived need on the part of politicians to reconcile the law with public opinion, which had been aroused by a series of well-publicized forgery trials and orchestrated by prototype penal reform pressure groups. As in the 1950s, when a series of sensational miscarriages of justice in murder cases began to shake the foundations of public and political support for the death penalty in Britain, seemingly irrational public responses to the plight of specific individuals had more impact on policy than either the 'scientific' arguments of intellectuals or the beliefs of religious factions.

Pressure group activists achieved further success in the 1860s with the abolition of public executions, although this time they were disappointed not to obtain a complete cessation of the death penalty. As mentioned earlier, the efficacy of the criminal code of the eighteenth century and earlier depended to a certain extent upon the visibility of punishment. A crowd was not merely a collection of onlookers; it was a significant player in its own right in the theatre of execution (Gatrell, 1996). Even—or especially—when the death penalty was only visited on murderers, the public nature of the punishment remained integral to its deterrent value. However, early nineteenth-century commentators periodically argued that the crowd at a hanging did not behave in the fashion desired by the authorities. Rather than observing the spectacle with respectful fear and awe, people seemed intent on enjoying themselves, pausing only momentarily—if at all—to reflect on the true meaning of the event (McGowen, 1986). By the 1840s instances when people in the crowds were killed or injured in the crush, and when large numbers of police officers had to be drafted in, only added to concern in government circles, and in 1856 a House of Lords committee recommended that executions no longer be held in public. After 12 more years and a further investigation by a Royal Commission, a parliamentary bill ending public hangings was passed in 1868.

Thus it was only by the late 1860s that a recognizably 'modern' system of punishment was starting to emerge in England and Wales, characterized by the centrality of prison as the default method of punishment. In the following decade the nationalization of local prisons, which were brought together with the convict system under the new Prison Commission, further emphasized the central position of incarceration in the official response to crime, and arguably the classic 'Victorian' form of imprisonment, which still has a strong grip on public imaginings of punishment, dates from the 1877–95 period. However, the heyday of the Victorian jail was extremely brief, as conditions were already in place for the second shift from a relatively simple and undifferentiated punishment regime to the adoption of a more extensive and varied range of disciplinary sanctions.

REVIEW QUESTIONS

1 What were the arguments put forward by supporters and opponents of the death penalty in the early nineteenth century?

2 After the legislation which ended public executions was passed, the campaign against the death penalty lost all momentum. Why do you think this happened?

The 'modern penal complex'

To a certain extent, the history of twentieth-century crime and punishment is only just now starting to be written. Partly this is because of restrictions on the availability of historical data, and partly because historians often prefer to place a distance of some decades between their own time and the period they are studying. However, thus far much of the work that has been done by historians, particularly that which is focussed on criminal justice policy, has chosen to engage in some way with the work of criminologist David Garland.

In *Punishment and Welfare* (1985) Garland argued that in the early decades of the twentieth century the relatively simple penal methods of the late Victorian era were replaced by a 'new penality'. He claimed that in the wake of a highly critical 1895 report by the government-appointed Gladstone Committee into the prison system the number of penal sanctions available to the courts doubled, and that new methods of control were subsequently developed. These new methods included placing offenders on probation rather than sending them to prison for short periods or (in the case of juveniles) giving them corporal punishment, as well as the novel—and ultimately unsuccessful—institutional regime of inebriate reformatories. The 'modern penal complex' also included the introduction of indeterminate and/or preventative sentences, which broke the connection between the seriousness of a crime and the length of the sentence it resulted in, a relationship of proportionality which had been so important to the theories of 'bloody code' opponents a century earlier. Garland characterized the 'new penality' as representing attempts (influenced by a new, 'scientific' criminology) to manage, rather than reform, social failure.

According to Garland, the 'modern penal complex' was characterized by features which allied it closely to the emerging institutions of the twentieth-century welfare state. It was no coincidence that, according to his schema, the 'modern penal complex' began to emerge in the first decade of the 1900s when legislative innovations included not only the establishment of juvenile courts, special youth prisons called borstals and a State-sanctioned probation system, but also old-age pensions and measures for the publicly subsidised feeding of school children. Of course this was not the first or the last time when the currents of welfare ran close to those of criminal justice, but the specific example of policy development in the early and mid-twentieth century has been subsequently labelled 'penal-welfarism'. Garland (1985) argued that there were four key influences on the 'new penality': 'scientific criminology', itself an outcome of the institutional opportunities that the prison had offered scientists by providing them with researchable subjects and data; the development of social work, especially the 'casework' approach which had been developed by charities working with the poorest classes and which had a strong influence upon the probation service; the evolution of welfare policies; and the development of eugenics, or 'Social Darwinism'.

Although Garland's analysis is powerfully constructed, like all generalizing approaches to the history of crime and criminal justice, it encounters challenges when set against empirical observations of historical events. Synergies between punishment and welfare are not unique to the post-1900 period, but are a recurring theme in the history of criminal justice, although they undoubtedly took new forms as the electoral franchise was widened to include the entire adult population in the early twentieth century. Timing inevitably throws up different interpretations: while Garland located the origins of the 'modern penal complex' in the post-1895 period, Wiener (1990) argues that some elements can be traced back to the 1870s, for example the origins of probation, which he associates with a growing aversion, caused by discourses of 'civilization', towards the application of violent, physical punishments for minor offences. Conversely, other scholars have highlighted the persistence of distinctly un-modern elements in twentieth-century penal methods, for example the continued use of the death penalty in Britain until the 1960s, and of corporal punishment as a judicial penalty for young offenders until 1948. Victor Bailey (1997: 293) offers more fundamental objections to Garland's and Wiener's theses when he argues that penal culture in the early twentieth century was more complex, and less dominated by the precepts of positivist criminology, than the two scholars in their different ways assumed. Once again, the pace of reform can easily be glossed over in grand narratives: as Bailey points out, the actual amount of progress in humanizing prison conditions in the wake of the supposedly revolutionary Gladstone report was 'glacial'; 'the debate on English prisons between 1895 and 1922 was framed by unchanging structures of a harsh prison system … the prison discipline meted out to the conscientious objectors during the [First World] War was almost identical to that suffered by Oscar Wilde, a quarter of a century before…' (Bailey, 1997: 322).

The debate over the 'modern penal complex' is important because most of the policies and institutions discussed within it are still recognizably part of the criminal justice landscape today. Twenty-first century governments remain committed to the notion of prison as a central and indispensable part of the penal system, while penal-welfarist strategies such as probation and community service are still vitally important elements of the criminal justice system. All these methods of punishment are today the subject of almost continual alterations in government policy, although their essential characteristics remain.

REVIEW QUESTIONS

1 How significant was the Gladstone Committee Report of 1895 in the history of the penal system in England and Wales?

2 How does 'penal-welfarism' influence the criminal justice system of the twenty-first century?

CONCLUSION

If there are general conclusions to be drawn from the above brief summary of developments in crime and punishment over the last 250 years, they are that crime and punishment remain fundamentally political and cultural matters, that there has undoubtedly been substantial change over the centuries, but that changes take place at paces and for reasons which are hard to capture in over-simplified narratives. Another overall conclusion is that people, as well as politicians, have played surprising roles in both crime and punishment over the centuries, and that popular opinions—as much as criminological theories—have had profound influence upon the criminal justice system which has emerged in the last two centuries. Thanks to the continued availability of historical sources, there is still much scope for research to be conducted into the history of crime and punishment.

QUESTIONS FOR DISCUSSION

1 To what extent can court records from the eighteenth and early nineteenth centuries (including those of the Old Bailey) be regarded as reliable evidence of crime and punishment in that era?

2 Discuss E.P. Thompson's theory of the 'moral economy' with reference to social and protest crime in the late eighteenth and early nineteenth centuries.

3 What were the effects of changing criminal justice practices in the nineteenth century upon the role of victims of crime?

4 Identify and discuss the causes and the consequences of the reform of the 'bloody code' in the early nineteenth century.

5 Critically examine the concept of a 'modern penal complex' as applied to criminal justice in England and Wales in the early twentieth century.

GUIDE TO FURTHER READING

Emsley, C. (2009) *Crime and Society in England, 1750-1900*. Harlow: Pearson.

Godfrey, B. (2005) *Crime and Justice, 1750-1950*. Collumpton: Willan.
These textbooks both provide an excellent introduction to the history of crime.

Archer, J. (2000) *Social Unrest and Popular Protest in England 1780-1840*. Cambridge: Cambridge University Press.
This is a succinct summary of research surrounding questions concerning social class, protest and crime.

Morris, N. and Rothman, D. (1995) *The Oxford History of the Prison: the Practice of Punishment in Western Society*. New York: Oxford University Press.
This contains several chapters of interest on prisons and related topics, including one on transportation to Australia.

D'Cruze, S. and Jackson, L. (2009) *Women, Crime & Justice in England since 1660*. Basingstoke: Palgrave Macmillan.

The topic of gender and crime is admirably covered in this history text.

Shore, H. (2002) *Artful Dodgers: Youth and Crime in Nineteenth-Century London*. Woodbridge: Boydell.

This monograph is a useful account of an important aspect of the history of crime.

WEB LINKS

http://www.legislation.gov.uk/

This website gives the original and the latest versions of Acts of Parliament mentioned in this chapter, including the Freedom of Information Act 2000 and the Vagrancy Act 1824.

http://hansard.millbanksystems.com/

Hansard is the historical record of all debates held in the UK parliament. It is an invaluable source for anyone researching the development of public policies including those for criminal justice.

http://www.oldbaileyonline.org/

As a 'fully searchable database' of criminal cases heard at London's Central Criminal Court between 1674 and 1913, this is an invaluable tool for researchers. However, it should be noted that London crime and criminal justice cannot be taken as representative of the country as a whole.

http://www.llgc.org.uk/index.php?id=criminals

A digitized register of criminals in a Welsh county 1897–1933, this collection includes unique photographs of offenders.

http://booth.lse.ac.uk/

This archive material from the papers of Charles Booth (1840–1916) who undertook extensive social investigations in late-nineteenth-century London includes his police notebooks.

http://www.nationalarchives.gov.uk/

A lot of useful resources can be accessed through the home page of the National Archives (NA), including registers of archival sources across the UK, the NA's own catalogue and some digitised sources. There are also guides for researchers on many topics including courts, trials and punishments.

REFERENCES

Archer, J. (1999) 'Poaching Gangs and violence: the Urban-Rural Divide in Nineteenth-century Lancashire', *British Journal of Criminology* 39, 1: 25–38.

Bailey, V. (1997) 'English Prisons, Penal Culture, and the Abatement of Imprisonment, 1895–1922', *Journal of British Studies* 36, 2: 285–324.

Bloch, M. (1954) *The Historian's Craft*. Manchester: Manchester University Press.

Devereaux, S. (1999) 'The Making of the Penitentiary Act, 1775–1779', *Historical Journal* 42, 2: 405–33.

Emsley, C. (1996) *The English Police: a Political and Social History*. London: Longman.

Emsley, C. (2005) *Crime and Society in England, 1750–1900*. Harlow: Pearson.

Foucault, M. (1977) *Discipline and Punish: the Birth of the Prison*. London: Penguin.

Garland, D. (1985) *Punishment and Welfare*. Aldershot: Gower.

Gatrell, V.A.C. (1996) *The Hanging Tree: Execution and the English People, 1770–1868*. Oxford: Oxford University Press.

Godfrey, B. (2008) 'Changing Prosecution Practices and their Impact on Crime Figures, 1857–1940', *British Journal of Criminology*, 48: 171–89.

Gray, D. (2007) 'The Regulation of Violence in the Metropolis: the Prosecution of Assault in the Summary Courts, c.1780–1820', *London Journal* 32, 1: 75–87.

Handler, P. (2005) 'Forgery and the End of the Bloody Code in Early Nineteenth Century England', *Historical Journal* 48, 3: 683–702.

Hughes, R. (2003) *The Fatal Shore: a History of the Transportation of Convicts to Australia, 1787–1868.* London: Vintage.

Ingram, M. (1984) 'Rough Music and the "Reform of Popular Culture" in Early Modern England', *Past and Present,* 105: 79–113.

King, P. (1989) 'Gleaners, Farmers and the Failure of Legal Sanctions in England, 1750–1850', *Past and Present*, 125: 116–50.

King, P. (2000) *Crime, Justice and Discretion in England 1740–1820.* Oxford: Oxford University Press.

Langbein, J. (1983) 'Albion's Fatal Flaws', *Past and Present*, 98: 96–120.

Langbein, J. (2003) *The Origins of Adversary Criminal Trial.* Oxford: Oxford University Press.

Lea, J. (1999) 'Social Crime Revisited', *Theoretical Criminology*, 3: 307–25.

Lewis, F. (1988) 'The Cost of Convict Transportation from Britain to Australia, 1796–1810', *Economic History Review* Second Series, XLI, 4: 507–24.

Logan, A. (2006) 'Professionalism and the impact of England's first women justices, 1920–1950', *Historical Journal* 49, 3: 833–50.

Marx, K (1842/1975) 'Debates on the law of the theft of wood' in Karl Marx and Frederic Engels: *Collected Works* (Volume One). London: Lawrence and Wishart.

McGowen, R. (1986) 'A Powerful Sympathy: Terror, the Prison and Humanitarian Reform in Early Nineteenth Century Britain', *Journal of British Studies*, 25, 3: 312–34.

McGowen, R. (1999) 'From Pillory to Gallows: the Punishment of Forgery in the Age of the Financial Revolution', *Past and Present*, 165: 107–40.

Melossi, D. and Pavarini, M. (1981) *The Prison and the Factory.* London: Macmillan.

Rock, P. (2004) 'Victims, Prosecutors and the State in Nineteenth Century England and Wales', *Criminal Justice* 4, 4: 331–54.

Slater, S. (2012) 'Street Disorder in the Metropolis, 1905–39', *Law, Crime and History* 1, 1: 59–91, available at http://www.pbs.plymouth.ac.uk/solon/journal.htm.

Storch, R. (1981) 'The Plague of Blue Locusts: police reform and popular resistance in Northern England 1840–57' in M. Fitzgerald *et al.* (eds) *Crime and Society: Readings in History and Theory.* London: Routledge.

Taylor, H. (1999) 'Forging the Job: a Crisis of Modernization or Redundancy for the Police in England and Wales, 1900–39', *British Journal of Criminology* 39, 1: 113–35.

Thompson, E.P. (1968) *The Making of the English Working Class.* Harmondsworth: Penguin.

Thompson, E.P. (1991) *Customs in Common.* Pontypool: Merlin.

Treadwell, J., Briggs, D., Winlow, S., and Hall, S. (2013) 'Shopocalypse Now: Consumer Culture and the English Riots of 2011', *British Journal of Criminology* 51, 1: 1–17.

3 What do crime statistics tell us?

Tim Hope

INTRODUCTION

Other chapters in this book explore the meaning of the concept of 'crime' (see Chapter 1). In this chapter, the definition of 'crime' refers to a category of human acts that are proscribed by law and for which those responsible, if found guilty, are liable to some form of judicial punishment. The custodian of these kinds of acts is, of course, the State. In this sense, then, crime is a 'property' of the State (Christie, 2004). So, too, are 'statistics'. Dictionary definitions point to the origins of the term, even before the adoption of numerical systems of accounting, as arising out of the act of administration and government itself. This is true still: even though other, non-government bodies can collect statistics (Statistics Commission, 2006), and alternative analyses and interpretations of statistics are possible, there is a real sense that 'statistics' are the 'arithmetic of politics' (Dorling and Simpson, 1999). In contemporary society, statistics have become an important medium of governance—simultaneously informing and obscuring the various risks, including crime, around which we increasingly orient our daily lives and from which we expect our governments to protect us (Rose, 1999). Thus, both 'crime' and 'statistics', as they will be discussed in this chapter, are bound-up fundamentally with the operation and function of the State itself. Crime statistics, then, are *the accounts* that the State compiles of the actions of its agencies concerning those acts which the law proscribes.

BACKGROUND

Broadly two views are held about crime statistics within criminology. First there is what we might call the *realist* view. This sees official records as an indicator of the true level of crime in society. Thus, while there may be a 'dark figure'—crime which is not recorded or reported—realists believe it remains possible to develop our statistics so that they aspire to, even if they never achieve, an accurate reflection of the underlying extent, patterns and trend of crime. Experience suggests that some measures—for example crimes recorded by the police—can be inaccurate and subject to biases of various kinds, some of which will be discussed later in this chapter. Other measures and estimation techniques have emerged, for example, *crime victimization surveys*, which promise improvements in accuracy and corrections of bias. There are two broad traditions of use. First, *administration*, where crime statistics provide government (and the electorate) with information that assists in the deployment and management of criminal justice resources. As the *Review of Crime Statistics for England and Wales*, one of several recent reviews of crime statistics notes: 'there is general agreement that the overarching purpose for collecting information on crime should be to reduce the impact of crime on society' (Home Office, 2000: 9). Second, *research*, which sees social statistics as 'social facts'—that is, indicators of the condition of society as a whole—the analysis of which reveals something about how society operates. The progenitor of this tradition is Emile Durkheim's classic nineteenth-century study of suicide (Durkheim, 1979).

Against the realist position, is the *constructivist* perspective stemming largely from Cicourel's study examining the organization of juvenile justice in an American city (Cicourel, 1968). Observing how officials and others saw the process, he concluded that official statistics could be understood only with reference to the ways the agencies collecting them carried out their work. In this view, official statistics tell us as much, if not more, about the organization that produces them than about the phenomenon—crime—they are supposed to measure. Because they are *social constructs*, statistics do not give a clear or objective view of the phenomena they purport to measure because they confuse details about crime with the way the relevant authorities react and deal with it.

Should the student of criminology bother with crime statistics at all? At one extreme, there are those who still believe that crime statistics can be used (more or less) as an objective measure of crime levels in society and wish to use crime statistics as true measures of the level of crime, or, even the moral health of society. While the public, media, and politicians may believe this, few criminologists take such an uncritical view of official statistics. Nevertheless they continue to be used in many studies, largely for *pragmatic* reasons. The questions asked of them are interesting and important. For example, how much crime is there, has it increased or declined? No more reliable ways are available and for all their faults, official statistics of crime are public records, whose collection is funded by the State. They have a comprehensive, standard coverage, and can be related to other official statistics, particularly those from the national Census of Population to provide profiles of crime in different communities. Criminologists will continue to use them in their work, not least in order critically to examine the ways in which they are used by governments—for example in the accounts they give to the public about trends in crime or as tools for measuring police performance.

At the other extreme are those who see official crime statistics as flawed, not just because they cannot measure crime separately from the actions of the agencies producing them, but because important social and cultural processes involved in defining and reacting to crime are not amenable to statistical measurement and analysis. In this view, quantitative measurement of cultural definitions, meanings and linguistic tropes about crime is impossible. Rather, the analysis of such phenomena has its own logic and canon of procedures that are inimical to the mathematically-based logic of statistics and risk analysis.

Criminology students must make up their own minds where they stand on these issues—after a careful reading of this and other chapters in this book! The stance taken here is pragmatic. It will be realistic enough to say that there are phenomena 'out there' that are capable of being measured in principle and that the careful use of statistics can illuminate many issues that may not be grasped properly by more subjective approaches. However, it also recognizes the constructivist argument that the various phenomena of crime in society cannot be divorced from the practices of the agencies that define, report and record them. This is an important area of social enquiry itself. If, philosophically, crime cannot be divorced from its control, statistics nevertheless can be used to illuminate the interplay between the two or, at the very least, the operation of control itself. Nor is this merely an academic exercise. The more politicians, government, and the media use and cite statistics in justification of their actions, or lack thereof, the more citizens—including students of criminology—will need to know about how those statistics are produced and how reliable they are as a basis for political decisions; especially if democracy is to work properly. Thus, this chapter will offer a brief 'consumers' guide' to some of the key issues concerning the construction of crime statistics.

Nature of crime statistics

What is a crime statistic?

This chapter will focus on one of the most popular of crime statistics—the *crime rate*—that gives an index of crime occurring in a particular jurisdiction for a specific time period. Police records have been the main source for constructing crime rates. However governments now look to other ways of collecting crime statistics—most significantly by commissioning large-scale crime victimization surveys. There are broadly two reasons for this. First, a realization that the various potential biases in agency records (discussed later) result in an inaccurate measure of the extent, scale and pattern of crime, causing particular problems when comparing jurisdictions, estimating trends over time, or explaining patterns and trends. Second, reliable statistics have become more important as governments assess the performance of criminal justices agencies, particularly the police, whose purpose is seen increasingly as a 'service' to the community, especially to reduce crime and provide security and protection for citizens (see, for example, Home Office, 2003).

As with all 'statistics' there are three different components or uses. These are:

- *Counts*—the number of offences occurring within a given referent of time and space—for example, the number of burglaries in England and Wales per year.
- *Frequencies*—how the counts of criminal offences are distributed amongst a population—for example, how many people are victims, and how frequently are they victimized?
- *Rates*—typically expressing the count of offences as a ratio of another population characteristic; for example, the rate of burglary per 10,000 households of the County of Staffordshire.

The following sections of this chapter will look, first, at the social and political context of statistics concerning 'the crime rate', and subsequently at each of these three 'statistics' in turn. Particular attention is paid to how they are defined and how their measurement is constructed.

REVIEW QUESTIONS

1 What is the difference between a 'realist' and a 'constructivist' view of crime statistics? What is the approach adopted here?

2 What are the three different components of a crime statistic?

What are the main types of crime statistics?

There are a number of different sources of crime data. The main official statistics are police-recorded crime and surveys.

Official statistics of police-recorded crime

In England and Wales police-recorded crime is composed of categories of crime that are outlined in the Home Office Counting Rules and known as 'notifiable offences'. These include: violence against the person, sexual offences, robbery, burglary, theft, handling stolen goods, fraud and forgery, criminal damage, drug offences, and 'other offences'. The coverage of available crime statistics is limited by the omission of most 'summary offences' from the published recorded data (in England and Wales) and the omission of data from certain specific police forces such as the British Transport Police (although the Smith Review, Home Office (2006), recommended that these should be included). Over time, there have been changes in the way that police have been asked to record crime such as amendments to the Counting Rules introduced in 1998 and the introduction of the National Crime Recording Standard (NCRS) in April 2002. The NCRS requires that the police record a crime if 'the circumstances as reported amount to a crime as defined by law and there is no credible evidence to the contrary'. The record is intended to stands unless evidence emerges to disprove that a crime has occurred. The NCRS was introduced to ensure standardization of police recording practices between types of complainant, types of incident, and within and between police forces. In Scotland, police-recorded crime statistics are more highly aggregated than those in England and Wales. Instead of the NCRS, Scotland has the Scottish Crime Recording Standard (SCRS), designed to reflect its distinct legal system. Northern Ireland adheres to the NCRS and follows similar principles to those in England and Wales.

In England and Wales, historically, the Home Office published an official, annual series of *Criminal Statistics*, though this was discontinued following a review (Home Office, 2000). Until 2012 a more limited range of police recorded statistics were presented as an annual 'snapshot of crime' in the *Home Office Statistical Bulletin* series, along with other statistical information, mostly from the British Crime Survey (BCS) (see later). In 2012, following a further review of the crime statistics by the Coalition government (Government Statistical Service (GSS) 2011), responsibility was transferred from the Home Office to the Office for National Statistics (ONS) (see also Chapter 19). Published summaries of official crime statistics are already available on the Internet (http://www.crimestatistics.org.uk) and, in future, the statistical information reported to the Home Office may also become available directly via the Internet. The ONS publishes a *User Guide to Crime Statistics for England and Wales* that provides a good description of the range and bases of the statistics published in this report (ONS, 2012).

Crime Victimization Surveys

There are a number of crime victimization surveys (CVS) within the UK. The largest of these is the BCS which in April 2012, was renamed the Crime Survey for England and Wales (CSEW) because since the mid-1980s it has only covered England and Wales, though here we will continue to refer to it as the BCS, reflecting its uses and findings over the past 30 years (Hough and Maxfield, 2007). This survey is currently annual, asking approximately 45,000 adults in private households about their experience of and attitudes to crime.[1] It asks about crimes the individuals have experienced within the last year, including those *that were not reported* to the police. This provides estimates of victimization at police service level and allows more robust estimates of those crimes less likely to be reported. While their original purpose was to provide an alternative means of estimating the amount of crime occurring (by finding out about unrecorded crime), surveys such as the BCS are also used increasingly as a means for government to assess the performance of criminal justice agencies, particularly the police (Allen, 2007).

The BCS also includes questions relating to attitudes to crime, such as the level of worry about crime, measures taken to avoid victimization and experiences of criminal justice agencies, although these are not all included in every sweep. It provides:

- a measure of crime victimization, independent of police-recorded crime statistics;
- a means of 'auditing' police-recorded crime statistics. Without the BCS it would not be possible to distinguish between trends in police figures generated by changes in crime and the public's propensity to report crime to the police, as opposed merely to changes in police recording practices;
- data on people's perceptions of crime such as worry and fear; and
- data to help policy makers identify those groups most likely to be at risk of crime.

Scotland was included in the first BCS, but since then, the Scottish Crime and Victimisation Survey has been independent of the BCS. Recent surveys—re-designated as the Scottish Crime and Justice Survey—now involve continuous data collection, with a much larger, rolling monthly sample of adults across Scotland that, as with BCS, involves adults over 16.

Other surveys have included:

- a Commercial Victimisation Survey run in 1994 and 2002. This survey involves crime against small and medium-sized retail and manufacturing premises in England and Wales; and
- the Offending Crime and Justice Survey, which examines the extent of offending, anti-social behaviour and drug use among the household population, and in particular, among young people aged from 10 to 25.

Administrative records

Police forces also collate and store statistical information on crime as a by-product of their administrative and operational activities. The police record information as it is reported to them by the public, via the emergency telephone system (the *999* number in the UK) and from other sources, including their own officers. Incoming calls for police service and assistance are usually logged as *incident data*, while attending and investigating officers may compile *crime reports* from them. As noted, some of this information is extracted, and recorded as notifiable offences. Police incident and crime report data are not usually published, though they may sometimes be accessible on request for research purposes (see later in this chapter) but were included in the 2011 review of crime statistics (Government Statistical Service, 2011) which showed that the number of reports of antisocial behaviour and other 'incidents' recorded by the police significantly outnumbered the official count of crime (see Chapter 19).

What are the purposes of crime statistics?

The uses to which governments put crime statistics have changed considerably. Whereas in the past official crime statistics were part of a system of national accounts of the condition of British society, now they are also used to manage the performance of criminal justice agencies and partnerships. This specifically instrumental definition of the use of crime statistics is a relatively new one, largely emerging as part of a political modernization agenda, and reflecting the policy priorities of the government, including police reform.

Understanding the purposes for which the public use crime statistics is difficult. One of the recent reviews of crime statistics (Statistics Commission, 2006; see also Fox *et al.*, 2006) suggested that private citizens might use them to:

- assess the performance of the authorities in tackling crime;
- understand policy development by government;
- understand the causes of crime, victimization and offending;
- determine personal risk and susceptibility to crime; and
- obtain information of criminal activity in their area.

The review suggested that although the public have some understanding of crime statistics, generally they do not keep abreast of crime trends. Further, it concluded statistics were only one of a number of sources of information the public used when making everyday decisions and they were not used to make precise calculations of crime risks. Indeed, although the public may use crime-related statistics to assess the performance of local agencies, or to decide whom to vote for, assessments of victimization risk are also strongly influenced by local factors. For example, anecdotal 'evidence' from friends and family is more likely to influence these perceptions than crime figures, which are not always robust, and which do not facilitate easy comparison of one area with another.

REVIEW QUESTIONS

1 How do police-recorded statistics differ from those obtained from crime victimization surveys?

2 How has the government's use of crime statistics changed?

3 How do the public perceive and use crime statistics?

Counting crime

What is counted?

Many things that people experience, witness or perpetrate could be classified as crime. Often people do not realize that these incidents are crimes. The retort 'I'll get you!' during a heated exchange between two irate neighbours could end up as an offence of 'threatening behaviour'. People may not want incidents to be considered as crimes, or more particularly do not want the police to intervene in what they see as their 'private' disputes, even if there is good reason that they should. For instance, the abused woman in a domestic violence scenario may be too afraid to report her abusive partner to the police while the abuser will not want his abusive behaviour to be known about or punished. Sometimes, people are not even aware they have been victims of crime—after all, the most successful confidence tricks or Internet scams are those where the victim remains completely oblivious, even while their pockets or bank accounts are being pillaged.

The police have little knowledge about most crime at the time it occurs and without victims or witnesses telling them about it they will remain ignorant. Thus, the BCS found that the police were present at the scene in only about 3 per cent of incidents experienced by respondents. Generally, there are more incidents and events in people's everyday lives that might warrant a police response than are ever brought to their attention.

Not only is there a 'dark figure' of unreported crime, but there is also a 'grey figure' (Bottomley and Pease, 1986)—the disparity between estimates of what members of the public say they report to the police and the number of crimes actually recorded. The difference is considerable. For instance, from estimates from the 1999 BCS, of the two-fifths of incidents experienced by victims that they said they had reported to the police, only slightly over half appear to have been recorded in the returns made by police to government (Kershaw *et al.*, 2000). Thus, there are two sources of 'bias' in police-recorded counts of crime—*the propensity of the public to report crime* and *the practice of the police in recording it.*

REVIEW QUESTIONS

1 What are the 'dark' and 'grey' figures of crime?

2 What are the three sources of statistical information about crime?

3 Who oversees crime statistics; who controls access to them?

Recording incidents as criminal offences

The police decision on whether to record a reported incident as an offence is a *negotiated outcome*, with the police balancing a number of considerations, usually with some permitted (and some acquired) discretion. There is only one reason for them to record a complaint or reported incident as a crime—*prima facie* evidence that an offence might have been committed—but there are a variety of reasons why the police do *not* record incidents.

Variation in discretionary police recording practice has most often been seen as the main influence on disparities in the recording (as distinct from the reporting) of crime.

The major overhaul of the Counting Rules that occurred in 1998 was an effort to improve the correspondence between numbers and types of incidents and recorded offences. Some of the disparity in recording is also due to different approaches taken when incidents are reported. The *Review of Crime Statistics for England and Wales* (Home Office, 2000) reported two distinct models of recording practice: a *prima facie* model which records as crime the details of all reported allegations; and an *evidential* model which subjects complaints to some investigative selection prior to recording (Burrows *et al.*, 2000); the former tending to produce a greater number of recorded crimes than the latter. In an example of how these approaches affected the counting of crime, Farrington and Dowds (1985) showed that the much greater crime rate of Nottinghamshire, compared to its surrounding counties, was due largely to zealous, *prima facie* recording of incidents, including the counting of series of milk-bottle thefts from door-steps as separate incidents! Efforts to standardize recording practices amongst police forces resulted in the implementation of the *National Crime Recording Standard* (NCRS), including further amendment of the Counting Rules, with effect from April 2002.

There are a number of reasons why a reported incident may or may not be recorded:

- The police decide there is insufficient evidence that a crime has occurred. For example, a mobile phone reported stolen may have been lost.

- There is little chance of an offender being detected and prosecuted successfully.

- The victim (complainant) withdraws the complaint and thus will not be willing to give evidence in court.

- The police exercise discretion in the recording of incidents as a result of police cultural prejudices and biases against certain types of complainant or complaint (Reiner, 1992).

- The police feel an obligation to record crime because other parties may require an official recognition of an incident. For instance, insurance companies usually require victims to report incidents to the police as a condition of meeting their claims regarding loss of property. Thus of BCS burglaries with loss reported to the police 98 per cent are recorded. In contrast, for attempted and no loss burglaries only 44 per cent are recorded.

- The police are under pressure to record, or not, as part of their individual or organizational performance (Bottomley and Pease, 1986). Until 2009, the government set targets for crime reduction, and used crime statistics as a measure of 'performance'. The 'clear-up rate', the proportion of recorded crimes detected or otherwise dealt with, also constitutes a measure of police performance, and has been criticized because it can also be manipulated through various recording practices (McCabe and Sutcliffe, 1978).

- The police may employ a range of 'covert' practices to massage the figures (for many reasons, including those noted earlier), generally known as cuffing (Bottomley and Coleman, 1981), where complaints are deliberately not recorded.

- Offenders frequently want their admissions to be 'taken into consideration'—that is, as TICs—in the hope of more lenient treatment in sentencing. Sometimes these admissions just affect the rate of detection. Sometimes, though, when offenders admit to committing offences that have not been recorded hitherto (known as *secondary detections*), they result in increasing the number of recorded offences as well.

Comparing counts of incidents and offences

As discussed earlier, for many years British police have kept a record—or log—of incidents attended by officers. Typically, calls for police service are received at a call centre, details taken, and available police officers assigned to investigate. Having conducted their enquiries and taken necessary action, the officers will confirm the nature of the incident, and if there is evidence that a crime has been committed, they will complete a *crime report* which will be entered onto the police crime recording information system. Numbers or details of incidents attended by the police are not usually published. Counts of *notifiable offences* are extracted from the police forces' crime recording systems and returned to the Home Office for processing, appearing in aggregate form in *Home Office Statistical Bulletins* (see the earlier discussion of police recorded crime and official statistics).

The computerization of police records and information systems has helped to provide a picture of how the profile of 'incidents' reported to and/or attended by the police matches the profile of 'crime' recorded by them. As the 2011 review of crime statistics (GSS, 2011) showed there is nothing like a perfect match. Yet what a comparison of incidents and crimes reveals is not whether the police are providing a good or bad service as the contrast between police work as a service to the public, and police work in the control of crime.

Basic differences between incident-based and crime-based profiles of police work were illustrated in a study (Hope *et al.*, 2001) carried out in an English county, comprising some 1.4 million residents, covering (for England) a large geographic area, with a representative spread of communities—from affluent to poor, including ethnic minorities—and land uses—from the densely urban to the sparsely rural. As part of the research project, access was given to data from both the incident and crime information systems for the calendar year 2000. In the research, the numbers of reported incidents and the number of recorded crimes were counted. Comparing incidents and crimes required grouping the two into broadly similar categories. This was not always easy, nor exactly equivalent, other than within broad classes. Nevertheless, the results are illustrated in Table 3.1.

Table 3.1 shows that there were over six times more incidents than there were recorded crimes. Just over a half of all reported incidents did not have crime equivalents, consisting

Table 3.1 Incidents reported ('calls') and notifiable offences ('crimes') recorded by an English County Constabulary for the year 2000 (percentages)

	Incidents	Crimes	Ratio of incidents to crimes
Nuisances and conflicts	24	30	4.9
Violence	9	9	6.0
Burglaries and thefts	14	58	1.5
Other incidents	41	–	
Other crimes	–	3	109.0
Roads and related incidents	11	–	
Total Number	733,695	118,503	6.2

Note: These records were compiled for a period before the changes brought in by the National Crime Recording Standard, implemented in April 2002.
Source: Hope *et al.* (2001).

of a wide and diverse range of incidents, accidents, other emergencies, and duties such as road traffic matters where a police presence was needed. Yet, even when comparing recorded crimes with incidents that could be construed as criminal, the respective profiles of incidents and recorded crimes differed quite considerably. It is possible that some of this disparity could have been due to multiple calls from the public about the same offence. Nevertheless, different types of criminal incident had different levels of 'excess' reporting, relative to the number of crimes recorded. Thus, anti-social and violent criminal incidents involving people, including incidents of nuisance, conflict and violence, comprised the majority of calls from the public to the police for incidents where an offence might have been committed (that is, 69 per cent of all possibly criminal incidents), while acquisitive property crime (largely burglaries and thefts of various kinds) comprised the majority of recorded crimes (58 per cent). Anti-social and violent incidents exceeded recorded crimes by a ratio of five reported incidents to one recorded crime, while acquisitive incidents exceeded crimes by only one-and-a-half to one. Thus, the profiles of public reporting and police recording differed both in volume and type of incident.[1]

As already noted, the police may be responding to the nature of the incident in question but they may also be responding to the different needs of the community. For example, concern about 'anti-social behaviour'—including noisy neighbours or young people scuffling in public—may be made by residents whose primary concern is for the police to control the situation by getting them to stop the upsetting behaviour. In these situations, an arrest (and crime report) may be the last resort when other means have failed. In sum, comparing the different profiles of incident and recorded crime statistics tells us something about the extent of crime, the public's demands on the police service, and the way in which the police respond to such demands.

REVIEW QUESTIONS

1 What are the reasons for the police under-recording crime?

2 What are meant by the 'prima facie' and 'evidential' approaches to recording crime?

3 To what kinds of incident are the police called most frequently? How does the profile of incidents differ from the profile of recorded crime?

Reporting crime to the police

We have seen how the recorded statistics of crime might be affected by police practices and discretion. Yet, since people do not report all the crime victimization they experience (see later), it is possible that some of the differences in official crime rates between communities, or their trends over time, reflect changes in the propensity to report. As noted earlier, crime victimization surveys, such as the BCS or the US National Crime Victimization Survey (NCVS), have developed as alternative measures of crime. Yet, if crime victimization surveys aim to give a more accurate estimate than recorded statistics, how accurate are they in turn?

Broadly, their accuracy depends upon two things: the *coverage* of the survey; and its accuracy of *measurement*.

Coverage of household crime victimization surveys

Crime victimization surveys may not measure all crime for the following reasons:

- They are surveys of *private individuals*, who are asked to report on both their personal crime victimization experiences and on property crime victimization suffered by their household. Hence crimes against *organizations*—firms, retailers, local authorities, hospitals and educational establishments—are not included.

- They are random samples of the population and may have *sample-selection biases*. Until recently the BCS did not interview individuals under the age of 16 and so the victimization experiences of this significant population group were missed. Current coverage of this group is still described as 'experimental'. It only interviews people in their homes, thus failing to reach both the homeless and those living in institutions. Furthermore certain population groups have lifestyles that lead them to be at home less than others, for example young people and inner-city dwellers. Telephone interviews, though cheaper than face-to face interviews, obviously relies on widespread telephone ownership.[2] Nowadays, the BCS uses a postal address system for sampling. Until 1992 surveys used the Register of Electors; however, non-registration to avoid the 'Poll Tax' during the 1980s and increasing non-voting led to the Electoral Register ceasing to be a reliable sampling frame. And some people, for a variety of reasons, simply refuse to take part. Unfortunately, research suggest that all these population groups tend to have substantial experience of crime victimization, thus leading to an under-estimation of crime in victimization surveys, and a biased profile of victimization risk for the population as a whole.

- Measurement of offences—because surveys rely upon the self-report method, they may not include offences where: victims are *unaware* they have been victimized (as in the case of some frauds, or crimes committed against them by corporate bodies); and so-called *victimless crimes*, such as prostitution or drug misuse.

- Rarity of crime—crime victimization is a relatively rare event, experienced by few people in the population at any one time (see the section on frequency). Thus, to obtain sufficient counts of victims and offences for reliable statistical analysis, it is necessary to have large samples, and long(ish) recall periods. Hence only central governments (and occasionally local or regional governments) can afford to commission such surveys on a regular basis. In 2000, the Home Office increased the sample size of the BCS to around 45,000 partly in an attempt to obtain reliable estimates of crime for each of the 43 police service areas of England and Wales.

- Geographic clustering—crime is not distributed equally amongst communities; the majority of victims, and of offences, occur in relatively few areas (see the section on rates). Alongside their large scale, surveys also have to selectively sample particular areas—usually 'inner city' residential areas—in order to obtain large enough samples of victims. Unfortunately, this means that the sample can become less representative

Table 3.2 Frequency distributions of self-reported crime victimization

Recalled-frequency crime distributions, previous 12 months—British Crime Survey (2002/03)
General adult population (percentages)

	Proportion of Non-victims	Proportion of victims experiencing two or more incidents
Property		
Burglary—households	96.6	18
Vehicle-related theft—vehicle owning households	89.2	19
Violence		
Mugging	99.9	10
Stranger	98.4	21
Acquaintance	98.6	28
Domestic	99.4	45

Notes: Adults in the BCS are persons over 15 years of age.
Source: Simmons and Dodd (ed.) HOSB 07/03

Recalled-frequency domestic violence distributions, previous 12 months—British Crime
Survey (2001) Adult women (percentages)

	Proportion of Non-victims amongst adult women	Proportion of victims experiencing two or more incidents
Domestic violence—threat or force	95.8	72
Domestic force	96.6	68
—minor	97.4	63
—severe	98.4	73

Source: Walby and Allen (2004).
Taken from Hope (2007a).

of the population as a whole, who are mostly non-victims, living in lower crime areas (see Table 3.2). Those crime victimization surveys that employ face-to-face interviewing usually select their samples in geographically-clustered areas to reduce survey costs, such as the travelling time for interviewers. Generally, although the clustering of respondents can produce biased estimates—because people living near each other are often similar in terms of their socio-demographic profile—these biases can be handled by statistical correction. However, there remains the potential for bias if the survey's cluster selection method 'misses' the geographical clustering of groups at-risk of crime victimization.

Accuracy of measurement in crime surveys

This set of issues and biases arises from the process of interviewing.[3]

- *Knowledge of incidents*—the BCS interviews one respondent per household to answer questions both about personal experiences of victimization and those of other household members. However, respondents may not know about, and so will not report, the crime experiences of others.

- *Not telling*—there are various reasons for respondents not telling interviewers about crime victimization, including: *load and fatigue*—too many victimizations or too many questions may make them reluctant to tell all; *concealing*, for instance, if there is a personal relationship between the victim and the offender (as in domestic violence) because of feelings of shame, or fear of reprisal, or if the victim feels culpable or responsible for the incident in some way. Ensuring greater anonymity, sympathy and/or confidentiality during the interview may help reduce concealment (for instance, the use of Computer Assisted Personal Interviewing (CAPI) by laptop, with an element of anonymous self-completion, may have increased the BCS count of domestic violence).

- *Memory decay*—the more distant the event, the less likely respondents are to remember it.

- *Telescoping*—conversely, especially serious or worrying events which occurred some time ago (that is, outside the survey's recall period) may be brought forward in time because they remain a worrying memory from which victims may not have recovered fully.

- *Education*—surveys ask questions, and rely on people's understanding and memory. Education trains people in understanding and remembering (all those exams!); so, the more educated you are, the more likely you are to recall incidents, and also to cooperate fully with the interviewer.

- *Multiple and series incidents*—in order to make their counts comparable to official crime counts, surveys try to measure crime as discrete, unrelated, incidents, but for some victims—(of domestic violence for example)—their experience of crime is such a feature of their everyday lives that it is nearly impossible to separate instances of these crimes into discrete incidents.

- *Interview conditions*—who the interviewer is, where the interview takes place, whether others are present, what procedures of recording (for example, the CAPI example noted), ensuring confidentiality and so on, are all likely to produce different responses, greater or less recall, different admission rates, etc.

What do crime surveys tell us about the reporting of crime?

In official reports based on crime victimization survey data the intrinsic characteristics of *incidents* are used to explain the differential reporting of incidents. Comparisons of reporting rates for different offences (for example, Kershaw *et al.*, 2001), alongside analyses of victims' responses to questions about their decisions to report (Mayhew *et al.*, 1993), point to respondents' assessments of the seriousness or triviality of the offence, as well as to the more ambiguous responses of perceived police ineffectiveness[4] and the ability to deal with matters privately (Coleman and Moynihan, 1996) as possible explanations. Where applicable, considerations of loss and validation of insurance claims also influence reporting decisions. Although, motor vehicle insurance against theft as well as damage is compulsory in the UK, according to the 1996 British Crime Survey, victims of motor vehicle theft reported 97 per cent of incidents to the police, while only 36 per cent of attempted vehicle thefts were reported.

Another explanation points to the 'discriminatory' nature of reporting decisions applied by, and recording practices applied to, particular *types of complainant.* Observational research on police-public encounters has generally found person-based selectivity on the part of the police in their decisions to record complaints and allegations from and against particular types of people, including selective treatment of particular social groups such as young people, members of ethnic minorities, the unemployed and economically disadvantaged (Reiner, 1992; Black, 1980; Reiss, 1971). Yet it is difficult to distinguish between what Reiner terms 'discrimination'— 'a pattern of exercise of police powers which results in some social categories being overrepresented as targets for police action' (1992: 157)—and 'differentiation'—a disproportionate exercise of police powers against some social categories relative to their presence in the population. A general difficulty is that 'social' selectivity in the types of incident, and person, coming to police attention—for instance, young members of Black and Minority Ethnic (BME) groups being out on the streets—is confounded with the potential for 'institutional bias' in police culture and practice in the way they respond to persons coming to their attention particularly while on patrol, or having been called by 'worried residents'.

A difficulty for research is separating out the *general propensity* of different population groups to report crime to the police, even if they are witnesses rather than victims (which may be due to differences in their confidence in the police, or their sense of public duty, or community spirit), from the specific *need* to report crime because they have been a victim (where victims are seeking some kind of service, or are obliged to report by their insurers). The BCS only asks victims about their actual reporting of their current incidents reported in the survey and not the general population about its general propensities in reporting incidents to the police. Likewise, 'incident-tracking' studies which audit the crime recording process retrospectively pre-select from amongst incidents already reported to the police 'those which either definitely, *or might have,* incorporated allegations of crime' (Burrows *et al.*, 2000, original emphasis; see also Farrington and Dowds, 1985).

The greater disparity between calls and crimes for incidents of nuisance and disorder, than for incidents of acquisitive crime (see Table 3.1), may reflect differences between the reporting of incidents witnessed by members of the public and the reporting of crime experienced by victims. A study of victims of property crime, identified in the BCS, used statistical techniques to estimate general propensities to report crime by taking into account differences in risk of victimization as well as incident-specific characteristics (MacDonald,

2001). Having done this, the research still found that younger, male or unemployed victims were less likely, while people of Indian Subcontinent ethnic origin were more likely, to report their victimization to the police. Further, victims who had a low opinion of police efficacy were less likely, while those who were worried about burglary were more likely, to report incidents. It would seem, at least with regard to their own personally-experienced victimization, that members of the public exercise a degree of choice—albeit constrained—over their decision to call the police and that this may reflect their perceptions of the likely response of the police to them as well as their own need to call.

Overview of counting crime

Much of the attention paid to the reporting and recording of incidents has been concerned with the bias in the resulting data. This reflects a particular, instrumental way of viewing these figures; that is, as an index of a *real* phenomenon (crime) calling for a specific control response by the State. Yet, since most of the incidents in the official accounts would not come to the attention of the State without being initiated by private citizens, these figures also represent a *social construction*, the 'policing of communications about risk in late modern society' (Ericson and Haggerty, 1997: 70). Here, the public are communicating their needs to the police as much as the police are collating evidence on behalf of the State of the need for crime control. Thus a *crime rate*, rather than being simply a record of police activity, or an indicator of the demand for crime control, may actually represent the aggregated outcome of the interaction of two processes—the *invocation of police authority* by the public in respect of difficult and troubling incidents—and the *criminalization of incidents* through the application of the criminal law by the police in respect of those incidents. In their own ways, both recorded criminal statistics and the crime victimizaton surveys that seek to supplement them, are each the outcome of *dialogues* between the citizen and the State; as with all dialogues, they reflect both what is being said, and how it is being received.

REVIEW QUESTIONS

1 What are the factors that lead to unrepresentative (biased) results from sample surveys of crime victimization?

2 What are the factors that affect the accuracy of measurement in crime victimization surveys?

3 What are the kinds of reasons victims have for reporting crime to the police?

The frequency of crime victimization

Sample surveys of general populations such as the BCS generate *counts* of crime-victimization events experienced by their respondents. Naturally, tabulations of responses to such questions yield frequency distributions for the number of crime victimizations experienced by respondents over the recall period. Typically also, those experiencing one or more incidents are usually considered to be 'victims', and thus distinguished from non-victims (that is, people not reporting any incidents), while persons reporting more than one incident have come to be termed 'multiple victims' or, following Farrell and Pease (1993), 'repeat victims'. Because the surveys are representative samples, so also have these categories come to be thought of as capturing the crime victimization experiences of the general population. Since the surveys also ask a range of questions about respondents' background, experiences and so on, these questions have been correlated with crime victimization frequencies and, in turn, have been considered as proxies for causal antecedents, used to support, substantiate or test various explanatory theories of crime victimization.

When the sampled count data of self-recalled crime victimization are arranged as a frequency distribution, they invariably display two characteristics: first, that crime victimization seems to be a *rare event*—that is, the majority of the sampled population do not report victimization over the recall period; and that the population distribution is *over-dispersed*—that is, the sample variance exceeds the sample mean, for example, that there are more higher-frequency crime victims than would be expected (in comparison with an appropriate theoretical statistical distribution), or conversely, that there are more non-victims (zeros) than would be expected. Frequency distributions of BCS data, illustrated in Table 3.2, show that these characteristics appear across a variety of types of crime and types of victim. Although these frequency rates differ between crime types—with property crime at one end of the spectrum and domestic violence at the other—the survey data nevertheless suggest a common pattern of multiple victimization, ranging from a fifth of victims of burglary to around three-quarters of victims of domestic violence. The difficulty, however, lies in working out what are the actual social and behavioural processes that might be producing the observed frequency distributions. Essentially, that is a matter for theory and further empirical research, though comparing observed frequency distributions with theoretical statistical distributions can help to suggest clues for further investigation (see Hope, 2007a).

REVIEW QUESTIONS

1 What is a frequency distribution?

2 What is 'over-dispersion' and how are crime victimization frequencies 'over-dispersed'?

The rate of crime victimization

A *crime rate* is an attribute of a specific population (in Table 3.2 the populations are, respectively, all adults and adult women). Even so, the conventional idea of a crime rate—usually expressed as the number of crimes divided by the size of the population in the area in which the crimes were counted—may be misleading (Bottomley and Pease, 1986). While a population denominator may serve the useful purpose of comparing rates across jurisdictions of different population sizes (on the natural assumption that, other things being equal, the bigger the population the greater the number of crimes committed), this particular way of conceptualizing a crime rate may also mask other characteristics of the distribution of crime amongst populations. For instance, a programme of research work during the 1990s sought to 'unpack' other features of the crime victimization rate (Trickett *et al.*, 1992; 1995) by employing the heuristic idea of crime-flux (Hope, 1995). The simple idea behind the notion of crime-flux is that the crime rate—called the crime incidence rate—can be decomposed arithmetically into two other distinct rates. Thus:

(1) The crime *incidence* rate = number of crimes (C) ÷ number in population (P) = C/P.

(2) The crime *prevalence* rate = number of victims (V) ÷ number in population (P) = V/P.

(3) The crime *concentration* rate = number of crimes (C) ÷ number of victims (V) = C/V.

Therefore, the crime incidence rate = prevalence × concentration = (V/P) × (C/V) = C/P.

This conceptual apparatus promised to provide a basis for both understanding changes in crime rates and for focusing resources to reduce crime incident rates. It suggests that the incidence rate can be tackled by either reducing the crime prevalence or by reducing crime incidence (or both). Since statistical tests on data such as those illustrated in Table 3.2 suggests that there are fewer victims than would be expected if crime victimization was randomly distributed amongst the population, then it was supposed that concentrating crime prevention effort on those fewer number of victims upon whom victimization appears to be concentrated—so-called 'repeat victims'—would produce a considerable efficiency gain relative to a more general crime prevention effort aimed at both victims and non-victims (Farrell and Pease, 1993). So, it is possible that efforts to reduce crime concentration rates would bring about reductions in the overall crime (incidence) rate. This possibility was so attractive to policy-makers that the goal of reducing repeat victimization was developed by the Home Office as a key performance indicator for the police in England and Wales (Laycock, 2001). Nevertheless, while the BCS shows that crime rates in England and Wales rose to a peak in the mid-1990s, and have fallen subsequently, Figure 3.1 suggests that changes in national crime rates—such as the volume crime of domestic burglary—may have been driven chiefly by changes in prevalence rates—that is, the number of victims in the population. During the period, the rate of crime concentration has remained relatively stable, apparently exerting a negligible influence on the trend in the burglary incidence rate.

It is possible that the two components of the crime incidence rate may be measuring different phenomena: as illustrated in Table 3.2 while prevalence may measure the *rate of exposure* to crime victimization amongst the general population, concentration may measure the *frequency rate* of crime victimization to those so exposed. Both rates are likely to be related in two ways: first, the arithmetic definition of the concentration rate (C/V) comprises both the total number of victims (the denominator V) as well as the number of victimizations (the numerator C). It follows that change in the rate of repeat victimization (as measured by the concentration rate) can be influenced both by changes in the prevalence of victims *as well as* by victimization frequency. Second, as is clear from Table 3.2, the proportion of repeat victims in the population is very rare. So, for the incidence rate to be determined by the concentration rate, a decline in the concentration rate would have to be very substantial indeed to overtake the effect of a reduction

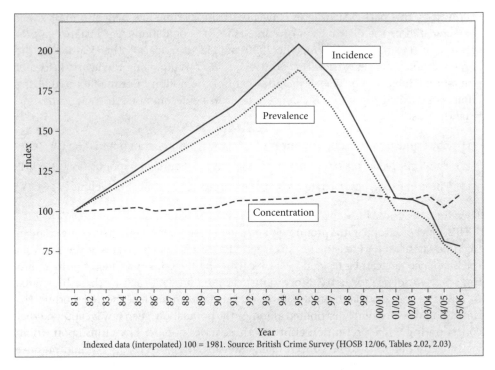

Figure 3.1 Burglary in England and Wales 1981–2006: incidence, prevalence, and concentration

Source: Hope T. (2007b) Copyright © 2007 by Criminal Justice Press. Used with permission by Lynne Rienner Publishers, Inc.

in the prevalence rate, since the latter may be simultaneously reducing the number of victims who would be exposed to further victimization. As there has been a reduction in the burglary incidence rate without a change in the concentration rate, the crime prevention benefits of targeting repeat victims may have turned out to have been less than policy-makers may have anticipated (Hope, 2007b).

REVIEW QUESTIONS

1 What is 'crime-flux'?

2 What are the two statistical components of the crime incidence rate?

3 Why might policy-makers be attracted to reducing 'repeat victimization', and would they be justified in targeting these victims for crime prevention?

CONCLUSION

A final point can be made about crime statistics from the data presented in the two previous sections. That is, the statistical analyses presented here are still essentially *descriptive*. Although they suggest intriguing areas of research enquiry, and practical investigation, they do not in themselves prove much about the various social processes that might be producing these observed statistical distributions. To undertake that task requires, initially, the formulation of hypotheses, drawn from theory, from which can be constructed *hypothetical models* that can then be tested against empirical data, and the results used subsequently to revise our theoretical, explanatory models. There are obvious dangers in leaving matters at the descriptive level without enquiring further as to what social-statistical processes might be producing the observed distributions—not least in drawing the wrong conclusions, as may have been the case with respect to the idea that crime prevention gains could be achieved by targeting repeat victims. Nevertheless, as Figure 3.1 suggests, hindsight may also help in solving hypotheses, which is another justification for maintaining regular statistical series. In sum, the production of reliable counts, frequencies and rates of crime is the start, rather than the end point, of statistical analysis.

To see crime statistics as a social construction in no way invalidates statistical research effort to investigate and explain them. The contemporary approach to the use of crime statistics differs from earlier uses. Rather than treating the statistics literally as an objective measure of a quantity called 'crime' that exists as a social fact 'out there'—what was once called in textbooks the *positivist* approach—the role of statistical analysis is to develop and test explanations (based upon hypothetical models) that best represent the observed (or sampled) data and which take into account, or treat as an object of statistical study in its own right, the various social processes that lie behind them, including how those statistics have been constructed socially. Crime statistics are the product of a dialogue between reporter and recorder, between citizen and State. Thus, rather than being an unfortunate set of biases that need to be circumvented, analysis of the various social processes leading to those biases tells us about the dialectic at the heart of criminology—the relationship between deviance and its regulation.

QUESTIONS FOR DISCUSSION

1 What does a comparison with either (a) police incident logs or (b) crime victimization surveys tell us about the reliability of official recorded crime statistics?

2 Do individual members of the public properly understand crime statistics, and should they care if they don't?

3 What does analysis of the frequency, and the rate, of crime victimization tell us about the distribution of crime?

GUIDE TO FURTHER READING

The following provide overviews of crime statistics and their relationship to criminology in Britain. They also contain information on other types of crime statistic not considered in this chapter:

Office for National Statistics (2012) *User Guide to Crime Statistics for England and Wales*. Newport: Office for National Statistics.

Maguire, M. (2007) 'Crime data and statistics', in M. Maguire, R. Morgan and R. Reiner (eds) *The Oxford Handbook of Criminology* (4th edn). Oxford: Oxford University Press.

Hough, M. and Maxfield, M. (2007) *Surveying Crime in the 21st Century: commemorating the 25th Anniversary of the British Crime Survey*. Crime Prevention Studies Volume 22. Monsey, NY, USA: Criminal Justice Press/Cullomptom, Devon, UK: Willan Publishing.

Statistics Commission (2006) *Crime Statistics: user perspectives*. Statistics Commission Report No. 30. London: Statistics Commission.

Bottomley, K. and Pease, K. (1986) *Crime and Punishment: Interpreting the Data*. Milton Keynes: Open University Press.

WEB LINKS

http://www.ons.gov.uk/ons

The Office for National Statistics now collates statistical information on crime and justice in England and Wales (an independent jurisdiction within the United Kingdom), containing data on crime, crime trends, criminal damage and anti-social behaviour, victims of crime, violent and sexual crime, criminal justice, police, and police personnel and resources. Links to this data can now be accessed under the 'Crime and Justice Theme'.

http://www.scotland.gov.uk/Topics/Statistics/Browse/Crime-Justice

Information on crime and justice statistics for Scotland (an independent jurisdiction within the United Kingdom).

http://www.ojp.usdoj.gov/bjs

Information on crime statistics for the USA from the Bureau of Justice Statistics, US Department of Justice.

http://www.europeansourcebook.org/

Information on crime statistics for European countries from the Council of Europe European Sourcebook of Crime and Criminal Justice Statistics.

http://www.unodc.org/unodc

Contains information on the United Nations Surveys on Crime Trends and the Operations of Criminal Justice Systems.

REFERENCES

Allen J. (2007) 'Survey assessments of police performance in the British Crime Survey.' In M. Hough and M. Maxfield (eds.) *Surveying Crime in the 21st Century*. Monsey, NY, USA: Criminal Justice Press/ Cullompton: Devon: Willan.

Black D. (1970) 'Production of Crime Rates'. *American Sociological Review*, 35: 733–48.

Black D. (1980) *The Manners and Customs of the Police*. New York: Academic Press.

Bottomley K. and Coleman C. (1981) *Understanding Crime Rates*. Farnborough: Gower.

Bottomley K. and Pease K. (1986) *Crime and Punishment: Interpreting the data*. Milton Keynes: Open University Press.

Burrows J., Tarling R., Mackie A., Lewis R. and Taylor G. (2000) *Review of Police Forces' Crime Recording Practices*. Home Office Research Study 204. London: Home Office.

Christie N. (2004) *A Suitable Amount of Crime*. London and New York: Routledge.

Cicourel A. (1968) *The Social Organisation of Juvenile Justice*. New York: Wiley.

Coleman C. and Moynihan J. (1996) *Understanding Crime Data: Haunted by the Dark Figure*. Buckingham: Open University Press.

Dorling D. and Simpson S. (1999) *Statistics in Society: the arithmetic of politics*. London: Arnold.

Durkheim E. (1979) *Suicide: A Study in Sociology*. London: Routledge and Kegan Paul.

Ericson R. V. and Haggerty K. D. (1997) *Policing the Risk Society*. Oxford: Clarendon Press.

Farrell G. and Pease K. (1993). Once Bitten, Twice Bitten: Repeat Victimisation and its Implications for Crime Prevention. Crime Prevention Unit Paper 46. London: Home Office.

Farrington D. and Dowds E. (1985) 'Disentangling criminal behaviour and police reaction.' In D. Farrington and J. Gunn (eds.) *Reactions to Crime*. Chichester: John Wiley.

Foster J. and Hope T. (1993) *Housing, Community and Crime: the impact of the Priority Estates Project*. Home Office Research Study No. 131. London: HMSO.

Fox C., Hope T. and Mackay S. (2006). 'The independent review of crime statistics'. *Community Safety Journal*, 5 (4): 4–12.

Government Statistical Service (2011). *National Statistician's Review of Crime Statistics*. Government Statistical Service.

H. M. Inspectorate of Constabulary (HMIC) (2000). *On the Record*, Thematic Inspection Report on Police Crime recording, the Police National Computer and Phoenix Intelligence System Data Quality. HM Inspector Keith Povey, July 2000.

Home Office (1967). *Report of the Departmental Committee on Crime Statistics*. (The Perks Committee). London: Home Office.

Home Office (2000) *Review of Crime Statistics: a discussion document*. London: Home Office.

Home Office (2003) *The National Policing Plan, 2004–2007*, November 2003. London: Home Office.

Home Office (2006) *Crime Statistics: an independent review carried out for the Secretary of State for the Home Department*. November 2006. London: Home Office.

Hope T. (1995) 'The Flux of Victimisation'. *British Journal of Criminology*, 35 (3): 327–42.

Hope T. (2007a). 'Theory and method: the social epidemiology of crime victims'. In S. Walklate (ed.) *Handbook of Victims and Victimology*. Cullompton, Devon: Willan.

Hope T. (2007b). 'The Distribution of Household Property Crime Victimisation: Insights from the British Crime Survey'. In M. G. Maxfield and M. Hough (eds.) *Surveying Crime in the 21st Century*. Crime Prevention Studies Vol. 22, Uffculme, Devon: Willan/New York: Criminal Justice Press.

Hope T., Karstedt S. and Farrall S. (2001) *The Relationship between Calls and Crimes*. Innovative Research Challenge Fund. Final Report to the Home Office.

Kershaw C., Budd, T,. Kinshott G., Mattinson J., Mayhew P. and Myhill A. (2000) *The 2000 British Crime Survey: England and Wales*. Home Office Statistical Bulletin 18/00. London: Home Office.

Kershaw C., Chivite-Matthews N., Thomas C. and Aust R. (2001) *The 2001 British Crime Survey: first results, England and Wales*. Home Office Statistical Bulletin 18/01. London: Home Office.

McCabe S. and Sutcliffe F. (1978) *Defining Crime: A Study of Police Decisions*. Oxford: Blackwell.

MacDonald Z. (2001) 'Revisiting the Dark Figure: a Microeconometric Analysis of the Under-reporting of Property Crime and its Implications'. *British Journal of Criminology*, 41: 127–49.

Mayhew P., Aye Maung N., and Mirrlees-Black C. (1993) *The 1992 British Crime Survey*. Home Office Research Study No. 132. London: HMSO.

Pease K. (1998) Repeat Victimisation: taking stock. Crime Detection and Prevention Series Paper 90. London: Home Office Police Research Group.

Reiner R. (1992) 'Police research in the United Kingdom: a Critical Review'. In M. Tonry and N. Morris (eds) *Modern Policing*. Crime and Justice: a review of research, Volume 15. Chicago: University of Chicago Press.

Reiss A. J. (1971) *The Police and the Public*. New Haven, Conn.: Yale University Press.

Simmons J. and Dodd T. (2003). '*Crime in England and Wales 2002/03*'. Home Office Statistical Bulletin, HOSB 07/03. London: Home Office.

Statistics Commission (2006). *Crime Statistics: user perspectives*. Statistics Commission Report No. 30. London: Statistics Commission.

Rose N. (1999) *Powers of Freedom: Reframing Political Thought*. Cambridge: Cambridge University Press.

Skogan W. G. (1986) 'Methodological issues in the study of victimisation'. In E. Fattah (ed) *From Crime Policy to Victim Policy*. Basingstoke: Macmillan.

Trickett A., Ellingworth D., Hope T. and Pease K. (1995) 'Crime Victimisation in the Eighties: Changes in Area and Regional Inequality'. *British Journal of Criminology*, 35 (3): 343–59.

Trickett A., Osborn D. R., Seymour J. and Pease K. (1992) 'What is Different About High Crime Areas?' *British Journal of Criminology*, 32: 81–9.

UKSA (2010). *Overcoming Barriers to Trust in Crime Statistics: England and Wales*. UK Statistics Authority.

1. The precise nature and scale of these disparities may have been peculiar to the police force in question, or have now changed as a result of Home Office effort to bring about consistent recording practice amongst police forces via the implementation (in April 2002) of the National Crime Recording Standard.

2. Although telephone ownership has greatly increased in Britain, poorer and more mobile households have tended not to have access to land-line telephones, at least until relatively recently; for this reason, the BCS has kept to face-to-face interviewing.

3. A good if somewhat dated guide to these methodological issues is Skogan (1986).

4. It is not clear from the wording of the question asked in the BCS whether this is a perception of police ineffectiveness *per se* or whether it is a perception restricted to the specific incident in question.

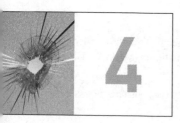

4

Theoretical criminology: a starting point

Keith Hayward and Wayne Morrison[1]

INTRODUCTION

Theoretical criminology is a vast, sprawling subject that straddles more than two centuries of intellectual thought and a range of academic disciplines. It is not therefore something that readily lends itself to summary in a short stand-alone chapter. Instead, our aim here is to offer those new to the subject a 'starting point', a very general (and hopefully gentle) introduction to some of the main criminological theories that have sought to explain and account for crime and criminality in the modern age. If this chapter is a starting point, then our first task must be to point the way forward to those interested in theorizing crime in more detail.

The following textbooks each provide excellent introductions to the rudiments of criminological theory:

Keith Hayward, Shadd Maruna and Jayne Mooney (2010) *Fifty Key Thinkers in Criminology*. London: Routledge.

This recent collection is an extremely useful resource in that it seeks to tell the story of criminological theory through the lives and times of the theorists themselves, whilst also setting the theories squarely against the historical and cultural backdrop in which they emerged. Cross-reference the key names mentioned in each of the following sections with the relevant entries in *Fifty Key Thinkers in Criminology*— this will help to bring the theories 'alive' through biographical narrative.

Robert Lilly, Francis Cullen and Richard Ball (2011) *Criminological Theory: Context and Consequences* (5th edn). London: Sage

John Tierney (2006) *Criminology: Theory and Context*. Harlow: Pearson Education

Mark Lanier and Stuart Henry (2004) *Essential Criminology*. Boulder, CO: Westview Press

Roger Hopkins-Burke (2009) *An Introduction to Criminological Theory* (3rd edn). Cullompton: Willan

Thomas Bernard, George Vold, Jeffrey Snipes, and Alexander Gerould (2010) *Vold's Theoretical Criminology* (6th edn). Oxford: Oxford University Press

David Downes and Paul Rock (2007) *Understanding Deviance*. Oxford: Oxford University Press

Katherine S. Williams (2008) *Criminology: A Textbook*. Oxford: Oxford University Press

Wayne Morrison (1995) *Theoretical Criminology: From Modernity to Postmodernism*. London: Cavendish

Claire Valier (2001) *Theories of Crime and Punishment*. London: Longman

If, after familiarizing yourself with some of these texts you feel you wish to explore the most up-to-date developments in the field of theoretical criminology, the following international journals provide some of the most exciting and cutting edge examples of contemporary criminological theory:

Theoretical Criminology: Creditably diverse in scope and content, *Theoretical Criminology* is a major interdisciplinary and international journal 'for the advancement of the theoretical aspects of criminological knowledge'.

Punishment and Society: A theoretical and empirical journal providing an 'interdisciplinary forum for research and scholarship dealing with punishment, penal institutions and penal control'.

Crime, Media, Culture: A cross-disciplinary journal that publishes research on the relationship between crime, criminal justice, media, and culture.

BACKGROUND

Perhaps the most important thing to highlight to those new to the subject is the overlapping nature of much criminological theorizing. Although our approach in this chapter is to break down theories into short, independent sections, it is important to recognize that criminological theory is not something that is easily compartmentalized. It is essential, therefore, to think critically about both the origins and the contemporary roles of criminological theories, rather than just repeating some learning of their basic outline/structure. One must also bear in mind that, whilst criminological theory is often viewed by many as an abstract, even esoteric enterprise (on this particular point see Valier, 2005), in reality its impact over the last century in areas such as crime control (see Chapters 19 and 20), juvenile justice (see Chapter 17), and public and penal policy (see Chapters 8, 24, and 25) has been profound and far-reaching. One need only think of the role played by criminological theory in such diverse policy initiatives as the 'welfarist' movement within youth justice during the 1970s, and the 'zero tolerance' policing phenomenon of the 1990s to recognize the influential, indeed potent, force of theory. In this sense, theoretical criminology should be seen as a vital, living subject, and not some historical or intellectual fancy. Finally, one should recognize that the collection of theoretical vignettes gathered together here is anything but exhaustive. A great number of other criminological theories abound from 'peacemaking' criminology (Quinney, 1991) to control-balance theory (Tittle, 1995), from routine activity theory (Felson, 2010) to 'constitutive criminology' (Henry and Milovanovic, 1996), all of which compete for attention against/with each other in the vibrant—if, at times, exasperating—world of criminological theory.

The theories—a beginner's guide

The founding doctrines

For much of modernity (roughly the last 250 years) social scientists believed that the problems of modern society would be overcome or at least managed by the careful, scientific pursuit of relevant knowledge and the application of this knowledge to a specific set of problems (for a good general introduction to the debates around modernity see Bocock and Thompson, 1992; Hall and Gieben, 1992). The basket of differing approaches that we may say collectively constitutes the discipline of criminology should thus be seen as part of this enterprise (see Beirne, 1993; Garland, 1994; Morrison, 2004). Certainly the discipline's two (contrasting) founding doctrines, the 'classical' and 'positivist' approaches to the study of crime, were fundamentally concerned with using the techniques and methods of enlightened science and philosophy to make good on their shared goal: the reduction and control of crime within modern, urban societies.

Classicism

The first sets of writings typically considered as criminology are labelled *classical criminology* and date from the late eighteenth century. It was a movement born of a combination of fear and optimism: fear of the breakdown of society, fear that there was no longer a God around which to centre things, and fear of the mob, the ragged, poverty-stricken masses that were increasingly drawn to the burgeoning cities of Western Europe; optimism in the sense of the steadfast belief that, as modernity unfolded, it would bestow social science with enlightened knowledge about the human condition. Classical scholars thus put their faith in these new 'sciences of man' in the belief that they would help create greater social stability.

Importantly, with classicism, the new intellectual instruments of modernity were employed not in a bid to understand the ultimate causes of human behaviour; rather, the task was to find ways of controlling and directing behaviour by affecting *rational motivation*. In other words, the underlying social conditions of crime were unimportant. Instead the emphasis was on administration, ordered systems that would free society from the arbitrary authority of monarchs and clerics and open it up so that the basic true forms of the human condition would become visible. To this end, classical scholars set about reforming the punishment system. A reasonably coherent, rational, intellectual structure was developed which legitimated the creation of a system of criminal justice based on equality and proportionality.

The central figure in classicism's development was the Italian, Cesare Beccaria (1738–94). In *On Crimes and Punishment* ([1764] 1963) Beccaria considered crime 'injurious to society'. It was this injury to society, rather than to the immediate individual(s) who experienced it (or, for that matter, the abstract sovereign), that was to direct and determine the degree of punishment. Beccaria claimed that criminal law should bind and guide society by laying out clear, rational rules. The rules are laid down by a legitimate body guided by a new science of decision making, namely *utilitarianism* (or the assumption that all social action should be guided by the goal of achieving the greatest happiness for the greatest number: see relatedly Hume, [1739] 1978). From this viewpoint, the punishment of an individual for a crime was justified, and justifiable only, for its contribution to the prevention of future infringements on the happiness of others. Accordingly, Beccaria reasoned that certain, transparent and quick, rather than severe, punishments would best accomplish these goals. Torture, execution, and other 'irrational' activities must be abolished. In their place there were to be quick and certain trials and, in the case of convictions, carefully calculated punishments determined strictly in accordance with the damage to society caused by the crime. Beccaria proposed that accused persons be treated humanely before trial, with every right and facility extended to enable them to bring evidence on their own behalf. (In Beccaria's time accused and convicted persons were detained in the same institutions, and subjected to the same punishments and conditions.)

Classicism was given further impetus by the British philosopher, Jeremy Bentham (1748–1832). Like Beccaria, Bentham insisted that prevention was the only justifiable purpose of punishment, and, furthermore, that punishment was too 'expensive' when it produced more evil than good, or when the same good could be obtained at the 'price' of less suffering. He recommended penalties be fixed so as to *impose an amount of pain in excess of pleasure that might be derived from the criminal act*. It was this calculation of pain compared to pleasure that Bentham believed would deter crime, it was his key for unlocking the functionality of human nature: 'Nature has placed mankind under the governance of two sovereign masters, pain and pleasure. It is for them alone to point out what we ought to do, as well as to determine what we shall do' (Bentham, [1789] 1982).

Famously, Bentham also attempted to radicalize imprisonment, an institution then used merely to hold persons awaiting trial or debtors. He spent much of his life trying to convince authorities that an institution of his design, called a 'Panopticon', would solve the problems of correction, of poverty, of idleness, and mental instability. There were three features to the panopticon. First, the architectural dimension; the panopticon was to be a circular building arranged so that every cell could be visible from a central observation tower providing a hierarchy of continuous surveillance. The omniscient prison inspector would be kept from the sight of the prisoners by a system of 'blinds unless ... he thinks fit to show himself'. Second, management by contract; the manager would employ the inmates in contract labour and he was to receive a share of the money earned by the inmates, but he was to be financially liable if inmates who were later released re-offended, or if an excess number of inmates died during imprisonment. Third, the panopticon was to be open to the inspection of the world. Bentham's panopticon idea was never fully implemented (although two prisons were built along his design in France and the US). The panopticon keeps its importance not for the institutions actually constructed, rather, for the type of disciplinary rationality the scheme displays (on this point see Chapter 21). Indeed, in many ways, the panopticon remains the physical embodiment of classicism.

In a bid to illustrate our earlier point that theoretical criminology is a vibrant, living subject, and not some historical fancy it is worth pointing out that many of the central ideas of classicism continue to endure within criminology today, not least the notion of rationality, which has been resuscitated in recent years by proponents of rational choice theory (see, for example, Clarke and Cornish, 1985; Roshier, 1989).

REVIEW QUESTIONS

1 What were the primary concerns of classical criminologists?

2 From where did classicism draw its ideas? In which areas of criminal justice did they hope to implement these ideas?

3 What has been the legacy of classicism within mainstream criminology?

Key readings

Beccaria, C. ([1764] 1963) *On Crimes and Punishments*. Indianapolis: Bobbs-Merrill.

Bentham, J. ([1791] 1999) *Collected Works of Jeremy Bentham*. Oxford: Oxford University Press.

Roshier, B. (1989) *Controlling Crime: The Classical Perspective in Criminology*. Milton Keynes: Open University Press.

Textbook reading/secondary source

See the entries on 'Cesare Beccaria' (by Majid Yar) and 'Jeremy Bentham' (by Pat O'Malley) in Hayward, K., Maruna, S. and Mooney, J. (2010) *Fifty Key Thinkers in Criminology*. London: Routledge.

Lanier, M. and Henry, S., Chapter 4 ('Classical, Neoclassical and Rational Choice Theories') in *Essential Criminology* (1998). Boulder, CO: Westview Press.

Criminological positivism

While positivism is a broad term which includes a number of differing applications (see Morrison, 1995: Chapters 6–9; Giddens, 1974), for the purposes of introducing criminological theory, we can say that it represents a field of criminological inquiry that emerged in the mid-nineteenth century which argued that criminality could be studied scientifically using methods derived from the natural sciences. Most famously, criminological positivism is associated with the Italian medical doctor, Cesare Lombroso (1835–1909). Lombroso laid claim to founding a new science—the 'science of criminology' that took as its focus not the criminal law or its related rational administrative practices (as with classicism), but the 'criminal [person]'. Thus, in sharp contrast to classicism, Lombroso's answer to the problems of criminal behaviour lay in *biology*, specifically a complex set of externally visible physiological variations that, he claimed, marked out certain individuals as predestined to commit crime. By observation and careful measurement of the bodily features of the criminal, Lombroso attempted to prove scientifically that those who broke the law were physically distinct from those who did not—this is the centrepiece of nineteenth-century criminological positivism.

Lombroso conducted thousands of post-mortem examinations and physiological studies of prison inmates and non-criminals. He concluded that the criminal existed, in the natural order of things, as a lower form of human evolution than the average man, with very distinct physical and mental characteristics (see editions of *L'Uomo delinquente*, first published in 1876). Lombroso proffered a four-fold classification:

(a) born criminal, those with true atavistic features;

(b) insane criminals, including idiots, imbeciles, and paranoiacs as well as epileptics and alcoholics;

(c) occasional criminals or criminaloids, whose crimes were explained largely by opportunity; and

(d) criminals of passion who commit crime because of honour, love, or anger. They are propelled by a (temporary) irresistible force.

Later, additional categories gave some allowance for the influence of social factors (on this particular point see the work of another Italian positivist, Enrico Ferri (1856–1929)) and he speculated somewhat as to the interaction of genetic and environmental influences (thus providing, to some extent, a precursor to socio-biological theories, see later). However, although Lombroso went some way to developing a multi-factorial approach, he never really moved beyond the principle that the true 'born criminal' was responsible for a large amount of criminal behaviour.

Importantly, Lombroso was not alone in his search for the 'criminal type' (see also the work of the aforementioned Ferri and Raffaele Garofalo (1852–1934))—there have been, and indeed still are (see later), a number of scholars and research projects dedicated to reducing the problem of crime to the problem of the criminal. For this reason, one should be aware that positivist criminology does not begin and end with the Italian deterministic tradition (*scuola positiva*). It also extends to include various other early schools of criminological thought. For example, the work of early nineteenth-century 'social ecology' scholars such as the Frenchmen André-Michel Guerry and the Belgian Adolphe de Quételet is also typically described as positivist in the sense that it sought to unearth objective, 'law-like' scientific knowledge about crime (in their particular case, via the moral analysis of early crime statistics and how they might help us better understand what they described as 'the social mechanics of crime', see Beirne, 1993: Chapters 3 and 4).

REVIEW QUESTIONS

1 What were the main methods employed by the nineteenth-century positivists?

2 What value can we place on this form of criminology?

3 Is the positivists' ultimate aim of a purely 'scientific' form of criminology a valid one?

Key readings

Lombroso, C. (2006) *Criminal Man*. Trans. Gibson, M. and Rafter, N. Durham, NC: Duke University Press.

Ferri, E. (2003) 'Causes of Criminal Behaviour' in Muncie, J., McLaughlin, E. and Hughes, G. (eds) *Criminological Perspectives: A Reader*. London: Sage.

Beirne, P. (1993) *Inventing Criminology: Essays on the Rise of 'Homo Criminalis'*. Albany, New York: State University of New York Press. Chapter 6.

Gibson, M. (2002) *Born to Crime: Cesare Lombroso and the Origins of Biological Criminology*. Westport: Praeger.

Textbook reading/secondary source

See the entries on 'Cesare Lombroso' (by Kate Bradley) and 'Enrico Ferri' (by Phil Carney) in Hayward, K., Maruna, S. and Mooney, J. (2010) *Fifty Key Thinkers in Criminology*. London: Routledge.

Morrison, W., Chapter 6 ('Criminological Positivism 1: The Search for the Criminal Man, or the Problem of the Duck') in *Theoretical Criminology: From Modernity to Postmodernism* (1995). London: Cavendish.

Individual perspectives

Biological and genetic explanations of crime

Biological explanations of crime appear to offer the promise that, if humans were examined like other animals, the 'laws of nature' that govern 'human behaviour' could be established and accounted for. Under this perspective, human behaviour is determined by factors that, while universal to the species, reside to a greater or lesser extent in the constitution of the individual—individuals are therefore, to an extent, predetermined into a life of crime. In this sense, this line of work can be seen as extending from the Italian positivist school inspired by Lombroso. The following are a small selection of some of the better-known examples of the biological approach to the study of crime:

William Sheldon's 'body type' theory—Sheldon's famous (1942) study attempted to link body-build and personality. He famously divided humans into three body types, or 'somatotypes' (see, relatedly, the slightly earlier work of the English criminologist, Charles Goring (1913) and the Harvard anthropologist, A.E. Hooton (1939)):

(a) endomorphs: a heavy, soft or round build; relaxed, sociable, extrovert personality;

(b) mesomorphs: well-developed, muscular, athletic build; active, dynamic, aggressive (sometimes violent) personality;

(c) ectomorph: small, lean, delicate/weak build; hypersensitive, intellectual, sensitive, introverted personality.

Some individuals are 'pure types', while others are 'hybrids' incorporating elements from two, or even three of the builds in their physique. Sheldon argued that delinquents were characterized by a preponderance of mesomorphs, some indication of endomorphy, and a marked lack of ectomorphs. Sheldon concluded this pattern differed from that found in non-criminal populations, demonstrating that there were differences in the physiques of delinquent and non-delinquent males. More recent studies, of course, have concluded that no such link between body type and crime actually exists. But, even today, this does not deter those who are desperate to reinstate constitutional factors (for example, Cortes and Gatti's 1972 study that argued that crime was caused by an interaction between biological and social factors (see also the 'New Directions in Criminological Theory' section in this chapter for more on the latest developments in 'biosocial criminology)).

Genetic transmission theory—Throughout the twentieth century a series of studies have tried to ascertain the *hereditary* nature of crime. Simply stated, this is the idea that certain criminal tendencies are inherited—a criminal is born not made. For example:

• In the 1920s, the German physician Johannes Lange began the tradition of 'twin studies', where the criminal records of identical and fraternal twins were contrasted. Work continues in this area today.

• Raymond Crowe (1974) and Barry Hutchings and Sarnoff Mednick's (1975) work in the area of 'adoption studies'. Here the aim is to compare the criminal behaviour of adopted children with that of their biological parents. If the behaviour of the children more closely resembles the biological parents rather than the adoptive parents, then there is a strong case for genetic transmission theory.

There have been numerous other specific biological theories, such as:

• the attention given to the 'XYY Syndrome' in the 1960s (a chromosomal abnormality that was controversially linked to violent crime) (for example, Sandberg *et al.*, 1961);

• research into biochemical and hormonal imbalances and criminality in the 1920s and 1930s (for example, Berman, 1921);

• the link between testosterone and aggression (for example, Moyer, 1971);

• Kathy Dalton's (1961) work on the relationship between PMT and female criminality.

Today there are still those who continue to try and reinstate constitutional factors into the study of crime. In their controversial work *Crime and Human Nature* (1985) James Q. Wilson and Richard Herrnstein devote several pages to reproducing diagrams and photography used by Sheldon, and conclude that 'wherever it has been examined, criminals on the average differ in physique from the population at large' (see 'Right Realism' in this chapter).

In conclusion, this body of work is inevitably plagued by the same problems encountered by the Italian positivists; specifically, it is constantly hampered by its inability to control for complex and interacting environmental and social influences. Thus, all informed scholars who claim that biology plays a strong role in criminality now no longer talk in terms of a dominating role; rather, a picture is drawn of behaviour resulting from the *interaction* of the biological make-up of the organism with the physical and social environment.

REVIEW QUESTIONS

1 Can criminality be inherited?

2 If we accept that crime is not a natural phenomenon but is socially constructed, is it possible to explain crime in terms of individual pathology?

3 How much emphasis can criminology afford to place on questions of biology? What are the possible pitfalls of such an approach?

Key readings

Ciba Foundation Symposium 194 (1996) *Genetics of Criminal and Antisocial Behaviour*. Chichester: Wiley.

Jeffrey, C.R. (1994) 'Biological and Neuropsychiatric Approaches to Criminal Behaviour' in Barak, G. (ed) *Varieties of Criminology: Readings From a Dynamic Discipline*. Westport, CT: Praeger.

Sheldon, W.H. (1942) *The Varieties of Temperament*. New York: Harper.

Wilson, J.Q. and Herrnstein, R. (1985) *Crime and Human Nature*. New York: Simon and Schuster.

Textbook reading/secondary source

Beaver, K. (2008) *Biosocial Criminology: A Primer*. Dubuque, IA: Kendall-Hunt Publishing.

Williams, K.S., Chapter 6 ('Influences of Physical Factors and Genetics on Criminality') in *Criminology: A Textbook* (2004). Oxford: Oxford University Press.

Psychological explanations of crime

The key psychological theories of crime and the relationship between psychology and criminology more generally are discussed in detail in Chapter 6.

Early sociological perspectives

The term 'sociological perspective' is used here to refer to a specific segment of criminological approaches that deal with crime from a distinctly social perspective. Namely, those theories rooted in functionalism that find their origins with Emile Durkheim (although he never referred to his own theories in these terms) but have undergone many transformations (particularly in the hands of Robert Merton) and were dominant from the 1920s to the 1950s.

Functionalist theories see society as an integrated whole, where ultimately all parts or subsystems operate in an integrated ('organic') and coordinated way. A healthy society is one where balance is achieved—which (according to this theory) is the natural tendency of social functioning. Individuals are perceived to undergo a process of 'socialization', where they are taught appropriate role behaviours and values that contribute to the overall functioning of the system as a whole. It is conventional today, of course, to attack functionalism for its inherent conservatism and assumption of consensus.

The influence of Emile Durkheim (1858–1917)

Durkheim's original thesis still appears quite shocking: namely, that a certain level of crime is not only inevitable but also functional to society. He argues that because crime produces a social reaction (that is, rituals of sanction and punishment, whether repressive or restitutive) it serves to rebind the various parts of society and its members into a strengthened whole. Further, in a social order predicated on stabilizing mechanisms and conformity, sources of innovation and change are rare, so deviance is also valuable in challenging established moral values.

Durkheim argued that crime is normal in society because there is actually no extra social, or natural, dividing line between criminal activity and other more acceptable activities. The dividing line is an ongoing process of demarcation and labelling, which serves to differentiate between acceptable and unacceptable behaviour. The use of the concept of crime is merely the strongest labelling procedure which works to maintain social solidarity. Its effectiveness actually comes from the process of punishment and social emotions which are engendered within society. For by observing the punishment of people, and engaging in the feeling of moral and social outrage at the offence, individuals become bound to the common perception of the justified and unjustified, *the right and wrong*. Punishment becomes inevitable. Durkheim's thinking in this area is illustrated in the following much-quoted passage: 'Imagine a society of saints, a perfect cloister of exemplary individuals. Crimes, properly so-called, will there be unknown; but faults which appear venial to the layman will create there the same scandal that the ordinary offence does in ordinary consciousness. If, then, this society has the power to judge and punish, it will define these acts as criminal and will treat them as such' (Durkheim, 1965: 68).

He therefore calls upon us to consider that crime is actually a factor in public health, an integral part of social organization. That does not mean to say that there are not (socially) abnormal or pathological levels of crime, but that both the absence of crime and a surplus of crime are socially pathological. A society in which there is no crime would be a rigidly over-policed, oppressive society. But a society which is experiencing too high a crime rate is a society in which the balance between regulation and individuality has broken down. Hence his conception of *anomie* (literally, the condition of normlessness), a condition in which individuals feel no identification with any system of values and thus have no reluctance to commit crime.

Durkheim argued that the economic structure of capitalism, with its strong emphasis on self-interested behaviour, was itself a major cause of *anomie*. Likewise, the forced division of labour associated with industrialized societies locates individuals in a structure of specialization and economic hierarchy where their position is not freely chosen but thrust upon each person by the accident of birth. As a result, many individuals find themselves estranged, resentful, and aspiring to social positions that are in fact arbitrarily closed off to them. Robert Merton was to call the reaction to this situation 'an anomie of injustice' (see later).

REVIEW QUESTIONS

1 What does Durkheim mean when he says that crime serves an important social function?

2 What assumptions about human nature are contained in Durkheim's theories?

3 What social factors might underpin anomie today?

Key readings

Durkheim, E., Chapter 3 ('Rules for the distinction of the normal from the pathological') in *The Rules of Sociological Method* ([1895] 1982). New York: Free Press.

Durkheim, E. (1970) *Suicide: A Study of Sociology.* New York: The Free Press.

Taylor, I., Walton, P. and Young, J., Chapter 3 ('Durkheim and the break with analytical individualism') in *New Criminology: For a Social Theory of Deviance* (1973). London: Routledge and Kegan Paul.

Textbook reading/secondary source

Downes, D. and Rock, P., Chapter 4 ('Functionalism, deviance and control') in *Understanding Deviance* (2007). Oxford: Oxford University Press.

Vold, G., Bernard, T. and Snipes J., Chapter 6 ('Durkheim, anomie, and modernization') in *Theoretical Criminology* (2002). Oxford: Oxford University Press.

Wilkinson, I., 'Emile Durkheim' in Hayward, K., Maruna, S. and Mooney, J. (eds) *Fifty Key Thinkers in Criminology* (2010). London: Routledge.

Strain theory—the work of Robert Merton (1910–2003)

In the hands of Robert K. Merton, functionalism was radically amended (along with the meaning of *anomie*). Under the Mertonian rubric, it was not that individual criminals did not have the same goals and aspirations as non-criminals, but rather that they lacked legitimate means to achieve them. Thus, the typical problem in modern societies is the *gap* between the ideal of a truly meritocratic society and the arbitrary realities of one's determining birth position (class, gender, ethnicity, and so on) within the social structure. Ironically, the rise of literacy and the onset of institutions of universal education serves to make this situation worse, making promises about opportunities that the society is not able to deliver. Merton famously articulated this situation in terms of a *strain theory* of deviance (1938), that is, the variable response of individuals' adaptations (including criminal ones) to tensions between a highly stratified social structure and the mass of cultural messages present in contemporary life (for example, advertisements for products that purport to instil identity, etc).

Merton's theorizing was a challenging moment because it considerably blurred the positivist boundary between 'them' (the criminal) and 'us' (the non-criminal). Following Merton, no longer was the criminal essentially different from the good citizen.

In turn, strain theory was taken a step further by Albert Cohen whose classic (1955) study, *Delinquent Boys*, included not only material goals but also social status, drawing on the idea of 'culture' as the realm of meaning as distinct from social structure. Culture, under this rubric, enables people to 'solve' problems created for them by the social structure by investing their lives—including their criminal activity—with an 'acceptable' meaning. For Cohen, for example, it allowed delinquent boys to lay claims to the great American value of achievement—if not at school, then in other (deviant) activities. Today the relevant value might be consumer culture, 'the fostering of the propensity to *consume* irrespective of the material possibilities of such a course' (Downes and Rock, 1988: 94; see also Hayward, 2004: Chapter 5).

The final step in this journey was the idea of subcultures (see Chapter 18). For is there not a problem in the assumption that everyone is part of the one overarching system of norms and values (white, middle class, imbued with the Protestant ethic)? Rather—and still maintaining the key theme that deviant actors *share the values* of the dominant culture—was it not more appropriate for theory to explore the diversity of cultures within any one set of national boundaries? Throughout this body of work (see also Cloward and Ohlin, 1960), the issue of conflict was less at the individual level and more portrayed as a clash of cultures. Occasionally teetering on the brink of racism (it took an incredible interest in immigrant groups in the US), subcultural theory became a huge industry in the 1960s, applied primarily to areas such as youth culture and sexuality.

REVIEW QUESTIONS

1 What are the similarities and differences between the way Durkheim and Merton understand crime?

2 What is meant by the term 'subculture'?

3 List some contemporary examples of 'deviant' subcultures. How relevant is sub cultural theory today?

Key readings

Agnew, R. (1992) 'Foundation for a general strain theory of crime and delinquency'. *Criminology*, 30: 47–87.

Cloward, R.A. and Ohlin, L. (1960) *Delinquency and Opportunity*. New York: The Free Press.

Cohen, A. (1955) *Delinquent Boys: The Culture of the Gang*. New York: Free Press.

Merton, R.K. (1938) 'Social structure and anomie'. *American Sociological Review*, 3: 672–82.

Textbook reading/secondary source

Downes, D. and Rock, P., Chapter 5 ('Anomie') in *Understanding Deviance* (2007) Oxford: Oxford University Press.

See the entries on 'Robert Merton' and 'Albert Cohen' (by Jock Young) in Hayward, K., Maruna, S. and Mooney, J (2010) *Fifty Key Thinkers in Criminology*. London: Routledge.

The Chicago School of Sociology

To understand the Chicago School it helps to know something of Chicago itself. By the 1930s, Chicago had expanded from humble beginnings as an obscure frontier outpost to a thriving city with a population of more than three million. One of the striking features of this phenomenal expansion was the extent to which the city had become home to a panoply of ethnic groups, both African-Americans escaping the rural poverty of the South and European immigrants.

The Chicago School's version of milieu—ecology—drew upon bio-ecological notions of plant adaptation and association that emphasized orderly spatial distribution as both enabling adaptation to the environment and maximizing the use of resources. Park (1925) postulated that human communities were closely akin to any natural environment in that their spatial organization and expansion was not the product of chance, but instead was patterned and could be understood in terms analogous to the basic natural processes that occur within any biotic organism. Thus, Park maintained that the city could be thought of as a *super-organism*; an amalgamation of a series of subpopulations, each unified at one level by race or income or business interests. Accordingly, each of these groups acted 'naturally' in that they were underpinned by a collective or organic unity. Furthermore, not only did each of these 'natural areas' have an integral role to play in the city as a whole, but each community or business area was interrelated in a series of 'symbiotic relationships'. Close observation of these relationships enabled Park to conclude that, just as is in any natural ecology, the sequence of 'invasion-dominance-succession' was also in operation within the modern city.

Such thinking was developed by Park's colleague Ernst Burgess (1925) in his concentric zone theory which contended that modern cities expanded radially from an inner-city core. Burgess identified five main concentric zones in Chicago—which he believed were applicable to all modern cities. At the centre was (1) the business district, an area of low population and high property values. This, in turn, was encircled by (2) the 'zone in transition'—crucial from the crime point of view—characterized by run-down housing, high-speed immigration, and high rates of poverty and disease. Then followed the belts of: (3) working-class housing; (4) middle-class housing; and, ultimately, (5) the affluent suburbs.

The (unfortunately named) 'invasion' aspect arises because, once immigrants establish themselves, they seek to leave the zone in transition and live in a more prosperous zone (typically zone 3). This makes the zone in transition itself a great place of flux and restlessness, not exhibiting a proper 'biotic balance' with its (always temporary) inhabitants. Also, it is itself always subject to invasion from the expansion of the core business district (and, in anticipation, property speculators hence keep the rents low, and the buildings unrepaired). The Chicagoans used the term 'social disorganization' to characterize the unstructured and fluid ethos of this social space with its disturbed social equilibrium, and to account for its higher rate of crime.

One influential study by Shaw and McKay (1931, 1942) mapped out juvenile court referral rates over time and found that these correlated closely to the zones, with the highest level in socially disorganized areas and progressively diminishing in the other zones— *irrespective of demographic/ethnic composition*. This was a momentous breakthrough that did much to dispel earlier criminological theories that located the root cause of crime in the individual (or populist racist theories of criminal ethnic minorities). Instead it was now the neighbourhood, the area, and the immediate environment that was the key factor in promoting delinquent values, largely through youth culture (rather than parent–child relations). Having established this important position, Shaw and McKay went on to claim that socially disorganized neighbourhoods perpetuate a situation in which delinquent behaviour patterns are *culturally transmitted* 'down through successive generations of boys, in much the same way that language and other social forms are transmitted' (1942: 166). This observation, along with Edwin Sutherland's (1939) theory of *differential association*, was an important strand in subsequent criminological theories that attempted to account for crime by reference to deviant subcultures.

Strongly related to their substantive arguments, the other important feature of the Chicago School was their *method*. Unlike Shaw and McKay who relied (perhaps naively) on official statistics, the majority of the Chicago School took their lead from Robert Park, a former newspaper journalist, who proceeded from the premise that the best way to study crime was through the close observation of the social processes distinctive to the city. In this they were positivists to the extent that they sought first-level facts or data through which to get to some underlying level of social reality (which would provide the explanatory connections). But their key contribution was in the area of *qualitative* methods—*participant-observation* and the *focused interview*. Such techniques enabled the Chicagoans to 'enter the world of the deviant' and compile ethnographic data on everything from hobos to 'taxi-dancers', racketeers to street-gang members (see, for example, Thrasher, 1927; Cressey, 1932; Anderson, 1975). The influence of this method can clearly be seen in subsequent writers of the labelling perspective, such as Howard Becker (see later).

The work of the Chicago School was criticized primarily at the explanatory level—whether its theories about social organization and disorganization did not rely on unexplored assumptions about consensual values, and whether the claim about the effect of environment was too strong (the so-called 'ecological fallacy'). What has survived most strongly (apart from their contribution, already noted, to qualitative methods and the study of social actions from the deviant's perspective) has been the observational tradition of collecting data about the spatial organization and distribution of crime. In Britain a number of area studies combined (uneasily) 'mini-ethnographies' of primarily working-class areas with a positivist search for definitive factors in the turn to crime. More recently, under the banner of administrative and environmental criminology (see Bottoms, 1994, 2007), the interest in area studies of the offender's *residence* has shifted to a concern with the location of criminal *offences*, and the notion of crime 'hot spots' (see Sherman *et al.*, 1989).

REVIEW QUESTIONS

1 Can locality itself be considered a causal factor in explaining crime and other social problems?

2 Was the ecological analogy useful or did it ignore some of the key forces that are present within city life?

3 What has been the legacy of the Chicago School within contemporary criminology?

Key readings

Park, R.E. 'The city: suggestions for the investigation of human behaviour in the urban environment' in Park, R.E., Burgess, E.W., and McKenzie, R.D. (eds) *The City* (1925) Chicago: Chicago University Press.

Shaw, C.R. and McKay, H.D. (1942) *Juvenile Delinquency and Urban Areas.* Chicago: University of Chicago Press.

Anderson, N. (1975) *The Hobo: The Sociology of the Homeless Man.* Chicago: University of Chicago Press.

Textbook reading/secondary source

See the entries on 'Edwin Sutherland' (by James Sheptycki), 'Clifford Shaw' (by Loraine Gelsthorpe) and 'Robert Park' (by Frank Bovenkerk) in Hayward, K., Maruna, S. and Mooney, J. (2010) *Fifty Key Thinkers in Criminology.* London: Routledge.

Vold, G., Bernard, T., and Snipes, J., Chapter 7 ('Neighbourhoods and crime') in *Theoretical Criminology* (2002) Oxford: Oxford University Press.

Hayward, K.J., 'The Chicago School' in *Sage Dictionary of Criminology* (2013), edited by Hayward, K. Maruna, S., and Mooney, J. London: Sage.

The 'labelling' perspective (including social interactionism)

'Labelling' is the term that the American sociologist Howard Becker, writing in the 1960s, used to describe the profound effect on a person of naming them as deviant. Such social 'proclamations' transform the doing of a deviant act into a core part of a person's identity—a symbolic reorganization of self—that, in a theatrical metaphor, 'pre-scripts' their future performances according to their new, conferred, role as deviant. Becker, and also Erving Goffman (1968), studied many examples of such roles, from 'becoming a marijuana user' to the 'sick role' involved in becoming a patient.

As a theoretical development, the labelling perspective proved devastating both to the whole positivist tradition of investigating the 'criminal', and to the established way in which criminology analysed the criminal justice system. These paradigms are challenged if we can no longer use words such as 'offender' or 'criminal or 'deviant'—all 'naming words'—simply as given, 'natural' categories describing the world as it just exists. What happens to these obvious vocabularies when we become aware of the social processing—the *work*, as Becker puts it—that has gone into creating the characterization of the person before us?

For Becker and fellow *symbolic/social interactionists*, the primary moments in this process were what was at stake in the labelling, and the individual's way of dealing with this. Such analysis drew upon a mix of theoretical frameworks, including the philosophical pragmatism of George Herbert Mead ([1934] 1962), and his distinction between the 'I' and the 'me' (I as observer/me as object of observation). For Mead, no (wo)man is an island; the self does not pre-exist interaction with others. Labelling as social or symbolic interactionism thus takes as its starting point the notion that people *lack* a strong sense of self—of who they are and what they can do—and rely on constant processes of social exchange and affirmation.

Equally important was the role of linguistic and visual components in the construction—*and* interactive negotiation—of meaning. Deviance, like any action or mode of being, only becomes deviance when it enters social life by receiving a linguistic response. Social control is thus not so much an external force but embedded in the very meanings we confer on acting and being. By the same token, the use of language also provides individuals with resources for 'negating' blame—what David Matza called 'neutralization techniques' by which we tell ourselves, for example, that 'everybody does it' or 'she was asking for it' (Sykes and Matza, 1957). Labelling theory can thus lead to strong associations with subculture theory when attention is paid to the elaboration of deviant 'worlds' with a sympathetic 'audience'.

For mainstream criminologists, more directly interested in formal social control and the criminalization process, labelling theory could also be absorbed in a straightforward causal way as part of the aetiology of 'the criminal' (and the formation of a criminal 'career'). This meant turning sociological theories on their head: it was not that deviance produced social control as a reaction but, rather, that social control produced deviance. Edwin Lemert (1951), for example, distinguished between 'primary deviance' (the original act—whose causes remained—were heuristically assumed to be unknown) and 'secondary deviance' (that is, deviance resulting from the labelling attached to the original act). Such re-incorporation of labelling theory reputedly caused Becker much distress, leading him to say that he wished that he had never invented the term. It must also be remembered that crime as such had not been the core focus of the theorizing but, rather, any mode that came to be seen as deviant. From this perspective, labelling theory leads away from the effects of criminalization on the individual and wonders instead what rules and labels tell us about society. Why do societies *react* the way they do, penalizing different particular acts and in different particular ways at different historical moments and parts of the world? (see Sumner, 1990; Cohen, 1972).

REVIEW QUESTIONS

1 How does the labelling perspective differ from both classicism and positivism?

2 Identify a significant 'label' by which you define yourself. How does that label condition how you act?

3 What is important about the distinction between deviant *acts* and deviant *people*?

Key readings

Becker, H.S. (1963) *Outsiders*. Free Press of Glencoe: Collier-Macmillan.

Goffman, E. (1968) *Stigma: Notes on the Management of a Spoiled Identity*. London: Penguin.

Matza, D. and Sykes, G. (1957) 'Techniques of neutralization: a theory of delinquency'. *American Sociological Review*, 22: 664–70.

Textbook reading/secondary source

See the entries on 'Howard Becker' (by Greg Snyder), 'Edwin Lemert' (by Shadd Maruna) and 'Erving Goffman' (by Phillip Hadfield and James Hardie-Bick) in Hayward, K., Maruna, S. and Mooney, J. (2010) *Fifty Key Thinkers in Criminology*. London: Routledge.

Lilly, R., Cullen, F., and Ball, R., Chapter 7 ('The irony of State intervention: labelling theory') in *Criminological Theory: Context and Consequences* (2011) London: Sage.

Downes, D. and Rock, P., Chapter 7 ('Symbolic interactionism') in *Understanding Deviance* (2007) Oxford: Oxford University Press.

Marxist/radical criminology

The late 1960s and 1970s saw dramatic changes in the study of crime. Moving on from the soft libertarianism of theories of deviancy and labelling theory, the emphasis was now on *political economy* of crime. Political economy implied a basic commitment to the idea that capitalism was criminogenic. Broadly, this meant a recognition that society was fundamentally organized around class-based structural antagonisms. Where more traditional criminology operated around naive consensual assumptions about shared values and socially functional processes, Marxism saw conflict not as social or individual pathology but as the social norm. In Britain, this turn to a Marxist inspiration was announced in Taylor, Walton and Young's groundbreaking work, *The New Criminology* (1973).

At the explanatory level, focusing on the 'political economy' of capitalism as criminogenic meant potentially two different aspects of causation. The first (more classically Marxist) was that the causes of criminal activity were to be found in the structure and operation of market relations, including the commodification of human labour—and to be studied at the direct level of the economy. Typical concerns would be the relation between unemployment and crime (Box, 1987) or the claim that crime reduces surplus labour by providing a black economy (Chambliss, 1975). Such issues have been developed (particularly in the USA) to encompass the interplay of different power economies (not only class, but also race and gender) notably in the work of James Messerschmidt (1993), who offers a version of the 'kick the dog' syndrome as a basis of crime (loosely, you pick on the person who is lower than you in the class hierarchy).

Second—and far more prominent in British theorizing (in turn reflecting the origins of this movement in deviancy and labelling theory) is the question of criminalization— what is criminalized and what forms does that criminalization take? This is where we find out what a society values as its core concerns and, more subtly (and this has to be acknowledged as a Durkheimian insight), what is also revealed by forms of social processing of infractions. Much of the most productive work on this theme looked at the past, partly inspired by the work of social historians such as E.P. Thompson (1975), Eric Hobsbawm (1972), and Marx's own great text on the criminalization of the theft of wood. The transition from feudalism to capitalism showed very dramatically how new social arrangements produced new criminalizations geared to the motor of a new economic system driven by the capitalist institution of private property as an alienable commodity (that is, that could—and must—only be bought and sold on the marketplace). As illustrated by the eighteenth-century introduction of legislation imposing capital punishment for poaching game, installing the new system and driving out the old one was simultaneously, (a) dramatically coercive on the part of the rising bourgeoisie; (b) complex in the mobilization of class resistance (with feudal aristocrats and 'their' peasants acting together in defence of the old way of life); and (c) subtle in its associated ways of disciplining the new factory workforce into an appreciation of the basic capitalist equation: time = money (see Thompson, 1968).

This kind of work in turn led in different directions. On the one hand, the conjunction of 'macro-power' (criminal law/coercion/death penalties) with 'micro-powers' was echoed in the work of Michel Foucault (1977) and Dario Melossi (1990) and to emphasize the continuities in disciplinary/policing mechanisms between prisons, factories, and schools (see Chapter 21). On the other hand, *The New Criminology*, reinforced by the tone of social historians' texts (such as Hobsbawm's *Bandits*) had an undeniable tendency to romanticize 'the criminal' as a proto-revolutionary or at least as a social critic—in Marxist terms, implying a degree of class-conscious warfare.

Finally, at the political and professional level, what was involved was a fundamental self-examination in which criminologists were urged to become aware of and, ideally, disengage from, their professional collusion with the State. Criminologists must stop being useful 'problem solvers' and become '*problem-raisers*' (Nils Christie). An important background paper of this period was Stan Cohen's (1981) 'Footprints in the Sand', which linked State recognition (and funding!) with professional criminologists' positivist tendencies towards measurable indices, in turn necessarily oriented to potential points of individual intervention. The target was identified as 'correctionalism'—the ideology and very real practices of dealing with crime as a problem of the individual law-breaker seen as in need of alteration. Adapting Marx's *Theses on Feuerbach*, the slogan was: 'the point is not to change the individual—the "criminal"—but to change society'.

REVIEW QUESTIONS

1 Should certain types of law-breakers be seen as class warriors?

2 In what different ways can crime and criminalization be explained by reference to political economy?

3 Why were historical studies so important to Marxist-inspired criminology?

Key readings

Taylor, I., Walton, P., and Young, J. (1973) *New Criminology: For a Social Theory of Deviance*. London: Routledge and Kegan Paul.

Quinney, R. (1974) *Critique of the Legal Order: Crime Control in Capitalist Society*. Boston: Little Brown.

Box, S. (1983) *Crime, Power and Mystfication*. London: Tavistock.

Chambliss, W. (1975) 'Toward a political economy of crime', *Theory and Society*, 2, 149–70.

Textbook reading/secondary source

See the entry on 'Karl Marx' (by John Lea) in Hayward, K., Maruna, S. and Mooney, J. (2010) *Fifty Key Thinkers in Criminology*. London: Routledge.

Jones, S., Chapter 10 ('Conflict, Marxist and Radical theories of crime') in *Criminology* (2001) London: Butterworths.

Lanier, M. and Henry, S., Chapter 11 ('Capitalism as a criminogenic society: conflict and radical theories of crime') in *Essential Criminology* (1998) Boulder, CO: Westview Press.

Gender and crime: the feminist perspective

Feminist-influenced writing started in criminology in earnest in the 1970s and has provided a fertile source of challenges and critiques to the mainstream criminological enterprise. Traditional and radical criminology stood accused not only of neglecting the study of women but falsely implying that the theories produced were theories of crime, rather than being what they actually were—theories of males committing crime. As a result, it was not surprising that women 'did not fit' the standard explanations. Even on the rare occasions when they have been considered, typically they have been portrayed in very stereotypical ways (for example, in the positivistic work of Cesare Lombroso, see earlier in this chapter).

As a preliminary exercise, let us begin with 'the facts' as given by crime statistics. The most striking fact is that women have always featured in these statistics to a much lesser extent than men. Typically, in the crime statistics for England and Wales, 80 per cent of crime is committed by men. Moreover, crimes committed by females tend to be less serious (for more on this point see Chapter 15). What implications, then, could be drawn from such analysis of statistics?

Traditional criminology dealt with these statistical facts in two different ways. On the one hand, it regarded them as fictional—a type of scepticism about statistics that identifies a huge reluctance on the part of men (whether as victims or criminal justice agents) to label women as criminals. While commentators such as Otto Pollak (1950) saw this as part of a system of oppression of women (an idealization that functions to keep them in their place, that is, the home), his deeply problematic depiction of women is itself 'backed up' with stereotypes about women as cunning deceivers excellent at concealing their true crime rate, especially in the home whose privacy provides many opportunities for abusing their families. On the other hand, the fact of women's non-delinquency was taken as correct; the key question about women being, why were they so conformist (Lombroso)? Here a further repertoire of stereotypes provided 'answers', concerning women's less individualized, non-achievement oriented natures. Consequently, those women who *did* commit crimes appeared as 'doubly deviant', departing from social and feminine norms—and often receiving explanations in terms of medical or psychological pathology.

This line of critique continued through the history of criminology, as one feminist writer after another set about documenting criminology's deficiencies in accounting for the gender divide in offending (for example, Heidensohn, 1968, 1996; Klein, 1973; Smart, 1976).

The question then was how should feminist criminology develop after critique? The dilemma posed was incorporation/assimilation or existing as a 'special topic'. On the one hand, should women be treated 'equally' and be subject to the same sorts of explanations as men? On the other hand, should there be special explanations relating to women's differences? Hence one dominant strand in feminist criminology unwittingly reproduced Lombroso's question (why are women so conformist?) while rejecting his (biologistic pseudo-evolutionary) answer. Posed in the language of social control theory (see later), women's non-deviance was to be understood in terms of the internalization of social norms *and* the nature of external informal controls, largely through family responsibilities, applied throughout women's lives (see Heidensohn, 1985; Cain, 1989).

Other approaches tended to step sideways, sometimes querying why feminism, in an era of radical critique, was so anxious to 'sign up' to categories such as 'criminality': why reproduce the most criticized categories of criminological theory? Alternatively, much attention was focussed on women as *victims* of crime, especially rape, including their 'second victimization' in the courtroom. Attention thus became more socio-legally oriented and also connected with campaigns to change criminal law or the law of (sexual character) evidence. Conventional victimology was also shown to be symptomatically deficient, especially, again in the area of rape (see Chapter 22).

One of the most vivid responses to the dilemma has been to argue that criminology was, in fact, correct all along to be studying men because men *are* the problem. But while past theories have been implicitly written from a male standpoint, they have not really confronted the issue of masculinity as such (see Messerschmidt, 1993; Jefferson, 1996; Collier, 1998, for specific attempts to correct this lacuna; for more on this particular point see also Chapter 9). The subject of gender and crime is discussed in more detail in Chapter 15 of this volume.

REVIEW QUESTIONS

1 Draw up a list of diverse crimes and account for how gender differences might account for different levels of involvement.

2 What have been the main achievements of feminist perspectives in criminology?

3 How has feminism transformed the discipline of criminology?

Key readings

Smart, C. (1976) *Women, Crime and Criminology*. London: Routledge.

Heidensohn, F. 'Gender and crime' in Maguire, M., Morgan, R., and Reiner, R. (eds) (5th edn) *The Oxford Handbook of Criminology* (2011) Oxford: Oxford University Press.

Gelsthorpe, L., 'Feminist methodologies in criminology: old wine in new bottles' in Gelsthorpe, L., and Morris, A., *Feminist Perspectives in Criminology* (1990) Milton Keynes: Open University Press.

Jefferson, T. 'Masculinities and crime' in Maguire, R., Morgan, M., and Reiner, R. (eds) (2nd edn) *The Oxford Handbook of Criminology* (1997) Oxford: Oxford University Press.

Textbook reading/secondary source

See the entries on 'Frances Heidensohn' (by Jane Mooney) and 'Carol Smart' (by Sandra Walklate) in Hayward, K., Maruna, S. and Mooney, J. (2010) *Fifty Key Thinkers in Criminology*. London: Routledge.

Hopkins-Burke, R., Chapter 11 ('Feminist perspectives') in *An Introduction to Criminological Theory* (2009) Cullompton: Willan.

Criminological realism

After the intellectual energy brought into the area by the labelling perspective, Marxism, and a host of other influences in the 1960s and 1970s, the mid-1980s saw a return to basics. Crime rates seemed to move upwards in the face of economic recession and the attempts of criminology to come up with workable theories designed to control/reduce crime. Writers from the political right, such as James Q. Wilson, asserted that the time had come to stop attempting to *explain crime* and simply concentrate instead on *controlling it* (a position that became known as right realism). At the same time, a 'nothing works' message came from several commentators who investigated the supposed success rates of penal measures and a general public perception surfaced in the US and UK that the criminal justice system had gone 'soft on the criminal'. Meanwhile, on the political left, many critical criminologists had become deeply disillusioned with the 'outdated' Marxism associated with radical criminology, not least its 'utopian' dreams of a revolutionary politics. In the face of an increasingly complex world, the desire for simplistic solutions reasserted itself—enter criminological 'realism'.

Right realism

Based largely around the work of the late James Q. Wilson (1985), right realism emerged in the US during the 1970s, as a direct response to the aetiological crisis in criminology. Unlike left realists (see later), right realists accept *prima facie* that crime has risen dramatically in the post-war era and that, furthermore, if left unchecked will continue to rise, irrespective of improved social conditions, unless governments change their overall approach to the problem of crime. Consequently, right realists are interventionists primarily interested in the issue of societal order. As a consequence, they rarely flinch from deploying those two old stalwarts of the right—incapacitation and criminal law—as a general deterrence and as a means of protecting the propertied.

The central plank of Wilson's thesis is that, at a community level, crime begets crime. Or to use his favourite analogy, if a window is smashed in a building and not replaced, it indicates to the immediate community that no one cares about the property; consequently it will only be a matter of time before other windows are smashed and the building falls prey to more serious criminals (Wilson and Kelling, 1982). Wilson describes this as the 'developmental sequence' of crime and disorder. This being the case, it is essential that governments acknowledge this pattern and implement specific policy initiatives to address it. Wilson further argues that governments should finally wake up to the fact that they can do little to attack the root cause of crime, and should strive instead for more 'realistic goals' and instigate a series of measures that will have a real and quantifiable effect on both recorded crime and importantly, the *fear of crime*—the measures to which he refers primarily centre around a new and somewhat controversial role for the police.

Wilson asserts that if inroads are to be made in areas of high crime and urban decay, then police work needs to be based around 'order maintenance' and 'crime prevention'. In other words a shift in police practices from 'incident-orientated policing' to 'community-orientated policing'. Briefly, this means expanding the practice of everyday police work to include certain social problems that he believes greatly affect levels of crime. In his own words: 'It means defining as a problem whatever a significant body of public opinion regards as a threat to community order. It means working with the good guys, and not just against the bad guys' (Wilson and Kelling, 1989). Effectively, then, the primary task for the police should be to establish order in problem areas by undertaking a systematic, hands-on, street level assault on anti-social behaviour—a policy referred to by some as 'zero tolerance policing'. Police officers are encouraged to 'sweep the streets of undesirables', and clamp down on behaviour like drunkenness, rowdiness, prostitution, begging, and vandalism. The theory behind this approach is that if significant inroads can be made in the level of lesser crimes in an area, then eventually more serious crimes will also 'cave-in' and neighbourhoods can begin to shed the skin of endemic criminality.

More controversial are views held by certain right realists concerning causality. While, originally, it was enough for right realists simply to refute the liberal orthodoxy that crime is a by-product of poor social conditions, more recently they have accounted for this by suggesting that criminality is in fact a complex composite of socio–environmental (especially familial), psychological, and contentiously biological factors. Drawing on the behaviourist psychology of Hans Eysenck (1970), Wilson and Herrnstein argue in *Crime and Human Nature* (1985) that certain personality traits—whether levels of intelligence or indeed levels of psychopathy—are the outcome of *genetic inheritance*. However, they are keen to point out that these traits do not in themselves result in criminal or deviant behaviour. What is of equal if not greater importance is the early 'social conditioning' and positive reinforcement that an individual experiences within key social environments (in this sense their ideas correspond with contemporary control theories, see later). The stress placed by Wilson on hereditary factors has resulted in this aspect of his work being decried as 'neo-positivism', and Wilson himself dismissed as an old-fashioned moral conservative. More controversial still was Herrnstein and Murray's 1994 book, *The Bell Curve*, in which it was suggested that black people and Latinos are over-represented within the US 'underclass' because of lower IQ and a resulting lack of 'self-control'. Other features, such as the experience of unemployment or location in the social hierarchy, are regarded as spurious and seen simply as a direct consequence of individual-level differences which are either inherited or caused by problematic family-school processes at an early age. Needless to say, such assertions were met with a considerable challenge by commentators from the political left.

REVIEW QUESTIONS

1 Why are right realists typically described as 'interventionists'?

2 What policing practices are associated with 'zero tolerance policing'? What is this approach to street crime hoping to achieve?

3 What mutual ground exists between right and left realists? (See later in this chapter.)

Key readings

Wilson, J.Q. (1985) *Thinking About Crime*. New York: Vintage Books.

Wilson, J.Q. and Kelling, G. (1982) 'Broken Windows' *Atlantic Monthly*, 29–38.

Wilson, J.Q. and Herrnstein, R. (1985) *Crime and Human Nature*. New York: Simon and Schuster.

Herrnstein, R. and Murray, C. (1994) *The Bell Curve*, New York: The Free Press.

Textbook reading/secondary source

See the entry on 'James Q. Wilson' (by Matt Delisi) in Hayward, K., Maruna, S. and Mooney, J (2010) *Fifty Key Thinkers in Criminology*. London: Routledge.

Lilly, R. Cullen, F., and Ball, R., Chapter 12 ('Bringing punishment back in: Conservative criminology) in *Criminological Theory: Context and Consequences* (2011) London: Sage.

Left realism

In the UK a movement called left realism, loosely grouped around members of Middlesex University, originated as a political platform with a message to the left to 'take crime seriously' as a pressing practical problem. In many ways, the emergence of left realism can be seen as a response to both the rise of the 'neo-positivism' of right realism and the significant political and cultural transformations that took place in the 1980s and 1990s—not least, the continued hegemony of capitalism and the subsequent fall of communist Eastern Europe. Although it would be doing a disservice to imply that left realism might simply be viewed as a way in which radical criminology sought to free itself from its limiting ideological roots, it is fair to state that left realism provided a more pragmatic, policy-oriented approach to the problem of crime than much previous critical criminology. Rather than the focus placed by Marxist (or radical) criminology on macro political theory and in particular the crimes of the powerful, left realism views crime from both ends of the social structure.

The disenchantment with Marxist criminology (or left idealism as left realists preferred to call it) came about for several reasons. First, as mentioned earlier, several of the leading lights of radical criminology had grown tired of the inherent Marxist 'utopianism' that underpinned 1970s British radical/critical criminology. Second (and by the same token), the move to left realism was mediated by several positions adopted within radical criminology that were perceived by realists as being either morally ambiguous or just plainly too liberal, in particular, radical penology's attempts to abolish the prison system and certain liberal positions adopted concerning drug use. Third, left realists took issue with the view asserted by many radical criminologists that there had been no real increase in levels of crime in the post-war era. (Radical criminology had always dismissed the 'aetiological crisis', claiming that the continued rise in recorded crime was a fallacy and that statistical evidence to that effect could be explained by police preference and anomalies in the recording processes.) Fourth, and most fundamentally, many former radicals upheld the belief that left idealism was 'failing to take crime seriously'. Left realists argued that because of its lopsided concern with the crimes of the powerful, radical criminology had lost touch with the reality of 'normal crimes'. Traditionally, left idealism upheld the view that offenders themselves were victims of social inequality and racial and class biases. Consequently, many radicals dismissed (and on occasions even celebrated) lower-class crime as political (or indeed quasi-revolutionary) action. Left realists, however, have tended to shy away from this position. While the realist approach does not lose sight of the fact that the working classes are often the victims of the crimes of the powerful ('the working-class is a victim of crime from all directions ... one sort of crime tends to compound another': Lea and Young, 1984: 264), they now place a greater emphasis on those members of society who are the *victims* of (normal) crime. Thus we see a significant shift in criminological attention away from the *working-class law-breaker to the working-class victim*.

Following this line of thought, left realists look at the social and symbiotic relationship between the victim, the offender, and both formal and informal controls in a bid to better understand both the anxieties of victims (and 'the fear of crime' generally) and offender motivations. This more comprehensive approach has a twofold purpose:

(a) it enables left realists to wrest the 'law and order' initiative out of the hands of the conservative right; and

(b) it produces a less ideologically tainted picture of contemporary crime.

This picture is made considerably clearer by undertaking a widescale empirical enquiry into levels of crime within society. For left realists the official crime statistics collated by the government are inaccurate indices that are not only highly subjective, but also corrupted by political and State agency bias. Instead, they favour (and indeed pioneered) the use of victim surveys and other types of localized crime surveys as a means of extracting more accurate data on the incidence of crime in a given locality (for example, Jones *et al.*, 1986).

As the name implies, left realism maintains that the best way to accomplish a reduction in crime is by developing common-sense policies that will have a quantifiable impact on crime and the fear of crime across all societal levels; but particularly among those most often victimized—the poor and the socially deprived. What is more, for maximum effectiveness, these 'realistic' initiatives should be implemented at local or 'community' level rather than nationally or regionally. As Lea and Young (1984: 267) explain: '[t]he organization of communities in an attempt to pre-empt crime is of the utmost importance'. In their emphasis on pragmatic community reform and crime prevention practices, left realists are very much reappropriating policies traditionally favoured by conservatives and right realists. Indeed, as noted earlier, many of the initiatives they advocate are often strikingly similar to those championed by right realists and administrative criminologists. However, left realists are keen to stress that these localized policies *are infused by an underlying socialist ethos*. This emphasis on community and the inclusion of marginalized and disenfranchised segments of society within localized crime-control initiatives is a central component of contemporary left realism (see Taylor *et al.*, 1996).

Needless to say, the main criticism of the left realist approach stems from the established Marxist and critical criminological tradition. For critical criminologists, the development of the left realist approach has been a major ideological step backwards.

REVIEW QUESTIONS

1 How does left realism differ from more traditional forms of Marxist criminology?

2 What are the key ideological differences between left realism and right realism?

3 What practical solutions might left realists employ in an effort to reduce crime on a troubled inner-city housing estate?

Key readings

Lea, J. and Young, J. (1984) *What is to be Done about Law and Order?* Harmondsworth: Penguin.

Currie, E. (1985) *Confronting Crime*. New York: Pantheon.

Kinsey, R., Lea, J., and Young, J. (1986) *Losing the Fight Against Crime*. Oxford: Blackwell.

Young, J. (1992) 'Ten points of realism', in Young, J. and Matthews, R. *Rethinking Criminology: The Realist Debate* (1992) London: Sage.

Textbook reading/secondary source

See the entry on 'Jock Young' (by Keith Hayward) in Hayward, K., Maruna, S. and Mooney, J. (2010) *Fifty Key Thinkers in Criminology*. London: Routledge.

Hopkins-Burke, R., Chapter 16 ('Left realism') in *An Introduction to Criminological Theory* (2009) Willan: Cullompton.

Control theory

American criminology, largely through the work of Travis Hirschi (1969), took up a reading of Durkheim's ideas and combined this with the assumption of classical criminology (that a tendency to crime is normal in any human being) to argue that criminal behaviour results from a failure of conventional social groups (family, school, social peers) to bind or bond with the individual. In other words, to maintain social order, society must teach the individual *not to offend*. Control theorists argue that we are all born with a natural proclivity to violate the rules of society; thus, delinquency is a logical consequence of one's failure to develop internalized prohibitions (controls) against lawbreaking behaviour.

In his early 'social bond theory', Hirschi focused on *how* conformity is achieved—this was a theory not of motivation, but of *constraint*. Put simply, *what is it that stops individuals from offending*? Hirschi outlined four major elements of the social bond:

(a) *Attachment*: the ties that exist between the individual and primary agents of socialization (parents, teachers, community leaders, etc). It is a measure of the degree to which law-abiding persons serve as a source of positive reinforcement for the individual.

(b) *Commitment*: investment in conformity or conventional behaviour and a consideration of future goals which are incompatible with a delinquent lifestyle.

(c) *Involvement*: a measure of one's propensity to participate in conventional activities (sports, pastimes, work, etc).

(d) *Belief*: acceptance of the moral validity of societal norms.

Delinquency was thus associated with weak attachments/bonds to conventional institutions and modes of conduct.

In 1990 Hirschi considerably updated and augmented social bond theory with the publication of *A General Theory of Crime* (co-written with Michael Gottfredson). In this work, the emphasis shifts from external to *internal* controls. In other words, in proposing a theory of low *self*-control, Hirschi moved away from his classic *social* bonding formulation to present differential rates of self-control as a set of *individual propensities* that give differing propensities to refrain from, or to commit crime, at all ages, and under all circumstances. Gottfredson and Hirschi's theory states that individuals with high self-control will be 'substantially less likely at all periods of life to engage in criminal acts' (1990: 89); while those with low self-control are highly likely to commit crime.

The source of low self-control is seen as ineffective or incomplete socialization, especially ineffective childrearing. Parents who are attached to their children, supervise their children closely, recognize the lack of self-control in their children, and punish deviant acts, will help to socialize children into social control. Such children will generally not become delinquent as teenagers or engage in criminal acts as adults. The explicit disapproval of parents or others about whom one cares is the most important negative sanction. School and other social institutions contribute to socialization, but it is the family in which the most important socialization takes place. Consequently, unlike with social-bond theory, peer groups are relatively unimportant in the development of self-control and in the commission of delinquency or crime (the four key elements of social bonding theory—belief, attachment, commitment, and involvement—are virtually absent from Gottfredson and Hirschi's later theory). Once formed in childhood, the amount of self-control that a person has acquired remains relatively stable throughout life.

The authors also spell out the policy implications of self-control. According to self-control theory, official actions taken to deter crime in adulthood are not likely to have much effect. Self-control, they contend, is already fixed, and therefore only preventative policies that take effect early in life (and have a positive impact on families) have much chance of reducing crime and delinquency.

These variants of control theory, however, have not gone uncriticized (see Morrison, 1995 for an extended critique of control theory). For example, commentators have pointed out the tautology in the self-control hypothesis; specifically, that propensity towards crime and low self-control appears to be one and the same. More accurately, Gottfredson and Hirschi do not identify operational measures of low self-control as separate from the very tendency to commit crimes that low self-control is supposed to explain. To avoid this tautological problem, conceptual definitions or operational measures of self-control must be developed that are separate from measures of crime or propensity towards crime. Unless that step is taken, this theory will remain untestable; much of the empirical work that picks up on the theory strives to develop indices of what self-control can be taken as.

REVIEW QUESTIONS

1 Describe what you consider is meant by the term 'self-control'. What are its constitutive elements?

2 Outline how control theories differ from other criminological theories you have studied.

3 What difficulties might be encountered when attempting to measure social control?

4 Control theory is predicated on a set of values—but whose values?

Key readings

Hirschi, T. (1969) *Causes of Delinquency.* Berkeley CA: University of California Press.

Gottfredson, M. and Hirschi, T. (1990) *A General Theory of Crime.* Stanford CA: Stanford University Press.

Reis, A.J. (1951) 'Delinquency as a failure of personal and social controls'. *American Sociological Review*, 16: 196–207.

Agnew, R. (1985) 'Social control theory and delinquency: a longitudinal test', *Criminology*, 23, 47–61.

Textbook reading/secondary source

See the entry on 'Travis Hirschi' (by Wayne Morrison) in Hayward, K., Maruna, S., and Mooney, J. (2010) *Fifty Key Thinkers in Criminology.* London: Routledge.

Vold, G., Bernard, T., and Snipes, J., Chapter 10 ('Control theories') in *Theoretical Criminology* (2002) Oxford: Oxford University Press.

Cultural criminology

Cultural criminology is a theoretical, methodological, and interventionist approach to the study of crime that places criminality and its control in the context of culture; that is, it views crime and the agencies and institutions of crime control as cultural products—as creative constructs. It emphasizes the centrality of meaning, representation and power in the contested construction of crime—whether crime is constructed as an everyday event or subcultural subversion, as social danger or state-sanctioned violence. From the perspective of cultural criminology, then, the subject matter of any useful and critical criminology must include not only 'crime' and 'criminal justice' as narrowly conceived, but related and diverse phenomena such as symbolic displays and media representations of transgression and control, the criminalized deviance of political and financial elites, the feelings and emotions that emerge within and as a result of criminal events, and the ideological foundations of public and political campaigns designed to define (and delimit) both crime and its consequences. This wider focus allows for a new sort of criminology—a *cultural* criminology—better attuned to prevailing social conditions, and so more capable of conceptualizing and confronting contemporary crime and crime control. This cultural criminology seeks both to understand crime as an expressive human activity, and to critique the perceived wisdom surrounding the contemporary politics of crime and criminal justice.

Although cultural criminology is a fairly recent development (dating from the mid-1990s; see Ferrell and Sanders, 1995), it actually draws heavily on a rich tradition of sociologically-inspired criminological work, from the early sub-cultural and naturalistic ideas of the Chicago School, to the more politically-charged theoretical analyses associated with the Marxist and critical criminology of the 1970s (see earlier). However, while it is the case that many of the key themes and ideas associated with cultural criminology have been voiced elsewhere in the criminological tradition (see Ferrell *et al.*, 2008: Chapter 2), it is clear that this dynamic body of work offers something new—primarily in the way it seeks to reflect the peculiarities and particularities of the *late modern socio-cultural milieu.*

With its focus on situated meaning, youth culture, identity, space, style, and media culture, along with its commitment to understand and account for the ongoing transformations and fluctuations associated with hypercapitalism, cultural criminology is an attempt to create a 'post' or 'late' modern theory of crime. Here criminal behaviour is reinterpreted as a technique for resolving certain psychic and emotional conflicts that are in turn viewed as being indelibly linked to various features of contemporary life (see, for example, Hayward, 2004 on the relationship between consumerism and certain forms of 'expressive criminality'). In other words, cultural criminology seeks to fuse a 'phenomenology of transgression' (see, for example, Katz, 1988; Lyng, 1990) with a sociological analysis of late modern culture (see, for example, Young 1999, 2007).

Such complex foci require the utilization of a wide-ranging set of analytical tools. No surprise, then, that cultural criminology is stridently inter-disciplinary, interfacing not just with criminology, sociology, and criminal/youth justice studies, but with perspectives and methodologies drawn from *inter alia* cultural, media and urban studies, philosophy, postmodern critical theory, cultural geography, anthropology, social movement studies, and other 'action' research approaches. To quote Jeff Ferrell, cultural criminology's goal is to be 'less a definitive paradigm' than an 'array of diverse perspectives' (Ferrell, 1999: 396). The strength of the 'cultural approach', then, is the way it tackles the subject of crime and criminalization from a variety of new perspectives and academic disciplines. In effect, its remit is to keep 'turning the kaleidoscope' on the way we think about crime, and, importantly, the legal and societal responses to it. (Cultural criminology and the relationship between crime, culture, and everyday life more generally are discussed in more detail in Chapter 7.)

REVIEW QUESTIONS

1 In what ways is deviance a cultural phenomenon?

2 Draw up a random list of crimes and identify the emotions that are integral to each. How does each crime differ in terms of specific emotions?

3 What does it mean when cultural criminologists suggest that much criminality can be understood as an 'array of reactions against mundane, secular, society'?

Key readings

Ferrell, J., Hayward, K., and Young, J. (2008) *Cultural Criminology: An Invitation*, London: Sage. (Note that the 2nd edition is currently in production for 2013.)

Ferrell, J. and Hayward, K. (2014) *Cultural Criminology: Theories of Crime*, Library of Essays in Criminological Theory. Farnham: Ashgate.

Ferrell, J., Hayward, K., Morrison, W., and Presdee, M. (2004) *Cultural Criminology Unleashed*. London: GlassHouse Press.

Ferrell, J. and Sanders, C.S. (1995) *Cultural Criminology*. Boston: Northeastern University Press.

Textbook reading/secondary source

Hayward, K. and Young, J., 'Cultural criminology' in Maguire, M. *et al.*, *The Oxford Handbook of Criminology* (2011) Oxford: Oxford University Press.

Morrison, W., Chapter 13 ('Culture and crime in the postmodern condition') in *Theoretical Criminology: From Modernity to Postmodernism* (1995) London: Cavendish.

New directions in criminological theory

One of the exciting aspects of theoretical criminology is that, rather than existing as a static set of perspectives, it is a field constantly evolving and expanding. This energy is reflected in a host of new approaches that now also compete for attention alongside the more established theories covered in this chapter. What follows is a selection of just a few of these alternative theories.

One of the more prominent current areas of theoretical exploration turns around the immediate experiences and subjective world views (including the justifications and rationalizations) of the offender himself. For example, the new field of 'narrative criminology' (Presser, 2009; Sandberg, 2009) looks at how offenders 'construct the self' through a series of 'narratives' (about crime, law, deviance, etc) that they use to make sense of their world and their surroundings. According to narrative criminologists, such narratives—whether true or false—can help us understand and analyse not only the complex and interconnected nature of individual values, emotions and identities, but also the wider social fabric that binds together cultures and communities. Operating on related intellectual terrain, the emerging field of 'existentialist criminology' (Crewe and Lippens, 2009; Hardie-Bick and Lippens, 2011) seeks to bring to bear the rich tradition of existential philosophy, from Nietzsche to Kierkegaard to Sartre, on questions surrounding crime, deviance, punishment and criminal justice. Questions of human agency and the immediate phenomenological foreground of crime (see, for example, Katz, 1988; Laub and Sampson, 2003) are also explored in new cognitive theories of 'desistance' from crime. Building on the long-standing tradition of 'criminal career research' (Blumstein *et al.*, 1988) and the empirical studies associated with 'life-course criminology' (for example, Farrington, 2003), criminologists such as Shadd Maruna (2001; Maruna and Roy, 2007) and Peggy Giordano and her colleagues (Giordano *et al.*, 2002) attempt to identify the different cognitive 'scripts' that exist between desisters and persistent offenders. Such thinking also features in a variant of radical criminology known as 'convict criminology' (Ross and Richards, 2003; Richards and Ross, 2001), a critical approach to the study of prisons and incarceration that gives voice to the experiences of convicted offenders (see the 'John Irwin' entry by Stephen Richards in *Fifty Key Thinkers in Criminology*). However, as Lilly *et al.* observe, it is unclear at this stage whether or not convict criminology actually represents a truly new theory, or whether it exists only as 'a small and insular paradigm within the discipline' (2011: 229).

A very different theoretical approach to the study of crime is that offered by researchers working within the field of 'biosocial criminology' (Beaver, 2008; Walsh and Beaver, 2008). Taking its lead from early biological and genetic explanations of crime (see earlier in this chapter), 'biosocial criminology' has emerged in recent years as shorthand vernacular for contemporary research linking developments in genetics and neurophysiology, with branches of epidemiology and, importantly, evolutionary psychology.

This merging of disciplines and intellectual perspectives is also present (albeit in a more socio-environmental form) in other areas of contemporary criminological theory, most noticeably in the 'constitutive criminology' of Stuart Henry and Henry Milovanovic (1996)—a conjuncture of theoretical approaches that includes everything from social constructionism to chaos theory—and the 'integrative criminologies' associated with the work of Gregg Barak (1998a; 1998b) and others.

Finally, it is worth remarking on another recent development in criminological theory: the extension of the field into related areas of analysis not constrained either by the term crime or by nation-state definitions of criminality and illegality. For example, in recent years, we have seen a growing theoretical body of work undertaken in the fields of 'criminology of war' (for example, Jamieson, 1998; Kramer and Michalowski, 2005; Green and Ward, 2009), 'criminology of genocide' (for example, Shaw, 2003; Cohen, 2003; Morrison, 2006) and the 'criminology of terrorism' (for example, Hudson and Walters, 2009; Grabosky and Stohl, 2010; Hayward, 2011; Cottee and Hayward, 2012; Poynting and Whyte, 2012). This focus on matters international and the interconnectedness and globalization of crime (see Findlay, 2000; Aas, 2007) is also much in evidence in related areas of criminological theory including John Braithwaite's ambitious work on international comparative peace building (Braithwaite *et al.*, 2012; Braithwaite, 2011) and recent intellectual forays into transnational and border studies (for example, Aas, 2011, 2012; Aas and Bosworth, 2013). It also infuses perhaps the most developed new direction in contemporary criminological theory, 'green criminology' (for example, White, 2008; South and Brissman, 2012); an approach that looks at the dangers posed to civil society by environmental crimes, harms, and threats. Such new thinking is illustrative of the continued energy and creativity that surrounds theoretical criminology.

Key readings

Hall, S. and Winlow, S. (2012) *New Directions in Criminological Theory*. Abingdon: Routledge

Aas-Franko, K. (2012) 'The earth is one but the world is not: criminological theory and its geopolitical divisions', *Theoretical Criminology*, 16 (1) 5–20.

South, N. and Brissman, A. (2012) *The Routledge Handbook of Green Criminology*. Abingdon: Routledge.

CONCLUSION

Trying to summarize 250 years of criminological thought in one short chapter was a difficult, daunting, and some might say rather foolhardy task. It was certainly very difficult deciding what to include and what to leave out. The trained criminological eye will inevitably point to certain gaps in the 'story', but we hope they will forgive us the broad sweep of our narrative. After all, as we state in the title, the chapter is meant purely as a 'starting point'. Moreover, much effort has been made to point the interested student to classic studies and further secondary readings for each of the chapter's various theoretical themes. We hope that you will, indeed we urge you to, follow these signposts, and not to read this chapter in isolation. All theories need to be unpicked and deconstructed if we are to understand what lies behind them and thus fully comprehend the political and social forces that brought them into existence. We feel that this chapter represents a decent starting point from which you can begin your own personal theoretical journey.

WEB LINKS

http://www.malcolmread.co.uk/JockYoung/

A website containing numerous articles by the British criminological theorist Jock Young. A useful resource for student essays.

http://www.crimetalk.org.uk/

The criminological website Crime Talk contains a number of short theoretical articles about crime and punishment.

http://blogs.kent.ac.uk/culturalcriminology/links/web-links/

This site houses key papers and news about conferences and publications in the area of cultural criminology.

http://www.asc41.com

The website of The American Society of Criminology. The ASC is the pre-eminent organization of academic, theoretical, and applied criminology in the United States.

http://tcr.sagepub.com/

Theoretical Criminology: An international journal for the advancement of the theoretical aspects of criminology.

http://pun.sagepub.com/

Punishment and Society: An interdisciplinary journal on punishment, penal institutions, and penal control.

http://cmc.sagepub.com/

Crime, Media, Culture: An international journal on the relationship between crime, criminal justice, media and culture.

http://www.crimeandjustice.org.uk/cjm.html

The website of the UK publication Criminal Justice Matters, which frequently publishes engaging and accessible articles debating theoretical matters within criminology.

REFERENCES

Aas, K.F. (2007) *Globalization and Crime*. London: Sage.

Aas, K.F. (2011) '"Crimmigrant" bodies and bona fide travelers: Surveillance, citizenship and global governance', *Theoretical Criminology* 15(3): 331–46.

Aas, K.F. and Bosworth, M. (2013) *Migration and Punishment: Citizenship, Crime Control, and Social Exclusion*. Oxford: Oxford University Press

Aas-Franko, K. (2012) 'The earth is one but the world is not: criminological theory and its geopolitical divisions', *Theoretical Criminology* 16(1): 5–20.

Anderson, N. (1975) *The Hobo: The Sociology of the Homeless Man*. Chicago: University of Chicago Press.

Barak, G. (1998a) *Integrating Criminologies*. Boston: Allyn and Bacon.

Barak, G. (1998b) *Integrative Criminology*. Aldershot: Ashgate.

Beccaria, C. ([1764] 1963) *On Crimes and Punishments*. Indianapolis: Bobbs-Merrill.

Beirne, P. (1993) *Inventing Criminology: Essays on the Rise of 'Homo Criminalis'*. Albany, New York: State University of New York Press.

Bentham, J. ([1789] 1982) *A Fragment of Government and an Introduction to the Principles of Morals and Legislation*. London: Methuen.

Berman, L. (1921) *The Glands Regulating Personality*. New York: Macmillan.

Blumstein, A., Cohen, J. and Farrington, D.P. (1988) 'Criminal career research: Its value for criminology', *Criminology* 26: 1–35.

Bocock, R. and Thompson, K. (eds) (1992) *Social and Cultural Forms of Modernity*. Buckingham: Open University Press.

Bottoms, A.E. (1994) 'Environmental criminology' in M. Maguire, R. Morgan and R. Reiner (eds) *The Oxford Handbook of Criminology*. Oxford: Oxford University Press.

Bottoms, A.E. (2007) 'Place, space, crime, and disorder' in M. Maguire, R. Morgan and R. Reiner (eds) *The Oxford Handbook of Criminology*. Oxford: Oxford University Press.

Box, S. (1983) *Crime, Power and Mystification*. London: Tavistock.

Box, S. (1987) *Recession, Crime and Punishment*. London: Macmillan.

Braithwaite, J. (2011) 'Partial truth and reconciliation in the *longue duree*', *Contemporary Social Sciences* 6(1): 129–46.

Braithwaite, J., Braithwaite, V., Cookson, M. and Dunn, L. (2010) *Anomie and Violence: Non-truth and Reconciliation in Indonesian Peacebuilding*. Canberra: ANU E Press.

Burgess, E.W. (1925) 'The growth of the city' in R.E. Park, E.W. Burgess and R.D. McKenzie (eds) *The City*. Chicago: University of Chicago Press.

Cain, M. (1989) *Growing Up Good*. London: Sage.

Chambliss, W.J. (1975) 'Towards a Political Economy of Crime', *Theory and Society* 2: 149–70.

Clarke, R.V.G. and Cornish, D.B. (1985) 'Modelling offenders' decisions: a framework for policy and research' in M. Tonry and N. Morris (eds) *Crime and Justice: An Annual Review of Research*, 6. Chicago: University of Chicago Press.

Cloward, R. and Ohlin, L. (1960) *Delinquency and Opportunity: A Theory of Delinquent Gangs*. New York: Free Press.

Cohen, A. (1955) *Delinquent Boys: the Culture of the Gang*. New York: Free Press.

Cohen, S. (1972) *Folk Devils and Moral Panics*. London: MacGibbon and Kee.

Cohen, S. (1981) 'Footprints in the sand: a further report on criminology and the sociology of deviance in Britain' in M. Fitzgerald, G. McLennan and J. Pawson (eds) *Crime and Society: Readings in History and Theory*. London: Open University Press.

Cohen, S. (2001) *States of Denial: Knowing about Atrocities and Suffering*. Cambridge: Polity Press.

Collier, R. (1998) *Masculinities, Crime and Criminology*. Buckingham: Open University Press.

Cornish, D.G. and Clarke, R.V.G. (1986) *The Reasoning Criminal: Rational Choice Perspectives on Offending*. New York: Springer-Verlag.

Cortes, J.B. and Gatti, F.M. (1972) *Delinquency and Crime: A Bio-psychological Approach*. New York: Seminar Press.

Cottee, S. and Hayward, K.J. (2011) 'Terrorist (e)motives: the existential attractions of terrorism', *Studies in Conflict and Terrorism* 34 (12): 963–86.

Cressey, P. (1932) *The Taxi-Dance Hall*. Chicago: University of Chicago Press.

Crewe, D. and Lippens, R. (2009) *Existentialist Criminology*. London: Routledge-Cavendish.

Crowe, R.A. (1974) 'An adoption study of anti-social personality', *Archives of General Psychiatry* 31: 785–91.

Dalton, K. (1961) 'Menstruation and crime', *British Medical Journal* 2: 1752–3.

Downes, D. and Rock, P. (1988) *Understanding Deviance*. Oxford: Oxford University Press.

Durkheim, E. (1965) *The Rules of Sociological Method*, trans. Solovay and Mueller. New York: Free Press.

Eysenck, H. (1970) *Crime and Personality*. London: Paladin.

Farrington, D.P. (2003) 'Developmental and life-course criminology: Key theoretical and empirical issues', *Criminology* 41: 221–55.

Felson, M. (2010) *Crime and Everyday Life*. Thousand Oaks, CA: Sage.

Ferrell, J. (1999) 'Cultural Criminology', *Annual Review of Sociology* 25: 395–418.

Ferrell, J. and Sanders, C.R. (eds) (1995) *Cultural Criminology*. Boston: Northeastern University Press.

Ferrell, J., Hayward, K.J., Morrison, W. and Presdee, M. (2004) *Cultural Criminology Unleashed*. London: GlassHouse.

Ferrell, J., Hayward, K.J. and Young, J. (2008) *Cultural Criminology: An Invitation*. London: Sage.

Ferri, E. (2003) 'Causes of Criminal Behaviour' in J. Muncie, E. McLaughlin and G. Hughes, *Criminological Perspectives: A Reader*. London: Sage.

Findlay, M. (2000) *The Globalization of Crime*. Cambridge: Cambridge University Press.

Foucault, M. (1977) *Discipline and Punish: The Birth of the Prison*. London: Penguin Books.

Garland, D. (1994) 'Of crime and criminals: the development of criminology in Britain' in M. Maguire, R. Morgan and R. Reiner (eds) *The Oxford Handbook of Criminology* Oxford: Oxford University Press.

Giordano, P.C., Cernkovich, S.A. and Rudolph, J.L. (2002) 'Gender, crime, and desistance: toward a theory of cognitive transformation', *American Journal of Sociology* 107: 990–1064.

Giddens, A. (1974) *Positivism and Sociology*. London: Heinemann.

Goffman, E. (1968) *Stigma: Notes on the Management of a Spoiled Identity*. London: Penguin.

Goring, G. (1913) *The English Convict*. London: Darling & Son.

Gottfredson, M. and Hirschi, T. (1990) *A General Theory of Crime*. Stanford, CA: Stanford University Press.

Grabosky, P. and Stohl, M. (2010) *Crime and Terrorism*. London: Sage.

Green, P. and Ward, T. (2009) 'The Transformation of Violence in Iraq', *British Journal of Criminology* 49(5): 609–27.

Hall, S. and Gieben, B. (1992) *The Formations of Modernity*. Cambridge: Polity.

Hardie-Bick, J. and Lippens, R. (2011) *Crime, Governance and Existential Predicaments*. Basingstoke: Palgrave-Macmillan.

Hayward, K.J. (2004) *City Limits: Crime, Consumer Culture and the Urban Experience*. London: GlassHouse Press.

Hayward, K.J. (2011) 'The critical terrorism studies-cultural criminology nexus: some thoughts on how to "toughen up" the critical studies approach', *Critical Studies of Terrorism* 4(1): 57–73.

Hayward, K.J., and Morrison, W. (2002) 'Locating "Ground Zero": caught between the narratives of crime and war' in J. Strawson (ed.), *Law After Ground Zero*. London: Cavendish.

Hayward, K.J. and Young, J. (2004) 'Cultural criminology: some notes on the script', *Theoretical Criminology* 8(3): 259–73.

Heidensohn, F. (1968) 'The Deviance of Women: a Critique', *British Journal of Sociology* 19.

Heidensohn, F. (1996) *Women and Crime*. London: Macmillan.

Henry, S. and Milovanovic, D. (1996) *Constitutive Criminology: Beyond Postmodernism*. London: Sage.

Herrnstein, R.J. and Murray, C. (1994) *The Bell Curve: Intelligence and Class Structure in American Life*. New York: The Free Press.

Hirschi, T. (1969) *Causes of Delinquency*. Berkeley: University of California Press.

Hobsbawm, E. (1972) *Bandits*. Harmondsworth: Penguin.

Hooton, E.A. (1939) *The American Criminal: An Anthropological Study*. Cambridge, MA: Harvard University Press.

Hudson, B. and Walters, R. (2009) 'Special Edition: Criminology and the War on Terror', *British Journal of Criminology* 49(5).

Hume, D. ([1739] 1978) *A Treatise on Human Nature*. Oxford: Oxford University Press.

Hutchings, B. and Mednick, S.A. (1975) 'Registered criminality in the adopted and biological parents of registered male criminal adoptees' in R.R. Fieve, D. Rosenthal and H. Brill (eds) *Genetic Research in Psychiatry*. Baltimore: Johns Hopkins University Press.

Jamieson, R. (1998) 'Towards a Criminology of War in Europe' in V. Ruggiero, N. South and I. Taylor, *The New European Criminology: Crime and Social Order in Europe*. London: Routledge.

Jefferson, T. (1996) 'Introduction to the masculinities', *Special edition of the British Journal of Criminology* 36.

Jones, T., MacLean, B. and Young, J. (1986) *The Islington Crime Survey*. Aldershot: Gower.

Katz, J. (1988) *The Seductions of Crime: Moral and Sensual Attractions in Doing Evil*. New York: Basic Books.

Kinsey, R., Lea, J. and Young, J. (1986) *Losing the Fight Against Crime*. Oxford: Blackwell.

Klein, D. (1973) 'The Etiology of Female Crime: a Review of the Literature', *Issues in Criminology* 8.

Kramer, R.C. and Michalowski, R.J. (2005) 'War, Aggression and State Crime: A criminological analysis of the invasion of Iraq', *British Journal of Criminology* 45(4): 446–69.

Lea, J. and Young, J. (1984) *What is to be Done about Law and Order?* Harmondsworth: Penguin.

Lemert, E.M. (1951) *Social Pathology*. New York: McGraw Hill.

Lilly, J.R., Cullen, F.T. and Ball, R.A. (2011) *Criminological Theory: Context and Consequences*. Thousand Oaks, CA: Sage.

Lombroso, C. (1876) *L'Uomo Delinquente*. Milan: Hoepli.

Lyng, S. (1990) 'Edgework: a Social Psychological Analysis of Voluntary Risk-Taking', *American Journal of Sociology* 95: 876–921.

McLaughlin, E. (2001) 'Functionalism' in E. McLaughlin and J. Muncie (eds) *The Sage Dictionary of Criminology*. London: Sage.

Maruna, S. (2001) *Making Good: How Ex-Convicts reform and Rebuild Their Lives*. Washington DC: American Psychological Association.

Maruna, S. and Roy, K. (2007) 'Amputation or reconstruction?: Notes on the concept of "knifing off" and desistance from crime', *Journal of Contemporary Criminal Justice* 23: 104–24.

Matthews, R. and Young, J. (1992) *Issues in Realist Criminology*. London: Sage.

Mead, G.H. ([1934] 1962) *Mind, Self, and Society: From the Standpoint of a Social Behaviorist*. Chicago: University of Chicago Press.

Melossi, D. (1990) *The State of Social Control*. Cambridge: Polity.

Merton, R.K. (1938) 'Social Structure and Anomie', *American Sociological Review* 3: 672–82.

Messerschmidt, J. (1993) *Masculinities and Crime*. Lanham, MD: Rowman and Littlefield.

Morrison, W. (1995) *Theoretical Criminology: From Modernity to Post Modernism*. London: Cavendish.

Morrison, W. (2004) 'Lombroso and the Birth of Criminological Positivism: Scientific Mastery or Cultural Artifice?' in J. Ferrell *et al.*, *Cultural Criminology Unleashed*. London: GlassHouse.

Morrison, W. (2006) *Criminology, Civilisation and the New World Order*. Abingdon: Cavendish-Routledge.

Moyer, K.E. (1971) 'The physiology of aggression and the implication for aggression control' in R.G. Green and E.I. Donnerstein (eds) *The Control of Aggression and Violence*. New York: Academic Press.

Park, R.E. (1925) 'The city: suggestions for the investigation of human behaviour in the urban environment' in R.E. Park, E.W. Burgess and R.D. McKenzie (eds) *The City*. Chicago: Chicago University Press.

Pollak, O. (1950) *The Criminality of Women*. New York: A.S. Barnes.

Poynting, S. and Whyte, D. (eds) (2012) *Counter-Terrorism and State Political Violence: The 'War on Terror' as Terror*. London: Routledge.

Presdee, M. (2000) *Cultural Criminology and the Carnival of Crime*. London: Routledge.

Quinney, R. (1991) *Criminology as Peacemaking*. Bloomington: Indiana University Press.

Presser, L. (2009) 'The narratives of offenders', *Theoretical Criminology* 13(2): 177–200.

Richards, S.C. and Ross, J.I. (2001) 'Introducing the new school of convict criminology', *Social Justice* 28(1): 177–90.

Roshier, B. (1989) *Controlling Crime*. Milton Keynes: Open University Press.

Ross, J.I. and Richards, S.C. (2003) *Convict Criminology*. Belmont, CA: Thomson.

Sandberg, A.A., Koepf, G.F., Ishiara, T. and Hauschka, T.S. (1961) 'An XYY human male', *Lancet* 262: 488–9.

Sandberg, S. (2009) 'A narrative search for respect', *Deviant Behavior*. 30(6): 487–510.

Shaw, C.R. and McKay, H.D. (1931) *Social Factors in Juvenile Delinquency*. Washington DC: Government Printing Office.

Shaw, C.R. and McKay, H.D. (1942) *Juvenile Delinquency and Urban Areas*. Chicago: University of Chicago Press.

Shaw, M. (2003) *War and Genocide: Organised Killing in Modern Society*. Cambridge: Polity Press.

Sheldon, W.H. (1942) *The Varieties of Temperament*. New York: Harper.

Sherman, L.W., Gartin, P.R. and Buerger, M.E. (1989) 'Hot spots of predatory crime: routine activities and the criminology of place', *Criminology* 27: 27–55.

Smart, C. (1976) *Women, Crime and Criminology: A Feminist Critique*. London: Routledge.

South, N. and Brissman, A. (2012) *The Routledge Handbook of Green Criminology*. Abingdon: Routledge.

Sumner, C. (1990) *Censure, Politics and Criminal Justice*. Milton Keynes: Open University Press.

Sutherland, E. (1942) *Principles of Criminology*. Philadelphia: J B Lippincott.

Sykes, G.M. and Matza, D. (1957) 'Techniques of neutralization', *American Sociological Review* 22.

Taylor, I., Evans, K. and Fraser, P. (1996) *A Tale of Two Cities: Global Change, Local Feeling and Everyday Life in the North of England: A Study in Manchester and Sheffield*. London: Routledge.

Taylor, I. Walton, P. and Young, J. (1973) *New Criminology: For a Social Theory of Deviance*. London: Routledge and Kegan Paul.

Thompson, E.P. (1968) *The Making of the English Working Class*. Harmondsworth: Penguin.

Thompson, E.P. (1975) *Whigs and Hunters*. London: Allen Lane.

Thrasher, F.M. (1927) *The Gang: A Study of 1,313 Gangs in Chicago*. Chicago: Chicago University Press.

Tittle, C. (1995) *Control Balance: Toward a General Theory of Deviance*. Boulder, CO: Westview Press.

Valier, C. (2005) 'Just theory: theory, crime and criminal justice' in C. Hale, K. Hayward, A. Wahidin and E. Wincup (eds) *Criminology*. Oxford: Oxford University Press.

Walsh, A. and Beaver, K. (2008) *Biosocial Criminology: New Directions in Theory and Research*. London: Routledge.

White, R. (2008) *Crimes Against Nature: Environmental Criminology and Ecological Justice*. Cullompton: Willan.

Wilson, J.Q. (1985) *Thinking About Crime*. New York: Vintage Books.

Wilson, J.Q. and Kelling, G. (1982) 'Broken windows', *Atlantic Monthly* 29–38.

Wilson, J.Q. and Herrnstein, R. (1985) *Crime and Human Nature*. New York: Simon and Schuster.

Young, J. (1999) *The Exclusive Society*. London: Sage.

Young, J. (2007) *The Vertigo of Late Modernity*. London: Sage.

NOTE

1. This chapter has been adapted from *Theoretical Criminology* (Hayward and Morrison, 2002), a subject guide used in connection with the University of London's External Laws Programme. Our thanks go to the University of London's International Programme for kindly allowing us to reproduce sections of that text here.

5 Researching crime and criminal justice

Emma Wincup

INTRODUCTION

Each chapter within this volume utilizes criminological research findings. Collectively these studies draw upon a range of disciplines and theoretical traditions and deploy a variety of research designs and methods to gather both qualitative and quantitative data. Criminological knowledge is produced when these data are analysed and subsequently disseminated, typically through academic publications but increasingly through other outlets in order to reach policy-makers, practitioners and the public. To make effective use of this knowledge, students need to adopt a critical stance when interpreting it; one which appreciates both its strengths and its limitations. This requires them to evaluate the studies on which it is based. This chapter aims to provide students with the necessary skills to appraise the studies they read.

The chapter is divided into three sections. The first outlines the range of options available to criminologists when researching crime and criminal justice. It identifies the key questions researchers need to ask when selecting a research design, outlines the different types of methods criminologists can select from, and explores the advantages and disadvantages of seeking to combine methods. In many respects, the discussion in the first section applies equally to social scientists interested in social phenomena other than crime. In contrast, sections two and three have been written specifically for criminologists. The second section seeks to identify some challenges faced by researchers interested in crime and criminal justice. It draws attention to the political nature of criminological research, the increased likelihood that criminologists will be exploring sensitive topics with consequent ethical implications, and the heightened need to manage risk during the research process. The final section considers recent methodological developments, considers the opportunities they present for researching crime and criminal justice.

BACKGROUND

This chapter focuses on the empirical research tradition within criminology, which can be defined as research based upon the analysis of data rather than conceptual analysis. It can be contrasted with theoretical research. Within criminology, there is a tendency for researchers to define themselves, or be defined by others, as either theorists or empirical researchers. As Bottoms (2007) argues, this form of specialization can be helpful in terms of building successful research careers; however, it tends to misrepresent the relationship between theory and data and fails to appreciate that criminologists cannot avoid theory. Empirical research needs to engage with theoretical debates so it can either test theory (for example, by testing hypotheses) or generate theory (for example, by generating concepts to make sense of the social world). Indeed, some of the most important theoretical insights within criminology have been derived from empirical studies; for example, Becker's (1963) study of marijuana users consolidated the development of the labelling perspective (see Chapter 4). Similarly, even if they do not conduct empirical research themselves, theorists still need to draw upon studies conducted by others.

The emergence of the empirical research tradition within criminology can be traced back to the nineteenth century when, positivism (see Chapter 4) rose to the fore and began to establish criminology as a 'scientific' discipline (Garland, 2002). Positivism is essentially concerned with emulating the approaches of the natural scientists in order to develop objective knowledge about crime. There is considerable variation in the work of positivist criminologists. For example, early positivists included the 'moral statisticians' (for example, Quetelet) who made use of official crime statistics, and linked them to social, economic, and environmental factors to suggest that crime rates are regular and predictable. Those who adopted an experimental approach to search for a criminal 'type' (most famously Lombroso; see Chapter 4) by comparing the physiological characteristics of 'offenders' and 'non-offenders' can also be described as early positivists. Despite these differences, three common characteristics of the work of positivist research are the search for cause and effect relationships, viewing crime in terms of either individual or social pathology, and a preference for quantitative (that is, numerical) data.

Criminologists soon came to realize the inherent weaknesses of the positivist approach, particularly its inability to appreciate the complex nature of criminal behaviour. In the twentieth century, they took inspiration from the emergent interpretivist tradition within the social sciences and explored different approaches to understanding the social world in general, and crime and criminal justice in particular. Interpretivism can be defined as a theoretical approach which seeks to explore the subjective meanings through which individuals understand the social world. This tradition was influential in exposing criminologists to a wider variety of approaches and methods for researching the social world. In particular, the work of the Chicago School (see Chapter 4) from the 1920s onwards was highly influential in establishing the ethnographic tradition. Ethnography can be defined as:

> the study of groups of people in their natural setting, typically involving the researcher being present for extended periods of time in order to collect data systematically about their daily activities and the meanings they attach to them. (Noaks and Wincup, 2004: 93)

In general terms, this involves the collection and analysis of qualitative data (that is, data which are not amendable to measurement and are textual, visual, or audio).

Making choices (1): choosing between research designs

The limited space available precludes a discussion of the development of the initial idea. Instead, readers are directed to King and Wincup (2007) which explores potential sources of inspiration; for example, the academic literature, personal experiences, and current policy concerns. They also discuss the process of turning initial ideas into researchable problems; a seemingly straightforward task which is surprisingly challenging and can be inordinately time-consuming. It involves thinking through what can realistically be done given the resources available and any requirements which must be fulfilled; for example, to obtain funding or an academic degree. It also requires imaginative thinking to develop a research question which contributes, even in a modest way, to criminological knowledge.

Once they have selected their research topic and developed their research question(s), criminologists need to focus their attention on the choice of research design and methods. This can be a challenging task because of the range of possibilities offered, and the methodological literature tends to confuse more than clarify in a number of respects. First, the distinction between research design and methods is not always apparent and often the terms are used interchangeably. For example, ethnography—a strategy for conducting research defined earlier in this chapter—is often conflated with participant observation—a research method defined later in this chapter. Second, the literature tends to focus more on specific research methods rather than more general issues of research design so that, as King and Wincup (2007: 23) argue, 'all too often new researchers make a serious mistake by moving straight from deciding the research question to choosing between methods' without thinking through how best to approach the study based upon both intellectual and pragmatic considerations. Third, whilst the methodological literature often presents neat typologies of research designs, in practice it can be difficult to attach a label to the chosen research design. Finally, the labels 'qualitative' and 'quantitative' are used to describe different research designs or methods rather than used more appropriately to characterize forms of data.

King and Wincup (2007) also outline some of the key questions for consideration when choosing a research design. Essentially these questions require the researcher to reflect upon three, albeit interrelated, issues: the relationship between research and theory; the relationship between research and policy; and the type of data needed to answer the research questions(s). We will now explore each of these issues in turn.

Theory and criminological research

Theory provides the researcher with a conceptual framework to make sense of the data. It should not be conflated with theories of criminal behaviour such as those discussed in Chapter 4. It guides, or at least it should guide, all aspects of the research process. The relationship between research and theory is complex and it is impossible to do justice to its intricacies within the confines of one chapter. It is, however, possible to make a distinction between research which is deductivist and aims to test theory, and research which is inductivist and aims to generate theory. In practice, this distinction over-simplifies the role theory plays in relation to criminological research (see Bottoms, 2007 for a more nuanced exploration of the relationship between theory and empirical observations in criminology). Nonetheless, the distinction helps us to draw out the implications for research design.

The starting point for deductivist research is to develop a theoretically informed hypothesis. A hypothesis is an 'untested assertion about the relationship between two or more variables' (Jupp, 2006: 137) and it is the task of the researcher to collect data which proves or disproves the hypothesis. Typically, this involves the collection of data from large samples using methods which form part of an experimental research design in order to assess the possibility of causality between independent (the 'cause') and dependent (the 'effect') variables. Emulating the approach of natural scientists, some criminologists have adopted this approach, although they have usually made compromises and conducted 'quasi' rather than 'true' experiments. Both involve comparing and contrasting data (usually quantitative) gathered from 'experimental' and 'comparison' groups, but only the latter involves the random allocation of research participants to each group.

For quasi-experiments, the comparison group may be the 'experimental' group prior to the intervention, allowing data to be collected before and after an intervention. Whilst 'true' experiments are the norm in scientific disciplines, criminologists have seldom adopted this approach. Experimental research designs are often viewed as more powerful than the alternatives due to perceived high levels of internal validity. Internal validity refers to the accuracy of any claims made, or indeed rejected, about causality between variables. 'True' experiments are viewed as the gold standard because the random allocation removes the possibility that similarities and differences between the 'experimental' and 'control' groups can be attributed to initial variation between the groups. This form of experiment also enables bold claims to be made about external validity, the ability of the research findings to be generalized beyond the group studied, because the sample achieved is a probability one (that is, all in the target population have an equal chance of being selected).

In contrast, inductivist research is exploratory rather than experimental in its approach. Rather than attempting to imitate the approach of natural scientists, it aims to generate theory through careful analysis of data gathered from researching in detail one aspect of the social world. Glaser and Strauss (1967) describe the outcome of this process as 'grounded theory'. In many respects, research can never be characterized as wholly inductivist because theory may inform the early stages of the research process. Hypotheses may be formulated at the outset, although when the chosen approach is to collect qualitative data, they are unlikely to be expressed in terms of causal relationships. Exploratory research designs are often subject to harsh and unfair criticism by those who favour experimental approaches. Criteria used to assess the quality of experimental research are rooted in positivist approaches to researching the social world. Consequently, exploratory approaches, which tend to involve the collection and analysis of qualitative data from non-probability samples, are often described as weak in terms of internal and external validity. In recent years, there has been increasing recognition of the need to judge different forms of research in another way (see, for example, Bryman *et al.*, 2012). Moving away from using quality criteria grounded in the positivist paradigm and using ones more appropriate to their interpretivist roots, we can appreciate that studies based upon exploratory research designs are of good quality if they can convey a high level of trust in the conclusions reached and contribute to the task of generalization through the development of theoretical concepts which merit exploration with other populations and/or within different settings.

The relationship between research and policy

The relationship between research and policy can take many forms and there is a long-standing history of social scientists trying to map out the range of possibilities (see Young *et al.*, 2002 for a recent five-fold typology of the relationship between research and policy). This relationship has been the subject of considerable academic debates during the past fifteen years, fuelled in part by the apparent shift under New Labour (1997–2010)—in rhetoric if not always in practice—towards evidence-based policy.

Policy-makers are often concerned with issues of effectiveness and therefore seek to commission evaluative rather than research studies. Research and evaluation are closely related but in some respects serve different purposes. It is important not to exaggerate the differences between research and evaluation: both involve choosing from the same 'menu' of research methods in order to collect and analyse data systematically. Evaluation can perhaps best be considered as a form of 'applied' research, which prioritizes solving practical problems over the generation of new knowledge (the core aim of 'basic' or 'blue-skies' research). Evaluative studies are most closely associated with experimental designs and the gathering of quantitative data. These data are collected as part of an attempt to measure 'what works' by considering inputs (for example, characteristics of participants), outputs (for example, proportion of participants completing the intervention), and outcomes (for example, the impact of the intervention on participants' behaviour). Qualitative data are sometimes gathered to provide an insight into processes, usually through interviews with key stakeholders or observation of interventions.

Data considerations

Taking into account the type of data needed to answer the research questions posed is essential when choosing between research designs. In this respect, considerations about the relative balance between breadth and depth are paramount. The narrow focus of a 'case study' approach is compensated for by the rich and detailed data gathered. In contrast, the broader focus of a 'survey' approach balances the somewhat decontextualized and superficial data gathered.

The term 'case' refers to a social unit with clear boundaries which can be studied holistically (Payne and Payne, 2004). The approach taken is exploratory rather than experimental and is often combined, therefore, with an ethnographic approach. The methods used tend to prioritize the collection of qualitative data. As Keddie (2006) outlines, a case can be an individual (for example, an offender), an event (for example, an urban riot), a social activity (for example, an offending behaviour programme), an organization (for example, a penal reform charity), or an institution (for example, a prison). Traditionally understood as the study of a single case (see, for example, Payne and Payne, 2004), an increasingly common approach is to incorporate multiple case studies into the research design. This helps to allay concerns about the lack of external validity (that is, the ability of the findings to be generalized beyond the particular case), particularly if care is taken to select a range of diverse cases. For example, a research study seeking to explore resettlement provision in prisons could make a stronger argument regarding generalizability if its research design included institutions accommodating prisoners serving different sentence lengths and could offer an even more robust defence if a women's prison was included. This case is a 'critical' one in the sense that women make up only a small proportion of the total prison population (see Chapters 15 and 25).

Surveys are often conflated with questionnaires, which is one of the main methods used by those who adopt a survey approach to collect predominantly quantitative data from a large, and ideally representative, sample. This sampling approach allows survey researchers to make bold claims about the generalizability of their findings if accompanied by a high response rate. It also enhances confidence in the results of any statistical techniques used to test hypotheses. Surveys can involve direct contact with research participants or indirect through post, email, the Internet, and telephone. They tend to adopt a structured and standardized approach so there is very limited flexibility once the survey is underway. Piloting of research instruments is used to ensure consistency of measurement (reliability).

A further consideration when designing a research study is whether cross-sectional or longitudinal data are needed. Often the data gathered are cross-sectional and provide a snapshot of a particular point in time, and this may be the only option to the researcher given the resources available. There are common exceptions, for example, studies which involve an ethnographic approach. There are few criminological studies which have adopted a long-term view and followed up research participants over a substantial period. These have tended to focus, at least initially, on young people and their pathways into crime (see Chapter 17 for examples). One compromise is to renew contact with research participants a matter of months after the initial contact. However, even this can be extremely resource-intensive.

Making choices (2): choosing between research methods

Criminologists have two options available to them when they are making decisions about how to obtain the data they need to answer their research question(s). First, they can make use of existing datasets, both qualitative and quantitative (secondary data). Many of these are held at the UK Data Archive (see the web links section at the end of the chapter) and at the time of writing (Autumn 2012), entering the term 'crime' into its search engine resulted in access to details of 918 studies. The archive includes large-scale studies, usually government funded. Criminologists can make use of specialist surveys such as the British Crime Survey (see Chapter 3) or more generic surveys such as the General Household Survey which provide data on issues related to crime such as poverty, unemployment, and alcohol use. Some researchers, and it is usually a requirement if funded by the Economic and Social Research Council, deposit their datasets in the archive. This has promoted access to qualitative datasets suitable for secondary analysis. Using existing datasets has obvious advantages. They make accessible to researchers data which it would not normally be possible to collect because of the high financial costs involved and these can be accessed relatively quickly and easily. Once research has been completed, rarely have all the analytical possibilities been exhausted, which opens up new avenues for other researchers to explore. With the data already available in a form suitable for analysis, researchers can devote all the available resources to this task. Alongside these advantages are some important drawbacks. Most importantly there is a danger that the data cannot answer the research questions posed. Secondary analysis of qualitative datasets is still in its infancy, and there are particular issues because reflexivity plays a key role when such data are gathered. Whilst depositors are required to provide detailed documentation to accompany their dataset, it is still difficult to reflect upon the context in which the data were gathered.

Second, criminologists can decide to collect their own (primary) data and there are four main research methods from which they can choose: questionnaires, interviews, focus groups, and observation. It is important to be clear that specific criminological research methods do not exist, although, as we will explore later in this chapter, when used to explore criminological issues each research method can present some unique challenges due to the subject matter. Criminologists therefore have to select from the same menu of research methods as their fellow social scientists and face similar constraints. Their chosen methods have to fit with the theoretical position and research design adopted, although researchers should resist rigid prescriptions about the incompatibility of particular methods with their chosen theoretical and methodological approach. Whilst researchers should not assume that 'anything goes', purist assertions, for example, that questionnaires cannot be used for exploratory research are unhelpful. Other considerations include the resources available and the expertise and ethical stance of the researcher (see King and Wincup, 2007).

Questionnaires (see Figure 5.1) are particularly suited to studies which require relatively straightforward data to be gathered from a large number of respondents who have good levels of literacy. Whilst it is not impossible to use questionnaires for sensitive topics (or for groups with low levels of literacy), extra care needs to be taken in these circumstances. A well-designed questionnaire with clear instructions can help to boost response rates, minimize the likelihood of incomplete answers, and reduce the possibility that respondents will not complete the questionnaires as intended. Getting the design right at the outset is important because questionnaires are an inflexible research method. Once the questionnaire has been distributed there is no scope to amend it, hence it is imperative to pilot the questionnaire in advance with a small sample.

Criticisms of questionnaires as a research method are numerous but tend to coalesce around response rates and the nature of the data gathered. Response rates, particularly for self-completion approaches, can be notoriously low, raising concerns that those who complete questionnaires may be different in some way from those who do not, thus compromising the representativeness of the sample. There is a tension between the researcher's desire to boost response rates (i.e. by designing a short questionnaire) and the need to gather sufficient data to answer the research questions. Even if a large number of questions are asked the data in some respects are inevitably superficial because the researcher

The term questionnaire describes a standardized research instrument used to collect data from respondents about a particular topic. This method relies on participants completing it themselves, although the term questionnaire is sometimes used to describe a highly structured interview schedule. Traditionally, administering questionnaires has required respondents to record their answer on paper copies distributed directly by the researcher or indirectly via a third party or post. Increasingly questionnaires are distributed and completed electronically. Questions are normally closed in the sense that the respondent has to select from a list of possible answers, thus the data gathered are quantitative. Asking open questions can produce qualitative data but answers tend to lack detail and responses are normally placed in categories allowing the data to be quantified.

Suggested further reading: Oppenheim (2000)
Example of a study using questionnaires: Hough and Roberts (2004)

Figure 5.1 Questionnaires

Interviews describe a data collection method based upon the posing of a series of questions, usually face-to-face but, as we will explore later in this chapter, technological developments now permit other forms of interaction. Interviews can be placed upon a continuum in terms of their degree of structure, ranging from highly structured interviews used in survey research to collect quantitative data using closed questions through to unstructured interviews most closely associated with ethnographic approaches which gather qualitative data through open questions. In between lie semi-structured interviews which combine the flexibility of more unstructured approaches with the standardization of more structured approaches. The data gathered using this type of interview are usually qualitative.

There are a number of techniques for recording interview data: interviewers may decide to take notes or record the discussion, allowing for the preparation of verbatim transcripts. The latter is often seen as the most desirable because it allows the interviewer to concentrate on the processes of listening and asking questions, and it facilitates analysis. However, transcribing is an extremely time-consuming task so interviewers need to assure themselves that that the benefits outweigh the costs.

Interviews normally involve only one participant but on some occasions it may be preferable to conduct group interviews, for example, if the interviewee requests that someone else is present. Group interviews are not synonymous with focus groups, discussed in Figure 5.3.

Suggested further reading: Arksey and Knight (1999)

Example of a study using interviews: Aldridge *et al.* (2011)

Figure 5.2 Interviews

has imposed limits on the nature of answers which can be given. This leads some social scientists to conclude that questionnaires cannot provide a complete understanding of the issue being investigated.

Interviews (see Figure 5.2) are the favoured method of many social scientists including criminologists. Their relative strengths and weaknesses depend upon the type of interview conducted. Highly structured interviews share many of the same advantages and disadvantages as questionnaires. However, response rates tend to be higher and the data may be more complete, but these advantages come at a greater financial cost. Less structured interviews have different merits, particularly because they present an opportunity for the interviewer to explore beyond the initial answers given. They also present possibilities to record non-verbal aspects which can either serve as data in their own right and/or be incorporated into a reflexive account of the research process. Unstructured interviews, in which the individual is treated as someone with a story to tell, provide the greatest prospect that new themes will emerge, making them ideally suited to exploratory research. However, the interviewer runs the risk that much of the data collected may not be relevant to the research questions and making sense of the data gathered can be difficult. Semi-structured approaches often emerge as the preferred option. They allow the interviewer to retain control over the interaction at the same time as responding to the interviewee by rephrasing questions, asking additional ones, or changing their order. This promotes some degree of consistency across transcripts, which simplifies the task of data analysis.

Focus groups take advantage of the dynamic interaction of groups to collect largely qualitative data. The discussion is participant-centred and the researcher takes on the role of moderator. They may be supported by an additional researcher with responsibility for recording data; a more challenging task in a group setting. Groups normally comprise of between six and eight participants: a sufficiently high number to generate discussion yet still providing opportunities for all to have a voice. To obtain the best data, groups need to gel quickly so participants are generally chosen because they are similar in some way. Homogeneity of participants is especially important if sensitive topics will be discussed (Morgan, 2006).

Suggested further reading: Bloor *et al.* (2001)

Example of a study using focus groups: Smithson *et al.* (2012)

Figure 5.3 Focus groups

Focus groups (see *Figure 5.3*) are an increasingly popular way to gather data. They have the potential to provide an effective way of establishing a large and diverse sample and their participant-led nature makes them ideal for exploratory studies. Many of the drawbacks of focus groups relate to practical considerations: they can be difficult to arrange and manage but careful planning can minimize the likelihood of problems arising. Focus groups may not be the preferred method for all studies. If the topic is a sensitive one, the privacy and confidentiality which can be afforded to research participants in a one-to-one interview might be more appropriate. Moreover, whilst focus groups provide an opportunity to observe group dynamics, they do so in an artificial environment. Consequently, if the research questions require a more contextualized understanding of these dynamics, then there is little substitute for observing research participants in their natural setting.

As for the use of interviews, the relative strengths and weakness of observation (see Figure 5.4) as a research method are highly dependent on the form selected. However, all forms allow researchers to observe directly what people *do* rather than rely on accounts of what people *say they do*. This can prove extremely resource-intensive, making it most appropriate for studies which deploy a case study design. The more structured and detached approaches are praised by some because they reduce researcher bias, encourage objectivity, and enhance the reliability of the data. For others, they unnecessarily restrict the data which can be recorded, resulting in a potential loss of some of the most interesting data. In contrast, less structured and more participative approaches provide the opportunity to collect rich and detailed data by allowing researchers to explore not only behaviours, but the meanings attached to them. Unsurprisingly, participant observation is the favoured method of ethnographers, often coupled with unstructured interviews. The act of participation makes it vulnerable to criticism because it raises the issue of whether the presence of the researcher fundamentally changes the research setting. It has also led to concerns being raised about whether the researcher can maintain a sufficient degree of academic detachment to facilitate analysis as they become increasingly familiar with the setting and its participants.

The three methods discussed so far as used to collect primary data. When conducting documentary research, it can be difficult to assess whether to treat the data as primary

Observation is a research method which involves watching and observing social activities. Often this takes place in a 'natural' setting although sometimes researchers seek to create situations which can be observed in the 'artificial' environment of a research setting. Criminological examples include observing the impact of media violence on children (see Chapter 7). Like interviews, observation can take many forms. Key sources of variation are the extent to which the observation is structured and the extent to which observers participate in the social setting they are observing. At the one extreme, observation can be highly structured, collecting largely quantitative data according to pre-specified criteria using a pro-forma. The observer in this instance takes on a detached role. At the other end of the spectrum, observers participate in the setting they are observing and record both their experiences and observations through compiling fieldnotes. The data gathered are typically qualitative.

Another key distinction between approaches to observation is the extent to which the observer takes on an overt or covert role. Strong objections to the latter are raised on ethical grounds, an issue we will return to later in this chapter. Unsurprisingly observation is usually carried out overtly.

Suggested further reading on participant observation, the favoured choice of criminologists: Spradley (1980)

Example of a study using participant observation: Becker (1963)

Figure 5.4 Observation

or secondary. Documentary research involves using existing sources of information, but researchers need to invest considerable time and energy converting this information into the data they need to answer their research questions. Denscombe (2010) distinguishes between three categories of documents: those which are in the public domain; those whose access is restricted; and secret documents. Applying this typology to documents which may be of interest to criminologists, the former might include newspapers, publications produced criminal justice agencies and those who monitor them (for example, the Independent Police Complaints Commission or HM Inspectorates), and parliamentary debates (published in Hansard). Increasingly, these documents can be accessed electronically. It is more difficult to think of criminological examples of secret documents for which access could ever be obtained, but personal correspondence and diaries would fall into this category. Often criminologists make use of documents which fall under the 'restricted access' heading, and they include records kept by criminal justice agencies and related organizations in the form of databases and individual files. These examples are numerical or textual in form, but documents may also include visual images.

Regardless of their form or their accessibility, the same criteria should be applied to documents to evaluate their utility as a source of data. Scott's (1990) four key criteria are the accepted starting point for this task and involve asking questions about authenticity, credibility, representativeness, and meaning. Together they require researchers to adopt a reflexive approach and consider the social context in which the documents were originally produced (Noaks and Wincup, 2004). Of especial importance is recognizing that the documents were initially created for another purpose. Once this task has been completed the researcher can move on to use these documents as source of qualitative and/or quantitative data. Sometimes this decision is obvious. For example, documents which contain largely numerical data will provide little in the way of qualitative data. Sometimes it is less so. For example, newspaper articles can be used to collect quantitative data on the proportion of space devoted to particular crimes and qualitative data on media representations of such crimes through a consideration of language, meaning, and so on (see Chapter 7 for a more detailed discussion).

Combining research methods

Increasingly criminologists combine methods when conducting research on crime and criminal justice. This practice is usually referred to as 'method' or 'technique' triangulation, although as Hoyle (2000) argues the term shrouds in mystery straightforward and sensible means of looking at the social world. A better term, which Walklate (2007: 325) advocates, is 'methodological pluralism'. The term 'triangulation' is based upon the belief that using different methods (or forms of data, theories, or researchers; see Noaks and Wincup (2004) for a more detailed discussion) can enhance the research findings. Before moving on to discuss the relative merits and demerits of combining methods, it is important to appreciate that at one level, all research is multi-method. For example, researchers interested in one aspect of the criminal justice process are likely to begin by conducting documentary research such as reading policy documents or other published material, although their study may be based upon observation.

Combining methods avoids the tendency for 'methodological pigeonholing' which Bottoms (2007: 81) describes as unhelpful. He warns against assuming that particular methods are incompatible with specific research designs. Such exclusionary practices, he argues, militate against the collection of the most appropriate data to answer the research questions posed. For instance, whilst a survey approach is typically accompanied by the use of methods which produce quantitative data from a large sample; for example, using questionnaires, there are good reasons for considering additional research methods which can be used to collect qualitative data. For instance, focus groups could be arranged to develop the questionnaire or to discuss the emerging findings.

Within the methodological literature, a common theme is that a multi-method approach enhances the validity of the research findings. As previously discussed, validity has multiple meanings when used by social scientists, but essentially it refers to the credibility and plausibility of the conclusions reached. We need to be wary about equating triangulation with a search for 'truth' to be achieved through the use of multiple methods which can compensate for each others' weaknesses and reduce bias. Instead, we should use the different methods available to us (if it is meaningful and pragmatic for us to do so, as we will discuss later) and take advantage of the opportunity this creates to look out for contradictions as much as confirmation between the data sets gathered using different techniques. The role of the researcher then becomes one of explaining apparent inconsistencies or complementary findings rather than seeking to establish 'facts'. Researchers often find themselves with the challenge of making sense of multiple versions of reality because different methods produce different findings, particularly if two or more techniques were deliberately chosen to explore different dimensions of the same issues; for example, 'paper' justice as articulated in policy documents and 'real' justice as reported by those involved in its delivery or recipients of it.

Researchers should approach the question about whether to combine methods with 'healthy cynicism' (Noaks and Wincup, 2004: 10) and only do so if convinced that a multi-method approach adds value to the study by enhancing understanding of the criminological issue being researched. In some instances it may detract from it. Some combinations of methods may not complement each other because they are based upon different assumptions of the social world. For instance, it is difficult to see what might be gained by selecting a research design which incorporated unstructured interviews and a questionnaire. There may be practical reasons too for not using multiple methods. The resources available (time, human, financial) may make this unrealistic, and a better approach is to use one method well and outline the possibilities for extending the research in the publications produced. In sum, researchers should not keep adding research techniques with the blind hope that it will produce a better outcome.

REVIEW QUESTIONS

1 What are the most important considerations when choosing a research design?

2 What are the most important considerations when choosing a research method?

3 What are the advantages and disadvantages of combining different research methods? You might find it helpful to think about triangulation with reference to a particular criminological issue; for example, students' experiences of criminal victimization.

Politics, ethics, and managing risk

The politics of criminological research

Criminological research is political in a number of senses. The term 'political' does not have to be reserved for references to politics at the level of government, although there is no doubt that the politics of law and order discussed in Chapter 19 can shape the research process from initial conception of the research idea through to the publication and dissemination (or not as the case may be) of results, either directly because the government is funding and/or conducting the research and/or indirectly because it shapes the context in which the research takes place. There are other ways in which criminological research can be viewed as a political endeavour. Research may be funded by other organizations such as research councils (principally the Economic and Social Research Council) and charitable foundations such as the Joseph Rowntree Foundation or Nuffield Foundation. Each has its own priorities and preferences in terms of the types of research designs they wish to fund and the substantive focus of potential research projects (see Morgan and Hough, 2007; Noaks and Wincup, 2004). Evaluating criminological knowledge therefore requires pertinent questions to be asked about the context in which the knowledge was produced.

We have noted some of the factors which influence the extent to which criminological research may be characterized as political. Beyond funding arrangements and the timing of the research, it is important to note the influence of the theoretical framework selected and the chosen subject matter. For some criminologists, those which Bottoms (2007) describes as political-activist criminologists, research and knowledge are viewed as part of the political process. Critical and feminist criminologists (see Chapter 4) fit most neatly into this category. Their stance is at the other end of the continuum from the positivist position which maintains that research can be wholly objective and value-free. They also challenge the reluctant acceptance of many criminologists that political influences shape research by actively engaging in the pursuit of political goals through research. Their choice of subject matter is influential in this respect. At the heart of critical and feminist criminological work lies a desire to challenge structural inequalities through researching discrimination and oppression of the powerless.

There is a further sense in which criminological research can be considered political. Political influences, in this instance, operate at a micro-level, although they are not disconnected from the macro-level political agendas. Criminologists often need to collect data in a range of settings which require relationships with the key players to be negotiated carefully in order to understand their different, and, sometimes opposing, perspectives. Researchers may find themselves confronted with the question 'whose side are you on?' (see Becker's (1967) classic essay on the subject). In relation to prison research, Liebling (2001) maintains that it is possible to understand the perspective of more than one 'side' and to do so without alienating opposing groups. She argues that attempting to synthesize different or competing perspectives (for example, between prisoners and prison officers, or between prison officers and prison governors) enhances the end product by sharpening the analysis. At the same time, she appreciates that this places the researcher in a precarious position as they try to keep everyone happy to maintain access.

The ethics of criminological research

In recent years, the issue of research ethics has come to the fore. Almost all learned societies in the social sciences have their own ethical code (see the web links section for details of how to access those most relevant to criminological research). There is now a burgeoning academic literature on research ethics, including specialist journals such as *Research Ethics Review*, and training on research ethics is firmly embedded in the curriculum of social science degrees at both undergraduate and postgraduate levels. To a greater extent than in the past, researchers are required to demonstrate that their research is ethically sound. Research proposals are subject to scrutiny by ethics committee at an early stage, certainly before the process of data collection commences, but sometimes before funding is sought. For criminologists working in academic institutions, this normally involves submitting the necessary documents to a committee operating at either department, faculty, or university level. There are, however, exceptions, and criminologists seeking to collect data which requires contact with NHS patients (for example, prisoners receiving health care services) or vulnerable people (for example, young offenders) may need to gain ethical approval from an external NHS or social services committee.

Ethical codes typically describe the professional standards to which researchers should adhere to ensure that they produce research which is high quality and methodologically sound whilst fulfilling their obligations to those involved in the research as colleagues, sponsors, and participants. The term 'sponsors' refers not only to those who provide financial support, but also to those who provide support in other ways; for example, 'gatekeepers' who facilitate access. Codes of ethics can vary but all aim to strike a balance between providing sufficiently detailed guidance to assist researchers and avoiding rigid prescriptions of what should and should not be done.

Criminological research has the potential to produce ethical dilemmas which are distinct in many respects from those which emerge when researching topics other than crime and criminal justice. Much depends on the subject matter, but there is a heightened likelihood that criminological research will require collecting data on sensitive issues (for example, offending behaviour or experiences of victimization) from individuals who might be described as 'vulnerable' in some way. These considerations have an impact on the researcher's ability to protect research participants from experiencing the research process as intrusive and a cause of harm. The current British Society of Criminology code of ethics (published in 2006) argues that researchers should make every effort to respect the rights of those they study, their interests, sensitivities, and privacy. It also briefly outlines strategies for preventing this, including referring research participants to support services.

Researching 'vulnerable' groups raises challenges in terms of obtaining informed consent. This involves the researcher providing as much detail about the research as necessary in a manner which is accessible to the potential research participant to allow them to make a decision about whether to participate. Obtaining consent occurs at the outset, but it should be viewed as a process rather than a one-off event with participants made aware that they can withdraw, either fully or partially (for example, by refusing to answer a question), at any point without adverse consequences. By virtue of their age (for example, children) or inability to understand the research process (for example, those with severe learning difficulties), sometimes consent needs to be obtained from an additional person (for example, a parent or social worker) as well as from the individual. For some criminological studies, obtaining informed consent can be difficult. Particular issues arise when conducting participant observation where it is not practical to obtain consent from all those present and there is a debate whether it is necessary to do so if the setting is a public one. Deliberately seeking to avoid obtaining consent is another matter and covert observation is only seen as ethically sound in exceptional circumstances; for example, when the subject matter would make an overt strategy impossible.

The final ethical issue which can prove particularly challenging for criminologists relates to privacy and confidentiality because there is a heightened potential that research participants may disclose that they themselves are at risk or that they pose a risk to others. Promises of absolute confidentiality that may need to be broken are therefore unwise, and research participants should be informed at the outset of any limitations to confidentiality so it can feed into their decision about whether to give consent.

Managing risk

The climate in which criminologists conduct research is changing and universities are now introducing risk assessment and risk management procedures, predominantly but not exclusively for those engaged in empirical research. These procedures are closely associated with the promotion of health and safety in the working environment, but also relate to other workplace agendas. Those who develop such procedures may adopt a broad definition of 'risk' and include questions about ethical *and* legal issues; for example, relating to data protection and the potential for an adverse impact on the reputation of the researcher, the university, or a third party (for example, members of an advisory body). Aside from ethical risks which were discussed in the previous section, the main issues for criminologists are risks to their own personal safety; theft, loss or damage to personal or university property; and the collection or processing of personal data. Unless the degree of risk is judged to be minimal, researchers are asked to provide further information about the nature and extent of the risk posed and to outline their strategies for protecting themselves, research participants, and the organizations involved (for example, their university or funding body) from harm.

In general terms, criminologists have paid more attention to promoting the health and safety of research participants than their own. The level and nature of risk, of course, varies from project to project and is dependent upon the subject matter, the extent to which it involves direct contact with research participants, and the setting in which it takes place. These factors all need to be taken into account and the comparative risks of different projects may not be as they first appear. For example, interviewing members of the public in their own homes might be considered more risky than interviewing offenders in prisons where there are multiple procedures in place to promote personal safety and offenders have been subject to risk assessments.

Despite criminologists' frequent exposure to risk, physical or emotional, there is surprisingly little attention paid in the criminological literature to the issue and a lack of guidance for criminologists to follow. It would be wrong, however, to deduce from this that criminologists are unaware of the risks or that they fail to take measures to protect themselves. They are and they do, but there may be considerable scope for improvement so that as far as possible the risks are fully appreciated in advance and strategies put in place to minimize them. When outlining the range of strategies they plan to adopt to ensure their own safety, in the absence of specific guidance, criminologists must turn to general guidance for social researchers (for example, the Social Research Association's *Code of Practice for the Safety of Researchers*) or advice relating to personal safety in the workplace (for example, from the Suzy Lamplugh Trust, http://www.suzylamplugh.org/). There is an urgent need for criminological researchers to share good practice in relation to promoting their safety and to develop professional guidance.

REVIEW QUESTIONS

1 Can research on crime and criminal justice be anything other than political?

2 Is it ever desirable to compromise on ethical principles when conducting research on issues of crime and criminal justice?

3 Why is it important that criminologists conduct risk assessments prior to commencing data collection?

New methodological developments: assessing the impact of technology on criminological research

Some of the most important methodological developments over the past three decades relate to the rapid expansion of technology. Most experienced researchers will be able to recount stories of how their research practices have been transformed in at least some respects by technological developments which have impacted upon all aspects of the research process. Most studies begin with a literature review, a task which is now much easier thanks to the advent of searchable databases such as *Criminal Justice Abstracts*, *ASSIA* (Applied Social Sciences Index and Abstracts), and *Web of Science*, and search engines which can be used to locate academic and policy literature plus statistics which are now increasingly available electronically via the Internet. Similarly the task of data analysis is now often more straightforward, particularly when large amounts of data are involved, due to the development of specialist software: usually *SPSS* (Statistical Package for the Social Sciences) for quantitative data and *NVivo* for qualitative data. It is, however, important to emphasize that such software only facilitates the analysis of data and the process is only meaningful if guided appropriately by the researcher. Technology has also simplified the dissemination process making it far easier to reach the intended audience(s) using the Internet to publish reports online or by creating bespoke websites. Research findings can also be disseminated in a more informal way through blogs, and for those who can crystallize their conclusions in less than 140 characters, Twitter. This, of course, leads to the issue of 'technological exclusion' because the reliance on electronic forms of publications has the potential to exclude those who are unable to access them, for example, those living in poverty or older people. Arguably some of the most interesting technological developments relate to their potential to alter radically the data collection process. The remainder of the section explores these with specific reference to researching crime and criminal justice.

Writing in 2007, Williams argues that whilst criminologists have made effective use of the Internet to retrieve information, for example, to obtain statistics, few have taken the opportunity to collect primary data online, and he goes as far as to claim that their use of the Internet for research 'remains largely parochial' (2007a: 476). In many respects, this claim is still valid. The Internet allows criminologists to use many of the 'traditional' methods in a different context. Using specialist websites, questionnaires can be designed and completed online. Interviews, particularly the more unstructured forms, could be conducted using instant messaging, although researchers would need to assess carefully whether the advantages (for example, the ability to interview people from across the world) outweigh the disadvantages (for example, the lack of face-to-face interaction) and consider how the disadvantages could be minimized (for example, through the use of Skype). Using online methods is very appealing, not least because they offer the potential of easy access to participants at low-cost.

The development of social networking websites such as *Facebook* also opens up possibilities for building up a sample of individuals who can be invited to complete an online questionnaire. Using snowball sampling, a form of non-probability (or non-random) sampling, through which each individual contacted is asked to identify other participants, a large sample can be established in a short space of time with minimal effort. It works, therefore, in a similar way to a chain letter (Oliver, 2006). Of course, the achieved sample will not be representative of a particular population because, for example, young people are likely to be over-represented. However, it offers a solution when achieving a sample through other means would be extremely difficult and is most effective when combined with alternative means to secure a more diverse sample.

The Internet also presents new opportunities to access virtual worlds and adapt 'traditional' methods to explore them. Williams (2007a, b) used a 'virtual ethnographic' approach based heavily upon participant observation to research a graphical online community, associated newsgroups, webpages, and email distribution lists. He also conducted focus groups online with community members. Reflecting upon his experiences, he is eager to point out that transferring 'traditional' designs and methods to a virtual setting involves encountering new challenges; for example, in terms of ethical practices or data analysis, for which there is little or no guidance. It also required revisiting methodological debates that had previously been held in relation to their usage for researching the 'actual' rather than 'virtual' social world.

REVIEW QUESTIONS

1 Evaluate the impact of technological developments on the processes of data collection.

2 Repeat the task with respect to the dissemination of research findings.

3 Reflect upon your own use of technology. Does this give you inspiration for research projects?

CONCLUSION

Like Chapter 4, which introduces students to criminological theory, this chapter was intended to be a starting point. Within the constraints of one short chapter, it has not been possible to do justice to the diversity of forms criminological research can take and the abundance of issues which arise throughout the research process. For instance, limited space has precluded a detailed discussion of core topics such as sampling (see Bryman, 2012) and data analysis (see Coffey and Atkinson, 1996 for qualitative data; and Bryman and Cramer, 2008 for quantitative data). We hope students will consult the more detailed texts outlined in the guide to further reading at the end of this chapter. Read in conjunction with this chapter, students should become skilled and confident evaluators of the studies they read and begin the process of designing their own small-scale studies if they are required to complete a dissertation or undertake project work.

QUESTIONS FOR DISCUSSION

1 Look at articles published in one of the leading academic journals, for example, *Criminology and Criminal Justice*, and focus on the articles which report the findings of empirical research studies. What does it reveal about the research designs and methods most frequently utilized?

2   Compare and contrast the codes of ethics produced by learned societies and professional associations which criminologists can draw upon. The web links section refers to some of the most important ones but you may wish to look at others, for example, the British Sociological Association, http://www.britsoc.co.uk/, or the British Psychological Society, http://www.bps.org.uk/.

3   Draw up a checklist of the main criteria you might use when evaluating a criminological study. Consider whether the criteria might be different depending upon the type(s) of data collected.

4   Select a criminological study, either a recent one or one regarded as a 'classic', and use your checklist to evaluate its contribution to criminological knowledge.

5   Repeat the activity in question 4 by selecting a study which used either a contrasting research design or different methods.

GUIDE TO FURTHER READING

Bryman, A. (2012) (4th edn) *Social Research Methods*. Oxford: Oxford University Press.

This leading textbook, and the companion website, explores in detail the main approaches and techniques in social research methods.

Jupp, V. (ed) (2006) *The SAGE Dictionary of Social Research Methods*. London: Sage.

This useful resource contains over 200 entries of key concepts associated with social research. For each, it provides a working definition, outlines its distinctive features, and evaluates the term. Links are made to other key concepts contained in the book, and readers are directed to key readings relating to the concept.

King, R. and Wincup, E. (eds) (2007) (2nd edn) *Doing Research on Crime and Justice*. Oxford: Oxford University Press.

This is one of the few texts which focus specifically on criminological research. Its main aim is to provide an honest account of the research process through the inclusion of chapters by established academics and new scholars.

Noaks, L. and Wincup, E. (2004) *Criminological Research: Understanding Qualitative Approaches*. London: Sage.

Focusing specifically on the collection and analysis of qualitative data on criminological topics, this textbook aims to provide a practically focused account of the research process.

Davies, P., Francis, P., and Jupp, V. (eds) (2010) (2nd edn) *Doing Criminological Research*. London: Sage.

Contextualizing research with real-life examples of crime and criminal justice, this book looks at the processes, practicalities and problems of doing criminological research.

WEB LINKS

http://www.britsoccrim.org/

The British Society of Criminology is a learned society which aims to further the interests and knowledge of both academic and professional people who are engaged in any aspect of work or teaching, research, or public education about crime, criminal behaviour, and criminal justice in the United Kingdom. Its Code of Ethics for Researchers in the Field of Criminology can be found on its website, alongside details of academics that can be approached for guidance on ethical matters.

http://www.slsa.ac.uk/

The Socio-Legal Studies Association brings together socio-legal scholars working in social scientific and humanities disciplines. Its website includes its statement of principles for ethical research practice.

http://www.the-sra.org.uk/

The Social Research Association aims to advance the conduct, development, and application of social research. Its members include academics and researchers working in a range of applied settings. Its ethical guidelines, code of practice for the safety of social researchers, and details of the training courses it offers can be found on the website.

http://www.esrc.ac.uk

The Economic and Social Research Council (ESRC) is the UK's leading research funding and training agency addressing economic and social concerns. Its website contains a copy of its Research Ethics Framework plus funding opportunities for research training.

http://www.data-archive.ac.uk/

The UK Data Archive (UKDA) is a centre of expertise in data acquisition, preservation, dissemination, and promotion, and is curator of the largest collection of digital data in the social sciences and humanities in the UK. It holds both quantitative data suitable for secondary analysis (for example, the British Crime Survey) and qualitative data (for example, data from Cohen's (1972) classic study of Mods and Rockers).

REFERENCES

Aldridge, J., Measham, F., and Williams, L. (2011) *Illegal Leisure Revisited: Changing Patterns of Alcohol and Drug Use in Adolescents and Young Adults*. London: Routledge.

Arksey, H. and Knight, P. (1999) *Interviewing for Social Scientists: An Introductory Resource with Examples*. London: Sage.

Becker, H. (1963) *Outsiders: Studies in the Sociology of Deviance*. New York: Free Press.

Becker, H. (1967) 'Whose side are we on?' *Social Problems* 14 (Winter): 239–47.

Bloor, M., Frankland, J., Thomas, M., and Robson, K. (2001) *Focus Groups in Social Research*. London: Sage.

Bottoms, A. (2007) 'The relationship between theory and empirical observations in criminology', in R. King and E. Wincup (eds) *Doing Research on Crime and Justice* (2nd edn) Oxford: Oxford University Press.

Bryman, A. (2008) (3rd edn) *Social Research Methods*. Oxford: Oxford University Press.

Bryman, A., Becker, S., and Sempik, J. (2008) 'Quality criteria for quantitative, qualitative and mixed methods research: a view from social policy' *International Journal of Social Science Research Methodology* 11(4): 261–76.

Bryman, A. and Cramer, D. (2008) (3rd edn) *Quantitative Data Analysis with SPSS 14, 15 and 16: A Guide for Social Scientists*. London: Routledge.

Coffey, A. and Atkinson, P. (1996) *Making Sense of Qualitative Data*. London: Sage.

Cohen, S. (1972) *Folk Devils and Moral Panics: The Creation of a Moral Panic*. London: MacGibbon and Kee.

Denscombe, M. (2010) (4th edn) *The Good Research Guide for Small-scale Social Research Projects*. Buckingham: Open University Press.

Garland, D. (2002) 'Of crimes and criminals: the development of criminology in Britain', in M. Maguire, R. Morgan, and R. Reiner (eds) *The Oxford Handbook of Criminology* (3rd edn) Oxford: Oxford University Press.

Glaser, B. and Strauss, A. (1967) *The Discovery of Grounded Theory*. Chicago: Aldine.

Hough, M. and Roberts, J. (2004) *Youth Crime and Youth Justice: Public Opinion in England and Wales*. Bristol: The Policy Press.

Hoyle, C. (2000) 'Being a "nosy bloody cow": ethical and methodological issues in researching domestic violence', in R. King and E. Wincup (eds) (2nd edn) *Doing Research on Crime and Justice*. Oxford: Oxford University Press.

Jupp, V. (2006) 'Hypothesis', in V. Jupp (ed) *The SAGE Dictionary of Social Research Methods*. London: Sage.

Keddie, V. (2006) 'Case study method', in V. Jupp (ed) *The SAGE Dictionary of Social Research Methods*. London: Sage.

King, R. and Wincup, E. (2007) 'The process of criminological research', in R. King and E. Wincup (eds) (2nd edn) *Doing Research on Crime and Justice*. Oxford: Oxford University Press.

Liebling, A. (2001) 'Whose side are we on? Theory, practice and allegiance in prisons research' *British Journal of Criminology* 41(3): 472–84.

McLean, C. (2006) 'Questionnaire', in V. Jupp (ed) *The SAGE Dictionary of Social Research Methods*. London: Sage.

Morgan, D. (2006) 'Focus group', in V. Jupp (ed) *The SAGE Dictionary of Social Research Methods*. London: Sage.

Morgan, R. and Hough, M. (2007) 'The politics of criminological research', in R. King and E. Wincup (eds) (2nd edn) *Doing Research on Crime and Justice*. Oxford: Oxford University Press.

Noaks, L. and Wincup, E. (2004) *Criminological Research: Understanding Qualitative Methods*. London: Sage.

Oliver, P. (2006) 'Snowball sampling', in V. Jupp (ed) *The SAGE Dictionary of Social Research Methods*. London: Sage.

Oppenheim, A. (2000) (2nd edn) *Questionnaire Design*. London: Continuum International Publishing Group Limited.

Payne, G. and Payne, J. (2004) *Key Concepts in Social Research*. London: Sage.

Scott, J. (1990) *A Matter of Record*. Cambridge: Polity Press.

Smithson, H., Ralphs, R., and Williams, P. (2012) 'Used and abused: the problematic usage of gang terminology in the United Kingdom and its implications for ethnic minority youth' *British Journal of Criminology* 53(1): 113–28. Published in 2013.

Spradley, J. (1980) *Participant Observation*. USA: Wadsworth/Thomson Learning.

Stewart, K. and Williams, M. (2005) 'Researching online populations: the use of online focus groups for social research' *Qualitative Research* 5(4): 395–416.

Walklate, S. (2007) 'Researching victims', in R. King and E. Wincup (eds) (2nd edn) *Doing Research on Crime and Justice*. Oxford: Oxford University Press.

Williams, M. (2007a) 'Cybercrime and online methodologies', in R. King and E. Wincup (eds) (2nd edn) *Doing Research on Crime and Justice*. Oxford: Oxford University Press.

Williams, M. (2007b) 'Avatar watching: participant observation in graphical online environments' *Qualitative Research* 7(1): 5–24.

6 Psychology and crime: understanding the interface

Keith Hayward and Craig Webber

INTRODUCTION

Many students new to academic criminology are often confused by exactly what role psychology plays in the contemporary criminological enterprise. Very often they have visions of a discipline preoccupied with offender profiling, forensic crime analysis, and the study of psychopathic or mentally impaired serial killers. This chapter aims to set the record straight by providing students with a brief introduction to some of the main points of interface between criminology and psychology. It combines a general review of some of the more prominent psychological explanations of criminal behaviour with some brief examples of how this work has come to be employed in criminological theory and practice. At various intervals, the chapter also adopts a more reflexive stance in a bid to develop some critical insights into the way that 'criminological psychology' is portrayed and perceived within the popular imagination. In this sense, the viewpoint taken here is very much that of a criminologist's perspective of psychology (for an opposite perspective see Hollin, 2012b).

BACKGROUND

It is a cliché to say that recent years have been marked by an increasing popular fascination with the subject of crime and criminality. Yet, in terms of understanding the ever-growing 'psychologistic preoccupation' among criminology students, it is worth pausing to consider some of the reasons behind this current 'fascination'. As Ian Taylor (1999: 2) pointed out, much of this interest is attributable to powerful cinematic and televisual representations of forensic or criminological psychology that serve both to popularize and legitimate various forms of 'analytically individualist criminology'. In Taylor's words, this 'is a form of common-sense criminology organized around 'the criminal', and particularly 'the criminal mind' as an 'object of analysis' (Taylor, 1999).

In these representations, criminal psychology is frequently portrayed in a very favourable light, almost as if it were a sort of 'secret science', its practitioners capable of feats of identification and detection that far exceed the laboured efforts of the police and other State agencies (Webber, 2010: 155; Ainsworth, 2000: 1–3). Moreover, in these accounts, the mundane, prosaic aspects of crime rarely feature. Instead we are offered up a steady diet of crimes that contain a highly charged emotional (typically pathological) dimension—rape, child abduction, stalking, hate crimes, sexual homicides and other forms of expressive violence.

The attraction of this type of fiction (and increasingly non-fiction; see, for example, the Channel Four documentary series *The Real Cracker* and the US A&E network's *Serial Killers: Profiling the Criminal Mind*) is that it suggests criminological psychology is capable of identifying and understanding 'uniqueness', of identifying whom we should trust and whom we should fear. Whether it is Robbie Coltrane's compelling portrayal of the forensic psychologist Fitz in the Granada Television series *Cracker,* or the mass of popu-lar crime-psychology titles that occupy the shelves of the 'Real Crime' section in high street bookshops, the message is always the same: that crime is about *individual difference* and that psychology holds the key to understanding that difference. We would argue that the impact of such representations of crime has been far-reaching, not least in the way it has contributed to how crime and criminality are currently perceived and understood within the contemporary socio-cultural imagination (Furedi, 2004: 30). Today, the popular image of the criminal as an 'emotionally disturbed' or 'psychologically distinct' individual not only provides entertainment, but feeds into student expectations of criminology courses, and the stereo-types of law enforcement agencies of a psychological approach to crime.

In stark contrast, criminology as an academic discipline has tended, in the main, to focus on wider questions concerning the complex relationship(s) that exist between crime, criminal justice and society—something that should immediately be apparent from the diverse range of chapters that comprise this volume. This is not to suggest that sociological criminologists discount the many impor-tant gains made by psychologists in understanding a whole range of abnormal and extreme criminal behaviour, both in terms of individual and collective action (see Gadd and Jefferson's (2007) work in the field of 'psychosocial criminology'). Rather, simply to point out that, in the majority of cases, most academic criminologists approach the subject of crime and criminality from a much broader perspec-tive that includes not just the 'causes of crime', but also questions about how crime is itself constructed (see Chapter 1), and how society and the State seek to both control and to respond to crime (*see* Chapters 20 and 21).

It should be obvious, then, even from this general introduction that, despite a shared interest in crimi-nal behaviour, criminology and psychology have often made rather uneasy bedfellows. Nevertheless, it should be remembered that this has not always been the case with key ideas in sociological criminol-ogy being drawn from psychology and psychoanalysis. For example, Albert Cohen's (1955) discussion of Freud's concept of reaction-formation, whereby young people denied access to the legitimate route to success attack and destroy that which they desire. Cohen used this idea to explain non-acquisitive crime such as vandalism. Cohen, in turn, was a student of Robert Merton, and Merton did not ignore the contribution of psychology either. Merton pointed out in an interview that "I have never, never taken… the polar position that if you're a sociologist, you dare not slip into considering questions of psychologi-cal process" (Cullen and Messner, 2007: 21). Another student of Merton, the sociologist W.G. Runciman, elaborated Merton's theory into the highly influential concept of relative deprivation. This concept relied on the social psychological idea of reference groups, something which once again has become popular in social psychology (Webber, 2007a).

The obvious question is, why did these two previously compatible disciplines drift apart? There are sev-eral reasons, but one of the most important is that psychological research has increasingly been funded by medical research councils, and so the discipline has become even more entrenched in a medical/individual model of behaviour. This does not reflect the broader sociological questions about poverty, inequality and social relationships. Nevertheless, one of the goals of this chapter is to remind those who already live with this gulf that it does not have to be unbridgeable, whilst at the same time, providing a discussion that suggests to those new to these disciplines that the division is not inevitable, and may not be beneficial (Webber, 2010; Putwain and Sammons, 2002: 2–3). In the next section, as attention turns to the main psychological explanations of criminal behaviour, we will make some intermittent comments about how this relationship has ebbed and flowed over the last 100 years or so.

Key psychological explanations of criminal behaviour

Introduction

Some brief historical context

Generally speaking, psychology and criminology emerged as distinct disciplines at a very similar historical moment—the latter half of the nineteenth century. Typically, one associates the birth of modern criminology with the work of Cesare Lombroso (1835–1909) and his fellow members of the Italian positivist school (*scuola positiva*; see Chapter 3, for a general introduction to positivism and other key moments in the historical development of criminology). At this point, of course, the nascent 'science of criminology' was still fundamentally preoccupied with matters relating to the individual actor, the so-called 'criminal person or type' (see Beirne, 1993: Chapters 2 and 3). Only later would it broaden its horizons to include wider social and economic factors in accounts of crime. Psychology, meanwhile, had begun to coalesce around the early experimental research of the German, Wilhelm Wundt (1832–1920)—the first person to call himself a psychologist—and the American, William James (1842–1940). (Sigmund Freud began his career as a neurologist and thus his early work was very much rooted in biology. It was not until slightly later that criminal psychologists took up his psychodynamic theory of personality; see later in this chapter.)

Such contemporaneous development is not surprising, for both disciplines should be seen as clear products of modernity's faith in enlightened science and philosophy. If modernity was about anything it was about the belief that society's failings would be overcome or at least managed (controlled) by the careful, scientific pursuit of relevant knowledge and the application of this knowledge to a specific set of problems. The then fledgling disciplines of criminology and psychology exemplified such ideals; protagonists of both 'sciences' steadfastly believing that rational scientific analysis could 'make sense' of human behaviour by identifying flaws and categorizing traits and types. No longer would there be talk of humans possessing a 'soul' or a 'spirit'—or indeed of 'good' and 'evil'. Instead, the psychologist and the criminologist would be the objective recorder of 'personality' and 'criminality' respectively—only later would these two sub-fields collide.

The nature versus nurture debate

Perhaps the most enduring (and over-simplified) controversy within psychology is the 'nature versus nurture debate'. In simple terms, the controversy revolves around the *origins* of individual human behaviour/personality. Carlson and Buskist neatly summarize the debate:

> 'Is it [personality] caused by biological or social factors?' 'Is it innate or learned?' 'Is it a result of hereditary or cultural influences?' 'Should we look for an explanation in the brain or in the environment?' Almost always, biology, innateness, heredity, and the brain are placed on the 'nature' side of the equation. Society, learning, culture, and the environment are placed on the 'nurture' side. Rarely, does anyone question whether these groups of items really form a true dichotomy ... most modern psychologists consider the nature-nurture issue to be a relic of the past. That

is, they believe that *all* behaviours, talents, and personality traits are the products of both types of factors: biological and social, hereditary and cultural, physiological and environmental. The task of the modern psychologist is not to find out which one of these factors is more important but to discover the particular roles played by each of them and to determine the ways in which they interact. (1997: 99–100)

Such is also the case with psychological understandings of criminality. While countless criminological psychologists have, over the years, sought to identify a single biological (that is, 'nature') explanation of crime, such attempts have borne little fruit (for a brief introduction to the some of the major biological and genetic explanations of crime— William Sheldon's 'body type' theory; genetic transmission theory; twin and adoptee studies, etc—see Chapter 3; see also Hollin, 2012a; Lanier and Henry, 1998: Chapter 5; Bartol, 2005: Chapter 3; and in more detail Jeffrey, 1994; Ciba Foundation, 1996). Indeed, the idea that human behaviour is determined by factors that, while universal to the species, reside to a greater or lesser extent in the *constitution of the individual*, is now distinctly unfashionable (cf. Mednick *et al.*, 1987; Raine, 1993 for attempts to reassert the role of genetics in criminal behaviour). To put it more bluntly, few psychologists still cling to the idea that certain individuals are somehow predetermined into a life of crime. Instead, the 'nature-nurture' dichotomy is seen to be less an absolute distinction and more an interacting framework for thinking about causal factors in the commission of crime.

In summary, criminological psychology is a multi-faceted discipline which, despite its overall goal of striving to understand, explain and predict criminal behaviour, typically tends to shy away from making any major pronouncements about there being a single or universal cause/explanation for deviant action. Moreover, since its emergence as a significant sub-discipline in the early 1960s, criminological psychology (along with its 'sister' discipline, forensic psychology (see Müller *et al.*, 1984; Bartol and Bartol, 1994; Kapardis, 1997; Gudjonsson and Hayward, 1998; Adler, 2004; Towl and Crighton, 2010) has proven to be of considerable practical use, both in terms of police work and to those working within the legal profession (see later in this chapter). Indeed, such has been the rise of criminological psychology as a disciplinary variant in its own right, that recent years have seen the publication of a whole host of excellent textbooks aimed at introducing the reader to the subject (for example, Hollin, 2012a, 1992; Blackburn, 1993; Feldman, 1993; Ainsworth, 2000; Putwain and Sammons, 2002; McGuire, 2004; Bartol and Bartol, 2005; Webber, 2010). Readers new to this area would do well to access one of these texts for a good general synopsis of the interface between psychology and criminology. Now, however, we wish to proceed by focusing on some of the main psychological theories of criminal behaviour. Again, we should point out that what follows is only the briefest of snapshots of some of the more prominent psychological explanations of crime.

Psychoanalytical theories of crime

Most readers will have some understanding of the term psychoanalysis and the work of the Austrian psychiatrist, Sigmund Freud (1856–1939). Freud's great achievement was to highlight the way that innate desires and repressed emotions shape individual human behaviour. For example, according to Freudian thinking, violent, aggressive or sexually

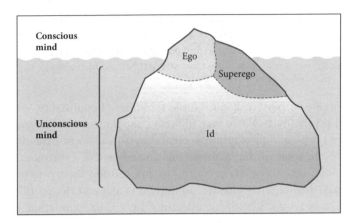

Figure 6.1 The 'pyramid' diagram of Freud's notion of the psyche

deviant acts should be seen as expressions of buried internal (psychic) conflicts that are the result of traumas or deprivations experienced during childhood.

Freud argued that the mind was comprised of three provinces: the *ego*, the *id* and the *superego* (Figure 6.1).

First, the id represents the primitive, instinctive, animalistic portion of the 'unconscious mind'. It is here that fundamental biological and physiological concerns reside, such as innate sexual urges (*libido*); the 'life instinct' (*Eros*) or drive for life; the destructive 'death instinct' (*Thanatos*); and the desire to eat, sleep, and be comfortable. The goal of the id is simple: to gratify instincts at all costs. According to Freud, the unconscious desires of the id are unresponsive to the demands of reality and are instead governed by what he termed 'the pleasure principle'. Consequently, such drives have been of considerable interest to criminal psychologists (see, for example, the work of Lorenz, 1966; Storr, 1970). Second, the ego relates (primarily) to the 'conscious mind', and acts as a 'mediating device' between the two opposing mental forces of the id and the superego. Because of the conscious recognition within the individual that 'every act has a consequence', Freud claimed that the ego was driven by the 'reality principle'. Finally, the (largely conscious) superego is the 'repository of moral values' and the seat of guilt within the individual. The superego can be thought of as a sort of internal 'nagging parent' or moral guardian. Importantly, especially for psychoanalytical theories of crime, the superego develops as a result of a series of early social experience(s) (and, for Freud at least, admonishments) that serve to engender in the individual an internal 'source of self-criticism based on the production of guilt'.

In crude terms, Freud maintained that human behaviour should be thought of as a 'struggle between the internalized psychic forces of the id and the superego'—with the ego constantly striving to maintain a suitable balance. Over time, and largely formed through learned behaviour, the ego strives to undertake a complex mental balancing act between the primeval desires of the id and the internalized conscience of the superego, whilst all the time seeking to work out the best way in which to actually 'serve' the id by meeting some of its requirements.

But what does all this mean in terms of understanding criminal behaviour? For proponents of psychoanalytical criminology, criminal behaviour can be understood as an expression of buried internal (mental) conflicts that are the result of traumas or deprivations experienced during childhood.

The importance of early childhood development on behaviour was further emphasized by a whole host of psychoanalysts—including most famously, the work of Aichorn (1925), Abramson (1944) and Alexander (Alexander and Staub, 1931; Alexander and Healy, 1935) on failure to control drives associated with the 'pleasure principle'; and Healey and Bronner's (1936) research into the Freudian concept of 'sublimation', or the way that 'unsatisfied instinctual desires' are often channelled into other forms of behaviour, including deviance. However, perhaps the most influential figure in this field was the British developmental psychologist, John Bowlby (1907–90). Bowlby's achievement was to solidify the link between *maternal deprivation* and antisocial behaviour (Bowlby, 1944; 1951). More specifically, what was important for Bowlby was the close, loving relationship between mother and child. Consequently, any rejection or separation between mother and child during early child development is likely to prove highly problematic. Indeed, according to Bowlby's sample groups, such ruptures in familial relations will be disproportionately represented in serious cases of delinquency in later life.

Bowlby's writings, along with other related research (for example, Little, 1965; Rutter, 1972), proved extremely effective in terms of influencing governments and generating policy initiatives. Not least, ideas about maternal deprivation and other later so-called 'broken home theories' were a central element in the rehabilitative 'welfarist' movement in youth justice of the 1960s and 1970s (see Chapter 16). However, many commentators objected strongly to the lack of scientific rigour associated with this early psychoanalytical criminology (specifically the '*tautological*', 'subjective' and 'untestable' nature of the intra-psychic Freudian approach). That said, the psychoanalytical approach to deviance went on to exert considerable influence within both psychology and criminology for many decades to come (see Garland, 1994: 42–60; Valier, 2006).

Social learning and behavioural theories of crime

In contrast to theories of crime that suggest the root cause lies with primitive instinctive drives and psychodynamic struggles, behavioural and social learning theories—as the name clearly implies—assert instead that crime and deviance are *learned responses*. One of the starting points for this expansive body of work was Edwin Sutherland's (1883–1950) sociological theory of 'differential association' (1947). For Sutherland, behaviour—including crime—is a social product, a result of different interactions and patterns of learning that occur in the intimate personal groups and surrounding social circumstances that encapsulate the individual. According to Sutherland, such groups teach 'definitions'—including special skills, motivations, norms and beliefs—either 'unfavourable' or 'favourable' to the violation of the law (that is, in the latter case, the *association* of an individual with a group, or indeed a community, that is both ingrained with criminal traits and norms, and also isolated from more positive anti-criminal traits and attitudes). Despite criticisms of differential association (not least questions about why, under shared conditions, individuals still tend to behave very differently from each other), Sutherland's work was extremely influential, ushering in a whole host of subsequent theories that sought to prove that the determinants of behaviour reside *outside the individual*.

This line of thinking inevitably chimed loudly with the shift already underway within American psychology towards 'behaviourism' (see, for example, Watson, 1913 for an early example). But as Clive Hollin makes clear, rather than making for harmonious relations between psychology and criminology, this apparent convergence in thinking surrounding the role of *external stimulants* in the development of behaviour, instead heralded a parting of the ways for the disciplines, as behavioural psychologists continued to focus their attention exclusively on the *individual behaviour* rather than the wider external circumstances in which that behaviour was forged. The uneven and, at times, strained relationship between psychology and criminology was now underway.

Psychological developments in learning theory meanwhile drew further strength from the behavioural research of B.F. Skinner (1904–90), and especially his principles of 'operant learning' (1938, 1953). Crudely stated, operant learning suggests that behaviour that leads to 'rewards' (that is, is 'positively reinforced') will increase, while behaviour that produces an unpleasant stimulus (that is, is 'punished') is avoided.

Among the first to suggest that criminal behaviour could be understood in terms of operant learning was C.R. Jeffrey (1965) and his *theory of differential reinforcement* (see also more recently Akers, 1985). By combining the principles of Skinner's operant learning with Sutherland's differential association, Jeffrey maintained that, although criminal behaviour might well be the result of pervasive socio-cultural norms and attitudes within a given locality (*à la* Sutherland), it is also greatly affected by the particular consequences (or 'reinforcements' in Skinnerian terms) that deviance produces for the individual. Such an approach has the advantage of overcoming the main problem associated with differential association. By focusing on *individual learning histories* (that is, unique reward and punishment experiences), differential reinforcement theory explains how, despite shared environmental conditions, individual actors ultimately behave very differently.

While Skinner and Jeffrey did not wholly discount the role of internal mental processes in their particular brand of behaviourism, neither did they feature prominently in their analyses. The first to actively integrate 'internal processes' into learning theory was the psychologist Albert Bandura (1973, 1977; also Rotter, 1954). Bandura's 'social learning theory' hypothesis was an uncomplicated one: individual behaviour is something learnt at the *cognitive level* by observing and then imitating the actions of others. Most famously, Bandura conducted an experiment in which a group of infants watched a film depicting an adult violently attacking an inflatable rubber 'Bobo' doll (see Figure 7.2). In subsequent tests, this group were significantly more likely to repeat the aggressive behaviour toward the doll than were the members of a control group who had not been exposed to the film—indeed, this second group behaved more passively throughout the whole experiment. Because of the emphasis Bandura placed on 'learnt aggression', his findings quickly found support within criminological psychology (for example, Nietzel, 1979).

Such experiments suggested that, not only does social learning take place at the familial and sub-cultural level, but also via the observation of cultural symbols and media 'role models' (see Chapter 7). 'For example, a child may learn to shoot a gun by imitating television characters. He or she then rehearses and fine tunes this behavioural pattern by practising with toy guns' (Bartol, 2002: 128). Naturally, just like other operant behaviour, cognitively learned behaviour is further 'reinforced' or 'punished' via the process of socialization. ('The behaviour is likely to be maintained if peers also play with guns and reinforce one another for doing so', Bartol, 2002.)

This interest in the relationship between wider social and cultural determinants and individual criminal behaviour could have heralded the onset of a productive, collaborative relationship between criminology and psychology. Not for the last time, however, this opportunity for disciplinary accord would be largely squandered. While behavioural and social learning theories continued to develop, by the end of the 1970s most criminal psychologists had turned their back on this approach, choosing instead to pursue a very different course based around theories of criminal behaviour concerned with the identification of individual *personality traits*.

Trait-based personality theories

The study of individual personality traits is nothing new in psychology (see, for example, Allport, 1937; Cattell, 1965). As we saw earlier, one could even view Freud's work as the study of personality development. Yet, while Freud saw abnormal behaviour as the product of unconscious desires and motivations, the new 'trait-based personality theories' set out to identify and classify particular personality characteristics, and to empirically measure how these traits become assembled differently in different people. The central figure in this shift towards understanding human behaviour via 'psychometric' statistical testing was Hans Eysenck (1916–97). Eysenck's work is especially pertinent to the current discussion as his goal was the creation of a general psychological theory of crime (1977; Eysenck and Gudjonsson, 1989).

Eysenck had little time for the 'sociological turn' in the study of crime and deviance. Instead he stressed the fundamental role of inherited genetic predispositions (especially in relation to the cortical and autonomic central nervous systems) in determining the way each individual responds to environmental conditioning. In other words, Eysenck subscribed to the view that an individual's personality—including those personality traits that he considered constitutive of the criminal personality—was largely the product of their genetic make-up. Yet, this was no simple return to biological determinism (see Chapter 3), rather, Eysenck's theory was a fusion of biological, socio-environmental and individual factors.

Because Eysenck spent much of his life's work constantly retesting and augmenting his theory of crime, his key assertions are not easily summarized, however, the following passages by Lanier and Henry provide a succinct general synopsis (for more detailed summaries see Eysenck, 1984; Bartol, 2002: 70–85; Hollin, 2012a):

> Eysenck claimed to show that human personalities are made up of clusters of traits. One cluster produces a sensitive, inhibited temperament that he called *introversion*. A second cluster produces an outward-focused, cheerful, expressive temperament that he called *extroversion*. A third dimension of personality, which forms emotional stability or instability, he labelled *neuroticism*; to this schema he subsequently added *psychoticism*, which is a predisposition to a psychotic breakdown. (Lanier and Henry, 1998: 119).

Eysenck plotted the personality traits of the individuals he studied on a very rudimentary graph that has since become one of the most famous diagrams in all psychology

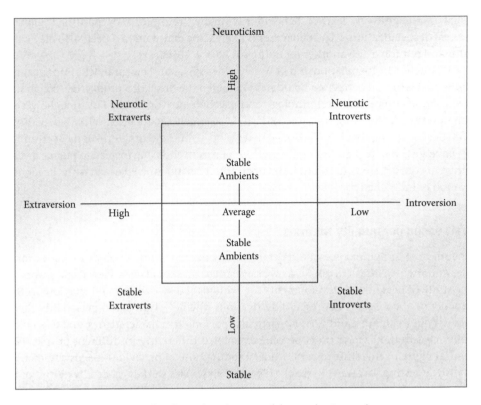

Figure 6.2 Eysenck's personality dimensions for neuroticism and extraversion

(Figure 6.2). Although something of an oversimplification, Eysenck concluded that most people in society would reside somewhere near the middle of the axis (that is, within the inner 'square'), but that what was important in terms of explaining criminal behaviour were those individuals who featured at the extremes of the diagram.

Taken at face value, Eysenck's theories seem convincing. Yet, a trawl through the mass of empirical research undertaken in an attempt to test his propositions reveals a more ambiguous picture—not least because many of these studies point to a number of significant methodological and theoretical flaws. Crucially, whilst there is general support for his contention that offenders will score highly on both the psychoticism and neuroticism dimensions, there is little evidence to support the crime-extroversion connection. Furthermore, a common charge often levelled at the trait-based approach is that it is inherently tautological: 'Stealing may be taken as an indicator of impulsiveness and impulsiveness given as the reason for stealing. Thus a recurrent criticism of trait-based theories is that they represent correlational rather than causal connections' (Lanier and Henry, 1998: 121).

These and various other criticisms aside, the wider influence of the trait-based approach to deviance can be seen in the continued growth of psychometric questionnaires and other related diagnostic devices that have emerged out of this field of research. These include early examples of so-called 'personality inventories' such as the Minnesota Multiphasic Personality Inventory (MMPI) (first proposed in 1939) to British equivalents like the British Maudsley Personality Index (MPI) and Eysenck-inspired self-report questionnaires such as the Eysenck Personality Inventory (EPI) and its subsequent iterations (see relatedly Boyle *et al.*, 2008). Basically, the idea here is that specific personality traits can be measured and assessed by asking the individual a battery of specially designed questions (or more recently, by testing responses to a series of images). Such assessments are then used to predict, prevent and treat future deviant behaviour.

Inevitably, many commentators have pointed out the intrinsic problems associated with statistical attempts to measure anything as complex and multifaceted as personality (see most famously, Taylor *et al.*, 1973: 44–61)—not least the all-too-familiar methodological pitfalls associated with self-report studies. Yet, most of this type of psychology has proceeded virtually oblivious to such methodological criticism and has continued to embrace empirical psychometric methods and other forms of quantitative analysis. This unflinching faith in psychology as a positivist science, coupled with the continued emphasis placed by Eysenck and his followers on the importance of *biological factors* in the development of personality, served to drive a deep wedge between psychology and criminology. For almost at the same moment that Eysenck's influence was being felt most acutely in psychology (the late 1960s and 1970s), criminology was dramatically affected by a new wave of Marxist-inspired research, as announced by Taylor, Walton and Young in the groundbreaking work *The New Criminology* (1973) (see Chapter 3: and relatedly the work of 'anti-psychiatry' movement writers such as Laing, Esterson, Cooper and Szasz). As (the majority of) criminology turned down the road towards theories of crime couched firmly in sociological and political economic terms, mainstream psychology continued down the experimental, empirical path. Such disharmony between the disciplines would only intensify, as psychology embarked on its next theoretical stage.

Cognitive theories of crime

Drawing on the early work of the Swiss child psychologist, Jean Piaget (for example, 1954), and Lawrence Kohlberg's (1969) notion of 'progressive moral development', cognitive theory is an attempt to understand the way people think via investigations of such concepts as intelligence, memory structure, visual perception and logical ability (see M.W. Eysenck and Keane, 1997; Lamberts and Goldstone, 2004; and Brown, 2006 for comprehensive overviews of mainstream cognitive psychology).

The first major cognitive study to make an impression on criminology was Yochelson and Samenow's infamous *The Criminal Personality* (1976; see Glueck and Glueck, 1950 for a precursor study). In an expansive three-volume work, Yocheslon and Samenow set themselves the ambitious task of 'mapping the criminal mind'. The positivist zeal with which they undertook this task is made clear in the following quote by Samenow:

> I shall expose the myths about why criminals commit crimes, and I shall draw a picture for you of the personality of the criminal just as the police artist draws a picture of his face from the description. I shall describe how criminals think, how they defend their crimes to others, and how they exploit programs that are developed to help them. (Samenow 1984: 5)

All this from a sample group of only 240 offenders, each one of whom had been adjudged 'not guilty by reason of insanity' and who, at the time of study, were institutionalized in a psychiatric hospital in Washington DC. After several thousands of hours of qualitative interviewing Yocheslon and Samenow identified '52 errors of criminal thinking' or 'problematic thinking styles' that, they claimed, taken together constituted 'the criminal personality'. These included *inter alia* 'chronic lying', irresponsible decision making, 'super optimism', 'distorted self-image', and a lack of empathy for others' (a trait that has since been made much of in contemporary cognitive-behavioural programmes for sex offenders; see later). According to Yochelson and Samenow, such 'cognitive distortions' ensure that 'criminals *think differently* from responsible people' and, moreover, that '[c]rime resides *within the person* and is "caused" *by the way he thinks, not by his environment*' (Samenow, 1984: xiv, cited in Lanier and Henry, 1998: 127, emphases added). Naturally, such assertions have implications in terms of how one treats the offender. Indeed it is within the sphere of contemporary treatment programmes that the influence of cognitive theory has been greatest—we will thus return to this subject in more detail later in this chapter. In the meantime, it is worth pausing to reflect on some of the much-voiced criticisms of Yochelson and Samenow's *The Criminal Personality*, as these critiques also serve to illustrate many of the problems associated with various other types of empirical psychology concerned with statistically measuring or 'mapping' the complexities of the human criminal personality.

To start with, little distinction is made between the various types of criminal studied. Thus, their assertion that all criminals share the same thought patterns/processes is highly problematic—does a violent offender, for example, share the same cognitive distortions as an embezzler? Second, by focusing so intently on internal thought process and dysfunctional cognitions, Yochelson and Samenow downplay the importance of both psychobiological *and* socio-environmental influences. Third, theories of crime that stress cognitive irregularities are seen as tautological in that certain behaviours are said to be indicative of cognitive processes, while these same cognitive processes are then used to explain away the behaviour. Fourth, and perhaps most obviously, Yocheslson and Samenow's sample was comprised only of *incarcerated* offenders. Yet, while one cannot deny the existence of these and several other theoretical and methodological flaws, it is hard not to be drawn to some of their ideas about cognitive reasoning, especially in relation to interpersonal relationships. Unsurprising, then, that many other psychologists have chosen to pursue this line of inquiry and in so doing have developed a body of work that not only greatly augments Yocheslson and Samenow's research, but which has since gone on to be enthusiastically received by practitioners working in the treatment arena.

A central assumption of *The Criminal Personality* is that a criminal's erroneous thinking can be corrected if they are first taught to construct a 'moral inventory' of their everyday thoughts, and then, by working with a practitioner, to identify and ultimately eradicate any dysfunctional cognitions (Samenow, 1984: 6–7). Although something of an oversimplification, this is the rationale behind the majority of cognitive therapeutic interventions that seek to correct problems experienced by offenders in their everyday lives. For example, such programmes typically concentrate on cognitive considerations such as:

- insufficient levels of *self-control* (that is, impulsivity or the failure to delay gratification) (for more on the role of self-control more generally within criminological theory, see Chapter 3);

- an inability *to feel empathy for others*—especially victims;

- deficits in basic *social problem-solving skills*—the type of skills we all employ to nego-tiate interpersonal relationships and everyday struggles;

- problems in the interpretation of *visual and situational cues* (for example, a great deal of research suggests that violent individuals not only perceive fewer social cues than non-violent people, but that they are also much more prone to interpret social cues in a hostile fashion);

- an inability to distinguish between which facets of personal life are subject to *internal control* (that is, are governed by one's own actions) and those which are subject to *external control* (that is, are governed by the actions of others).

Cognitively inspired treatment programmes are currently very popular within the UK criminal justice system, being employed in increasing numbers both within the prison setting and as an alternative to custody. However, while these correctional programmes have often proved successful at reducing certain forms of persistent offending, ulti-mately they remain fundamentally limited in scope—primarily in the sense that they never really offer a full and inclusive explanation of why someone becomes involved in criminality (or, for that matter, decides to stop; on this point see the interesting article by Shadd Maruna (2000) 'Criminology, desistance, and the psychology of the stranger'). That said, perhaps this is not really the point. These cognitively inspired programmes make little attempt to consider traditional criminological concerns such as the inequali-ties associated with class, race, gender and socio-economic deprivation. Instead, the goal is the distillation of crime and criminality to rigid 'narratives of feeling' and formalized, reductionist understandings of the social world. Only when this process is complete, it is asserted, will the individual offender then be in a position to assume responsibility for his or her actions. As Wayne Morrison (1995: 63) has pointed out, such psychothera-peutic practices represent the new wave of governmental and institutional weapons in the fight against crime, a discourse preoccupied solely with strategies of pacification and control (Garland, 2001; O'Malley, 2004, 2008 for general introductions to criminologi-cal thinking in this area)—with the psychologist as independent arbiter of acceptable behaviour and intention.

REVIEW QUESTIONS

1 Outline the main differences and similarities that exist between the four psychological explana-tions of crime outlined in this chapter.

2 Draw up a list of diverse crimes that range in seriousness from petty street crime through to murder. Which of the theories described in this chapter do you think best accounts for each type of crime?

3 Given what you have just read, how would you describe the historical relationship between the disciplines of psychology and criminology? What have been the main points of agreement and contestation?

Theory into practice: some examples of the way psychology is employed within criminal justice

The second half of this chapter will focus on some of the more prominent practical applications of psychology within the sphere off criminal justice (see Webber, 2010 for a general introduction). Students should recognize that, once again, what follows here is only an introduction and that many other practical interfaces abound.

Recent psychological developments in rehabilitation and treatment

The most obvious place to start is with psychological attempts at rehabilitation, as the various treatment programmes put forward by psychologists naturally draw heavily on many of the psychological theories and principles outlined earlier in this chapter. The key point here is that psychologically based rehabilitation models operate on very different principles to traditional judicial sanctions such as imprisonment or fines. To start with they are less concerned with *punishing the offender* than with reducing the 'risk' of reoffending. We have chosen here to concentrate on what is perhaps the most common initiative—*cognitive behavioural treatments for offending* based on cognitive and social learning theories.

As Anne Worrall and Rob Canton make clear in their chapter on offender management in this volume (Chapter 24), the nature of probation intervention has changed radically in the past two decades. The disillusionment and pessimism encapsulated in Robert Martinson's infamous 1974 remark that 'nothing works' in penal interventions (see Chapter 22) epitomized the lack of confidence in the efficacy of established offender treatment/supervision modalities, heralding a 'crisis in confidence' both in the National Probation Service specifically and the 'welfarist' treatment paradigm more generally. This loss of confidence lasted until the early 1990s and the emergence (initially in North America) of cognitive behavioural programmes based in large part on a new wave of psychological research (see Lipsey *et al.*, 2004 for recent commentaries on developments in this area).

Rather than attempting to change the whole personality or circumstances of an offender, cognitive behavioural programmes focus on specific unacceptable behaviours and seek to modify these by correcting distortions in the way offenders think about their crimes. The practitioner's primary goal therefore is to get the offender to 'face up' to their crimes and accept responsibility for their actions (instead of blaming the victim or their social circumstances). Likewise, treatment programmes also concentrate both on correcting problem behaviours (such as anger management, drunk driving or deviant forms of sexual arousal), and the acquisition of new social and inter-personal skills that will help the offender better deal with certain situations that, previously, had triggered antisocial or criminal behaviour. Typically, these strategies are bundled together in the form of a treatment/correction 'programme'.

Since their emergence in the UK in the early 1990s, the use of such programmes has grown exponentially. Jill Peay, for example, estimated that, as early as 2001, 'over 100 prisons were running such programmes, with five specific programmes in prisons and nine in the probation service having been accredited' (2002: 775). The interesting thing to note here about such growth is the way that cognitive behavioural programmes are now employed as a 'mainstream application' within the contemporary probation system. No longer are they employed simply as a means of treatment for chronic offenders with various personality disorders, or as a way of assessing, managing and ultimately *reducing the risk of re-offending* among sexual and violent offenders (see Kemshall, 2001; Jones, 2000: 151–6; and Kemshall, 2003 more generally). Increasingly, these programmes are offered to offenders involved in a much more general range of so-called 'antisocial behaviours' (see McGuire, 2004: Chapter 6). Clearly, this is more evidence of the widening of what Wayne Morrison (1995: 163–4) has described as the net of 'governmental structures' of 'self-reflection and self-examination'.

Nevertheless, a significant number of these therapies have proven highly successful in the treatment of both adult and juvenile offenders. It is for this reason that many psychologists and practitioners are highly optimistic about the future potential of cognitive-behavioural rehabilitative strategies (Vennard and Hedderman, 1998). However, we need also to consider the concerns of many criminological researchers that the current enthusiasm for cognitive behavioural practices could result in the further marginalization of 'traditional' programmes such as basic literacy and social skills. Moreover, commentators such as Pat Carlen have pointed to the problematic way in which many of the programmes that constitute the 'What works' movement are assessed and evaluated:

> The verity of the 'programmer's' claims to 'success' are often 'proven' by dubious self-report questionnaire evidence from prisoners that a programme 'works'—usually in terms of changing prisoners' understanding of their offending behaviour. (Indeed, in view of all these 'programmers' and 'counsellors' claiming to have found the philosopher's stone in relation to changing offenders' behaviour, it is truly amazing that the prisons have not been emptied by now!) (Carlen, 2002: 120)

Psychology and police work

In the modern police force, psychology seems to play an ever-expanding role (see Reiser, 1973; Bull *et al.*, 1983; Ainsworth and Pease, 1987; Hollin, 2012a; Webber, 2010). For example, there has been much research in the following areas:

- the selection and training of police recruits;
- analysing the values, norms and perceptive skills of police officers as they proceed through their careers;
- training and ultimately improving the way officers conduct interviews with witnesses (see for example, Geiselmen *et al.*, 1985 on the idea of the 'cognitive interview'; McGurk, 1993);
- understanding the way police officers deal with work-related stressors such as complaints made against them by the public or being faced with a violent or dangerous confrontation (see, for example, Terry, 1981);
- improving the ability of police officers to retrieve, recall and interpret events that may have a bearing on a criminal investigation (see Clifford and Bull, 1978);

- improving interrogation techniques (Gudjonsson, 1992); conversational relations with uncooperative suspects (Mortimer and Shepherd, 1999); and the detection of lies and false statements (Vrij, 2008);

- understanding and improving officer decision making in riot and firearm situations;

- and, of course, most famously (and perhaps most contentiously) as a key component in the construction of offender profiles.

Of course, just because the police are studied, it does not mean that the techniques that have been proven successful will actually be implemented or maintained over the long term. Moreover, a theme of this section is that police use of psychological research can have the unintended effect of short-circuiting the more traditional police techniques for investigation, namely knocking on doors and asking questions (De Lint, 2003).

Perhaps the most celebrated application of psychology within police work is the notion of the *offender profile* (see Jackson and Bekerian, 1997; Ainsworth, 2001; Holmes and Holmes, 2002). Certainly the role of the 'offender profiler' has, over the last decade or so, become a major theme within the mass entertainment industry, featuring in a slurry of TV shows and hit movies such as *Manhunter* and *The Silence of the Lambs*. Consequently, the idea of the so-called 'mind hunter' now holds something of a fascination with both the general public, and a great many students new to academic criminology—a number of whom often labour under the misapprehension that an undergraduate degree in criminology could lead to a formal 'job' as an offender profiler. In reality, in the UK in 2010, there were only five full time 'profiling' positions, known as Behavioural Investigation Advisors (BIAs) (Webber, 2010; Alison *et al.*, 2010; and Gudjonsson and Copson, 1997 for a guide to what profilers actually do). It is difficult to predict if the cut in police numbers since the financial crisis will lead to more or less use of BIAs. There are increasing opportunities for those trained in psychology to get work with the police, but the cinematic representation of the role is very much a myth in the UK, and heavily distorted in the US.

'The best way to become a profiler is to become a chartered forensic psychologist or a chartered forensic psychiatrist, and then, after you've done that, wait ten years and then wait to be asked.' Dr Julian Boon, the British psychologist and offender profiler (*The Real Cracker*, Channel 4 TV, 2001)

The purpose of offender profiling is to provide a way to limit the possible suspects in a particular criminal case, thereby improving the police use of their resources. This drive to efficiency is one of the main reasons why criminologists and psychologists are finding work in law enforcement, it saves the police money. However, the problem is the way that this can result in short cuts being taken in the investigation. One example of this is the investigation of the murder of Rachel Nickell on Wimbledon Common in 1992. Colin Stagg, a local man, became a prime suspect based on a profile provided by the psychologist Paul Britton. An approach was suggested whereby a female police officer would go undercover to befriend Stagg in the hope that he would confess. The officer recorded their increasingly intimate conversations until the police felt they had a case. However, the judge threw it out because it amounted to entrapment. The case went cold because no other leads were followed. In 2008, Robert Napper pleaded guilty to the murder, Napper was at the time serving life for the murder of Samantha Bissett and her four-year-old daughter Jazmine. They were killed a year after Rachel Nickell was killed in front of her three-year-old son. In an earlier case, David Canter, regarded as a more scientifically-led investigative psychologist, provided a profile of the Railway Killer, a serial sex offender and murderer later identified as John Duffy. Canter suggests that his profile was accurate, and in his own words 'the reflections led us to the man' (Canter, 1994: 70). This may well be true, but Duffy was not the only man involved, he had an accomplice, David Mulcahy, who was convicted in 2000. The evidence suggested that he was the first to escalate the attacks to murder. In the absence of forensic scientific evidence, profiling might be a method that helps to focus the police investigation, but it must be treated with caution. One of the key questions surrounding profiling concerns which crimes are suitable to be profiled (Pinizzotto, 1984; Stevens, 1995). While some maintain that profiling is only applicable in crimes that indicate a high degree of psychological abnormality (such as violent, sexual assaults or seemingly 'motiveless' murders), others claim that the practice could be extended to include a range of other crimes that do not necessarily involve personal contact or clinical disorders. David Canter suggests that his approach can even be used for what he calls 'volume crimes' such as burglary (Canter, 2004; Bennell and Jones, 2005). Again, it remains to be seen if this is something that will be pursued in an era of cuts to police resources.

There are two major approaches to profiling: the crime scene analysis approach favoured by the FBI Investigative Support Unit (formerly the Behavioural Science Unit), and the 'investigative psychology' approach as favoured by the British psychologist David Canter and his various proponents (see Ainsworth, 2001: Chapters 6 and 7 for introductions to these different approaches).

Essentially, the FBI's approach is to cross-reference crime scene evidence (such as levels of violence or mutilation, timing of the offence, body disposal/position, or levels of premeditation and so on) with established 'offender typologies' to determine a working personality profile of the perpetrator(s), thus enabling the authorities to better focus their investigations. However, these typologies inevitably rely upon the 'subjective judgements' of the individual profiler (see Ressler and Shachtman, 1992). Such reliance upon individual intuition has led many to question the empirical value of this approach, with critics such as David Canter (1994) and Philip Jenkins (1994) asserting that individual hunches and rigid typologies based primarily on interviews with notoriously distrustful offenders are no basis for a systematic science.

The second approach is different in that it eschews the so-called informed speculation—or what David Canter has described as the 'flash of insight'—that is a key feature of the FBI approach. Instead it seeks to construct a situational/geographic profile of the offender(s) based on the assumption that the offender, like most people, acts consistently over time (the criminal consistency hypothesis). It is for this reason that the investigative psychology approach is not limited solely to crimes such as murder and rape, and that it can also be used to profile a whole range of more prosaic 'volume' crimes (see, for example, Canter and Alison, 2000). The goal of this form of profiling is to identify intelligible patterns between things like time and location of offence (Canter and Larkin, 1993; Canter and Gregory, 1994), factors surrounding victim selection and, if the victim survived (for example, non-homicidal rape cases) a close analysis of the offender's behaviour (Canter and Heritage, 1990) and speech patterns. Canter's goal, then, is the rigorous application of applied psychological principles to the study of offender profiling.

Canter's work was originally based on five aspects of the interaction between the victim and the offender—the five-factor model:

(1) *Interpersonal coherence* assumes that offenders will deal with their victims in a manner similar to the way they treat people in their day-to-day lives.

(2) *The significance of time and place* may provide analysts with clues about the offender's mobility and even his residence.

(3) *Criminal characteristics* are used by researchers and analysts to place offenders into broad categories, from which subcategories can be selected or developed.

(4) *Criminal career* is an assessment as to whether the offender may have engaged in criminal activity before and what type of activity it most likely was.

(5) *Forensic awareness* draws in part from Step 4, criminal career. It is an assessment of the scene and evidence to determine if the offender has any special knowledge of evidence gathering procedures used by the police.

Source: Criminal Investigation (Chapter 8) by Swanson, C.R., Chamelin, N.C. and Territo, I. (2002) New York: McGrawHill.

Despite optimistic noises about the growing 'scientific' rigour of offender profiling, significant doubts still remain about its empirical legitimacy—not least the problem of how one measures the accuracy and thus the ultimate value of profiles. Two of the most well-known American authors writing on the subject present, perhaps, the most damning indictment when they state that 'a tremendous amount of interest surrounds the field of profiling. But, we must remember that it is only one tool and by itself has never solved a murder case despite the statements made by some' (Holmes and Holmes, 2002: 3).

Psychology and the courtroom

The last two decades have witnessed a growing mass of psychological research produced on various aspects of the legal process. A detailed account of what is often referred to as legal psychology is beyond the compass of this chapter. Instead we have chosen here to introduce three key areas of overlap between psychologists and those working in the legal profession: the pre-trial role of psychologists and psychiatrists in the assessment of mentally disordered offenders; the psychological research into eyewitness testimony; and the decision-making strategies and psycho-social dynamics of jurors/juries. Let us look at each in turn.

Mental disorder and criminal responsibility

The question of whether or not mentally disordered offenders should be incarcerated in prisons and institutional facilities or cared for within the community is an incredibly complex and contentious one (see Peay, 2002 for an excellent summary). The key problem in this area is one of definition: 'Mental disorder' ... is a term of acute terminological inexactitude. Definitions of mental disorder act like a concertina, expanding and contracting in order to accommodate different client groups with little or no coherence. Their mismatch frequently results in uncertainties and anomalies' (2002: 753). Inevitably, these definitional problems ensure that there is a ready need for the assessment expertise of the psychiatrist, not least in relation to *mens rea* (the notion of criminal intent) and the thorny question of whether or not the offender was in a sound psychological state of mind when committing the criminal act (Prins, 1986).

Such clinical testimony, along with various other courtroom roles played by the psychologist—such as the expert witness (see MacKay *et al.*, 1999) and the role of adviser to counsel—ensure 'that psychiatric and psychological evidence is increasingly prevalent and influential in criminal proceedings' (Peay, 2002: 766). Indeed, the wealth of empirical studies undertaken within psychology into abnormal behaviour, in tandem with the long history of predominantly medical diagnoses proffered by psychiatrists, have served as the catalyst for the modification of the law's approach to a number of issues concerning criminality and mental health.

The psychology of eyewitness memory

Witnesses to a crime are often asked to recall the details of the event, whether by witness statement or police interview, or perhaps even via an artist's impression, photo-fit or identity parade (Putwain and Sammons, 2002: 111–19). In every case, it is essential that the police and other authorities be provided with accurate and reliable information. To assist in this process, a body of work has emerged based on the psychology of eyewitness memory (and testimony) (Loftus, 1979; Gudjonsson, 1992; Ainsworth, 1998; Heaton-Armstrong *et al.*, 1999 for comprehensive overviews). The goal of these studies is to better understand the processes and problems associated with memory. Unlike an audio-visual recorder, our memories can be altered, manipulated, and lose information (Putwain and Ammons, 2002: 97).

By way of summary, one can state that the psychology of eyewitness memory focuses on three stages of the memory process: *acquisition, retention,* and *retrieval* (see Cohen, 1999):

(a) *Acquisition (or encoding) stage—the witnessing of the incident*: This stage can be affected by time factors like the length of time spent witnessing the event; the time of day when the event took place (studies show that witnesses recall more details about crimes that took place in daylight than at night); the nature of the incident witnessed (for example, the so-called 'weapon focus effect', where victims of gun-related crime often recall intimate details about the firearm, but very little about other aspects of the crime).

(b) *Retention (or storage) stage*: Research in this area has shown that this stage of the memory process can be affected by the duration of time that passes between witnessing a crime and the request to retrieve the details; and whether the witness discusses the events with others prior to giving evidence—the so-called contamination effect.

(c) *Retrieval stage—the process of giving evidence*: Studies around the retrieval of information have highlighted that memory can be affected by subtle changes in the way the questions are worded/inferred; or by the process of *expectation*, where witnesses often tend to report what they expected to see (on such points, see the large body of work by the psychologist, Elizabeth Loftus).

Psychology of the jury

As with other areas of the legal process, criminological psychology has had much to say about courtroom dynamics and, in particular, the way that juries arrive at their decisions (see Ainsworth, 2002: Chapter 7). Importantly, one should point out that because of the obvious inherent practical and ethical difficulties of studying actual jury decision-making strategies, much of the psychological research in this area is the product of experiments conducted on mock juries/trials. Summarized below are a few of the main research areas:

(a) *Eyewitness testimony*: Research suggests that juries place considerable emphasis on eyewitness testimony when weighing their decisions—even when counsel has cast doubt on the veracity of the eyewitness (see Loftus, 1974).

(b) *The effects of pre-trial publicity on the jury*: Experimental studies in this area have found clear evidence to suggest that juries are prejudicially affected by exposure to pre-trial publicity, a process that does not appear (in mock trials at least) to be offset by judicial instruction.

(c) *Levels of confidence displayed by witnesses*: Perhaps unsurprisingly, research indicates that jurors tend to place most faith in witnesses who display a confident manner when testifying.

(d) *The extent to which jurors perceptions about defendant characteristics such as attractiveness, gender, race, age, status/qualifications and demeanour affect their decision-making*: See Fife-Schaw, 1999.

(e) *Jury selection procedure*: In the US the 'screening out' of jurors who counsel believe may have the 'wrong type of personality' to try a particular case has become a major area of psychological research (see Kassin and Wrightsman, 1983). Indeed, this practice of *voir dire* has become a specialism of certain trial lawyers—as illustrated most publicly in the trial of O.J. Simpson.

(f) *The social dynamics of how a group of twelve jurors arrive at their verdict.*

(g) *The problems associated with children's testimony.*

REVIEW QUESTIONS

1 What are the limitations of psychologically-based rehabilitation programmes?

2 Is offender profiling a systematic science or just intuitive guesswork?

3. What psychological factors might affect eyewitness memory/testimony?

CONCLUSION

It is hoped that this chapter has provided the reader with a solid introduction to the various ways in which psychological research has contributed to our understanding of crime and the criminal justice system. On the way, we hope it has also helped to shatter some of the popular myths and 'media-created' assumptions about criminological psychology. In particular, our goal has been to dispel the erroneous conception of criminal psychology as a sort of 'secret science', wherein its practitioners are capable of identifying and detecting something as specific and observable as a psychologically distinct criminal mind or personality.

We have also seen that, despite the fact psychological research has frequently served as an important driver of change in society's attitudes and responses to crime, there still exists a slightly uneasy relationship between criminology and psychology. Certainly, we still find ourselves in a situation where researchers in one discipline are often working independently of those in the other. In part this is due to the disciplinary schisms that are an intrinsic part of the history of Western social sciences. That said, we have endeavoured to highlight some of the more productive interactions between these areas of ongoing research. It remains to be seen if a more conciliatory approach may lead to a greater consensus or convergence in 'scientific knowledge'.

QUESTIONS FOR DISCUSSION

1 What early behavioural characteristics/traits might be listed as predicators of violent crime? Do you agree with the statement that 'most psychological problems have their roots in some sort of trauma yet to be resolved'?

2 Think about some of your own characteristics, traits and behaviours. To what extent have these behaviours been learned, either via 'positive reinforcement', 'differential association' or via the observation of cultural symbols and media 'role models'?

3 Is it really possible to empirically map something as complex as the human personality? Are our personalities stable or changeable?

4 What are the social and cultural factors behind the public's fascination with criminal psychology?

GUIDE TO FURTHER READING

Ainsworth, P. (2002) *Psychology and Policing*. Cullompton: Willan.
A good general introductory account of the way in which psychological principles and practices are applied to policing.

Bartol, C.R. and Bartol, A.M. (2005) *Criminal Behaviour: A Psychosocial Approach*. Upper Saddle River, NJ: Pearson Education.
An engaging and helpfully frequently updated introduction to the role of psychology in understanding criminal behaviour.

Blackburn, R. (1993) *The Psychology of Criminal Conduct: Theory, Research and Practice*. Chichester: Wiley.
A detailed and comprehensive account of many of the themes discussed in this chapter.

Hollin, C.R. (2012) *Psychology and Crime: An Introduction to Criminological Psychology*. London: Routledge.
This newly revised book provides one of the most comprehensive and accessible reviews of the literature on criminological psychology.

Kapardis, A. (1997) *Psychology and Law: A Critical Introduction*. Cambridge: Cambridge University Press.
A general introduction to psychology's various contributions to criminal justice and socio-legal studies.

Webber, C. (2010) *Psychology and Crime*. London: Sage.
Webber's *Psychology and Crime* provides a good overview of both these areas, as well as an analysis of the consequences of crime for victims, offenders, and wider society. It also includes a range of practical devices to support the learning process. The book is also useful in that it discusses some of the more thoughtful critiques of psychology by writers such as Nicholas Rose and Michel Foucault.

WEB LINKS

http://www.clas.ufl.edu/users/gthursby/psi/
Link to the *Psychology World Wide Web Virtual Library*, a site that keeps track of psychology related websites.

http://www.psychology.org/
The Encyclopaedia of Psychology website.

http://www.psychologyinfo.com
A private US internet resource run by Donald J. Franklin, Phd, that provides general and accessible information about the practice of psychology, see more specifically http://www.psychologyinfo.com/forensic/

http://faculty.washington.edu/eloftus/
The homepage of Elizabeth Loftus, one of the leading researchers in eyewitness testimony and other aspects of legal psychology. The site has various links to her books and articles.

http://www.freudfile.org/
A website dedicated to the life and work of the psychoanalyst Sigmund Freud.

http://www.bps.org.uk/index.cfm
Website of the British Psychological Society.

REFERENCES

Abrahamson, D. (1944) *Crime and the Human Mind*. New York: Columbia University Press.

Adler, J.R. (2004) *Forensic Psychology: Concepts, Debates and Practice*. Cullompton: Willan.

Aichorn, A. (1925) *The Wayward Youth*. New York: Meridian Books.

Ainsworth, P.B. (1998) *Psychology, Law and Eyewitness Testimony*. Chichester: Wiley.

Ainsworth, P.B. (2000) *Psychology and Crime: Myths and Realities*. London: Longman.

Ainsworth, P.B. (2001) *Offender Profiling and Crime Analysis*. Cullompton: Willan.

Ainsworth, P.B. and Pease, K. (1987) *Police Work*. London: Methuen.

Akers, R. (1985) *Deviant Behaviour: A Social Learning Approach*. Belmont, CA: Wadsworth.

Alexander, F. and Healy, W. (1935) *Roots of Crime*. New York: Knopf.

Alexander, F. and Staub, H. (1931) *The Criminal, The Judge and the Public*. New York: Macmillan.

Alison, L., Goodwill, A., Almond, L., van den Heuvel, C., and Winter, J. (2010), 'Pragmatic solutions to offender profiling and behavioural investigative advice', *Legal and Criminological Psychology* 15: 115–32.

Alison, L. and Kebbell, M. (2006) 'Offender profiling: limits and potential' in M. Kebbell and G. Davies (eds) *Practical Psychology for Forensic Investigations and Prosecutions*. Chichester: Wiley.

Alison, L., Smith, M.D., and Morgan, K. (2003) 'Interpreting the accuracy of offender profiles', *Psychology, Crime and Law* 9 (2): 185–95.

Allport, G.W. (1937) *Personality: A Psychological Explanation*. New York: Holt.

Ayllon, T. and Milan, M. (1979) *Correctional Rehabilitation and Management: A Psychological Approach*. New York: Wiley.

Baars, B.J. (1986) *The Cognitive Revolution in Psychology*. New York: Guildford Press.

Bandura, A. (1973) *Aggression: A Social Learning Analysis*. Englewood Cliffs, NJ: Prentice Hall.

Bandura, A. (1977) *Social Learning Theory*. New York: Prentice Hall.

Bartol, C.R. (2002) *Criminal Behaviour: A Psychosocial Approach*. Upper Saddle River, NJ: Prentice Hall.

Bartol, C.R. and Bartol, A.M. (1994) *Psychology and Law*. Pacific Grove, CA: Brooks/Cole. Albany, NY: State University of New York Press.

Bartol, C.R. and Bartol, A.M. (2005) *Criminal Behaviour: A Psychosocial Approach*. Upper Saddle River, NJ: Pearson Education.

Bekerain, D.A. and Jackson, J.L. (1997) 'Critical issues in offender profiling' in J.L. Jackson and D.A. Bekerian (eds) *Offender Profiling: Theory, Research and Practice*. Chichester: Wiley.

Bennell, C. and Jones, N.I. (2005) 'Between a ROC and hard place: a method for linking serial burglaries by *modus operandi*', *Journal of Investigative Psychology and Offender Profiling* 2(1): 23–42.

Blackburn, R. (1993) *The Psychology of Criminal Conduct: Theory, Research and Practice*. Chichester: Wiley.

Boon, J.C.W. (1997) 'The contribution of Personality Theories to psychological profiling' in J.L. Jackson and D.A. Bekerian (eds) *Offender Profiling: Theory, Research and Practice*. Chichester: Wiley.

Bowlby, J. (1944) 'Forty-four juvenile thieves: their characters and home life', *International Journal of Psycho-Analysis* 25: 19–52 and 107–27.

Bowlby, J. (1951) *Maternal Care and Mental Health*. World Health Organization: London: Her Majesty's Stationery Office.

Bowlby, J. (1973) *Separation: Anxiety and Anger. Volume 2 of Attachment and Loss*. London: Hogarth Press.

Boyle, G.J., Matthews, G., and Saklofske, D.H. (2008) *Handbook of Personality Measurement and Assessment* (Vols 1 and 2). Thousand Oaks, CA: Sage.

Bull, R.H.C., Bustin, B., Evans, P., and Gahagan, D. (1983) *Psychology for Police Officers*. Chichester: Wiley.

Brown, C. (2006) *Cognitive Psychology*. London: Sage

Burbeck, E. and Furnham, A. (1985) 'Police Officer Selection: a Critical Review of the Literature', *Journal of Police Science and Administration* 13: 58–69.

Canter, D. (1994) *Criminal Shadows*. London: Harper Collins.

Canter, D. (2004) 'Offender profiling and investigative psychology', *Journal of Investigative Psychology and Offender Profiling* 1(1): 1–16.

Canter, D. and Alison, L. (2000) *Profiling Property Crimes*. Aldershot: Ashgate.

Canter, D. and Gregory, A. (1994) 'Identifying the Residential Location of Rapists' *Journal of the Forensic Science Society*, 34: 169–75.

Canter, D. and Heritage, R. (1990) 'A Multivariate Model of Sexual Offence Behaviour: Developments in Offender Profiling', *Journal of Forensic Psychiatry* 1: 185–212.

Canter, D. and Larkin, P. (1993) 'The environmental range of serial rapists', *Journal of Environmental Psychology* 13: 63–69.

Carlson, N.R. and Buskist, W. (1997) *Psychology: The Science of Behaviour*. Boston, MA: Allyn and Bacon.

Cattell, R.B. (1965) *The Scientific Analysis of Personality*. Harmondsworth: Penguin.

Ciba Foundation (1996) *Ciba Foundation Symposium 194: Genetics of Criminal and Antisocial Behaviour*. Chichester: Wiley.

Clifford, B.R. and Bull, R. (1978) *The Psychology of Person Identification*. London: Routledge.

Cohen, G. (1999) 'Human memory in the real world' in A. Heaton-Armstrong, E. Shepherd and D. Wolchover (eds) *Analysing Witness Testimony*. London: Blackstone.

Colman, A.M. and Gorman, L.P. (1982) 'Conservatism, dogmatism, and authoritarianism in British police officers', *Sociology* 16: 1–11.

Cook, P.M. (1977) 'Empirical survey of police attitudes', *Police Review* 85: 0142, 1078, 1114, 1140.

Copson, G. (1995) *Coals to Newcastle? Part 1: A Study of Offender Profiling*. London: Police Research Group Special Interest Series/Home Office.

De Lint, W. (2003), 'Keeping open windows: police as access brokers', *The British Journal of Criminology* 43(2): 379–98.

Evans, B.J., Coma, G.J., and Stanley, R.O. (1992) 'The police personality: Type A behaviour and trait anxiety', *Journal of Criminal Justice* 20: 429–41.

Eysenck, H. (1977) *Crime and Personality*. London: Routledge.

Eysenck, H. (1984) 'Crime and Personality' in Müller, D.J. *et al.* (eds) *Psychology and Law*. Chichester: Wiley.

Eysenck, H. and Gudjonsson, G. (1989) *The Causes and Cures of Criminality*. New York: Plenum Press.

Eysenck, M., and Keane, M. (1997) *Cognitive Psychology: A Student's Handbook*. Hove: Psychology Press.

Feldman, P. (1993) *The Psychology of Crime*. Cambridge: Cambridge University Press.

Fife-Schaw, C. (1999) 'The influence of witness appearance and demeanour on witness credibility' in A. Heaton-Armstrong, E. Shepherd, and D. Wolchover (eds) *Analysing Witness Testimony*. London: Blackstone.

Freud, S. (1935) *A General Introduction to Psychoanalysis*. New York: Liveright.

Fridel, L.A. and Binder, A. (1992) 'Police Officer Decision Making in Potentially Violent Confrontations', *Journal of Criminal Justice* 20: 385–99.

Furedi, F. (2004) *Therapy Culture*. London: Routledge.

Gadd, D. and Jefferson, T. (2007) *Psychosocial Criminology: An Introduction*. London: Sage.

Garland, D. (1994) 'Of crimes and criminals: the development of criminology in Britain' in M. Maguire, R. Morgan, and R. Reiner (eds) *The Oxford Handbook of Criminology*. Oxford: Oxford University Press.

Garland, D. (1997) '"Governmentality" and the Problem of Crime: Foucault, Criminology and Sociology', *Theoretical Criminology* 1(2): 173–214.

Garland, D. (2001) *The Culture of Control*. Oxford: Oxford University Press.

Geiselman, R.E., Fisher, R.P., MacKinnon, D.F., and Holland, H.L. (1985) 'Eyewitness Memory Enhancement in Police Interview: Cognitive Retrieval Mnemonics Versus Hypnosis', *Journal of Applied Psychology* 70: 401–12.

Glueck, S. and Glueck, E. (1950) *Unravelling Juvenile Delinquency*. New York: Harper and Row.

Gudjonsson, G.H. (1992) *The Psychology of Interrogations, Confessions and Testimony*. Chichester: Wiley.

Gudjonsson, G.H. and Adlam, K.R.C. (1983) 'Personality Patterns of British Police Officers', *Personality and Individual Differences* 4: 507–12.

Gudjonsson, G.H. and Copson, G. (1997) 'The role of the expert in criminal investigation' in J.L. Jackson and D.A. Bekerian (eds) *Offender Profiling: Theory, Research and Practice*. Chichester: Wiley.

Gudjonsson, G.H. and Hayward, L.R.C. (1998) *Forensic Psychology: A Guide to Practice*. London: Routledge.

Healy, W., and Bronner, A.F. (1936) *New Light on Delinquency and its Treatment*. New Haven, CT: Yale University Press.

Heaton-Armstrong, A., Shepherd, E., and Wolchover, D. (eds) (1999) *Analysing Witness Testimony*. London: Blackstone.

HM Prison Service and the National Probation Service (2003) 'Driving Delivery: A strategic framework for psychological services in prisons and probation' HM Prison Service, NPS, London: Applied Psychology Group.

Hollin, C.R. (1992) *Criminal Behaviour: A Psychological Approach to Explanation and Prevention*. London: Falmer Press.

Hollin, C.R. (2012a) 'Criminological psychology' in M. Maguire *et al.* (eds) *The Oxford Handbook of Criminology* (5th edn) Oxford: Oxford University Press.

Hollin, C.R. (2012b) *Psychology and Crime: An Introduction to Criminological Psychology* (2nd edn). London: Routledge.

Holmes, R.M. and Holmes, S.T. (2002) *Profiling Violent Crimes: An Investigative Tool*. London: Sage.

Jackson, J.L. and Bekerian, D.A. (eds) (1997) *Offender Profiling: Theory, Research and Practice*. Chichester: Wiley.

Jeffrey, C.R. (1965) 'Criminal Behaviour and Learning Theory', *Journal of Criminal Law, Criminology, and Police Science*, 56: 294–300.

Jeffrey, C.R. (1994) 'Biological and Neuropsychiatric Approaches to Criminal Behaviour' in G. Barak (ed) *Varieties of Criminology: Readings from a Dynamic Discipline*. Westport, CT: Praeger.

Jenkins, P. (1994) *Using Murder: The Social Construction of Serial Homicide*. New York: Aldine de Gruyter.

Jones, S. (2000) *Understanding Violent Crime*. Maidenhead: Open University Press.

Kapardis, A. (1997) *Psychology and Law: A Critical Introduction*. Cambridge: Cambridge University Press.

Kassin, S.M. and Wrightsman, L.S. (1983) 'The construction and validation of a juror bias scale', *Journal of Research in Personality* 17: 423–42.

Kemshall, H. (2001) *Risk Assessment and Management of Known Sexual and Violent Offenders: A Review of Current Issues.* Police Research Series Paper 140. HMSO.

Kemshall, H. (2003) *Understanding Risk in Criminal Justice.* Maidenhead: Open University Press.

Kline, P. (1984) *Psychology and Freudian Theory.* London: Metheun.

Kohlberg, L. (1969) 'Stage and sequence: the cognitive-developmental approach to socialization' in D.A. Gosling (ed) *Handbook of Socialization Theory and Research.* Chicago: Rand McNally.

Lamberts, K. and Goldstone, R. (2004) *Handbook of Cognition.* Thousand Oaks, CA: Sage.

Lanier, M., and Henry, S. (1998) *Essential Criminology.* Boulder, CO: Westview Press.

Lipsey, M.W., Landenberger, N.A., and Chapman, G.L. (2004) 'Rehabilitation: an assessment of theory and research' in C. Sumner (ed) *The Blackwell Companion to Criminology.* Oxford: Blackwell.

Little, A. (1965) 'Parental deprivation, separation and crime: a test on adolescent recidivists', *British Journal of Criminology* 5: 419–30.

Loftus, E.F. (1974) 'The Incredible Eyewitness', *Psychology Today,* December 117–19.

Loftus, E.F. (1979) *Eyewitness Testimony.* Cambridge, MA: Harvard University Press.

Lorenz, K. (1966) *On Aggression.* New York: Harcourt Brace World.

McGuire, J. (ed) (1995) *What Works: Reducing Reoffending.* Chichester, John Wiley.

McGuire, J. (2000) *Cognitive Behavioural Approaches: An Introduction to Theory and Research.* London: HMSO.

McGuire, J. (2004) *Understanding Psychology and Crime.* Maidenhead: Open University Press.

McGuire, J., Mason, T., and O'Kane, A. (eds) (2000) *Behaviour, Crime and Legal Process: A Guide for Practitioners,* Chichester: John Wiley.

McGurk, B.J., Carr, M., and McGurk, D. (1993) *Investigative Interviewing Courses for Police Officers,* London: Home Office.

Mackay, R.D., Colman, A.M., and Thornton, P. (1999) 'The admissibility of expert psychological and psychiatric testimony' in A. Heaton-Armstrong, E. Shepherd, and D. Wolchover (eds) *Analysing Witness Testimony.* London: Blackstone.

Maruna, S. (2000) 'Criminology, desistance and the psychology of the stranger' in D. Canter and L. Alison (eds) *The Social Psychology of Crime: Groups, teams and Networks.* Aldershot: Ashgate.

Mednick, S.A., Moffitt, T.E., and Stack, S.A. (1987) *The Causes of Crime: New Biological Approaches.* Cambridge: Cambridge University Press.

Morrison, W. (1995) *Theoretical Criminology: from Modernity to Post-modernism.* London: Cavendish.

Morrison, W. (2004) 'Lombroso and the Birth of Criminological Positivism: Scientific Mastery or Cultural Artifice?' in J. Ferrell *et al., Cultural Criminology Unleashed.* London: GlassHouse.

Mortimer, A. and Sheperd, E. (1999) 'Frames of mind: schemata guiding cognition and conduct in the interviewing of suspected offenders' in A. Memon and R. Bull (eds) *Handbook of the Psychology of Interviewing.* Chichester: Wiley.

Müller, D.J., Blackman, D.E., and Chapman, A.J. (eds) (1984) *Psychology and Law.* Chichester: John Wiley and Sons.

Nietzel, M.T. (1979) *Crime and its Modification: A Social Learning Perspective.* New York: Pergamon.

O'Malley, P. (2004) *Risk, Uncertainty and Government.* London: GlassHouse.

O'Malley, P. (2008) 'Governmentality and risk' in J. O. Zimm (ed) *Social Theories of Risk and Uncertainty: An Introduction.* Oxford: Blackwell.

Peay, J. (2002) 'Mentally disordered offenders, mental health and crime' in M. Maguire *et al.* (eds) *The Oxford Handbook of Criminology* (3rd edn) Oxford: Oxford University Press.

Piaget, J. (1954) *The Construction of Reality in the Child.* New York: Basic Books.

Pinizzotto, A.J. (1984) 'Forensic psychology: criminal personality profiling', *Journal of Police Science and Administration* 12: 32–40.

Prins, H. (1986) *Dangerous Behaviour, the Law and Mental Disorder.* London: Tavistock.

Putwain, D. and Sammons, A. (2002) *Psychology and Crime.* London: Routledge.

Raine, A. (1993) *The Psychopathology of Crime: Criminal Behaviour as a Clinical Disorder.* San Diego, CA: Academic Press.

Raynor, P. (2002) 'Community penalties: probation, punishment and "What Works"' in M. Maguire *et al.* (eds) *The Oxford Handbook of Criminology* (3rd edn) Oxford: Oxford University Press.

Reiser, M. (1973) *Practical Psychology for Police Officers.* Springfield, Ill: C.C. Thomas.

Ressler, R. and Shachtman, T. (1992) *Whoever Fights Monsters*. New York: St Martins.

Rider, A.O. (1980) 'The firesetter: a psychological profile', *FBI Law Enforcement Bulletin* 4 (6): 6–13.

Roberts, P. (1996) 'Will you stand up in court? On the admissibility of psychiatric and psychological evidence', *Journal of Forensic Psychiatry* 7: 63–78.

Rotter, J.B. (1954) *Social Learning and Clinical Psychology*. Englewood Cliffs, NJ: Prentice Hall.

Rutter, M. (1972) *Maternal Deprivation Reassessed*. Harmondsworth: Penguin.

Samenow, S.E. (1984) *Inside the Criminal Mind*. New York: Times Books.

Skinner, B.F. (1938) *The Behaviour of Organisms*. New York: Appleton.

Skinner, B.F. (1953) *Science and Human Behaviour*. New York: Macmillan.

Stevens, J.A. (1995) 'Offenders in profile', *Policing Today*, August.

Storr, A. (1970) *Human Aggression*. Harmondsworth: Penguin.

Strentz, T. (1988) 'A terrorist psychological profile', *Law Enforcement Bulletin* 57: 11–18.

Sutherland, E. (1947) *Principles of Criminology*. Philadelphia: Lippincott.

Swanson, C.R., Chamelin, N.C., and Territo, L. (1984) *Criminal Investigation*. New York: McGraw-Hill.

Terry, W.C. (1981) 'Police Stress: the Empirical Evidence', *Journal of Police Science and Administration* 9: 61–75.

Towl, G.J. (2004) 'Applied psychological services in Prisons and Probation' in J.R. Adler (ed) *Forensic Psychology*. Cullompton: Willan.

Towl, G.J. and Crighton, D.A. (2010) *Forensic Psychology*. Oxford: Blackwell.

Valier, C. (2006) 'Psychoanalytic Criminology' in E. McLaughlin and J. Muncie (eds) *The Sage Dictionary of Criminology*. London: Sage.

Vennard, J. and Hedderman, C. (1998) 'Effective Interventions with offenders' in P. Goldblatt and C. Lewis (eds) *Reducing Offending: An Assessment of Research Evidence on Ways of Dealing with Offending Behaviour*. Home Office Research Study No. 187, London: Home Office.

Vrij, A. (2008) *Detecting Lies and Deceit: The Psychology of Lying and the Implications for Professional Practice*. Chichester: John Wiley and Sons.

Watson, J.B. (1913) 'Psychology as the behaviorist views it', *Psychological Review*, Vol. 20(2), Mar 1913, 158–77.

Webber, C. (2010) *Psychology and Crime*. London: Sage.

Yochelson, S. and Samenow, S. (1976) *The Criminal Personality*. New York: Jason Aronson.

Yuille, J.C. (1986) *Police Selection and Training: The Role of Psychology*. Dordrecht: Martinus Nijhoff.

7

Crime and media: understanding the connections

Chris Greer

INTRODUCTION

The contemporary era—whether we term it the information society, the knowledge society, the network society, the image world, postmodernity, or late modernity—is a fundamentally mediatized era. It is also an era in which high crime rates and high levels of concern about crime have become accepted as 'normal'. The rapid and relentless development of information and communication technologies (ICTs) over the past 100 years has shaped the modern age, transforming the relations between space, time and identity. Where once 'news' used to travel by ship, it now hurtles across the globe at light speed and is available 24 hours-a-day at the push of a button. Where once cultures used to be more or less distinguishable in national or geographical terms, they now mix, intermingle and converge in a constant global exchange of information. Where once a sense of community and belonging was derived primarily from established identities and local traditions, it may now also be found, and lost, in a virtual world of shared values, meanings and interpretations. In short, the media are not only inseparable from contemporary social life; they are, for many, its defining characteristic. Understanding the connections between crime and the media is central to understanding the cultural place that crime and media occupy in our social world.

This chapter is an introduction to the investigation of crime and media. My main aim is to present a summary of major themes and debates which have shaped the research agenda, but I also want to sharpen the focus of investigation on some less well rehearsed issues such as the changing global communications marketplace, the development of new media technologies, and the significance of these for understanding the connections between crime and media. The chapter is divided into four main sections. The first offers some background information and addresses the crucial question of why exploring media images of crime and control is important. The second section considers how scholars have researched crime and media, and presents an overview of the main findings. The third section examines the dominant theoretical and conceptual tools which have been used to understand and explain media representations of crime. The final section considers the evidence for the influence of media representations, both on criminal behaviour and fear of crime. Finally, I will suggest some areas for future research.

BACKGROUND

Though sections of the popular press may suggest otherwise, most of us have little first-hand experience of serious criminal victimization. Our understanding of the crime problem—how much crime is out there, what types of crime are most prevalent, who is most at risk, what are the best responses—derives mostly from sources other than personal experience. Paramount among these are the media. The media, then, are key producers and purveyors of 'knowledge' about crime, disorder and control. For this reason alone, media representations are worthy of in-depth investigation.

But precisely what kinds of knowledge do these representations generate, and to what effect? Some key questions which have perplexed students of crime and media include:

- Is it possible to discern a coherent picture of 'the crime problem' from the media and, if so, does this picture bear any resemblance to what we may claim, however tentatively, to know of the 'reality' of crime and criminal justice?

- Do the media merely reflect, objectively and impartially, what happens in the world, or are they active agents in socially constructing 'mediated realities' in which certain values, interests and beliefs are promoted, while others are downplayed, or even actively suppressed?

- Do the media reproduce and reinforce prejudice and the stereotyping of marginalized groups, or actively challenge it?

- Do the media undermine or fortify the existing structures of power and authority?

- Does violence in the media make us more aggressive, more fearful, or both?

Concern about the pernicious influence of the media is perennial, and academic research exploring media representations of crime dates back to the early 1900s (Pearson, 1983). Yet despite literally thousands of studies, these key questions have generated few conclusive answers. The media *are* a multiplicity of institutions, organizations, processes and practices which are hugely diverse in composition, scope and purpose. Today there are more media forms (television, newspapers, magazines, radio, the Internet) and greater levels of diversity within each individual form (satellite, cable and digital television) than ever before. Understanding media, therefore, requires a critical and reflexive appreciation both of the diversity of forms and formats involved and of the complexity with which images, texts, messages and signs are produced, transmitted and consumed.

One of the key points to grasp—and one of the issues I want to communicate most forcefully—is that we do not all use, interpret, and respond to media representations in the same way. Images of violent crime, for example, may repel some and attract others, disturb some and excite others, frighten some and anger others. Readers are encouraged to look beyond the instinctive desire to tackle complex dilemmas with simplified accounts and generalizations. The relationship between media images and the world around us is so fascinating precisely because it is complex and hard to pin down.

Researching crime and media

Research on crime and media covers three principal areas of interest: content; production; and consumption and influence. Each area has its own particular research methods and approaches (Greer, 2010). Media content analysis can be split between studies which are primarily either quantitative or qualitative. Quantitative analyses are concerned first and foremost with measuring the *amount* of crime, violence or control in the media—for example, the number of crime stories reported in a newspaper, or the number of violent incidents appearing in a television programme. The 'media picture' of crime is then usually compared with the 'real world' picture, normally derived from official criminal statistics. Quantitative approaches traditionally have predominated in research on media content. Qualitative content analyses, by contrast, are concerned primarily with investigating the *nature* of media representations of crime, violence and control. Though they may incorporate some quantitative component, qualitative research is more interested in untangling the complex processes through which media images are produced, exchanged and interpreted—for example, by exploring the use of language, the forces and constraints that shape media production, or the wider influence of the economic, political, moral and cultural environment. Both quantitative and qualitative analyses may be equally concerned with media influence.

Each approach has its strengths and weaknesses, but some of the limitations of purely quantitative research are particularly noteworthy. Official statistics are a very poor indicator of crime rates and may reveal more about the reporting and recording practices of the public and the police than they do about actual levels of offending (Maguire, 2012). Quantitative claims about the relationship between media images and the statistical 'reality' of crime, therefore, need to be treated with caution. More fundamentally, because quantitative analyses cannot tackle the crucial issue of meaning, for many they can only ever provide a surface description of media representations of crime rather than a deeper understanding, which would generally be the favoured research outcome. Nevertheless, quantitative research can offer important insights into changing patterns and trends in the representation of crime, as well as generating useful data on which deeper qualitative investigations can be based (see, for example, Jackson *et al.*, 2013).

Content analyses of media representations of crime—whether news, film, television drama, magazine articles or Internet sites—are the key method of establishing 'how' various forms of media represent crime. Content analysis alone, however, cannot explain 'why' media images take the particular forms that they do. It is only through a focus on media production that representations can be explained. Research on media production is necessarily more qualitative in nature, since it is concerned with the 'social processes'—commercial, political, moral—that shape media content. These processes are too complex to be captured as statistical data. The majority of research has sought to understand media production 'at a distance' by analysing, for example, the 'news values' that determine which crimes are newsworthy and which are not, or the impact of the wider socio-political environment on the representation of crime and justice in film or television drama (Soothill and Walby, 1991; Sparks, 1992; Reiner *et al.*, 2000; Soothill *et al.*, 2002; Seal, 2009). A minority of researchers have sought to understand media production 'up close'. In addition to considering the structural determinants of media production and the wider socio-political environment, they have also employed interviews—with journalists, editors and producers, police and probation officers, and victims and offenders—and ethnography (for example, exploring crime journalism through shadowing news reporters). The aim here is to gain a deeper, interpretive understanding of media production by engaging directly with those involved in the production process (see Chibnall, 1977; Ericson *et al.*, 1987, 1989, 1991; Schlesinger and Tumber, 1994; Kitzinger and Skidmore, 1995; Greer, 2012).

The third principal area of interest is media consumption and influence. Much media criminology is underpinned by an often implicit assumption of media influence: the media distortion of crime and deviance has a significant impact on society, and this impact is somehow detrimental. On the political right, the concern has been that media glamorize crime and encourage criminality. On the political left, it has been that media increase fear of crime, encouraging political acquiescence to the status quo and strengthening support for authoritarian measures of control and containment. However, with the important exception of studies on media and fear of crime, criminologists have actually conducted very little research to 'evidence' the nature of media influence. Thus there is a fundamental tension within media criminology: much is assumed, but little is researched and evidenced empirically. What research does exist on media consumption and influence has, like content analysis, tended to be quantitative in nature. It has been situated not within sociological criminology, but within a psychological positivism which foregrounds classification ('this is violence, this is not') and counting (the number of violent acts in a given film, newspaper article, website) over a more nuanced, in depth understanding of what media 'mean' to active consumers. Before discussing the pros and cons of this type of research, it is useful to consider in greater detail the content of media representations of crime and control.

The nature and extent of crime in the media

A virtually universal finding in the literature is that media representations exaggerate both the levels of serious interpersonal crime in society and the risk of becoming a crime victim. This is the case for studies of newspapers (Marsh, 1991), television (Gunter *et al.*, 2003) and radio content (Cumberbatch *et al.*, 1995), across both news and entertainment media (Reiner *et al.*, 2000), and literary crime fiction (Knight, 2004). The representation of crime is largely event-oriented in that it focuses on specific criminal cases and incidents rather than wider debates around causes, prevention, or policy (Rock, 1973; Greer, 2012). All media forms focus overwhelmingly on violent or sexual offences.

Calculations of the proportion of news space devoted to crime vary considerably depending on the definition of 'crime' adopted, and the types of material included and excluded on that basis. Some studies, for example, may only include news reports of particular criminal events or court cases (Ditton and Duffy, 1983; Smith, 1984). Others, in addition to considering news reports, may also include feature items, editorial pieces and letters to the editor (Hall *et al.*, 1978; Ericson *et al.*, 1987; Greer and McLaughlin, 2012). Studies may also expand the definition of 'crime' to explore a wider range of deviant acts, such as corporate offending (Cavender and Mulcahy, 1998; Knotterus *et al.*, 2006; Machin and Mayr, 2013), environmental crime (Lynch *et al.*, 2000; Joosse, 2012), and State violence (Cohen, 2002; Herman and Chomsky, 1994). 'Popular' (normally tabloid) news outlets are generally found to include a greater proportion of crime stories reported in a more sensational style than 'quality' (broadsheet) ones (Graber, 1980; Schlesinger *et al.*, 1991). Estimates of the proportion of crime in the UK news media have ranged from 4 per cent in one study (Roshier, 1973) to 13 per cent in another (Williams and Dickinson, 1993). A summary of content analyses in the US found the proportion of crime news to range from just over 1 per cent, to more than 30 per cent (Marsh, 1991). In the entertainment media, an average of around 25 per cent of US and UK prime-time television programming, and around 20 per cent of film releases are crime-centred (Allen *et al.*, 1997).

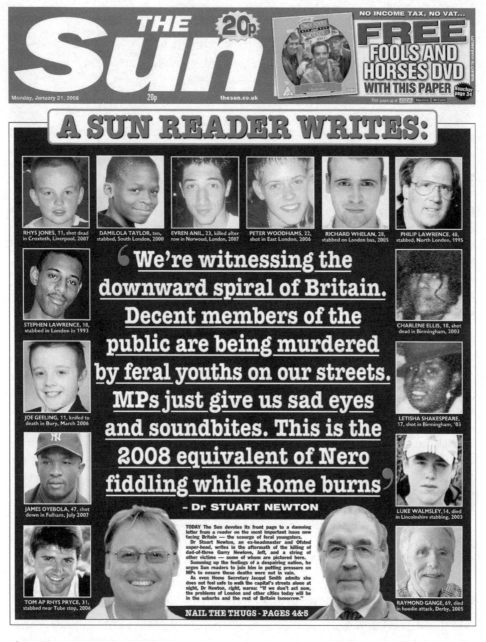

Figure 7.1 A *Sun* Reader Writes…

Source: © *The Sun.*

This section has provided a brief review of the research literature on the content of media representations of crime and criminal justice. The aim of the next section is to establish a clearer picture of the forces and influences that might shape that content.

REVIEW QUESTIONS

1 Why is it both important and useful to study crime and the media?

2 What are the main differences between quantitative and qualitative methods of content analysis and what are their respective strengths and weaknesses?

3 Can a coherent picture of the crime problem be discerned from media representations? If so, what is it, and is it accurate?

Theorizing crime and media

Crime news is not simply plucked out of thin air; nor does it exist in a vacuum. It is the end result of a complex process of selection, processing and prioritization, and is shaped by interactions between journalists, editors, their working conditions, the wider environment and, crucially, news sources. News sources are those individuals, organizations and institutions that provide the information on which journalists often base their stories. In relation to crime news, key sources include the police, probation, prison and court services, politicians, penal reform groups, victim organizations, and a host of other interested parties.

Reporting crime takes time, money and effort. Editors and producers seek to maximize the efficiency and cost-effectiveness of this process by concentrating limited resources around sources that can offer consistently reliable and reportable crime material within the rhythms of the news production process. Powerful criminal justice institutions like the police and the judiciary routinely produce a significant volume of reportable information, and therefore are extremely useful to crime reporters. For this reason, they enjoy what Hall *et al.* (1978) refer to as 'privileged access' in the media: that is, they usually find it easier than less powerful, or less useful (in news terms), organizations to have their views or version of events publicized. This 'privileged access' is further enhanced by the credibility and cultural authority—the 'expert status'—associated with official agencies on matters of crime and control (Ericson *et al.*, 1989, 1991). That journalists are to an extent reliant on powerful institutional sources is undeniable. The consequences of this reliance, however, and the wider implications for the democratic flow of information and the objectivity and impartiality of the news product, may be interpreted very differently depending on the theoretical approach adopted.

Media theory and crime news production

Traditional theorizations of news media production can be broadly distinguished according to two opposing positions: radical and liberal pluralist. Radical approaches are influenced by the theories of Karl Marx and Antonio Gramsci, among others, and stress the unequal distribution of economic and cultural power throughout society, and its impact on media production. Liberal pluralist interpretations are underpinned by the ideals of classical liberal theory, and emphasize the principles of freedom, choice and democracy, and their impact on media production. There are numerous variations on each perspective, but in their simplest terms, radical readings see the mass media as controlling the people, while liberal pluralist readings see the mass media as serving the people. Some of the most relevant examples of each position will now be outlined.

At the radical extreme, the 'propaganda model' views the media as an extension of the State's apparatus of ideological control. Herman and Chomsky (1994) have argued that economic, political, military and cultural elites conspire to control the content and flow of media information, filtering out or delegitimizing dissenting views to protect ruling class interests. Through analysing news coverage of 'terrorism' and the media's alleged collusion in the 'criminalization' of non-friendly regimes, the authors argue that the key actors in the news production process are not journalists, who are seen as largely powerless, but media owners, who share interests in common with other elite groups. In this critical materialist interpretation the function of the news media is to 'manufacture consent' around elite ideas in the name of the 'national interest' and, in so doing, to engender political compliance and acceptance of the established order.

An arguably more nuanced approach is the 'hegemonic model', based on the neo-Marxist writings of Antonio Gramsci (1971). Here the media are viewed not as the direct mouthpieces of the powerful, but as sites of contestation on which alternative viewpoints actively compete for ideological dominance, or hegemony. Due to their privileged access, however, criminal justice institutions are able to advance a 'primary definition' of crime-related issues, which frames the terms for any ensuing debate and subverts competing viewpoints, though these may still be heard, to marginal status (Hall *et al.*, 1978). Journalists may think they are autonomous, but in practice they are constrained to reproduce the elite 'ideas' of the dominant sources on which they rely, in turn helping to make these the 'ideas' of everyone. This is why, it is suggested, crime reporting tends to favour an elite (conservative) portrayal of the crime problem—an issue of working-class, minority youth offending (not white collar corruption or State violence), requiring greater punishment and control of particular groups (not government accountability and corporate regulation) (Barlow *et al.*, 1995).

The radical perspective in its various guises contrasts with liberal pluralist media theory (Gans, 1980; Hetherington, 1985). Liberal pluralists concede that certain official interests are advantaged in the media, but they insist that any significant source bias or pressure from media owners is offset by journalistic professionalism, the requirements of objectivity and balance, the ideological and stylistic diversity of the media, and what is viewed as open and equal competition between a wide range of groups for media access and influence. Journalists insist, indeed pride themselves, upon maintaining high levels of professional autonomy and are actively encouraged in this pursuit by colleagues who share the same system of values (Gans, 1980). Any pressure to follow a particular line, apply a particular 'spin', suppress a particular piece of information, or in some other way distort the 'truth status' of the news will be forcefully resisted. Nor does the 'privileged access' of powerful institutions guarantee definitional control. Journalists and other social actors both can and do challenge the established order. This is clear, for example, when the high-profile exposure of scandal (political, sexual, economic) forces senior politicians to resign from office (Thompson, 2000), or the credibility of criminal justice agencies is undermined by media exposés evidencing corruption, incompetence, or institutional racism. In the liberal pluralist view, then, the media expose injustice and hold the powerful to account. They provide a voice for marginalized groups and, in so doing, defend the integrity of the democratic process (Blumler and Gurevitch, 1995).

In practice, the power relations between journalists and sources are more fluid than radical scholars have tended to argue, but more constraining than liberal pluralists suggest (Greer, 2012). With the proliferation of media and the transformation of the information landscape in recent decades, both theoretical approaches have come under fire for being too rigid and deterministic, incapable of capturing the fluidity and unpredictability of power and information flows in multi-mediated societies. Many postmodernists argue that in societies where images, signs and codes are constantly recycled through the media, it is no longer possible to distinguish with any certainty between 'image' and 'reality', the 'represented' and the 'real' (Baudrillard, 1983; Poster, 1990); *how* crime policy is presented becomes more important than *what* the policy actually is.

The emergence of a highly diversified, 24/7 globalized media environment has changed the terrain upon which struggles over media power and influence are played out. At the national level an already fragmented government struggles to control the crime news agenda, but is repeatedly beaten down by adversarial journalists intent on increasing sales by taking scalps. Rather than routinely controlling the news agenda, Home Secretaries, Police and Crime Commissioners, entire public institutions become the target for press exposés of scandal and corruption (Greer and McLaughlin, 2010, 2012b). In a context of declining deference to authority and an increasingly competitive and unpredictable communications marketplace, 'trial by media' becomes a means of journalistic advancement and economic survival (Greer and McLaughlin, 2011, 2012a, 2012c). Dissatisfied and vociferous victims and victim groups now routinely employ professional PR advisers to make the public articulation of their cases more 'media-friendly', and therefore more widely disseminated. Media audiences, tired of the 'permanent crisis in criminal justice', are actively encouraged to participate in the news production process by emailing, texting or phoning in their views and concerns.

At the global level, faced with ecological disaster, government corruption, police repression, torture and economic meltdown, activists organize themselves into resistance movements and turn increasingly to social media to bring attention to their growing discontent. Facebook is used to schedule protests, Twitter to coordinate events, and the world is simultaneously informed, enthralled and scandalized through YouTube and Wikileaks (Hamm and Greer, 2011). The ongoing military presence in Afghanistan continues to attract moral opprobrium from sections of the press and public, making discursive closure around the 'war on terror' an impossibility. Botched surveillance operations at home are reported alongside the mounting deaths of troops and the abuse of prisoners abroad (Hamm, 2007; Carrabine, 2011). In an age of media proliferation, political spin, ubiquitous public relations operatives, and ever-more sophisticated media audiences, communication power may shift from story to story, and the balance of definitional influence becomes increasingly unstable and unpredictable.

News values and newsworthiness

Only a tiny fraction of events, criminal or otherwise, are deemed sufficiently 'newsworthy' to merit media attention. News values are the criteria that determine 'newsworthiness'. They enable journalists and editors to decide which stories to run and which to drop, which are headliners and which are fillers, which are the most important details and which are the least. Having 'a good nose for a story', then, may equally be interpreted as having a well-honed appreciation of news values.

Table 7.1 outlines three different but overlapping interpretations of what it is that make events in general, and criminal events in particular, worthy of media attention.

News values help to explain the broad profile of media representations of crime and control. Interpersonal crimes of sex and violence can be more easily presented as dramatic and titillating than non-violent crimes—for example, most property and white collar offences—particularly when they have high levels of proximity (spatial nearness and cultural meaningfulness) to the consumer. By focusing on people (as victims and offenders) and events rather than abstract issues and debates, crime reporting is individualized and simplified, which also contributes to the common association of crime with individual pathology rather than wider social-structural influences. In line with the growth of celebrity culture (Rojek, 2012), crimes are more newsworthy if they involve famous or notable people. Although names will generally be included where possible, one of the most compelling figures in crime stories is the 'unknown' predatory stranger. As the producers of reality television shows like *Crimewatch UK* or *America's Most Wanted* and countless newspaper editors know only too well, few stories capture the public imagination as forcefully as the killer on the loose, especially when the (potential) victims are children. In addition to their inherent drama, individualization, violence and proximity, such narratives possess an unnerving sense of immediacy and a palpable risk of further attacks. They have a clear capacity to fulfil that vital, commercially driven journalistic imperative; the requirement to shock (Greer, 2012).

This imperative is increasingly realized by capitalizing on the highly visual nature of contemporary culture (Carrabine, 2012). As the experience of crime and control has become more mediatized, so too has it become more image-oriented. Stories are more readily personalized and individualized, they more easily invoke empathy, disdain, shock, when accompanied by visual images. Today 'crime stories are increasingly selected and 'produced' as *media events* on the basis of their visual (how they can be portrayed in images) as well as their lexical-verbal (how they can be portrayed in words) potential' (Greer, 2007: 29). The availability of an image may determine whether or not a story is run or dropped. The availability of the right image can help elevate a crime victim or offender to national or even global iconic status (Greer and McLaughlin, 2012c).

The previous sections have reviewed the literature on the nature and extent of representations of crime and control in the media, and offered an overview of some of the main theoretical and conceptual tools used to understand why media representations take on the form that they do. The next section considers the evidence for media influence and effects.

REVIEW QUESTIONS

1 What are the principal characteristics of the radical and liberal pluralist readings of news production? How does each reading view journalistic freedom and source power?

2 How useful are radical and liberal pluralist approaches to understanding media in an age of media proliferation, diversification and saturation?

3 What is it that makes some crimes so eminently reportable, while others are scarcely mentioned?

Table 7.1 Criteria of newsworthiness

Galtung and Ruge (1965)	Chibnall (1977)	Jewkes (2011)
Threshold (level of importance required to achieve news visibility)		Threshold (level of importance required to achieve news visibility)
Unexpectedness (novelty)	Novelty (unexpectedness)	
Negativity (violent, harmful, deviant, sad)		Violence
Unambiguity (clear and definite)	Simplification (removing shades of grey)	Simplification (removing shades of grey)
Dramatization (action)		
Frequency (timescale, fit within news cycle)	Immediacy (the present, fit within news cycle)	
Elite-centricity (powerful or famous nations or people)	Personalization (notable individuals, celebrities)	Celebrity or high-status (notable individuals)
	Structured Access (experts, officials, authority)	
Composition (balance, fit with other news)		
Personification (individual focus or causality)	Individual pathology (individual causality)	Individualism (individual focus or causality)
Continuity (sustainability)		
		Children (young people)
	Graphic presentation	Spectacle or graphic imagery
	Visible/spectacular acts	
Meaningfulness (spatial and cultural relevance)	Proximity (spatial and cultural relevance)	
Consonance (fit with existing knowledge and expectations)	Conventionalism (hegemonic ideology)	Predictability (expectedness)
	Titillation (exposés, scandal)	
		Risk (lasting danger)
	Sexual/political connotations	Sex
	Deterrence and repression	Conservative ideology or political diversion (deterrence, distraction from wider problems)

Sources: Galtung and Ruge (1965); Chibnall (1977); Jewkes (2004).

Problematizing crime and media

Few today would suggest that media representations have no influence on their audiences. Rather, the debate is about the nature, extent and significance of that influence. As noted earlier in this chapter, the concern on the political right has been that media images glamorize crime and violence, undermining respect for authority and the rule of law and encouraging criminality. On the left it has been that media images of crime and deviance increase public fears and anxieties, helping to win support for authoritarian measures of control and containment.

Media violence and the problem of 'effects'

Research on media effects has for decades sought to demonstrate a causal relationship between media violence and violent thoughts and behaviours in the real world. Typically, subjects (most often children) are exposed to some aggressive stimulus (say, a short violent film) within a controlled setting (frequently a laboratory or office), and then observed to see if they think or behave more aggressively than a control group not exposed to the aggressive stimulus (Bandura *et al.*, 1963 is the classic experimental design). Myriad variations have been conducted on this 'stimulus-response' format, variously controlling for participant characteristics, type of violence shown, duration of exposure, whether the violence is punished or rewarded, and so on. In a frequently quoted statistic, more than 70 per cent of studies claim to demonstrate that media violence does cause real life violence (Andison, 1977; Howitt, 1998).

Such 'evidence' of criminogenic media effects is regularly cited by right-wing moral campaigners as justification for greater controls and censorship. However, effects research

Figure 7.2 Bandura's Bobo doll experiment

Source: With permission of Albert Bandura.

has been criticized at the levels of both method and theory. Gauntlett (2001), and others (Livingstone, 1996; Greer and Reiner, 2012), have identified a number of problems with the 'effects model'. Some of the most pertinent are summarized here.

- Counting 'units' of violence in accordance with the pre-established definitions of the researcher ('this is violence, this is not'), ignores the different meanings that people attach to acts and behaviours and implicitly assumes not just that we all think the same way, but that we all think the same way as the researcher.

- It is dubious to suppose that how subjects behave in controlled experimental environments (where they know they are being observed), sometimes toward inanimate objects (for example, an inflatable doll), reflects how they will behave in the real world toward real people.

- There is an assumption that only certain types of person are susceptible to the influence of media violence—mostly children, who are considered helpless victims, but sometimes also 'uneducated' or 'working class' populations, who apparently lack the maturity and sense most people take for granted.

- Different forms of violence—for example, in cartoons, soap operas, and horror movies—are often conflated, treated as equal in weight, and reduced to statistical data lacking any sense of plot or context. Whether violence is rewarded or punished, realistic or humorous, perpetrated by a 'hero' or a 'villain', may influence its impact profoundly.

- A correlation—violent people enjoy violent media—is not the same as a causal relationship—people are violent *because* of violent media. Media representations may provide technical knowledge about committing violent crimes, but that does not mean they also motivate people to use it.

- Whether intended or not, effects studies play into the hands of moral conservatives who wish simplistically to blame the media for society's ills, rather than addressing more intractable sources of crime like social inequality.

- Media influence, short-term or cumulative, can never be disaggregated entirely from other social, psychological and cultural influences, yet studies routinely search for a 'pure' (negative) media effect. Pro-social images, though rarely considered, may be just as powerful as anti-social ones, and perhaps even more so.

While psychological positivism searches for direct 'media effects' on more or less 'passive subjects', sociological and media researchers focus on media use and interaction among 'active consumers'. Here, the reception and interpretation of media images are considered, not in isolation, but as part of an ongoing process of interaction, both with other media forms and with the 'material and social realities of people's lives' (Kitzinger, 1999: 11; Hunt, 1997; Buckingham, 2000). Kitzinger (2004) has conducted in-depth interviews and focus groups with media practitioners, interest groups and consumers to explore the role of media representations in shaping understanding of sex crime as a contemporary social problem. With the development of 'creative methods' in media studies (Buckingham, 2009), researchers empower young people by allowing them to illustrate with the use of new media technologies their understandings of crime and disorder, violence and power, and how these understandings shape their everyday experiences (Thornham and Myers, 2012).

Media and fear of crime

Fear of crime first registered on the policy agenda in the early 1980s, when the British Crime Survey suggested it was becoming as big a problem as crime itself (Hough and Mayhew, 1983). Its consequences may range from not walking home alone at night to withdrawing from society altogether (Ferraro, 1995). Given the centrality of fear of crime in the public and political imagination, understanding its origins is an important criminological undertaking. Fear of crime is influenced by a range of social and demographic variables—perceptions of risk and vulnerability, age, social class, geographical location, ethnicity, and experience of criminal victimization (Box *et al.*, 1988; Hale, 1996). Media representations, though enormously diverse, are only one possible influence among many. As such, their significance remains a matter for debate.

Probably the best known research in this area is the 'cultivation analysis' of Gerbner *et al.*, which over several decades has employed content analyses and survey questionnaires to assess quantitatively the influence of violence on prime-time US television (Gerbner and Gross, 1976; Gerbner *et al.*, 1994). The central finding is that 'heavy' television viewers (those who watch most TV—more than four hours per day in Gerbner's studies) cultivate a world-view which more closely resembles the 'television message' than 'light' television viewers (those who watch less than two hours per day). Because television overstates both the seriousness and risk of criminal victimization, portraying the world as 'mean and scary', heavy viewing is said to cultivate higher fear of crime. Fearful citizens, it is argued, tend to be depoliticized, more dependent on established authority, more punitive, and more likely to acquiesce to authoritarian measures of control.

While supported in some studies (Hawkins and Pingree, 1980; Morgan, 1983), others have failed to replicate the cultivation effect (Gunter, 1987; Cumberbatch, 1989), and a number of empirical and theoretical weaknesses have been identified, including: the simplification and de-contextualizing of the categories 'media', 'violence' and 'fear'; the attempts to quantify the creative and highly variable processes of interpretation and influence; and the search for a straightforward causal connection between media and fear of crime (Sparks, 1992; Ditton *et al.*, 2004). Though more recent studies, including revised work by Gerbner, have sought to address these shortcomings, evidence for an isolated 'cultivation effect' remains inconclusive.

Exploring the extent to which images of crime and violence resonate with consumers' lives appears crucial to understanding their impact. Schlesinger *et al.* (1992), for example, found that women may be particularly sensitive to images of interpersonal attacks. Partly on this basis, concerns have been expressed that the highly unrepresentative focus on 'real' violent and sexual interpersonal crimes in the BBC's long running reality show *Crimewatch UK* may increase levels of fear in sections of the viewing audience (Jewkes, 2011). Research on US television news concluded that local crime coverage generates more fear than national coverage, particularly within individuals who have experienced victimization and perceive television accounts to be realistic (Chiricos *et al.*, 2000; see also Eschholz *et al.*, 2003). Ditton *et al.*'s (2004: 607) combination of quantitative questionnaires and qualitative interviews revealed that it is not the 'objectively determined randomness, localness or sensationalism that is important, but rather the interpretation of media content as relevant to and by the consumer'. Finally, some have questioned the tendency to characterize fear of crime in purely negative terms, and asked if some level of 'functional fear'—as opposed to 'dysfunctional worry'—might in fact be 'a motivating force that encourages vigilance and stimulates precautionary activity', such as taking additional measures to safeguard one's self and personal belongings (Jackson and Gray, 2010).

Moral panics and multi-mediated societies

The term 'moral panic' refers to the disproportionate and hostile social reaction to a group or condition perceived as a threat to societal values. It involves sensational and stereotypical media coverage, public outcry and demands for tougher controls. As the name suggests, the panic may subside as rapidly as it erupted. Moral panics have most often emerged around youth-related issues, particularly subcultural expressions of identity—for example, punk, rave and the wider drugs culture—but football hooliganism, the re-housing of sex offenders in the community, knife crime and terrorism have also been the source of recent panic (Jenkins, 1992; Silverman and Wilson, 2002; Cohen, 2011).

In the original analysis, Cohen (1972) problematized the social reaction to the Mods and Rockers disturbances in 1964, when boredom and bad weather one Bank Holiday resulted in a few fights, lots of noise and some windows being smashed. Though the damage was minor, the national press exaggerated and sensationalized the disturbances using phrases like 'day of terror' and 'hell-bent on destruction'. News reports predicted further violence, demanded tighter controls, and portrayed Mods and Rockers as 'folk devils'—a symbol not just of youth delinquency, but of wider permissiveness and social decline. Cohen (1972) demonstrates how the labelling and marginalization of Mods and Rockers and the emphasis on mutual antagonism created a 'deviancy amplification spiral' that resulted in further disturbances. These disturbances seemed to justify initial fears, resulting in more media coverage, more public outcry, more policing, and thus the spiral of reaction and deviancy amplification continued. The moral panic occurred at a time of rapid social change. In particular, the increase in youth spending power and sexual freedom, defiantly flaunted by young people, blurred moral and class boundaries and challenged the traditional ethics of hard work and sobriety, generating resentment and hostility among 'respectable society'. The 'creation' of Mods and Rockers provided scapegoats or 'folk devils'—a deviant minority against whom the conforming (nostalgically reactionary, adult) majority could unite at a time of uncertainty, conflict and change.

In a radical, Gramscian analysis of 'hegemonic crisis' at a time of economic recession, political decline and class unrest in 1970s Britain, Hall *et al.* (1978) argue that the State orchestrated a moral panic around 'mugging', and cast the young black street criminal in the central role. The creation of this 'folk devil', again providing a unifying focus for 'respectable' outrage, tapped into escalating fears around crime, race and social decline, and allowed the State to reassert and relegitimize itself—'policing the crisis', crucially with public consent, by stamping down hard on the problem from above (see *Crime, Media, Culture*, 2010: 4, 1, 2012: 7, 3).

Critics of moral panic theory have questioned the attribution of 'disproportionality' to the social reaction because this assumes a superior knowledge of both the objective reality of the issue and of what a 'proportionate' reaction would look like (Waddington, 1986). Left realists (see Chapter 3), in committing to 'take crime seriously', insisted that crime and fear of crime cannot simply be dismissed as groundless media-induced hysteria (Matthews and Young, 1992). Others have gone further, suggesting that in multi-mediated, risk societies the concept of moral panic needs to be reformulated (McRobbie and Thornton, 1995; Garland, 2008). While folk devils were once helpless against their demonization, they may now find themselves being vociferously supported in the same media that castigate them. In the chaotic 24/7 global mediasphere, they may also provide counter-definitions and explanations in any number of alternative media outlets. While moral panics were once rare, they are now commonplace, and even commercially desirable. One of the best ways of promoting (and selling) records, clothes, books, films—most popular cultural commodities, in fact—is to court controversy and proactively generate a little 'panic'.

REVIEW QUESTIONS

1 What does the media 'effects' model propose, and how has media effects research been criticized?

2 Compile a list of factors, other than media representations, which might influence fear of crime, and rank them in order of importance.

3 Can you think of any recent moral panics? On what basis would you say that the term 'moral panic' is sociologically justified in these instances?

Contemporary dimensions in crime and media

Today, sensational crime and justice events are webcast as they happen, high-profile 'celebrity' trials are tweeted live, riots and revolutions are orchestrated with social media, and the growth in 'reality' programming continues to erode the boundaries between news and entertainment, fact and fiction. From the 'live broadcast' destruction of New York's twin towers on 11 September, 2001 (Castells, 2004), through the 'shock and awe' invasions of Afghanistan and Iraq (Ullman and Wade, 1996), to the carefully 'staged and scripted' executions of Western kidnap victims (Ferrell *et al.*, 2005), global conflicts have become hyper-mediatized contests of strike and counter-strike, claim and counter-claim, in a manner unimaginable in the industrial modern era. As Castells (2004: 139) argues, 'The media, local and global, are the means of communication through which the public mind is formed. Therefore, action has to be media-oriented, it has to be spectacular, provide good footage, so the whole world can see it: like a Hollywood movie because this is what has trained the human mind in our times.'

This process of hyper-mediatization extends to other spheres of crime and criminal justice, in turn looping back to connect again with defining twenty-first century fears and insecurities. With millions of operational surveillance cameras, the UK has the dubious distinction of containing the highest ratio of CCTV cameras to people anywhere in the world (Home Affairs Committee, 2008). While some level of surveillance is necessary for the smooth running of any democracy—for example, postal services and electoral systems could not function without an up-to-date record of every citizen's name and address—the exponential increase in surveillance has generated concerns about the erosion of civil liberties and the boundaries between public and private in a 'surveillance society' (Doyle *et al.*, 2011; Norris and Armstrong, 1999; McCahill, 2002). Considered alongside the massive growth in personal data gathering in the private and public sectors—travel, credit, store loyalty and identity cards; mobile phones; online banking, shopping and social networking facilities; predictive customer profiling systems—the benefits of surveillance cannot eclipse its potential problems. There are real risks of data loss and abuse by those in power, the criminal appropriation of confidential personal information, and the data-driven stereotyping of whole sections of society (Coleman, 2005; Lyon, 2009). Such stereotyping spans the spectrum of deviance, from controlling everyday youthful transgression by banning hooded tops, or 'hoodies', from shopping centres (Hayward and Yar, 2006), to the ongoing 'war on terror' (Mythen and Walklate, 2006).

Globalized access to the Internet generates unprecedented opportunities for social networking and the creation of virtual communities (Greer, 2004), but also new forms of criminality and criminal victimization. The spread of hate sites (Franko Aas, 2006), cyberstalking (Wykes, 2007), viral victimization (Brown, 2003), cyberbullying (Shariff, 2008) and the online 'grooming' and sexual abuse of children (Martellozzo, 2012), have all come under the criminological gaze. Across the 24/7 global mediasphere, the conceptualization, definition and experience of crime and control are changing. The challenge is for media criminologists to keep up.

CONCLUSION

This chapter has provided an overview of some of the main issues and debates that continue to inform the scholarly investigation of crime and media. You should now have a sense of the nature and extent of crime, violence and control in media content, an understanding of some of the dominant theoretical and conceptual tools used to explain and understand media representations, a working knowledge of the evidence for and against media effects, and an awareness of new developments in crime and media research. Equipped with this knowledge and insight, you can now explore in greater detail any issues which have challenged your assumptions, tested your critical faculties, or stimulated your imagination.

Today, image and representation penetrate all areas of social existence. Media tap into and reinforce social and political concerns. They help shape individual and collective identities, sensibilities, fears, anxieties and appetites. They provoke public outcry and, at times, generate moral panics. They serve as ideological weapons in the ongoing struggle for hegemony. They impart important but often mixed messages about the nature and extent of 'the crime problem', how we should think and feel about it, who is most at risk, and what is to be done. They indicate, however inaccurately, the state of the nation, but they also entertain. 'Crime talk' (Sasson, 1995), in whatever form, simultaneously elicits fear and fascination; it is a major source of concern, but also of distraction, resistance, escapism, and moral reassurance (Sparks, 1992; Ferrell *et al.*, 2008). Crime sells. It always has.

Whether as news, fiction, or that expanding cultural form that lies somewhere in between, the sheer quantity of crime in the media illustrates that we have an insatiable appetite for narratives of deviance and control. And there is evidence to suggest we are growing hungrier (Reiner *et al.*, 2000). Given the close interrelationship between the political, commercial and cultural significance of crime and disorder, it is small wonder it features so prominently across all media and markets. As the boundaries between fact and fiction, the represented and the real, become increasingly diffuse and uncertain, so the importance of understanding the connections between crime and the media becomes more concrete.

QUESTIONS FOR DISCUSSION

1   Design and conduct your own content analysis of newspaper crime reporting. Make sure you include quantitative and qualitative considerations and consider both words and images.

2   Compare coverage of the same crime or justice event in at least three different media forms (newspaper, Internet, television, radio, Twitter). How and why does representation differ between media forms?

3   Watch an episode of your favourite crime drama or a recent film and note the portrayal of policing and criminal justice. Are the representations favourable or critical?

4   Keep a 'crime diary' for a week and record your thoughts and feelings about crime and personal safety. Do media representations have any impact on your fear of crime?

5   Compile a list of all the ways in which you are subject to surveillance in a typical day.

GUIDE TO FURTHER READING

Greer, C. (2010) *Crime and Media: A Reader.* London: Routledge.
This book provides the only comprehensive collection of key and classic readings on crime and media in one volume.

Jewkes, Y. (2011) *Media and Crime* (2nd edn) London: Sage.
This highly accessible textbook offers a book length analysis of many of the issues discussed in the chapter you have just read.

Greer, C. and Reiner, R. (2012) 'Mediated Mayhem: Media, Crime and Criminal Justice' in M. Maguire, R. Morgan and R. Reiner (eds) *The Oxford Handbook of Criminology* (5th edn) Oxford: Oxford University Press.
An alternative overview of many of the issues covered in this chapter.

Cohen, S. (2002) *Folk Devils and Moral Panics: The Creation of Mods and Rockers* (3rd edn) London: Routledge.
This classic text presents the original development of 'moral panic'—one of the most widely used (and often misused) concepts in the sociology of deviance, crime and social control.

Crime, Media, Culture: An International Journal. London: Sage.
This international journal provides a forum for researchers working at the interface between criminology, media studies and cultural studies.

WEB LINKS

http://www.lexisnexis.com

Lexis Nexis is a useful resource for searching news and other print media from around the world. However, beware that data are returned structure, style and image free. Use LexisNexis to locate the coverage. Then obtain the original copy to research it!

http://www.ccms-infobase.com

The Communication, Cultural and Media Studies Infobase contains a wide range of salient links, definitions, and issues for debate—pitched at an introductory undergraduate level—which are easy to navigate.

Web of knowledge

Accessible through most university websites, the Web of Knowledge is one of the most comprehensive searchable databases for scholarly research articles on a host of topics, including crime and media. The web address varies depending on the university system being used to access it.

Newspaper and news websites

Literally thousands of news websites provide a rich source of data for news media criminologists to conduct content and semiotic analyses of crime reporting.

REFERENCES

Allen, J., Livingstone, S., and Reiner, R. (1997) 'The Changing Generic Location of Crime in Film: A Content Analysis of Film Synopses', *Journal of Communication* 47: 89–101.

Andison, E. (1977) 'TV Violence and Viewer Aggression: A Cumulation of Study Results, 1956–1979', *Public Opinion Quarterly* 41, 3: 314–31.

Bandura, A., Ross, D., and Ross, S. (1963) 'Imitation of Film-Mediated Aggressive Models', *Journal of Abnormal and Social Psychology* 66: 3–11.

Barlow, M., Barlow, D., and Chiricos, T. (1995) 'Economic Conditions and Ideologies of Crime in the Media: A Content Analysis of Crime News', *Crime and Delinquency* 41, 1: 3–19.

Baudrillard, J. (1983) 'The Precession of the Simulacra' in T. Doherty (ed) *The Postmodern Reader*. Hemel Hempstead: Harvester Press.

Blumler, J. and Gurevitch, L. (1995) *The Crisis of Public Communication*. London: Routledge.

Box, S., Hale, C., and Andrews, G. (1988) 'Explaining Fear of Crime', *British Journal of Criminology* 28: 340–56.

Brown, S. (2003) *Crime and Law in Media Culture*. Buckingham: Open University Press.

Buckingham, D. (2000) *The Making of Citizens: Young People, News and Politics*. London: Routledge.

Buckingham D. (2009) '"Creative" visual methods in media research: possibilities, problems and proposals', *Media, Culture & Society* 31, 4: 633–52.

Carrabine, E. (2012) 'Just Images: Aesthetics, Ethics and Visual Criminology', *British Journal of Criminology* 52, 3: 463–89.

Carrabine, E. (2011) 'Images of Torture: Culture, Politics and Power', *Crime, Media, Culture* 7, 1: 5–30.

Castells, M. (2004) *The Power of Identity* (2nd edn) Oxford: Blackwell.

Cavender, G. and Mulcahy, A. (1998) 'Trial by Fire: Media Constructions of Corporate Deviance', *Justice Quarterly* 15, 4: 697–719.

Chermak, S. (1995) *Victims in the News: Crime and the American News Media*. Boulder, CO: Westview Press.

Chibnall, S. (1977) *Law and Order News: An Analysis of Crime Reporting in the British Press*. London: Tavistock.

Chiricos, T., Padgett, K., and Gertz, M. (2000) 'Fear, TV News, and the Reality of Crime', *Criminology*, 38, 3: 755–85.

Cohen, S. (2011) 'Whose side were we on? The undeclared politics of moral panic theory', *Crime Media Culture* 7, 3: 237–43.

Cohen, S. (1972) *Folk Devils and Moral Panics: The Creation of the Mods and Rockers*. London: MacGibbon and Kee.

Cohen, S. and Young, J. (eds) (1981) *The Manufacture of News: Social Problems, Deviance and Mass Media* (revd edn) London: Constable.

Coleman, R. (2005) 'Surveillance in the City: Primary Definition and Urban Spatial Order', *Crime, Media, Culture: An International Journal* 1, 2: 131–48.

Cumberbatch, G. (1989) 'Violence in the Media: The Research Evidence', in G. Cumberbatch and D. Howitt (eds) *A Measure of Uncertainty: the Effects of the Mass Media*. London: John Libbey.

Cumberbatch, G., Woods, S., and Maguire, A. (1995) *Crime in the News: Television, Radio and Newspapers: A Report for BBC Broadcasting Research*. Birmingham: Aston University, Communications Research Group.

Ditton, J., Chadee, D., Farrall, S., Gilchrist, E., and Bannister, J. (2004), 'From Imitation to Intimidation: A Note on the Curious and Changing Relationship Between the Media, Crime and Fear of Crime', *British Journal of Criminology* 44, 4: 595–610.

Ditton, J. and Duffy, J. (1983) 'Bias in the Newspaper Reporting of Crime', *British Journal of Criminology* 23, 2: 159–65.

Doyle, A., Lippert, R. and Lyon, D. (2011) *Eyes Everywhere: The Global Growth of Camera Surveillance*. London: Routledge.

Ericson, R., Baranek, P. and Chan, J. (1987) *Visualising Deviance: A Study of News Organisation*. Milton Keynes: Open University Press.

Ericson, R., Baranek, P., and Chan, J. (1989) *Negotiating Control: A Study of News Sources*. Milton Keynes: Open University Press.

Ericson, R., Baranek, P., and Chan, J. (1991) *Representing Order: Crime, Law and Justice in the News Media*. Milton Keynes: Open University Press.

Eschholz, S., Chiricos, T., and Gertz, M. (2003) 'Television and Fear of Crime: Programme Types, Audience Traits and the Mediating Effect of Perceived Neighbourhood Racial Composition', *Social Problems* 50, 3: 395–415.

Ferraro, K. (1995) *Fear of Crime: Interpreting Victimisation Risk*. New York: State University of New York, Albany.

Ferrell, J., Greer, C., and Jewkes, Y. (2005) 'Hip Hop Graffiti, Mexican Murals, and the War on Terror', *Crime Media Culture: An International Journal* 1, 1: 5–9.

Ferrell, J., Hayward, K., and Young, J. (2008) *Cultural Criminolgoy: An Invitation*. London: Sage.

Franko Aas, K. (2006) 'Governance and the Internet' in Y. Jewkes (ed) *Crime Online*. Cullompton: Willan.

Galtung, J. and Ruge, M. (1965) 'Structuring and selecting news' in S. Cohen and J. Young (eds) (1981) *The Manufacture of News: Deviance, Social Problems and the Mass Media* (revd edn) London: Constable.

Gans, H. (1980) *Deciding What's News*. London: Constable.

Garland, D. (2008) 'On the Concept of Moral Panic', *Crime, Media, Culture: An International Journal* 4, 1: 9–30.

Gauntlett, D. (2001) 'The Worrying Influence of "Media Effects" Studies' in M. Barker and J. Petley (eds) (2001) *Ill Effects: The Media/Violence Debate* (2nd edn) London: Routledge.

Gerbner, G. and Gross, L. (1976) 'Living with Television: the Violence Profile', *Journal of Communication* 26, 1: 173–99.

Gerbner, G., Gross, L., Morgan, M., and Signorielli, N. (1994) 'Growing up with Television; The Cultivation Perspective' in J. Bryant and D. Zillman (eds) *Media Effects*. Hillsdale, NJ: Lawrence Erlbaum.

Graber, D. (1980) *Crime, News and the Public*. New York: Prager.

Gramsci, A. (1971) *Selections from the Prison Notebooks*. London: Lawrence and Wishart.

Greer, C. (2004) 'Crime, media and community: grief and virtual engagement in late modernity' in J. Ferrell, K. Hayward, W. Morrison, and M. Presdee (eds) *Cultural Criminology Unleashed*. London: Cavendish.

Greer, C. (2007) 'News Media, Victims and Crime' in P. Davies, P. Francis, and C. Greer (eds) *Victims, Crime and Society*. London: Sage.

Greer, C. (2010) *Crime and Media; A Reader*. London: Routledge.

Greer, C. (2012) *Sex Crime and the Media: Sex Offending and the Press in a Divided Society*. London: Routledge.

Greer, C. and Jewkes, Y. (2005) 'Extremes of Otherness: Media Images of Social Exclusion', *Social Justice (special edition on Emerging Imaginaries of Regulation, Control and Oppression)* 32, 1: 20–31.

Greer, C. and McLaughlin, E. (2010) 'We Predict a Riot: Public Order Policing, New Media Environments and the Rise of the Citizen Journalist', *British Journal of Criminology* 50, 6: 1041–59.

Greer, C. and McLaughlin, E. (2011) 'Trial by Media: Policing, the 24-7 News Mediasphere, and the Politics of Outrage', *Theoretical Criminology* 15, 1: 23–46.

Greer, C. and McLaughlin, E. (2012a) 'Trial by Media: Riots, Looting, Gangs and Mediatised Police Chiefs, in J. Peay and T. Newburn (eds) *Policing, Politics, Culture and Control: Essays in Honour of Robert Reiner*. Oxford: Hart Publishing.

Greer, C. and McLaughlin, E. (2012b) 'This is not Justice: Ian Tomlinson, Institutional Failure and the Press Politics of Outrage', *British Journal of Criminology* 52, 2: 274–93.

Greer, C. and McLaughlin, E. (2012c) 'Media Justice: Madeleine McCann, Intermediatisation and "Trial by Media" in the British Press', *Theoretical Criminology* 16, 4: 395–416.

Greer, C. and Reiner, R. (2012) 'Mediated Mayhem: Media, Crime and Criminal Justice', in M. Maguire, R. Morgan, and R. Reiner (eds) *Oxford Handbook of Criminology* (5th edn) Oxford: Oxford University Press.

Gunter, B. (1987) *Television and the Fear of Crime*. London: John Libbey.

Gunter, B., Harrison, J., and Wykes, M. (2003) *Violence on Television: Distribution, Form, Context and Themes*. London: Lawrence Erlbaum.

Hale, C. (1996) 'Fear of Crime: A Review of the Literature', *International Review of Victimology*, 4, 2: 79–150.

Hall, S. Critcher, C. Jefferson, T. Clarke, J. and Roberts, B. (1978) *Policing the Crisis: Mugging, the State and Law and Order*. London: Macmillan.

Hamm, M. (2007) 'High Crimes and Misdemeanors: George Bush and the Sins of Abu Ghraib', *Crime, Media, Culture: An International Journal* 3, 3: 259–84.

Hamm, M. and Greer, C. (2011) 'Into the Future Darkly', *Crime Media Culture: An International Journal* 7, 1: 3–4.

Hawkins, R. and Pingree, S. (1980) 'Some Processes in the Cultivation Effect', *Communication Research* 7, 2: 193–226.

Hayward, K. and Yar, M. (2006) 'The "Chav" Phenomenon: Consumption, Media and the Construction of a New Underclass', *Crime. Media, Culture: An International Journal* 2, 1: 9–28.

Herman, E. and Chomsky, N. (1994) *Manufacturing Consent: The Political Economy of the Mass Media*. New York: Pantheon.

Hetherington, A. (1985) *News, Newspapers and Television*. London: Macmillan.

Hough, M. and Mayhew, P. (1983) *The British Crime Survey*. Home Office Research Study 76. London: HMSO.

Howitt, D. (1998) *Crime, the Media and the Law*. London: Wiley.

Hoyle, C. (2012) 'Victims, the Criminal Process, and Restorative Justice' in M. Maguire, R. Morgan, and R. Reiner (eds) *The Oxford Handbook of Criminology* (5th edn) Oxford: Oxford University Press.

Hunt, D. (1997) *Screening the Los Angeles 'Riots'*, New York: Cambridge University Press.

Jackson, J. and Gray, E. (2010) 'Functional Fear and Public Insecurities About Crime', *British Journal of Criminology*, 50, 1: 1–22.

Jackson, J., Bradford, B., Stanko, E., and Hohl, K. (2013) *Just Authority? Trust in the Police in England and Wales*. London: Routledge.

Jenkins, P. (1992) *Intimate Enemies: Moral Panics in Contemporary Great Britain*. Hawthorne, NY: Aldine de Gruyter.

Jewkes, Y. (2002) *Captive Audience: Media, Masculinity and Power in Prisons*. Cullompton: Willan.

Jewkes, Y. (ed) (2003) *Dot. Cons: Crime, Deviance and Identity on the Internet*. Cullumpton: Willan.

Jewkes, Y. (2011) *Media and Crime* (2nd edn) London: Sage.

Joosse, P. (2012) 'Elves, environmentalism, and "eco-terror": Leaderless resistance and media coverage of the Earth Liberation Front', *Crime, Media, Culture* 8, 1: 75–93.

Kitzinger, J. (1999) 'A sociology of media power: key issues in audience reception research' in G. Philo (ed) *Message Received*. London: Longman.

Kitzinger, J. (2004) *Framing Abuse: Media Influence and Public Understanding of Sexual Violence Against Children*. London: Pluto.

Kitzinger, J. and Skidmore, P. (1995) 'Child Sexual Abuse and the Media', Summary Report to ESRC. Award no. R000233675. Report available from Glasgow Media Group.

Knight, S. (2004) *Crime Fiction 1800–2000*. Basingstoke: Palgrave Macmillan.

Knotterus, D., Ulsperger, J., Cummins, S., and Osteen, E. (2006) 'Exposing Enron: Media Representations of Ritualised Deviance in Corporate Culture', *Crime, Media, Culture: An International Journal* 2, 2: 177–95.

Livingstone, S. (1996) 'On the Continuing Problem of Media Effects' in J. Curran and M. Gurevitch (eds) *Mass Media and Society*. London: Arnold.

Lynch, M., Stretesky, P., and Hammond, P. (2000) 'Media Coverage of Chemical Crimes, Hillsborough County, Florida, 1987–1997', *British Journal of Criminology* 40, 1: 112–26.

Lyon, D. (2009) *Identifying Citizens: ID Cards as Surveillance*. Cambridge: Polity.

Machin, D. and Mayr, A. (2013) 'Corporate Crime and The Discursive Deletion Of Responsibility: The Case Study of The Paddington Rail Crash', *Crime, Media, Culture: An International Journal* 9: 63–82.

Maguire, M. (2012) 'Criminal Statistics and the Construction of Crime' in M. Maguire, R. Morgan, and R. Reiner (eds) *The Oxford Handbook of Criminology* (5th edn) Oxford: Oxford University Press.

Manning, P. (2001) *News and News Sources: A Critical Introduction*. London: Sage.

Marsh, H.L. (1991) 'A Comparative Analysis of Crime Coverage in Newspapers in the United States and Other Countries From 1960–1989: A Review of the Literature', *Journal of Criminal Justice* 19, 1: 67–80.

Martellozzo, E. (2012) *Online Child Sexual Abuse: Grooming, Policing and Child Protection in a Multi-Media World.* London: Routledge.

Matthews, R. and Young, J. (1992) (eds) *Rethinking Criminology: The Realist Debate.* London: Sage.

McCahill, M. (2002) *The Surveillance Web: The Rise of Visual Surveillance in an English City.* Cullompton: Willan.

McNair, B. (2009) *News and Journalism in the UK* (5th edn) London: Routledge.

McRobbie, A. and Thornton, S. (1995) 'Rethinking "Moral Panic" for Multi-Mediated Social Worlds', *British Journal of Sociology* 46, 4: 559–74.

Miller, D. (1993) 'Official Sources and "Primary Definition": The Case of Northern Ireland', *Media, Culture and Society* 15, 3: 385–406.

Morgan, M. (1983) 'Symbolic Victimisation and Real World Fear', *Human Communication Research* 9, 2: 146–57.

Mythen, G. and Walklate, S. (2006) 'Communicating the Terrorist Risk: Harnessing a Culture of Fear', *Crime, Media, Culture: An International Journal* 2, 2: 123–42.

O'Connell, M. and Whelan, J. (1996) 'The Public Perceptions of Crime Prevalence, Newspaper Readership and "Mean World" Attitudes', *Legal and Criminal Psychology.* 1: 179–95.

Pearson, G. (1983) *Hooligan: A History of Respectable Fears.* London: Macmillan.

Poster, M. (1990) *The Mode of Information: Poststructuralism and Social Context.* Cambridge: Polity Press.

Potter, W., Vaughan, M., Warren, R., Howley, K., Land. A., and Hagemeyer, J. (1997) 'Aggression in Television Entertainment: Profiles and Trends', *Communication Research Reports* 14: 116–24.

Reiner, R., Livingstone, S., and Allen, J. (2000) 'Casino culture: media and crime in a winner-loser society' in K. Stenson and D. Cowell (eds) *Crime, Risk and Justice.* Cullompton: Willan.

Rock, P. (1973) 'News as eternal recurrence' in S. Cohen and J. Young (eds) (1981) *The Manufacture of News: Social Problems, Deviance and the Mass Media* (revd edn) London: Constable.

Rojek, C. (2001) *Celebrity (FOCI).* London: Reaktion Books.

Rojek, C. (2012) *Fame Attack: The Inflation of Celebrity and its Consequences.* London: Bloomsbury.

Roshier, R. (1973) 'The Selection of Crime News by the Press' in S. Cohen and J. Young (eds) (1981) *The Manufacture of News: Deviance, Social Problems and the Mass Media* (revd edn) London: Constable.

Sasson, T. (1995) *Crime Talk: How Citizens Construct Social Problems.* Hawthorne, NY: Aldine de Gruyter.

Schlesinger, P., Dobash, R.E., Dobash, R., and Weaver, C.K. (1992) *Women Viewing Violence.* London: British Film Institute.

Schlesinger, P. and Tumber, H. (1994) *Reporting Crime: The Media Politics of Criminal Justice.* Oxford: Clarendon Press.

Schlesinger, P., Tumber, H., and Murdock, G. (1991) 'The Media Politics of Crime and Criminal Justice', *British Journal of Sociology* 42, 3: 397–420.

Seal, L. (2009) 'Issues of Gender and Class in the Mirror Newspaper's Campaign for the Release of Edith Chubb', *Crime Media Culture* 5, 1: 57–78.

Shariff, S. (2008) *Cyberbullying: Issues and Solutions for the School the Classroom and the Home.* London: Routledge.

Silverman, J. and Wilson, D. (2002) *Innocence Betrayed: Paedophilia, the Media and Society.* Cambridge: Polity Press.

Smith, S. (1984) 'Crime in the News', *British Journal of Criminology* 24, 3: 289–95.

Soothill, K. and Walby, S. (1991) *Sex Crime in the News.* London: Routledge.

Soothill, K., Peelo, M., Francis, B., Pearson, J., and Ackerley, E., (2002) 'Homicide and the Media: Identifying the Top Cases in *The Times*', *Howard Journal of Criminal Justice* 41, 5: 401–21.

Sparks, R. (1992) *Television and the Drama of Crime: Moral Tales and the Place of Crime in Public Life.* Buckingham: Open University Press.

Thompson, J.B. (2000) *Political Scandal: Power and Visibility in the Media Age.* Cambridge: Polity.

Thornham, H. and Myers, C. (2012) 'Architectures of Youth: Visibility, Agency and the Technological Imaginings of Young People', *Social and Cultural Geography* 13, 7: 783–800.

Waddington (1986) 'Mugging as a Moral Panic: A Question of Proportion', *British Journal of Sociology* 37, 2: 245–59.

Williams, P. and Dickinson, J. (1993) 'Fear of Crime; Read All About It; The Relationship Between Newspaper Crime Reporting and Fear of Crime', *British Journal of Criminology* 33, 1: 33–56.

Winston, R. (2004) 'Seeing is Believing', *The Guardian, G2,* 7 January 2004.

Wykes, M. (2001) *News, Crime and Culture.* London: Pluto Press.

Wykes, M. (2007) 'Constructing Crime: Culture, Stalking, Celebrity and Cyber', *Crime, Media, Culture: An International Journal* 3, 2: 158–74.

Part II
FORMS OF CRIME

8 Drugs, alcohol, and crime

Emma Wincup and Peter Traynor

INTRODUCTION

Drug and alcohol use are frequently offered as explanations for crime. The use of so-called 'hard' drugs such as heroin and crack cocaine is cited as one of the causes of a range of crimes, particularly acquisitive crimes; excessive alcohol use is perceived as closely connected with anti-social and violent behaviour. For many members of the general public and the media, the relationship between drug or alcohol use and criminal activity is clear and the solutions straightforward. This contrasts sharply with the findings of research studies which identify the need for a more complex understanding and consequently, a multi-faceted response.

This chapter is divided into two main parts. The first part focuses on drug use and addresses three key issues: (a) the nature and extent of drug use; (b) the relationship between drug use and crime; and (c) strategies for reducing drug-related crime. In the second part, we explore the same issues in relation to alcohol use. Exploring the relationship between drugs, alcohol, and crime is a huge task and it is necessary to impose some editorial boundaries: first, we will be concentrating predominantly on England and Wales; and second, space precludes a detailed consideration of organized crime relating to drug and contraband alcohol markets or the policing of these markets.

Part one: Drugs and crime

BACKGROUND

Attempts to control drug use date back to the Pharmacy Act 1868 which confined the sale of opium to pharmacists. Throughout the twentieth century, other statutes were passed to strengthen the drugs laws including a succession of Dangerous Drugs Acts. The 1971 Misuse of Drugs Act consolidated earlier statutes and laid the foundations for existing and future controls on the import, export, possession, use, manufacture, and distribution of 'controlled' drugs. We should pause for a moment and reflect upon the language utilized within the legislation, because it is revealing about the ideological assumptions underpinning the Acts and offers an insight into shifting conceptions of drug use across time. By 1971, the language of danger, with its moralistic overtones, had been replaced by the language of control which emphasized the need to control drugs by preventing their inappropriate use at the same time as permitting their correct use in medical contexts. The 1971 Act divided controlled drugs into three categories (see Table 8.1) according to official perceptions of their relative harmfulness when misused. The level of control is expected to be proportionate to official definitions of harmfulness.

Although a series of statutes have been passed since, the 1971 Act continues to be cornerstone of drug legislation. There have been repeated calls for the classification system to be overhauled, most

Table 8.1 The Misuse of Drugs Act 1971

Category	Examples of controlled drugs
Class A (judged to be the most harmful)	Cocaine (crack and powder), ecstasy, hallucinogens (LSD, magic mushrooms), opiates (heroin, methadone)
Class B	Amphetamines (unless in injectable form, then Class A), cannabis (in all forms)
Class C (judged to be the least harmful)	Anabolic steroids, ketamine, minor tranquillisers

recently by the UK Drug Policy Commission (2012) who argue that the 40-year-old ABC classification system has significant weaknesses, and for many people it lacks credibility. Legislation is based upon official perceptions of the harm caused by drugs, which may not be shared by all members of society. This is illustrated vividly by the debate about the class in which cannabis should be placed or whether it should be included at all: between 2004 and 2009, cannabis was moved from Class B to Class C and back again. The growth of 'legal highs', designed to mimic the effects of illegal drugs, has added a further level of complexity. Since March 2012 a number have been banned on a temporary basis whilst evidence is gathered of the harm they might cause. It remains to be seen whether potentially harmful drugs can moved from being legal to illegal and back again if it is deem that they 'safe'.

A number of classic criminological studies illustrate vividly the plurality of perceptions of the harm-fulness of illegal drugs (Becker, 1963; Young, 1971). These qualitative studies were shaped by symbolic interactionism (see Chapter 4) and focused on cannabis use. They emphasized the plurality of societal norms and values and identified the processes by which drug use was socially constructed as a 'deviant' act and drug users portrayed as belonging to a counter-culture. More recently, criminological work has drawn attention to the 'normalization' of drug use, or more accurately recreational drug use (defined in the next section). Its strongest advocates, Howard Parker and his colleagues (Parker *et al.*, 1998), argue that drug use is no longer confined to atypical subcultural groups. Instead it forms part and parcel of growing up in contemporary Britain and is one of a number of ordinary, unremarkable activities. They argue that drugs are widely available and are accommodated within youth culture; levels of drug trying are high (although few people will engage in long-term use); young people are open-minded about their future drug use; and their knowledge of drugs is extensive. The 'normalization thesis' has been criticized for being simplistic (Shildrick, 2002) and exaggerating the extent of drug use by young people (Shiner and Newburn, 1999). Nonetheless it usefully draws attention to the plurality of norms and values which continue to surround illegal drugs.

The drug 'problem' has been officially defined as a law and order, social, medical, and public health 'problem'. These different interpretations have, at different times, influenced the development of UK drug policy. During the 1980s and most of the 1990s, the UK adopted a public health approach to drug policy, initially concerned with reducing the risk drug users pose to themselves and later with risks to wider society (Harman and Paylor, 2002). The public health approach was a response to the realization that unsafe injecting practices could transmit HIV. As the new millennium drew close, a new approach to drug policy was adopted: problem drug use and offending became increasingly interlinked. *Tackling Drugs to Build a Better Britain* (President of the Council, 1998), a ten-year strategy launched in 1998, included reducing crime and anti-social behaviour among its four overarching aims. Critics of the shift in policy emphasis are numerous, and it has been described as a 'war on drug users' (Buchanan and Young, 2000: 409). An updated drug strategy published in 2002 (Home Office, 2002) brought about a further strategic orientation through accelerating the introduction of criminal justice interventions, all with the aim of channelling and coercing drug-using offenders to undergo treatment in the hope it would promote desistance from crime. The 2008 drugs strategy furthered this approach but was short-lived. Shortly after gaining power, the Coalition government published its own strategy (HM Government, 2010a), promising one that was fundamentally different from its predecessors. Whilst this is true in some respects, as we will explore later in the chapter, it did little to reverse the policy emphasis on severing the links between drug use and crime.

The nature and extent of drug use

Commonly used terms to describe drug use include experimental, recreational, and problem, but these are based more on individual opinion than accepted definitions. In one sense, all drug use is problematic due to the health risks involved and because it can lead to contact with criminal justice agencies. The difficulties of defining categories of use adequately have been commented on elsewhere (Barton, 2003); however, we offer some working definitions here. Recreational drug use is characteristically centred on the use of cannabis and 'dance drugs' (for example, ecstasy), and whilst these drugs may be used frequently on a recreational basis, unlike problem drug use, recreational use does not involve dependency, regular excessive use, or use which exposes users to serious health (for example, through injecting) or other risks (social, psychological, physical, or legal). Problem drug use typically involves consuming Class A drugs (especially heroin and crack cocaine) and has the strongest links with offending behaviour.

Estimating the extent of illegal drug use is extremely difficult and there is no comprehensive data source. Criminologists seeking to understand the nature and extent of drug use have to piece together data from official statistics, self-report studies, and academic studies.

Official statistics

Obtaining accurate data on drug use is challenging since the majority of episodes of drug use form part of a 'dark figure', unknown to criminal justice or other agencies who work with drug users. National data on the number of drug users seeking drug treatment sheds some light on the 'problem'. The latest data demonstrate that just over 195,000 individuals received drug treatment in England between April 2011 and March 2012 (National Treatment Agency for Substance Misuse, 2012), but this represents the 'tip of the iceberg' since it excludes drug users who were unable to or did not wish to access treatment. Given these limitations, researchers have developed elaborate models to estimate the prevalence of problem drug use using data gathered from various agencies that problem drug users are likely to make contact with; for example, criminal justice agencies, GP surgeries, and hospital accident and emergency departments. The latest estimate is that in 2011–12 there were approximately 306,150 problem drug users (defined as those using opiates and/or crack cocaine) in England (Hay *et al.*, 2011). Data on recreational drug use are best obtained via self-report studies given that this form of drug use is unlikely to reach the attention of official agencies.

Self-report studies

Self-report studies have become the most commonly used means of assessing how many people use, or have used, drugs. The main study which provides data on drug use for England and Wales is the Crime Survey for England and Wales. Established in 1982 as the British Crime Survey, the survey involves face-to-face interviews with 35,000 adults living in a representative cross-section of private households in England and Wales. Whilst the main focus of the survey is on experiences of crime, data have been collected on drug use since 1994. Respondents enter their answers directly into a laptop computer so that sensitive information can be kept confidential and refusal rates kept to a minimum. The 2011–12 survey (Home Office, 2012) estimated that 37 per cent of 16- to 59-year-olds have used one or more illicit drugs in their lifetime, and 16 per cent have used a Class A drug at least once. Levels of drug use within the past year were lower with only 9 per cent of all 16- to 59-year-olds admitting to taking an illicit drug and 3 per cent to using a Class A drug. Levels of drug use within the past month are lower still, and this is illustrated in Table 8.2. The data show that usage varies tremendously between drug types and provides evidence of a strong relationship between drug use and age. Comparing patterns of drug use over the past five years reveals that, with the exception of a growth in the use of cocaine powder and methadone, drug use has fallen considerably, but levels have now stabilized (Home Office, 2012).

The BCS does have its limitations as a survey of drug use. The BCS is a household survey, and therefore excludes some of the groups most likely to be involved in drug use such as homeless people or those living in institutions (for example, prisons). Nor does it include young people aged under 16. Surveys of young people's (aged 11 to 15) use of drugs (plus alcohol and tobacco) are commissioned by the Department of Health (see Fuller, 2011). Drug use is largely confined to cannabis or sniffing glue, gas, aerosols, and solvents.

Table 8.2 Prevalence of drug use in the last month by age group

Type of drug	% used (16- to 24-year-olds)	% used (16- to 59-year-olds)
Cannabis	9.2	4.1
Any stimulant	4.9	2.5
Any Class A drug	3.2	1.5
Any illicit drug	11.1	5.2

Source: Crime Survey for England and Wales 2011/12 (Home Office, 2012).

Academic studies

Academic studies have captured the diversity of the drug-using population by exploring different populations, such as homeless people (Wincup et al., 2003); care leavers (Ward *et al.*, 2003); young offenders (Hammersley *et al.*, 2003); and sex workers (Cusick *et al.*, 2004). These studies identify that levels of drug use are far more prevalent among these groups. Together these studies support the conclusion that certain groups are more vulnerable to becoming problem drug users and that it is important to understand the risk factors associated with the onset of problem drug use to develop effective approaches to drug prevention (Lloyd, 1998).

Lloyd (1998) reviewed studies which have sought to identify the risk factors associated with problem drug use. He concluded that risk factors can relate to the family (for example, parental or sibling drug use, family disruption, poor attachment or communication with parents and child abuse); school (for example, poor educational performance, exclusion); involvement in crime and other conduct disorders (for example, truancy); mental disorder; social deprivation; and young age of onset for drug use. He suggests that these factors are highly connected and best viewed as a 'web of causation' (Lloyd, 1998).

Academic research has also drawn attention to the link between social divisions and drug use. Both theoretical work (Ettore, 2007) and empirical research (for example, Taylor, 1993) has pioneered the development of a feminist understanding of women's drug use and argued for the development of gender-sensitive policy responses. Research on the links between ethnicity and crime is less developed which has hindered the attempts of drug treatment agencies to respond to the diverse needs of the minority ethnic population (Fountain *et al.*, 2003). The available evidence from Britain (see Bennett and Holloway, 2007 for a review) suggests that there are clear ethnic differences in patterns of drug use, with the white population reporting the highest levels of drug use. There is a growing literature on the interconnections between social exclusion and problem drug use, which recognizes that whilst drug experimentation is widespread, problem drug use is largely confined to the most disadvantaged sectors of the population requiring multi-faceted policy responses to tackle the range of problems they face (Foster, 2000; Neale, 2006). The importance of looking at drug careers in context, both in term of geography and socio-economic status, is vividly illustrated in a series of ethnographic studies on the lives of young people growing up in Britain's poor neighbourhoods (MacDonald and Marsh, 2005).

REVIEW QUESTIONS

1 What are the main sources of data on drug use?

2 What are the strengths and weaknesses of the main data sources?

3 What factors are most closely associated with drug use?

Exploring the links between drug use and crime

There have been multiple attempts to conceptualize the links between drug use and crime. This is a complex task because both drug use and crime encompass a wide range of behaviours. Unsurprisingly, therefore, some academics have restricted their analysis to particular forms of crime (for example, violence (Goldstein, 1985) or acquisitive crime (Seddon, 2000)) and/or drug use (for example, non-recreational' (that is, problem) drug use (Seddon, 2000)). Essentially the literature consists of a number of typologies which have been developed to make sense of the relationship between drug use and crime (Bean, 2008; Bennett and Holloway, 2005, 2007; Hammersley, 2008). The number of categories within them varies but, broadly speaking, all begin by exploring initially whether a clear relationship between drug use and crime exists and if so, which behaviour is the cause and which is the effect. From this starting point, two ways of understanding drug-crime connections emerge. The first is that drug use leads to crime. Taking this further, Bennett and Holloway (2005) outline psychopharmalogical, economic, and lifestyle explanations for this link. Drug use can be criminogenic due to the impact of drugs on drug users' behaviour, their need to generate income to support their drug use, or due to crime being embedded in drug networks. At their most basic, these explanations are deterministic and suggest that crime is an inevitable consequence of drug use. More sophisticated analyses acknowledge the role of mediating and moderating factors. They also recognize the need to explore evidence which challenges accepted wisdom; for example, that drug use is linked with victimization.

The second main way of understanding drug-crime connections is to explore the counter view that crime causes drug use. Bennett and Holloway (2005) propose that the three types of explanations just described can be used to understand how involvement in crime can lead to the development of a drug-using career. Psychopharmalogical explanations propose that drugs may be used to celebrate offending or used to facilitate committing an offence (through the provision of 'dutch courage'). Economic explanations identify that surplus proceeds from crime allow drugs to be purchased, whilst lifestyle explanations argue that drug use is a systemic part of a criminal lifestyle.

Whilst the two main ways of understanding the drug-crime connections described helpfully draw out the different ways in which drug use and crime are connected, neither are satisfactory in isolation. Consequently, academics have attempted to identify alternative ways to conceptualize the links between drug use and crime. Most discussions are accompanied by a warning that explanations are often undeveloped and in need of further research. Nonetheless, they have shifted thinking away from direct, causal understandings of the relationship between drug use and crime. These conceptualizations are now described.

- Interactive (or reciprocal) approach: the relationship between crime and drug use is bi-directional as criminal/drug-using careers develop in parallel (see Edmunds *et al.*, 2008; Pudney, 2002).

- Shared (or common) cause approach: crime and drug use are both caused by a single reinforcing factor, which may be psychological, social, or environmental (see Bennett and Holloway, 2005).

- Multivariate approach: both crime and drug use are linked to a complex set of macro and micro factors which may be socio-economic, cultural, or individual (see Seddon, 2000).

- Spurious (or coincidence) approach: involvement in crime and drug use are unconnected and are merely behaviours which occur simultaneously.

Each model has its strengths and weakness. None of them are satisfactory in their own right. Crucially, it is important to recognize that for many drug users, especially those engaged solely in recreational drug use, their involvement in crime is largely restricted to possession and use of a controlled drug. Offering a comprehensive review of the available literature, which may or may not offer support for these models, is beyond the scope of this chapter. This ambitious task has been taken on by Bennett and Holloway, (2005, 2007) who have drawn upon their own extensive research with arrestees alongside empirical studies from across the globe. In a nutshell, we can reasonably conclude that for a small proportion of drug users there appears to be a close relationship between their involvement in (problem) drug use and (prolific) offending but it is problematic to assume that the relationship is unidirectional or causal.

REVIEW QUESTIONS

1   Critically evaluate the different ways in which the relationship between drug use and crime has been understood.

2   Consider the following drug policies. What impact might they have on crime?

   • Drug treatment for offenders

   • Drug education targeted at socially excluded young people

   • More intensive policing of drug markets

3   Refer to Chapter 17. How similar are the risk factors for problem drug use and youth crime?

Breaking the links

A strategic response to the drug 'problem' in the UK first emerged in the mid-1990s (Lord President of the Council, 1995). Fifteen years later, a further four drug strategies have been published, which continue to operate in three spheres: prevention, treatment, and enforcement despite heavy criticism of this tripartite approach. It has been suggested that it can result in duplication of effort and missed opportunities for partnership working with individuals and communities to tackle drug problems (UK Drug Policy Commission, 2012). The latest strategy (HM Government, 2010a) is structured around three themes: reducing demand, restricting supply and building recovery in communities in order to meet two overarching aims: reducing illicit and other harmful drug use and increasing the numbers recovering from their dependence. The strategy argues that it places clear water between its approach and that adopted by its predecessors in a number of respects. These are set out in the introduction to the strategy. Perhaps most significantly, given our concern with both drugs and alcohol in this chapter, is its focus on all forms of drug dependence including alcohol. However, whilst it is important not to underplay the distinctive aspects of the 2010 Drug Strategy, we should note that it leaves untouched the emphasis upon breaking the links between drug use and crime. Consequently, the criminal justice process remains a key site for targeted intervention through the provision of treatment from the point of arrest through to release from prison. Since 1993, these interventions have been coordinated across England (and more recently Wales) through the Drug Interventions Programme (DIP). DIP aims to provide an integrated approach for adult users of Class A drugs from the point of arrest through to beyond sentencing. Explicitly focussed on reducing reoffending through the provision of treatment, DIP involves police forces, the criminal courts, probation trust, and prisons working in partnership with providers of drug treatment and social support (for example, housing).

Broadly speaking criminal justice interventions involve drug testing, drug treatment, or both. At the pre-trial stage, individuals arrested for 'trigger' offences (that is, those often deemed to be drug-related such as forms of acquisitive crime) are required to undergo testing following the introduction of the Drugs Act 2005. Testing on arrest is currently operational in all DIP-intensive areas (that is, those with the greatest levels of problem drug use) in England (and supplements police powers to test upon charge which were introduced in April 2003). Those testing positive for heroin, crack, and cocaine are required to undergo an initial and follow-up assessment. Failure to comply, without good cause, is a criminal offence. Test results are also used to inform court decisions such as whether to grant bail. Similarly the police can use the information for their own purposes; for example, they can attach a drug rehabilitative condition to a caution (for adults only). Failure to comply in this instance can lead to an individual being prosecuted for the original offence.

At the sentencing stage, courts now have access to tailored sentences for drug-using offenders. Courts, in this instance, refers mainly to Magistrates' and Crown Courts, although dedicated drug courts have been piloted in England and Wales and have existed in Scotland since 2001 (see McIvor, 2010). The introduction of the Drug Treatment and Testing Order across the UK following the Crime and Disorder Act 1998 paved the way in this respect. These were replaced following the introduction of the Criminal Justice Act 2003 in 2005 (in England and Wales and Northern Ireland but not Scotland) by drug rehabilitation requirements attached to a generic community order (see Chapter 24). They continue to be used widely (see Ministry of Justice Offender Management Statistics (Quarterly)), especially for women, and typically in combination with supervision by a probation officer.

Those sentenced to custody are also afforded opportunities to seek treatment for their drug use through Counselling, Assessment, Referral, Advice and Treatment (CARAT) schemes. However, offering treatment alongside measures such as mandatory drug testing and increased security measures to prevent circulation of drugs and drug paraphernalia within prisons is fraught with contradictions (Duke, 2003). Drug policy within prison has to balance concerns with 'control', 'order', and 'punishment' alongside harm minimization and treatment. Additionally the vision to provide continuity of treatment for drug-using prisoners is not always realized in practice, especially for short-sentence prisoners (Paylor et al., 2010). For some prisoners, control will extend beyond the prison gate as the Criminal Justice and Court Services Act 2000 permitted a drug testing requirement to form part of a condition of release from prison.

Whilst drug users are required to take part in some of these interventions, principally those limited to drug testing, others are voluntary. However, drug users are 'coerced' into participating in the sense that failing to comply results in less favourable outcomes; for example, it could lead to being remanded in custody rather than being granted bail or being given a custodial sentence rather than a community penalty. The notion of 'coerced treatment' no longer attracts the controversy it did in the past and the debate is now largely focused on whether coerced drug treatment is effective (see Stevens, 2010). The debate has also become more nuanced, focusing on the appropriateness of substitute medication, the form of treatment typically offered to drug-using offenders, namely substitute medication (see Monaghan, 2012).

Whilst evidence on the impact of criminal justice interventions on drug-using and offending behaviour is far from unequivocal, it is certainly the case that the number of drug users receiving treatment has increased rapidly in recent years but is now levelling off. Whilst this has undoubtedly had a positive impact on drug users, families, and potential victims of crime, Reuter and Stevens (2007) argue that this is unlikely to have a substantial and measurable impact on overall levels of problem drug use and crime. They note that many problem drug users do not engage in treatment, treatment programmes vary in terms of their effectiveness, and rates of relapse are high plus new problem drug users replace those who have abstained (Reuter and Stevens, 2007).

REVIEW QUESTIONS

1 Why has drug treatment become firmly embedded in the criminal justice process?

2 What concerns have been expressed about drug treatment for offenders?

3 What impact can the provision of drug treatment for offenders have on crime rates?

Part two: Alcohol and crime

BACKGROUND

Attempts to restrict alcohol use date back to the Licensing Act 1872. Since then legislation has been introduced periodically to prevent or reduce the problems associated with excessive alcohol consumption with significant changes made during the last decade. The Licensing Act 2003 represented an ambitious attempt by the (New Labour) government to simplify, rationalize, and build upon the accumulated legislation. This was a challenging task because alcohol occupies an ambiguous position in contemporary Britain, associated with pleasure but also individual and social harms (Newburn and Shiner, 2001). Britain is often described as having a 'wet' culture; in other words, drinking alcohol is widespread and socially accepted as a legitimate and pleasurable activity (Newburn and Shiner, 2001): indeed, alcohol remains Britain's 'favourite drug' (Aldridge et al., 2011). Alcohol and related industries are seen as important in economic terms, playing an important role in regenerating urban centres, alongside providing employment and government revenue.

We referred earlier to 'problem drinking' but what this actually means is a source of debate, and a variety of terms are used to describe different kinds of drinking and levels of consumption. For example, New Labour's alcohol strategy (HM Government, 2007) distinguished between drinking that was sensible, harmful or classed as binge drinking. The current strategy (HM Government, 2012) no longer includes a 'sensible drinking' category based on the assumption that any form of drinking is potentially harmful. Consequently, it divides drinkers into three risk categories: lower-risk, increasing-risk, and higher-risk drinkers and notes that even drinking *at* recommended levels can have a negative effect on health and well-being. Binge drinking is still considered a problem and involves drinking similar or higher daily amounts to high-risk drinkers (drinking at more than twice the recommended levels) but in short, irregular periods.

Undoubtedly, problem drinking has health and public order implications. Reviews of the literature from criminological perspectives have explored how problem drinking can lead to drink-driving, drug use and violence, from minor assaults through to domestic violence to homicide (Deehan, 1999; Finney, 2004a, b, c), whilst longitudinal studies suggest that binge drinking in adolescence is related to an increased risk of adult alcohol dependence, illicit drug use, homelessness, criminal conviction, and school exclusion (Viner and Taylor, 2007). Academic, political and media attention has focused in particular on the extent of alcohol-related violence and disorder in urban centres (Academy of Medical Sciences, 2004; Finney, 2004a; Hobbs *et al.*, 2003; Mistral *et al.*, 2006). In post-industrial cities, urban regeneration has resulted in the rapid development of the night-time economy as cities have re-invented themselves as sites of consumption and leisure (Hobbs, 2003). Binge drinking places heavy demands on the resources of criminal justice agencies, although policing is increasingly pluralized and the night-time economy is now 'policed' by both public and private sector personnel (Hobbs *et al.*, 2003; Hadfield *et al.*, 2009).

The nature and extent of alcohol use

The majority of adults in England consume alcohol and most confine their drinking to reasonable levels. Data on alcohol consumption can be obtained from a variety of sources. The General Lifestyle Survey (formerly known as the General Household Survey) provides data annually on alcohol use for those aged 16 and over based upon face-to-face interviews with individuals from over 13,000 households. Since 2006 the survey has used two measures of daily consumption to estimate levels of problem drinking. The first asks whether people have exceeded the recommended weekly benchmarks to capture harmful drinking and the second measure explores whether people have engaged in binge drinking by questioning them about the maximum amount drunk on any one day in the week prior to being interviewed. This takes into account the number of units that people drank, reflecting the fact that alcohol is now often stronger than it was in the past and that measures of alcohol, especially wine, are more generous than previously. Despite this methodological improvement, the present authors warn that the data need to be treated with caution because social surveys in general consistently record lower levels of consumption than is indicated from data on alcohol sales. This is partly because of the fact that people often underestimate how much alcohol they have consumed, especially when they have consumed alcohol at home, because the quantities are not measured in the same way they are in licensed premises.

In England, in 2010, two-thirds of men and half of women (aged 16 and over) reported drinking an alcoholic drink on at least one day in the week prior to interview (Dunstan, 2012). Like its predecessors, the 2010 study noted the persistence of significant gender differences. Men remain more likely than women to have engaged in both harmful and binge drinking, although the gender difference is less marked for the 16–24 age group. The proportion of adults who reported drinking in the week prior to interview has decreased since 1998. Similarly, the proportion of adults drinking on five or more days in the previous week has also decreased since 1998 as has the amount they actually consume. Overall, the proportion of the public who report either harmful and/ or binge drinking has fallen during the past decade but there is still cause for concern. Approximately one-quarter of men and one-sixth of women still drank more than the recommended weekly limit. Similarly, whilst the majority of women and men do not binge drink, in the week prior to interview just over one-third of men and just under one-third of women did. The data also revealed that involvement in problem drinking is not restricted to the younger age groups (although those aged 65 and over were the most likely to drink sensibly). This contrasts with media images which focus on the drinking of young people. The context in which the different age groups drink may be significant here with binge drinking in public space, predominantly by young people, being more visible than the same behaviour by older age groups within the private sphere.

There are various other sources of information on young people's alcohol consumption. The annual schools-based survey—*Smoking, Drinking and Drug Use among Young People in England*—provides data on alcohol use for young people aged between 11 and 15. Analysis of the 2010 data (Fuller, 2011) found that girls and boys were equally likely to have drunk alcohol in the last seven days and tended to drink similar amounts. There has been a decline in recent years in the recorded prevalence of drinking among this age group. In 2001 one-quarter of pupils said they drank alcohol in the previous week, which had halved by 2010. The amounts consumed are difficult to compare but appear to have remained relatively steady and high. The average weekly consumption among pupils who drank in the previous week is high at 12.9 units, a slight increase on the year before and close to the level recorded for adults. The small proportion of heavy underage drinkers remains a cause for concern and their behaviour contrasts sharply with the growing intolerance of underage drinking and drunkenness. In 2010 approximately one-third agreed that it was acceptable for someone of their age to drink alcohol once a week compared with just over two-fifths in 2003.

REVIEW QUESTIONS

1 What are the main strengths and weakness of the different data sources?

2 How can we explain higher levels of alcohol consumption among men? (You might find it helpful to refer to Chapter 15.)

3 What are the possible implications of young people's patterns of alcohol use?

Exploring the links between alcohol use and crime

The link between alcohol use and crime has been explored extensively. Collins (1982) concluded that there was sufficient evidence to justify the inference that alcohol is sometimes causally implicated in the occurrence of serious crime although this conclusion has been the source of considerable debate. Numerous attempts have been made to develop typologies for understanding the relationship between drinking and offending behaviour and whilst these vary, all agree that the link between alcohol and crime is multi-faceted. A useful starting point is offered by Hayes (1993) who suggests that the relationship can be characterized in three ways. First, the relationship may be causal because an offender has committed an alcohol-defined offence, an alcohol-induced offence (for example, assaulting someone when drunk) or an alcohol-inspired offence (for example, shoplifting to obtain alcohol). Second, the relationship between alcohol and crime may be contributory: alcohol provides 'dutch courage' to commit an offence, acts as a catalyst, or is offered later as an excuse for offending behaviour. Finally, there may be no relationship between alcohol and crime with the two behaviours simply co-existing as separate activities.

Similarly, Purser (1995) developed a functional model of the alcohol and crime relationship, distinguishing between the different roles alcohol plays in the offence. His five categories are listed here:

(a) offences which specifically mention alcohol;

(b) offences against the licensing law;

(c) offences committed while under the disinhibiting effects of alcohol where alcohol has affected the person's self-control or judgement;

(d) offences resulting from an alcohol problem where alcohol need not have been consumed immediately prior to the offences being committed;

(e) offences where alcohol is used an excuse.

Both approaches are helpful, but tend to oversimplify the relationship between alcohol and crime. Hayes' typology runs the risk of attributing causality more readily than appropriate whilst Purser's model tends to assume that alcohol and crime are always related, even if alcohol is not always a causal factor in crime. Research on the relationship between alcohol and crime is voluminous and difficult to interpret. A number of researchers have reviewed the available literature (Deehan, 1999; Newburn and Shiner, 2001; Ramsay, 1996; Sumner and Parker, 1995). Rather than repeat their efforts, we will focus here on the two key studies, which illustrate the complexities of the relationship between alcohol and crime.

The Crime Survey for England and Wales (formerly the British Crime Survey) explores among other things alcohol-related violence, which it categorizes as woundings, assaults with minor injury, assaults with no injury, and robberies where the offender was thought to be under the influence of alcohol. According to analysis of the 2009–10 data (Flatley et al., 2010), victims of violence believed the offender(s) to be under the influence of alcohol in half of all violent incidents, representing 986,000 violent incidents. These findings reveal the co-existence of alcohol use (but not necessarily drunkenness) and crime, but cannot provide an insight into whether alcohol was a contributory factor. However, when coupled with the accounts of offenders they enhance our understanding of the relationship between alcohol and crime.

The 2004 Offending, Crime and Justice Survey (Matthews et al., 2006) begins to illustrate the complex relationship between alcohol use and youth offending. Among 10- to 17-year-olds, those who drank at least once a month committed offences more often than those who drank less frequently or not at all. This applied to all offences, but particularly to violent offences. Similarly, 10- to 17-year-olds who drank at least once a week (14 per cent of respondents) were responsible for a disproportionate amount of crimes (just over one-third of all offences) committed by this age group. Those who drank at least once a week or more frequently were more likely to admit involvement in crime and/or disorder during or after drinking, especially arguments, fights, and criminal damage. They were also more likely to engage in other forms of risky or illegal behaviour, including smoking and drug use.

In some respect surveys provide only a superficial insight into the relationship between alcohol and crime and qualitative studies can add further depth of analysis. Focusing more narrowly on persistent offenders, Parker (1996) conducted in-depth interviews with 66 young people aged between 18 and 25 subject to probation supervision. The majority of these (52) were current drinkers and just under half of these (24) stated their use of alcohol caused problems, typically relating to involvement with crime and contact with the police. The entire sample felt alcohol was sometimes part of the explanation for their offending, but even the heavy drinkers did not perceive alcohol as central to their explanations of their own offending behaviour. Parker argued that the search for a simple correlation between alcohol use and offending is not 'good criminology' (Parker, 1996: 291). He found that through analysis of their qualitative motivational accounts, other variables emerged relating to illegal drug use and the desire to pursue a preferred lifestyle, thus attempts to isolate alcohol use as a key variable are misguided. Parker concluded that for persistent young adult offenders alcohol is both an accessory to crime and to a lawful good time, and in the latter respect they are no different to so-called law-abiding young adults.

REVIEW QUESTIONS

1 Can you think of examples of crime which fit each of Purser's categories?
2 What are the challenges of exploring the relationship between alcohol use and crime?
3 What forms of drinking have been linked to crime?

Breaking the links

Concerns about alcohol-related crime and disorder have moved up the political and public agendas in recent years, linked in with wider concerns about anti-social behaviour. Media images, particularly those broadcast through 'fly-on-the-wall' TV documentaries, paint a picture of lawless city centres characterized by binge drinking and associated crime. As a result, both the present and previous governments have generated a great deal of research, legislation and regulatory frameworks around alcohol. New Labour responded to concerns about an increasingly disordered night-time economy with an unprecedented array of initiatives, regulation, and legislation designed to completely change the licensing landscape. The Licensing Act 2003 represented a significant 'shake up' of existing legislation and defined public safety, the prevention of crime, disorder, and public nuisance and the protection of children as key objectives for local authorities. A range of measures were introduced, including the controversial extension of drinking hours. The following year the first of two detailed strategies was published. The *Alcohol Harm Reduction Strategy for England* (Prime Minister's Strategy Unit, 2004) set out the broad framework in which local authorities and partners were obliged to work together to tackle problematic alcohol use. Its key priority was tackling alcohol-related crime and disorder, particularly in town and city centres 'blighted by alcohol misuse at weekends' (2004: 5). There was also a commitment to tackling harms to public health. The follow-up, *Safe, Sensible, Social—Next Steps in the National Alcohol Strategy* (HM Government, 2007) was published three years later. It acknowledged that despite substantial effort a small yet significant proportion of violence was still being committed around pubs and clubs (17 per cent in 2005–6). As a result, *Next Steps* built on the original strategy and set out three key objectives:

1. to ensure laws and licensing powers were being used widely and effectively to crack down on crime and disorder, tackle irresponsible management of licensed premises and protect young people;

2. to sharpen the focus on the minority of drinkers who were seen to be causing the most harm including under-age drinkers, young binge drinkers and harmful drinkers); and

3. to shape an environment that actively promoted sensible drinking.

New Labour's principal objective was to reduce alcohol-related harms. Whether it fully achieved this is debatable. The extension of licensing hours reflected one of the broader aspirations of the strategy which was a change in national culture and a move towards a more continental approach to drinking which was viewed (erroneously for some) as being more measured, relaxed, and peaceable. Longer hours would, in theory, lead to less binge drinking and reduce violence by staggering closing times. However, in practice, whilst alcohol-related violence reduced at what were the traditional closing times (11pm for pubs and 2am for clubs), studies found that alcohol-related violence had actually increased in some areas and was spread more throughout the night (Newton *et al.*, 2007). Despite these commitments, however, alcohol remained the 'poor relation' to drugs in terms of funding, and for some the effectiveness of this approach was hampered by the close relationship between the government and alcohol producers/retailers and over-optimism about the capacity to impose a continental café-style culture on the social terrain of the UK.

In its *Programme for Government* (Cabinet Office, 2010) the nascent Coalition government committed among other things to tackling late night alcohol-related disorder and under-age drinking. It has since produced a number of documents and initiatives aimed at honouring these commitments. In 2010 the consultation document *Rebalancing the Licensing Act* (HM Government, 2010b) proposed two new measures which were subsequently included in the Police Reform and Social Responsibility Act 2011. The first is the Early Morning Restriction Order (EMRO), a measure originally designed by the New Labour government, which from October 2012 has local areas restrict alcohol sales late at night if they are causing problems. The second is the 'Late night levy' on businesses providing alcohol and related services in the late-night economy. In 2012 the government published its *Alcohol Strategy* (HM Government, 2012) in which it committed to, among other things, a review of minimum pricing; enhancing tools and powers so that local agencies and partnerships are able to tackle alcohol disorder more effectively; working with industry to increase social responsibility and improving health resources to support individuals make informed choices about drinking. In doing these a number of outcomes are set out:

- a change in what is seen as acceptable drinking behaviour;
- a reduction in alcohol-related crime;
- a reduction in those drinking above recommended drinking levels (including binge drinking);
- a reduction in alcohol-related deaths;
- a reduction in the number of 11–15-year-olds drinking and the amounts they consume.

The consultation and subsequent strategy were both critical of the previous government's commitment to 'café culture' and its failure to effectively tackle alcohol-related disorder. Nonetheless, many of the proposals in the document are extensions of or amendments to earlier legislation and approaches rather than radical innovations. Likewise, an emphasis on changing attitudes, strengthening local partnerships and working with rather than against industry were all key elements of New Labour's approach. The latter might seem especially optimistic given the findings of an independent review of social responsibility within the drinks industry which found considerable evidence of poor practice across England including 'inducements to people to drink more and faster, and to allow under-age people entry to premises, and blatantly serving intoxicated people' (Home Office/KPMG, 2008: 10). Nonetheless, there are a number of notable departures: the review of alcohol pricing promises to tackle the sale of cheap alcohol in supermarkets, something New Labour never quite got to grips with.

It would be inappropriate to give the impression that prior to the launch of New Labour's wider ranging agenda there were few attempts to reduce levels of crime related to problem drinking. A wide range of interventions are described by Alcohol Concern (1999) and Deehan (1999) with most being attempts to change the environment in which drinking takes places through a variety of situational crime prevention (SCP) measures including the use of plastic glasses, serving food with alcoholic drinks, reduced prices for low- and non-alcohol drinks, and the abolition of 'happy hours'. Local Community Safety Partnerships are increasingly using such measures as part of a toolkit to tackle alcohol-related disorder. Other innovations have included sophisticated data analysis which allows disorder 'hotspots' to be identified, the use of CCTV and taxi marshalling schemes to promote public safety at specific locations. Furthermore, Pubwatch and Best Bar schemes have been developed. The former are local partnerships between licensees and enforcement agencies, aimed at reducing crime and anti-social behaviour on licensed premises, through, for instance, the identification and exclusion of problematic individuals; the latter is a national award scheme, aimed at encouraging responsible management and operation of licensed premises, and supported by the Home Office. Whilst SCP approaches offer a potentially effective means of reducing alcohol-related harm, they are only part of the solution. Criminologists have been urged by Hayward (2004) to adopt a cultural perspective and ask why the majority of violent assaults in the UK involve the use of alcohol in one form or another. As we have noted, successive governments have embarked upon the ambitious task of promoting cultural change but have yet to make any significant inroads.

Alongside SCP measures, there are opportunities to work with offenders as they progress through the criminal justice process. The Drug Intervention Programme, described earlier in this chapter, currently focuses on problem drug use, but there is support for it to be tailored to work with those whose offending is judged to be related to problem alcohol use. Current provision is most developed for convicted offenders, although it has expanded through the piloting of arrest referral schemes which include mandatory referral routes through conditions attached to bail or cautions (Blakeborough and Richardson, 2012). Following the implementation of the Criminal Justice Act 2003 in 2005, the criminal courts in England and Wales can now require adult offenders to undergo alcohol treatment as part of a community order or suspended sentence order. The requirement to engage with alcohol treatment is typically combined with supervision (see Ministry of Justice Offender Management Statistics (Quarterly)).

REVIEW QUESTIONS

1 How do measures to tackle alcohol-related crime compare to those used to tackle drug-related crime?

2 What are the strengths and weaknesses of using situational crime prevention measures as a means to tackle alcohol-related crime and disorder?

3 What might a cultural perspective add to our understanding of how best to reduce alcohol-related crime? (You may find it helpful to refer to Chapter 18.)

CONCLUSION

In this chapter, we have pieced together the available evidence, and acknowledged its limitations, to present a picture of drug and alcohol use in England and Wales. We have noted that alcohol use and, to a lesser extent, drug use is widespread but problematic use is confined to a minority. Males, especially young males, are most likely to be engaged in problem drug or alcohol use and therefore more likely to come into contact with criminal justice agencies.

We have explored the dangers of relying upon deterministic explanations and suggested that 'chicken and egg' arguments about whether drug (or alcohol) use leads to crime or vice versa are both simplistic and unhelpful. Instead, we have argued for a more complex understanding of the relationship between drugs, alcohol and crime which locates it within its social, economic, political, and cultural context.

Finally, it is important to note that the material on drugs and alcohol has been presented separately to aid understanding of a challenging criminological issue. This approach runs the risk of glossing over the fact that both the causes and effects of problem drug and alcohol use may be similar, that alcohol is often a common element in polydrug use among offenders (Boreham et al., 2006). Whilst the latest drug strategy does recognize this, strategic responses to alcohol remain largely separate.

QUESTIONS FOR DISCUSSION

1 Look at newspaper reporting of crime. To what extent are drug and alcohol use offered as explanations for offending?

2 Is it possible to obtain an accurate figure of the nature and extent of drug and alcohol use?

3 How can we respond to the commonly held view that the relationship between drugs (or alcohol) and crime is straightforward?

4 What are the main differences between policy responses to drugs and alcohol?

5 Is more legislation likely to reduce levels of drug-related and alcohol-related crime?

GUIDE TO FURTHER READING

Bennett, T. and Holloway, K. (2005) *Understanding Drugs, Alcohol and Crime*. Buckingham: Open University Press.

This text provides a succinct overview of current theory and research on the links between drugs, alcohol and crime.

Dingwall, G. (2006) *Alcohol and Crime*. Cullompton: Willan Publishing.

This book seeks to understand the nature of the connection between alcohol and crime, and the way the criminal justice system responds to the problem.

Hammersley, R. (2008) *Drugs & Crime*. Cambridge: Polity Press.

Challenging simplistic and misguided thinking about drugs and crime, this text argues that the relationship between drug problems and crime needs to be examined in their complex social and psychological contexts.

Simpson, M., Shildrick, T., and MacDonald, R. (2007) (eds) *Drugs in Britain: Supply, Consumption and Control*. Basingstoke: Palgrave Macmillan.

An edited collection which explores the distribution and consumption of illicit drugs and debates surrounding the policing of drugs and the care and control of drug users.

Measham, F. and South, N. (2012) 'Drugs, Alcohol and Crime' in M. Maguire, R. Morgan, and R. Reiner (eds) (5th edn) *The Oxford Handbook of Criminology*. Oxford: Oxford University Press.

This chapter covers similar ground to the chapter you have just read, but offers a more detailed discussion of trends in drug and alcohol use and strategies to tackle both the demand for, and supply of, drugs.

WEB LINKS

http://www.drugscope.org.uk
DrugScope is an independent centre of information and expertise on drugs and aims to inform policy development and reduce drug-related harms.

http://www.alcoholconcern.org.uk
Alcohol Concern is the national voluntary agency on alcohol misuse, acting as an umbrella body for 500 local agencies tackling alcohol-related harm.

http://www.ukdpc.org.uk

The UK Drug Policy Commission is an independent body providing objective analysis of UK drug policy. It aims to improve political, media, and public understanding to develop a rational and effective response to problems caused by illegal drugs.

http://www.drugs.homeoffice.gov.uk

Aimed at professionals, this site offers the latest news and guidance from the government about the drugs strategy.

http://www.dh.gov.uk

The Department of Health website includes details of the government's health policies on alcohol misuse and access to a wide range of statistical information on alcohol use mainly for England.

REFERENCES

Academy of Medical Sciences (2004) *Calling Time: The Nation's Drinking as a Major Health Issue*. London: Academy of Medical Sciences.

Alcohol Concern (1999) *Proposal for a National Alcohol Strategy for England*. London: Alcohol Concern.

Aldridge, J., Measham, F., and Williams, L., (2011) *Illegal Leisure Revisited: Changing Patterns of Alcohol and Drug Use in Adolescents and Young Adults*. Sussex: Routledge.

Barton, A. (2003) *Illicit Drugs: Use and Control*. London: Routledge.

Bean, P. (2008) *Drugs and Crime* (3rd edn) Cullompton: Willan Publishing.

Becker, H. (1963) *Outsiders: Studies in the Sociology of Deviance*. New York: Free Press.

Bennett, T. and Holloway, K. (2005) *Understanding Drugs, Alcohol and Crime*. Buckingham: Open University Press.

Bennett, T. and Holloway, K. (2007) *Drug-Crime Connections*. Cambridge: Cambridge University Press.

Blakeborough, L. and Richardson, A. (2012) *Summary of Findings from Two Evaluations of Home Office Alcohol Arrest Referral Pilot Schemes*, Research Report 60. London: Home Office.

Buchanan, J. and Young, L. (2000) 'The War on Drugs—A War on Drug Users', *Drugs: Education, Prevention and Policy* 7 (4): 409–22.

Cabinet Office. (2010) *The Coalition: Our Programme for Government*. London: HM Government.

Hall, P. and Innes, J. (2010) 'Violent and sexual Crime' in J. Flatley, C. Kershaw, K. Smith, R. Chaplin, and D. Moon (eds) *Crime in England and Wales 2009/10: Findings from the British Crime Survey and Police Recorded Crime*, Home Office Statistical Bulletin 12/10 (3rd edn) London: Home Office.

Collins, J. (1982) *Drinking and Crime; Perspectives on the Relationship between Alcohol Consumption and Criminal Behaviour*. London: Tavistock.

Cusick, L., Martin, A., and May, T. (2003) *Vulnerability and Involvement in Drug Use and Sex Work*, Findings 207. London: Home Office.

Deehan, A. (1999) *Alcohol and Crime: Taking Stock*, Crime Reduction Research Series Paper 3. London: Home Office.

Duke, K. (2003) *Drugs, Prisons and Policy-Making*. Basingstoke: Palgrave Macmillan.

Dunstan, S. (ed) (2012) *General Lifestyle Survey Overview: A Report on the 2010 General Lifestyle Survey*. London: Office for National Statistics.

Edmunds, M., May, T., Hearnden, I, and Hough, M. (1998) *Arrest Referral: Emerging Lessons from Research*, Drug Prevention Initiative Paper 23. London: Home Office.

Ettore, E. (2007) *Revisioning Women and Drug Use: Gender, Power and the Body*. Basingstoke: Palgrave Macmillan.

Finney, A. (2004a) *Violence in the Night-time Economy: Key Findings from the Research*, Findings 214. London: Home Office.

Finney, A. (2004b) *Alcohol and Sexual Violence: Key Findings from the Research*, Findings 215. London: Home Office.

Finney, A. (2004c) *Alcohol and Intimate Partner Violence: Key Findings from the Research*, Findings 216. London: Home Office.

Foster, J. (2000) 'Social Exclusion, Crime and Drugs', *Drugs: Education, Prevention and Policy* 7(4): 317–30.

Fountain, J., Bashford, J., Winters, M., and Patel, K. (2003) *Black and Minority Ethnic Communities in England: A Review of the Literature on Drug Use and Related Service Provision*. London/Preston: National Treatment Agency for Substance Misuse/Centre for Ethnicity and Health.

Fuller, E. (ed) (2011) *Smoking, Drinking and Drug use Among Young People in England 2010*, published online by NHS Information Centre for Health and Social Care, available at http://www.ic.nhs.uk/pubs/sdd10fullreport

Goldstein, P. (1985) 'The Drugs/Violence Nexus: A Tripartite Conceptual Framework', *Journal of Drug Issues* Fall: 493–506.

Hadfield, P., Lister, S., and Traynor, P. (2009) 'This Town's A Different Town Today: Policing and Regulating the Night-time Economy', *Criminology and Criminal Justice* 9(4): 465–85.

Hammersley, R. (2008) *Drugs and Crime*. Cambridge: Polity Press.

Hammersley, R., Marsland, L., and Reid, M. (2003) *Substance Use by Young Offenders: The Impact of the Normalisation in the Early Years of the 21st Century*, Home Office Research Study 261. London: Home Office.

Harman, K. and Paylor, I. (2002) 'A Shift in Strategy', *Criminal Justice Matters*, 47: 8–9.

Hayes, P. (1993) 'A View from the Probation Service' in J. Russell (ed) *Alcohol and Crime: Proceedings of a Mental Health Foundation Conference*. London: Mental Health Foundation.

Hay, G., Gannon, M., Casey, J., and Millar, T. (2011) *National and Regional Estimates of the Prevalence of Opiate and/or Crack Cocaine Use 2009/106: A Summary of Key Findings*. London: National Treatment Agency for Substance Misuse.

Hayward, K. (2004) *City Limits: Crime, Consumer Culture and the Urban Experience*. London: Glasshouse Press.

HM Government (2007) *Safe, Sensible, Social: Next Steps in the National Alcohol Strategy*. London: HM Government.

HM Government (2008) *Drugs; Protecting Families and Communities: The 2008 Drug Strategy*. London: HM Government.

HM Government (2010a) *Drug Strategy 2010: Reducing Demand, Restricting Supply and Building Recovery: Supporting People to Live a Drug Free Life*, London: HM Government.

HM Government. (2010b) *Rebalancing the Licensing Act*. London: HM Government.

HM Government. (2012) *The Government's Alcohol Strategy*. London:

Hobbs, D. (2003) *The Night-Time Economy*, Alcohol Concern Research Forum Papers. London: Alcohol Concern.

Hobbs, D., Hadfield, P., Lister, S., and Winlow, S. (2003) *Bouncers: Violence and Governance in the Night-time Economy*. Oxford: Oxford University Press.

Home Office (2002) *Updated Drug Strategy 2002*. London: Home Office.

Home Office/KPMG (2008) *Review of the Social Responsibility Standards for the Production and Sale of Alcoholic Drinks, Volume 1*. London: Home Office.

Home Office (2012) *Drug Misuse Declared: Findings from the 2011/12 Crime Survey for England and Wales*. London: Home Office.

Hough, M., Clarke, R., and Mayhew, P. (1980) 'Introduction' in R. Clarke and P. Mayhew (eds) *Designing Out Crime*. London: Home Office.

Lloyd, C. (1998) 'Risk Factors for Problem Drug Use: Identifying Vulnerable Groups', *Drugs: Education, Prevention and Policy* 5(3): 217–32.

Lord President of the Council (1995) *Tackling Drugs Together: A Consultation Document on a Strategy for England 1995–98*. London: HMSO.

Matthews, S., Brasnett, L., and Smith, J. (2006) *Underage Drinking: Findings from the 2004 Offending, Crime and Justice Survey*, Findings 277. London: Home Office.

McDonald, R. and Marsh, J. (2005) *Disconnected Youth? Growing up in Britain's Poor Neighbourhoods*. London: Palgrave Macmillan.

McIvor, G. (2010) 'Drug courts: lessons from the UK and beyond' in A. Hucklesby and E. Wincup (eds) *Drug Interventions and Criminal Justice*. Buckingham: Open University Press.

Mistral, W., Velleman, R., Templeton, L., and Mastache, C. (2006) 'Local Action to Prevent Alcohol Problems: is the UK Community Alcohol Prevention Programme the Best Solution?', *International Journal of Drug Policy* 17(4): 278–84.

Monaghan, M. (2012) 'The Recent Evolution of UK Drug Strategies: From Maintenance to Behaviour Change?', *People, Place and Policy Online*, 6(1), http://extra.shu.ac.uk/ppp-online/issue_1_300312/article_4.html.

National Treatment Agency for Substance Misuse (2012) *Facts and Figures*. Available at http://www.ntas.nhs.uk/facts.aspx.

Neale, J. (2006) 'Social Exclusion, Drugs and Policy' in R. Hughes, R. Lart, and P. Higate (eds) *Drugs: Policy and Politics*. London: Longman.

Newburn, T. and Shiner, M. (2001) *Teenage Kicks? Young People and Alcohol: A Review of the Literature*. York: Joseph Rowntree Foundation.

Newton, A., Sarker, S., Pahal, G, van den Bergh, E., and Young, C. (2007) 'Impact of the New Licensing Law on Emergency Hospital Attendances: A Cohort Study', *Emergency Medical Journal* 24(8): 532–4.

Paylor, I. Hucklesby, A., and Wilson, A. (2010) 'Drug interventions in Prison' in A. Hucklesby and E. Wincup (eds) *Drug Interventions and Criminal Justice*. Buckingham: Open University Press.

Parker, H. (1996) 'Young Adult Offenders, Alcohol and Criminological Cul-de-sacs', *British Journal of Criminology* 36(2): 282–98.

Parker, H., Aldridge, J., and Measham, F. (1998) *Illegal Leisure: The Normalization of Adolescent Recreational Drug Use*. London: Routledge.

President of the Council (1998) *Tackling Drugs to Build a Better Britain: The Government's Ten Year Strategy for Tackling Drug Misuse*. London: The Stationery Office.

Prime Minister's Strategy Unit (2004) *Alcohol Harm Reduction Strategy*. London: Cabinet Office.

Pudney, S. (2002) *The Road to Ruin? Sequences of Initiation into Drug Use and Offending by Young People in Britain*, Home Office Research Study 253. London: Home Office.

Purser, R. (1995) *Alcohol and Crime*, Submission to the All Party Group on Alcohol Misuse.

Ramsay, M. (1996) 'The Relationship between Alcohol and Crime' in C. Bryon (ed) *Home Office Research and Statistics Directorate Research Bulletin No. 38*. London: Home Office.

Reuter, P. and Stevens, A. (2007) *An Analysis of UK Drug Policy*. London: UK Drug Policy Commission.

Seddon, T. (2000) 'Explaining the Drug-Crime Link: Theoretical, Policy and Research Issues', *Journal of Social Policy* 29(1): 95–107.

Shildrick. T. (2002) 'Young People, Illicit Drug Use and Questions of Normalization', *Journal of Youth Studies* 5(1): 35–48.

Shiner, M. and Newburn, T. (1997) 'Definitely, Maybe Not: The Normalisation of Recreational Drug Use amongst Young People', *Sociology* 31(3): 1–19.

Sumner, M. and Parker, H. (1995) *Low in Alcohol: A Review of the International Research into Alcohol's Role in Crime Causation*. London: The Portman Group.

Taylor, A. (1993) *Women Drug Users: An Ethnography of a Female Injecting Community*. Oxford: Clarendon Press.

UK Drug Policy Commission (2012) *A Fresh Approach to Drugs: The Final Report of the UK Drug Policy Commission*. London: UK Drug Policy Commission.

Viner, R.M. and Taylor, B. (2007) 'Adult Outcomes of Binge Drinking in Adolescence: Findings from a UK National Birth Cohort', *Journal of Epidemiology and Community Health* 61: 902–7.

Ward, J., Henderson, Z., and Pearson, G. (2003) *One Problem Among Many: Drug Use among Care Leavers in Transition to Independent Living*, Home Office Research Study 260. London: Home Office.

Wincup, E., Buckland, G., and Bayliss, R. (2003) *Youth Homelessness and Substance Use: Report to the Drugs and Alcohol Research Unit*, Home Office Research Study 258. London: Home Office.

Young, J. (1971) *The Drugtakers*. London: Paladin.

9

Violent crime

Larry Ray

INTRODUCTION

This chapter is an introduction to criminological and sociological analysis of violence that will provide you with an overview of some of the main debates and issues along with suggestions for further reading. It begins by raising the question 'what is violence?' which is itself subject to debate. It then examines a key theoretical approach to violence developed by the sociologist Norbert Elias that has placed the understanding of violence in historical context as well as providing a theory accounting for the gradual but uneven diminution of interpersonal violence in modern societies. The chapter then presents summary data on the prevalence of violence in the UK based largely on information from the British Crime Survey (BCS). Next it examines specific issues—aggression and masculinity, violence in the private sphere, racist violence, and homicides. For each type of violence a summary of the data, its prevalence, and discussion of some key explanatory frameworks is given. The chapter ends with some general questions for discussion and a guide to further reading and Internet sources.

BACKGROUND

What is violence? There is no simple answer to this question. The sociological analysis of violence has focussed on criminal forms—especially homicide, assault, child abuse, sexual violence and intimate violence—with the result that a research literature has developed that is specialized but lacks overall theoretical coherence (Jackman, 2002). Except for specialist studies of war, revolution and social movements, the sociology of violence has tended to focus on interpersonal rather than collective or state violence, although this is changing with recent publications including Malešević (2010), Ray (2011), Wieviorka (2009) and Žižek (2008). 'Violence' tends to be separated from 'legitimate force' so that the killing of a police officer by a civilian is considered 'homicide' (that is, violence) whereas the killing of a civilian by a police officer 'in the line of duty' is generally not. Similarly, the exposure of workers to hazardous working conditions that result in death or injury is not considered violence, either because the hazard level is within the law or because the motives of the corporation cannot be verified within legal notions of premeditated intent. Indeed, the definition of violence is contested and this dispute itself is part of the process of identifying ways of resisting violence and the structures that give rise to it (Hearn, 1998). We could say that violence is behaviour that intentionally threatens or does physical harm, and more generally 'involves the infliction of emotional, psychological, sexual, physical and material damage' (Stanko, 1994: 38). Kelly's (1987) famous definition, developed in the context of **domestic violence**, is a continuum of verbal, emotional and sexual abuses of power. This definition extends violence to include abusive behaviour that might not inflict direct physical harm but ties the concept to 'abuse of power', which is a theme that will be discussed here. For many writers violence forms a continuum of types of threatening and harmful behaviour including name-calling, stalking, vandalism and intimidation. On the other hand, for Collins (2008) it is essential to separate violence as physical harm from situations of confrontation and threat, the majority of which do *not* lead to actual violence, because in his view violence is difficult and requires overcoming deep aversion grounded in an evolutionary-psychological desire to form social bonds. There are quite different approaches here to the definition of violence.

Like any other behaviour, violence is embedded in complex ways in social relations and values. Although violence is often described as 'meaningless', and violent offenders are imagined to be 'out-of-control' and psychologically disturbed, violence is virtually never without purpose and often takes place between people who know each other. Violence is generally embedded in social relations where its use has meaning to victims and perpetrators. For example one of the common triggers for a violent incident can be a situation where someone responds to taunts and harassment in an unexpected way—by rejecting a subordinate role and resisting. Finally, it is mainly men who perpetrate violence. Most offenders in England and Wales are male (accounting for about 90 per cent of stranger attacks) and in 66 per cent of attacks on women the assailant is male. 'More than anything else', says Oliver James, 'violence is caused by not being female' (James, 1995: 75).

REVIEW QUESTIONS

1 What is violence?

2 Try to list as many forms of harm as you can and decide whether they would be considered to be 'violence' or not. Give reasons for your answer.

3 Why is violence enacted by the State likely to be judged differently from violence against the State?

Violence, the body and the civilizing process

Violence is about relationships to and around the body and more particularly about pain, emotions, control and discipline. As such it is an intensely emotional experience, variously invoking among other things, hatred, pleasure, fear and threat. Hence understanding emotions and their social consequences is central to the process of management and control of violence on interpersonal and wider levels. Recently there has been increased attention to the importance of emotion, and in particular shame, in social life, in opposition to the dominant cognitive focus in the human sciences (for example, Scheff and Retzinger, 2001), and such concern echoes earlier sociological theories such as those of Simmel, Goffman and Elias. It is beyond the scope of this introductory chapter to do this, but there is a need for broader conceptualizing of various forms of hurt, injury and threat within a common theoretical framework, which Ray (2011) attempts to provide.

Norbert Elias (1897–1990) famously proposed the thesis of a **'civilizing process'**. This occurred during the transition between European medieval and modern societies during which complex social, cultural and psychological changes occurred that resulted in a reduction in interpersonal violence. This thesis aimed to reverse the view that industrialization and urbanization are inseparable from *rising* violence. Elias claims that the growth of increasingly mannered social interaction was accompanied by increased public intolerance of violence and cruelty. Repugnance towards physical violence increased with advancing thresholds of shame and embarrassment surrounding the body—acts once performed publicly, such as defecation and sexual intercourse, become intensely private. Most people now regard carnivals of violence, such as public executions, or the torture of animals, as deeply repugnant. Underlying this cultural and psychological shift there is a deepening and widening of interdependencies between people which Elias calls 'figurations'.

In medieval society war was the normal state of society and pleasure was derived from cruelty, destruction and torment evidenced, for example, in the mutilation of prisoners of war, burning heretics, public torture and executions. In modern societies there is a concentration of the means of violence in the state. This pacification of everyday life Elias says, moulds 'effects and the standards of the economy of instincts'. (Elias, 1994: 201) By this he means that emotional and instinctual sources of aggression are increasingly restrained and result in more self-controlled behaviour. Elias argued that with the centralization of State power there was a growth in personal restraint and mannered conduct, initially in court society, gradually spreading more widely along with the expansion of trade, urban life, a more complex division of labour, and the formation of 'civil society'. The longer and denser were networks of interdependence, the more people were obliged to attune their actions to those of others and the less their interactions will be marked by overt violence. Elias (1994: 368) suggests an example of these changes, in the difference between a medieval and modern journey. A medieval journey was a difficult and dangerous undertaking, along muddy roads on which there were few other travellers and risk of collision was low. However, the medieval traveller had to be alert to dangers posed by animals, other travellers and bandits. This state of alertness required a volatile temperament and eager readiness to fight and a personality that would be impulsive and resort quickly to violence. On the other hand on modern roads the danger of physical attack is low but the risk of collision high. In this context (typical of the interconnected and complex nature of modern society) the development of control systems based on self-regulation, constant vigilance, foresight and self-control is crucial. These require personalities that are not impulsive but rational, calculating, technically competent.

However, in modern society people still feel the need for excitement—which is provided by institutionalized and regulated activities such as sport, in which rules reduce the risk of injury but gratify need for excitement. Sport institutionalizes calculated violence (especially in contact sports such as rugby) without loss of self-control, while spectators have the opportunity to vicariously enjoy the excitement of contest without the actual violence of earlier spectacles such as gladiatorial struggle. This analysis does raise the issue, though, of how to explain actual violence among rival spectators, which has become a major topic of research pursued particularly by followers of Elias such as Dunning *et al.* (1987). Their work points to factors such as a change in social composition of spectators and decontrolling emotional controls in explaining spectator violence.

Elias argues that over several hundred years there developed increased sensitivity and repugnance towards violence. Is there any evidence for this? Pinker (2011) argues, with reference to Elias, that there has been a historical 'decline of violence' that is 'visible at the scale of millennia, centuries, decades, and years'. It applies over several orders of magnitude of violence, from genocide to war to rioting to homicide to the treatment of children and animals. Pinker cites in support evidence from historical criminologists such as Eisner (2001) for a declining rate of homicide between the thirteenth and twentieth centuries, which is illustrated in Figure 9.1. Eisner (2003) proposes an explanation for this long-term violent crime decline.

These observations are consistent with the view that with modernization came a long-term decline in interpersonal violence although many factors might produce short-term fluctuations such as the rising rates of violent crime in particular years or decades. However, long-range data should be interpreted with caution because of the inadequacy of records over much of this period, changes in key juridical concepts such as *mens rea*, changing rules of evidence and so on. There is evidence that although Britain, for example, became less violent during the first half of the twentieth century than it had been in the nineteenth, levels of interpersonal violence rose again in the latter half and serious violent assaults rose between 1975 and 1996 (see Figure 9.2). However, changes in reporting rules make it appear that there was a steep increase in violent crime in 1998–99, but this is largely a consequence of the National Crime Recoding Standard. By contrast, the BCS (now Crime Survey for England and Wales)[1] data shown in Figure 9.2 indicates a declining trend in interpersonal violence during the same period. Further, Elias was most concerned to show the fragility of the 'civilizing process' by situating it historically. Since it emerged historically it could be subject to reversals and there will remain places 'cultures of violent solutions' in which where its use is commonplace.

Elias' thesis has been influential and offers insight into the formation of the modern self through regulation of violence, in ways that for Smith (1999) parallels Michel Foucault's work on similar themes. Elias describes the formation of a personality structure governed by self-control and foresight combined with feelings of shame, repugnance and embarrassment towards our own and others' behaviour. The pressures of surviving within highly interdependent social networks lead us to treat others and ourselves as a 'danger

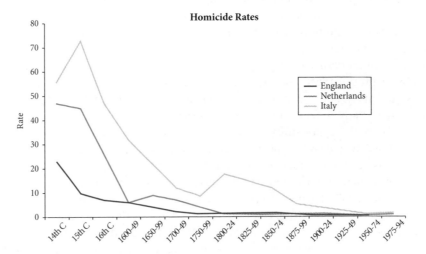

Figure 9.1 Long-term trends in homicide rates for selected countries

Source: Adapted from Eisner (2001).

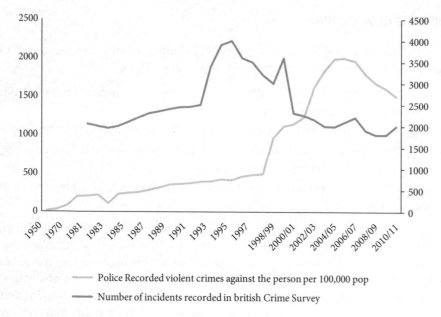

Police Recorded violent crimes against the person per 100,000 pop

Number of incidents recorded in british Crime Survey

Figure 9.2 Trends in violent crime in England and Wales

Source: Crime in England and Wales 2010, Home Office, © Crown Copyright.
NOTE - In 1998/99 [*] there is a steep increase in police recorded violent crime following the National Crime Recording
Standard that changed reporting rules and included offences such as 'common assault' not previously included in violent
crime statistics.

zone'—we feel anxiety about our vulnerability to other's behaviour and to our own
inner drives (Elias, 1994: 445). The experience of these tensions has two consequences
in particular. First, modern human beings draw tight boundaries between themselves
and whatever is 'outside', to the point of doubting the 'reality' of our perceptions of the
outside world. Second, there is the tendency to see ourselves as free and unique sovereign
individuals and to deny that we are shaped by the figurations into which we are born.
Thus, renunciation of violence forms the modern self as individuated and subject to
internal and external techniques of control. This in turn has structured how violence
tends to be viewed in sociological and criminological literature as a threat arising in
some sense from 'outside'—either from somewhere spatially separate, such as transitory
spaces (deserted trains, subways, night metro stations) or from 'below' (the threat to
social order from the dispossessed and dark places of our inner psyche). However, one
theme in recent studies of violence has been to suggest its routine or habitual nature such
that its origins lie within, not outside, and nowhere is safe.

REVIEW QUESTIONS

1 What is the 'civilizing process'?

2 Why is interpersonal violence less in modern than medieval societies?

3 Is it true that the modern person feels repugnance at public displays of violence?

Patterns of violence

Violent crime measured by the BCS is subdivided into a typology of four groupings based broadly on the relationship between suspect and victim:

- domestic violence—including all violent incidents involving partners, ex-partners, household members or other relatives;
- mugging—comprising robbery, attempted robbery and snatch from the person;
- acquaintance violence—includes wounding and assaults in which the victim knew one or more of the offenders, at least by sight;
- stranger violence—includes common assaults and wounding in which the victim did not know the offenders in any way.

Currently available evidence from the BCS suggests that violent crime in England and Wales is still rare (accounting for about 4 per cent of all crimes), although it rose during the 1980s and has fallen fairly consistently since the mid-1990s. According to the BCS, perpetrators and victims often know each other—either as intimates or acquaintances, although the pattern is clearly gendered, with men being represented highly in incidents of stranger violence and women in domestic violence. Victims are most often men aged 16 to 24 (15.1 per cent of that group in the past 12 months), single people living alone (8.9 per cent), single parents (8 per cent), people living in private rented accommodation (7.4 per cent), those living in 'disordered areas' (7.3 per cent) and women between the ages of 16 and 25 (6.9 per cent). Moreover, ethnic minorities—especially Afro-Caribbean and Pakistani British—have twice the risk of being victims of violent crimes than other Britons.

Fear of violence generally exceeds its statistical risk (Croall, 1998: 93–5) and is likely to give rise to anger about threats of crime (Ditton *et al.*, 1999). Yet young men, who are most at risk from assault, express least worry about it while the elderly (who are least at risk) worry most (Croall, 1998: 93–5). There are problems, however, with these kinds of risk assessments. Questions about fear of crime in the BCS do not relate people's answers to their locality which, for example, may have higher than average crime. On the other hand the possibility of risk factors being compounded (for example, if many single parents also live in 'disordered areas' or if many men aged 16–24 are single) is not addressed in these surveys.

Where does violence take place? Violence takes place in all settings although different types are predicted by their location, often in unsurprising ways. Masculine confrontation violence is most common in public leisure areas (such as pubs and clubs) and in the workplace. In fact 25 per cent of reported incidents in England and Wales occur at work and of these 75 per cent are perpetrated by members of the public on practitioners and service providers (ESRC, 2002). High-risk professions include the police, public transport, medical, public transport, bouncers and teachers. Domestic violence takes place largely in the home, where it is still under-reported—for example the BCS consistently finds reported prevalence rates for domestic violence around five times higher in self-completion modules (where the respondent completes an electronic questionnaire) than in face-to-face interviews (Home Office, 2009: 55). This suggests a continuing reluctance amongst victims to report experience of violence directly to other people. However, national level data can obscure how the risk of violence is distributed through geographical space where it is closely related to patterns of inequality and exclusion. In economically abandoned areas of cities the rate of recorded violence quadrupled between 1960 and 2000 (Rosen, 2003: 33) and Castells (1998: 138) argues that there is a systematic relationship between the structural transformations of capital, the growing dereliction of the ghetto and the emergence of a global, yet decentralized criminal economy. In London the rate of recorded assaults in the most deprived tenth of wards is, at 30 per 1,000 of the population, twice the average and five times the rate in the least deprived tenth (Home Office, 2009: 146). These relationships are analysed further in Ray (2011: 63–82).

REVIEW QUESTIONS

1 Why might BCS data be a more reliable indication of the prevalence of violence than prosecution rates?

2 What forms of violence are most common?

3 Who is most at risk from violent assault?

Aggression and masculinity

Steve Hall comments that 'the claim that men commit most acts of physical violence is possibly the nearest that criminology has come to producing an indisputable fact' (Hall, 2002). Crime, especially violent crime, is an overwhelmingly masculine activity. This gender pattern is not new—males have been over-represented in all major violent crime categories since the collection of crime statistics began and the same pattern is found in all countries. According to the UK National Statistics office in 2006, 1.42 million offenders were sentenced for criminal offences in England and Wales, the majority of whom (80 per cent) were male and of these seven per cent were aged less than 18 years old. In the teenage years the gap between girls and boys in delinquency, broadly defined, is relatively small, although the gap in more serious offending is considerably wider (Smith *et al.*, 2001). Offending is highly gender and age related.

Explaining male violence

While it is often taken for granted that (especially young) men do more crime than women, recent work has undertaken more complex analysis of the nature of masculinity and its relationship with violent crime. A division has appeared between bio-social, evolutionary approaches on the one hand and sociological explanations on the other.

Evolutionary lag

Evolutionary explanations point out that for 99 per cent of our history humans have lived in small hunting groups in which violence was natural rather than pathological since it aided survival. Masculine violence aided hunting success and maximized food supply while men competed with one another for reproductive mates. However, this violence would be balanced by a need to preserve the size of the group, thus cultural norms of reciprocity and reconciliation emerged to limit violence (Hatty, 2000: 50). However, in modern societies violence has become dysfunctional and is no longer restrained by environmental pressures. Pinker (2011) kind of sits in both camps—claiming both that aggressiveness has psycho-environmental bases, but also that increased social complexity and learned social influences have led to long-term diminution of violence.

While evolutionary psychology is becoming increasingly influential, it is problematic to suggest that human aggressiveness is a kind of biosocial lag from an earlier developmental state. In a wide-ranging comparative study of violence among humans and other primates, Eric Fromm (1979) argued that human violence has become pathological (detached from self-defence and hunting) and that 'man is the only mass murderer'. Evolutionary theory attempts to explain aggressiveness in terms of a *continuation* of primal tendencies, when in fact humans display *more* destructive violence than other primates do. Evolutionary accounts pay little regard to the symbolic and culturally mediated forms that violence can take (for example in rituals) and cannot easily explain why rates of violence vary among locales and countries. If there is an underlying biological tendency towards masculine violence this should manifest similarly in different cultures and places, which it clearly does not. Further, James (2002) has taken issue with evolutionary theories of human aggression, arguing that family influences are critical. He claims that children born to violent parents but raised in peaceable households are no more likely to have violent criminal records than those born to non-violent parents.

Social theories and 'hegemonic masculinities'

There are many social and cultural theories of violent behaviour that emphasize social learning, youth sub-cultures, economic inequality and the potential thrill and enjoyment of violence (see for example Katz, 1988). Through the process of gender socialization (how we learn the attributes of 'masculine' and 'feminine' behaviour) violence may acquire different meanings for men and women. Through violence men may attempt to affirm a positive self-concept, enhance self-esteem and reclaim personal power, while women on the other hand may see violence as a failure of self-control. Further Campbell (1993) suggests that men tend to engage in justifications for violence that minimize their use of violence while women are more likely to express guilt. Justifications for violence are learned speech acts that prepare ground for violence and deploy wider available narratives in society.

In these terms excess male violence reflects patterns of socialization in which the male role involves greater readiness to use violence as a means of control and assertion of power. In Connell's (1995) and Messerschmidt's (1993 and 1997) theory of 'hegemonic masculinities', masculinity is viewed as a crucial point of intersection of different sources and forms of power, stratification, desire and identity.[2] Unlike socialization theories, Connell and Messerschmidt emphasize performance and choice rather than passively learnt behaviour. Violent behaviour is *chosen* while calling upon dominant discourses of masculinity for support and legitimation. Connell thus sees crime as a way of 'doing gender'; which manifests differently in social situations structured by the influences of race, class and age. Violence is a resource that men can call upon based in prevailing idealized cultural conceptions involving the dominance over women, heterosexuality, the pursuit of sexual gratification, and independence.

Criminal behaviour is seen here as a resource for 'masculine validation'. For example, white, middle-class boys can achieve masculinity through moderate academic success, sports, and preparation for a career. But schools are repressive and authoritarian, so these boys will deviate outside of school through for example vandalism, drinking and petty theft. This is 'opposition masculinity' that demonstrates to peers dominance, control, and aggressiveness. White, working-class boys on the other hand tend to demonstrate opposition masculinity outside of school, but also in school, through fighting, vandalism and so on. They do still have opportunities in the labour market, however, whereas disadvantaged (racial minority and lower-class) boys have even fewer conventional opportunities to achieve the normative ideas associated with masculinity (they perceive no future in schooling or good job prospects in the real world), and are more likely to use illegal means like robbery and crimes of violence to demonstrate their masculinity. They are more likely to engage in serious crime in and out of school.

How useful is the concept of **hegemonic masculinity** for explaining the predominance of men in violent crime figures? This approach has the advantage of avoiding reification of 'masculine' and 'feminine' traits and emphasizing the active process of 'doing gender'. But one limitation is that it does not explain the meaning of crime perpetrated by women, while at the same time 'over-predicting' male criminality (see Miller, 2002). There are problems with specifying what performance of masculinity is hegemonic since this will vary by class, ethnicity and generation (Demetriou, 2001). Connell and Messerschmidt (2005) respond to these and other critiques but present a reformulated concept of hegemonic masculinity that is explicitly ambiguous. Further, there is not a great deal of empirical support for the theory. One exception is Krienert (2003) who undertook a study of 704 offenders in Nebraska and found that masculine traits alone failed to predict violent events. But men with very high 'masculine' traits and few acceptable outlets to assert masculinity (such as education, marital status, children, employment and income) *were* more likely to have been involved in violent incidents. Even so, the theory lacks a subjective or motivational account of the meanings of violence for perpetrators, and Messerschmidt cannot show why some men are violent and (most) others are not. Like many theories of crime it over-predicts incidence since if the theory were straightforwardly true, then the incidence of violent behaviour would be much higher than it is.

'Crisis of masculinity'

Dominant forms of masculinity are at various historical periods thrown into crisis, a process also related to violent behaviour. Suzanne Hatty (2000: 6) comments, 'Violence is the prerogative of the youthful male especially when confronted by the contradictions and paradoxes of thwarted desire and personal and social disempowerment'. This account suggests that unemployment and decline of traditional working class male occupations combined with increasing women's equality provokes a **'crisis of masculinity'**.

Whereas the fathers and grandfathers of today's young men spent their lives in male spaces of manual work and associated leisure activities, young working-class men are often unemployed and spend time at home or on the street. However, home is still a female space, whereas the street offers opportunities for alternative experiences of dominance and risk-taking—joyriding, theft, burglary, competition and 'business'—drugs and organized crime. At the same time youth cultures emerge that emphasize and exaggerate features of traditional white working-class masculine appearance and behaviour. Nayak (1999) argues that skinhead culture, for example, represents a consolidation of masculinity, sexuality and white ethnicity in working-class culture. Similarly Hebdige (1987) regarded skinheads as expressing a nostalgic exaggeration of white working-class characteristics and 'mime of awkward masculinity' that was a macho, working-class, white (often racist) 'geometry of menace'. The uniform—boots, braces and cropped hair—represented a caricature of the traditional dress mode of a working man.

Philippe Bourgois' (1996) study of Puerto Rican migrants to the USA exemplifies this argument. This is an ethnographic study of street-level drug dealers in East Harlem (USA) who had found that the work they had migrated to do was disappearing but they would not take work in the service sector, which was regarded as 'women's work'. However, their wives did take this work and gained more financial independence than they had previously had, thereby threatening the basis of male dominance in the household. The men often took refuge in the drug economy where there were very violent norms of gang rape, sexual conquest, abandonment of families and 'real manhood' based on devotion to group membership. Thus, the crisis of masculinity is more acute at lower socio-economic locations where violence is way of confirming status in a street culture. Moreover, this is more consistent with the dynamics of shame and violence described by Scheff and Retzinger (2001) than an outcome of the confidence of enjoying 'hegemonic' power.

Rich insight into changing cultural representations of masculinity and violence can be found in popular culture and especially the film. Post-World War II masculine heroes showed little emotional sensitivity and were prone to impulsivity and anger. War was 'what good men do' and its portrayal was unproblematic especially since in the war zone sexual differentiation was reaffirmed. In the later genre of 'hard body' films such as *Rambo First Blood Part Two* (1985) and *Die Hard* (1988) violence and single-handed rescue fantasy is unproblematic and unchallenging but also exaggerated, suggesting uncertainty about real life masculine roles. Hard masculine body cinematic representations of combat—robotic masculinity of *Robocop* and *Judge Dredd*—concealed a growing crisis in masculinity, in which an alienated individual experiences potency through experiencing and inflicting pain. This idea becomes thematic in later films and is often related to violence. For example in *Falling Down* (1993) a middle-class man, 'D-Fens' (Michael Douglas) divorced and unemployed, unable to visit his children, engages in an escalating spree of violence that ends with his own demise. Playing to the theme of compromised masculinity, D-Fens is successfully pursued by Detective Prendergast of the LAPD (Robert Duvall) who took a 'safe' desk job some years back to placate his 'bossy' wife. The denouement in which D-Fens is shot while carrying only a toy gun compounds the sense of masculine aggression as impotent rage. David Fincher's *Fight Club* (1999) offers a more complex exploration of the crisis of masculinity and violence. Though sometimes regarded as an overtly masculine film, the powerful white masculinity of the 1980s and hard body films of the 1990s is absent. It features Jack (the narrator) and Tyler Durden his destructive alter ego whom we find first in a support group for men recovering from testicular cancer ('remaining men together') where following chemotherapy, one character, Bob, has lost his testicles and grown breasts symbolizing masculinity's demise. Jack's addiction to self-help groups has replaced his addiction to consumerism (again 'feminized' activity), which is then replaced by a search for authentic masculinity in the self-inflicted violence of the fight club. But the sole woman character Marla Singer (Helen Bonham-Carter) is dominant in the unfolding plot and enables Jack to renounce violence. However, when the film looks as though it has reverted to a familiar hero-rescue fantasy Jack is unable to prevent the terrorists of Project Mayhem from blowing up large commercial buildings, their falling symbolizing the failure of the masculine corporate world. Multiple cultural representations of masculinity and femininity are then available and these can be deployed in various ways—but one contemporary theme is that violence may be an outcome of a perceived *failure* to perform traditional masculine roles rather than necessarily an emanation of power. These kinds of filmic representations resonate with analysts who suggest that violence is a manifestation of (perceived) powerlessness rather than of power.

REVIEW QUESTIONS

1 Why is violent crime predominantly 'masculine'?

2 What do you understand by 'hegemonic masculinities'?

3 Is there a 'crisis of masculinity'? If so, why should it manifest in violence?

Violence in the private sphere

Closely related to masculinity and violence is the issue of violence against women and children within the family, which can take many different forms, including physical assault, rape and sexual violence, psychological or emotional violence, torture, financial abuse including dowry-related violence, and control of movement and of social contacts. For centuries domestic violence was not considered a serious problem. For example, it is sometimes claimed that in 1782 the English Judge Francis Buller ruled it permissible to beat a wife with a stick no wider than a thumb. There is some doubt as to whether the ruling was ever given, but English common law sanctioned violence against women and it is only from the 1980s that the police have seriously begun to pursue offenders. This change in perceptions of seriousness of domestic violence arose from at least four developments (Pahl *et al.*, 2004):

- feminist activism in the 1970s identified this as an issue that would give practical expression to their more general concern about the position of women;

- the opening of women's refuges made visible what had previously been hidden;

- the growth of Women's Aid, as a coordinating body for the growing number of refuges, brought the activists together to share ideas and experience and to work for increased political visibility for their analysis;

- feminist scholars and activists were energetic in researching the issue and in pressing for more effective and appropriate action by relevant agencies.

How extensive is domestic violence? Despite the widespread association of violence with public street crime, domestic violence represents a significant proportion of crimes known to the police. The London Metropolitan Police Service (MPS) receives around 100,000 domestic violence calls each year, accounting for one in 20 notified offences (Ray, 2011: 110). BCS data records experience of domestic violence both during the past 12 months and during a lifetime. In answer to the question 'have you experienced domestic violence during the past twelve months?', 4.2 per cent of women *and* men experienced assault, although twice as many women as men had been injured, suffered repeated violence and frightening threats. Although this may create the impression that men and women experience domestic violence roughly equally, victimization takes two distinct patterns. One, accounting for about 10 per cent of cases, which both women and men perpetrate is marked by occasional anger and aggression; the other, which is more likely to be 'male', is characterized by severe escalating violence and terrorization (Mirrlees-Black, 1999). This second type is more widespread. When asked about lifetime prevalence, a ratio of 1:4 women report being assaulted by male partner, 1:8 women have been assaulted repeatedly; while 1:6 men reported occasional assault and 1:20 repeated assaults. Further, domestic violence typically escalates so that previous violence is a predictor of further violence—35 per cent of second incidents occur within five weeks of first and domestic violence has the highest rate of repeat victimization of any violent crime (MPS, 2003).

Reported domestic violence varies considerably worldwide (ranging between 10 and 69 per cent of violent offences in different countries) and definitions vary considerably too, along with levels of culturally accepted violence. Statistics alone offer only limited insight into the issue. Questions such as 'have you ever been abused?' or even behaviourally specific questions might fail to take account of the atmosphere of terror in violent relationships and its effects on children. Some men may enjoy inflicting violence. One of the women interviewed by Hanmer (2000: 12) reported that 'the more violence he did to me the happier he would be ... After he had hit me, he would say "Sit there in front of me, if I see any tears in your eyes then see what happens"'. At the same time men may blame women for provoking violence and adopt the posture of victims (Glasser, 1998), which is a common feature of other violent offenders (Ray *et al.*, 2003). Some estimates suggest that many fathers in violent families also abuse children in the home and even those who do not suffer abuse will be witnesses to violence. Such children are likely to suffer from confused and torn loyalties; they may feel ashamed, guilty, isolated and alone; they may respond by trying to protect their mothers, by phoning the police, or most dangerously, by trying to restrain their fathers (Krug *et al.*, 2002).

The World Health Organization (WHO) indicates that the triggers for domestic violence are remarkably consistent across all countries and cultures (Krug *et al.*, 2002: 120). These include:

- 'not obeying the husband'
- 'arguing back'

- 'not having food ready on time'
- 'not caring adequately for children or home'
- 'questioning about money and girlfriends'
- 'going out without permission'
- 'refusing sex'
- pregnancy.[3]

One of the conclusions that can be drawn from this is that domestic violence is primarily about the exercise of power and a response to perceived challenges to male power. Even so, domestic violence occurs more in some settings and places than others and this patterning still requires more specific explanation.

Explanations

Many explanations of domestic violence follow the patterns of explanations of violence in general. There are explanations that focus on individual pathologies (for example, paranoid or narcissistic disorders), socialization (many abusers have come from dysfunctional and violent families) and social structural (for example, poor education, unemployment, low income and so on). There is an association between domestic violence and low socio-economic status (as there is for violence in general) and Finney (2004–05: 9) found that 'indicators of socio-economic status such as household income, vehicle ownership, tenure type and council/non-council areas, suggest fairly consistently that higher prevalence rates of intimate abuse are associated with relatively lower levels of socioeconomic status'. Similar findings are reported in as Walby and Allen (2004). It is true that these accounts do not explain middle-class domestic violence (for example, Pahl *et al.*, 2004) and feminist researchers suggest that rather than look for specific pathologies amongst perpetrators we should recognize that domestic violence is ubiquitous and a routine means of maintaining patriarchal power and authority. Feminist researchers emphasize factors such as:

- the historically subordinate position of women within marriage;
- women's responsibility for childcare (and consequent exclusion from the labour market and weak economic position in the household);
- patriarchy that reproduces male power/female dependence at all levels—social, cultural and economic;
- machismo cultures and the tacit or explicit approval of male violence.

However, one weakness of these explanations is that, like the theory of hegemonic masculinities, they encounter the problem of over-prediction. If violence were routinely inscribed into intimate heterosexual relations then we would expect to find a higher incidence than we do, even allowing for significant under-reporting. A broader approach that incorporates feminist analysis would be a more multi-factorial one that estimates the risk of domestic violence across a number of dimensions. The model set out in Table 9.1 based on the WHO report on violence and health (Krug *et al.*, 2002: 98) attempts to

Table 9.1 Risk factors in domestic violence

LEVEL	Individual	Relationship	Community	Societal
FACTOR	• Young	• Conflict	• Weak community sanctions	• Traditional gender norms
	• Alcohol abuse	• Marital instability	• Poverty	• Social norms supportive of violence 'machocultures'
	• Depression Personality disorder	• Economic stress	• Low social capital	
	• Low educational attainment	• Dysfunctional families		

Source: Krug *et al.* (2002: 98)

combine individual, relationship, community and societal levels of analysis while identifying markers of risk, rather than causes of violence. In this model poverty causes stress, inadequacy, a 'crisis of masculinity' while making it more difficult for women to leave abusive relationships. Social capital refers to social trust that facilitates coordination and cooperation for mutual benefit, so that people believe that a benefit granted now will be repaid indirectly within a community in the future. While this model may explain why some societies and individuals are more violent than others, we do not know the specific and relative weights to give the factors nor how they operate on different levels. However, these factors suggest that the dynamics of power and powerlessness in domestic violence might be complex and as Schrock and Padavic (2007) argue, 'men who harm women often do so when their sense of traditional manhood—such as being a breadwinner or having women meet their often-unspoken needs—is threatened'.

REVIEW QUESTIONS

1 How widespread is domestic violence?

2 Why might official figures under-represent its actual prevalence?

3 What are the causes of domestic violence?

Racist violence

Racist violence in the UK came under sharp public scrutiny following the murder of a black teenager, Stephen Lawrence, by a gang of racist white youths in 1993 and the

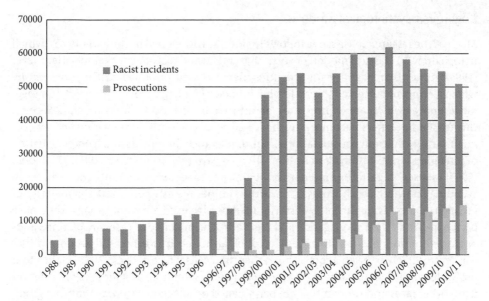

Figure 9.3 Racist incidents reported to the police in England and Wales

Sources: Home Office Racist Incident Reports, CPS Reports 1997–2011 and Statistics on Race and the Criminal Justice System 2010 http://www.justice.gov.uk/downloads/statistics/mojstats/stats-race-cjs-2010.pdf

subsequent public inquiry that reported in 1999 (Macpherson, 1999).[4] Criticism of the police investigation and wider suggestion that the police were 'institutionally racist' resulted in widespread scrutiny of institutional practices in the police and other public organizations of ways in which racism might be inscribed in routine practices and beliefs.[5] Among the UK police it resulted in the creation of many new practices, training, and requirements to report, record and act on allegations of racist harassment and assault. Moreover, the targeting of racist violence, along with domestic and homophobic violence is part of a wider social and legal agenda to tackle 'hate' or bias crimes where the victim is selected on the grounds of their social status. Partly as a result of this, the numbers of recorded racist incidents in England and Wales rose from 15,000 in 1988 to 25,000 in 1999, and 57,902 in 2006 (see Figure 9.3).

However, the dramatic increase in reporting of racist incidents (within which increasing proportions are serious assaults) was accompanied by slow increases in convictions, although these rose between 2006 and 2007 and 2010–11. The 'proportion of successful convictions across all types of **hate crime** has increased from 76.8% to 82.8%, while the number of prosecutions has also increased from 12,535 to 15,284' (CPS, 2011: 4).

Explaining racist violence

The existing data provide several causal models of racist violence. These are generally multivariate models although there is again little attempt to weight the various factors cited and they are all usually assumed to be relevant.

Cognitive psychological models

Much of the research in this area follows hypotheses developed in the early 1990s, which in turn drew on classical models of authoritarianism and racism. For example, Heitmeyer (1994) argues that hostility towards foreigners is based on an identifiable process by which feelings of perceived threat develop into racist violence. First, feelings of 'estrangement' appear which are expressed as 'an attitude of distance' and 'contempt'. Second, this fear of foreigners becomes overshadowed by a 'competitive stance fuelled by economic and/or cultural considerations'. Third, tolerance disappears and 'complete hatred of foreigners' arises resulting in hostile 'offensive struggle' (Heitmeyer, 1994: 17). Bjørgo (1994) focuses on patterns and motives of violence towards immigrants and refugees in Scandinavia where youth gangs often with criminal records perpetrate the majority of racist incidents. Though not necessarily members of extreme right groups, they have been exposed to their propaganda and methods. The majority of cases are planned and/ or carried out under the influence of alcohol, although it is generally recognized that this is most likely to be an aggravating rather than causal factor. Beck (2000) claims that pro-violent attitudes towards black and Asian people stem from archaic belief in inferiority of other races and women that are perpetuated by allegiance to wider cultural group experience. These models regard the racist offender as having a distinctive personality that predisposes them to both racism and violence. Violent racism arises from poor and problematic moral reasoning, cognitive defects, inability to accept the impact of violence on the victim, a predisposition to resort to violence and a 'distorted worldview'. These explanatory models inform many current intervention programmes in the UK probation service.

Social process models

There is considerable evidence that perpetrators' racist views are shared by the communities to which they belong and provide a source of reinforcement and justification of their behaviour, at least by not condemning it (for example, Sibbitt, 1997 and Ray *et al.*, 2003). This illustrates how human behaviour is not simply 'caused' but is embedded in systems of belief, legitimation and justification within which it appears to be acceptable. Sibbitt (1997) argues that prejudice permeates whole communities that have entrenched problems of socioeconomic deprivation and crime and 'spawn' violent perpetrators through mutually supportive relationships between the perpetrator and the wider community (1997: 101). Hence she speaks of 'perpetrator communities' that scapegoat their problems onto visible minorities who serve to provide an external focus for their dissatisfaction, frustration and alienation. Sibbitt developed a typology of different groups, stratified by generational experiences:

- the pensioners—long-term residents who feel that the area has been 'invaded';
- the 'people next door'—insecure adults who latch onto their parents' racialization of problems;
- the 'problem family'—with poor mental or physical health, who behave abusively towards children who in turn are low achievers and learn racist abusive behaviour;

- racist and antisocial behaviour is then transmitted to younger age groups who, although they will have black friends at school, learn to participate in racist violence and bullying.

Ray *et al.* (2003) further found that racist offenders tended to scapegoat South Asians for community problems of unemployment, the decline of local manufacturing, and (somewhat paradoxically) for the rise in local crime. There was evidence here of the kind of 'crisis in masculinity'; noted elsewhere in this chapter. Ray *et al.* (2003) found a contrast between the global city image of central Manchester and the isolated and deprived life on outer-city housing estates from which many racially motivated offenders came. The latter expressed hostility at exclusion that was projected onto South Asians as symbols of an apparently cosmopolitan culture.

A conclusion of these studies is that there are links between deprivation, social and personal disorganization and racist violence. Similar themes arise in the inquiry reports into the disturbances in English towns in 2001, which identify a territorial mentality, residential segregation and the deep fracturing of communities on racial, generational and religious lines. Home Office reports into the disturbances put considerable weight on residential segregation, which is in turn symptomatic of several underlying structural conditions (Home Office, 2002: 12). These include:

- systematic disadvantage in that many members of ethnic minorities can only afford cheaper housing;
- higher unemployment than in the majority community, especially in Bangladeshi and Pakistani communities;
- cultural cohesion and choice amongst minority communities, which is possibly linked to fear of racist attacks and hostility from the surrounding areas;
- discrimination in council housing allocation that has been a major cause of residential segregation.

These residential concentrations though could themselves be responses to racism and exclusion.

Cultural factors

Racism is not confined to areas of deprivation—it also affects rural, suburban and prosperous areas as well as blighted inner-city locales (Bowling and Phillips, 2002: 115). It can increase during periods of higher consumption, as it did during the 1990s. In addition to deprivation as a cause of racist violence, there are cultural logics in which deeply rooted fears and beliefs about 'contamination' by other cultures are crucial. One study of racist Internet chat rooms found no reliable connections between unemployment and racist hate but did find a correlation with politicized mobilization, which was associated with fears of threats to integrity and in particular of interracial marriage (Glasser *et al.*, 2002). Again Back (2002) found that white supremacist Internet sites were preoccupied with fears of cultural 'pollution' manifest in 'White Singles' dating pages. These cultural fears are in turn rooted in the colonial past of European nations and a belief in the cultural and 'civilizational' inferiority of ethnic minorities that paradoxically pose a threat because of their supposed global power. Such views are of course part of articulated racist worldviews and other evidence indicates that these are relatively rare even amongst racist offenders (Ray *et al.*, 2003). Nonetheless, these assumptions and fears may be part of the cultural background of racism even when they are not explicitly articulated.

REVIEW QUESTIONS

1 Why did recorded racist incidents in the UK rise during the late 1990s and 2000s?

2 How do you explain racist violence?

3 Are there links between 'hegemonic masculinity' and racism?

Homicides

The most extreme form of violence is homicide. This is rare in the UK and in most other developed countries—generally ranging between one and two per 100,000 of the population per annum (Ray 2011: 126). Like any other crime homicide is patterned by class, gender and ethnicity. Men are more likely to be both victims and offenders than are women and men are more likely to be killed by strangers—the highest risk of victimization in the UK is among Afro-Caribbean men aged between 21 to 25. Women are more at risk from spouses or former spouses with 20 per cent of all murders occurring among spouses (Metropolitan Police Service, 2003). Key factors in explaining homicide rates have been shown to include multiple deprivation, low social mobility, income inequality, a high proportion of 19- to 29-year-olds in a locality, and a high correlation between inequality measured by the Gini coefficient and homicide (Ray, 2011: 113–47).[6] The relationship between income inequality and homicide rates is remarkably consistent cross-nationally (Daly *et al.*, 2001) although it is unlikely to be sufficient to explain variations in the rate, and other factors will be relevant.

Messner's (1989) now famous study claimed that there was a close relationship between inequality and homicide rates. Savolainen (2000) argues (using anomie theory) that the effect of economic inequality on the level of lethal violence is limited to nations characterized by relatively weak collective institutions of social protection (such as welfare states). He tests this hypothesis with two cross-national data sets drawn from Finland and Mexico. Both settings suggest that the effects of income inequality on homicide can be mitigated by the strength of the welfare state. Nations that protect their citizens from the vicissitudes of market forces appear to be immune to the homicidal effects of economic inequality. This suggests that it is the social disorganization caused by sharp inequality rather than the inequality itself that is the determining factor. Similarly, Kawachi *et al.* (1999) argue that the degree of cohesiveness in social relations among citizens, measured, for instance, by indicators of 'social capital', affects the level of violent crimes, including homicides, that were 'consistently associated with relative deprivation (income inequality) and indicators of low social capital'. Social capital here refers to the extent of voluntary groups, involvement in the community, social networks and levels of social trust. The process that is suggested by studies like these is that relative poverty causes feelings of stress, inadequacy, 'crisis of masculinity' and undermines social capital. This in turn creates a context conducive to risk taking, criminality and increasingly violent competition for resources such as street business and dominance. However, other factors will be relevant too. Messner (1989) pointed out that in addition to inequality; an aggravating factor would be the mechanism by which inequality was reproduced—so that for example inequality based on racist exclusion would result in high levels of diffuse hostility and a high homicide rate. It is worth noting in this context that South Africa, where there is a long and bitter history of apartheid, has one of the highest homicide rates in the world at 600 per million per annum (Ray 2011: 142) These factors may also be compounded by cultural attitudes towards violence. Commenting on higher rates of homicide in southern as opposed to northern states in the USA, Cohen and Nisbett (1997) argue that southerners articulate and transmit attitudes that legitimate and encourage violence, especially violence in defence of personal and familial honour.

REVIEW QUESTIONS

1 How is the homicide rate related to inequality?

2 Who is most at risk from homicide?

3 How relevant are cultural factors in explaining the homicide rate?

CONCLUSION

One consequence of the civilizing process is an increased sensitivity to and fear of violence, which constitutes a threat to the integrity of the controlled and individualized self. There is evidence for a gradual diminution of interpersonal violence in modern societies and social and political agendas around the control of violent emotions, such as **hate crime** legislation, illustrates how the civilizing process has increased repugnance towards violence and its causes. At the same time violence and its threat is a routine part of everyday life for large numbers of people in settings of the street, home, neighbourhood, workplace and leisure activities. A great deal of research focuses on interpersonal violence and is accompanied by theoretical explanations that address the circumstances of individual perpetrators. Clearly, however, violence has multiple manifestations—and most of the theories discussed here point at least implicitly towards wider societal issues. In each type of violent behaviour examined here, explanations raise issues of power and dominance, but also powerlessness and inequality, the effects of which are mediated by broader cultural contexts. In order to develop a more comprehensive theory of violence we need to elaborate the ways in which power and exclusion, and the consequences of increasingly complex patterns of inequality intersect with emotional life and forms of socialization. There is clearly an important issue around masculinities and violence that is receiving increasing attention in the literature along with recognition that 'masculinity' cannot (any more than 'femininity') be viewed as a simple construction, but has multiple cultural and psychosocial manifestations. Once we begin to unravel the complex links between social, economic and cultural reproduction, gender socialization and the intersecting dimensions of identity and class—we may begin to understand how violence is embedded in everyday life.

QUESTIONS FOR DISCUSSION

1   What is violence and how are definitions linked to power? Consider different forms of harm to people and whether these would be considered 'violence' or not. Why?

2   Why do you think violent crime increased in the UK and many other countries in the later twentieth century? Do explanations of violence outlined here account for this?

3   What is the relationship between masculinity and violence? Is there a 'crisis of masculinity' and how might this be connected with violent behaviour?

GUIDE TO FURTHER READING

Bowling, B. (1998) *Violent Racism: Victimisation, Policing and Social Context*. Oxford, Clarendon Press.

This is a detailed analysis of official documents and historical origins of racist violence. Bowling uses a case study to analyse the language of white supremacy and the experience of racist victimization.

Collins, R. (2008) *Violence—A Macro-Sociological Theory*. Oxford: Princeton University Press.

This is a major study of the microdynamics of aggression and violence with detailed case studies that aims of develop a general theory of violence as a situational process. His core thesis is that violence is difficult and its enactment has to overcome deep inhibitions—the interaction processes of which are the main focus of the book.

Messerschmidt, J. (1993) *Masculinities and Crime*. Lanham, MD: Rowman & Littlefield.

This has become a key text in theorizing the relationship between masculinities and crime and uses the theory of 'hegemonic masculinities'.

Ray, L. (2011) *Violence and Society*. London: Sage.

This is an interdisciplinary text that draws on evidence from sociology, criminology, primate studies and archaeology to shed light on arguments about the social construction and innate nature of violence.

Scheff, T.J. (2000) 'Shame and the social bond: A sociological theory', *Sociological Theory* 18(1): 84–99.

Develops a theory of the links between social solidarity, emotions, anger and violence. Links with work inspired by John Braithwaite on shame and reintegrative shaming.

Wilson, D. (2007) *Serial Killers: Hunting Britons and their Victims, 1960–2006*. Winchester: Waterside Press.

A scholarly account of serial killing in the UK but based on the victims of serial killers, rather than the 'medical-psychological' tradition of understanding the motivation of the serial killer.

WEB LINKS

http://www.worldbank.org/poverty/inequal/abstracts/violence.htm

World Bank Poverty Net website. This is a portal into articles, discussions and other material on the relationship between inequality and violence.

http://www.who.int/violence_injury_prevention/violence/world_report/en/

World Health Organization. World report on violence and health.

http://www.norberteliasfoundation.nl /

The Norbert Elias Foundation. Access to Figurations an on-line journal with discussions and reviews and other Elias related material.

http://www.disastercenter.com/crime/

US crime statistics 1960–2006

http://projects.nytimes.com/crime/homicides/map

New York Times (2010) 'Murder: New York City' (A map showing yearly and cumulative homicides 2003–11)

REFERENCES

Beck, A. (2000) *Prisoners of Hate*. New York: Harper Collins.

Bjørgo, T. and Witte, R. (eds) (1994) *Racist Violence in Europe*. London: St Martin's Press.

Bourgois, P. (1996) *In Search of Respect*. Cambridge: Cambridge University Press.

Bowling, B. and Phillips, C. (2002) *Racism, Crime and Justice*. London: Longman.

Campbell, B. (1993) *Men, Women, Aggression*. London: Basic Books.

Castells, E. (1998) *End of Millennium, The Information Age: Economy, Society and Culture* Vol. III. Oxford: Blackwell.

Cohen, D. and Nisbett, R.E. (1997) 'Field experiments examining the culture of honor: The role of institutions perpetuating norms about violence', *Personality and Social Psychology Bulletin* 23, 11: 1188–99.

Collins, R. (2008) *Violence—A Macro-Sociological Theory*. Princeton: Princeton University Press.

Connell, R. and Messerschmidt, J. (2005) 'Hegemonic Masculinity—Rethinking the Concept', *Gender and Society* 19, 6: 829–59.

Connell, R. (1995) *Masculinities*. Cambridge: Polity Press.

CPS (2011) *Hate crime and crimes against older people report 2010–2011* http://www.cps.gov.uk/publications/docs/cps_hate_crime_report_2011.pdf.

Croall, H. (1988) *Crime and Society in Britain*. London: Pearson.

Daly, M., Wilson, M., and Vasdev, S. (2001) 'Income Inequality and Homicide rates in Canada', *Canadian Journal of Criminology* 43, 2: 19–36.

Demetriou, D.Z. (2001) 'Connell's concept of hegemonic masculinity: a critique', *Theory and Society* 30, 3: 337–61.

Ditton, J., Farrall, S., Bannister, J., Gilchrist, E., and Pease, K. (1999) 'Reactions to Victimisation: Why Has Anger Been Ignored?', *Crime Prevention and Community Safety: an International Journal* 1, 3: 37–54.

Dunning, E., Murphy, P., and Williams, J. (1987) *The Roots of Football Hooliganism*. London: Routledge.

Eisner, M. (2001) 'Modernization, Self-control and Lethal violence. The Long-term Dynamics of European Homicide Rates in Theoretical Perspective', *British Journal of Criminology* 41, 4: 618–38.

Eisner, M (2003) 'Long-Term Historical Trends in Violent Crime', *Crime and Justice; A Review of Research*, 30: 83–142.

Elias, N. (1994) *The Civilizing Process*. Oxford: Blackwell.

ESRC (2002) *ESRC Violence Research Programme—Taking Stock*. Royal Holloway: HMSO.

Finney, A. (2006) *Domestic Violence, sexual assault and stalking: findings from the British Crime Survey*. Home Office Online Report 12/06 http://www.homeoffice.gov.uk/rds/pdfs06/rdsolr1206.pdf.

Fromm, E. (1979), *Anatomy of Human Destructiveness*. London: Cape.

Glasser, J., Dixit, J., and Green, D.P. (2002) 'Studying Hate Crime with the Internet: What Makes Racists Advocate Racial Violence?', *Journal of Social Issues* 58, 1: 177–93.

Glasser, M. (1998) 'On Violence: a Preliminary Communication', *International Journal of Psycho-Analysis* 79, 5: 887–902.

Hall, S. (2002) 'Daubing the drudges of fury—Men, violence and the piety of the 'hegemonic masculinity' thesis', *Theoretical Criminology* 6, 1: 35–61.

Hanmer, J. (2000) 'Domestic violence and gender relations: contexts and connections' in J. Hanmer and C. Itzin (eds) *Home Truths About Domestic Violence*. London: Routledge, 9–23.

Hatty, S. (2000) *Masculinities, Violence and Culture*. London: Sage Publications.

Hearn, J. (1998) *The Violences of Men*. London: Sage.

Hebdige, D. (1987) *Subculture—Meaning of Style*. London: Methuen.

Heitmeyer, W. (1994) 'Hostility and violence towards foreigners in Germany' in Børgo and Witte. *Racist Violence in Europe*, 17–28.

Home Office (2002) *A Report of the Independent Review Team Chaired by Ted Cantle*. London: Home Office.

Home Office (2009) *Crime in England and Wales 2008/09* vol 1 Edited by: Walker, A., Flatley, J., Kershaw, C. and Moon, D. http://www.homeoffice.gov.uk/rds/pdfs09/hosb1109vol1.pdf.

Jackman, M.R. (2002) 'Violence in Social Life', *Annual Review of Sociology* 28: 387–415.

James, O. (1995) *Juvenile Violence in a Winner-Loser Culture*. London: Free Association Books.

James, O. (2002) *They F*** You Up*. London: Bloomsbury.

Katz, J. (1988) *Seductions of Crime—moral and sensual attractions in doing evil*. NY: Basic Books

Kawachi I., Kennedy B.P. and Wilkinson, R.G. (1999) 'Crime: Social Disorganization and Relative Deprivation', *Social Science and Medicine* 48, 6: 719–31.

Kelly, L. (1987) *Surviving Sexual Violence*. Cambridge: Polity.

Krienert, J.L. (2003) 'Masculinity and Crime: A Quantitative Exploration of Messerschmidt's Hypothesis', *Electronic Journal of Sociology* http://www.sociology.org/content/vol7.2/01_krienert.html.

Krug, E.G., Dahlberg, L.L., Mercy, J.A., Zwi A.B., and Lozano, A. (eds) (2002) 'World report on violence and health', Geneva: World Health Organization.

Macpherson, W. (1999) *The Stephen Lawrence Inquiry. Report of an Inquiry by Sir William Macpherson of Cluny* (Cm 4262). London: The Stationery Office http://www.archive.official-documents.co.uk/document/cm42/4262/sli-00.htm.

Malešević, S (2010) *The Sociology of War and Violence*. Cambridge: Cambridge University Press.

Messerschmidt, J. (1993) *Masculinities and Crime*. Lanham, MD: Rowman & Littlefield.

Messerschmidt, J. (1997) *Crime as Structured Action*. London: Sage.

Messner, S. (1989) 'Economic Distribution and Homicide Rates: Further Evidence on the Cost of Inequality', *American Sociological Review* 54, 4: 597–612.

Metropolitan Police Service (2003) *Findings from the Multi-Agency Domestic Violence Murder Reviews in London*. London: Metropolitan Police Service.

Miller, J. (2002) 'The strengths and limits of 'doing gender' for understanding street crime', *Theoretical Criminology* 6, 4: 433–60.

Mirrlees-Black, C. (1999) *Domestic Violence—Findings from a new BCS self-completion questionnaire*. Home Office: RDS.

Nayak, A. (1999) '"Pale warriors": skinhead culture and the embodiment of white masculinities' in A. Brah, M. Hickman, and M. Mac an Ghaill *Thinking Identities*. London: Macmillan, 71–99.

Newburn, T. and Stanko, E.A. (eds) (1994) *Just Boys Doing Business? Men, Masculinities and Crime*. London. Routledge.

Pahl, J., Hasanbegovic, C., and Yu, M-K. (2004) 'Globalisation and Family Violence' in V. George and R. Page (eds) *Global Social Problems and Global Social Policy*. Cambridge: Polity Press.

Pinker, S. (2011) *The Better Angels of our Nature*. New York: Viking.

Ray, L.J. (2011) *Violence and Society*. London: Sage.

Ray, L., Smith, D., and Wastell, L. (2003) 'Understanding racist violence' in E. Stanko (ed) *The Meanings of Violence*. London: Routledge, 112–29.

Rosen, A. (2003) *The Transformation of British Life, 1950–2000: a social history*. Manchester: Manchester University Press.

Savolainen, J. (2000) 'Inequality, welfare state, and homicide: Further support for the institutional anomie theory', *Criminology* 38, 4: 1021–42.

Scheff, T.S. and Retzinger, S.M. (2001) *Emotions and Violence—Shame and Rage in Destructive Conflicts*. Lincoln, NB: Backprint.

Schrock, D.P. and Padavic, I. (2007) 'Negotiating hegemonic masculinity in a batterer intervention program', *Gender & Society* 21, 5: 625–49.

Sibbitt, R. (1997) *The Perpetrators of Racial Harassment and Racial Violence*. London: Home Office.

Smith, D. (1999) 'The Civilizing Process and the History of Sexuality: Comparing Norbert Elias and Michel Foucault', *Theory and Society* 28, 1: 79–100.

Smith, D. J., McVie, S., Woodward, R., Shute, J., Flint, J., and McAra, J. (2001) 'The Edinburgh Study of Youth Transitions and Crime' http://www.law.ed.ac.uk/cls/esytc/findreport/wholereport.pdf.

Stanko, E. (1994) *Perspectives on Violence*. London: Quartet Books.

Walby, S. and Allen, J. (2004) *Domestic Violence, Sexual Assault and Stalking: Findings from the British Crime Survey*. Home Office Research Study 276, RDS http://rds.homeoffice.gov.uk/rds/pdfs04/hors276.pdf.

Wieviorka, M. (2009) *Violence: A New Approach*. London: Sage.

Žižek, S. (2008) *Violence*. London: Profile Books.

NOTES

1. This is a survey of experience of crime in England and Wales with a sample of around 50,000 people aged 16 and over living in private households. See http://www.homeoffice.gov.uk/science-research/research-statistics/crime/crime-statistics/british-crime-survey/.

2. 'Hegemony' refers to the ways in which the dominance of a group is sustained through culture. Hegemonic masculinity refers to cultural representations of dominant cultural ideals of masculinity that reinforce the subordination of women and marginal masculinities such as gay and racialized minorities (Connell, 1995: 77ff).

3. The ESRC's Violence Research Programme found that 2.5 per cent of pregnant women had suffered assault in the last 12 months and lifetime prevalence was 13.4 per cent. Women were ten times more likely to be assaulted in pregnancy if they had experienced violence in the last 12 months (ESRC, 2002).

4. After a very long campaign for a re-trial led by Stephen's parents, on 3 January 2012, two of his murderers (Dobson and Norris) were convicted.

5. The report defined institutional racism as: 'the collective failure of an organisation to provide an appropriate and professional service to people because of their colour, culture or ethnic origin. It can be seen or detected in processes, attitudes and behaviour which amount to discrimination through unwitting prejudice, ignorance, thoughtlessness, and racist stereotyping which disadvantage minority ethnic people'.

6. The Gini coefficient measures the percentage difference between a hypothetical model of perfect equality (the Lorenz curve) and actual income inequality—so higher Gini coefficients indicate greater income inequality.

10

Sex crime

Terry Thomas

INTRODUCTION

As a category of criminal activity, **sexual offending** has long been seen as somehow 'different' to other crimes. Crimes of a sexual nature are particularly invasive and exploitative as well as being accompanied by deception or a latent or manifest violence. The victims are usually women or children and the offenders invariably men; the recognition and study of women who commit sexual offending is opening up. Within the prison community there has been a history of other offenders regarding the sexual offender as 'different' and 'by tradition *nonces* are expected to know their place and keep out of the way of "straight cons"' (Sparks *et al.*, 1996: 179).

In the UK and North America the 'problem' of the sex offender has long been high on the political agenda. Other countries have followed suit as politicians realize the swell of popular anger directed at such offenders and that 'doing nothing' is not an option. Reforms have been made within the criminal justice system in terms of police investigation of sexual offences and the prosecution of the offenders; sentences have been introduced specifically aimed at the sex offender. In the civil arena attempts to improve public protection have been introduced in such forms as registration and better monitoring of known sex offenders in the community.

This chapter examines the nature of sexual offending and the forms it takes as well as the enhanced social response now being made.

BACKGROUND

When the UK decided to overhaul its laws on sexual offending at the turn of the century it particularly stated that its guiding principle was 'that the criminal law should not intrude unnecessarily into the private life of adults' (Home Office, 2000: para.07). This was recognition that sexual activities are usually left to the participants involved and to them alone. How, then, have we reached a position where some sexual behaviour simply cannot be left to the participants and where levels of public intervention in the otherwise private areas of life are required?

In the 1970s the feminist movement helped reveal the degree to which women had to contend with being victims of male violence and sexual offending and the apparent cultural blindness of the criminal justice system and its constituent agencies to recognize the problems involved. In the 1980s social workers and health care professionals drew attention to the sexual abuse of children and the degree of such abuse within families. During the 1990s there was a punitive 'push' toward all forms of offenders driven by forms of 'popular punitivism' which were always going to have sexual offending at the fore. Encouraged by a rampant tabloid press interventions became more prompt and punishments became heavier. In a world beset by changing values, there was some security to be had in knowing that, whatever else might change, sexual offences against children, for example, were going to be a constant 'wrong' and the perpetrators the constant 'wrongdoer'. The paedophile became the 'folk devil' of our times.

Sexual offending: consent and prohibited activities

Sexual offending is deemed to have taken place when a person has not consented to the activities in question or when those activities have been prohibited by law whether or not **consent** is present.

Sexual activities are premised on the idea that it is an activity between consenting adults. The adults know the full consequences of their behaviour and are under no duress and subject to no deceptions as to what they are consenting to. Sexual offending takes place when consent has not been given to the activities. This would be a charge of rape or sexual assault (Sexual Offences Act 2003 ss. 1–3).

Consent may be withheld by adults in full command of their faculties. It may also be missing because an adult lacks the capacity to consent due to learning disabilities or other intellectual impairments. Adults may also be unable to give a free consent if their decision making is impaired by alcohol or drugs having been consumed. UK law defines 'consent' simply as follows: 'a person consents if he agrees by choice, and has the freedom and capacity to make that choice' (Sexual Offences Act 2003 s. 74).

Children are said to lack an adult capacity to consent. The UK and most other developed countries protect children from sexual activities by having an 'age of consent'. In the UK that age is 16 years but in other countries it varies from 14 (Germany), 15 (Denmark), and other ages in other countries. The UK chose 16 in 1885 when it was moved up from 13 years.

Consent by 'underage children' is immediately flawed and sex with children under 13 in the UK—even with consent—can result in a charge of rape (Sexual Offences Act 2003 s. 5). The age of consent for homosexual activities is also 16 and this was fixed in law in 2000.

Certain sexual activities have been declared illegal because they have been prohibited by law; the question of consent is irrelevant. These include sex with children under 13 (see earlier) but also incestuous relationships within families between brother and sister or father and daughter (Sexual Offences Act 2003 s. 25).

Sexual relationships are also prohibited between teachers, care workers and others employed in positions working with children even if those children are young people over the age of 16. These positions are regarded as 'positions of trust' that should preclude the development of sexual relationships (Sexual Offences Act 2003 ss. 16ff).

Forms of sexual offending

Within the parameters of consent being absent or certain activities being declared 'prohibited', jurisdictions define their own sexual offences. When the 1996 Consultation Paper appeared outlining the idea of a UK **sex offender register** it listed 33 sexual offences as possibly leading to registration (Home Office, 1996). When the Sex Offender Act appeared in 1997 that list had diminished to 12 for England and Wales and other lists had to be produced covering Scotland and Northern Ireland with their own laws (see Sex Offender Act 1997 Sch. 1).

Sexual offences can be created and repealed with a simple change in the law. The Sexual Offences Act 1967 had decriminalized homosexual activities just as the Criminal

Justice and Public Order Act 1994 had made the rape of a man by another man an offence for the first time.

In general terms sexual offences are committed by two groups of people; those who already know their victim and those who do not. Offences against children are more likely to be committed by adults who know them or are part of their extended family than by people who do not know them. Adult rapes have sometimes been divided into those where the perpetrator is known to the victim (acquaintance rapes) or those where they are not (stranger rapes).

Adults who persistently target children for sexual activities may be described as 'paedophiles' or 'child molesters' although neither term is recognized in legal terms and some people dislike the term 'paedophiles' because it implies a quasi-medical condition that excuses the behaviour as being something the perpetrator has no control over and therefore he bears no responsibility for his actions.

The commercial exploitation of children has been recognized as a form of sexual offence committed by those purchasing the services and policies have turned to exit strategies for the children concerned, who are now seen as the victims of abuse.

The production, dissemination and ownership of pornography are considered sexual offences especially when that pornography has featured images of children. The rise of the Internet has become the favoured form of dissemination since its inception in the mid-1990s. The point is often made that each pornographic image is a picture of a child being abused and that although the viewer might be far removed from that child, the demand for child pornography has helped 'cause' the crime.

REVIEW QUESTIONS

1 Do you agree that the paedophile is the 'folk devil' of our time? Give three reasons for your answer.

2 Discuss the meaning and importance of 'consent'.

3 Do you think that the age of consent is too high compared to the age of consent in other European countries?

Criminal processes

The criminal justice system processes sexual offenders just as it processes all offenders. A police investigation is followed by a decision to prosecute—or not; a fair and open trial, a finding of guilt—or not; and, if necessary, the passing of an appropriate sentence of punishment.

Investigating sexual offences

The police have been criticized in the past for their lack of interest in investigating sexual crimes. A notorious television documentary in 1982 showed male officers of the Thames Valley Police dismissing a woman's reported rape as fairy tales and a cover up for consensual activity. The public criticism that followed led to Home Office circulars to the police and internal activity by the police themselves leading to better interviewing techniques and more sensitive investigations. More training was introduced and better reception facilities made available for women victims.

The result was more victims coming forward and a rise in the reporting of sexual crimes. Research confirmed a threefold increase in reporting between 1985 and 1996 (Harris and Grace, 1999). When the police became custodians of the sex offender register in 1997 (see later in this chapter) together with more multi-agency work in this area, their awareness of sexual offending increased.

Another report commissioned by the Home Office in 2005 confirmed that all was not well. Reporting was increasing but successful prosecution was falling and only one in 18 rapes (6 per cent) reported to the police ended with the suspect being punished. The figure of 6 per cent was a much quoted statistic as a reason for changes to be made. This study tracked 3,500 rape cases through the courts and interviewed 228 rape victims. Both the police and Crown Prosecution Service (CPS) (see later) were said to be over-estimating the number of false allegations and the report identified a 'culture of scepticism' about rape complaints (Kelly *et al.*, 2005).

A study of eight police forces in England and Wales in 2007 was designed to look at the attrition rate again. This study looked at 676 cases and successful prosecutions were found to have risen to 13 per cent with the factors leading to the best chance of getting to court listed as:

> that the assault was linked to sexual offence against a separate victim; the victim's medical history was obtained; the offender threatened the victim; forensic evidence was recovered; and, where witnesses were present. The presence of any of these variables increased the odds of an offence resulting in getting to court and resulting in a conviction. (Feist *et al.*, 2007: ii)

The study concluded that implications for the police included better care for victims to encourage them not to withdraw their complaints, the encouragement of reporting to be as early as possible after the event and a greater emphasis on getting medical evidence. The police were also encouraged to look more at the alleged offender and better record and use intelligence in their investigative work; a move away from the victim and more toward the offender.

The report also found that attrition could be reduced when:

- Call handling systems are more responsive.
- Specially trained officers or their equivalents have been widely introduced.
- Training for police and prosecutors is improved.
- Access to sexual assault referral centres (SARCs) is either in place or planned in all forces.
- Use of early evidence kits is widespread.

Prosecuting the people who commit sexual offences

At the completion of a police investigation and the gathering of evidence the CPS begin the process of taking the case into court for prosecution. This has long been a matter of concern because many cases are 'discontinued' at this point for various reasons and the CPS has been the subject of some criticism for their performance in prosecuting alleged sexual offenders (see, for example, Harris and Grace, 1999; Home Office, 2000; Kelly *et al.*, 2005). The CPS has recognized the problem and responded by publishing a joint Protocol between the Police and Crown Prosecution Service in the Investigation and Prosecution of Allegations of Rape (available at http://www.cps.gov.uk/publications/agencies/rape_protocol.html#_01, last accessed 19 March 2012).

A fair and open trial

A person accused of a sexual crime has the same rights as any other defendants in a criminal court to defend themselves while receiving a fair and open trial. The particularly sensitive nature of sexual crime, however, has led to various provisions in the court to help victims of sexual crime to give evidence in what can be an intimidating environment. These provisions have to be balanced against the defendant's right to a fair and open trial.

In 1976 victims of alleged rapes were given the right to anonymity and this right was extended to victims of all alleged sexual offences in 1992. Defendants were also granted anonymity in 1976 but this was withdrawn in 1988.

One of the prime criticisms of the way in which women victims of sexual crime have been treated by the criminal justice system has been the manner in which they have been 'smeared' in court and painted by the defendant's lawyers as at least partly responsible for their own fate. Laws have been passed to try and minimize this 'smearing' and especially to prevent the woman's sexual history being used against her to discredit her evidence. These laws started in 1976 but were often evaded in practice; they were strengthened by the 1999 Youth Justice and Criminal Evidence Act ss. 41–43.

The same 1999 Act also introduced 'special measures' to help vulnerable and intimidated witnesses give evidence in court. Screens may be brought in to shield the woman witness from the defendant and video links and video pre-recordings may be used. These measures drew on similar arrangements for child witnesses that had been introduced in 1992 to improve the quality of their evidence to the court.

Punishing the people who commit sexual offences

The sentencing of convicted sex offenders has become progressively more severe over the last 20 years. The tone was set by the 1990 Home Office statement that it wished to give courts the powers 'to give custodial sentences longer than would be justified by the seriousness of the offence to persistent violent and sexual offenders, if this is necessary to protect the public from serious harm' (Home Office, 1990: para.3.13).

The Criminal Justice Act 1991 s. 2(2)(b) duly introduced these stronger provisions and the later Crime (Sentences) Act 1997 allowed for automatic life sentences for persistent serious offenders including those committing rape, attempted rape, and intercourse with a girl under 13; these sentences were known colloquially as the 'two strikes and out' provisions.

One of the more contentious provisions brought in to deal with sex offenders was the sentence of 'Imprisonment for the Public Protection' (IPP). This measure was introduced by the Criminal Justice Act 2003 ss. 224–236 and effectively committed an offender to an open ended period of custody wherein release was dependent on the prisoner being assessed as no longer a risk to the public. The Home Office estimated only a few IPP orders would be made annually, but in practice far more were made than had been anticipated and not all of them on sexual offenders.

A major blow to the IPP came in 2008 when some prisoners challenged their validity in court. If a prisoner's detention was dependent on demonstrating they were no longer a risk to society, they argued that the Home Office through the Prison Service should be providing treatment facilities and help for them to achieve that lower level of risk. In many prisons no such help was available to IPP prisoners. The courts agreed (Jacobson and Hough, 2011).

The IPP was also partly blamed for the overcrowding in UK prisons and the new Coalition government started to re-examine the whole *raison d'être* of the IPP. In 2011, the government announced its intention to replace the IPP with 'a clear tough predictable system of long determinate sentences' (Hansard HC Debates, 29 June 2011 col. 1062).

REVIEW QUESTIONS

1 Explain why there are so few successful prosecutions for the offence of rape.

2 Has the police service of England and Wales improved its handling of rape cases?

3 The sentencing of convicted sex offenders has become progressively more severe over the last 20 years. Explain why this is the case.

Civil measures for public protection

Running parallel to the criminal justice system and its provisions to investigate, prosecute and punish people for sexual offending are the arrangements now put in place to better protect the public from sex offenders. Public protection has become a major commitment from successive governments since the early 1990s and not least when it comes to protection from sex offenders. These arrangements include sex offender registers, multi-agency public protection arrangements, restrictions on travel for sex offenders, and other restrictions that may be imposed.

The registration and monitoring of sex offenders

The registration of sex offenders started in the USA in 1947 and a number of individual states introduced their own versions of registration through the 1950s and 1960s. People who committed a designated sexual offence were required to report their circumstances to the police and notify the police when any changes took place, and in particular changes of address. This would continue for a specified period of time, but sometimes would be on an indefinite basis; failure to comply with these requirements would be an offence in itself. The idea was to provide the police with more accurate and up to date information on the 'known' sex offenders in their jurisdiction.

In 1994 the Federal Jacob Wetterling Crimes against Children and Sexually Violent Offender Registration Act required all 50 US states to introduce a sex offender register or risk losing Federal funding; all 50 had complied by 1996 and in that same year new Federal laws required the FBI to start work on a national US register that would draw on data held in all the individual state registers.

At the same time the Home Office proposed creating a sex offender register for the UK. A Consultation Document stated the rationale for the register as being something that would 'help police identify suspects after a crime', something that 'could help to prevent crimes' and something that 'might act as a deterrent' (Home Office, 1996: para.43). The UK's 1997 Sex Offender Act created a sex offender register for England, Wales, Scotland and Northern Ireland; the law is now to be found in the Sexual Offences Act 2003 Part Two.

The UK law requires only those convicted or cautioned to appear on the register. Some critics wanted to include those suspected of sexual offending but they were overruled. Others wanted the register to be retrospective and include those convicted before 1997 but that too was ruled out.

Where the USA and the UK have led others have followed. Sex offender registers now exist in Canada, Australia, South Africa, Kenya and Jamaica and within Europe in France, Germany and the Republic of Ireland (Thomas, 2011).

An evaluation of the UK register in 2000 found a compliance rate of 94 per cent amongst those required to notify the police of their circumstances and also reported on the much better working relationships being developed between local police and probation services as a result of the register (Plotnikoff and Woolfson, 2000: 5 and 45). What the evaluation could not say was whether or not the register was successful in reducing the incidence of sexual offending or making communities any safer (Plotnikoff and Woolfson, 2000: 34). At the same time the Criminal Justice and Court Services Act 2000 now required formal cooperation between the police, probation services and other agencies within an area in what was to be termed the Multi-Agency Public Protection Arrangements or MAPPA (see later in this chapter).

In 2001 another review of the register reported the compliance rate to have risen to 97 per cent. In an introduction to this review the Home Secretary of the time claimed the register 'had proved a valuable tool in helping protect the public'—even though there was little evidence to support this claim—but that nonetheless 'experience in implementing it has suggested that aspects could be strengthened'. Some 15,000 people were now reported to be registering with the police (Home Office/Scottish Executive, 2001).

The strengthening of the register duly took place with shorter time periods being allowed for the notification of changes (14 days down to three days) and more powers given to the police to photograph, fingerprint, and take DNA samples from those required to register. Annual verification reporting to the police was introduced even if no changes had taken place in a person's circumstances. The police were given a new duty to risk assess all those on the register (Criminal Justice Act 2003 ss. 325–327) and obtained powers to force entry to premises if this was necessary to carry out a risk assessment on a registered sex offender (Violent Crime Reduction Act 2006 s. 58). The UK sex offender register was on a trajectory designed to close all perceived loopholes that an offender might try to use to continue offending despite being monitored; such exercises in 'strengthening' gave the register a 'function creep' of its own causing one observer to believe 'the community's protection [had become] in effect the sex offender's punishment' (Kemshall, 2008: 21; see also Thomas, 2008).

Periodic legal challenges to the sex offender register made virtually no inroads into its provisions until 2010 when two people convicted of sexual offences requiring them to be registered for the rest of their life argued that they should at least be allowed a right of appeal if they no longer posed a risk of further offending. They accepted that some people might need to be registered for life but equally some people did not and there was no appeal mechanism in the law.

The Supreme Court agreed with them and declared that aspect of registration to be incompatible with the European Convention on Human Rights (Article 8). The Home Office responded for England and Wales with a proposal for a limited form of appeal to the police but the joint House of Lords and House of Commons Human Rights Committee has already declared the proposals to be wanting (House of Lords/House of Commons, 2011).

The numbers on the UK sex offender register have grown steadily. In August 1999 after just two years the number stood at 8,608 (Plotnikoff and Woolfson, 2000: 5) but by the end of 2009 this figure had risen to 32,336 (CJJI, 2010: 22). Having successfully withstood legal challenges in the Supreme Court the US Federal government now required a strengthened version of the register in every state. The Adam Walsh Act 2006 was duly passed. The 2006 Act was, in fact, so strong and complex that by the date set for implementation of the new registration provisions in July 2009, not one state had implemented the law. The first state to actually do so was Ohio in September 2009, some two months past the deadline, followed by Delaware and then Florida in May 2010. All the other registration jurisdictions had requested and were granted extensions to 27 July 2011 but even by that date, only 14 out of the 50 states had implemented the SORNA requirements.

REVIEW QUESTIONS

1 Explain the development of the sex offender register.

2 Explain the advantages and disadvantages of the sex offender register.

3 Should sex offenders be monitored?

Multi–agency Public Protection Arrangements (MAPPA)

One of the major differences between registers in the USA and in the UK was that the American registers were open to the public. Policies of 'community notification' had started in Washington State in 1990 and spread slowly to other states and most notably to New Jersey in 1994 where the law was called Megan's Law after eight-year-old Megan

Kanka who had been assaulted and killed by a man with previous convictions against children who lived in the same street as the Kanka family. The idea was that families should know if such men lived in their area in order to better protect their children (for more on 'community notification' see later in this chapter).

In the UK, a test case in North Wales had ruled that US-style 'community notification' could not take place in any routine 'blanket' fashion. The public disclosure of police held conviction records could take place, however, but only on an individualized basis when a particular offender was considered 'high risk' and it was in the interests of crime prevention for those in his or her immediate vicinity to be informed (*R v Chief Constable of North Wales ex p Thorpe* (1998) *The Times* 23 March).

The assessment of who was 'high risk' was to be taken by the police as custodians of the register. In turn the police started to make ad hoc arrangements to consult with agencies such as probation and social services to help them make decisions on risk. These initially informal multi-agency arrangements were to become formalized in 2000.

The Criminal Justice and Court Services Act 2000 (ss. 67–68) required the police and probation service (as the 'responsible authorities') to form Multi-Agency Public Protection Panels and to draw in other agencies such as social services, health and housing authorities (sometimes known as the cooperating agencies); the prison service was later added as a third 'responsible authority'. Together they would form the Multi-Agency Public Protection Arrangements (MAPPA), based around the Panels, which has oversight for three categories of people:

(1) Those required to register as sex offenders;
(2) Those who had been imprisoned for more than 12 months for violent or sexual offences;
(3) Those considered to pose any form of risk to the community

The people concerned were risk assessed and divided into three management levels from one to three; level one were the least likely to re-offend and level three the most likely.

The Panels themselves would focus on the very high-risk offenders referred to as 'the critical few'; the Panels would produce annual reports on their activities to keep their local communities informed and a national report would be published annually by the Home Office. The Home Office (and later the Ministry of Justice) would also provide the local MAPPA with detailed guidance on how they should conduct themselves (see, for example, Ministry of Justice *et al.*, 2009).

In what appears to have been a response to continuing demands for 'community notification' in the UK, the MAPPA now has lay members of the public working with the Panels at a strategic level; the lay members do not, however, have any access to individual names of people being considered by the MAPPA and this does not constitute a form of 'community notification' (see later). The lay member scheme has been the subject of some criticism in its lack of clarity (Home Office, 2007: 16) and its impact seems to be quite limited (see also CJJI, 2011: para.6.6).

Overall the MAPPA appears to have been well received and has assisted joint work between agencies even if it is reportedly better at exchanging information than in clearly identifying lead agencies ensuring management plans are implemented (CJJI, 2011).

Some US states have Sex Offender Management Groups which bear a resemblance to the UK MAPPA arrangements but they are more policy-orientated than the UK version with their hands-on decision making about individuals.

Sexual Offences Prevention Orders

The aim of the Sexual Offences Prevention Order (SOPO) is to protect the public from 'serious sexual harm' and if the qualifying criteria are met, the court makes the Order which contains a set of prohibitions on a person's behaviour.

The SOPO evolved from what was originally called a Sex Offender Order (SOO) (Crime and Disorder Act 1998 ss. 2–3); part of this initial thinking was that it might compensate for the fact that the UK sex offender register that had started in 1997, was not retrospective and this Order might add some past sex offenders to the register (CJJI, 2011: para.2). The SOO in turn became the SOPO (Sexual Offences Act 2003 ss. 104–113).

The use of the SOPO to restrict a sex offender's movements is as far as the UK goes in this direction; the UK has not considered the more universal sex offender 'residence restrictions' used by many states in the USA (Nieto and Jung, 2006).

The SOPO was premised on the use of the civil law as a 'first step' to create the Order, complemented by the criminal law as a 'second step' if there was non-compliance.

The SOPO is applied for by the police in a civil court; it may also be imposed by a criminal court at the time of sentencing. Failure to comply with the Order could result in criminal procedures and a fine of up to £5000 or imprisonment for up to five years. SOPOs can be made on anyone who is a 'qualifying offender' which means they have been convicted of one of the sexual offences listed in the Sexual Offences Act 2003 Sch. 3.

Police applying for a SOPO have to demonstrate that the person is a 'qualifying offender' and that they have been acting in such a way that a SOPO is believed necessary. The Home Office has provided guidance to the police on how to assess the latter including evidence that a sexual offence will be committed, the nature and pattern of the concerning behaviour, the current circumstances of the offender, etc. (Home Office, 2010: 51–3).

The 'negative prohibitions' are deemed necessary for the purpose of protecting the public; the Order cannot list any 'positive requirements'. The person made subject to the SOPO is required to desist from the activities listed; the activities in themselves may or may not be criminal acts. The SOPO leads to automatic inclusion on the sex offender register if the person was not already on it (that is, their convictions pre-date the register, which is not retrospective).

Concern has been expressed about what exactly constitutes a 'negative prohibition'. In particular the right of police entry to the home of someone subject to a SOPO could not be made because that would have been a 'positive requirement' rather than a 'negative prohibition'. The police, however, could simply re-word this 'right of entry' and make it a 'negative prohibition' by saying the person concerned 'must not deny access' to a police officer. The Appeal Court described such police semantics as 'draconian' because it effectively created a continuing search warrant lasting at least five years—the length of the SOPO (*Thompson* [2009] EWCA Crim 3258). It also conflicted with new powers given to the police in 2006 to apply for a specific 'right of entry' on anyone on the sex offender register if the police were being obstructed from completing a risk assessment (Violent Crime Reduction Act 2006 s. 58; see earlier in this chapter).

The travelling sex offender

As jurisdictions have put domestic 'public protection' measures in place including registers, civil orders and multi-agency arrangements, attention has been turned to the person who travels across international borders and commits sexual offences; these travellers include both those already convicted and 'known' to the authorities and those who may be going to offend for the first time and are currently 'unknown' to the authorities.

The term 'sex tourist' appeared in the early 1990s to refer to those men from 'Western' developed countries who travelled to the more under-developed areas of the world where poverty had driven women and children into prostitution; the same areas often had less rigorous laws and law enforcement, and children could be commercially exploited with relative ease. Countries such as Thailand and Cambodia became known as destination countries for these tourists.

The term 'sex tourist' was somewhat misleading because it often included people who were not strictly 'tourists', but travellers for business purposes, military forces working overseas, diplomats and governmental employees posted abroad and expatriates residing abroad. Some people travelled without the intent to commit offences but still committed them on their arrival.

In its widest sense the 'travelling sex offender' could also include those who just wanted to escape from their domestic registration and monitoring arrangements and those who wanted to just be anonymous and able to commit offences where they were not known. Some international travellers were people looking for employment with children in schools or children's homes in order to use their access to those children to commit sexual offences.

Attempts to regulate the behaviour of people who might be travelling to commit sexual crimes have focused mainly on the 'known' and registered sex offenders. In both the USA and the UK anyone required to register as a convicted sex offender must notify the authorities if they intend to travel abroad. The UK introduced such notification in 2001 for anyone leaving the country for eight days or more; this was later reduced to three days in 2004 and proposals have been made that it should apply to anyone on the register going abroad for *any* period of time (Home Office, 2011).

On being notified of the travel the police make an assessment of the risk of sexual harm that may be posed and decide if they, in turn, are going to notify the police of the destination country; if information is passed through, then any further action is at the discretion of the country concerned.

The UK police can also decide that the risk of harm is so great that the travel should not be allowed. They can apply to a magistrates' court for a Foreign Travel Order which, if granted, prevents the person leaving the country for any time period up to five years (Sexual Offences Act 2003 ss. 114–122 as amended).

The opposite side of the coin to regulating those leaving the country is for the authorities to be aware of those who might be coming *into* the country as convicted sexual offenders or registered sex offenders whether as foreign nationals or people returning home. The police and immigration authorities may or may not be aware of such arrivals and the exchange of intelligence between authorities at this point is critical. Recent initiatives within the European Union to automatically notify each Member State when their citizens are convicted of any offence—not just sexual offences—may ease this problem and will also enable better and more comprehensive vetting of people wanting to work with children (EU Framework Decision 2009/315/JHA; Coroners and Justice Act 2009 s. 144 and Sch. 17; Jacobs and Blitsa, 2008).

Sex offenders arriving in the UK may be included on the UK register—if not already registered—by means of a Notification Order granted by magistrates (Sexual Offences Act 2003 ss. 97–103).

The grooming of children for sexual purposes

The practice of befriending and enticing children into sexual activities has been termed 'grooming' and has become a recognized preliminary to exploitative child sexual abuse. Since the arrival of the Internet this has sometimes taken place in 'chat-rooms' and through other social networking arrangements with examples found of adults pretending to be children. Since 2003 the UK police have been able to apply for a Risk of Sexual Harm Order (RSHO) if they have evidence of patterns of behaviour that can be interpreted as 'grooming' behaviour; the Order requires the adult in question to stop the concerning behaviour (Sexual Offences Act 2003 ss. 123–129). The RSHO is another Civil Order (first step) with criminal proceedings (second step) if there is non-compliance.

The RSHO seeks to prevent adults from initiating contact with children to 'groom' them in order to initiate the sexual abuse of a particular child or group of children. The RSHO was an attempt to prevent preparatory interactions between adult and child from taking place whether on-line or off-line.

The application for an RSHO has to demonstrate that a person has on at least two occasions been:

(a) engaging in sexual activity involving a child or in the presence of a child;

(b) causing or inciting a child to watch a person engaging in sexual activity or to look at a moving or still image that is sexual;

(c) giving a child anything that relates to sexual activity or contains a reference to such activity;

(d) communicating with a child, where any part of the communication is sexual (Sexual Offences Act 2003 s. 123(3)).

The first two items on this list of required evidence—(a) and (b)—are actually offences documented in the Sexual Offences Act 2003. Critics believe, therefore, that they are acts that could have led to a prosecution but have not done; possibly because of lack of evidence for the higher standard of proof criminal proceedings would require. In effect the civil RSHO was arguably being used as a 'softer' alternative to prosecution (Craven *et al.*, 2007).

The need for evidence of 'sexual communication' (item (d)) also suggests Internet grooming is getting a greater priority in the law than its lower rate of incidence warrants, compared to face-to-face grooming (Craven *et al.*, 2007).

The same critics also suggest that RSHOs could have offered a more exact definition of 'grooming' and point out that:

> [I]t is extremely difficult to distinguish between sexually motivated grooming behaviours and perfectly normal child/adult interactions that have no sexual motivations. (Craven *et al.*, 2007)

Guidance has been provided by the Home Office on what the police should examine to suggest the person is likely to harm a child or group of children (Home Office, 2010: 67–9).

An RSHO can be made on anyone and there is no necessity that the person already be 'known' and convicted for earlier sexual offences, as is the case with the SOPO. Applicants have only to demonstrate the behaviour patterns just listed; this is a tacit widening of the scope of just who might be a sex offender by now saying in effect *anyone* could be a potential child sexual offender.

A variation on this form of individual 'grooming' has been identified as 'localized grooming' whereby groups of young men have targeted vulnerable girls in a given locality and drawn them into situations of sexual exploitation. The UK research on this behaviour is limited but a CEOP study has found:

> grooming is used to manipulate victims, distance them from families and friends, and place them under the control of the offender. Offenders will often use flattery and attention to persuade victims to view them as a 'boyfriend'. (CEOP, 2011:10)

Public access to the 'register'?

A disputed aspect of the sex offender register has been the degree to which it should be open to the public and not just to law enforcement authorities. Federal law in the USA since 1996 has required all 50 states to have a form of public access to the register; this policy is often referred to as Megan's Law or 'community notification' with the aim of better informed parents being better able to protect their children (see, for example, Thomas, 2003; Fitch, 2006). Other jurisdictions with registers around the world have not given public access in such a universal manner often because of public order fears of vigilante behaviour.

The UK has selective forms of public access to certain people either through its 'discretionary disclosure scheme' and since 2011 through its 'child sex offender disclosure scheme'. The 'discretionary disclosure scheme' is an administrative arrangement carried out by police that generally works well (Cann, 2007); the 'child sex offender disclosure scheme' is a statutory scheme rolled out 2010–11 that requires the police to have a 'presumption to disclose' previous convictions to safeguard children (Criminal Justice and Immigration Act 2008 s. 140 amending Criminal Justice Act 2003 (s. 327A and B)). The latter has a low take-up but again early evaluations suggest it is working well (Kemshall and Wood, 2010).

Mental health and sexual offending

People diagnosed as having a mental illness who also commit sexual offences have prompted particular problems for the policy makers. If people were to be taken compulsorily into hospital the UK legislation in the form of the Mental Health Act 1983 required—amongst other things—a 'treatability' test to be applied. This meant that if admitted, their mental health condition was susceptible to improvement—or at least there should be a prevention of deterioration. The long-standing paradox was that some sexual offenders and paedophiles were generally considered unlikely to change their behaviour and were—to the general public—in effect 'untreatable'. On that basis 'known' sex offenders—often now being referred to as having 'severe personality disorders'—could not be compulsorily admitted to hospital and if they had committed no offence could not be detained by the police.

The government attempted to square this circle with the Mental Health Act 2007. This act amended the 1983 Act by removing the so-called 'treatability' test as it then stood and replacing it with the concept of 'appropriate medical treatment'. This might include nursing which in turn might enable a form of 'containment' for some people considered 'dangerous' even if their hospitalization and treatment led to no reduced risk. The fear for some critics was that this might result in some hospitals masquerading as prisons; the new law commenced in November 2008.

REVIEW QUESTIONS

1 Explain the role of Multi-Agency Public Protection Panels.

2 What are the advantages and disadvantages of the Sexual Offenders Prevention Order?

3 Should the sex offender register be open to the public? Give reasons for your answer.

CONCLUSION

Sexual offending continues to be a high-profile form of offending drawing headlines usually of a salacious and unhelpful kind. In autumn 2012 the press and other media reported widely on the 'grooming' of vulnerable children and young girls in Rochdale followed by their systematic abuse in prostitution rings. The police and social services seemed to have missed numerous opportunities to intervene and protect these children. They appeared unwilling to listen to the girls when they came for help or dismissed them as having chosen prostitution as a 'life-style' choice (see, for example, Norfolk, 2012).

Widespread press reporting also took place when a schoolteacher in Sussex was accused of an 'abuse of trust' by abducting a 15-year-old pupil in his school and taking her to France. A prurient interest evolved with the press claiming the publicity was only helpful in helping track the couple down and returning the child to her family.

And at the same time allegations of child sexual abuse were made about the former TV personality Sir Jimmy Savile who had died in October 2011: a broadcast television documentary made the allegations on ITV (Halliday, 2012). All these cases show the fine line between public outrage and public interest in anything sexual.

The UK, the USA and other jurisdictions have made strenuous efforts over the last two decades to investigate, prosecute and punish people who commit sexual offences more effectively. Similar efforts have been made to better protect the public from possible sexual crimes. The 'requirements' and 'obligations' placed on those on the sex offender register, for example, have strengthened incrementally over the years despite there being little evidence to demonstrate that the register makes any difference to levels of sexual offending.

Much of the drive to improve public protection has been underpinned by a governmental need to 'protect children'. In this context, the changing nature of society/State relations with and status of family/children within it is important to understand. Class differences and social hierarchies maintain the 'social distance' between individuals and contribute to a perceived breakdown in social/interpersonal trust in society reducing the levels of social cohesion and social capital. The sex offender becomes the archetypal 'other' criminal to be avoided and contained.

Government and professional risk-based policies are seen not as a probability calculus, but seeking to avoid the 'worst case' scenario; a precautionary logic takes over to ensure we do everything possible to minimize future risk posed by sex offenders (Hebenton and Seddon, 2009).

Whether a more punitive approach to sex offenders or ever more embracing public protection arrangements actually make any difference is hard to tell because so many other variables enter the picture when re-offending and re-conviction rates are looked at. The 'public protection' from sex offenders is one of those policies that is far removed from being 'evidence-based'.

QUESTIONS FOR DISCUSSION

1 Why has sexual offending become such a priority over the last 20 years compared to earlier years?

2 What forms does sexual offending take?

3 How could we improve the reporting levels of sex crime?

4 Are people who commit sexual offences 'treatable'?

5 Is it possible to improve the public protection arrangements against sex offenders?

GUIDE TO FURTHER READING

Harrison, K. (ed.) (2010) *Managing High Risk Sex Offenders in the Community: risk management, treatment and social responsibility*. Cullompton: Willan Publishing is a collection of chapters looking at all aspects of sexual offending and the management and treatment of sex offenders in the community.

Harrison, K. (2011) *Dangerousness, Risk and the Governance of Serious Sexual and Violent Offenders*. Abingdon: Routledge is authoritative and up to date on sexual offending from a political and legal stance.

Ireland, J. L., Ireland, C. A. and Birch, P. (eds) (2009) *Violent and Sexual Offenders: assessment, treatment and management*. Cullompton: Willan Publishing is another collection of papers examining the assessment, treatment and management of sexual offending.

Thomas, T. (2005) *Sex Crime: sex offending and society* (2nd edn). Cullompton: Willan Publishing takes a wider criminological view of all aspects of sexual offending and the social response to it both currently and historically over the last 100 years.

Thomas, T. (2011) *The Registration and Monitoring of Sex Offenders: a comparative study.* Abingdon: Routledge focuses solely on the registration of sex offenders in the USA, UK and other jurisdictions that have introduced registers; it challenges the value of registration.

WEB LINKS

http://www.nota.co.uk/

The National Organisation for the Treatment of Abusers (NOTA)—a UK-based organization for practitioners working with people who have committed sexual offences; contains details of publications, conferences, etc.

http://www.stopitnow.org.uk/

Stop it Now! is an organization that sees sexual offending s a preventable public health issue that encourages potential offenders to come forward for help.

http://www.atsa.com/

Association for the Treatment of Sexual Abusers—the US equivalent to the UK's NOTA.

http://www.iatso.org/

International Association for the Treatment of Sex Offenders—an international forum for the discussion of global developments in this work.

http://www.csom.org/

Center for Sex Offender Management (CSOM)—a US based centre supported by the Department of Justice. A source of many papers on all aspects of sex offender management.

REFERENCES

Cann, J. (2007) *Assessing the extent of discretionary disclosure under the Multi-Agency Public Protection Arrangements (MAPPA),* Home Office on-line report 13/07 (available at http://www.homeoffice.gov.uk/rds)

CEOP (Child Exploitation and Online Protection Centre) (2011) *Out of Mind, Out of Sight: breaking down the barriers to understanding child sexual exploitation* (Executive Summary) June, London.

CJJI (Criminal Justice Joint Inspection) (2010) *Restriction and Rehabilitation: getting the right mix—an inspection of the management of sexual offenders in the community.* June, London.

CJJI (Criminal Justice Joint Inspection) (2011) *Putting the Pieces Together: an inspection of Multi-Agency Public Protection Arrangements,* November 2011, London: HM Inspectorate of Probation/HM Inspectorate of Constabulary.

Craven, S., Brown, S., and Gilchrist, E. (2007), 'Current Responses to Sexual Grooming: Implication for Prevention', *Howard Journal of Criminal Justice* 46(1): 60–71.

Feist, A., Ashe, J., Lawrence, J., McPhee, D., and Wilson, R. (2007). *Investigating and detecting recorded offences of rape.* London: Home Office Research Development and Statistics Directorate.

Fitch, K. (2006) *Megan's Law: does it protect children?* (2) London: NSPCC.

Halliday, J. (2012) 'Jimmy Savile was interviewed by police over sexual assault allegations', *Guardian* 1 October.

Harris, J. and Grace, S. (1999) *A Question of Evidence: investigating and prosecuting rape in the 1990s* Home Office Research Study 196. London: Home Office.

Hebenton, B. and Seddon, T. (2009) 'From Dangerousness to Precaution: managing sexual and violent offenders in an insecure and uncertain age', *British Journal of Criminology* 49(3): 343–62.

Home Office (1996) *Sentencing and Supervision of Sex Offenders—a consultation document* Cm 3304 London: HMSO.

Home Office (2000) *Setting the Boundaries: reforming the law on sex offences* (vol. 1), July, London.

Home Office (2010) *Guidance on Part 2 of the Sexual Offences Act 2003,* October, London.

Home Office/Scottish Executive (2001) *Consultation Paper on the Review of Part 1 of the Sex Offenders Act 1997* July, London.

House of Lords/House of Commons (2011) *Proposal for the Sexual Offences Act 2003 (Remedial) Order 2011* Joint Committee on Human Rights 19th Report of Session 2010–12, HL paper 200/HC 1549, October TSO.

Jacobs, J. and Blitsa, D. (2008) 'Major "minor" progress under the Third Pillar: EU Institution Building in the Sharing of Criminal Record Information', *Chicago-Kent Journal of International and Comparative Law* 111–65.

Jacobson, J. and Hough, M. (2010) *Unjust Deserts: imprisonment for public protection*. London: Prison Reform Trust.

Kelly, L., Love, J. and Regan, L. (2005) *A Gap or a Chasm? Attrition in reported rape cases* Home Office Research Study, February. London: Home Office.

Kemshall, H. (2008) *Understanding the Community Management of High Risk Offenders*. Maidenhead: McGraw Hill/ Open University Press.

Kemshall, H. and Wood, J. with Westwood, S., Stout, B., Wilkinson, B., Kelly, G. and Mackenzie, G. (2010) *Research Report 32: Child Sex Offender Review (CSOR) Public Disclosure Pilots: a process evaluation*, March. London: Home Office.

Nieto, M. and Jung, D. (2006) *The Impact of Residency restrictions on Sex Offenders and Correctional Management Practices: a literature review*. Sacramento: California Research Bureau.

Ministry of Justice, National Probation Service, HM Prison Service and Association of Chief Police Officers (2009) *MAPPA Guidance 2009 Version 3*, National Offender Management Service, Public Protection Unit, London.

Norfolk, A. (2012) 'Abuse Report reveals catalogue of missed chances', *The Times* 27 September.

Plotnikoff, J. and Woolfson, R. (2000) *Where are they Now? An evaluation of sex offender registration in England and Wales* Police Research Series Paper 126. London: Home Office.

Sparks, R., Bottoms, A. and Hay, W. (1996) *Prisons and the Problem of Order*. Oxford: Clarendon Press.

Thomas, T. (2003) 'Sex Offender Community Notification: the American Experience', *Howard Journal of Criminal Justice* 42(3): 217–28.

Thomas, T. (2008) 'The Sex Offender Register: a case study in function creep', *Howard Journal of Criminal Justice* 47(3): 227–37 (July).

Thomas, T. (2011) *The Registration and Monitoring of Sex Offenders: a comparative study*. Abingdon: Routledge.

Williams, R. (2012) 'Missing school girl Megan Stammers found "safe and well" in France', *Independent* 28 September.

11 Corporate crime

Steve Tombs

INTRODUCTION

Not least in the wake of the financial crises which erupted across many of the most advanced economies from 2007 onwards, evidence of immoral and illegal practices on the part of corporations seems ubiquitous. That said, political and popular responses to corporate crimes almost never take the form of calling for a 'war' or crackdown—as has occurred with illegal drugs or 'anti-social behaviour'. In this we see mutually reinforcing links between popular understanding of crime and criminality, the distribution of power in capitalist societies, the proclivities of political elites, and the differential responses of criminal justice systems to different kinds of offending and offenders. Thus, albeit discussing **white-collar crime** rather than **corporate crime** *per se*, Levi argues that several factors mitigate against the development of the kinds of moral panics which are periodically generated and sustained in relation to some forms of conventional offending:

> Most questionable corporate practice and personnel are able to maintain a subterranean existence characterized by low visibility to outsiders. In this, they are aided by the 'softly, softly' approach of the enforcement agencies, media averse to the genuine risk of libel suits, and governments and public almost superstitiously afraid of meddling with the market. (Levi, 2009: 49)

Moreover, even where folk-devils, moral outrage and panic emerge, there often remains a chasm between what are recognized as immoral and illegal practices and real *'crimes* with the requisite "mental element"' (Levi, 2009: 50). This is signalled by the words we use in relation to corporate crimes: mis-selling, scandals, and so on. As argued at length in this chapter, a rather impermeable, if not absolutely unbreakable, tautology emerges: corporate crimes are not real crimes and do not need treating as such; because corporate crimes are not treated as real crimes they are not real crimes.

This chapter explores corporate 'impunity', a product of the fact that corporate crime remains *relatively* free of critical political, popular and (still) academic scrutiny. It begins by examining the emergence and nature of 'corporate crime', before focusing on its various dimensions, its relative invisibility, diverse aetiologies, and issues in its effective control. The central aim is to mark out corporate crime as a legitimate area of criminological concern.

BACKGROUND

In his Presidential Address to the American Sociological Association in 1939, and subsequent publications, Edwin Sutherland (1940, 1945, 1983) introduced the idea of 'white-collar crime'—'a crime committed by a person of respectability and high social status in the course of his occupation' (Sutherland, 1983: 7). He thus challenged the stereotypical view of the criminal as lower class since 'powerful business and professional men' also routinely commit crimes. The main difference between the crimes of the upper and lower classes is in the implementation of the law: 'upper class' criminals often operate undetected; if detected they may not be prosecuted; and if prosecuted they tend to receive relatively lenient (and overwhelmingly financial) penalties.

Sutherland's definition of crime was based upon what is punishable rather than actually punished by law, thereby incorporating offences that went undetected, or, if detected, were not acted upon. Further, he extended the term 'crime' to cover activities beyond those proscribed by criminal law. He recognized that a large number of activities that could be criminalized were in fact subject to forms of State response different from normal criminal processing. For Tappan (1947), these leaps beyond a narrow definition of crime were highly problematic: Sutherland's over-extended definition of crime denied due process and obscured very real differences between 'criminal' and 'harmful' behaviour. Yet Sutherland stressed that differences in offence types—criminal or otherwise—were contingent, an effect of relations of power. Further, he was clear that the differential interpretation and enforcement of law against 'white-collar crime' is partly because legislators, judges and administrators within the criminal justice system are either subject to material and ideological influences of business people, or share their ideological and/ or cultural worldviews (Sutherland, 1945: 137–8).

Sutherland's writings were intended as a 'clarion call' to criminologists to focus upon the crimes of the powerful, as well as those of the powerless. In many respects this went unheeded. One obstacle to academic study of corporate crime can be traced back to Sutherland's own work on 'white-collar' crime, which generated theoretical and conceptual confusion since, having defined the field in terms of people, he proceeded to study corporations (Cressey, 1989). Considerable disagreement remains (Friedrichs, 1992), not least, in a renewed, contemporary form, in the debate over merits of studying **social harm** rather than crime (Hillyard *et al.* (eds), 2004).

In this chapter, corporate crimes are viewed as 'illegal acts or omissions, punishable by the State under administrative, civil or criminal law, which are the result of deliberate decision making or culpable negligence within a legitimate formal organisation' (Pearce and Tombs, 1998: 107–10). This definition encompasses a range of companies, from the smallest limited liability company such as John Barr and Sons (a butchers involved in an E-coli outbreak leading to 21 deaths) to large multinationals such as Apple or BP. Further, it incorporates Sutherland's insight that distinctions between different forms of illegality—whether classed as criminal, civil, administrative—to a great extent reflect the ability of the powerful, including corporations, to have activities in which they may be implicated classified as less serious (Pearce and Tombs, 2003).

To cut through some of the confusion caused by Sutherland's terminology and operationalization of the concept of white-collar crime: corporations are legal constructs and do not literally 'act'. They are represented by real people, through CEOs, Boards of Directors, senior management, and chains of command, on the basis of standard operating procedures, strategies and policies, and organizational cultures. But to be clear about the relationship between the corporate form, individual action, and corporate crime, individuals may promote, connive in or turn a blind-eye to illegality for a variety of reasons. To the extent that this actually does, or is designed to, further the goals of the corporate entity, then such actions (and omissions) can be viewed as corporate crime—even if they also benefit the individual(s). By contrast, where individuals act contrary to the operating goals of, norms or interests of a corporation, and do so simply for their own benefit, this is considered white-collar crime, and is not the subject matter of this chapter: a high-profile example of the latter is Asil Nadir's looting of some £29 million from his company Polly Peck, for which he received a ten-year jail sentence in 2012 (BBC, 2012).

Finally scholars in the US have developed the term **state-corporate crime**. First used in 1990, Kramer and Michalowski (2006: 15) defined it as 'illegal or socially injurious actions that occur when one or more institutions of political governance pursue a goal in direct co-operation with one or more institutions of economic production and distribution'. Such crimes, they argue, are produced at the 'intersection' of business and government, either initiated or facilitated by states. An important conceptual development in the study of the **crimes of the powerful**, 'state-corporate crime' allows the capture of crimes committed in the context of increasingly complex relationships between states and the private sector, where private providers increasingly work alongside public authorities. Such contexts are diverse (see Chambliss *et al.*, 2010); they include the delivery of health care or the running of railway systems, the building of large infrastructure projects (schools, hospitals) through the 'Private Finance Initiative', specific high-profile collaborative activities such as the winning of large, overseas defence contracts, or even the 'war on terror' and the conflicts in Iraq and Afghanistan; and, as several contributors to this volume demonstrate, are also increasingly pervasive in the delivery of criminal justice (**Chapters 22, 23, 24, and 25 (Victims; Policing; Community sentences and offender management for adults; Prisons))**.

The problem of corporate crime

Dimensions of corporate crime

Corporate crime remains a broad term, covering a large range of offences of omission and commission with differing types of modus operandi, perpetrators, effects and victims. Because 'corporate crime' refers to a wide range of events and processes, it is often classified into 'types', one common classification covering financial offences, those against consumers, employees and the natural environment.

Academic studies have focused upon a range of financial crimes, including: illegal share dealings, mergers and takeovers; tax evasion; bribery; and illegal accounting practices. Enron, a classic example of the last, joins a list of offenders—including Guinness (illegal share dealings in the 1980s (Punch, 1996: 167–80) and BCCI (a global bank systematically involved in fraud, money laundering and bribery (Punch, 1996: 9–15)—whose crimes are symbolic of the term 'financial crime'. These may target other companies, shareholders, governments, or consumers. Consumers have been victims of three recent waves of offences in the UK, involving many of the same (well-known) financial services companies: in the 1980s, personal pensions frauds emerged, in which as many as 2.4 million victims lost their pensions after replacing their occupational schemes with high-risk private schemes (Slapper and Tombs, 1999); the endowment mortgage frauds of the 1990s—mis-selling a particularly risky mortgage product to high-risk customers—created as many as five million victims (Fooks, 2003); a decade later, the 'mis-selling' of payment protection insurance generated an estimated 2.75 million successful claims for compensation (BBC, 2011).

A second class of corporate crimes is those committed directly against consumers: illegal sales/marketing practices; the sale of unfit goods; conspiracies to fix prices and/or carve up market share; and various forms of false/illegal labelling. One academic focus here has been the diverse offences associated with 'food crime'—crimes at all stages of food production, distribution, preparation and sale which may ultimately result in consumers being over- or wrongly charged, misled, made ill or even killed (Croall, 2007). Also well documented are crimes associated with health care products (see Braithwaite, 1984). One example emerged in December 2011, when the French government recommended that women with breast implants from the manufacturer Poly Implant Prothese have these removed—they were filled with industrial rather than the approved medical silicone. Some 300,000 had been sold across 65 countries in Europe and South America (Sage, 2012). The case had echoes of silicone breast implants marketed by the US company Dow Corning in the 1990s (Dodge, 2005).

Third are a series of offences arising from the employment relationship. These include sexual and racial discrimination, violations of wage laws, of rights to organize and take industrial action, and various occupational health and safety offences. Again, these illegalities are varied and widespread. For example, in the UK at least 3,000 building workers were on a 'blacklist', preventing them gaining employment, mostly as a result of trade union health and safety activity (Ewing, 2009). Also in the UK, there are 1,200–1,500 work-related fatal injuries annually (Tombs and Whyte, 2008)—and the best estimate is that up to 75 per cent involve some violation of the law by an employer, even if most never result in prosecution (Tombs and Whyte, 2007)—and fatal occupational diseases, with up to 50,000 deaths *per annum* in the UK (Palmer, 2008). Internationally, high-profile disasters such as that at Bhopal may result in tens of thousands of deaths (Pearce and Tombs, 2012). And in this category we can also see the significance of relationships between legal and illegal organizations—while the 23 undocumented Chinese workers killed in Morecambe Bay were employed illegally by a 'gangmaster', this organized crime was nevertheless linked into a legitimate food processing, manufacturing and retail supply chain which puts ready meals in many of our microwaves (Tombs and Whyte, 2007: 26–9).

The final category, crimes against the environment, includes illegal emissions to air, water, and land, hazardous waste dumping, and illegal manufacturing practices. Pollutants are a key cause of death and disease. For example, in the UK, the Department of Health estimates at least 24,000 deaths every year can be attributed environmental air pollution (cited in Whyte, 2004). Separating corporate from individual sources of environmental pollution (the key example of the latter being personal vehicle emissions) is not easy. However, official data indicate that the largest known killers are nitrogen oxide, fine particles emissions and sulphur dioxides, which tend to be produced by commercial activity (Whyte, 2004). Without underestimating the harm caused by motor vehicles, it can be confidently assumed that corporations cause most deadly environmental pollution.

Even from this brief review, the difficulties of quantifying the scale of corporate crime are apparent. Nonetheless, on the basis of available data, two unequivocal conclusions can be reached.

First, corporate crime entails enormous costs. Many have physical costs—deaths, injuries, ill-health—arising out of dangerous workplaces, polluted environments, unsafe goods and services, and so on. Furthermore governments, taxpayers, consumers, workers, and other companies incur economic costs; the best available evidence indicates these far outweigh those associated with 'conventional' or 'street' offending (Slapper and Tombs, 1999). Whilst recognizing the difficulty in estimating the 'costs' of any form of crime this conclusion is difficult to contest. Even studies of 'single' cases of corporate crime—such as the collapse of Christmas club Farepak, estimated to have cost savers upwards of £50 million (Spalek, 2007)—support this general conclusion.

Second, the range of work that exists on corporate crime, case-studies of particular offences or categories of offences by type or industry, as well as more limited efforts at quantifying its scale and ubiquitousness, shows clearly that such offending is not a peripheral activity of a few 'bad apples' in the business world. Rather, it is endemic: corporate crimes are not simply widespread, they are routine and pervasive (Slapper and Tombs, 1999: 36–84).

REVIEW QUESTIONS

1 Can you think of other examples of the different categories of corporate crimes?

2 What evidence exists to indicate that corporate crime is widespread and pervasive?

The relative invisibility of corporate crime

While we know something of corporate crime, much of it, as with other forms of crime discussed in this volume, remains hidden from popular and legal scrutiny. This section is concerned with the particular ways corporate crime evades such scrutiny.

It should be emphasized that this is a *relative*, not an absolute, invisibility: corporate crime remains obscured but not entirely buried. Indeed, the whiff of corporate wrong-doing pervading the financial crisis and its austere aftermath makes plausible the suggestion that corporate crime has achieved a greater political and popular salience in recent years. The UK phone hacking scandal continues to enmesh staff at News International and senior figures from various branches of the State; the incessant TV adverts inviting pursuit of claims for 'mis-sold' personal protection insurance when taking out loans or credit cards are a constant reminder of corporate illegalities; and the seemingly unending stories—such as the manipulation of interest rates via LIBOR by senior bankers, or HSBC's alleged involvement in global money laundering—only confirm the public's steadily growing sense of a post-financial crisis banking system where illegal practices are routine. To this we could add a seemingly endless list of companies associated with some form of corporate wrongdoing, from Apple to Adidas, Walmart to Worldcom.

Why might this greater salience have arisen? Certainly the role of popular campaigns against corporate illegality—often using direct action designed to maximize publicity, further facilitated by widespread use of social media—is part of the story; the Occupy movement and UK Uncut, have both been relatively effective movements in demonstrating, amongst much else, how a different system of law appears to apply to corporations compared to 'us'.

More fundamental, however, may be the now-ubiquitous presence of private corporations in all aspects of our lives, a direct result of three decades of neo-liberalism. Across four Conservative governments between 1979 and 1997, literally hundreds of publicly owned companies were privatized or deregulated: British Aerospace, telecommunications, gas, electricity and water supply, coal, steel, atomic energy, bus and train services, shipbuilding, freight and ports, and postal services. Subsequent Labour administrations continued to open almost every area of the public sector to private providers. Traffic management, refuse collection, health and social care, higher education, criminal justice and even national security and war are all to some extent marketized sectors where private corporations are significant if not dominant players. Moreover, many of these companies are multinationals operating internationally across a range of sectors. G4S, for example, infamous for a series of scandals from the death of Jimmy Mubenga to its failure to provide adequate security at the London Olympics, has almost 700,000 employees across 125 countries working in a diverse range of sectors. The sheer scale and ubiquity of its presence makes it more vulnerable to exposés of wrongdoing.

There are numerous routes by which corporate violations may become known—and State surveillance may be amongst the least significant. There are many examples of investigative journalism exposing corporate offending—most recently the tenacity of Nick Davies and others at *The Guardian* newspaper uncovered the systematic hacking of phones and computers by journalists at the *News of the World*, leading to its demise, two Parliamentary Select Committee Inquiries, the Leveson Enquiry on The Culture, Practice and Ethics of the Press and a string of arrests and prosecutions. An alternative but often related route is through whistle-blowers—those inside organizations who expose wrongdoing, often at great personal danger and cost and often after failing to have their concerns acted upon by the organization's senior management prior to 'going public'. Third are efforts by local campaigners, communities or others affected by corporate wrongdoing—bullied employees, housing estates affected by pollution, patients experiencing side-effects of a prescribed treatment or drug—to have their victimization recognized. Again, an aim is often to attract media attention. Finally, specific incidents often cast the spotlight on a particular company or industry only to reveal further examples of offending: a series of multiple fatality train crashes in the UK through the 1980s and 1990s revealed the common practice of ignoring red stop signals and the dire state of privatized, sub-contracted maintenance work; somewhat differently, televised abuse of vulnerable residents of a Bristol care home focused attention on the dangers of contracting out social care.

Ultimately all of these routes to exposure lead to the State and its regulatory functions in respect of private business. Responding to corporate crime, as well as proactive attempts to prevent it, falls to State regulators, the laws they have to enforce and the resources and political support at their disposal. These are crucial elements in the explanation of the relative invisibility of corporate crime, a series of mutually reinforcing social processes which in combination contribute to removing such offences from dominant definitions of 'crime, law and order' (Slapper and Tombs, 1999).

At the formal political level—for example, the location of regulatory agencies outside the Ministry of Justice and Home Office, resources allocated, and in legislation for 'light touch' **enforcement**—the marginalization of corporate crime as crime is underlined. This is reinforced through the political rhetoric of crime, law and order, where 'zero tolerance', being 'tough on crime, tough on the causes of crime' and furthering the 'rights' of victims are always deployed in the context of street or traditional crimes (see Chapters 18 and 21) but never to corporate offending—even though perfectly applicable (Geis, 1996).

Through the application of law and legal regulation, corporate crimes are consistently filtered out from processes of criminalization (see, for example, Tombs and Whyte, 2008). Thus, in the very framing of the substance and parameters of legal regulation, its enforcement, the extent and ways of investigation of potential offences and offenders, the prosecution of offences, and the use of sanctions, most corporate offences are relatively decriminalized.

This filtering out is reproduced in 'crime data': Home Office crime statistics ignore corporate crimes, focusing on the conventional; and it is revealing to compare the Home Office's response to problems in official recording of conventional crimes, the annual British Crime Survey (see Chapter 3), with the complete absence of any analogous initiative to uncover the hidden figure of corporate crime. Independent efforts to piece together official data on specific types of corporate crimes are fraught with problems (Levi and Burrows, 2008; Tombs and Whyte, 2007). If, as Maguire notes, 'a salient feature of almost all modern forms of discourse about crime is the emphasis placed upon terms associated with its quantification and measurement' (Maguire, 1994: 236), it is hardly surprising that corporate crimes 'do not feature in ... debates about the "crime problem"'(Nelken, 1994: 355).

These absences cannot be understood without reference to the legitimacy which attaches to business and the difficulties of viewing them as (potential) offenders (Snider, 2000). 'Conventional criminals' are represented as a burden upon society in a way corporations are not. Where organizations engage in criminal activity, this is represented as an aberration from their routine, legitimate activities, and tends to be cast as involving technical infringements of law, rather than real crimes. BAE Systems remains Britain's national champion in the international arms industry. Its various long running involvements in bribery to secure contracts—and several legal actions against it in the US and the UK (*The Guardian*, nd)—have hardly dented its pride of place. One recent high-profile case in the UK was settled when it admitted to what were agreed to be 'accounting irregularities' (Evans and Leigh, 2010), a euphemism for fraud and corruption hardly likely to generate a criminal label!

This contrast with 'real' crime and criminals, is reflected in and reinforced through the media. Whether in fictional or documentary treatments of crime on TV, newspaper or other print coverage, while there may be some attention to corporate crime, representations of crime converge to produce 'blanket' conceptualizations that reinforce dominant stereotypes of crime and the criminal (Chibnall, 1977). Although corporate crime is represented, its presence is vastly outweighed by treatments of conventional crime, it is treated in lesser profile outlets or formats, and it is represented in the sanitizing language of mis-selling, scandals, disasters and accidents, rather than crime (Tombs and Whyte, 2001).

If corporate crime is an ongoing part of our lived experience, few of us are consciously aware of it as we go about our lives as workers, consumers, or residents. Thus, many victims of corporate crimes may never be aware of their victimization (Snell and Tombs, 2011). If people overpay for goods because of price-fixing between retailers, or are duped into buying inappropriate pensions or mortgages by illegal means, they may never be aware of their victimization. Even if they are aware, acting upon it is often extremely difficult (Snell and Tombs, 2011)—they may know that their community's health is declining, but not be able to pinpoint the exact source of illegal pollution; or, if a factory or industrial process is identified, may feel the organization too big, or that support from public bodies (the Environment Agency or the local council) is lacking, to make pursuing the matter worthwhile.

None of the mechanisms whereby corporate crimes are rendered relatively invisible are particularly remarkable in isolation. What is crucial is their mutually reinforcing nature—that is, they all work in the same direction and to the same effect, removing corporate crime from 'crime law and order' agendas.

REVIEW QUESTIONS

1 In what ways do political processes contribute to the obscuring of corporate crimes?

2 In what ways do various media contribute to the relative invisibility of corporate crime?

Explaining corporate crime?

One of the most intriguing characteristics of criminology is that the vast majority of teaching and research simply assumes that 'crime' refers to those illegal activities on which the State focuses most of its crime control resources (Hillyard *et al.* (eds), 2004). Thus, virtually all forms of criminological theorizing (see Chapter 4) have been developed to explain conventional offending—but this is not to say none of this theory is applicable to corporate crime.

Classicism sought to develop a rational, just system of penality, albeit aimed at conventional crimes. Its key claim was that 'the criminal' chooses, more or less freely, to commit crime, a choice based on a calculative reasoning, weighing the benefits of a criminal act against the likelihood and consequences of detection. If such rational calculation under-explains the incidence of conventional crime (Taylor *et al.*, 1973), it may better approximate what corporations, or their directors and managers, actually do. One of the defining characteristics of a corporation is the potential for rational action, based upon strategic calculation, including the ability to anticipate and to predict external responses to its actions—all in order to maximize its long run profits, the corporate *raison d'être*. If we add the fact of relatively weak regulation (see later in this chapter), we have exactly the combination of factors that, according to classicist logic, will produce criminality. There might, therefore, be real potential for deterrent-based strategies for controlling corporate crime, even if these have manifestly failed with respect to 'traditional' offenders (Pearce and Tombs, 1998: 292–305).

Turning to the variety of individual positivisms within criminology, we find attempts to identify the abnormalities that either propel individuals into crime, or ensure that they are more predisposed to committing crime than the general population. Yet one of the most interesting features about individuals involved in corporate offending is their normality, there being an almost total lack of meaningful differences between them and non-offenders (Snider, 1993: 61). Indeed, where individuals involved in corporate offences appear not to be 'normal', this is unlikely to be cast negatively, as pathology; rather, this becomes a mark of distinctiveness to be aspired to, characterized by success, wealth, hard work, and entrepreneurship, personified by Branson, Jobs, Sugar, and other celebrities from the world of business.

Thus, some have sought to identify those 'personality' factors associated with success in the business world, highlighting features such as being innovative, ambitious, shrewd, aggressive, impatient, and possessing a 'moral flexibility' (see Snider, 1993). Robert Hare—developer of the 'Psychopathy Checklist' and long-term adviser to the FBI—has also written of those with 'psychopathic' tendencies valued in work organizations (Babiak and Hare, 2006). Moreover, it is clear how the personality traits through which these authors define 'psychopathy' may allow individuals to become involved in corporate illegalities. Leaving aside the problematic nature of 'psychopathy', such observations tell us something about how we might explain many forms of corporate crime—if corporations recruit people with these characteristics, and if the higher up the corporate hierarchy the more likely these are to be accentuated, then we need to know something about the culture and functioning of the corporation itself, as well as the environments within which it operates, to understand how its employees, from the most senior downwards, act, think and rationalize. We shall return to these issues later.

If individual positivism failed to consider corporate offenders, then so too did the tradition dominant since the 1930s, sociological positivism. However, there are some notable exceptions. A leading member of the Chicago School, Sutherland, attempted to develop a general, sociological, theory of crime causation, claiming 'differential association' could explain both upper-class and lower-class crimes: crime arises from an excess of definitions favourable to law violation over definitions unfavourable to such violation. Criminal activity—motivations, *post hoc* rationalizations and techniques of commission—is, like all behaviour, learnt. This learning emerges out of our associations—associations which vary by frequency, duration, priority and intensity.

This seems to have validity for understanding the willingness of individuals to engage in crime within and on behalf of corporations. Our associations with individuals within a corporation are hardly fleeting; we spend a significant amount of time at work, sometimes for the same company, often in the same kind of industry. Further, many of us invest our work with significance—either instrumentally, seeing work as sheer necessity, or (for the lucky few) more expressively, as part of our identity. Moreover, all companies and jobs have their accepted 'ways of doing things', and employees learn these; presumably, if this holds for legal activity, it holds for illegal activity too. For example, within retail butchery, it is common knowledge that frozen poultry can be defrosted in a particular way to make it resemble fresh poultry—then sold at a higher price, defrauding the consumer. Further, there may be generalized knowledge that 'everyone' in the trade is doing it—which not only provides a motivation, since not to do so is to place one's own business at a competitive disadvantage, but also because it is so generalized it is acceptable, not really criminal, an instance of the 'techniques of neutralisation' which can aid understanding motivation (Matza and Sykes, 1957; Box, 1983: 54–7).

Differential association has been subjected to stringent criticism (Taylor *et al.*, 1973: 125–30). It is of interest, however, precisely because it attempted to incorporate corporate crime within a general theory of crime. While other variants of sociological positivism have not done so in such an explicit manner, some aspects may still be useful. For example, Merton linked lower-class crime and deviant behaviour to the disjunction between institutionalized aspirations and the availability of legitimate opportunity structures; Passas argues that there is no compelling reason why this anomie cannot apply to corporate deviance: 'people in the upper social reaches' are 'far from immune to pressures towards deviance' (Passas, 1990: 158). Similarly, Box (1983) identified structural pressures to succeed for business in terms of maximization of profit, growth and efficiency, all furthered through predictable operating environments—with deviant methods often the most effective means of achieving these.

Finally, forms of criminology placing an understanding of power at the centre of their theorizing also have the potential for insights regarding the nature and incidence of corporate crimes which are, after all, made possible on the basis of relative power. Ironically, the labelling perspective, while it sought to examine how processes of criminalization operated with respect to individuals from certain social groups, failed to ask very obvious converse questions: why are certain kinds of crime not subject to social opprobrium, and why are certain kinds of offenders able successfully to resist the processes of criminalization to which lower-class offenders seem highly vulnerable? (Nelken, 1994).

Various forms of critical criminologies—including Marxism and feminism—have made important contributions to our knowledge of corporate crime causation: Pearce (1976) has argued that corporations, with the connivance of the American state, act systematically to control the markets within which they operate; Hills' (1987) edited collection contains a series of empirical and theoretical case studies of how the drive for profit systematically produces injury and death; and Szockyj and Fox's (1996) *Corporate Victimisation of Women* is an anthology documenting the myriad ways in which corporations exploit constructions of gender to victimize female consumers, workers and recipients of health care (only an understanding of patriarchy and dominant ideologies of body image that circulate within patriarchal societies can explain how women are in the position to become victims of toxic breast implants, see earlier in this chapter).

Whilst there are clear differences between the labelling perspective, Marxisms and feminisms, they share the theoretical commitment to move beyond the narrowest confines of criminology, to deconstruct dominant categories of crime and to view these constructions, and the criminal justice systems based upon them, as an effect of, but also a means of reproducing power. From the preceding, it should also be clear that to understand corporate crime causation we must take into account a series of factors ranging from the individual through to the structural.

At the individual level we need to take account of personality and other characteristics, not least the kinds of personalities that are valued within companies, as well as 'individual' factors that are socially constructed as relevant, such as rank/position within hierarchy, age, gender, and ethnicity. For example, it is relevant to enquire whether an organization is one where being female diminishes one's social power, or in which time served adds authority.

At the level of the immediate work-group or sub-unit within the organization, we must take account of inter-personal dynamics, the culture of the work-group (and the extent to which this coheres or clashes with the culture of the wider organization), its location within the overall organization, both structurally and geographically—that is, is it relatively autonomous or highly supervised, part of one large organizational complex, or geographically isolated?

There are also key sets of issues relating to the organization itself. We need to understand its structure, its internal lines of decision-making and accountability, its geographical scope of operations and the nature, volume and complexity of internal transactions. Issues of organizational culture must be addressed: is the organization risk-taking or risk-averse; gendered; authoritarian; dominated by a blame culture? The products or services that are the focus of the organization are also relevant: are these opaque or transparent, are they sold to consumers or other organizations, is their production labour-or capital-intensive? Further we also need to know something of levels of profitability, how that is calculated, and how that relates to rewards systems.

Lastly, there are key questions regarding the wider economic, political and social environments within which the organization operates. Amongst these are: the nature of the market structure; the size and scope of the market; the nature and level of regulation; the general nature of State-business relationships; and the dominant form of political economy, and concomitant societal values, including the nature and degree of pro- or anti-business sentiment. Again, the overall economic 'health' of the economies in which the corporation operates is of relevance.

This is only a brief summary of an extensive and complex inter-related, set of factors. The need for such a wide-ranging integrated explanatory framework has long been recognized (Coleman, 1987), though theoretical development remains at an early stage.

REVIEW QUESTIONS

1 How might we apply classicism and individual positivism to an understanding of corporate crime causation?

2 What forms of sociological positivism have been used in the explanation of corporate crime?

3 What factors need to be incorporated into an adequate explanation of corporate crime?

'Controlling' corporate crime

Understandings of the causes of corporate crime inevitably influence arguments regarding its control. As we have seen, the various forms in which corporate offending may be brought to light—such as whistle-blowing or investigative journalism—are also potentially forms of social control of corporate activity. That said, each leads in its own way to the main *formal* mechanisms intended to control corporate crime, namely the enforcement of law through regulatory bodies via inspection and monitoring systems. It is these, and their limitations, which are the subject of this section.

It is in the area of **regulation** that there is perhaps the most significant body of academic research. Numerous studies—mostly nationally based, but some with useful cross-national comparative work—examine the practices of a range of regulatory bodies (for a review see Clarke, 2000: 136–61). These allow broad generalizations to be made about the practices and effects of regulatory enforcement agencies: non-enforcement is the most frequently found characteristic; enforcement activity tends to focus upon the smallest and weakest individuals and organizations; and sanctions following regulatory activity are light (Snider, 1993: 120–4).

Most commonly, such studies identify a cooperative approach as predominant: regulators seek to enforce through persuasion—they advise, educate, and bargain, negotiate and reach compromise with the regulated (see Pearce and Tombs, 1998: 223–46). When violations become known, inspectors engage in a dialogue with management, prioritizing compliance for the most serious offences, usually on the basis of an agreed timetable, whilst accepting that others, deemed less serious, may take longer to correct. This dialogue clearly takes into account the priorities of the inspectorate along with the commitment, motivation and resources of the regulated (see Hawkins, 2002).

This is not to say more punitive methods are not used. Indeed, much academic work on regulation is concerned to identify the most appropriate, context-dependent, combination of cooperation and punitiveness—'the regulatory mix'. The most influential work here remains that of John Braithwaite and colleagues. Their starting point is a consideration of self-regulation, on the basis that State regulators will never have the resources to effectively enforce regulatory law, and that internal regulators enjoy technical and social advantages over outsiders (Braithwaite and Fisse, 1987). Self-regulation is described (and prescribed) on a 'carrot and stick' basis: where it proves ineffective, the next preferred regulatory move is 'enforced self-regulation', requiring the company to develop a tailored set of rules by which it intends to comply with the law. Once approved by regulators, they are 'enforced' internally; where evidence of non-compliance emerges, the potential for punitive external intervention remains (Ayres and Braithwaite, 1992: 102–16). Enforcement is thus conceived of in terms of potential escalation, where non-compliance may lead to ever more interventionist and punitive modes of enforcement. In essence, this is an incrementalist and compliance-oriented strategy based on the principle of deterrence. It is also one that targets resources on recalcitrant businesses—assumed to be a small minority—and is increasingly allied to techniques of risk-based regulation, now predominant in the UK, whereby regulators make assessments on the basis of various forms of 'intelligence' as to where to concentrate limited resources (Black, 2005).

By contrast, a more marginal body of work exploring alternatives to cooperative approaches advocates a more punitive approach—though not suggesting that every violation of the law be prosecuted. A starting point is that corporate crime is viewed as real crime, and subject to more adversarial, punitive and interventionist forms of regulation (Pearce and Tombs, 1998: 280–316). If such an approach has failed to gain traction in academic and policy circles, there is evidence of the success of this approach where it has been attempted in specific instances (Pearce and Tombs, 1998: 286–92). Moreover, under very specific social, political and economic conditions, it remains possible that it can be generalized (Alvesalo, 2003).

Fundamentally at issue in these different views of regulation are distinct understandings of the corporation: of the extent to which corporate entities can and do act morally, have some sense of social responsibility, with concern for their reputations, are capable of being trusted, and the ways in which concerns of profitability interact with these sentiments. For some, these issues, particularly of trust, need to be explored much more fully, especially in an era where regulatory resources are likely to be diminished further—as does the potential for regulation 'beyond the state', where non-governmental actors such as insurers, trade associations, consultants, lawyers and NGOs play potentially key roles in regulation (Hutter, 2011). For others, to place trust in trust overlooks the legal duties owed by managements to shareholders to maximize profits, to disregard the short-term horizons of those who own and control corporations and the realities of the stock market pressures upon them, and to under-estimate the intimate relationships between corporations and states.

Notwithstanding these disputes, a key issue remains—namely, what sanctions can be most usefully imposed upon an offending corporation?

By far the most common sanction is the monetary fine, generally considered to be low. For example, the average fine for all HSE health and safety convictions for 2010–11 was £27,420 (Freedom of Information Request Reference No: 2011110416, December 2011). Such averages mask the occasionally much higher fine—but even these tend to be insignificant when set against a company's annual profits or turnover. The record fine for a health and safety offence in the UK was £15 million, levied on Transco Plc in August 2005 following the deaths of Andrew and Janette Findlay and their two children when a gas explosion destroyed their home. When sentencing, the judge commented on Transco's long history of safety offences, while pouring scorn on its defence that the gas leak had been internal to the property, effectively seeking to blame the deceased themselves. Yet even this fine was less than 2 per cent of Transco's previous year's after-tax profit, and just 0.16 per cent of turnover— the equivalent of fining someone earning £25,000 a year just £36 (Tombs and Whyte, 2007: 174-8; see also Walters, 2010: 877).

While some recent fines for high-profile offences—for example, by July 2012, the total costs of fines and compensation for BP following the explosion at its Deepwater Horizon facility in the Gulf of Mexico was estimated at $38 billion (Press Association, 2012)—are so large as to be virtually unimaginable, it is important to reach some sense of what any fine means to the company in question. Thus, even apparently staggeringly high fines may not be all bad news. For example, when the British-based bank, Standard Chartered, negotiated a penalty with the New York Department of Financial Services (DFS) of $340 million (£220 million) in August 2012, following allegations that it broke international sanctions by hiding trades of some $250 *billion* with Iran, its share price *rose* by 3 per cent—even though it expected other US regulators subsequently to seek to impose penalties for the offences, committed between 2001 and 2007. Crucially, the settlement had not only protected the bank's US licence to operate but, according to one group of analysts:

> The aggregate of this fine, plus any additional recompense to other regulators, could total less than 1% of Standard Chartered's equity and the DFS fine represents around 6% of our current earnings forecast for Standard Chartered, suggesting the company will be able to absorb this cost and still deliver a 10th successive year of record profits. (cited in Treanor, 2012)

Now, it might be argued that were fines to be raised to levels sufficient to have a deterrent effect, this might be counter-productive: the company may pass costs on to workers, consumers, or both, rather than to shareholders, and some levels of fines might even lead to firm closure, affecting employees, suppliers and consumers. These are not reasons against using large fines, but indicate the need to use them sensitively. Moreover, fines need not simply be a direct monetary penalty—the equity fine involves the confiscation of a block of shares. Moreover, even if we accept that there are problems with the use of monetary sanctions, sentencing of corporations and/or individuals involved in corporate crime is an area in which there now exists a range of imaginative proposals, some having had limited introduction, others remaining at the proposal stage. They include:

- disqualification of individual directors of the offending firm (used in the case of financial crimes, but rarely beyond this context);
- withdrawal of licences to operate or the barring of convicted companies from bidding for government-related contracts;
- use of community service or restitution orders, whereby a convicted company makes good damage caused, or uses its resources to provide goods and services to a victimized community;
- use of probation and rehabilitation orders, requiring a company to hire outside 'experts', for example, to reform safety training or financial reporting systems;
- use of adverse publicity and 'shaming', naming an offending company in appropriate media or other outlets.

All of these have drawbacks and each is more or less appropriate for particular types of corporation following specific forms of offence (Slapper and Tombs, 1999). While there are clearly difficulties developing effective sanctions in the case of corporate crime, these are more political than technical (Etzioni, 1993). Determining 'appropriate' sentencing is based upon a view of what and how big the problem is, and what sanctioning regimes can and should seek to achieve (Macrory, 2006). The 'problem' of sentencing is very much an effect of a political refusal to treat corporate crime as real crime.

REVIEW QUESTIONS

1   What are the attractions and limitations of self-regulation?

2   What are the main problems associated with the use of fines as a sanction against corporations?

CONCLUSION

The central aim of this chapter has been to mark out corporate crime as a crime problem, in effect to reiterate Sutherland's demand, made over half a century ago—that corporate crime be given greater attention within the discipline of criminology. This also raises awareness of the economic, political and social obstacles to so doing: at issue here is power—for exposing corporate crime means exposing crimes associated with powerful organizations, ones with which States (local, regional, national) have increasingly intimate relationships (Tombs and Whyte, 2003).

There has, of course, been progress since Sutherland's 'clarion call'—even if, as this chapter has indicated, this has been rather faltering. The very existence of this chapter in an introductory undergraduate text is, perhaps, one manifestation of that progress. And, as we write, what we referred to as the increased salience of corporate crime *may* make this a watershed period in the political, popular *and academic* scrutiny to which corporate illegalities are subject.

But there still remains significant legal, political and social distance between corporate entities and their crimes and those of 'real' criminals. There are numerous reasons for this persistent chasm in our understanding of what crime is and who criminals are. Corporations are fictional entities—staffed by real people, but lacking arms, legs, brains, so on a very basic level they do not fit the image of a criminal with which we all grow up (Hillyard and Tombs, 2004). Moreover, those actual men (and, to a lesser extent, women) who manage them retain, for the most part, a status, respectability and a life-style which does not cohere with a 'criminal' image. Many of us, through choice or necessity, still use their goods or services—virtually every high street bank has some record of recent offending, as does every major oil company. And crucially, these *corporate* entities are not treated as real criminals by criminal justice systems or political elites.

This last point is particularly significant, and can perhaps be best illustrated by the banking scandals in the UK over the past five years. The recession engendered by the financial crisis led to widespread negative reaction. But there were several intriguing patterns to this. One was the vilification of a handful of individuals—the folk-devilling of some high-profile bankers such as Fred Goodwin and Bob Diamond. But as folk devils these were represented as *rogue individuals*. Somewhat differently, while social reaction did stray into the realm of systemic practices, such reaction rarely included capitalist activity *per se*: notably there emerged distinctions between 'crony' and 'moral' capitalism, or 'predator' versus 'producer' capitalism, always with the implicit notion that 'good' capitalism can outweigh the bad. Another response to the crisis has been to present it as an uncontrollable force for which no-one in particular was responsible—the use of the term 'tsunami' has been widespread and instructive. Somewhat differently, the costs of the bailout have been recast as a public debt for which 'we' are all somehow responsible, having lived beyond our means, with other analogies, such as the need to balance the household budget or the 'maxed-out' credit card, being invoked. Within all of these social reactions, what is missing is any sense that corporate crime is routine and systematic—a fact this chapter has sought to document. And the dominance of such discourses is important—they crucially underpin systems of regulation which, while varying across nation-states and indeed across different areas of social protection, remain predicated upon the assumption that most companies most of the time are essentially law-abiding, not least through having some form of social responsibility—a view still dominant amongst academic scholars of regulation.

While it is too soon to make any definitive judgement, at present there is little evidence that corporate crime scholarship has been significantly kick-started by the new popular and political salience of this phenomenon. But aside from the scale and significance of corporate crime *per se*, rendering it a necessary object of sustained academic scrutiny, corporate crime research is also worthwhile in that it can perform an important role for the discipline of criminology: such work can encourage criminological reflexivity. A focus upon corporate crime entails continual scrutiny of the coverage and omissions of legal categories, the presences and absences within legal discourses, the social constructions of these categories and discourses, their underpinning of, treatment within and development through criminal justice systems, the ways in which particular laws are enforced (or not), interpreted, challenged, and, of no little significance, the contours of the discipline of criminology itself. If the criminological imagination can shed important light upon corporate crime (White, 2003), then there is no doubting that the study of corporate crime is itself one means of reinvigorating that same criminological imagination (Alvesalo *et al.*, 2006).

QUESTIONS FOR DISCUSSION

1 The (in)visibility of corporate crime

Select one broadsheet and one tabloid newspaper from the same day, then search for stories related to (a) conventional crime, and (b) corporate crime; 'count' the stories devoted to each type of crime; note the prominence (page and/or section) of the stories; and consider the tone/nature of the two types of stories. Are there differences between the coverage of these two types of crime; are there differences between the two newspapers?

2 Explaining corporate crime

Select a case study of corporate crime. How might we apply the following criminological perspectives to understand the genesis and nature of this case?

- classicism;
- individual positivism;
- sociological positivism;
- labelling;
- Marxist/critical criminologies.

3 The problem of enforcement

One of the arguments against the more punitive enforcement of law against business is that this will be counter-productive—it will generate opposition from business and ultimately prevent the regulators doing their job. Discuss how likely you consider this reaction to be and what forms it may take. How can it be countered? How would such arguments be received if they were applied to conventional criminals?

4 Sentencing corporate offenders

There are several well-recognized limitations in the use of monetary fines against corporations convicted of crime: how might these weaknesses apply to the use of fines for conventional criminals?

Aside from monetary fines, what other sanctions might be applied—and what are the strengths and weaknesses of these other sanctions? How might these considerations of strengths and weaknesses apply to conventional criminals?

GUIDE TO FURTHER READING

Academic texts

Box, S. (1983) *Power, Crime and Mystification*. London: Tavistock, Chapter 2.

Over 60-plus pages, Box's classic introduction to this area of study explores the scale of corporate crime, its invisibility, ways in which it must be explained, and issues of regulation and control.

MacSheoin, T. (2010) 'Chemical Catastrophe: from Bhopal to BP Texas City', *Monthly Review*, 62, (4), September, http://monthlyreview.org/2010/09/01/chemical-catastrophe-from-bhopal-to-bp-texas-city

A forensic, accessible account of 'disasters' which contain many of the routine features of corporate crimes: the denial of responsibility, blaming victims, a-moral management, and neglect by state regulators.

Pearce, F. and Snider, L. (eds) (1995) *Corporate Crime: contemporary debates*. Toronto: University of Toronto Press.

Across 19 chapters, this edited text covers a range of theoretical and empirical issues related to the incidence, nature, and regulation of corporate crime, including contributions by most of the leading corporate crime scholars across the English-speaking world.

Szockyi, E. and Fox, J.G. (eds) (1996) *Corporate Victimisation of Women*. Boston, Mass.: Northeastern University Press.

The eight chapters here take a gendered view of corporate crime, covering theoretical debates around corporate crime, case studies of particular industries and forms of crime, and discussing the nature of regulation as well as prospects for regulatory reform.

Whyte, D. (ed) (2009) *Crimes of the Powerful: a reader*. Maidenhead: Open University Press.

Contains 45 abridged extracts from a wide range of texts not just focusing upon, but providing key social scientific contexts for, the study of corporate crime, complete with original Section Introductions.

Other material

The Corporation (M. Achbar, 2004)

A wide-ranging diagnosis of the modern corporation as psychopathic; best viewed alongside a read of Joel Bakan's (2004) book of the same name.

Crude: The Real Price of Oil (J. Berlinger, 2009)

Documents the legal and political struggles of the indigenous people of the Ecuadorian Amazon with the US oil giant Texaco over claims of deadly levels of pollution.

Enron—the Smartest Guys in the Room (A. Gibney, 2005)

Charts the rise, demise and pursuit through the criminal justice system of Enron, itself based upon a 2004 book by McLean and Elkind

Iraq for Sale: The War Profiteers (R. Greenwald, 2006)

Portrays occupied Iraq as a free for all, where private companies rushed to provide security and infrastructural services at vastly inflated prices, with the support of key US politicians.

Inside Job (C. Ferguson, 2010)

Based upon interviews with almost all of the key players—politicians, regulators and academics—this provides an overview of the conditions which produced the economic crisis of 2008, and how they look set to stay in place.

Walmart: the High Cost of Low Price (R. Greenwald, 2005)

A wide-ranging focus upon the world's largest retailer, demonstrating its involvement in a range of illegalities and harms.

WEB LINKS

http://www.business-humanrights.org/Home

The Business and Human Rights Resource Center provides access (through links) to a wide range of materials relating to business and human rights across the globe.

http://www.corporatewatch.org/

A campaigning site, bringing together the work of activists and researchers seeking both to expose illegal and unethical corporate activity and to explore business-government relations in general; it has a US counterpart, although they are not formally linked, see Corporate Watch (US) at http://www.corpwatch.org/trac/about/about.html

http://www.open.gov.uk/

The Open Government website, which contains links to all regulatory bodies in England and Wales.

http://paulsjusticepage.com/elite-deviance.htm

An excellent source of corporate crime material, maintained by Paul Leighton, co-author of Jeffrey Reiman's *The Rich Get Richer the Poor Get Prison*.

REFERENCES

Alvesalo, A. (2003) *The Dynamics of Economic Crime Control*. Espoo, Finland: The Police College of Finland.

Alvesalo, A., Tombs, S., Virta, E., and Whyte, D. (2006) 'Re-Imagining Crime Prevention: controlling corporate crime?', *Crime, Law and Social Change* 45: 1–25.

Ayres, I. and Braithwaite, J. (1992) *Responsive Regulation. Transcending the Deregulation Debate*. Oxford: Oxford University Press.

Babiak, P. and Hare, R. (2006) *Snakes in Suits: When Psychopaths Go to Work*. New York: HarperCollins.

BBC (2011) 'What Now for Payment Protection Insurance?', 13 June, http://www.bbc.co.uk/news/business-13143819

BBC (2012) 'Asil Nadir Jailed for 10 Years for Polly Peck Thefts', 23 August, http://www.bbc.co.uk/news/uk-19352531

Black, J. (2005) 'The Emergence of Risk Based Regulation and the New Public Management in the UK', *Public Law*, Autumn: 512–49.

Box, S. (1983) *Power, Crime and Mystification*. London: Tavistock.

Braithwaite, J. (1984) *Corporate Crime in the Pharmaceutical Industry*. London: Routledge and Kegan Paul.

Braithwaite, J. and Fisse, B. (1987) 'Self-Regulation and the Control of Corporate Crime' in C.D. Shearing and P.C. Stenning (eds) *Private Policing*. Beverly Hills: Sage, 221–46.

Chambliss, W, Michalowski, R., and Kramer, R. (eds) (2010) *State Crime in the Global Age*. Cullompton: Willan.

Chibnall, S. (1977) *Law-and-Order News. An Analysis of Crime Reporting in the British Press*. London: Tavistock.

Clarke, M. (2000) *Regulation. The Social Control of Business Between Law and Politics*. London: Macmillan.

Cressey, D. (1989) 'The Poverty of Theory in Corporate Crime Research' in F. Adler and W.S. Laufer (eds) *Advances in Criminological Theory*. New Brunswick, NJ: Transaction, 31–55.

Coleman, J.S. (1987) 'Toward an Integrated Theory of White-Collar Crime', *American Journal of Sociology* 93: 406–39.

Croall, H. (2007) 'Food Crime' in P. Beirne and N. South (eds) *Issues in Green Criminology*. Cullompton: Willan, 206–29.

Dodge, M. (2005) 'Breast Implants' in L. Salinger (ed) *Encyclopedia of Corporate and White-Collar Crime*, Volume 1. Thousand Oaks, Ca/London: Sage, 107–9.

Etzioni, A. (1993) 'The US Sentencing Commission on Corporate Crime: a critique' in G. Geis and P. Jesliow (eds) *White-Collar Crime. Special Issue of the Annals of the American Academy of Political and Social Science*, 525, January. Newbury Park, Ca: Sage.

Evans, R. and Leigh, D. (2010) 'BAE Admits Poor Accounting as Part of Corruption Case Plea Bargain', *The Guardian*, 23 November.

Ewing, K. (2009) *Ruined Lives. Blacklisting in the UK construction industry*. Liverpool: Institute of Employment Rights.

Fooks, G. (2003) 'Contrasts in Tolerance: the Peculiar Case of Financial Regulation', *Contemporary Politics*, 9, (2): 127–42.

Friedrichs, D. (1992) 'White-Collar Crime and the Definitional Quagmire: a Provisional Solution', *Journal of Human Justice*, 3, (2): 5–21.

Geis, G. (1996) 'A Base on Balls for White Collar Criminals' in D. Shichor and D.K. Sechrest (eds) *Three Strikes and You're Out. Vengeance as Public Policy*. Thousand Oaks, Ca: Sage.

Hawkins, K. (2002) *Law as Last Resort. Prosecution Decision-making in a Regulatory Agency*. Oxford: Oxford University Press.

Hills, S. (ed) (1987) *Corporate Violence. Injury and death for profit*. Totowa, NJ: Rowman & Littlefield.

Hillyard, P., Pantazis, C., Tombs, S., and Gordon, D. (eds) (2004) *Beyond Criminology? Taking Harm Seriously.* London: Pluto Press.

Hillyard, P., Sim, J., Tombs, S., and Whyte, D. (2004) 'Leaving a "Stain Upon the Silence": contemporary criminology and the politics of dissent', *British Journal of Criminology* 44, (3): 369–90.

Hillyard, P. and Tombs, S. (2004) 'Beyond Criminology?' in P. Hillyard *et al.* (eds) (2004) *Beyond Criminology? Taking Harm Seriously.* London: Pluto Press.

Hutter, B. (2011) 'Understanding the New Regulatory Governance: Business Perspectives', *Law & Policy* 33, (4): 459–76.

Kramer, R. and Michalowski, R. (2006) 'The Original Formulation' in Michalowski, R. and Kramer, R. (eds) *State-Corporate Crime.* New Jersey: Rutgers University Press.

Levi, M. (2009) 'Suite Revenge? The Shaping of Folk Devils and Moral Panics about White-Collar Crimes', *British Journal of Criminology* 49, (1): 48–67.

Levi, M. and Burrows, J. (2008) 'Measuring the Impact of Fraud in the UK: a conceptual and empirical journey', *British Journal of Criminology* 48, (3): 293–318.

Macrory, R. (2006) *Regulatory Justice: making sanctions effective.* Final Report. London: Better Regulation Executive.

Maguire, M. (1994) 'Crime Statistics, Patterns, and Trends: changing perceptions and their implications' in M. Maguire *et al.* (eds) *The Oxford Handbook of Criminology,* 233–91.

Matza, D. and Sykes, G.M. (1957) 'Techniques of Neutralization: a theory of delinquency', *American Sociological Review,* 22, December: 667–70.

Nelken, D. (1994) 'White-Collar Crime' in D. Nelken (ed) *White-Collar Crime.* Aldershot: Dartmouth.

Palmer, H. (2008) 'The Whole Story', *Safety and Health Practitioner,* 10 December.

Passas, N. (1990) 'Anomie and Corporate Deviance', *Contemporary Crises* 14: 157–78.

Pearce, F. (1976) *Crimes of the Powerful: Marxism, Crime and Deviance.* London: Pluto.

Pearce, F. and Tombs, S. (1998) *Toxic Capitalism: corporate crime and the chemical industry.* Aldershot: Dartmouth.

Pearce, F. and Tombs, S. (2003) 'Multinational Corporations, Power and "Crime"' in C. Sumner (ed) *The Blackwell Companion to Criminology.* Oxford: Blackwell, 359–76.

Pearce, F. and Tombs, S. (2012) *Bhopal: Flowers at the Altar of Profit and Power.* North Somercotes: CrimeTalk Books.

Press Association (2012) 'BP Adds $847m to Deepwater Horizon Costs', *The Guardian,* 31 July, http://www.guardian.co.uk/business/2012/jul/31/deepwater-horizon-bp-847m-dollars

Punch, M. (1996) *Dirty Business. Exploring Corporate Misconduct. Analysis and Cases.* London: Sage.

Sage, A. (2012) 'Special Report: The French breast implant scandal', Reuters, 2 February, http://www.reuters.com/article/2012/02/02/us-breast-implants-mas-idUSTRE8110WY20120202

Slapper, G. and Tombs, S. (1999) *Corporate Crime.* London: Longman.

Snell, K. and Tombs, S. (2011) '"How Do You Get Your Voice Heard When No-One Will Let You?" Victimisation at work', *Criminology & Criminal Justice* 11, (3): 207–23.

Snider, L. (1993) *Bad Business. Corporate Crime in Canada.* Toronto: University of Toronto Press.

Snider, L. (2000) 'The Sociology of Corporate Crime: an Obituary. (Or, Whose Knowledge Claims Have Legs?)', *Theoretical Criminology* 4, (2): 169–206.

Spalek, B. (2007) *Farepak Victims Speak Out: an exploration of the harms caused by the collapse of Farepak.* Centre for Crime and Justice Studies/Unison.

Sutherland, E. (1940) 'White-Collar Criminality', *American Sociological Review* 5: 1–12.

Sutherland, E. (1945) 'Is "White-Collar Crime" Crime?', *American Sociological Review* 10: 132–39.

Sutherland, E. (1983) *White-Collar Crime. The Uncut Version.* New Haven: Yale University Press.

Szockyj, E. and Fox, J.G. (eds) (1996) *Corporate Victimisation of Women.* Boston, Mass.: Northeastern University Press.

Taylor, I., Walton, P., and Young, J. (1973) *The New Criminology. For a Social Theory of Deviance.* London: RKP.

Tappan, P. (1947) 'Who Is the Criminal?', *American Sociological Review* 12: 96–102.

The Guardian (nd) 'The BAE Files', http://www.guardian.co.uk/world/bae

Tombs, S. and Whyte, D. (2001) 'Media Reporting of Crime: Defining Corporate Crime Out of Existence?', *Criminal Justice Matters* 43, Spring: 22–3.

Tombs, S. and Whyte, D. (eds) (2003) *Unmasking the Crimes of the Powerful: scrutinizing states and corporations.* New York: Peter Lang.

Tombs, S. and Whyte, D. (2007) *Safety Crimes*. Cullompton: Willan.

Tombs, S. and Whyte, D. (2008) *A Crisis of Enforcement: the decriminalisation of death and injury at work*. London: Centre for Crime and Justice Studies.

Treanor, J. (2012) 'Standard Chartered Shares Rise as US Regulator Drops Licence Threat', *The Guardian*, 15 August, http://www.guardian.co.uk/business/2012/aug/15/standard-chartered-shares-rise-licence-threat

Walters, R. (2010) 'Eco-Crime and Air Pollution' in Brookman *et al.* (eds) *Handbook on Crime*, 867–83.

White, R. (2003) 'Environmental Issues and the Criminological Imagination', *Theoretical Criminology* 7, (4): 483–506.

Whyte, D. (2004) 'Regulation and Corporate Crime' in J. Muncie and D. Wilson (eds) *Student Handbook of Criminal Justice*. London: Cavendish.

12

Cybercrime

Matthew Williams and David Wall

INTRODUCTION

The Office of Cyber Security and Detica reported in 2011 that the annual cost to the UK economy from cybercrime was £27 billion (Detica and Cabinet Office, 2011). Regardless of the accuracy of this estimate the British Crime Survey and Eurostat ICT survey evidence that cybercrime is now the typical volume property crime in the UK, impacting on more of the public than traditional acquisitive crimes such as burglary and car theft (Anderson *et al.*, 2012). Because of its global nature similar estimates of the prevalence and losses of cybercrime are found in most other countries. The big problem, however, with the subject of cybercrimes is that whilst everyone agrees that they are one of the greatest crime challenges of modern times, few seem to agree what they are, how many there are, how they actually impact upon society and what is to be done about them (Wall, 2007).

This chapter examines cybercrime, its contemporary manifestations and what it means for criminology. Part one maps the evolution of the Internet as an environment for the emergence of cybercrime. The second part dwells upon the various conflicting definitional problems of cybercrime and offers a method of resolving them. The third part of the chapter outlines the problems with measuring cybercrime before providing an indication of the scale of the problem. In the fourth part, we briefly explore how those problems are being resolved. The fifth part looks at the governance and regulation of cybercrime, while the final section provides an overview of the various theoretical explanations.

BACKGROUND

The Internet, technological change and cybercrime: 1969–2012

The advent of networked computer technologies in the latter half of the twentieth century opened up new deviant and criminal opportunities to both the classical offender and those previously ill-equipped potential offenders. The specific characteristics of the Internet have opened up a new 'virtual criminal field' (Capeller, 2001). New technologies are both facilitating traditional criminal activities and creating avenues for new and unprecedented forms of deviance; some still to be rationalized in legal discourse. The devolution of computer network access to the domestic arena can be seen as a milestone in cyber criminal and cyber deviant entrepreneurship. During the Cold War, in response to the launch of Sputnik in 1957, the US established the Advanced Research Projects Agency (ARPA), the birthplace of what is know commonly known as the Internet. ARPA's remit was to develop a networked computer infrastructure for use by the military that could survive a nuclear attack. The need to expand the network beyond the military and private sector to universities was quickly realized resulting in the establishment of ARPANET in 1969. During the latter years of the 1980s the Internet was slowly being devolved from the private and university sector to the domestic arena. Since this time the Internet has experienced exponential growth. In 1997 only 2 per cent of the UK's population had access to the Internet compared to 84 per cent in 2012 (ONS, 2012).

In the infancy of the Internet, cyber criminal activity was the avocation of a small number of computer programmers and others with similar technical expertise. These were the game hackers and hacker/crackers of the 1980s (Taylor, 2001). The impetus behind cyber criminal activity was usually non-malignant and based on a utopian idealism of non-centralized computer hardware and software access. The illicit activities of these individuals were not widely detected or publicized. During this time law enforcement was far from capable of either proactively or reactively tackling the problem. A decade on, the pervasiveness of communications technology and the advancements in field of human computer interaction meant that the network user no longer needed the esoteric knowledge of a computer programmer to become a cyber criminal.

Cyber criminal activity was not considered a significant problem by statutory authorities until the mid-1990s. As businesses and domestic users increasingly adopted the technology, reports of the misuse of the Internet began to emerge. Online community members, newsgroup users and website owners began to complain of online harassment and defamation, breaches of decency due to the online dissemination of 'obscene' materials, instances of vandalized web pages, and even cases of 'virtual rape' (Mackinnon, 1997). A clear shift occurred from the relatively benign cyber deviant activity of the 1980s to the more Machiavellian cyber criminal activity of the mid- to late 1990s.

The turn of the millennium brought with it several technological and criminal transformations that re-shaped the cybercrime landscape. These included the emergence of Web2.0 and social media networks, the automation of malware and the increasing organization of cyber criminal entrepreneurship. These transformations saw the beginning of 'mass digital victimization'. While many of these cases are classed as *de minimis* (too trivial for legal intervention), the potential for victimization at the scale of populations is particularly characteristic of twenty-first century cybercrimes.

As data on cybercrimes became more readily collected and consumed in this period it became apparent that criminals were targeting three distinct populations: the domestic population, the business population and the State. In relation to the domestic population the proliferation of automated scam and scareware (for example, adverts for anti-virus software that appear on a user's computer warning them of a virus infection or the like that is entirely fictional, which once downloaded delivers its own malware) has seen millions of domestic Internet users victimized and financially and psychologically harmed by organized cyber criminals. Less organized, but no less harmful are the opportunist 'cyber-bullies' and 'cyber-haters' of the twenty-first century. The advent and exponential spread of social media has seen the unprecedented propagation of harmful content on digital social networks. In particular, the practice of 'trolling' (the posting of defamatory and antagonistic messages aimed at eliciting an emotional response) has resulted in several high-profile arrests and the call for clear guidelines for prosecutors (BBC, 2012). The widespread uptake of social media networking, which shows no sign of abating with Facebook's members now amounting to over one billion (Tate, 2012), has the potential to expose whole communities to harmful, antagonistic and potentially socially disruptive content.

In relation to the business population, contemporary cyber-threats are no longer confined to hacking and viruses. Criminals (both organized and opportunists) have also begun to make use of social media technologies to command the crowd in processes known as 'crime-sourcing' and 'flash-mobbing/robbing'. As Goodman (2011) describes, 'groups of individual criminals, who may or may not even know each other, are organizing themselves online and suddenly descending into unsuspecting stores to steal all that they can in a flash. The unsuspecting merchant has little he can do when 40 unruly strangers suddenly run into his shop and run off with all his merchandise'. Similar problems also affect the State where social media has been implicated in mass public unrest and protest. The HMIC (2011) report *Policing Public Order* highlighted how mass public disorder had taken on a new dimension which involved the use of Internet communications on fixed and mobile platforms. In particular social networking sites (such as Twitter and Facebook) were implicated in the UK Uncut and university tuition fees protests in London in late 2011 and the August riots. At the extreme end of the spectrum, social media use was also associated with the Tunisian and Egyptian Revolutions (Lotan, 2011).

At the most grievous level, the development of 'super-viruses', such as Flame, Zeus and Spy-Eye (which created botnets—large global networks of 'zombified' computers under the control of organized criminals) and Stuxnet (a suspected State-sponsored virus designed to penetrate top secret computer systems that control nuclear enrichment plants in Iran) evidence that cybercrime can cause significant harm to whole populations, and to the extreme extent cause international conflicts and even cyberwar. The contemporary problem of cybercrime is now perceived to be so acute that governments are establishing contingency plans in the event of cyber-terrorist attacks, and are creating specialized national and international law enforcement agencies to tackle cyber criminal phenomena (Wall, 2007).

REVIEW QUESTIONS

1 How were cybercrimes characterized during the infancy of the Internet?

2 How did cybercrimes change in the mid- to late 1990s?

3 To what extent have Web2.0 technologies such as social media changed cybercrimes?

Defining cybercrime

There is no common definition of cybercrime. Developing a fixed definition is difficult due to a combination of factors including the technology neutral stance of many bodies of law and the rapidly changing technological landscape. Furthermore, the various private and public actors involved in the regulation of cybercrime produce divergent viewpoints. For example, computer security experts warn about potential and actual risks to hardware and software and suggest a range of strategic and tactical solutions— often their own products and services. Meanwhile, the legal/administrative community stresses the potential harms to individuals and define what is (and is not) supposed to happen by establishing and clarifying the rules that identify boundaries of acceptable and unacceptable Internet behaviour. The criminological and general academic community endeavour to provide an informed analysis about the wider societal implications of cybercrime in terms of aetiology, consequence and regulation. Concerns about cybercrime are therefore expressed through a range of voices that do not articulate a common understanding of the phenomenon.

Yet this dilemma has not prevented the proliferation of terms for cybercrimes invented by Internet users and professionals. Identity theft (phishing), cyberterrorism, information warfare, spams, denial of service attacks, hacking and cracking, hacktivism, e-frauds, auction fraud, click fraud, scams, hate crime, cyber-bullying, illegal online gambling, extreme pornography, viruses, worms and Trojans are just some of the terms that now come under the umbrella of 'cybercrime' (Williams, 2010). While many of these terms are entering the modern lexicon, there remains some confusion between those crimes that are wholly reliant upon the Internet and those, such as the more traditional crimes, that merely use the Internet as a means to target victims in new ways. Cybercrime can be understood more clearly if it is mapped out in terms of a) whether the victim groups are individual users, corporate entities or nation-states; b) their level of mediation by technology; and c) the type of offending behaviour (for example, crimes against system integrity, using computers to commit crimes and crimes relating to computer content).

Defining cybercrime by victim

A particularly confusing aspect of the debate over cybercrime is that it is constituted of a combination of a number of different deliberations that each relate to quite different victim groups. The debate over the personal Internet security of individual users is very different in substance to the debate over corporate victims of cybercrime in terms of risk of victimization and degree of loss, which in turn is different to the debate over national security where the nation-state and its citizens are the victims. The manifestation of cybercrimes varies by victim targets. Domestic users are most likely to be victims of more *minor* cybercrimes, such as micro-frauds (via technologies that read keyboard strokes—keyloggers—delivered by malware) and online harassment and bullying (via social media networks such as Facebook and Twitter). Corporate victims tend to suffer more serious cybercrime, such as Denial of Service attacks (repeated requests made of a computer server intended to slow down service or prevent service altogether) and insider misuse/proprietary information theft, while the State may suffer life-threatening attacks against its critical national infrastructure (for example, energy, water and emergency services). It is therefore analytically productive to tease out these differences between victims when attempting to establish the contours of cybercrime.

Defining cybercrime by technological mediation

Cybercrimes have evolved alongside networked digital technology. If cybercrimes are understood as mediated or shaped by networked technology, then they can be categorized in terms of these technologies. By applying a 'transformation test'—simply thinking about what happens if the Internet is removed from the activity—three generational levels of cybercrime can be identified that each display different combinations of informational, networked and global mediation by technology. At the *first* level are the traditional or ordinary crimes that use computers. Initially they were crimes, such as banking frauds, that took place within discrete (usually mainframe) computing systems, although they might now also include crimes that involve using computers as a method of communication, such as drug trafficking, or to gather precursor information to help commit or organize a crime, such as murder. The point is that, although they can be quite serious in their impact, they are nevertheless low-end cybercrimes since the behaviour will persist if the Internet is removed from them. Offenders will simply revert to other forms of dishonesty or using other forms of available communication or information sources (Wall, 2007).

At the *second* level are the hybrid **cybercrimes**: 'traditional' or legislated crimes for which network technology has created entirely new global opportunities. They are distinguished from the first level by the fact that they are committed across networks (such as auction frauds). Take away the Internet and the behaviour will continue by other means, but not on such a global scale or across such a wide span of jurisdictions and cultures. At the *third* level are the **true cybercrimes**. Solely the product of the Internet, they are high-end cybercrimes that are not possible without it. They include spamming, phishing (identity theft) and pharming (hijacking browsers) and variations of online intellectual property piracy (see Table 12.1) (Wall, 2007).

Defining cybercrime by offending behaviour

In addition to generational levels of cybercrime, there are different types of substantive criminal behaviours that fall under the cybercrime rubric. This behaviour falls into three basic categories that can also be linked to existing bodies of law and associated professional experience: 1) *Crimes against the machine/Computer integrity crimes*: these include hacking and cracking, cyber-vandalism, spying, DDOS (distributed denial of service) attacks and viruses. Each crime assaults the integrity of computer network access mechanisms. Computer integrity crimes often pave the way for more serious forms of offending, such as phishing. Crackers, for example, may use Trojans or other malware to install 'back doors' that are later used to facilitate other crimes, possibly by spammers who

Table 12.1 Cybercrime matrix

Cybercrime matrix	Crimes against the machine	Crimes using machines	Crimes in the machine
Level 1: Ordinary crimes (Assisting existing or 'traditional' crime)	E.g., Hacking within systems ALSO using internet to inform traditional crime (e.g. murder)	E.g., Fraud within banking systems	E.g., Storing extreme pornography
Level 2: Hybrid cybercrimes (New global opportunities for existing or 'traditional' crimes)	E.g., Hacking across networked computer systems	E.g., Fraud across banking systems and Networks	E.g., Distributing extreme pornography/ hate crime/
Level 3: True cybercrimes (New opportunities for new types of crime)	E.g., Automated hacking across networks—Phishing/DDOSA/ Spammed Viruses/Drive-by downloads/Scareware	E.g., Micro-frauds across networks/ Theft of virtual artefacts	E.g., Networked content delivery of e. pornography/hate crime

Source: adapted from Wall, D. S. (2005) 'The internet as a conduit for criminals' in A. Pattavina (ed) *Information Technology and The Criminal Justice System* Thousand Oaks, CA: Sage.

have bought lists of the infected addresses. 2) *Crimes using machines/Computer-assisted (or related) crimes*: these include phishing or advanced fee frauds, a form of social engineering that uses networked computer systems (often legitimately) to engage victims with the intention of dishonestly acquiring cash, goods or services. 3) *Crimes in the machine/Computer content crimes*: these cybercrimes relate to the illegal content of computer systems and include the trade and distribution of pornographic, hate crime materials or materials that intend to deceive.

The distinctions made here between the level of technological mediation and type of criminal behaviour provide important reference points for policy formation. When they are cross-tabulated against each other, the resulting mental map or 'matrix' usefully demonstrates the differences between the types of cybercrime that can be used for organizational or analytical purposes, for example, for collecting data, the assessment of risk or allocation of resources. Remember that the implications will vary according to the intended victim group (individual user, corporate entities, and nation-states) (Wall, 2005–10: 4).

REVIEW QUESTIONS

1 What are the key problems with defining cybercrime?

2 How can we define cybercrime by technological mediation?

3 How can we define cybercrime by offending behaviour?

Counting cybercrime

A key problem to better understanding and controlling cybercrimes is the lack of reliable data on their prevalence and impact upon individuals, businesses and nation-states. Several papers provide insightful reasons why existing data are flawed (see Anderson *et al.*, 2008; 2012; Casper, 2007; and Sommer and Brown, 2011). The data issues identified include information asymmetries, the lack of data sharing protocols, confidentiality and anonymity of respondents, failure to adopt gold standard data collection practices, and knowledge and perception of victimization.

Anderson *et al.* (2012) identified over 100 different attempts to collect data on cybercrime to date. The sources of data include reports of attack trends (for example, from Symantec and McAfee); security breach disclosure reports from the Information Commissioner's Office; reports by trade bodies (for example, from the British Chambers of Commerce, the Federation of Small Businesses, and banking trade associations), and surveys (for example, British Crime Survey, Offending Crime and Justice Survey, Commercial Victimisation Survey, Information Security Breaches Survey, Oxford internet Survey and Eurostat).

By far the most voluminous sources of data on cybercrimes are vendor databases of malicious code activity (for example, Symantec's Threat Assessment Report). For example, Sophos estimated that there were approximately 10 million cybercrimes in 2011 (Sophos, 2012: 3). This estimation is in stark contrast to the low levels of prosecutions: for example, the 300 or so successful prosecutions in the UK since the introduction of the Computer Misuse Act 1990 (also reflected in other jurisdictions) (Wall, 2007: 54). Vendor data understandably focus on cybercrimes such as botnet activity and subsequent spam levels that are technologically measurable by vendor specific software (that is, in the process of data generation, persons are not asked if they experienced a breach). This approach, while valuable in identifying overall trends, does not represent all the populations of interest (for example, the business community and domestic users). Essentially they cannot provide the detail required on prevalence of cybercrimes within each sector or region (where the unit of analysis is an organization or individual), the perceived or actual impact of cybercrimes, and the reaction of business or individuals to attack. Furthermore, the origin of such statistics raises important questions of perceived impartiality. In terrestrial terms, such sources of data would be comparable to data produced by private security companies who provide services to local communities and businesses. Objectivity suffers in the face of economic drivers inherent in such enterprises.

Police data on reported cybercrimes are potentially the most impoverished source. A review of police cybercrime recording evidenced that the practices of individual police services varied enormously, with only a few including computer crime markers on crimes committed via computer networks (Hyde-Bales *et al.*, 2004). More recent recording practices have been guided by the Association of Chief Police Officers' (ACPO) eCrime strategy (ACPO, 2009) which recommended that the National Fraud Reporting Centre become the hub for all recorded cybercrimes. While this has the benefit of harmonizing recording practices across forces, the criminal justice system as a whole is restrained by the criminal law which is largely technology neutral. The detail required by analysts (for example, the nature of an electronic attack such as denial of service, distributed denial of service, insider unauthorized access, etc.), common to other cybercrime sources, is often missing in police data.

National surveys on cybercrime identify the organization or individual as the unit of analysis. That is to say an employee (usually the person with responsibility for IT security) is asked about security issues and attacks in relation to their organization, or a member of the general population is asked similar questions in relation to the home. These surveys capture instances of 'known' victimization where the respondent directly experiences a cybercrime or has been made aware of the attack by software (for example, virus checker) or by another person. In contrast to vendor data, these surveys not only identify prevalence of 'known' cybercrimes, but also capture data on impact and response. Impact questions vary by survey, but often include length of system downtime, financial losses, potential reputational damage and anxiety in relation to possible future attack (in relation to surveys of the general public). Response questions include reporting and system upgrade behaviour, among other topics.

The majority of the surveys on business cybercrimes adopt non-random sampling. The resulting data pool is biased towards knowledgeable victims from sectors where IT security is well embedded (that is, there is an IT security manager to answer the survey questions). Those respondents who are reluctant to respond, due to a lack of knowledge or interest or fear of reputational damage from notification of a cybercrime, are absent from the dataset, leaving a skewed picture of the cybercrime problem. Unlike in some American states, where business cybercrime notification is required by law (see Anderson *et al.*, 2008), the UK picture from the perspective of surveys adopting non-random samples is partial and biased at best.

While surveys that adopt random probability approaches to surveying cybercrimes produce the most representative data, conceptual issues with question wording and with knowledge assumption can undermine the reliability and validity of data produced. Such problems led the European Commission i2010 High Level Group to conclude many of the questions in the Community Surveys on ICT Usage relating to business cyber-crimes were unreliable. They also reported similar problems in relation to their domestic surveys (i2010 High Level Group, 2006).

Large-scale random probability national surveys, such as the British Crime Survey, the Offending Crime and Justice Survey, and the Commercial Victimisation Survey, have sometimes included questions on cybercrime victimization and perpetration in their questionnaires. However, surprisingly few respondents reported cybercrime experiences, and in the light of other data on anxiety about identity theft and the prevalence of security breaches, response validity is open to question. Furthermore, questions on e-victimization are sparse, often only focusing on a very limited range of completed e-fraud. Given the problems outlined, it is apparent that the cybercrimes data pool is currently unfulfilled, both in terms of quality and quantity. The largest databases produced by vendors are likely to be partial and biased, while the best quality data from national surveys adopting random probability sampling techniques, suffer from poor conceptualization and a paucity of detailed questions on the topic.

Cybercrime trends

The 'best' data on business cybercrime available in the UK prior to 2010 was the Information Security Breaches Survey (ISBS). The ISBS adopted probability sampling and adhered to standardized and well-conceptualized questions. In the domestic domain, the Oxford internet Survey (OIS) represents the gold standard. The OIS adopts a random sampling technique and includes a good range of cybercrimes questions that the general public understand. Figure 12.1 shows trends in business cybercrimes over the last decade in the UK and the US. What is clear in the UK is that the trend in cybercrime has reversed from a general decline since 2004 to a sharp increase from 2010. This is contrary to trends in the US where a general decline in cybercrime has been recorded since 2000 by the CSI Computer Crime & Security Survey.[1]

Figure 12.2 shows ISBS recorded breaches over time disaggregated by cybercrime type. Malware attacks show the most marked decrease in breaches between 2004 and 2008, followed by theft and fraud, and insider misuse. The reported prevalence of unauthorized access (including hacking) remained relatively stable in the same period. Reports in 2010 indicate a sharp increase in prevalence for malware infection, insider misuse and unauthorized access, and a slightly modest increase in reports of theft and fraud. Reports of insider misuse and unauthorized access peak at new all-time highs (42 and 49 per cent, respectively), while malware attacks return to near their peak prevalence in 2004.

Figure 12.3 details trends over time in domestic cybercrime collected by the OIS. Given the public's limited understanding of many e-crime types, this survey adopts more colloquial terms to ensure robust data collection. Unfortunately this precludes

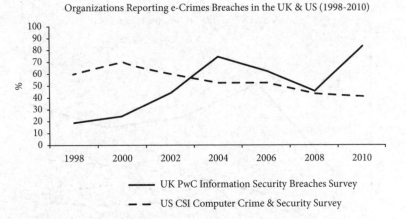

Figure 12.1 Organizations reporting e-crimes breaches in the UK & US (1998–2010)

Source: Compiled from the Information Security Breaches Survey 1998 to 2010, PriceWaterhouseCoopers, and the US Computer Crime & Security Survey 1998–2010, Computer Security Institute.

a forensic comparison with business cybercrime trends. However, the pattern of those members of the public experiencing virus attacks is similar to the patterns of business malware attacks. A decline is evident from 2005 to 2009, with a definite upward trend in 2011 (an increase of 7 per cent compared to 2009). Similarly, there is an upward trend in recorded domestic phishing attempts, indicating, as with business recorded

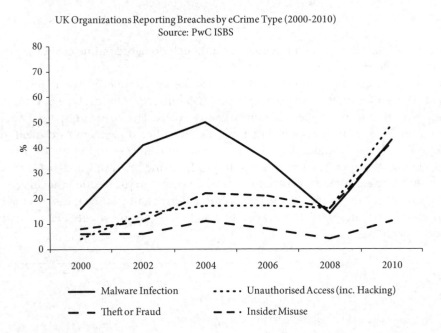

Figure 12.2 UK organizations reporting breaches by e-crime type (2000–10)

Source: Compiled from Information Security Breaches Survey 2000 to 2010, PriceWaterhouseCoopers.

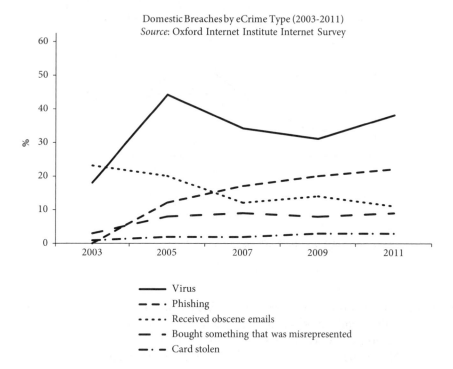

Figure 12.3 Domestic breaches by e-crime type (2003–11)

Source: Compiled from the Oxford Internet Survey 2003–11, Oxford Internet Institute.

cybercrime, that eFraud is on the increase (although domestic online credit card theft remains stable at 3 per cent).

The British Crime Survey only routinely includes cybercrime questions relating to fraud. The last incarnation showed 4 per cent had suffered from this type of victimization, twice that who experienced burglary or car theft. The 2010 Eurostat ICT survey shows the 5 per cent of respondents from the UK suffered payment card fraud, placing it first in rank compared to all other European countries in the survey. The UK placed second for financial losses caused by phishing and pharming attacks (Anderson *et al.*, 2012). These domestic cybercrimes data add weight to the position that in general trends are on the rise in the UK and that online *property* victimization is now overtaking its terrestrial counterparts. The next section addresses the governance and regulation of cybercrime.

REVIEW QUESTIONS

1 What are the problems with counting cybercrimes?

2 What are the various methods used to count cybercrime?

3 Describe the cybercrime trends over the last decade.

Governance and regulation of cybercrime

Law and public policing

The use of existing laws to deal with cybercrime can be seen as a distal (offline) node of governance (Wall and Williams, 2007). While law is generally slow to respond to escalating online threats it has been utilized in several cases to prosecute cyber offenders. Yet law only serves the purpose up to a point. A key challenge is the *de minimis* **trap** (Wall, 2007). A common characteristic of many cybercrimes is that they lead to low-impact, bulk victimizations that cause large aggregated losses which are spread globally, potentially across all known jurisdictions. This creates the problem of *nullum crimen* legal disparities in inter-jurisdictional cases. Protocols, including the COE Cybercrime Convention and the establishment of multi-agency partnerships and forums, assist in facilitating inter-force cooperation, but they rely upon the offence in question being given similar priority in each jurisdiction. If, for example, a case is clearly a criminal offence for which the investigation carries a strong mandate from the public, such as the investigation of online child pornography, then resourcing its investigation is usually fairly unproblematic from a police point of view. However, where there is not such an implied mandate, such as with offences other than child pornography, then resourcing becomes more problematic, especially if the deviant behaviour in question is an offence in one jurisdiction but not another. Of course, the other inter-jurisdictional problem is that there may be cultural differences in defining the seriousness of specific forms of offending, or some offences may fall under civil law in one jurisdiction and criminal law in another, as with the theft of trade secrets, which is a criminal offence in the US, but a civil offence in the UK.

Cybercrime and the challenges for public policing

Dealing with cybercrime poses significant challenges to British policing. Police services have historically suffered from insufficient technical and legal knowledge and a lack of investigative resources. Reports of cybercrime to the police have been faced with inconsistent record keeping and recording practices, often resulting in records that lack the electronic element in the *modus operandi* (Hyde-Bales *et al.*, 2004). In an attempt to combat this shortfall some local forces attach a computer crime marker to command and control incident records, crime desk records and crime related intelligence logs. These practices however are far from systematic and significant gaps still remain in the recording process. Therefore, denial of service attacks, hacking, malware infection and the like, are unlikely to be easily identifiable from police data. Over time however, police cybercrime recording may improve given the ACPO eCrime Strategy recommended that the National Fraud Reporting Centre become the responsible authority for recording all cybercrimes reported to the police (ACPO, 2009). This strategy is being reviewed in late 2012 and is likely to change in light of the establishment of the National Crime Agency (late 2013) which will take a strategic lead on cybercrime.

Problems for criminal justice agencies also arise from the local, national and international political demands placed upon them to respond to cybercrime. Such demands are regularly inflamed by the apparent disparity between the cybercrime waves portrayed by the news media and the relatively few arrests and prosecutions of so-called cybercriminals. One explanation for this disparity is the fact that local police forces in most jurisdictions tend to work within tightly prescribed budgetary parameters defined by their routine activities and therefore find it difficult to cope with demands to investigate the crimes arising from globalized electronic networks. However, the disparity also arises because traditional law enforcement agencies only play a very small part in the overall policing of cyberspace. Law enforcement agencies are understandably focused on crimes posing a perceived greater level of threat, such as child pornographers, fraudsters and those who threaten infrastructure, such as terrorists and the vengeful hacker.

However, this is not to say that cyberspace goes unpoliced, nor that police activity is either inefficient or ineffective. Rather, law enforcement activity is carried out within the broader and largely informal networked and nodal architecture of Internet policing. This is comprised of Internet users and user groups; digital environment managers and moderators; network infrastructure providers; corporate security organizations; non-governmental, non-police organizations; governmental non-police organizations and public police organizations (see Wall, 2007: Chapter 8). Each of these regulatory groups uses different combinations of moral, contractual (economic), technological and legal sanctions to maintain order online.

Technological regulation

While the same technology that creates cybercrimes can also be used to regulate them, the need to balance security with privacy creates new legal and political challenges. Software technology can be far more potent than law as a regulator of digital environments since it not only controls their architecture but can also shape any behaviour that takes place within them. When applied to cybercrimes, this simply means that the more a criminal behaviour is mediated by a new technology, the more it can be policed by that same technology. However, since technological interventions tend to raise new sets of ethical and legal issues—for example, whether they are legal or whether they infringe privacy—any successful interventions will have to be set within acceptable moral, ethical, social, economic and technological frameworks.

Spam filters are a good example of a successful technological solution to a cybercrime problem. Yet there has been very little critical discussion about the application of spam filters into the networked delivery mechanisms, especially with regard to technological knock-on effects such as filtering out legitimate information sources. Not only do spam filters restrict some communications (for example, some legitimate emails from, for example, Nigeria or China), but they also can contravene the long-standing, although changing, end-to-end principle of the Internet, which is freedom of movement across the network to its nodes while leaving choice and mode of receipt to the end users. Of equal concern is the unbridled use of software techniques designed to entrap criminals, such as 'honeypots' and 'honeynets'. For example, false hyperlinks purporting to lead to websites hosting pornographic images of children can be used to gather intelligence regarding criminal Internet users. While they may be successful in their mission, they raise a range of moral, ethical and legal concerns, including allegations of entrapment.

Social control

A range of social control mechanisms are currently being employed to govern online behaviour. For example, virtual worlds such as Secondlife and online marketplaces such as Ebay and also Facebook, utilize reputation management systems to tarnish the identities of those who break rules. Williams (2006) shows how these social control systems can draw upon shaming as a form of regulation (Braithwaite, 1989). He argues that there is little doubt that complex social relationships are played out within online spaces such as virtual worlds and social media networks. Markham (1998) and Mnookin's (1996) accounts of social interaction online show how individuals developed complex interdependencies, characterized by social and emotional bonds. These online interdependent social networks provide a fertile ground for the use of shaming in Internet deviance reduction. While the constraining effects of the family are absent within virtual worlds (unless family members are also present online), the bonds to other citizens and online community can be as significant as offline ties. For example, strong relations within purely social worlds, such as SecondLife, are important to sustaining positive reputation and status. Acts of shaming online invariably draw on these ties, attempting to either humiliate the wrongdoer or draw upon their classical conditioning in an attempt to induce feelings of guilt (Braithwaite, 1989). In a now classic example Mackinnon (1997) shows how a socially disruptive and sexually aggressive character in the virtual world LambdaMOO was eventually controlled via shaming techniques by online community members, following the failure of technological controls (eviction from the virtual world, deletion of account, etc). Such findings evidence the need for a plural response to the control of cybercrime and deviance, with misdemeanours being dealt with by *proximal* **control** mechanisms (social and technological controls) and more serious transgressions dealt with by *distal* mechanisms (the law and policing of a particular terrestrial jurisdiction) (Wall and Williams, 2007).

REVIEW QUESTIONS

1   How does cybercrime challenge existing policing practices?

2   How can cybercrime be controlled via technology?

3   How can cybercrime be controlled socially?

Theoretical explanations

The small amount of factual knowledge currently available about virtual offenders comes from offender surveys, such as the UK-based OCJS (Allen *et al.*, 2005; Wilson *et al.*, 2006). These sources suggest that offender profiles are like those of most offenders—young and male—but they possess rather different, if not opposing, characteristics found in the criminologies of street criminals. They are more likely to be introverted and more likely to share a much broader range of social characteristics. Perhaps more significant is that their use of the Internet enables them to commit crimes at a distance and also crimes that would previously have been beyond their means. Consequently, when combined with the offenders' relative isolation from others, these characteristics reduce the amount of available criminal intelligence about them and makes the law enforcement job harder.

The generalizability of these observations will, of course, vary further according to the types of crime involved and the available opportunities to offend. Such is the view of the situational crime prevention theorists (see Newman and Clarke, 2003). However, while this may easily explain computer-mediated thefts, it sits less comfortably with computer integrity and computer content crimes. McQuade (2006: 113–35) gives a very useful overview of offender profiles, but acknowledges the problems in so doing because: '[i]n reality, cybercriminals carry out different types and combinations of illicit actions in the course of committing abuse, attacks and/or crimes, thus underscoring the difficulty and limitations of categorising offenders'.

If the construction of offender profiles is problematic, so too is the ability to isolate offender motivations. Normally in criminology we may turn to the more complex theories of criminalization for some guidance here. McQuade (2006), for example, applied six criminological theories to cybercrimes, which each outline different motivational factors. They are classical choice theories, based upon rational decision-making; trait theories, which focus upon psychological imperfections in the individual; social process theories, which explore how individuals learn criminal behaviour; social structure theories, which consider the individual's social and economic position in society; conflict theories, based upon non-consensual, pluralistic and conflict views of social organization. He also observed a sixth, integrated theories, which combine aspects of the previous five. The problem McQuade identifies is that criminologists have long tended not to consider the impacts of technology in the commission of crime. Furthermore, the field of study is currently unfolding—especially where an act of cybercrime involves a number of forms of offending behaviour.

One powerful theory of motivation, which Wall (2007) builds upon and which begins to explain the transformative impacts of the Internet is based upon social structure/alienation theory, but also integrates themes from other criminological theories. Presdee's 'carnival of crime' thesis expresses a broader concern about the criminalization of everyday life in which: 'everyday responses to modern, highly commodified society become themselves defined as criminal' (Presdee, 2000: 15). He argues that much of the crime occurring in society, especially that relating to social disorder, is a product of the fact the existing relationships of production encourage us to live two lives. Our 'first life' is our official life characterized by work and imposed order, which sustains our physical existence. In contrast, our 'second life' is where we live out our fantasies and obtain emotional fulfilment (not to be confused with the website of the same name). It runs counter to the alienation caused by the 'rhythms of production' in the 'first life', by working to restore some meaning to our lives and control over our existence (Presdee, 2000: 62). During the course of living out this 'second life', which Presdee calls our 'carnival of leisure', the boundaries of order are frequently crossed. We, in effect, consume crime, not just through our diet of entertainment, but also when the 'commodification of excitement' that characterizes much of our leisure is taken that one step further.

Presdee's main concern is that the 'bulk of crime is created, through the criminalisation and policing of social behaviour as against dishonest behaviour and that it is a crime to be many things including poor, young, disadvantaged, to fail and even at times to be creative' (Presdee, 2000: 162). This explanation of second-life fulfilment can go a long way to explaining much of the Internet's broader popularity but also offending and victimization. In Presdee's view, the Internet has become a '"safe site" of the second life of the people' (Presdee, 2000: 54) and it certainly does provide an environment 'where we can enjoy in private immoral acts and emotions' (Presdee, 2000: 64). But, he is also right when he states that the days when the consumption of crime, as he puts it, has become 'a blissful state of "non-responsibility", a sort of never-ending "moral holiday", are long gone, if they ever existed, especially on the internet'.

Other scholars have also attempted to apply social theories designed for the terrestrial world to cyberspace. Williams (2006) applied Social Control Theory (Hirschi, 1969) to cyberspace. He took the core concepts of attachment, involvement, commitment and belief and tested them in the virtual environment Cyberworlds. *Attachment* refers to the capacity of individuals to form effective relationships with other people and institutions, for example, parents, peers and school. When attachments are strong, individuals are more likely to be concerned with the opinions and expectations of others and thus more likely to behave in accordance with them. *Commitment* relates to the amount and time invested into conventional lines of activity, such as attaining an education, developing a career or simply building a reputation. 'Rational' deviants, who weigh up the costs of committing crimes, risk losing these when they break from group norms. *Involvement* in conventional acts and avocations is one of the more mundane elements of a social bond to society. The assumption is that a person may simply be too busy to even consider committing a deviant act if they are involved in conventional lines of activity. The final component of a control theory is one's *belief* in the values, norms and laws of society. Control theory assumes that there exists an accepted universal belief system at work in society. The deviant rationalizes their behaviour so they can simultaneously still believe in its wrongful nature while committing the act. Most notably Sykes and Matza (1957) term this process 'techniques of neutralisation'. The individual drifts in and out of states of delinquency depending upon the circumstances and requirements of the moment.

Williams found that a lack of attachment to other online community members, community founders, and institutions, such as the Peacekeeper Core (the online community police service) was an important factor in explaining anti-normative cyber behaviour. The application of commitment to the online setting was relatively non-problematic given the similarities in social structure. At the simplest level individuals who became *citizens* (paying members of the community) had more at stake (their citizenship) than tourists (non-paying members) when they deviated from community rules. Aspirations to join the Peacekeeper Core and the time invested in building virtual property were also identified as elements of commitment that prevented individuals from committing deviant acts online. Similarly, those involved in building property (a time intensive activity), organizing social events and volunteering for the Peacekeeper Core were less likely to veer into antisocial activity than those who had no static online vocation or avocation. Finally, those that shared the common value system of the online community were less likely to deviate than those who did not. Williams noted however, that his successful application of Control Theory to cyberspace was only possible because he examined an online community. While his findings might be replicated in other online communities, it is doubtful that the components of Control Theory will be as analytically fruitful in an explanation of cyber deviance outside of online community structures.

Yar (2005) applied routine activities theory to cybercrime. He found that with respect to the 'central core of three concepts', 'motivated offenders' and 'capable guardianship' could be treated as largely similar between cyber and terrestrial settings. However, the application of 'suitable targets' produced certain asymmetries, with respect to the components of 'inertia', 'visibility' and 'accessibility'. The complexities of applying this theory to cyberspace related largely to the distinctive *spatial-temporal* differences between online and terrestrial spaces. Time-space distanciation (Giddens, 1990) is an acute characteristic of online spaces. In relation to criminal activity this means that individuals are able to attack their victims at a distance and in compressed and extended periods of time. For example, a fraudulent transaction can take place over thousands of miles in milliseconds while a harasser can subject their victim to derisory discourse at great distance in real time. This causes problems for routine activities as the theory holds that the 'organization of time and space is central for criminological explanation' (Felson, 1998: 148), yet cyberspace is spatio-temporally *disorganized*. Yar concluded routine activity theory (and other ecologically oriented theories of crime causation) appears of limited utility in an environment that defies many of our taken-for-granted assumptions about how the socio-interactional setting of routine activities is configured.

Joinson (2003) explored the application of the social psychological theory of deindividuation (Festinger *at al.*, 1952) to the Internet. The theory advances that anonymity and disinhibition within social situations can lead to individuals acting in ways counter to conventional behaviour. Prentice-Dunn and Rogers (1982) suggest that deindividuation results in a reduced awareness of the public component of one's own behaviour and is caused by a reduction in accountability cues (for example, anonymity and membership of a group) and reduced private self-awareness. The power of the crowd has been used to show how an individual's behaviour can be shaped by these processes to produce anti-normative outcomes. Essentially people behaving in crowds are less likely to feel individually judged by others and are hence more likely to break rules. The August 2011 London riots can be used as an example of deindividuation. Normally law-abiding individuals were temporarily provided with a justification by the crowd to embark on looting sprees. When applied to the Internet Kiesler *at al.* (1984) argue that the anonymity afforded to individuals online can result in deindividuating effects, similar to the effect of the crowd. Other social psychological explanations of online deviant activity include the Reduced Social Cues model, the Two-Component Self-Awareness model and the Social Identity Explanation of Deindividuation Effects model (see Joinson, 2003).

REVIEW QUESTIONS

1 What criminological/sociological theories can be used to explain cybercrime?

2 What psychological theories can be used to explain cybercrime?

3 Do we need a specific theory of cybercrime?

CONCLUSION

Cybercrime will continue to evolve, bringing fresh challenges for criminological understanding. The emergence of the first generation of cybercrimes in the 1980s and 1990s was met with inadequate criminological insight. Criminologists were simply not prepared for the digital re-engineering of terrestrial crimes. The same can be said for the police, the legal system and victims. However, this is not an isolated happening. Throughout history criminals have been the first to capitalize on opportunities when they arise, often leaving institutions lagging behind. Yet this repeated pattern has been no more acute than with the development and proliferation of the Internet and associated cybercriminal activity. Our ability as criminologists, with our terrestrial based methodological and theoretical tools, to understand this phenomenon is complicated by the ways in which networked technology alters commonsense notions of space and time, and in turn how offenders, victims, the police and the public interact in these new orderings. Cybercrime definition, prevalence, regulation, and aetiology have all confounded the criminological imagination, calling for a re-evaluation of how we conduct research and the bodies of disciplinary knowledge we draw upon.

QUESTIONS FOR DISCUSSION

1 To what extent are cybercrimes different from 'terrestrial' crimes?

2 Do the profiles of cyber criminals and cyber victims differ from their 'terrestrial' counterparts?

3 Does cyberspace need to be regulated?

4 What are the implications of regulation upon cyber rights and liberties?

5 How have criminologists attempted to explain cybercriminal behaviour?

GUIDE TO FURTHER READING

Jewkes, Y. (ed) (2007) *Crime Online*. Cullompton: Willan.
This book provides an overview of the key issues drawing upon a range of internationally known experts in the field of cybercrime. It includes chapters on cyber homicide, identity theft/duplication, child pornography, piracy, football hooliganism and cyberstalking.

Joinson, A. N. (2003) *Understanding the Psychology of the Internet*. New York: Palgrave Macmillan, Chapter 3.
This is an excellent introductory chapter on the psychology of cyber criminality. It provides an overview of the key psychological theories that attempt to explain why people are more likely to behave in deviant and criminal ways online.

Wall, D. S. (2007) *Cybercrime: The transformation of crime in the information age*.
Cambridge: Polity.
Wall draws on empirical research findings and multidisciplinary sources to argue that we are beginning to experience a new generation of automated cybercrimes, which are almost completely mediated by networked technologies that are themselves converging. An excellent book on the nature of cybercrime and its regulation.

Williams, M. L. (2006) *Virtually Criminal: Crime, Deviance and Regulation Online*. London: Routledge.

Williams provides a criminological analysis of deviance and regulation within an online community. The book explores the causes, impactions and regulation of deviance within virtual worlds through an application of control theory, speech act theory and reintegrative shaming.

Yar, M. (2006) *Cybercrime and Society* (2nd edn, 2013) London: Sage.

Yar locates cybercrime in the wider contexts of social, political, cultural and economic change. The book draws upon perspectives spanning criminology, sociology, law, politics and cultural studies. Chapter topics include hacking, intellectual property theft, cyber fraud and scams, obscene materials and cyber stalking.

WEB LINKS

http://www.cardiff.ac.uk/socsi/resources/Levi%20Williams%20eCrime%20Reduction%20 Partnership%20Mapping%20Study.pdf

Link to the findings from the Nominet Trust *eCrime Reduction Partnership Mapping Study* (2012) by Mike Levi and Matthew Williams. The report is the first to attempt to map the cooperation of the wide array of internet regulators.

http://www.homeoffice.gov.uk/publications/science-research-statistics/research-statistics/ crime-research/hosb0612/hosb0612?view=Binary

A link to the most recent (at time of press) Home Office/Office for National Statistics analysis of cybercrime questions in the British Crime Survey/Crime Survey for England and Wales.

http://www.ukcert.org.uk/

A link to the UK Computer Emergency Response Team webpage. Provides up-to-date information on existing security threats to business, academia and government.

http://www.hmso.gov.uk/acts/acts1990/Ukpga_19900018_en_1.htm

Link to the Computer Misuse Act 1990.

http://conventions.coe.int/Treaty/en/Treaties/Html/185.htm

Link to the Council of Europe Convention on Cybercrime.

REFERENCES

ACPO (2009) *ACPO e-Crime Strategy*. ACPO: London, http://www.acpo.police.uk/documents/ crime/2009/200908CRIECS01.pdf (accessed 9 October 2012).

Allen, J., Forrest, S., Levi, M., Roy, H., and Sutton, M. (2005) 'Fraud and technology crimes: findings from the 2002/03 British Crime Survey and 2003 Offending, Crime and Justice Survey', *Home Office Online Report* 34/05, http:// www.homeoffice.gov.uk/rds/pdfs05/rdsolr3405.pdf (accessed 9 October 2012).

Anderson, R., Boehme, R., Clayton, R., and Moore, T. (2008) *Security Economics and the Internal Market*. Crete: ENISA.

Anderson, R., Barton, C., Boehme, R., Clayton, R., Levi, M., Moore, T., and Savage, S. (2012) *Measuring the Cost of Cybercrime*, paper presented at the WEIS Conference, Berlin.

British Broadcasting Corporation (BBC) (2012) *Tom Daley 'abuse' tweet: Legal rethink on online rules*. http://www. bbc.co.uk/news/uk-19660415 (accessed 20 Septembet 2012).

Braithwaite, J. (1989) *Crime, Shame and Reintegration*. Cambridge University Press: Cambridge.

Capeller, W. (2001) 'Not Such a Neat Net: Some Comments on Virtual Criminality', *Social and Legal Studies* Vol. 10, no. 2, 229–42.

Casper, C. (2007), *Examining the Feasibility of a Data Collection Framework*. Crete: ENISA.

Detica and Cabinet Office (2011) *The Cost of Cyber Crime: A Detica and Cabinet Office Report In Partnership With The Office Of Cyber Security And Information Assurance In The Cabinet Office*. http://www.baesystemsDeticaand CabinetOffice.com/uploads/resources/THE_COST_OF_CYBER_CRIME_SUMMARY_FINAL_14_February_2011.pdf (accessed 9 October 2012).

Felson, M. (1998). *Crime and everyday life* (2nd edn) Thousand Oaks, CA: Pine Forge Press.

Festinger, L., Pepitone, A., and Newcomb, T. (1952) 'Some consequences of deindividuation in a group', *Journal of Social Psychology* 47, 382–9.

Giddens, A. (1990) *The Consequences of Modernity*. Cambridge: Polity.

Goodman, M. (2011) 'From crowdsourcing to crime-sourcing: The rise of distributed criminality: How criminals are applying crowdsourcing techniques', *O'Reilly Radar*. http://radar.oreilly.com/2011/09/crime-sourcing.html (accessed on 21 September 2012).

Hirschi, T. (1969) *Causes of Delinquency*. Los Angeles: University of California Press.

HMIC (2011) *Policing Public Order: An overview and review of progress against the recommendations of Adapting to Protest and Nurturing the British Model of Policing*. London: HMIC.

Hyde-Bales, K., Morris, S., and Charlton, A. (2004) *The Police Recording of Computer Crime*. London: The Stationery Office.

i2010 High Level Group (2006), *Benchmarking Framework*. Brussels: European Commission.

Joinson, A. N. (2003) *Understanding the Psychology of Internet Behaviour*. London: Palgrave Macmillan.

Kiesler, S., Siegel, J., and McGuire, T. W. (1984) 'Social Psychological Aspects of Computer-Mediated Communication', *American Psychologist* 39:10, 356–70.

Lotan, G., Graeff, E., Ananny, M., Gaffney, D., Pearce, I., and Boyd, D. (2011) 'The Revolutions Were Tweeted: Information Flows During the 2011 Tunisian and Egyptian Revolutions', *International Journal of Communication* (5) Feature: 1375–405.

MacKinnon, R. (1997) 'Virtual rape', *Journal of Computer Mediated Communication*, 2 (4). http://www.ascusc.org/jcmc/vol2/issue4/mackinnon.html (accessed 9 October 2012).

Markham, A. (1998) *Life Online: Researching Real Experience in Virtual Space*. California: Sage.

McQuade, S. (2006) *Understanding and Managing Cybercrime*. Boston: Allyn & Bacon.

Mnookin, J. (1996) 'Virtual(ly) Law: The Emergence of Law in LambdaMOO', *Journal of Computer-Mediated Communication* 2:1. http://www.ascusc.org/jcmc/vol2/issue1/lambda.html (accessed 9 October 2012).

Newman, G. R. and Clarke, R. V. (2003) *Superhighway Robbery: Preventing e-commerce crime*. Cullompton: Willan.

Office for National Statistics (2012) *Statistical bulletin: Internet Access - Households and Individuals, 2012*. London: ONS http://www.ons.gov.uk/ons/rel/rdit2/internet-access—households-and-individuals/2012/stb-internet-access-households-and-individuals–2012.html (accessed 9 October 2012).

Prentice-Dunn, S. and Rogers, R. (1982) 'Effects of public and private self-awareness deindividuation and aggression', *Journal of Personality and Social Psychology* 43(3), 503–13.

Presdee, M. (2000) *Cultural Criminology and the Carnival of Crime*. London: Routledge.

Sommer, P. and Brown, I. (2011) *Reducing Systemic Cybersecurity Risk*. London: OECD.

Sophos (2012) 'Security Threat Report 2012', *Sophos*. http://www.sophos.com/en-us/medialibrary/PDFs/other/SophosSecurityThreatReport2012.pdf.

Sykes, G.M. and Matza, D. (1957) 'Techniques of Neutralization: A Theory of Delinquency', *American Sociological Review* 22, 664–70.

Tate, R. (2012), 'Facebook Hits 1 Billion Users, Here's How It Hits $141 Billion in Value', *Wired*. http://www.wired.com/business/2012/10/facebook-case-for-optimism/ (accessed 5 October 2012).

Taylor, P. (2001) 'Hacktivism: in search of lost ethics?' in D.S. Wall (ed) *Crime and the Internet*. London: Routledge, 59–73.

Wall, D.S. and Williams, M. (2007) 'Policing diversity in the digital age: maintaining order in virtual communities', *Criminology and Criminal Justice* Vol. 7, no. 4, 391–415.

Wall, D.S. (2007) *Cybercrimes: The Transformation of Crime in the Information Age*. Cambridge: Polity.

Wall, D.S. (2005–10) 'The internet as a conduit for criminals' in A. Pattavina (ed), *Information Technology and The Criminal Justice System*. Thousand Oaks, CA: Sage, 77–98. Revised in 2010. http://papers.ssrn.com/sol3/papers.cfm?abstract_id=740626 (accessed 9 October 2012).

Williams, M. (2006) *Virtually Criminal: Crime, Deviance and Regulation Online*. London: Routledge.

Williams, M. (2010) 'Cybercrime' in F. Brookman, T. Bennett, M. Maguire, and H. Pierpoint (eds) *Handbook of Crime*. Cullompton: Willan.

Wilson, D., Patterson, A., Powell, G., and Hembury, R. (2006) 'Fraud and technology crimes: findings from the 2003/04 British Crime Survey, the 2004 Offending, Crime and Justice Survey and administrative sources,' *Home Office Online Report 09/06*. http://www.homeoffice.gov.uk/rds/pdfs06/rdsolr0906.pdf (accessed 9 October 2012).

Yar, M. (2005) 'The novelty of 'cybercrime': an assessment in light of routine activity theory', *European Journal of Criminology* 2: 407–27.

NOTE

1. The data for the ISBS 2010 presented in Figure 12.1 is derived from the responses from small to medium-sized firms as they represented the largest group of respondents. It is important to note reports of e-crimes breaches from large firms were far in excess of those reported by SMEs, making the sharp increase in e-crimes attacks in Figure 12.1 a conservative estimate.

13 Terrorism and the politics of fear

Frank Furedi

INTRODUCTION

Since the destruction of the World Trade Center in September 2001, terrorism has become one of the defining issues of the twenty-first century. Billions of dollars have been devoted to the so-called 'war against terror'. New technologies and laws have been created to assist the crackdown of what according to official accounts constitutes the gravest risk to our existence. Unfortunately, in the discussion of terrorism, what divides fact from fiction and information from propaganda is inexact. This chapter attempts to address this problem. It starts by casting doubt on simple, typically very narrow, definitions of terrorism, before then going on to deconstruct the climate of fear currently surrounding the majority of research in this area. Finally, the chapter casts a critical eye on current counter-terrorism measures and recently invoked anti-terrorist legislation, arguing that, if governments continue to adopt a cavalier attitude towards civil liberties, they will surely face the risk of playing into the very hands of those who promote and perpetrate political violence.

BACKGROUND

The inexplicable behaviour of apparently irrational terrorists is often tenuously linked to events whose causes are not known. Incomprehensible events are readily presented as the consequence of the actions of agents we do not understand. As Jenkins (2003) observes, even with the best will in the world, government officials are not in the position to inform the public of all the facts. When it comes to terrorism, official agencies 'have a powerful vested interest in not revealing the full extent of the information available to them'. Indeed, transmitting misinformation is part of the job description of anti-terrorist agencies. 'Since so much official action involves clandestine methods or sources, even the most reputable and responsible agencies will on occasion present less than the full truth, or actively give false information in order to protect their methods or sources', writes Philip Jenkins (2003: 6).

Of course, official statements that are designed to provide misleading information are not confined to the crime of terrorism. Information about crime statistics and specific crimes is often conveyed through statements that seek to gain political advantage through manipulating the facts. However, when it comes to conventional crimes, the questioning academic researcher is often in a position to demystify the official version of events and offer a plausible alternative. Matters are much more complicated when it comes to analysing terrorism. As Jenkins (2003) argues, it is easy to know when a particular act constitutes a crime such as robbing a bank. It is much more difficult to be certain that a particular deed is an act of terrorism. For often, it is not the deed but the motives that inspired it that turns a particular event into an act of terrorism. A random shooting may be the act of a psychopath or of a politically motivated activist; as Jenkins remarks, 'before we know whether the act falls within the scope of terrorism, we have to know both who did it, and why they did it' (2003: 6). These are very difficult questions to answer and unless we have direct access to the individual accused of a terrorist crime it is difficult to offer an alternative to the official version of events.

Interpreting terrorism

'Traditionalist' versus 'social constructionist' conceptions of terrorism

Although the terms 'terrorism' and 'terrorist' are widely used, it is far from evident what these words actually mean. Until recently, terrorism tended to be associated with the tactics of individuals or organizations who were waging unconventional warfare against legitimate authority through targeting non-combatants and spreading fear through the populace (Wilson, 2003: 119). Since the turn of the century, the term terrorism is often used to connote a distinct identity or ideology of an individual or organization. Thus, the widely used phrase 'war on terror' suggests that there is more to this problem than the violent tactics carried out by illegitimate clandestine organizations. Implicit in this phrase is the idea that terrorism represents a way of life, a political outlook as well as a physical and military threat.

The unusual degree of controversy that surrounds the discussion on terrorism stems from the fact that acts of political violence encourage people to take sides. The vocabulary used to express acts of political violence is continually contested. It is not simply the case that 'one person's freedom fighter is another one's terrorist'. Are members of organizations like Hamas or ETA, militants, guerrillas, or terrorists? And are they fighting a war or committing crimes? Most of the time the answers to these questions are influenced by one's attitude to the particular conflict. Whether or not an act of political violence is represented as a crime is linked to beliefs about its legitimacy.

The literature on terrorism is sharply divided between the 'traditionalists' who perceive it as a distinct form of violence that can be understood in its own terms and those who perceive it as the product of social construction. Paul Wilkinson's classic traditionalist account, *Political Terrorism*, is devoted to the task of elaborating the fundamental features of this crime. According to Wilkinson the 'key characteristics common to all forms of political terror' are 'indiscriminateness, unpredictability, arbitrariness, ruthless destructiveness and the implicitly amoral antinomian nature of a terrorist's challenge' (Wilkinson, 1976: 17). Most supporters of the idea that terrorism is a distinct form of crime argue that its essential feature is the pursuit of violence for political ends. 'What distinguishes terrorism from both vandalism and non-political crime is the motivated violence for political ends', writes Crozier (1974). Political motivation, randomness, and the targeting of innocent non-combatants are the characteristics most often cited by contributors who seek to represent terrorism as a distinct form of violence (for a useful overview of these definitions see Thackrah, 2004: 66–71).

The main alternative to the project of representing terrorism as a distinct form of political violence that can be understood in its own terms is the social constructionist approach. This approach is oriented towards exploring how terrorism is constructed as a problem. As Jenkins argues, a social constructionist perspective does not necessarily imply that terrorism does not exist and that it is an invented problem. Nor does it imply a particular political stance towards the question (Jenkins, 2003: 14–15). However, by suggesting that terrorism is not a self-evident concept most constructionist contributors tend to question the dominant consensus and representation of this subject.

Some constructionists claim that the attempt to portray terrorism as a distinct form of political violence represents an attempt to objectify it. Oliverio argues that 'terrorism as a construct is given an objective formation because it is accepted by most scholars as a special form of political violence' (1998: 27). According to Oliverio the objectification of the terrorist construct is inextricably associated with the imperative of legitimating the authority of the State. She claims that the 'construct of terrorism is typically adopted discursively by the State to represent threats against its sovereignty' (Oliverio, 1998). Many constructionists regard the problematization of terrorism as a self-serving attempt by the State to consolidate its power. For example, Tomis Kapitan appears to be more concerned with deconstructing the official rhetoric on terrorism than with the phenomenon of political violence itself. From this perspective it is difficult to avoid the conclusion that the promotion of the rhetoric of terrorism constitutes a problem that is at least as significant as the acts of political violence by those labelled as terrorist.

Problem of definition

Terrorism is an unusually controversial concept. Most leading contributions in this field recognize the difficulty that social scientists have had in defining this concept (see for example Gurr, 1979: 24, or Wilkinson, 1977: 52). One study reviewed 109 definitions of terrorism that covered 22 definitional elements (Schmid and Jongman, 1988: 5–6). Walter Laqueur, a well-known expert on the subject, has counted over 100 definitions. He has concluded that the only 'general characteristic generally agreed upon is that terrorism involves violence and the threat of violence' (Laqueur, 1999: 6). But of course the use and threat of violence is not confined to terrorism. The deployment and the threat of violence is also practised by institutions that are deemed to be legitimate—particularly those of the State (Blakeley, 2009).

One reason why there may be so much confusion surrounding the definition of this term is due to the fact that it is not simply an objective analytical concept but also a moral statement on the behaviour of the terrorist. 'Thus in attempting to determine whether a specific action (or series of actions) is terroristic or not, the scholar should be aware that he is making a value judgement about the perpetrators of the alleged act, and about the circumstances of their actions', writes Wilkinson in his classic account of the subject (1974: 21). The normative dimension of this concept is evident in the political controversies that surround the issue of terrorism. Since so often debates about terrorism are linked to taking sides, the controversy that surrounds it is likely to be far more inflated than the kind of arguments that occur around other forms of deviant behaviour in the social sciences. The moral and political concerns that surround discussion on this subject mean that the concept is rarely used consistently and objectively.

The term terrorist is a loaded one—highly subjective, with aggressive connotations. It has acquired extremely negative associations. In the West, only the crime of paedophilia can compete with the act of the terrorist as a symbol of evil (Filler, 2003). The terrorist label serves as a health warning; it suggests that those to whom it is attached are morally inferior individuals. 'To identify someone as a terrorist is to render judgement on them, not simply to make a discovery' writes Claudia Card (2003: 178). Frequently, the attempt to represent an individual or a movement as terrorist is part of a propaganda war designed to discredit opponents. Not surprisingly, academic discussion of terrorism is not entirely detached from the propaganda battle for hearts and minds (Bonn, 2009).

Often the definition of terrorism that is adopted is self-consciously designed to undermine the legitimacy of those promoting political violence. According to the RAND Corporation, the aim of its definition is to criminalize the acts it deems to be terrorist. 'In separating terrorist tactics from their political context, the intent clearly was to criminalize a certain mode of political expression' (Jackson, 1999: v). Not surprisingly, when a definition serves in part as a political statement it is likely to become a focus for controversy.

Most serious contributions on the subject acknowledge that they have difficulty in defining terrorism. Often this difficult problem is side-stepped through attempting to enumerate a list of features that distinguish this form of crime. However, the attempt to construct a list of characteristics that are specific to terrorism is undermined by the fact that they can be found in other areas of violent activities. For example Wilkinson (1974: 13) claimed that 'a major characteristic of political terror is its indiscriminate nature'. The insistence that the indiscriminate quality of terrorist violence is one of this phenomenon's distinct features is accepted by many specialists on the subject. Images of the Washington D.C. 'Beltway snipers' (John Allen Muhammad and Lee Boyd Malvo) terrorizing passers-by during their killing sprees in the summer of 2002 or of pedestrians blown to bits in Tel Aviv by a hidden bomb lend weight to the argument that this form of violence is distinguished by its indiscriminate character. However, as the American sociologist Joel Best (1999) argues in his *Random Violence*, many of today's high-profile crimes have a capacity to scare the public precisely because they are perceived to be carried out indiscriminately. It is random violence that characterizes the acts of the serial killer, the perpetrator of road rage, or the paedophile preying on innocent children. Indiscriminate violence is not the sole property of terrorism. Indeed it is associated with many of the high-profile crimes that excite the public's imagination.

The claim that terrorism is premeditated, politically motivated violence that targets innocent non-combatants is widely accepted by specialists as important features of this phenomenon. Those who object to this definition raise questions about the nature of political motivation or of the meaning of innocence. 'This definition, however, begs the question of who is innocent and by what standards is innocence determined' notes Record (2003). Record and others contend that innocent non-combatants are frequently the victims of State-sponsored violence. He points to the firebombing of Japanese cities in 1945 and to the terrified inhabitants who were not involved in the war effort.

Many critics of conventional definitions of terrorism believe that its emphasis on the actions of non-State actors obscures the role of the State in promoting acts of political violence. In some cases, critics tend to represent political violence exercised by the State as another form of terrorism. Writing in this vein, Sterba (2003: 24) condemns the past misdeeds of the US and argues that 'the United States surely needs to take steps to radically correct its own wrongdoing if it is to respond justly to the related wrongdoing of Bin Laden and his followers'. Likewise, Record criticizes the traditional definitions because 'they exclude state terrorism, which since the French Revolution has claimed far more victims—in terms of millions—than terrorism perpetrated by non-state actors' (Record, 2003: 7).

Whatever definition one supports it is difficult to make a fundamental distinction between the violence and attributes of terrorism and the acts of others. For example, the objective of terrorizing the enemy is widely practised by conventional military forces. 'Shock and Awe' was the term used by the Bush administration to describe its massive hi-tech air strike against the Iraqis during the Second Gulf War. Its aim was clearly to strike terror in the minds of the enemy population. But those who supported this campaign did not regard it as an act of terror for the simple reason that they believed that this was a legitimate operation against a legitimate opponent. Definitions of terrorism involve the making of judgements of value. They also involve an element of selection. (Furedi, 2007: xxvii–xxxi).

Definitions of terrorism are fluid because ideas are continually changing about what forms of acts are legitimate or illegitimate. For example, violence against abortion clinics in the US was not considered as an act of terrorism until 1994.

In the 1980s, Americans tended to view terrorism as a Middle Eastern phenomenon, whereas in the 1990s the threat was perceived 'at least as much domestic as foreign' (Jenkins, 2003: 57; see also Hamm, 2002; 2004a). In recent years there has been a tendency on the part of Western governments and institutions to widen the definition of terrorism. In Britain, until recently the official definition was based on the one contained in the 1989 Prevention of Terrorism (Temporary Provisions) Act. According to this Act, terrorism 'means the use of violence for political ends and includes any use of violence for the purpose of putting the public or any section of the public in fear'. A review of terrorism legislation, carried out by Lord Lloyd in 1996, claimed that this definition was far too narrow since it did not encompass acts carried out by promoters of religious and single issue causes. The definition adopted in s. 1 of the Terrorism Act 2000 reflected these concerns and includes action that involves the 'use or threat of action' designed to 'influence the government or to intimidate the public or section of the public'. Violent acts committed against scientists conducting experiments on animals or in association with a hate crime (Chakraborti, 2010) are thus now frequently described as forms of terrorism.

Since 9/11 there has been a radical re-conceptualization of the meaning of terrorism. Official anxiety about the growing threat of home-grown extremism represents a radical departure from the way that terrorism was conceptualized in the past. Today terrorism is understood as not merely a physical threat. It is not simply the capacity of the terrorist to wreak mass destruction that worries society. Terrorism is also endowed with moral and ideological power that it is able to exercise over significant sections of the domestic population. The influence that the cause of the terrorist is able to exercise over the minds of sections of the public endows this threat with unparalleled danger. Sir David Omand, the former UK Security and Intelligence Coordinator goes as far as to state that the 'most effective weapon of the terrorist at present is their ideology' (cited in Furedi, 2007: 90). The model of a terrorist as an effective purveyor of ideas represents a significant departure from the way this threat was perceived in the past. Indeed the idea that a terrorist can appeal to people's heart and minds and not just merely scare the public is fundamentally inconsistent with traditional definitions of this threat. Until recent times the danger of terrorism was interpreted through its capacity to inflict fear on its target population. It is only in recent times that terrorism is conceptualized as an effective ideological competitor.

State terrorism

One of the most frequent criticisms made against the mainstream definitions of terrorism is that by focusing on non-State actors it overlooks the far more important problem of State-sponsored violence (Blakeley, 2009). Critics argue that the focus on the violence of the individual overlooks the fact that the real threat to humanity is destructive acts of State institutions. Gearty argues that the language of terrorism has become 'the rhetorical servant of the established order, whatever and however heinous its own activities are' (2002: 36–7). According to this perspective, the term terrorist is a label that the powerful use to stigmatize the activities of the powerless. 'It is easy for the politically satisfied and militarily powerful to pronounce all terrorism evil regardless of circumstance, but, like it or not, those at the other end of the spectrum are bound to see things differently' argues one critic (Record, 2003: 8). The belief that the promotion of the ideology of terrorism has helped to minimize the crimes of the powerful has led many to insist that the political violence exercised by the State should be viewed as another form of terrorism. Some contributors to the debate emphasize the association of terrorism with the State because they believe that this powerful institution is responsible for far more violence than that which has been perpetrated by non-State actors (see Morrison, 2004, 2006; and relatedly Cohen, 2001). According to one account 'state terrorism' should be given 'pride of place' because it 'has been responsible for more killings, more tortures, and more disappearances than all other forms' of crime (Williams, 2004: 499).

Historically, the terms terror and terrorism have been associated with both individuals and States. Regimes such as those of revolutionary France, Stalinist Soviet Union, or Nazi Germany are just some of the States associated with terrorism. In more recent times Western governments adopted the term 'State-sponsored terrorism' to denounce regimes deemed to be responsible for supporting and promoting terrorist activities. Nevertheless, in recent decades 'the anti-state sense of the term has become paramount' (Thackrah, 2004). Today, the terrorist threat is predominantly associated with non-State networks of activists.

Although the problem of State violence is an important issue requiring serious analysis and deliberation, it does not follow that it should be characterized by the same label as the one that is used to describe the bombing of a nightclub in Bali in October 2002 or the indiscriminate killing of railway commuters in Madrid in March 2004. There are problems in using a single concept of terrorism to account for all forms of politically influenced violence or threat of violence.

State violence is of course widespread and is a subject in its own right (see Hagan, 1997 for a general criminological introduction). However, its context and social dynamics make it a very different type of activity to those pursued by non-State actors. States possess a monopoly over the means of coercion and apply force and violence against some of their citizens as well as those from other societies. Historically the right of the State to exercise force has rarely been questioned. In all societies a distinction is usually made between the use of violence by the State and by others. Unlike civilians, in certain circumstances police and military personnel are allowed to shoot and kill. Some may have ethical objections to this double standard regarding the application of violence. But it is worth remembering that this double standard is integral to the institutionalization of authority in the modern nation-state.

Approaching the problem

The downside of conceptualizing terror as a form of violence associated with non-State actors is that it can easily be absorbed into an ideology that criminalizes individuals or groups who may have a legitimate cause to promote. However, the frequent manipulation of the terrorist label requires that we exercise care when we discuss the problem. Given the value-laden and subjective character of the construction of the problem of terrorism, it is tempting to avoid using the term altogether. This was the conclusion drawn by the BBC's World Service, when in the aftermath of 9/11 it decided not to use the word terrorist since to do so implied an 'improper value judgement' (cited in Jenkins, 2003: 18). Yet the problems that lead to the conceptualization of terrorism ought not to be defined out of existence. Yes, there is a problem with the label terrorist—it is often used to mystify rather than clarify. But nevertheless there are a range of disturbing practices that need to be conceptualized through a distinct category. Twenty-first century terrorism has distinct features which will be discussed in the rest of this chapter.

Whilst any definition is unlikely to solve the problem of how to distinguish this form of political violence from others, it is possible to outline some of the significant features that are associated with contemporary terrorism. As many official and non-official definitions of this subject suggest, contemporary terrorism is self-consciously directed at non-combatants. These individuals are not hurt or killed by accident but are intentionally targeted. It is violence that is randomly directed at civilians. However, those who are killed are not the targets of terrorism. As Jackson notes, 'the identities of the actual targets or victims of the attack often were secondary or irrelevant to the terrorist objective of spreading fear and alarm or gaining concessions' (Lesser *et al.*, 1999: v). This form of violence is directed at civilians in order to create fear in others.

REVIEW QUESTIONS

1 Why are definitions of terrorism a continuous focus of contestation?

2 What do we mean when we say that 'terrorism is a social construction'?

Contemporary terrorism

Understanding the threat

Political violence has been around throughout most of history. Although often condemned, politically motivated violence is not always considered to be a crime. The right to armed resistance against oppressive and coercive regimes is recognized by most political traditions. The case for a morally justifiable resort to political violence against a tyrannical regime is acknowledged within both the Christian and Western legal tradition and also within the Islamic worldview. Terrorism is a form of political violence that does not enjoy this legitimacy. Although terrorist tactics are sometimes linked to revolt and resistance, terrorism is generally regarded as a violation of prevailing moral norms.

As Fred Halliday (2004) remarks, the stigma attached to terrorism has been 'remarkably resilient and universal'. He notes that 'the killings of women and children, of prisoners, or of groups of civilians are actions widely recognized in all cultures, religions and contexts as invalid in principle' (Halliday, 2004: 6).

While non-State terrorist movements have been active since the nineteenth century, it is only in the recent period that they have been perceived as a significant if not principal threat to global stability. Since the end of the 1980s, the process of globalization has been experienced as one that encourages uncertainty, instability and the promotion of destructive forces. According to some accounts, global change has led to the disintegration of previously stable countries and State systems. This development has stimulated the rise of religious, ethnic, and other forms of internal conflicts, which in turn have helped consolidate a climate of global instability (Staten, 1999: 8). The fragmentation of the structural integrity of many societies has been linked to the rise of a variety of transnational or non-State actors and to the emergence of a new breed of international terrorists. It has been suggested that this new breed of 'postmodern' terrorists is particularly dangerous because for the first time such malcontents are able and are likely to access weapons of mass destruction (WMD) (see Laquer, 1996). The British House of Commons Select Committee on Defence has also expressed the view that society faces a new kind of terrorist. It noted that:

> while the UK may be regarded as well geared up to deal with traditional terrorist threats in general, new forms of terrorism and other aspects of asymmetrical warfare such as the use of hostages, environmental degradation, cyberwar, black propaganda etc, may find us rather less well prepared. (Select Committee on Defence 2001, para. 74)

The releasing of the nerve agent *sarin* in the Tokyo underground system in March 1995 marked an important watershed in the conceptualization of the global terrorist. After Tokyo, terrorism 'was said to have made a qualitative leap' since for the first time a terrorist organization was prepared to discharge materials of mass destruction (Zanders, 1999). Yet, the impact of this experience on the conceptualization of asymmetric threat pales into insignificance in comparison to the way in which the events of 11 September have come to define the problem. The tragic events of 11 September have served to lend credence to the claim that terrorist threats represent the major challenge to global stability. As Delpech (2002) noted: 'to think that the leading world power would have found itself in the extraordinary position of needing to mobilize four aircraft carriers and 400 planes to oppose a non-State actor is astonishing' (Delpech, 2002).

There is a substantial body of opinion that equates the threat of terrorism with WMDs, particularly chemical and biological weapons (CBWs). This diagnosis of the problem clearly has an anticipatory character. The experience until now provides little evidence that non-State actors have the capability to deploy WMDs. It is in the sphere of information technology that new forms of techno-terrorism have been most successful. Although the significance of cyber-terrorism is often exaggerated, a variety of radical organizations have been successful in manipulating and destroying their opponents' information systems. More importantly, the easy availability of information technology has facilitated the mobility of networks devoted to the pursuit of political violence. 'The latest communications technologies are thus enabling terrorists to operate from almost any country in the world, provided they have access to the necessary IT infrastructure' argues an authoritative contribution on this subject (Zanini and Edwards, 2001: 38).

Is there a new terrorism?

There is a substantial literature that insists that terrorism today is fundamentally different to the way it worked in previous times and that society is confronted with a new species of terrorism (Laqueur, 1999). However there is very little that is genuinely 'new' about terrorism. Those devoted to the pursuit of political violence have always sought to use the latest technologies in order to maximize the destructive impact of their operation. More than four decades ago in 1972 a group of terrorists belonging to a right-wing sect called the Order of the Rising Sun were arrested after they were found to be in possession of a large quantity of epidemic typhus pathogens with which they wanted to poison the water supplies of cities in the Mid-West of the US. Nor is there anything new about official concern about the proliferation of WMDs. For almost half a century officials have been discussing how to deal with a catastrophic terrorist attack. In all this time there is little empirical evidence of a qualitative transformation of this threat.

The one event that promoters of the new terrorism constantly allude to as proof of the arrival of a new era of terrorism was the attempt by members of the Japanese cult Aum Shinrikyo to launch a sarin attack on the Tokyo subway in March 1995. Although this millenarian sect sought to inflict mass casualties on Tokyo commuters, fortunately due to its inability to design an effective delivery system only 12 passengers lost their lives. In one sense the failure of the release of the nerve agent sarin to cause mass casualties can be interpreted as a good news story. It points to 'the difficulties in developing, producing and deploying biological agents' (Durodie, 2004: 1). It is worth noting that although Aum was a relatively sophisticated organization with access to scientific expertise and significant financial resources it still failed to realize its objectives. One important assessment of this experience concluded that 'the probability of a major biological attack by either a state or a sophisticated terrorist group seems remote' (Parachini, 2001: 5).

The evidence so far indicates that those oriented towards inflicting violence on civilians appear to choose conventional weapons to create mass casualties. Superficially the experience of 9/11 can be interpreted as confirmation of the catastrophic terrorism thesis. Yet one of the principal defining features of the new terrorism—the use of WMDs—was conspicuously absent during this event.

In retrospect it is evident that the destruction of the World Trade Center was the consequence of tactics that have been deployed by terrorists for a very long time. As Gearson observes, 'instead of technologically sophisticated weapons of mass destruction, the superterrorists of 11 September utilised the long-established terrorist approach of careful planning, simple tactics and operational surprises to effect the most stunning terrorist "spectacular" in history' (Gearson, 2002: 7).

One of the most persuasive arguments used to distinguish the new from the traditional form of terrorism is the claim that today it is far more brutal, destructive, and indiscriminate in its attitude to human life. Specialists on this subject frequently counterpose the traditional terrorist who was relatively selective in choosing targets to today's perpetrator of catastrophic acts of mass casualty. However, this argument has been repeatedly restated since at least the 1970s. Acts of apparently indiscriminate violence have a long history. This trend is illustrated by examples such as the simultaneous bombings of the US and French barracks in Lebanon in 1983 which resulted in the deaths of 367 people, the destruction of Pan Am Flight 103 over Lockerbie that killed 270 people, and the bombing of an Air India plane by a Sikh group that resulted in 329 deaths. Another characteristic attributed to new terrorism is the motive of religious fanaticism. Yet from Sicarii of the Jewish Zealot movement of biblical times there have been numerous violent sects who were inspired by religious and millenarian impulses (see Griset and Mahan, 2003: Chapter 1).

At first sight it is far from evident what has changed about terrorism. Virtually every characteristic that is associated with this new breed of destructive behaviour has been linked with terrorism in the past. However, the very fact that contemporary terrorism is perceived as very new, uniquely dangerous and the greatest threat to global stability renders it a distinct phenomenon. What is important about terrorism as a social phenomenon is how society responds to it. And the more dangerous that terrorism is perceived the more dangerous it becomes. It is the normalization of the expectation of catastrophic mass casualty events that transforms perceptions of terrorism into a global threat of unprecedented magnitude.

The one dimension of terrorism that is genuinely 'new' is the way it is conceptualized. On the one hand this is very much the case of reinterpreting old concerns and re-branding them as existential threat. On the other hand the meaning of terrorism has expanded and is used to account for a variety of threats. In recent decades a growing range of global threats have been assimilated into a narrative of new terrorism. The conceptual inflation of terrorism has been noted in an important study by Crelinsten who remarked that the 'tendency to place disparate phenomena into the same security basket' is 'reflected in recent analyses of terrorism' (Crenlisten, 1998: 390). A key development in this conceptual inflation was the shift from perceiving terrorism as a specific local phenomenon to one that was globally connected and therefore constituted a worldwide threat. During the 1970s a variety of disparate terrorist incidents in the West and in the Third World were interpreted as an integral part of a common global threat. 'All these events were increasingly incorporated into a single overarching narrative of "international terrorism"' notes Carr (2006: 198). One consequence of the perception of terrorism as an international phenomenon is that it becomes uprooted from any historical, cultural, and social context. As an international phenomenon it exists in its own right and terrorism can be readily interpreted as a stand-alone problem of apocalyptic dimensions.

The shifting narrative since 9/11

Since the start of the twenty-first century, there has been a dramatic shift in the way that the threat of terrorism has been understood and dramatized.

At the beginning of the century, terrorism was conceptualized as something that had its origins 'over there'—usually in the Middle East. However, since 9/11 it has become increasingly difficult to ignore the fact that the threat may not simply be an external one, but a domestic one, too. In America and Europe, the realization that there are people who do not like their societies, who do not want to be American or Dutch or whatever, has made the terror threat feel more intimate. And in response to this realization, the cultural narrative has shifted its focus on to 'home-grown terrorists' and the radicalization of young people who feel existentially distant from their societies. In recent years, almost seamlessly, the discussion about home-grown terrorism has mutated into a debate about the threat posed by 'the lone wolf' terrorist (see Michael, 2012; Spaaij, 2011). It was American law enforcement agencies that pioneered the construction of a new threat facing Western society—that is, from people referred to by the FBI as HGVEs (home-grown violent extremists).

Perceptions of the terrorist threat facing the United States have evolved significantly over the past ten years, and they are still evolving. The main threat now emanates from within the borders of the US, in the form of these HGVEs. A further development has been the emergence of the so-called lone wolf: an individual malcontent with no connection to any organized group, someone who is entirely off the radar; indeed, someone who could be anyone. The concept *leaderless resistance* (Kaplan, 1997), which originated amongst American White Supremacists is now used by law enforcement agencies to understand this threat.

The label was subsequently embraced by law enforcement agencies and the media to refer to individuals who, acting on their own initiative, attempt to inflict terror on their fellow citizens. So the Oklahoma City bomber, Timothy McVeigh, and the army officer Nidal Malik Hasan, who shot and killed 13 of his fellow soldiers at Fort Hood in Texas in November 2009, have been referred to as 'lone wolves'. And since last July, with the massacre of 77 Norwegians by Anders Behring Breivik, the concept has become Europeanized.

Indeed, in the aftermath of the terrible attacks in Norway, the European Union exhorted Member States to be wary of 'lone-wolf terrorism'. 'The issue of "lone-wolf" terrorism [requires] increasing attention', declared the EU. Numerous European security agencies have subsequently become preoccupied by the lone-wolf terrorist. In February 2012, the London-based Royal United Services Institute warned that the UK faces a growing threat from lone-wolf terrorists returning from fighting with radical Muslim groups overseas. Apparently, returnees from 'wars in Somalia, Yemen or Nigeria' might apply their experiences to the streets of the UK. (See http://www.bbc.co.uk/news/uk-16920643.) In response to these claims, the Home Office confirmed that it would do more to try to pre-empt the activities of lone wolves.

From a sociological perspective, it seems clear that threat assessments of lone wolves express a concern about the failure of society to win the loyalty of its citizens. Americans who kill fellow Americans, like Norwegians who shoot their neighbours, do not just murder individuals—they also raise fundamental questions about the integrity of the communities that they inhabit.

The characteristic feature of non-State terrorists

Although terrorist organizations are the product of a wide variety of circumstances and exist throughout the world, it is the Middle Eastern variety that appears to personify the problem. Frequently the threat posed by terrorism is ascribed to the power of religious ideology, especially that of Islam. 'Islamic fundamentalism represents a deep and coherent ideology stretching back fourteen centuries, and that is interiorized into the souls of millions of people' (Phillips, 2003: 101–2). The success of many Islamist movements notwithstanding (see Gerges, 2011 on the vacillating fortunes of Al-Qaeda), it is important not to interpret terrorism as an essentially religious phenomenon. As Halliday (2004) notes, the politics of terrorism has its roots in 'modern secular politics' and not in the distant past. It is both a product of and a revolt against modernity.

Unfortunately, the discussion and analyses of non-State actors is relatively underdeveloped and constitutes a weak link in the conceptualization of the problem. Many commentators cannot resist the temptation of using essentially moral or highly subjective categories to make sense of these individuals. Steele (1998) writes that 'when all is said and done, most men, and especially men from non-western cultures and less-developed areas, are capable of taking great pleasure in great evil' (Steele, 1998: 79). Many other observers adopt the perspective of regarding 'them' as our moral opposites. Dunlap claims that 'likely future adversaries will be unlike ourselves'. He characterizes opponents as members of 'The New Warrior Class' 'who have acquired a taste for killing, who do not behave rationally, who are capable of atrocities that challenge the descriptive powers of language, and who will sacrifice their own kind in order to survive' (Dunlap, 1996: 2). Numerous observers promote the view that terrorists are behaving irrationally. For example it has been suggested that the great practitioners of terror—Stalin, Hitler, Pol Pot, Osama Bin Laden, whom Robins and Post (1998) call charismatic terrorists—suffer from a personality disorder. Apparently they have low self-esteem and end up blaming others.

It is difficult to ascribe a single cause or motive that can account for the pursuit of political violence. These acts are committed by a wide variety of individuals who often have very specific and sometimes very individual reasons for adopting this course of action (see Cottee and Hayward, 2011). It is worth noting that empirical research carried out on terrorists and suicide bombers does not support the idea that they are mentally unstable and irrational people. Scott Atran's (2003) research on the phenomenon of suicide bombers provides powerful evidence that suggests that these individuals are not irrational crazed people, but are frequently well-educated and stable members of their community (see also famously Crenshaw (1981) on the normal state of mind of terrorists).

From the previous analysis it should be evident that the abstract counterposition drawn between rational and irrational can lead to a mis-assessment of the dynamic of global terrorism. Even suicide bombing—which many in the West find incomprehensible—is motivated by the rational calculation that such tactics are likely to weaken the morale of the target population. As Sprinzak (2000) argues 'the perception that terrorists are undeterrable fanatics who are willing to kill millions indiscriminately just to sow fear and chaos belies the reality that they are cold, rational killers who employ violence to achieve specific political objectives' (Sprinzak, 2000: 4). Labelling such individuals as zealots and fanatics can lead to an underestimation or at least a misunderstanding of the problem (see Pape and Feldman, 2010 in relation to the phenomenon of suicide bombing). Sprinzak notes that the experience of 11 September indicates that 'some of the best and the brightest among the enemy would rather sacrifice themselves' for their cause. According to Sprinzak (2001) the people responsible for 9/11 can be seen as 'innovators' and 'developers' who are 'incessantly looking for original ways to surprise and devastate the enemy'.

One reason why the demonization of individuals engaged in political violence is counterproductive is that it helps transform them into omnipotent and unstoppable threats. Such an approach transforms them into a far more frightening and dangerous threat than is warranted by their capabilities. One possible consequence of this approach is to inflate public anxieties and thereby indirectly empower them.

Too great an emphasis on cultural differences—religion, value systems, morality—fails to take account of the fact that many individuals drawn towards terrorism are products of modern technologically advanced societies or have had considerable contact with life in Western cultures. To take a few examples: members of the Rajneeshee cult, who employed biological agents to incapacitate many of the inhabitants of a small town in Oregon in 1984, were often American university-educated individuals; the *sarin* attack on the Tokyo underground in 1995 was carried out by a Japanese sect, whose members possessed considerable scientific and technological expertise; likewise, some of the individuals involved in the first terrorist attack on the World Trade Center were beneficiaries of American university education. Individual terrorists such as the 'Oklahoma bomber' Timothy McVeigh, an American Gulf War hero turned mass murderer, was no less prepared to inflict indiscriminate terror than his counterparts from different cultures. Similarly, the notorious 'una bomber', Theodore Kaczynski, is a former university professor with an Ivy League degree. Neither the British nail-bomber, David Copeland, nor his fellow citizen, Richard Reid, the alleged Al-Qaeda operative, were brought up as members of a 'New Warrior Class'.

The problem of terrorism today is constituted through actors who are products of important changes within the global and domestic environment. One of the characteristic features of the so-called new terrorists is that they appear to be free of many of the constraints that curbed similar acts of violence in the past. The weakening of systems of State structures, the erosion of legitimate institutions and of shared values have played a significant role in the shaping of asymmetric threat (Kilcullen, 2009). The process of globalization has provided new opportunities for non-State actors to develop powerful networks to sustain their operations. Halliday (2004) is right to draw attention to the fact that terrorism has emerged in 'rich and poor countries alike, as part of a transnational model of political engagement'. The global networks that underpin some of the terrorist organizations serve to enhance their influence. Hoffman claims that the problem is no longer confined to small groups of isolated individuals. The Al-Qaeda network can mobilize 4,000–5,000 individuals scattered throughout the globe. He believes that 'the appearance of these different types of adversaries—in some instances with new motivations and different capabilities—accounts largely for terrorism's lethality in recent years' (Hoffman, 1999: 9).

Campbell (1997) believes that one of the distinguishing features of 'post-modern' terrorists is that they are 'free of constraints provided by sponsoring nation-states'. Many associated terrorist organizations have the character of free agents, whose activities transcend national boundaries and cultures. They are often mobile members of diasporic organizations who are unconnected to any formal State institutions. As a result they are freed from the geopolitical calculations that State actors are forced to make. These actors are not only less connected to formal institutions—they are often freed from account-ability to a community and other forms of conventional networks. The erosion of a consensus around fundamental values about life also diminishes communal restraint. Throughout the world—and especially in the West—there has been a weakening of the prevailing value systems (see Hayward and Morrison, 2002: 146–50 for an account of this process in relation to contemporary terrorist activity). This has undermined many societies' ability to integrate and socialize its members. As a result many individuals drawn towards political violence are less restrained by such values and are therefore less accountable to conventional forms of behaviour than was the case in the past. The wider social and cultural disagreements about values actually free potential activists from hav-ing to justify their actions according to a specific ethos accepted by their community.

At a time of weakening State systems, the erosion of a sense of community and shared values, it makes little sense to attempt to label terrorists according to conventional politi-cal labels. In the past terrorist organizations could be labelled along ideological lines—conservative, revolutionary, religious, or nationalist. Since the 1990s, as Sprinzak (2001) argues, this typology has been rendered obsolete. Although these groups are 'not politi-cally blind—they remain apolitical'. Since the end of the Cold War, the erosion of the distinction between left and right has rendered ideologically driven politics problematic. Tucker (2001) insists that because today's 'most pernicious terrorists are not motivated by political ideology on the far left or right' they are 'more likely to be extremists on the fringe of traditional religions or idiosyncratic cults with an apocalyptic mindset'. This shift of focus from political objectives is also stressed by Carter (2002). He argues that 'not in all cases, but at least in some important cases, the motivation for mass ter-ror is a vengeful or messianic one, rather than a politically purposeful one'. As a result the actions of many radical movements has become less predictable and less oriented towards seeking political change. Instead of ideology, some movements have adopted a morally sanctioned worldview where ideas of evil and salvation influence behaviour. Such forms of behaviour often characterize movements involved in the so-called 'cul-ture wars'. It also affects contemporary violent protest movements, for example, animal rights campaigners. What unites Western-bred individuals like Timothy McVeigh and David Copeland with Islamic militants is the belief that their cause cannot be subject to conventional forms of restraint. As Tucker (2001) notes, today's terrorists 'experience fewer constraints on the use of violence to inflict indiscriminate casualties'. 'In these instances, the weakening of social capital lends individual grievances a cultural form.'

From research carried out by social psychologists, we know that individuals 'acting under the auspices of a group may feel that their personal accountability for the group's violent actions is diminished'. It is also suggested that, as a result, this diminished responsibility may lower individual thresholds of acceptability for violent behaviour (Pynchon and Borum, 1999: 345–6). What distinguishes some members of violent pro-test organizations from those of the past is that individual thresholds of acceptability for violent behaviour may become even lower in circumstances that prevail today (on this specific point see Chapter 8). With the intensification of social, institutional, and community fragmentation, the actions of militants are less contained by conventional norms and sanctions. This reduction in accountability is particularly the case for mobile transnational diasporic actors.

Finally, it is important to point out that the process of social fragmentation also encourages that of *individuation*. The general loosening of restraints also affects individual behaviour and may stimulate individual resentment to acquire a wider moral form. This may endow contemporary individual terrorism with a potentially more violent dimension. Developments in information technology help connect such individuals with one another and provide them with access to resources and ideas about how to conduct their affairs (see relatedly Chapter 6).

Conceptualizing the global problem of terrorism as the product of an estrangement from and rejection of modernity helps link this phenomenon to the wider social dynamic at work. The causes of individual cases of political violence are too numerous to be explained by a single set of variables. But it is not the existence of terrorism that represents a unique feature of the early twenty-first century. Rather, it is its ability to significantly destabilize individual societies and the prevailing global order that constitutes the nub of the problem. And that is not merely the result of the actions of the terrorist but of the powerful forces of globalization that work to diminish the sense of common purpose in many societies.

REVIEW QUESTIONS

1 How do we account for the significance that contemporary society attaches to the problem of terrorism?

2 Discuss the concept of a 'post-modern' terrorist.

3 Is terrorism just politics pursued by other means?

4 Is State-sanctioned violence just another form of terrorism?

CONCLUSION

The relationship between political violence and the criminal justice system has always been an uneasy one. It is important to note that not every form of political violence is criminalized and certainly not to the same extent. An analysis of the US media noted that the Irish Republican Army (IRA) got a better press than the Puerto Rican FALN (Hewitt, 2003: 112). And while the Reagan administration refused to describe anti-abortionist violence as terrorist, the Clinton one did. It is only in the past decade that the terrorist label has been applied to violent single-issue campaigns such as the targeting of laboratories conducting animal experimentation or abortion clinics

Since terrorism is such a highly charged politicized concept there are considerable difficulties in treating it as a crime. Certainly, it is rarely treated as an ordinary crime. Since it is perceived as representing a threat to the security of society and the authority of the State, it is usually dealt with under special emergency powers. The official response to terrorism often exists in a state of tension between treating it as a crime—that is, as a normal law and order problem—or responding to this threat in a more militaristic fashion through the application of special anti-terrorist legislation (see Hamm, 2004b for a recent criminological critique of this approach in relation to the US Patriot Act). In fact almost every violent act associated with terrorism could be prosecuted through the normal laws of the criminal justice system. Since the stated aim of these laws is to protect the public from harm, it stands to reason that they ought to be applied in all circumstances. However, advocates of special anti-terrorist legislation claim that extraordinary powers are necessary for dealing with the unique threat posed by terrorism. But, it can be argued that the very act of treating terrorism as a special, unique, and formidable threat serves to empower the terrorist as someone that cannot be dealt with through the normal institutions of society. It can also be argued that the use of special legislation serves to affirm the claim of those who argue that they are being persecuted for their beliefs rather than for their acts.

Although most governments and societies represent terrorism as a crime, they treat it as a problem that is quite distinct and one that requires special measures. Unlike a criminal who is seen to represent a threat to the well-being of the public, terrorism is perceived as a unique danger that threatens the very fabric of society. As a result, organizations that are deemed dangerous are formally banned and membership in them is considered to be a criminal offence. For example, in February 2001, 21 international organizations were banned under the UK Terrorism Act 2000. These include organizations such as Al-Qaeda, The Kurdistan Workers Party, and Palestinian Islamic Jihad. One of the objectives of terrorist legislation is to curb the international activities of terrorists, particularly acts that transcend national boundaries. A variety of such acts—inciting terrorism abroad, financing terrorists overseas—are now prosecuted under special legis-lation on both sides of the Atlantic. Such legislation is frequently justified on the ground that the domestic criminal justice system is inappropriate for dealing with global threats to the functioning of society.

Anti-terrorist legislation is different to normal criminal legislation in that it actively seeks to pre-empt and not simply catch the perpetrators of a terrorist act. As a result such laws can turn into criminal offences people's beliefs, organizational affiliation, possession of certain literature and otherwise legal substances. Anti-terrorist legislation also allows authorities to detain and interrogate suspects in cir-cumstances that are very different to what is acceptable under the criminal justice system. While such unusual powers appear to be necessitated by the extraordinary threat represented by the terrorist, the application of special anti-terrorist measures can be seen to represent a threat to civil liberties. Numerous commentators have pointed to the problem of enacting laws that have the potential for undermining the established liberties of a democratic society in the name of protecting freedom. As Wilkinson (1974: 109) noted a long time ago:

> [I]f the government is provoked into introducing emergency powers, suspending habeas corpus, or invoking mar-tial law, it confronts the paradox of suspending democracy in order to defend it. There is always the risk that by using heavy repression to crush the terrorist campaign the authorities may alienate the innocent mass of citizens caught up in the procedures of house-to-house searches and interrogations.

There is also the danger that a heavy-handed anti-terrorist policy could also end up repressing legitimate forms of dissent (see the 2007 documentary *Taking Liberties*, Dir. Chris Atkins). Most governments have found it difficult to resist the temptation of adopting special powers to pre-empt and contain terrorism. Yet if governments adopt a cavalier attitude towards civil liberties they will surely play into the very hands of those who promote and perpetrate political violence.

QUESTIONS FOR DISCUSSION

1 Discuss the statement that 'terrorism is in the eyes of the beholder'. Does the label terrorist necessarily represent a judgement of value?

2 How do we distinguish terrorism from other forms of violent crime?

3 What are the distinct features of twenty-first-century terrorism?

4 Provide your definition of terrorism and explain the reasons for your choice.

5 Why and how could government over-reaction play into the hands of the terrorist?

GUIDE TO FURTHER READING

The following texts each provide interesting accounts of the debates and issues surrounding contemporary terrorism discussed in this chapter. They also, to varying degrees, attempt to confront the rhetoric and politics of fear that often surround these debates:

Arquilla, J. and Ronfeldt, D. (2001) *Networks and Netwars: The Future of Terror, Crime, and Militancy*. Santa Monica, CA: RAND.

Carter, A. Deutch, J. and Zelikow, P. (1998) 'Catastrophic Terrorism; Tackling the New Danger', *Foreign Affairs*, November/December.

Filler, D.M. (2003) 'Terrorism, Panic, and Pedophilia', *Journal of Social Policy and the Law*, Spring.

Furedi, F. (2007) *Invitation To Terror: The Expanding Empire of the Unknown*. London: Continuum Press.

Hewitt, C. (2003) *Understanding Terrorism in America: From The Klan To Al Qaeda*. London: Routledge.

Jenkins, P. (2003) *Images of Terror: What We Can and Can't Know about Terrorism*. New York: Aldine de Gruyter.

Laqueur, W. (1999) *The New Terrorism: Fanaticism and the Arms of Mass Destruction*. New York: Oxford University Press.

Wilkinson, P. (1974) *Political Terrorism*. New York: Macmillan.

WEB LINKS

http://www.security.homeoffice.gov.uk
The Home Office counter-terrorism website: these pages provide information for the public on the threat from international terrorism and accounts of what the government is doing to protect, prevent, and prepare for terrorist attacks.

http://www.terrorism.com
Website of the Terrorist Research Center

http://www.start.umd.edu/start/
National (US) consortium for the study of terrorism and responses to terrorism. Very useful site for finding terrorist-related government reports.

http://www.hri.org/docs/USSD-Terror
US Department of State: Patterns of Global Terrorism Reports.

http://jihadology.net/2011/11/18/articles-of-the-week-1112-1118/
Jihadology: a clearing house for material on Islamic terrorism.

REFERENCES

Atran, S. (2003) 'Genesis of Suicide Terrorism', *Science* 299. March 7.

Best, J. (1999) *Random Violence; How we Talk about New Crimes and new Victims*. Berkeley: University of California Press.

Blakeley, R. (2009) *State terrorism and neoliberalism*. Abingdon: Routledge.

Bonn, S. (2010) *Mass Deception: Moral Panic and the U.S. War on Iraq*. New Jersey: Rutgers University Press.

Campbell, J. (1997) *Weapons of Mass Destruction—Terrorism*. New York: Interpact Press.

Card, C. (2003) 'Making War on Terrorism in Response to 9/11' in J.P. Sterba (2003) (ed) *Terrorism and International Justice*. New York: Oxford University Press, 178.

Carr, M. (2006) *Unknown Soldiers: How Terrorism Transformed the Modern World*. London: Profile Press.

Carter, A. (2002) in 'Understanding Terrorism; A Harvard Magazine Roundtable', *Harvard Magazine* January–February 2002.

Chakraborti, N. (2010) *Hate Crime: Concepts, Policy, Future Directions*. Cullompton: Willan.

Cohen, S. (2001) *States of Denial: Knowing About Atrocities and Suffering*. Oxford: Polity.

Cottee, S, and Hayward, K. J. (2011) 'Terrorist (e)motives: the existential attractions of terrorism', *Studies in Conflict and Terrorism*, 34 (12): 963–86.

Crelinsten, R. (1998) 'The Discourse and Practice of Counter-Terrorism in Liberal democracies'. *Australian Journal of Politics and History*, Vol. 44, no. 1.

Crenshaw, M. (1981) 'The Causes of Terrorism', *Comparative Politics* 13 (4).

Crozier, B. (1974) *A Theory of Conflict*. London: Hamish Macmillan.

Delpech, T. (2002) 'The Imbalance of Terror', *The Washington Quarterly*, Winter 2002.

Dunlap, C. (1996) 'Sometimes The Dragon Wins; A Perspective on Information-Age Warfare' http://www.intowar.com/MIL_C4I/DRAGON.html-ssi.

Durodie, B. (2004) 'Facing the possibility of Bioterrorism', *Current Opinion in Biotechnology*, Vol. 15.

Filler, D.M. (2003) 'Terrorism, Panic, and Pedophilia', *Journal of Social Policy and the Law*, Spring issue.

Furedi, F. (2007) *Invitation To Terror; The Expanding Empire Of The Unknown*. London: Continuum Press.

Gearson, J. (2002) 'The Nature of Modern Terrorism', *The Political Quarterly*.

Gearty, C. (2002) 'Terrorism and Morality', *European Human Rights Law Review*.

Gerges, F (2011) *The Rise and Fall of Al-Qaeda*. Oxford: Oxford University Press.

Griset, P. and Mahan, S. (2003) *Terrorism in Perspective*. Thousand Oaks, CA: Sage.

Gurr, T. (1979) *Violence in America*. New York: Sage Publications.

Hagan, F.E. (1997) *Political Crime*. Needham Heights, MA: Allyn and Bacon.

Halliday, F. (2004) 'Terrorism in historical perspective', *Open Democracy*, 22 April.

Hamm, M. (2002) *In Bad Company: America's Terrorist Underground*. Boston: Northeastern University.

Hamm, M. (2004a) 'Apocalyptic violence: the seductions of terrorist subcultures' *Theoretical Criminology* 8 (3) Special Edition: Cultural Criminology.

Hamm, M. (2004b) 'The US Patriot Act and the politics of fear' in J. Ferrell, K. Hayward, W. Morrison, and M. Presdee (eds) *Cultural Criminology Unleashed*. London: GlassHouse.

Hayward, K.J. and Morrison, W. (2002) 'Locating Ground Zero: caught between the narratives of crime and war' in J. Strawson (ed) *Law After Ground Zero*. London: Cavendish Press.

Hewitt, C. (2003) *Understanding Terrorism in America; From The Klan To Al Qaeda*. Routledge: London.

Hoffman, B. (1999) 'Introduction' in I.O. Lesser, B. Hoffman, J. Arquilla, D. Ronfeldt, M. Zanini, and B. Jenkins (1999) *Countering The New Terrorism*. Santa Monica, CA: RAND, MR–989.

Jackson, B.M. (1999) 'Foreword' in I.O. Lesser, B. Hoffman, J. Arquilla, D. Ronfeldt, M. Zanini, and B. Jenkins (1999) *Countering The New Terrorism*. Santa Monica, CA: RAND, MR–989.

Jenkins, P. (2003) *Images of Terror: What We Can and Can't Know about Terrorism*. New York: Aldine de Gruyter.

Kaplan, J. (1997) 'Leaderless Resistance', *Terrorism and Political Violence*, vol. 9, no. 3: 80–95.

Kilcullen, D. (2009) *Accidental Guerrilla*. London: Hurst.

Laqueur, W. (1996) 'Postmodern Terrorism', *Foreign Affairs*, September–October.

Laqueur, W. (1999) *The New Terrorism: Fanaticism and the Arms of Mass Destruction*. New York: Oxford University Press.

Lesser, I.O., Hoffman, B., Arquilla, J., Ronfeldt, D., Zanini, M., and Jenkins, B. (1999) *Countering The New Terrorism*. Santa Monica, CA: RAND.

Michael, G. (2012) *Lone Wolf Terror and the Rise of Leaderless Resistance*. Nashville: Vanderbilt University Press.

Morrison, W. (2004) 'Criminology, genocide and modernity' in C. Sumner (ed) *The Blackwell Companion to Criminology*. Oxford: Blackwell.

Morrison, W. (2006) *Criminology, Civilisation and the New World Order*. Abingdon: Cavendish-Routledge.

Oliverio, A. (1998) *The State of Terror*. Albany: State University of New York Press.

Pape, R.A. and Feldman, J.K. (2010) *Cutting the Fuse: The Explosion of Global Suicide Terrorism and How to Stop It*. Chicago: Chicago University Press.

Parachini, J. (2001) *Combatting Terrorism: Assessing The Threat Of Biological Terrorism. Before the House Subcommittee on National Security, Veteran Affairs and International relations, Committee on Government Reform, US House of Representatives*, 12 October, Washington D.C.

Phillips, R.L. (2003) 'The war against pluralism' in J.L. Sterba (ed) *Terrorism and International Justice*. Oxford: Oxford University Press.

Pynchon, M.R. and Borum, R. (1999) 'Assessing Threats of Targeted Group Violence: Contributions from Social psychology', *Behavioral Sciences and the Law*, Vol. 17.

Record, J. (2003) *Bounding The Global War On Terrorism*. Carlisle, PA: Strategic Studies Institute, available at http://www.carlisle.army.mil.

Robins, R.S. and Post, J.M. (1998) *Political Paranoia: The Psychopolitics of Hatred*. New Haven, CT: Yale University Press.

Schmid, A. and Jongman, A. (1988) *Political Terrorism: A New Guide to Actors, Authors, Concepts, Data bases, Theories, and Literature*. New Brunswick, NJ: Transaction Books.

Select Committee on Defence (2001) *Eight-Report*, para. 74. London: HMSO.

Spaaij, R. (2011) *Understanding Lone Wolf Terrorism: Global Patterns, Motivation and Prevention*. Springer Briefs in Criminology.

Sprinzak, E. (2000) 'Rational Fanatics', *Foreign Policy*, September/October.

Sprinzak, E. (2001) 'The Lone Gunmen', *Foreign Policy*, November.

Staten, C.L. (1999) 'Asymmetric Warfare, the Evolution and Devolution of Terrorism: The Coming Challenge for Emergency and National Security Forces', *Journal of Counter-Terrorism and Security International*. vol. 5, no. 4: 8.

Sterba, J.L. (ed) (2003) *Terrorism and International Justice*. Oxford: Oxford University Press.

Steele, R.D. (1998) 'The Asymmetric Threat to the Nation,' Defence Daily Network (http://www.defensedaily.com/reports/takedown.htm). 22 June.

Thackrah, J.R. (2004) *Dictionary of Terrorism*. London: Routledge.

Tucker, J. (2001) 'The Proliferation of Chemical and Biological Weapons Materials and Technologies to State and Sub-State Actors'. *Testimony before the Subcommittee on International Security, Proliferation, and Federal Services of the U.S. Senate Committee on Governmental Affairs*. 7 November 2001.

Williams, K.S. (2004) *Textbook on Criminology*. Oxford: Oxford University Press.

Wilkinson, P. (1974) *Political Terrorism*. New York: Macmillan.

Wilkinson, P. (1976) 'Terrorism versus Democracy: The Problem of Response', *Conflict Studies*, no. 76.

Wilkinson, P. (1977) *Terrorism and the Liberal State*. London: Macmillan.

Wilson N.B. (2003) 'Bibliographical Essay on Fear', *The Hedgehog Review*, Fall, Vol. 5, no. 3: 119.

Zanders, J.P. (1999) 'Assessing the Risk of Chemical and Biological Weapons Proliferation to Terrorists', *The Nonproliferation Review*, Fall.

Zanini, M. and Edwards, S. (2001) 'The Networking of Terror in the Information Age' in J. Arquilla, and D. Ronfeldt (eds) (2001) *Networks and Netwars: The Future of Terror, Crime, and Militancy*. Santa Monica, CA: RAND.

Part III
SOCIAL DIMENSIONS OF CRIME

Economic marginalization, social exclusion, and crime

14

Chris Hale

INTRODUCTION

This chapter reviews the long-standing debates around the relationships between the economy, poverty, inequality, and crime. Beginning by summarizing what criminologists and others have said about these issues it then considers evidence for links between unemployment, and more fruitfully the broader labour market, and crime. A more focused discussion of the links between poverty, inequality, and crime follows, examining concepts such as the underclass and social exclusion. This will raise political issues of how to deal with these problems. For many, integrating people into work is central to combating social exclusion and this links back to the discussion of the relations between the labour market and crime. At the centre of this debate lie not only matters of power and inequality, but also the need to question the nature of paid work and the position it takes within capitalist society.

BACKGROUND

> 'The devil makes work for idle hands'
> 'Poverty is the mother of crime'

As with all folklore these proverbs both contain a kernel of truth, but as with much 'common sense' they need careful interpretation.

The first suggests that work, gainful employment, is important in preventing crime. Thus those who do not have jobs, the idle hands, are more likely to become involved in criminal pursuits, partly, perhaps, to provide for their daily needs and partly because they lack the discipline and structure employment provides. As will be seen later in this chapter, the relationship between unemployment and crime provokes much debate amongst criminologists. However, this is not the complete picture since it ignores the 'idle rich' and few suggest that they might benefit from the discipline of the workplace!

The second suggests that poverty causes crime—the poor are more likely than the rich to be criminal. Again this seems sensible—those lacking in material resources may resort to illegal behaviour to provide their daily bread. Further, they may have less to lose than the better off and so be less afraid of the consequences if their offending is discovered. Again it is silent about the crimes of the rich and the powerful where greed rather than need is more relevant. Space precludes examining the relationship between the economy and crimes of the powerful, but the interested reader is referred to Box (1987) and Chapter 11.

So while this chapter focuses primarily on the debate around economic hardship and crimes such as burglary, vehicle theft, and robbery, it should be remembered that this debate is a product of ideological emphasis on types of crime more likely to be committed by the powerless than by the powerful.

There are theoretical arguments and empirical evidence to support the hypothesis that crime and the economy are related. Some, but not all, studies of the relationship between unemployment and crime have found a link. Other studies show that the poor and unemployed form a significant proportion of known offender populations. More broadly work linking crime with wider economic changes in the structure of economy can be cited.

Critics of these positions will object that this is labelling all the poor and unemployed as criminals, whereas most are law-abiding citizens. Further, they will suggest that during the economic depression of the 1930s, when poverty was widespread and severe, crime was much lower than it has been throughout the period since 1945 when the standards of living of everyone in industrialized countries have improved considerably. Against this could be set the massive increase in recorded crimes in England and Wales during the severe recession between 1989 and 1992 and the fact that between 1993 and 2008, the UK, along with many other countries had an unprecedented 15 years of steady economic growth accompanied by a steady decline in crime whether measured by police statistics or the British Crime Survey. This signals the danger of seeking a single explanation for crime. Social relationships are historically contingent; what may hold in one period may not in another because of broader social and cultural changes. In particular how problems related to economic hardship are dealt with, both formally and informally, how inequality and wealth are viewed will affect the relationship between crime and economic conditions.

REVIEW QUESTIONS

1 In what ways might being unemployed or poor increase the likelihood of engaging in crime?

2 In what ways might being in work or rich increase the likelihood of engaging in crime?

3 What were the differences between the 1930s and the 1960s in terms of crime and unemployment?

Why might economic conditions affect the level of crime?

What does social theory have to say about the relationship between economic conditions and crime? Despite being 25 years old, Box (1987) remains an excellent review, so his approach is summarized and developed here. As he notes, many theories can be read in ways that predict more crime when unemployment increases and income inequalities widen. What follows is a brief, selective look at what some have said.

Strain theory

Strain theory tackles motivation—why would anyone want to commit crimes? It argues people would conform to prevailing norms and laws but for stresses and contradictions in their lives. Two variations are identified, anomie leading to 'thwarted ambition' and relative deprivation caused by material inequalities in wealth.

Durkheim's concept of *anomie* (Durkheim, 1893 (1985)) describes a society where rules are breaking down, are blurred and confused so that people do not know what to expect of each other producing feelings of isolation and a sense of meaninglessness in life. Durkheim was writing in the late nineteenth century after the massive upheavals of the Industrial Revolution transformed predominantly rural agricultural societies into urban communities dominated by manufacturing industry. For Durkheim, anomie arises during periods of rapid social change and leads to dissatisfaction, conflict, and deviance. This is likely to happen during economic recessions, but can also occur during periods of prosperity. Many observers see recent changes, where industrialized countries have seen declining manufacturing sectors and concomitant rises in service industries, as producing similar effects.

Merton adapted anomie as the basis of strain theory (Merton, 1938). Unlike Durkheim, he does not argue the problem is sudden social change. Instead crime is one possible response to strains produced by unequal opportunities for achieving success. Where the dominant culture values success in terms of material goods and economic status, crime would be expected to increase whenever legitimate opportunities to achieve such success are restricted. In supposedly meritocratic societies, education and hard work are the major ways of attaining material success. In an economic recession, when unemployment rises and inequality widens, more people will experience a sense of failure to achieve these culturally defined goals and will become more likely to attempt to achieve them by resorting to illegal activities. Note however that for Merton crime is only one of five possible responses to strain (see Chapter 4). Strain theory is a structural theory that posits disjuncture between culturally prescribed goals of success and the means available to achieve them. Moreover the theory would suggest crime would be a lower-class phenomenon since they will have similar goals as middle and upper classes, but will lack the means to achieve them.

Relative deprivation is related to, but distinct from strain. As the name suggests, it refers to relative, rather than absolute poverty, hence to the distribution of wealth and income across society. Wealth and income can be increasing for all individuals, but relative deprivation will also increase if the gap between rich and poor increases. For example, one objective measure often used is to compare the income of the top 10 per cent income earners with that of the lowest 10 per cent. To take an artificial example, if the income of the top 10 per cent triples while that of the bottom only doubles, then inequality has increased.[1] Clearly the UK is a richer society today than 100 years ago, and not just in terms of economic wealth but also in matters such as health and education. However, whether or not it is a more equal society is a different matter. At an individual level it is possible to be well off and still feel relatively deprived. For example, I feel poor when comparing myself to Bill Gates but rich when considering the homeless in my local town. As well as the objective situation, an awareness of one's position is important. Today people are continually bombarded by media images and definitions of the 'good life' that only add to the sense of deprivation of those unable to afford designer labels and expensive holidays. Similarly in urban areas, with the process of gentrification that follows when the middle classes move into poorer areas, the stratification of neighbourhoods is less marked than previously. Relative deprivation has become a popular explanation for crime, because for long periods in the second half of the twentieth century—in the industrialized economies at least—rising living standards have been accompanied by rising crime. Note that, unlike strain theory, relative deprivation does not necessarily suggest that crime is a lower-class phenomenon, amongst societies' 'losers', since it accepts that discontent 'can be felt anywhere in the class structure where people perceive their rewards to be unfair compared to those with similar attributes' (Young, 2001). Nevertheless, a sense of relative deprivation is likely to be more pronounced for those whose economic position is least secure especially during periods of economic recession when unemployment increases and wage levels are likely to be depressed.

Social disorganization theory—the Chicago School

The Chicago School is famous for the links it established between environmental factors and crime (Chapter 4; Hayward, 2001). An important part of this is the idea of a zone of transition within cities, characterized by run-down housing, high residential mobility, high levels of poverty, and poor health. It is the first home for new immigrants, who remain only long enough to become economically established before moving to more prosperous neighbourhoods. So the 'zone of transition' is a place of constant change, where communal ties are difficult to establish and most relationships impersonal. Such neighbourhoods were described as socially disorganized and as a consequence were likely to be low in informal methods of social control and high in crime. In Chicago, Shaw and McKay (1942) tested this hypothesis and found that delinquency rates were 'at their highest in run-down inner city areas and progressively declined the further one moved into the prosperous suburbs' (Hayward, 2001: 31). Generalizing these ideas, it seems a logical step to posit that in times and neighbourhoods where unemployment is high or economic prospects are poor it will be difficult to muster the necessary resources to combat social disorganization and maintain informal social control. Hence, again an argument suggests deteriorating economic conditions will lead to increasing levels of crime.

Economic theory: rational economic (wo)man

This posits individuals who choose between crime and legitimate work depending on the opportunities, rewards, and costs of each. Thus, individuals choose to work or to commit a crime depending on the chances of getting a job and the wages in the legitimate market compared with opportunities for illegal earnings, the risk of being caught and the probability and severity of punishment if caught (for an alternative to this calculating approach that emphasizes crime's expressive attraction, see Chapter 18). Whilst originally this was posited as choice between legitimate and illegitimate work (Becker, 1968; Ehrlich, 1973) more recently it has been extended to allow for individuals to engage in both crime and legitimate work during the same period of time. It will be argued later that this is particularly important in periods when many jobs are part-time, low quality, have little or no security, and are poorly paid. Again this theory suggests that as economic returns from paid employment deteriorate or disappear, crime will increase.

Control theory

Avoiding implicating social structure, control theory's focus on individual responsibility appeals to those of a conservative bent. It asks not why people commit crime, but rather, how they are constrained not to offend, seeing offending as a natural human instinct. Individuals and their internalization of moral rules and codes become a key focus. One variant, Hirschi's social bond theory (Hirschi, 1969), emphasizes how social bonds to family, school, work, everyday activities, and beliefs insulate people against deviant behaviour. The theory argues that those who:

- are high in *attachment*, with close emotional links to others;
- have a strong *commitment* to the future in that they believe conventional behaviour will lead to immediate or long-term rewards;
- have *involvement* so that they are kept busy in conventional activities such as school or work;
- hold the 'right' *beliefs* about what is permissible or not, that is beliefs that coincide with conventional rules and norms

are less likely to be involved in deviant or unlawful behaviour. At first sight this does not look hopeful for those seeking theoretical arguments relating unemployment and poverty to crime.

However, as Box (1987) argues, economic recession and unemployment can be expected to weaken social bonds leading to increased levels of crime. Consider first *attachment*. Unemployment and increasing inequality are unlikely to improve family relationships. Rather, they will create increased tension, anger, and sullenness against society that may well lead to family breakdown. Fracture of attachment within the family may lead some to become involved in crime as they care less about what others think of them. Turning to *commitment*, Box (1987: 45) suggests unemployment 'casts a long shadow' over institutions that are supposed to prepare people for employment. He has in mind particularly schools, that risk being delegitimated if their role in preparing pupils for the discipline of work seems redundant with prospects of future employment reduced. Next he argues that individual *beliefs* in the legitimacy of conformity will weaken as recession undermines families and schools and this will damage the ability of one generation to impress its values on the next. Alert readers will have spotted that *involvement* has been missed. Surprisingly, Box does not consider this in his discussion, although it seems straightforward to integrate it. With more unemployment, shorter working hours and more part-time work, people will have less involvement in conventional activity and social bond theory would suggest that crime would increase.

Later work by Hirschi developed, or many would argue restricted, control theory most notably in his 1990 collaboration with Gottfredson under the rather grand title of *A General Theory of Crime* (Gottfredson and Hirschi, 1990). This rejected social bond theory, conceiving of control instead as 'a permanent internal state' (Lilly *et al.*, 2002). As these authors note, this was part of a broader trend during the 1980s to prioritize individual, rather than structural, explanations of social problems. According to Gottfredson and Hirschi self-control, developed during early childhood, is the key factor that restrains people from engaging in crime. For them self-control depends on the quality of parenting during a child's early years. Ineffectual and neglectful parents will raise children who 'tend to be impulsive, insensitive, physical (as opposed to mental), risk-taking, shortsighted and nonverbal, and they will tend therefore to be engage in criminal and analogous acts' (Gottfredson and Hirshi, 1990). This somewhat depressing picture suggests that nothing can be done to correct traits already set firm in early years. And what of unemployment and recession? Harriet Wilson's work on socially deprived families in inner Birmingham (Wilson, 1980) looked at the degree of 'chaperonage' parents gave to their children. She found a:

> very close association between lax parenting methods [and] severe social stress. Lax parenting methods are often the result of chronic stress, situations arising *from frequent or prolonged spells of unemployment* [emphasis added], physical or mental disabilities among members of the family and an often permanent condition of poverty . . . It is the position of the most disadvantaged groups in society, and not the individual which needs improvement in the first place.

So again, control theory is combined with a strong structural analysis. But the implications for the relationship between unemployment and crime are different. Parenting might be expected to deteriorate in times of recession. However, the effect on crime would not be immediate. Rather, it would impact in perhaps eight to ten years' time. Dealing with today's crime problems would have required action a decade ago.

Opportunity and routine activity theory

These theories argue that, in order for a crime to occur, three things are needed—a motivated offender, a suitable target, and a lack of guardianship (see Chapter 4). Cantor and Land (1985) suggest rising unemployment has two effects tending to increase both the numbers of motivated offenders and the level of guardianship. The reasons behind the first effect have already been rehearsed. According to Cantor and Land (1985: 350) the second arises with increased numbers of unemployed—more individuals will be at home and this reduces both the risks of their property being burgled and provides more informal social control within neighbourhoods. Further, the fact that the unemployed are not involved in daily travel to and from work may reduce their risk of becoming victims of street crime. Hence they argue unemployment has two opposite effects on crime. On one hand, crime will tend to rise as unemployment potentially causes the numbers of motivated offenders to rise. On the other hand, more unemployed will mean increased levels of guardianship that will tend to cause crime to fall.

Having briefly reviewed theories that suggest crime is related to economic conditions—mainly the level of unemployment—the next step is to consider what, if any, evidence exists to support of refute the hypothesis.

REVIEW QUESTIONS

1 What is meant by anomie?

2 What are the differences between relative and absolute deprivation?

3 Why might crime fall as unemployment increases?

What is the evidence for a relationship between crime and the economy?

It is worth beginning with some observations of Radzinowicz. In two classic papers (Radzinowicz, 1939; 1971) he suggests the more multifaceted the economic structure of society becomes, the harder it is to measure cycles of depression or prosperity. While relatively straightforward in a simple agricultural community, in a complex industrial society measuring economic change is more complicated and relating these changes to trends in crime a more demanding task. Hence it will be necessary to use multiple economic indices rather than relying on single measures such as unemployment. Radzinowicz counsels that economic change may not influence crime at once but at some time in the future—there will be a lagged effect. Further, he makes the important point that economic conditions appear to affect certain types of crime more than others. He suggests property crime is the most sensitive and likely to decrease in times of prosperity. Conversely, crimes against the person seem to go up in times of economic growth.

Unemployment and crime

It has proved difficult to reach anything approaching a consensus on the unemployment-crime (U-C) relationship. As well as reviewing the evidence it is hoped to persuade the reader that a broader view of economic influences than just unemployment is needed. Others factors that need considering include the quality of work, wage rates, and the precariousness of employment.

Two major surveys of statistical work on unemployment and crime are Chiricos (1987) and Box (1987). Both concluded that the evidence slightly favoured a positive relationship, that is, rises in unemployment increased crime. However, as Chiricos comments, the period covered by most of the studies were dominated by the years up to the 1970s when unemployment was much lower than during the following two decades. Further, he also noted that the evidence for a positive relationship was stronger in studies that focused on property crimes.

As noted earlier, Cantor and Land (1985) use opportunity theory to explain why negative relationships may arise as unemployment leads to increased guardianship. Positive U-C relationships can be explained by the increased motivation to offend as unemployment grows. Hence, in any particular study crime may rise, remain constant or fall as unemployment rises depending on the relative strengths of the two effects. Whatever the merits[2] of their argument Cantor and Land alert us to the need to take a more nuanced approach to unemployment and crime.

Other approaches to the relationship between the economy and crime

Recent studies have questioned the focus on the U-C link when examining the relationship between the economy and crime. Pyle and Deadman (1994) argue that unemployment may not be the best indicator of the state of the economy. The definition and measures of unemployment underwent numerous revisions in recent years making it difficult to construct a consistent data series. (The changes always reduced the numbers of unemployed entitled to benefit!) Further, they argue unemployment lags behind the business cycle by between six and 12 months. A recession will affect the labour market first through reduced overtime, more part-time work, and falling wages. If property crime increases in response to worsening economic conditions, the time lag before unemployment rises suggests it may not capture this effect. Instead Pyle and Deadman suggest using other economic indicators that more closely track the business cycle, such as **Gross Domestic Product** (GDP) or Consumers' Expenditure.

In a classic study Field (1990) found consumer expenditure was the best economic indicator for explaining crime. As well as economic variables, he considered a wide range of demographic, criminal justice, and environmental effects using multivariate statistical techniques. He concluded that economic factors had a major influence on both property crime (including burglary, theft, robbery, vehicle crime, criminal damage, and fraud) and personal crime (including violence against the person, thefts from the person (excluding robbery) and sexual offences).

For property crime he found two opposite effects. In the short run, year-on-year changes in consumption were negatively related to changes in crime. Field ascribes this to a motivational effect with individuals switching in and out of criminal activity as their economic position declines or improves. Longer term, over a period of several years he found a positive or direct relationship between crime and growth in consumption. He interpreted this as an opportunity effect since in a growing economy there will be more goods and money available to steal.

Field found that personal crime was quite different to property crime. In both the short and the long term he found that personal crime was positively related to consumer expenditure. He suggested that increased consumption leads to an increase in the amount of time spent outside the home and so increases the likelihood of being the victim of a personal attack. This is (probably) also linked to increased alcohol consumption as incomes rise (see Chapter 8). Again care must be taken in generalizing these findings. Consider domestic violence: are decreasing incomes and increasing unemployment likely to lead to less partner abuse?

Pyle and Deadman (1994) and Hale (1998) confirmed Field's findings of short-run linkages between the economy and property crime: other things being equal, it increases as economy declines. This held whether the economic indicator used was GDP, personal consumption or unemployment. Moreover, for burglary and theft they found positive long-run relationships between crime and economic growth, indicating that for the period under consideration (1950–91), the growing economy led to increased crime. The importance of exploring the use of alternative economic indicators has been emphasized by the work of Rosenfeld (2009) and Detotto and Otranto (2012).

A tentative conclusion may be that while the U-C relationship is likely to be important in many circumstances it is important to look at broader economic factors than unemployment.

Crime and the changing labour market

Hale (1999) uses data from England and Wales to explore the impact of broader labour market changes on crime between 1946 and 1994. He argues that the UK economy, and particularly its labour market, has undergone fundamental changes in this period. There has been:

- a shift in employment from manufacturing to the service sector;
- an increase in part-time employment and an accompanying increase in numbers in temporary and untenured jobs;
- a shift in the patterns of employment from men to women.[3]

A dual labour market has developed with a primary or core sector and a secondary or periph-eral sector. The primary sector consists of skilled workers usually working full-time for large organizations with good employment and benefit rights. Conversely, those in the secondary sector are either unemployed or have a high probability of being unemployed at some time. They have low skills, and when working, low wages. They are more likely to be employed part-time and have few rights to sickness benefits, holidays or pensions. The secondary sec-tor is characterized by high labour turnover among the least skilled workers. Thus:

> Employment in the 1990s has become far more unstable. The penalties attached to job loss, jobless duration, and the reduced wages on return have risen. Hence, the secondary labour market has become far riskier. However this new insecurity has been concentrated on a minor-ity for whom jobs for life will become the stuff of legends. (Gregg *et al.*, 1996: 89)

Hale (1999) concentrated on de-industrialization, the shift from manufacturing to serv-ice sector jobs. This approach is linked to that of Allen and Steffensmeier (1989), who show that for juveniles it is the *availability* of employment that matters whereas for young adults the *quality* of employment is important as part-time work with low pay leads to higher rates of property crime. Kapuscinski *et al.* (1998) looked at the impact on crime in Australia of the increased participation of women in the labour market. They contend that increased female employment may lead to increased crime in a patriarchal society if appropriate measures are not introduced to '"take up the slack" in the traditional female role of guardianship' (Triggs, 1997). The mechanisms they identify for this link between crime and female employment include:

- supervision—women in traditional roles: (a) guard their own homes and those of neighbours during the day; (b) look after children who, if unsupervised, are more likely to be both offenders and victims;

- opportunity and motivation—women in the labour force may have more oppor-tunity to commit crime; conversely, of course, their motivation might decrease. Victimization of working women might increase if they are out more or if domestic tensions increase. Conversely, of course, domestic tensions might decrease if the household economic situation improves via female wage contribution.

For similar results using US data see Witt and Witte (1998) and for the UK Hale (1999). Hansen (2003) argues that increased female labour market participation is likely to have had two further effects which are likely to increase crime. First, increasing the supply of labour will tend to lower wages rates. Second, given the increased employment of women is mainly in part-time unskilled work, this is likely to increase male unemployment, par-ticularly amongst young, less well-educated men most likely to commit property offences. Using cross-section data from England and Wales, she shows that areas with higher rates of female labour force participation are likely to have higher levels of recorded crime.

Crime and inequality

Since the neo-liberal resurgence from the late 1970s, there has been considerable inter-est in the impact of inequality on various social problems (for excellent discussions see

Wilkinson and Pickett, 2009 and Dorling, 2011). Crime is no exception. This work may be divided broadly into those that look at variations in inequality and crime across countries, those that consider variations across areas within a single country, mainly the USA, and those that look at changes over time. The focus for much of the first two bodies of work has been on violent crime and homicide in particular (see also Chapter 9). For cross-national studies of homicide the consensus seems to be that there is a positive relationship with inequality while for cross-section data from the USA absolute rather than relative poverty is more significant. The reasons for these different findings have been the subject of some debate. Messner *et al.* (2010) suggest that in cross-national studies the mediating effect of variations in welfare provision is a possible explanation for the lack of relationship between homicide and absolute poverty. In the USA the welfare state is relatively underdeveloped and so absolute poverty serves as a reasonable measure of material well-being (Messner *et al.*, 2010). Pridemore (2011) uses child mortality as a measure of absolute poverty and Messner *et al.* (2010) argue that this captures broader social disadvantage beyond just the material. This suggests that social exclusion, a more multi-dimensional concept than just financial, might be a more useful approach and we discuss this further later in this chapter.

In the UK inequality has been growing since the late 1970s. One popular measure is the Gini Coefficient which ranges from 0 to 1 and the higher its value the greater the level of inequality. During the 1960s and 1970s it was around 0.26 but during the 1980s it grew significantly to reach 0.34 by 1990 (Institute for Fiscal Studies (IFS), 2012). As well as being the most rapid rise in recent UK history it was also more rapid than that experienced by other industrialized nations (Atkinson and Micklewright, 1992). In the 1990s and 2000s it remained stable around this high level.

In his statistical modelling of recorded property crime in England and Wales from the 1950s, Hale (1999) used two separate measures for inequality. The first was the Gini Coefficient and the second the ratio of the share of income going to the highest 10 per cent of earners with that going to the lowest 10 per cent. He found that the second measure was positively related to growth in burglary.

The growing polarization between 'work rich' and 'work poor' households has reinforced patterns of poverty and inequality. For example by 2009 the proportion of households that were workless had roughly quadrupled since the late 1960s and of households with children, 18.6 per cent were workless (Gregg and Wadsworth, 2011b).[4]

Wage inequality[5] in the UK is now significantly higher than it was in the early 1970s. The biggest increases occurred in the 1980s with the rises in the 1990s and 2000s being more muted. A key factor in this increased inequality was the rapid deterioration in the labour market position of less-skilled workers at the bottom end of the wage distribution. The economic model of crime argues that individuals will choose between legal and illegal work on the basis of their relative rewards. Many individuals, whilst in work, now find their jobs insecure, low-paid, and low-skilled. Often they are in part-time or temporary work and they are on the economic and social margins. Many of the theoretical arguments presented earlier for why unemployment and crime might be related apply equally well to that between low-wage, low-skill employment. The importance of exploring these issues in any model of crime is underlined by the results of analyses by Reilly and Witt (1996), Witt, *et al.* (1998, 1999) and Machin and Meghir (2004). Witt *et al.* (1998) found a positive relationship between widening (male) wage inequality and crime.

Recent work using US data has looked at the statistical relationship between crime and low wages. Gould *et al.* (2002) reported significant negative relationships across areas between changes in wages and changes in recorded burglary, aggravated assault, and robbery. Grogger (1998) showed that falling wages explain not only rising youth crime, but also age and ethnic differences. For England and Wales, Machin and Meghir (2003) analyse property crime (burglary plus theft and handling) at the police force area level from 1975 to 1996. They show that over this period falls in the wages of unskilled workers led to increases in property crime.

In a similar vein Hansen and Machin (2003) examined the impact of the introduction of the minimum wage in England and Wales in April 1999. This gave a pay increase to an estimated two million low-paid workers. Within an economic model of crime this would decrease the relative benefits of criminal as opposed to legal activity and so might be expected to persuade those on the margins not to engage in criminal activity and hence to reduce crime. Police force areas that gained most were those with the highest proportions of workers paid less than the new minimum prior to April 1999.[6] Hansen and Machin examined crime rates before and after its introduction. They looked at total crime, property crime, vehicle crime, and violent crime (violence against the person) and found that, on average, areas that benefited most from the minimum wage saw the greatest decreases in crime.

As well as wages, social security benefits might be expected to have an impact on crime levels by mediating the effects of unemployment and economic recession. If welfare payments are cut, or their eligibility criteria tightened, then the economic benefits from crime would increase. Machin and Marie (2004) consider the impact of the introduction of the Jobseekers Allowance (JSA) in Britain in October 1996. Replacing both unemployment benefit and income support, it brought about major changes in benefit entitlement. The period of non-means-tested contributory benefits was reduced to six months and requirements tightened by stopping benefit where individuals were judged not to be actively seeking work. Although the idea behind the JSA is to persuade people back to work, Machin and Marie point out unemployment may fall not by getting people back to work (or into education or training), but because they move off benefits and suffer an income cut. In such circumstances they are likely to find crime more attractive. They present evidence that crime rose by more in the areas more affected by JSA. Hence they argue that the benefits sanctions may have caused individuals previously on the margins to turn to crime.

Thus far the focus has been on the economic circumstances of offenders and the relationship between crime and the business cycle. What of the economic situation of victims? In England and Wales the best source of information on this are the British Crime Surveys (BCS)[7] now more appropriately called the Crime Survey for England and Wales (for details see Chapter 3). Simmons and Dodd (2003) use data from the 2003 BCS to examine how crime victimization risks vary across neighbourhoods. The highest risk areas for burglary are: (a) urban areas whose residents are well off professional singles and couples; and (b) council estates with elderly, lone parent or unemployed residents. For both the risk is 5 per cent, compared to 3 per cent across households as a whole. Within the second group, households on estates with the greatest hardship have a burglary victimization risk of 6.9 per cent—over twice the national risk. For vehicle-related thefts

11 per cent of all vehicle-owning households were victims but this rose to 21 per cent in the highest risk areas, described as multi-ethnic low-income neighbourhoods. Again the highest risk of violence, at 7 per cent, was to adults in multi-ethnic low-income areas compared to the overall average of 4 per cent.

More generally the risk of crime victimization is unequally spread across society and follows the pattern suggested by Ulrich Beck in *The Risk Society*:

> The history of risk distribution shows that, like wealth, risks adhere to the class pattern, only inversely; wealth accumulates at the top, risks at the bottom. To that extent, risks seem to strengthen, not to abolish the class society. Poverty attracts an unfortunate abundance of risks. By contrast, the wealthy (in income, power or education) can purchase safety and freedom from risk. (Beck, 1992: 35)

In a series of papers researchers from the University of Manchester Quantitative Criminology Group analysed the unequal distribution of victimization across neighbourhoods. Their work, combining BCS and Census data, shows around 20 per cent of the victims of household property crime in England and Wales live in the 10 per cent of residential areas with the highest crime rates and account for over a third[8] of the total of household property crime (see, for example, Hope, 2001, 2003). Twenty per cent of communities in England and Wales have over a third of all property crime victims and suffer over half of all property offences. At the other end of this spectrum, the 50 per cent least victimized areas suffer only 15 per cent of the crime and contain just 25 per cent of the victims. Moreover, when Census data on income and deprivation are considered a stark picture emerges of crime risk increasing markedly with area deprivation. Crime adds to the disadvantage suffered by the least well off groups in society and adds to their social exclusion. What is more, Trickett *et al.* (1995) show that during the 1980s, a decade when the long-term trend to greater equality of wealth, income and opportunity was rapidly reversed, inequality of victimization also became more marked.

This redistribution of crime victimization can also be seen in the regional figures. The North-South divide in terms of economic and demographic trends—with economic and population growth in the latter at the expense of the former, exacerbated by de-industrialization—was again inversely reflected in patterns of crime victimization. During the 1980s the North's disproportionate share of property crime increased relative to the South and to Greater London in particular (Trickett *et al.*, 1995: 353). Hence, crime contributes to the very inequality and social exclusion that are seen as its causes.

Crime, the underclass, and social exclusion

Crime and its relationship to poverty re-appeared in the last decades of the twentieth century as part of a politically right-wing response to the perceived failings of the welfare state that cushioned the poor so they became 'welfare dependent', unable to stand on their own two feet. Crime and other social problems were seen as the product of individual characteristics rather than the result of structural factors. Criminality was voluntaristic, committed by individuals with no self-control who chose crime as well as unemployment and poverty.

Particularly relevant here is Charles Murray (1984, 1990), and his notion of the under-class.[9] For Murray the important distinguishing characteristic of the underclass is not that they are poor, but that they are not respectable.

> Their homes were littered and unkempt. The men in the family were unable to hold a job for more than a few weeks at a time. Drunkenness was common. The children grew up ill-schooled and ill-behaved … (Murray, 1990: 1)

Murray essentially sees a segregated society. On the one hand are those sectors uphold-ing traditional values of hard work, sobriety, and family; on the other the morally weak underclass who are unemployed, involved in crime, and drug addiction and have ille-gitimate children raised by single mothers living on welfare. He sees this as a matter of choice and believes the solution is to reduce welfare payments for unmarried mothers, encouraging the avoidance of pregnancy without supportive working fathers and to cut unemployment benefits to encourage those capable of work to seek employment. The problem of crime in Murray's view is that increasing numbers of young men are being brought up without positive male role models and are avoiding the civilizing institutions of marriage, family, and work, preferring to live on welfare and/or illegal activities.

The definitive sign that an underclass has developed is that 'large numbers of young healthy, low income males *choose* not to take a job' (Murray, 1990: 17) (emphasis added). The key word here is 'choose' as Murray believes that, as well as unemployed workers actively seeking work, there is a large group of 'economically inactive' people who have opted not to work.

The notion of the underclass is not unique to Murray and indeed under another name 'socially excluded' (see the earlier discussion on inequality) is prominent in the writings of those of the left and was central to much of New Labour thinking when in power (see Chapter 21). The terms are different, but the people in Murray's underclass are the same as those regarded as socially excluded. Social exclusion covers not just poverty but also political and spatial exclusion and the notion that the excluded are denied access to 'information, medical provision, housing, policing, security etc' (Young, 2002: 457). These factors interact and reinforce each other to the extent that those who experience the exclusion are denied the chance to participate fully as citizens. Whilst the symptoms of the underclass and the socially excluded are similar, the latter implies the issue is a structural problem, driven by economic globalization that has led to the rapid changes in the labour markets of industrialized countries driven by the decline in manufacturing and the rise of precarious employment in the service sector previously discussed.

Whilst accepting the arguments that social exclusion is a structural problem, the last Labour government nevertheless adopted policies that blamed the victim by locating solutions at the individual level. The Social Exclusion Unit (SEU) set up in 1997, and replaced by the Coalition government's Office for Civil Society in 2010, looked to tackle a wide range of issues including deprived neighbourhoods, unemployment, drug use, teenage pregnancy, truancy, school exclusion—a list of the classic symptoms of social exclusion. The SEU is clear that social exclusion is a major factor in both crime and fear of crime, and that in turn these are part of the interlinked facets of the problem (Social Exclusion Unit, 2001). Whilst acknowledging the (global) economic and social changes that have taken place, they saw the problem of crime and social exclusion as related to issues of socialization, and lack of control in young people as related to poor parenting and inadequate schooling, together with drug and alcohol abuse. Having first identified the problems at a structural level the emphasis, as Matthews and Young (2003) point out, shifted to an implicit control theory. Central to this strategy of combating social exclusion, and hence being tough on the causes of crime, was entry into work. So the focus was on persuading the unemployed and excluded back to work by threatening to cut benefits and offering re-training programmes. Evidence that suggested work *per se* is not the answer; that poorly paid work or part-time work with little security and sense of worth does not reduce crime in the long run, has been reviewed earlier in this chapter. Currie (1998) has shown inclusionary policies that focus on work involving long and inflexible hours serve to undermine family and community, to weaken rather than strengthen social control. As explored in Chapter 21 this was coupled with a political emphasis on being tough on crime that has increased rather than decreased social exclusion by pushing crime and disorder to the margins of society (see also the references to Trickett *et al.*, 1995 later in this chapter).

REVIEW QUESTIONS

1 Why might an increase in female employment cause crime to rise?

2 What are the differences between the concepts of the 'underclass' and 'social exclusion'?

3 Will creating more part-time, low paid jobs necessarily reduce crime?

The crime drop

It came as some surprise to American criminologists that the crime drop they observed in the USA from the early 1990s was not unique (see *inter alia* Zimring, 2007). Indeed, beginning at more or less the same time in the early to mid-1990s recorded crime began to fall around the world (Van Dijk *et al.*, 2007, Tseloni *et al.*, 2010). For example in England and Wales recorded crime peaked in 1992 and declined more or less thereafter (more definite statements are not possible due to the changes in recording rules in 1998 and 2002, see Chapter 3 and Figure 19.1 in Chapter 19). For crimes covered by the BCS the estimated number of offences peaked at just over 19 million in 1995 and declined relatively consistently to 9.5 million in the 2011/12 survey, 50 per cent of its peak level and the lowest estimate since the BCS began in 1981 (Office for National Statistics, 2012).

It would seem sensible therefore to look for explanations not in the exceptionalism of any one country but in factors that they might have in common. With the increasing global interdependency of national economies one obvious candidate is the economic expansion[10] that occurred in most countries from the early 1990s and was unprecedented in its duration before coming to an abrupt end in 2008 with the financial crisis triggered by the sub-prime mortgage market problems in the USA.

Evidence to support this link between the economy and crime is available for the USA (see *inter alia* Arvanites and Defina, 2006; Rosenfeld and Fornago, 2007) and from an international perspective in Rosenfeld and Messner (2009).

The question that remains unanswered is whether this fall will now reverse given the recession that affected a significant proportion of the world's States post-2008. In the UK for example the annual BCS estimates have not increased since 2008–09 rather, they have remained relatively static. One argument, the 2011 riots across the UK notwithstanding, is that we have still to see the full impact of the economic downturn. Gregg and Wadsworth (2011a) argue that while the latest recession has inflicted the largest cumulative loss of any post-war recession, unemployment remains lower than would have been expected. Furthermore the full impact of the Coalition government's plans to cut the cost of welfare provision have yet to be felt. The last time an economic recession was accompanied by a major restructuring of the welfare state was during the 1980s, the decade that saw the largest increases in crime ever recorded.

CONCLUSION

This chapter has considered the impact of economic conditions on crime. Inevitably some topics of importance have not been discussed. As noted earlier, the focus has been on crimes such as burglary and theft rather than those that might be described as corporate and white collar. That is not to imply that in times of economic downturn these will not also increase as competitive pressures increase the incentives for individuals and businesses to cut corners and bend and break the law in order to survive (see Chapter 11). Indeed the notion that market economies based on competition and rewarding risk taking might encourage criminality has not been developed. Finally, violent crime might also have been considered, but for constraints on space. Again the evidence suggests that the long-term trend has been for violence to decline as countries' economies develop. Broadly speaking, comparative analysis suggests that rates of violence in industrialized countries are lower than in less-wealthy economies. However, in the short run it seems that economic booms lead to increased levels of violence fuelled at least in part by increased alcohol consumption (see Chapters 8 and 9).

Turning to work, on balance both the theoretical arguments and the empirical evidence reviewed support the hypothesis that deteriorating economic circumstances will lead to increased property crime. Unemployment, poverty, inequality, and low wages have all been found to be related to property crime in one study or another. Other work suggests that the quality of work available may also be key.

The growth in the secondary labour markets, with precarious employment in low-paid, part-time work, that has been the consequence of the process of globalization and economic restructuring over the last 40 years have had an impact on crime similar to that of the nineteenth century when the Industrial Revolution caused major ruptures in the established structures of society. However, the work reviewed here also questions whether strategies to combat social exclusion based on encouraging people back to paid employment will necessarily succeed since it is not work *per se* that is important but its quality and the satisfaction it provides.

QUESTIONS FOR DISCUSSION

1 What do the main criminological theories have to say about the relationship between crime and the economy?

2 Compare and contrast the policy approaches of the New Right to the underclass with those of New Labour to social exclusion.

3 Is unemployment the main factor to consider when examining the relationship between crime and the economy?

4 Why might corporate crime increase during economic recessions?

GUIDE TO FURTHER READING

Box, S. (1987) *Recession, Crime and Punishment*. London: Macmillan.
This remains an excellent and still relevant overview of this field.

Gregg, P. and Wadsworth, J. (eds) (2011) *The Labour Market in Winter: The State of Working Britain*. Oxford: Oxford University Press.
Provides a very useful discussion of labour market changes in the UK.

Hagan, J. and Peterson, R.D. (eds) (1995) *Crime and Inequality*. Stanford: Stanford University Press.
Another book that provides an overview of a wide range of issues.

Taylor, I. (1995) *Crime in Context: A Critical Criminology of Market Societies*. Cambridge: Polity Press.
Provides an excellent discussion of broader issues of crime in market economies.

Young, J. (2002) 'Crime and social exclusion' in M. Maguire, M. Morgan, and R. Reiner (eds) *The Oxford Handbook of Criminology* (3rd edn) Oxford: Oxford University Press.
Jock Young's chapter is a good introduction to social exclusion.

WEB LINKS

http://www.jrf.org.uk/home.asp
The website for the Joseph Rowntree Foundation. This contains useful information on poverty and deprivation.

http://www.poverty.org.uk/intro/index.htm
The Joseph Rowntree Foundation also supports this New Policy Institute site dedicated to monitoring poverty and social exclusion.

http://www.ifs.org.uk/
The site of the Institute of Fiscal Affairs. It has good reports on poverty and inequality and more generally on the economy.

http://www.tuc.org.uk
This is the website of the Trades Union Congress. It provides links to recent research and has discussion of labour market trends.

REFERENCES

Allen, E.A. and Steffensmeier, D.J. (1989) 'Youth, Underemployment, and Property Crime: Effects of the Quantity and Quality of Job Opportunities on Juvenile and Young Adult Arrest Rates', *American Sociological Review*, 54: 107–23.

Arvanites, T.M. and Defina, R.H. (2006) 'Business Cycles and Street Crime', *Criminology* 44: 139–64.

Atkinson, A.B. and Micklewright, B. (1992) *Economic Transformation in Eastern Europe and the Distribution of Income*. Cambridge: Cambridge University Press.

Beck, U. (1992) *Risk Society, Towards a New Modernity*. London: Sage.

Becker, G. (1968) 'Crime and Punishment: An Economic Approach', *Journal of Political Economy* 76: 175–209.

Box, S. (1987) *Recession Crime and Punishment*. London: Macmillan.

Bruegel, I. (2000) 'No more Jobs for the Boys? Gender and Class in the Restructuring of the British Economy', *Capital and Class* 71: 79–102.

Cantor, D. and Land, K.C. (1985) 'Unemployment and Crime Rates in Post World War II United States: a Theoretical and Empirical Analysis', *American Sociological Review* 50: 317–32.

Chiricos, T.G. (1987) 'Rates of Crime and Unemployment: An Analysis of Aggregate Research Evidence', *Social Problems*, 34: 187–211.

Currie, E. (1998) *Crime and Punishment in America*. New York: Metropolitan Books.

Detotto, C and Otranto, E. (2012) 'Cycles in crime and Economy: Leading, Lagging and Coincident Behaviours', *Journal of Quantitative Criminology* 28: 295–317.

Dorling, D. (2011) *Injustice: Why Social Inequality Persists*. Bristol: The Policy Press.

Durkheim, E. (1893) *The Division of Labour in Society*, 1984 edition translated by W.D. Halls, with an introduction by Lewis Coser. Basingstoke: Macmillan.

Ehrlich, I. (1973) 'Participation in Illegitimate Activities: a Theoretical and Empirical Investigation', *Journal of Political Economy* 81: 521–63.

Farrell, G., Tseloni, A., Mailley J., and Tilley N. 'The crime drop and the Security Hypothesis', *Journal of Research in Crime and Delinquency* 48(2): 147–75.

Field, S. (1990), 'Trends in Crime and their Interpretation: A Study of Recorded Crime in Post-war England and Wales', *Home Office Research Study No. 119*, Home Office, London.

Gottfredson, M. and Hirschi, T. (1990) *A General Theory of Crime*. Stanford: Stanford University Press.

Gould, D., Mustard, D.B., and Weinberg, B.A. (2002) 'Crime Rates and Local Labor Market opportunities in the United States: 1979–1997', *Review of Economics and Statistics* 84: 45–61.

Greenberg, D.F. (2001) 'Time Series Analysis of Crime Rates', *Journal of Quantitative Criminology* 17: 291–327.

Gregg, P., Hansen, K., and Wadsworth, J. (1999) 'Workless households', chapter 5 in P. Gregg and J. Wadsworth (eds) *The State of Working Britain*. Manchester: Manchester University Press.

Gregg, P. and Wadsworth, J. (2011a) 'The Labour Market in Winter: The 2008-2009 Recession', chapter 1 in P. Gregg and J. Wadsworth (eds) *The Labour Market in Winter: The State of Working Britain*. Manchester: Manchester University Press.

Gregg, P. and Wadsworth, J. (2011b) 'Workless households', chapter 5 in P. Gregg and J. Wadsworth (eds) *The Labour Market in Winter: The State of Working Britain*. Manchester: Manchester University Press.

Grogger, J. (1998) 'Market Wages and Youth Crime', *Journal of Labor Economics* 16(4): 756–91.

Hale, C. (1998) Crime and the Business Cycle in Post-war Britain Revisited, *British Journal of Criminology* 38(4): 681–98.

Hale, C. (1999) 'The labour market and post-war crime trends in England and Wales', in P. Carlen and R. Morgan (eds) *Crime Unlimited: Questions for the 21st Century*. Basingstoke: Macmillan.

Hale, C. and Sabbagh, D. (1989) 'Testing the Relationship between Unemployment and Crime: A Methodological Comment and Empirical Analysis using Time Series data from England and Wales', *Journal of Research into Crime and Delinquency* 28: 400–17.

Hansen, K. (2003) 'The Impact of Increasing female Labour Force Participation on Male Property Crime', Paper presented at the British Society of Criminology Conference, Bangor, July.

Hansen, K. and Machin, S. (2003) 'Spatial Crime Patterns and the Introduction of the UK National Minimum Wage', *Oxford Bulletin of Economics and Statistics* 64: 677–98.

Hayward, K. (2001) 'Chicago School of Sociology' in E. McLaughlin and J. Muncie (eds) *The Sage Dictionary of Criminology*. London: Sage.

Hirschi, T. (1969) *The Causes of Delinquency*. Berkeley: University of California Press.

Hope, T. (2000) 'Inequality and the Clubbing of Society' in T. Hope and R. Sparks (eds) *Crime, Risk and Insecurity*. London: Routledge.

Hope, T. (2003) 'Private Security and Crime Victimisation in Risk Society', Paper delivered at the conference *Per Una Società Più Sicura: il contributo conoscitivo dell.informazione statistica*, ISTAT, Rome, Italy, 3–5 December 2003.

Kapuscinski, C.A., Braithwaite, J., and Chapman, B. (1998) 'Unemployment and crime: resolving the paradox', *Journal of Quantitative Criminology* 14: 215–44.

Lilly, J.R., Cullen, F.T., and Ball, R.A. (2002) *Criminological Theory: Context and Consequences* (3rd edn) London: Sage.

Machin, S. (2011) 'Changes in UK Wage Inequality over the last 40 years', chapter 11 in P. Gregg and J. Wadsworth (eds) *The Labour Market in Winter*. Manchester: Manchester University Press.

Machin, S. and Marie, O. (2004) 'Crime and Benefit Cuts', Paper presented to the Annual Conference of the Royal Economic Society, Swansea, April.

Machin, S. and Meghir, C. (2004) 'Crime and Economic Incentives', *Journal of Human Resources* 39: 958–79.

Matthews, R. and Young, J. (2003) *The New Politics of Crime and Punishment*. Cullompton: Willan.

Merton, R. (1938) 'Social Structure and "Anomie"', *American Sociological Review* 3: 672–82.

Messner, S.F., Raffalovich, L.E., and Sutton, G.M. 'Poverty, Infant Mortality and Homicide Rates in Cross national perspective: Assessments of Criterion and Construct Validity', *Criminology* 48(2): 509–37.

Murray, C. (1984) *Losing Ground*. New York: Basic Books.

Murray, C. (1990) *The Emerging British Underclass*. London: Institute of Economic Affairs.

Office for National Statistics (2012), *Trends in crime: a short story 2011/12* Office for National Statistics http://www.ons.gov.uk/ons/rel/crime-stats/crime-statistics/period-ending-march-2012/trends-in-crime--a-short-story.html.

Pyle, D. and Deadman, D. (1994) 'Crime and the Business Cycle in Post-war Britain', *British Journal of Criminology* 34: 339–57.

Radzinowicz, L. (1939), 'The Influence of Economic Conditions on Crime', *Sociological Review* 33: 139–53.

Radzinowicz, L. (1971), 'Economic Pressures', Chapter 34 in Radzinowicz, L. and Wolgang, M.E., *Crime and Justice Volume 1: The Criminal in Society*. New York: Basic Books.

Reilly, B. and Witt, R. (1996) 'Crime, Deterrence and Unemployment in England and Wales: an Empirical Analysis', *Bulletin of Economic Research* 48: 137–59.

Rosenfeld, R. (2009) 'Crime is the Problem: Homicide, Acquisitive Crime, and Economic Conditions', *Journal of Quantitative Criminology* 25: 287–306.

Rosenfeld, R. and Fornango, R. (2007) 'The Impact of Economic Conditions on Robbery and Property Crime: The Role of Consumer Sentiment', *Criminology* 45, 735–68.

Rosenfeld, R. and Messner, S.F. (2009) 'The Crime Drop in Comparative Perspective: The impact of the economy and imprisonment on American and European burglary rates', *The British Journal of Sociology* 60(3): 445–71.

Shaw, C.R. and McKay, H.D. (1942) *Juvenile Delinquency and Urban Areas*. Chicago: University of Chicago Press.

Simmonds, J. and Dodd, T. (2003) *Crime in England and Wales 2002/2003*. Home Office Statistical Bulletin.

Social Exclusion Unit (2001) *Preventing Social Exclusion*. London: Stationery Office.

Trickett, A., Ellingworth, D., Hope, T., and Pease, K. (1995) 'Crime Victimisation in the Eighties', *British Journal of Criminology* 35: 343–59.

Triggs, S. (1997) *Interpreting Trends in Recorded Crime in New Zealand* http://www.justice.govt.nz/pubs/reports/1997/crime, New Zealand Ministry of Justice.

Tseloni, A., Mailey, J., Farrell, G., and Tilley, N. (2010) 'Exploring the international decline in crime rates', *European Journal of Criminology* 7(5): 375–94.

Van Dijk, J., van Kesteren, J., and Smidt, P. (2007) *Criminal Victimisation in International Perspective: Key Findings from the 2004-2005 ICVS and EU ICS*, The Hague: Boom Juridische Uitgevers.

Wilkinson, R. and Pickett, K. (2009) *The Spirit Level: Why equality is better for everyone*. London: Penguin Books.

Wilson, H. (1980) 'Parental Supervision: A Neglected Aspect of Delinquency', *British Journal of Criminology* 20.

Witt, R., Clarke, A., and Fielding, N. (1998) 'Crime, Earnings Inequality and Unemployment in England and Wales', *Applied Economics Letters* 5: 265–7.

Witt, R., Clarke, A. and Fielding, N. (1999) 'Crime and Economic Activity: A Panel Data Approach', *British Journal of Criminology* 39: 391–400.

Witt, R. and Witte, A.D. (1998) 'Crime, Imprisonment and Female Labour Force Participation: A Time Series Approach', *Journal of Quantitative Criminology* 16: 69–86.

Young, J. (2001) 'Relative Deprivation' in E. McLaughlin and J. Muncie (eds) *The Sage Dictionary of Criminology*. London: Sage.

Young, J. (2002) 'Crime and Social Exclusion' in M. Maguire, M. Morgan and R. Reiner (eds) *The Oxford Handbook of Criminology* (3rd edn) Oxford: Oxford University Press.

Zimring, F.E. (2006) *The Great American Crime Decline*. New York: Oxford University Press.

NOTES

1. The definition of poverty used in the UK refers to the numbers of families who earn less than 60 per cent of median income. Hence poverty here is a relative concept and tackling it requires reducing inequality as well as increasing low incomes.

2. See Hale and Sabbagh (1989) and Greenberg (2001) for methodological critiques of their statistical approach.

3. See also Breugel (2000) for a discussion of the feminization of employment in Britain.

4. Labour Force Survey estimates give 8.2 per cent households workless in 1977, 16.4 per cent workless in 1987, 18.2 per cent workless in 1997, and 17.3 per cent workless in 2009 (Gregg and Wadsworth, 2011b: Table 5.1).

5. See also amongst others Machin (2011) and the data and sources on wage inequality given therein.

6. To take two extremes, in areas where everyone was paid more than the minimum wage to begin with, then no one would be better off when it was introduced. Conversely, in areas where all workers earned less than the new minimum, then all would benefit.

7. Similar information for Scotland can be obtained from the Scottish Crime Surveys (SCS).

8. The point being that some households are victimized more than once. See Chapter 4 for further discussion of this point.

9. As he himself pointed out, it was not a new idea. It has resonance with Victorian notions of respectable and unrespectable, the deserving and undeserving poor.

10. Alternative, if not competing explanations, are the increased and improved security available to protect property (see Farrell *et al.*, 2011, and for the exclusionary impact of this, Tseloni *et al.*, 2011) and the possibility that this has led, with the opportunities available via the Internet, to displacement to new types of offending that goes largely unrecorded.

15 Gender and Crime

Azrini Wahidin

INTRODUCTION

The aim of this chapter is to explore the relationship between **gender** and crime and show how gender permeates throughout the criminal justice system. This chapter will begin by deconstructing the concept of sex and gender. It will then demonstrate how feminist perspectives have played a significant role in understanding the relationship of gender and crime by making visible the experiences of women who come into conflict with the law as offenders or as victims. The chapter will then turn its attention to the area of masculinities in examining how and why the 'maleness' of crime has been taken for granted in the discipline of criminology.

Crime is largely a male activity and there is a general assumption that women are sentenced and punished more leniently than men. The differences in treatment are all too evident as this chapter will show. But the question the reader needs to ask is whether or not differential treatment can be justified.

BACKGROUND

> Women are typically non-criminal: they have lower rates of crime in *all* nations, *all communities* within nations, for *all age groups, for all periods of recorded history,* and for practically all crimes. (Leonard, 1982: 1, emphasis in original)

> Crime is an activity disproportionately carried out by young men living in large cities. There are old criminals, and female ones, and rural and small town ones, but to a much greater degree than would be expected by chance, criminals are young urban males (Wilson and Hernstein, 1985: 26).

In understanding the differences between men and women, we must first make a basic distinction between sex and gender. Clearly women are biologically different from men. There is disagreement about the exact nature and consequence of the difference. The term sex refers to the biological determined, chromosomal, chemical, anatomical structures that make us either male or female. The term gender will be used to describe the cultural and social constructions of masculinity and femininity which relate to expectations about appropriate social roles. The term gender informs us that the differences are a reflection of the complex social processes rather than being biologically determined. The social constructions of masculinity and femininity vary across cultures, over historical time, among men and women, within any one culture, and over the life course (Oakley, 1972). This means that masculinity and femininity are not constant or common to all men and women. In this sense, we must speak of masculinities and femininities in recognition of the continuum of masculinities, femininities and gender identities (Connell, 1987; Kimmel, 2000) and through this distinction, it is made clear that gender subordination is neither inborn nor inevitable.

Connell (1995) argues that as a society there is a gender order, which consists of a hierarchy of masculinities and femininities. At the top of this hierarchy is **hegemonic masculinity**, where upon heterosexuality is pivotal to hegemonic masculinity. The hegemonic ideal emphasizes masculine characteristics producing social relationships based on degrees of domination and subordination (Jefferson, 1994: 12). Other forms of 'subordinated masculinity' exist, notably that of 'homosexual masculinity', which is subordinated by practices of exclusion and discrimination. In such a system, 'successful' masculinity and 'successful' femininity depend upon the extent to which one adopts the image of masculinity and femininity. Although Connell (1995) made few observations about the criminality of males, his insights have been adopted in an attempt to understand the offending behaviour of boys and men (see Messerschmidt 1993, 1997, 2000). Thus the male 'over-involvement' in crime-related activity can be argued not as an essential characteristic of men and boys but as a reflection of a 'wide range of activities which need to be understood within the context of gender relations' (Newburn and Stanko, 1994: 4).

In comparison, women's lower involvement in crime-was not generally questioned because crime was associated with male behaviour. This chapter will demonstrate that gender is a key factor in the involvement of offending behaviour, yet as the next section will show gender has not always been recognized in criminological thought. Indeed, the development of criminological knowledge has always proceeded on the assumption that 'crime was men's work not women's' (Walklate, 2001: 26). So the study of the 'criminal man' has dominated the development of criminological thought, and 'criminal women' have been largely excluded, neglected and ignored. Similarly, criminology as a discipline has been dominated by male academics and male perspectives. As Hearn (1996) points out, the history of criminology has been largely a history of men but one which the 'maleness' of crime, crime control, and crime analysis has been taken for granted as to be rendered invisible.

Sex, gender, and criminology

To understand the current debates concerning sex, gender, crime, and justice, it is first necessary to examine the historical development of the discipline of criminology and the emergence of feminist theorizing. The study of female crime was traditionally a neglected area, invisible in the discipline of criminology and 'malestream' theories of crime. Explanations of female crime were rooted in theories derived from late nineteenth-century biological positivism put forward by Lombroso and in particular his work with Ferrero in their book (1895), *The Female Offender.* Lombroso and Ferrero assumed that all criminals were less developed than the non-criminal. They argued, that 'women are big children … their moral sense is deficient', and the female criminal was masculine, showing 'an inversion of all the qualities which specifically distinguished the normal woman; namely reserve, docility and sexual apathy' (Lombroso and Ferrero, 1895: 153). In contrast, other theories began to see female crime as pathological, such as Thomas in his (1907) text, *Sex and Society*; while Freud (1933) asserted that the criminal woman was unable to come to terms with her essential femininity and suggested that delinquency is driven by 'penis envy', and/or the desire to be a man (Klein, 1973: 89). Even as late as 1968, Cowie, Cowie and Slater argued that, though delinquency in boys may be caused by social factors, delinquency in young women was most likely to be caused by a chromosome imbalance that made delinquent young women emulate men. These explanations of female crime are given in terms of women failing to comply with their supposedly natural biological socio-sexual expectations dictated by biological attributes. As Carlen *et al.* (1985: 1) states, 'in both criminological and lay explanations, criminal women have always been presented as being "other": other than real women, other than real criminals and other than real prisoners'. Mainstream criminology has, until recently, been committed to what Garland (2002) described as the 'Lombrosian project'. The idea of the Lombrosian project aimed 'to develop an etiological, explanatory science, based on the premise that criminals can somehow be scientifically differentiated from non-criminals' (Garland 1992: 18).

Criminology, like feminism, encompasses disparate and sometimes conflicting perspectives that is evidence of its vitality as a mode of critique and one which changes with the times. The broad approaches are: Liberal Feminism; Marxist Feminism; Socialist Feminism, Radical Feminism, and Post-Modernism Feminism (see Walklate, 2001, for an overview). Yet, despite the different stances, feminist theory is concerned generally with a 'woman-centred description and explanation of human experience and the social world' (Danner, 1989: 51). It asserts that gender and gender relations order social life and social institutions and is directed towards social change and, in particular, towards challenging **sexism** and patriarchy. Sexism refers to oppressive attitudes and behaviours directed towards either sex but, in particular, the concept has been used to refer to discriminatory practices aimed primarily at women. Patriarchy, on the other hand, refers to a system of social structures and practices in which men dominate. Patriarchy has long been an important object of social and political theory and in feminist literature it has come to mean male domination in general, and this is now the main way it is used in sociology. Within feminist literature there are a number of different approaches to patriarchy.

However, the main underlying thread of feminist contributions to criminology incorporate the following:

1. To feminists, the question of women is central and the problem of gender in criminology is central to the feminist debate.
2. An examination of women as offenders and victims.
3. A critique of the gender-blindness in criminology.
4. Developing feminist epistemologies and methodologies.
5. The examination of the intersectionality of class, ethnicity, and sexuality on gender and crime.
6. Theories of crime should examine both men's and women's criminal behaviour and victimization.

It was not until Smart published *Women, Sexuality and Social Control* in 1977 that the first critique of criminology in Britain was published. Heidensohn (1997) described the book as a turning point in criminology and claimed that issues raised by Smart 'were firmly on the agenda for all criminologists' (1977: 393). From this period onward there has been a plethora of work that examines women's lawbreaking and criminalization (see in particular, Daly and Chesney-Lind, 1988; Gelsthorpe and Morris, 1990). Smart argues that 'criminology and the sociology of deviance must become more than the study of men and crime if it is to play any significant part in the development of our understanding of crime, law and the criminal process (Smart, 1977: 185). Smart inspired a plethora of studies and writings on the subject of 'women and crime', which served to render 'women visible' and ensured that they were no longer represented as a 'mere gargoyle-like stereotype' (Heidensohn, 1996: 17). However, it became increasingly apparent that attempts to construct women as a 'unitary subject' (Carrington, 1998:80) served to erase the 'intra-sex specificities among women' (Carrington, 2002: 119). The increasing awareness of the need to locate female offending with regard to age, class, race, status, power, and so on, alerts us to the complexity and multiplicity of experiences that precipitate criminality. Indeed the endeavours of black feminist criminology (Arnold, 1990) is a reminder of the need to widen the criminological lens to not only incorporate gender, but also the diversity of experiences that 'gender' can encapsulate. It is as Gelsthorpe and McIvor (2007: 323), eloquently state: 'we are rarely just men or women, black or asian or white, but rather situate ourselves on a number of social and cultural planes'.

The next section will examine the development of feminist theory in understanding women and crime.

REVIEW QUESTIONS

1 Discuss the advantages of using the concept of gender rather than sex in understanding crime.

2 Explain why the study of criminology has focused mainly on men.

3 What can the study of masculinity bring to the discipline of criminology?

Women, femininities, and crime

Feminist theory is likely to dismantle the long-standing dichotomy of the devilish and daring criminal man and the unappealing inert conforming woman. The threat it poses to a masculine criminology is therefore considerable (Naffine, 1987: 133).

There is now a large body of work on women, femininities, and crime and this section provides an overview of the main debate. The rise of feminist criminology lies in the liberation movements of the 1960s and that of the civil rights movement. The feminist movement challenged discrimination around reproduction, economic, and social discrimination. They questioned the underlying problem of sexism. Criminology up to this point remained positivist in terms of methods and methodology. But because the vast majority of crimes were committed by men, criminologists focused on men and it was women's low crime rate that was the phenomenon to be explained. Connell (1993: x) states, 'it was women's lack of criminality that was seen as the intellectual problem'. Men were taken as the norm and women as departures from it, 'deviants from the deviance so to speak'. Even in the 'great creative explosions in "modern sociology"' (Heidensohn,

1996: 128) emanating from the University of Chicago in the 1920s, women were marginalized and the belief that 'the delinquent is a rogue male' (Cohen, 1955: 140) was still prevalent and meant that a 'cavalier androcentrism', remained a defining feature of the criminological endeavour (Chesney-Lind and Pasko, 204: 15). Indeed, seminal studies addressing juvenile gangs (Thrasher, 1927); social disorganization (Shaw and McKay, 1942); strain theory (Merton, 1938), did not question whether women had either the same means or same goals; subcultural theory (Cloward and Ohlin, 1960; Cohen, 1955) ignored the question of gender and the use of different spaces occupied by girls and women (McRobbie and Garber, 1976); control theory (Hirschi, 1969) and differential association theory (Sutherland and Cressey, 1978) all made girls and women invisible by focusing on the delinquent male. Even labelling theory (Matza, 1964) failed to explore women's transgressions.

Four key early feminists changed the face of criminology by questioning criminology's underlying silence, invisibility and marginalization of women and crime and the pervasive androcentrism within the discipline (see Bertrand, 1967; Heidensohn, 1968; Klein, 1973; Smart, 1977). It was not until Carol Smart published *Women, Crime, and Criminology* in 1977 that feminist perspectives gained recognition. This line of work was continued by Leonard (1982), Heidensohn (1985), Morris (1987), and Naffine (1987). All these texts addressed in their own way the 'woman and crime problem'. Smart introduces her book by questioning the invisibility of women by stating:

> [Considering] the overwhelming lack of interest in female criminality displayed by established criminologists and deviancy theorists ... it became obvious to me that, as a first step at least, what was required was a feminist critique of existing studies of female criminality. (Smart 1977: xiii–xiv)

Over the past three decades feminist criminological studies have multiplied and courses calling for texts and collections of articles on women and crime began appearing. By the mid-1980s victimological studies had begun to develop (see Walklate, 1989) which developed new theories about, and policies for, women and children as victims and as survivors of violent, sexual, and other crimes. Feminist epistemologies, methods and methodologies started to change the face of research acknowledging the diverse range of standpoints. But it was only by the mid-1970s that it was possible to talk about a feminist agenda and by this time the authors cited earlier were now witnessing the second phase of the development within criminology as 'consolidating and expressing key ideas more confidently (Heidensohn, 1994: 1013). It is evident that the study of gender is complex and feminist influences, range and breadth are as fragmented as they are diverse. Feminism has impacted on the way we ask the gender question and in recognition of some of the key achievements of the feminist agenda—it has put women on the criminological map; critiqued the traditional essentialist and sexualized view of women; promoted justice campaigns for women and other victims; explored the possibilities of founding a feminist criminology; investigated the potential of feminist jurisprudence; and called for the re-envisioning of feminist thinking on crime and justice and the political difference it has made to date.

The foregoing discussion reflects the transformative debates that occurred because of the feminist agenda—debates which are still ongoing. It is as Gelsthorpe and Morris (1990: 4) argued: that introducing 'feminist perspectives in criminology [is] *a project under construction*' (original emphasis). By attending to the question of female criminality and deviance, our understanding of existing social practices within the legal and penal systems will be enhanced and it may then be possible to move towards the formulation of proposals for radically reforming our systems of justice. However, Heidensohn has repeatedly criticized criminologists for not taking the feminist critique seriously by, for example, 'tacking on' women as an afterthought and not taking up the challenge of integrating the subject of gender (Heidensohn, 1996). Incorporating gender into the discipline has been a piecemeal process, but without doubt, the feminist enterprise has enriched the discipline by challenging biological determinism and by exploring the social construction of gender. It is only by exploring the intersections of gender and crime that we can begin to gain a deeper understanding of the relationship between the two. Without such an exploration there will be no progress made in understanding male and female criminality or the gendered experiences of crime and victimization which still remain a problem in society today.

REVIEW QUESTIONS

1 Provide three reasons as to why female crime is a neglected area.

2 Give three reasons as to why 'malestream' criminology marginalized the experiences of women.

3 How has feminist theorizing influenced criminological understandings of women and crime?

The following section will examine the ways in which an analysis of the relationship between men, masculinities, and crime can lead to a greater understanding of men's involvement in crime related activities.

Men, masculinities, and crime

What is it about men, not as working class, not as migrant, not as underprivileged individuals, but as men that induces them to commit crime? Here it is no longer women who are judged by the norms of masculinity and found to be 'the problem'. Now it is men and not humanity who are openly acknowledged as the objects and subjects of investigation. (Grosz, 1987: 5)

This quote demonstrates a turning point in criminological theory, where the question now focuses on the relationship between men, masculinity/ies, their relationships with other men, women and criminal activity. By the late 1980s onwards, research on gender and social issues across the humanities and social sciences began to focus on masculinities and within the field of 'masculinities studies' there has been a recognition of plurality of masculinities and masculine identities.

This section will show how some male criminologists have taken on board 'the transgression of criminology' called for by feminist scholars (Cain, 1990). The literature on masculinity has increased markedly over the last 20 years, and has emerged from feminist work on gender, lesbian and gay studies and men's involvement in feminism. In 1977 Andrew Tolson wrote a seminal book entitled *The Limits of Masculinity*, exploring the plurality of masculinities and questioning whether it was possible to have a unitary form of masculinity which could only be understood as the opposite to femininity. He argued that masculinities varied across cultures and between generations and was a product of gender relations rather than sex roles. Morgan (1992) argues that femininity and masculinity were part of a broader continuum of gender relations. He goes on further to argue that gender relations must be examined in relation to the concept of power and difference and how patriarchy, oppression, exploitation, and domination impacts on the performativity of gender in society. In Connell's (2005) *Masculinities*, he clearly argues that masculinity is a configuration of practice or performance within a system of gender relations which is subject to disruption and change. Connell (1987, 1995, 2002) makes a significant contribution to our understanding of the relationship between different types of masculinity, identity, and crime. He argues that there is no universal male experience but rather, there is a diversity and difference among men which varies through time and space and in turn defines and structures the different expressions of femininities and masculinities (see Connell, 1987).

He applies the term 'hegemonic masculinity' to explain the spectrum of masculinities. The concept of **hegemony** is borrowed from Gramsci (1971) referring to the way in which one class or group can dominate a society by consent. According to Connell (1987), hegemonic masculinity 'is constructed in relation to various subordinated masculinities as well as in relation to women (1987: 183).

Jefferson (2001, cited in Walklate 2007: 152) defines it as:

> the set of ideas, values, representations and practices associated with being male which is commonly accepted as the dominant position in gender relations in a society at a particular historical moment.

Hegemonic masculinity is about a socially dominated ideal of 'manhood', which serves to provide individual men with a sense of self while downgrading other types of masculinity and femininity (ies). The 'successful' male identity can be found in the dominant notion of the male as breadwinner (from the gender division of labour); it is found in the definition of homosexuality (from the gender relations of heterosexuality); and it is found in the objectification of women. Normative heterosexuality is that form of masculinity that is prioritized over 'non-male' characteristics and defines both the structure and the form of those who either live up to the power of this image or those who choose not to engage in the struggle (Stoltenberg, 2000). Thus while many men strive for the hegemonic ideal, some may not succeed and will be placed in a position of subordinated masculinity. Although Connell made few observations about the criminality of males, his insights have been used to garner a better understanding of the offending behaviour of boys and men. For example, Messerschmidt (1993, 1994, 1997, 2000), explored how criminal activity reinforced different types of masculinity and in turn structures relationships between men and women and other men. As Messerschmidt (1993: 76) states, 'it defines masculinity through difference from, and desire for women'.

Thus male involvement in crime-related activities can be 'understood not as an essential characteristic of men and boys but as enacted by practices, which need to be understood within the context of gender relations' (Newburn and Stanko 1994: 4). Masculinity is 'accomplished' in many differential ways, but under dominant patriarchal ideologies.

In criminology, Connell has been drawn upon to highlight the complex and nuanced relationship between masculinities and crime. Messerschmidt (1993) goes on to offer one of the most thorough descriptive accounts in which 'race', ethnicity, age, and socio-economic status class interact in particular with the social construction of youthful masculinities and crime. He highlights how men who cannot access economic and material resources commit crime as a method of 'doing masculinity' rather than arguing that these factors push men into crime. In his work, we can see the ways in which socially organized power differences between men produce different constructions of masculinity.

'Research reveals that men construct masculinities in accord with their position in social structures and therefore their access to power and resources' (Messerschmidt, 1993: 119).

Various studies have shown how men who lack societal power may create a sense of themselves as men through creating 'compensatory measures' by their involvement in crime-related activities and other forms of 'risk' and pleasure seeking behaviour (see Katz, 1995; Hobbs *et al.*, 2003; Winlow, 2004). Katz (1995) examines how in post-industrial society hegemonic masculinity has been challenged by the lack of traditional forms of gendered employment and changing roles of masculinity. The response to these pressures has led to exaggerated forms of masculine expression involving the physical body as a mode of aesthetic and actual power. Other writers have also suggested that socio-economic changes have led to hyper-masculinity expressed through violent behaviour (Winlow, 2004). Winlow (2004) argues that the 'involvement of predominantly young men in crime-related activities needs to be examined in relation to their economic social status and as the means of validating their masculinity. Such an analysis of masculinity and that of '"underclass" masculinities' (Winlow, 2004: 19) provides an important contribution to understanding male criminality and the doing of gender. However, while the nature of the economy may explain why some men resort to crime, it cannot be applied to all male offending.

Jefferson (1997) advanced the psycho-social approach and viewed the idea of hegemonic masculinity as limited. He argued that Connell failed to look towards understanding masculinity by examining the inter-subjectivity of the subject in relation to other men. The psycho-social approach allows for an examination of the 'seductions' of crime and the intersections of masculinity.

What this discussion demonstrates is that by giving up the notion of biological determinism and by exploring the constructive nature of gender, we begin to gain a deeper understanding of the intersections of gender and crime. Without such an exploration there will be a limited understanding of male and female criminality and the gendered experiences of crime and victimization.

The following section will examine why differences on the basis of gender occur in the treatment of women who come into conflict with the law.

REVIEW QUESTIONS

1 Do women and men commit crimes for different or similar reasons?

2 Is there a relationship between crime and masculinity? Give two reasons for your answer.

3 How would you evaluate the argument that masculinity is related to certain types of crime?

Gender and the criminal justice process

Women account for a small proportion of all known offenders and the differences between female and male rates of crime has been termed as 'the gender gap' or 'sex crime ratio'. The numbers of women appearing before the court are few and are often seen as doubly deviant. They have not only come into conflict with the law but have also transgressed gender norms. Double deviance, in short, can lead to 'judicial paternalism' or chivalrous attitudes towards women (Allen 1987). Official statistics do point to the fact that males are more likely to be arrested, convicted, and, if convicted, given a custodial sentence. The literature on sentencing has also drawn attention to the possibility that women are treated less severely than men by the courts because of chivalrous feelings towards women.

However, when the defendant's previous record and the nature of the offence are taken into account, this position is less certain and studies which have controlled for legal variables have found that males and females are treated similarly—the 'equal treatment hypothesis' (Farrington and Morris, 1983). Although there is little evidence to support the chivalry thesis, Allen's study (1987) suggests that violent women offenders received a more lenient approach for serious crimes than men.

Feminist writers have challenged the 'chivalry and equal treatment hypothesis' and have argued that the criminal justice system discriminates against women on the basis that women who come into conflict with the law have always been presented as being '"other"': other than real women, other than real criminals and other than real prisoners' (see Carlen, 1985: 1). They argue that females are treated more harshly than males for similar offences and are punished for breaching criminal law and sex role expectations—known as the 'double deviance hypothesis' (see Howe, 1994 for an overview). In Eaton's work (1986) she demonstrates the ways in which social controls operate in the treatment of women defendants in magistrates' courts based on the perceived domestic roles of women and familial obligations. She noted that women conforming to conventional roles received better treatment than single mothers or lesbians. Carlen (1983) found that Scottish sheriffs differentiated between 'good' and 'bad' mothers and were prepared to sentence them accordingly. All of these examples demonstrate, as Gelsthorpe and McIvor (2007) have pointed out, how the sentencing of women has been overshadowed by stereotypical constructions of womanhood. They argue:

Accumulated research evidence suggests that sentencers treat women differently from men due to chivalry or paternalism, familial protection, or enforcement of gender appropriate behaviour. But what is also clear is that sentences operate a bifurcated system of sentencing which distinguishes between those women who conform to gender stereotypes, and those who do not. (Gelsthorpe and McIvor, 2007: 59)

This suggests that women who come into conflict with the law find themselves in double jeopardy (Carlen, 1998) and that gender-related factors do impact on sentencing decisions and can in turn explain why differences in treatment occur.

There is a general assumption that women are sentenced and punished more leniently than men. The differences in treatment are all too evident. But the real question is whether or not such differential treatment can be justified. National crime figures show that men outnumber women in all major crime categories. Arrest data for 2008–09 shows that 83 per cent of adult men were arrested for committing violence against a person; 97 per cent for sexual offences; 91 per cent for robbery; 92 per cent for burglary; 78 per cent for theft and handling stolen goods (Ministry of Justice, 2010). Women on the whole commit less serious crimes and are less likely to persist in crime than males (McIvor, 2004). The idea of chivalrous treatment as an example of 'reverse discrimination' that has been evidenced in sentencing statistics revealing that women are far less likely than men to receive a custodial sentence, are more likely than men to receive probation or discharges, and if given a custodial sentence, are generally given shorter sentences (see Hedderman and Hough, 1994; Gelsthorpe, 2001). Gelsthorpe and Loucks' (1997) study found that magistrates treated females more leniently than males, viewing women as 'troubled' rather than 'troublesome', or maddened or misguided victims of maligned circumstances. Belknap (2001: 132) argues that chivalrous treatment is part of a 'bartering system' or exchange relationship in which lenient treatment is extended only to certain kinds of female, according to the nature of the offence, but also according to adherence to 'proper' gender roles. As Gelsthorpe (1986) concludes, those women who conform to stereotypical conceptions of 'ladies' seem to receive different sentences to those who breach these expectations.

The theme of punishment for breaching sex role expectations, has been identified in much of the literature on women and crime, and it has been argued that the sentencing of women reflects notions of the 'ideal' woman, related to family and domestic considerations, leading to differentiation between women. Carlen (1983) in her seminal book, *Women's Imprisonment: A Study of Social Control*, shows how women prisoners are treated *differently* from male prisoners. Traditionally, the training of female prisoners was directed towards equipping them to perform the work they were thought most likely to do when released, namely housework, sewing, and hairdressing. Women were not being equipped with skills which would lead to employment in non-gender appropriate roles. Moreover, studies have shown that women in prison are placed under greater surveillance and regulation than men (Sim, 1990). In 2001, women were charged with offences against a discipline rate of 224 offences per 100 women compared with 160 per 100 men (Butler and Kousoulou, 2006). Genders and Player in their study on female youth custody centres (now young offender institutions), found how the 'mad not bad' stereotype of female offenders influences the type of regimes. They assert that:

an important part of the treatment and training of young women serving youth custody relates to the building of self-confidence and self-esteem, the lack of which is deemed responsible for much of the attention- and approval-seeking which causes many girls to come into conflict with the law. The skills which are taught in youth custody centres, however, continue to permit success mainly within the boundaries of stereotypical female roles. The concentration upon personal hygiene and appearance, through training in beauty care and hairdressing, and the development of domestic skills, such as cleaning, cooking and household budgeting, makes clear those areas in which delinquent young women are expected to develop feelings of self- worth. (Genders and Player, 1986: 368)

However, other writers still argue that there is no monolithic male or female experience and some men and some women are dealt with in a discriminatory manner—the 'selectivity hypothesis'. This view considers the interaction of gender with other aspects of social experience and points to the ways in which constructions of age, ethnicity, class, and sexuality affect how males and females are treated.

Thus, being married and having dependent children may lead to lenient treatment. However, in the last decade sentencing for women has taken a punitive turn and there has been a marked rise in the women's prison population.

As prisoners, women suffer from the same deprivations and violations of civil rights as male prisoners but the problems amongst female prisoners are more acute, even though their offending presents less of a threat to public safety. Female prisoners are more likely to have a history of physical and sexual abuse and more likely to face issues relating to care of their children. Additionally, as women in prison, they suffer from sexist and racist discriminatory practices which results in receiving fewer leisure, work, and educational opportunities, greater surveillance and more control by drugs than male prisoners. The impact of imprisonment on women's lives is qualitatively different from that of male imprisonment and the Corston Report (2007) illustrated the 'catastrophic' impact of women's imprisonment.

The final section will draw on the police service to highlight the machismo cop culture, but also how diversity is influencing policy and practice.

REVIEW OF QUESTIONS

1 Explain how the construction of femininity impacts on sentencing decisions.

2 Give three reasons as to why certain women are treated more punitively by the criminal justice system.

3 Give two reasons that support the 'chivalry' argument and two reasons against.

Who are the professionals in the criminal justice system?

The culture of policing

The police organization and the canteen culture/cop culture of the police service (Waddington, 1999), represents a type of masculinity which leads to the police service being viewed as a male profession; membership of which requires the characteristics of men (Morris, 1987: 135). The police service has not only been perceived as being resistant to change, but a central feature of police culture is 'hegemonic masculinity', as discussed earlier. Campbell elaborates further upon this point (1993: 20) and has described the police service 'as the most masculinised enclave in civil society'.

The Sex Discrimination Act 1975; the creation of the British Association of Women Police; and the Gender Agenda Initiative (which aims 'to have a woman's voice in influential policy fora' focusing on both internal and external service delivery) are all signs that things can and might change in the police organization. This change is evident in the increased number of women serving in English and Welsh forces—from 8.6 per cent in 1981 to 11 per cent in 1990 (Brown, 1997) to 26 per cent in 2010 (Ministry of Justice, 2010).

A five-year trend analysis shows that the proportion of female police officers in post has increased year on year since 2005–06 (see Table 15.1).

However, female officers continue to be under-represented in senior ranks which are, for the most part, still male dominated. There have been increases over a five-year period in the proportion of women employed as senior police officers: 9 per cent of Superintendent and above grades at 31 March 2005 were women. By 31 March 2010, the proportion had risen to 13 per cent (see Table 15.2). Police management scholars have highlighted that women's limited advancement in the police profession is problematic because of the

Table 15.1 Percentage of police officers in post (full-time equivalents) by gender, as at 31 March 2005–06 to 2009–10

	2005/06	2006/07	2007/08	2008/09	2009/10
Females	22.3	23.3	24.2	25.1	25.7
Males	77.7	76.7	75.8	74.9	74.3
Total	141,523	141,892	141,859	143,770	143,734

Source: Statistics on Women and the Criminal Justice System A Ministry of Justice publication under Section 95 of the Criminal Justice Act 1991 (Ministry of Justice, 2010).

Table 15.2 Percentage of senior police officers in post (full-time equivalents) by gender, as at 31 March 2005–06 to 2009–10

	2005/06	2006/07	2008/09	2009/10
Females	9.3	10.1	12.0	13.0
Males	90.7	89.9	88.0	87.0
Total	1,689	1,662	1,713	1,725

Source: Statistics on Women and the Criminal Justice System A Ministry of Justice publication under Section 95 of the Criminal Justice Act 1991 (Ministry of Justice, 2010).

cultural barriers faced by female officers emanating from the police organization and managerial structure (Walklate, 1993, 1995; Fielding, 1994).

The issue of sexism as a cultural barrier came to the fore when Alison Halford, the Assistant Chief Constable of Merseyside, brought a sex discrimination case against the force on the grounds that she had been turned down on nine occasions for promotion while male officers with less experience were being promoted over her. Merseyside Police agreed a settlement and in return she dropped all charges of sexual discrimination. In 1993, a Home Office Study found that nearly all the women officers surveyed had experienced some form of sexual harassment from fellow colleagues and in the same year a report by Her Majesty's Inspectorate concluded that breaches of equal opportunities policies were a common occurrence.

The move away from the cult of masculinity with the feminization of policing has and should lead to a more varied police service that reflects the needs of a diverse community. This is most evidently seen in the policing of gender-based crimes and responses to women survivors of sex-related crimes. For example, the number of recorded incidents of rape has increased, although convictions are still low. This is attributable to changing attitudes towards rape and changes in police practice. Another good example of changing practices is the way in which the police respond to domestic violence which was once seen as not 'real' police work and viewed as 'domestic disputes' (Faragher, 1985). To challenge this view and effect a cultural change within the police service, between 1986 and 1990, the Metropolitan Police created a dedicated Domestic Violence Unit. This cultural change was given further impetus by the Home Office circular 60/1990 which stated:

> The Home Secretary regards a violent or brutal assault and threatening behaviour over a period of time by a person to whom the victim is married or with whom the victim lives or has lived as seriously as violent assault by a stranger.

This statement is telling and far reaching and indicative of a cultural and ideological change in the response to **intimate violence**. By 2004, the Domestic Violence Crime and Victims Act 2004 extended police powers to allow arrests to be made for common assault (which previously was not an arrestable offence). Much more work is required to change attitudes in responding to domestic violence and rape but the examples given are illustrative of a move in the right direction.

It should be noted that although we have focused on rape in heterosexual terms, rape and intimate violence also occurs between men and between women. In addressing issues of gender and race, sexual orientation has been left off the agenda and hence the issue of sexuality is only now beginning to challenge the view that criminal justice work is hetero-normative and male. However, homophobia, **racism**, and sexism still exist and impact on those who choose these professions (Burke, 1993). It was only in 1991 that a Lesbian and Gay Police Association, covering every rank up to Chief Superintendent, was launched to raise awareness around sexual orientation and to prevent discrimination against lesbian and gay officers. What is clear is that although attempts are being made to challenge stereotypes, prejudice and discriminatory behaviour, sexism, racism, ageism, and homophobia are not confined to policing but are prevalent throughout the criminal justice system.

REVIEW QUESTIONS

1 Explain why the police service is viewed by some as a male profession.
2 Discuss the advantages of having a more inclusive police service.
3 In what ways can the 'cult of masculinity' be challenged?

CONCLUSION

This chapter has examined some of the salient issues in relation to sex, gender, and crime. It began by documenting the relationship between sex, gender, and crime and argues that although the role of gender and crime is of importance, it has not always played a key role in the development of criminological thought. This was achieved by highlighting the deficiencies within 'malestream' criminology.

This chapter also examines the role of feminist approaches in understanding gender and crime illustrating how feminist theorizing has not only contributed to the development of criminological thought but has placed the gender question firmly on the criminological agenda by critiquing the long held assumption that men commit more crime than women. Furthermore, feminist approaches question the idea that men's involvement in crime is due to 'masculine' traits such as aggressiveness in comparison to women and associated characteristics of femininity. Indeed Wooton (1959: 32), states that 'if men behaved like women, the courts would be idle and the prisons empty' (cited in Walklate 1995a: 20). In so doing feminists have questioned the male-centredness of criminology, and centralized the lived experience of women thus making the voices of women heard. An important contribution made by feminist theorizing was to 'dismantle or fracture the limitations of existing knowledge, boundaries and traditional methodologies' (Gelsthorpe, 2003: 8).

It is through the work of feminist criminologists exploring the role of gender and crime that there has been a move to question the construction of masculinities and femininities and its subsequent relationship to crime related activities. By examining how gender is played out in the criminal justice process from sentencing to imprisonment, we can see how 'criminal' women are constructed as doubly deviant (for not only committing an offence but also going against their essential nature) and how the law and its application is not gender neutral.

Even at the time of writing in the spring of 2012, after decades of campaigning work to address the needs of women who come into conflict with the law, there are still unanswered questions related to gender and crime. What emerges overwhelmingly from the discussion is that it is only by locating female and male offending within the inter-sectionality of class, age, ethnicity, sexual orientation, masculinities, and femininities that we can begin to examine how men and women are treated differently by the criminal justice system and how their social experiences as offenders and victims differ. As Walklate (1995: 192) argues:

> Gender may hold some of the clues to the 'crime problem', but it would be misguided to think that it holds all of the answers. A gendered lens certainly helps us see some features of the crime problem more clearly perhaps; but how and under what circumstances is that clarity made brighter by gender or distorted by it?

Indeed, as this chapter has shown, a series of seminal studies have not only served to destabilize criminological theorizing around women and crime (Heidensohn, 2006: 3), but also to challenge 'malestream' assumptions within the discipline. Much more work is needed and Heidensohn (2003), Naffine (2003), and Scraton (1990) suggest that questions of gender, ethnicity, and sexuality still remain peripheral to mainstream criminology and criminological theory. In the 1980s David Morgan believed that the reason for the marginalization of women was because of 'academic machismo' (the competitive display of masculine skills) and 'male homosociability' (the processes of discrimination and exclusion of women). Three decades later these two variables are still in play and the feminist project of reconstructing knowledge so that it no longer reflects exclusively a male social reality (Naffine, 1987: 127), is still a project under construction. To reiterate the point made by Carol Smart:

> Criminology and the sociology of deviance must become more than the study of men and crime if it is to play any significant part in the development of our understanding of crime, law and the criminal process and play any role in the transformation of existing social practices. (Smart, 1977: 185)

QUESTIONS FOR DISCUSSION

1 Outline the strengths and weaknesses of feminist perspectives in criminology.
2 Do you think women are treated differently to men in the criminal justice system?
3 Can we understand criminal behaviour through a gendered lens?
4 Give reasons as to why there are fewer women in high ranking positions.

GUIDE TO FURTHER READING

Smart, C. (1977) *Women, Crime and Criminology*. London: Routledge and Kegan and Paul.
This text made an important contribution to the development of criminology and is one of class in the area of women and crime.

Heidensohn, F. and Gelsthorpe, L. (2007) 'Gender and Crime' in M. Maguire, R. Morgan and R. Reiner (eds) *The Oxford Handbook of Criminology* (4th edn) Oxford: Clarendon Press.
Written by two of the most influential feminist criminologists, this chapter demonstrates how gender informs criminology and evaluates the impact of feminist perspectives on the discipline of criminology.

Heidensohn, F. (2006) *Gender and Justice: New Concepts and Approaches*. Cullompton: Willan Publishing; Basingstoke: Macmillan.
This edited collected brings a range of issues together, examining both offending behaviour and official responses to it.

Newburn, T. and Stanko, E.A. (1994) *Just Boys Doing Business, Men, Masculinities and Crime*. Tottowa, NJ: Rowman and Littlefield.
An edited collection examining the relationship between the role of masculinity, masculinities and crime. The chapters describe the importance of theorizing masculinities in understanding men's involvement in crime, their experiences of victimization and the responses of criminal justice agencies.

Silvestri, M. and Crowther-Dowey, C. (2008) *Gender and Crime*. London: Sage.
A good introduction covering a range of issues, examining the relationship between gender and crime and human rights.

WEB LINKS

http://www.cleanbreak.org.uk/

Clean Break was set up in 1979 by two women prisoners who believed that theatre could bring the issues facing women in prison to a wider audience. Clean Break has produced award winning plays which dramatize women's experiences of, and relationships to, crime and punishment.

http://www.asc41.com/dir4/

The American Society of Criminology has a division on Women and Crime. It developed out of the growing interest in the study of gender and women as offenders, victims, and criminal justice professionals.

http://www.fawcettsociety.org.uk/

The Fawcett Society campaigns on issues that highlight the gender gap. The website details its work, on women as victims, offenders and criminal justice professionals.

http://www.womeninprison.org.uk

Women in Prison was established in 1983 by Chris Tchaikovsky (a former prisoner), Women in Prison (WIP) is an organization which supports and campaigns for women affected by the criminal justice system. WIP is the only women-centred, women-run organization that provides specialist services to women affected by the criminal justice system both in prison and in the community throughout England.

http://www.justice.gov.uk/publications/womencriminal justicesystem.htm.

The Ministry of Justice website includes an annual report which brings together data produced by a range of criminal justice agencies relating to the experiences of women in the criminal justice system.

REFERENCES

Allen, H. (1987) *Justice Unbalanced: Gender, Psychiatry and Juridical Decisions*. Milton Keynes: Open University Press.

Arnold, R. (1990) 'Processes of victimisation and criminalisation of black women', *Social Justice: Feminism and the Social Control of Gender* (Fall) 17,3 (41): 153–166.

Belknap, J. (2001) *The Invisible Woman: Gender, Crime and Justice* (2nd edn) Belmont, CA: Wadsworth.

Bertrand, M.A. (1967) 'The myth of sexual equality before the law', Proceedings of the fifth research conference on Delinquency and Criminality. Montreal: Quebec, Society of Criminology.

Brown, J. (1997) 'European policewomen: a comparative research perspective', *International Journal of the Sociology of Law* Vol. 25: 1–19.

Burke, M. (1993) *Coming out of the Blue: British Police Officers Talk about their Lives in 'The Job' as Lesbians, Gays and Bisexuals*. London: Cassell.

Butler, P. and Kousoulou, D. (2006) *Women at Risk: The Mental Health of Women in Contact with the Judicial System*. London: London Development Centre.

Cain, M. (1990) 'Realist Philosophy and Standpoint Epistemologies or Feminist Criminology as a Successor Science' in L. Gelsthorpe and A. Morris (eds) *Feminist Perspectives in Criminology*. Milton Keynes: Open University Press, 124–41.

Campbell, B. (1993) 'Too much of a woman for the boys in blue', *The Independent*, 1 June: 20.

Carlen, P. (1983) *Women's Imprisonment: A Study in Social Control*. London: Routledge and Kegan Paul.

Carlen, P. (1985) 'Law, Psychiatry and Women's Imprisonment: A Sociological View', *British Journal of Psychiatry*: 618–21.

Carlen P. (1998) *Sledgehammer: Women's imprisonment at the millennium*. Basingstoke: Macmillan.

Carlen, P, Hicks., J, O'Dwyer, J., Christina, D. and Tchaikovsky, C. (1985) *Criminal Women: Autobiographical Accounts*. Oxford: Blackwell.

Carrington, K. (1998) 'Postmodern and feminist criminologists: fragmenting the criminological subject' in P. Walton and J. Young (eds) *The New Criminology Revisited*. London: MacMillan; New York: St Martin's Press.

Carrington, K. (2002) 'Feminism and Critical Criminology: Confronting Genealogies' in K. Carrington and R. Hogg (eds) *Critical Criminology: Issues, Debates, Challenges*. Cullompton: Willan, 114–45.

Chesney-Lind, M. and Pasko, L. (2004) 'Girls' troubles and "female delinquency"' in M. Chesney-Lind and L. Pasko *The Female Offender: Girls, Women and Crime* (2nd edn) Thousand Oaks, CA, London and New Delhi: Sage Publications, 10–33.

Cloward, R.A. and Ohlin, L.B. (1960) *Delinquency and Opportunity: A Theory of Delinquent Gangs*. New York: Free Press.

Cohen, A.K. (1955). *Delinquent Boys*. New York: Free Press.

Connell, R.W. (1987) *Gender and Power*. Oxford: Polity.

Connell, R.W. (1993) 'Forward' in J.W. Messerschmidt, *Masculinities and Crime: Critique and Reconceptualisation of Theory*. Lanham, MD: Rowman and Littlefield.

Connell, R.W. (1995–2005) *Masculinities*. Oxford: Polity.

Connell, R.W. (2000) *The Men and the Boys*. Oxford: Blackwell.

Connell, R.W. (2002) *Gender*. Oxford: Blackwell.

Corston, J. (2007) *The Corston Report: a review of women with particular vulnerabilities in the criminal justice system*. London: Home Office.

Cowie, J, Cowie, V. and Slater, E. (1968) *Delinquency in Girls*. London: Heinemann.

Daly, K. and Chesney-Lind, M. (1988) 'Feminism and criminology', *Justice Quarterly* 5 (4): 101–43.

Danner, M. (1989) 'Socialist feminism: a brief introduction' in B. MacLean and D. Milovanovic (eds) *New Directions in Critical Criminology*. Vancouver: The Collective Press.

Eaton, M. (1986) *Justice for Women? Family, Court and Social Control*. Milton Keynes: Open University Press.

Faragher, T. (1985) 'The police response to violence against women in the home' in J. Pahl (ed.) *Private Violence and Public Policy: The Needs of Battered Women and the Response of the Public Services*. London: Routledge and Kegan Paul.

Farrington, D.P. and Morris, A.M. (1983) 'Sex, sentencing and reconviction', *British Journal of Criminology* Vol 23, No. 3: 229–49.

Fielding, N. (1994) 'Cop canteen culture' in T. Newburn and E. Stanko (eds) *Just Boys Doing Business? Men, Masculinities, and Crime*. London: Routledge, 46–64.

Freud, S. (1933) *New Introductory Lectures on Psychoanalysis*. New York: W.W. Norton.

Garland, D. (1992) 'Criminological Knowledge and Its Relation to Power—Foucault's Genealogy and Criminology Today', *British Journal of Criminology* Vol. 32: 403–22.

Garland, D. (2002) 'Of Crimes and Criminals: The Development of Criminology in Britain' in M. Maguire, R. Morgan, and R. Reiner (eds) *Oxford Handbook of Criminology* (3rd edn) Oxford: Clarendon Press, 11–45.

Gelsthorpe, L. (1986), 'Towards a sceptical look at sexism', *International Journal of the Sociology of Law* 14, 2: 125–52.

Gelsthorpe, L. (2001) 'Critical decisions and processes in the criminal courts' in E. McLaughlin and J. Muncie (eds) *Controlling Crime*. London: Sage/Open University.

Gelsthorpe, L. (2003) 'Feminist perspectives on gender and crime: making women work', *Criminal Justice Matters* 53: 8–9.

Gelsthorpe, L. and Louks, N. (1997) 'Justice in the making, key influences on decision-making' in C. Hedderman and L. Gelsthorpe (eds) *Understanding the Sentencing of Women*. London: Home Office Research Study, 170.

Gelsthorpe, L. and Morris, A. (eds) (1990) *Feminist Perspectives in Criminology*. Buckingham: Open University Press.

Gelsthorpe, L. and McIvor, G. (2007) 'Difference and diversity in probation' in L. Gelsthorpe and R. Morgan (eds) *Handbook of Probation*. Cullompton: Willan.

Genders, E. and Player, E. (1986) 'Women's Imprisonment: The Effects of Youth Custody', *British Journal of Criminology* 35: 188–200.

Gramsci, A. (1971) *Selections from the Prison Notebooks*. London: Lawrence and Wishart.

Grosz, E.A. (1987) 'Feminist Theory and the Challenge to Knowledge', *Women's Studies International Forum* Vol. 10, No. 5: 208–17.

Harding, S. (1987) *Feminism and Methodology: Social Science Issues*. Bloomington: University of Indiana Press.

Hearn, J. (1996) 'Is masculinity dead? A critique of the concept of masculinity' in M. Mac an Ghail (ed) *Understanding Masculinities*. Buckingham: Open University Press, 202–18.

Hedderman, C. and Hough, M. (1994) *Does the Criminal Justice System Treat Men and Women Differently?, Research Findings 10*. London: Home Office, Research and Statistics Department.

Heidensohn, F. (1968) 'The Deviance of Women: A Critique and an Enquiry', *British Journal of Sociology* 19 (2): 160–75.

Heidensohn, F. (1985–96) *Women and Crime* (2nd edn) Basingstoke: Macmillan.

Heidensohn, F. (1994) 'From Being to Knowing: Some Reflections on the Study of Gender in Contemporary Society', *Women and Criminal Justice* 6(1): 13–737.

Heidensohn, F. (2003) *Gender and Policing* in T. Newburn (ed), *Handbook of Policing*. Cullompton: Willan.

Heidensohn F. (ed) (2006) *Gender and Justice: New concepts and Approaches*. Cullompton: Willan.

Heidensohn, F. and Gelsthorpe, L. (2007) 'Gender and Crime' in R. Reiner, R. Morgan, and M. Maguire (eds) *The Oxford Handbook of Criminology* (4th edn) Oxford: Oxford University Press, 381–421.

Heidensohn, F. and Silvstri, M. (2012) 'Gender and Crime' in R. Reiner, R. Morgan, and M. Maguire (eds) *The Oxford Handbook of Criminology* (5th edn) Oxford: Oxford University Press, 337–69.

Hirschi, T. (1969) *Causes of Delinquency*. Berkeley: University of California Press.

Hobbs, D., Hadfield, P., Lister, S., and Winlow, S. (2003) *Bouncers: Violence and Governance in the Night-time Economy*. Oxford: Oxford University Press.

Howe, A. (1994) *Punish and Critique*. London: Routledge.

Jefferson, T. (1994) 'Theorising masculine subjectivity' in T. Newburn and E. Stanko (eds) *Just Boys Doing Business? Men, Masculinities and Crime*. London: Routledge, 10–32.

Jefferson, T. (1997) '"Tougher than the rest": Mike Tyson and the destructive desires of masculinity', *Aean Journal* 6: 89–105.

Katz, J. (1995) 'Advertising and the construction of violent, white masculinity' in G. Dines and J. Humaz (eds) *Gender, Race and Class in Media*. London: Sage, 349–59.

Kimmel, S. M. (2000) *The Gendered Society*. Oxford: Oxford University Press.

Klein, D. (1973) 'The Aetiology of Female Crime: A Review of the Literature', *Issues in Criminology* 8 (2): 3–30.

Leonard, E.B. (1982) *A Critique of Criminology Theory: Women, Crime and Society*. London: Longman.

Lombroso, C. and Ferraro, W. (1895) *The Female Offender*. London: T. Fisher Unwin.

Matza, D. (1964) *Delinquency and Drift*. New York: John Wiley and Sons Inc.

McIvor, G. (ed) (2004) *Women Who Offend, Research Highlights in Social Work*. London: Jessica Kingsley.

McRobbie, A. and Garber, J. (1976) 'Girls and Subcultures' in S. Hall and T. Jefferson (eds) *Resistance Through Rituals*. London: Hutchinson, 177–89.

Merton, R.K. (1938) 'Social Structure and Anomie', *American Sociological Review* 3: 672–82.

Messerschmidt, J. (1993) *Masculinities and Crime: Critique and Reconceptualisation of Theory*. Lanham, MD: Rowman and Littlefield.

Messerchmidt, J. (1994) 'Schooling masculinities and youth crime by white boys' in T. Newburn and E. Stanko (eds) *Just Boys Doing Business? Men, Masculinities and Crime*. Tottowa, NJ: Rowman and Littlefield, 81–100.

Messerschmidt, J. (1997) *Crime as Structured Action*. London: Sage.

Messerschmidt, J. (2000) *Nine Lives*. Boulder, CO: Westview.

Ministry of Justice (2010) *Statistics on Women and the Criminal Justice System A Ministry of Justice publication under Section 95 of the Criminal Justice Act 1991*. London: Ministry of Justice, http://www.justice.gov.uk/publications/womencriminaljusticesystem

Morgan, D. (1992) *Discovering Men*. London: Routledge.

Morris, A. (1987) *Women, Crime and Criminal Justice*. Oxford: Basil Blackwell.

Naffine, N. (1987) *Female Crime: The construction of women in criminology*. London: Allen and Unwin.

Naffine, J. (2003) 'The "Man Question" of Crime, Criminology and Criminal Law' , *Criminal Justice Matters* 53: 10–11.

Newburn, T. and Stanko, E.A. (1994) *Just Boys Doing Business, Men, Masculinities and Crime*. Tottowa, NJ: Rowman and Littlefield.

Oakley, A. (1972) *Sex, Gender and Society*. Aldershot: Gower.

Scraton, P. (1990) 'Scientific knowledge or masculine discourses? Challenging patriarchy in criminology' in L. Gelsthorpe and A. Morris (eds) *Feminist Perspectives in Criminology*. Buckingham: Open University Press, 10–26.

Shaw, C.R. and McKay, H.D. (1942) *Juvenile Delinquency in Urban Areas*. Chicago: Chicago University Press.

Sim, J. (1990) *Medical Power in Prisons*. Buckingham: Open University Press.

Smart, C. (1977) *Women, Crime and Criminology*. London: Routledge and Kegan Paul.

Smart, C. (1990) 'Feminist approaches to criminology or post-modern woman meets atavistic man' in L. Gelsthorpe and A. Morris (eds) *Feminist Perspectives in Criminology*. Milton Keynes and Philadelphia, PA: Open University Press.

Sutherland, E.H. and Cressey, D. (1978) *Criminology* (10th edn) Philadelphia, PA: Lippincott.

Stoltenberg, J. (2000) *Refusing to be a Man: Essays on Sex and Justice*. London: Routledge.

Thomas, I. (1907) *Sex and Society*. Boston, MA: Little Brown.

Tolson, A. (1977) *The Limits of Masculinity*. London: Routledge.

Thrasher, F.M. (1927) *The Gang*. Chicago: Chicago University Press.

Waddington, P.A.J. (1999) 'Police canteen culture—an appreciation', *British Journal of Criminology* Vol. 39, No. 2: 286–309.

Walklate, S. (1989) *Victimology: The Victim and the Criminal Justice Process*. London: Unwin Hyman.

Walklate, S. (1993) 'Policing by women, with women, for women', *Policing* Vol. 9: 101–15.

Walklate, S. (1995a) *Gender and Crime: An Introduction*. Hemel Hempstead: Prentice Hall.

Walklate, S. (1995b) 'Equal opportunities and the future of policing' in F. Leishman, B. Loveday, and M. Savage (eds) *Core Issues in Policing*. Longman: London, 191–203.

Walklate, S. (2001) *Gender, Crime and Criminal Justice*. Cullompton: Willan Publishing.

Walklate S. (2007) 'Men, victims and crime' in P. Francis, P. Davies, and C. Greer (eds) *Crime, Victims and Social Control*. London: Sage, 142–65.

Wilson, J.O. and Hernstein, R.J. (1985) *Crime and Human Nature*. New York: Touchstone

Winlow, S. (2004) 'Masculinities and Crime', *Criminal Justice Matters* 55: 18–19.

Wooton, B. (1959) *Social Science and Social Pathology*. London: George, Allen and Unwin.

16 'Race', ethnicity, and crime

Marian FitzGerald

INTRODUCTION

This chapter starts by exploring notions of 'race' and ethnicity since these terms are frequently used in the context of crime with very little attempt to define what is meant by either. Then it provides some background on how particular groups have come to be defined as 'ethnic minorities' in Britain and what the official statistics on these groups currently tell us about the differences between them—with particular reference to known risk factors for offending.

After outlining the history of these groups' relations with the police and public perceptions of their involvement in crime and disorder, it looks at trends in the official statistics on ethnicity and offending. Despite the promises made by New Labour following the Macpherson Report of 1999 to reduce the over-representation of Black people at all stages of the criminal justice system, the picture has worsened. The very diverse 'Asian' group has also started to be over-represented, albeit not to the same extent as Black people; but popular perceptions have recently developed of some minority White groups as disproportionately involved in crime even though these cannot be identified from the available statistics.

In the light of this, the chapter concludes by looking critically at the pitfalls of taking such figures at face value, including the risk that this will legitimate negative stereotyping—as illustrated by the government's use of the data to highlight the very significant over-representation of Black people in the riots of August 2011. It argues that criminologists must therefore interpret such statistics in the light of relevant criminological theories rather than giving primacy to explanations which treat the experiences of different 'ethnic' groups as if they were unique.

Definitions

The terms 'race' and ethnicity are often used very loosely and even interchangeably; but their precise meaning is also contested. Academics have coined different (and sometimes competing) definitions of each for many decades.

'Race' and racism

For present purposes the notion of 'race' rests on assumptions that human beings can be divided into broad groups which are in some way distinguished on the basis of inherently different biological characteristics.

On the one hand, it is true that certain groups of people with common ancestry and/or geographic origins may share some genetic characteristics which, for example, make them more susceptible to some types of disease. However, it is now well established that each individual has their own unique biological makeup within an overarching biological framework which is common to *all* human beings. That is, the genetic patterns which are specific to particular groups have minimal significance compared to the characteristics they share with others. Also, such differences are themselves not permanent and immutable. They blur as people from different groups mate with each other, and individuals within the same family vary in the extent to which they are affected by inherited characteristics.

On the other hand, the term 'race' is rarely used in this very limited scientific sense but more commonly as a way of categorizing people whose shared genetic characteristics mean they *look* broadly similar to each other and members of other groups see them as different. These distinctions are usually very crude—and they are often in the eye of the beholder.

The reason why 'race' is such a contested term (and therefore written here in inverted commas) is because it has sometimes been used *as if* these crude distinctions were scientifically based and, in particular, because this pseudo-scientific usage has given spurious legitimacy to negative stereotypes of some groups. Thus, in previous centuries notions of 'racial' difference were used to divide human beings into separate species and rank them 'according to inborn worth' (Gould, 1981). Importantly, this type of thinking has given rise to genocidal ideologies, as epitomized in the notion of a 'Master Race' which underpinned Nazism.

There are, though, many situations in which it is convenient to describe people according to some group characteristics, including whether, for example, they are male or female, young or old, Black or White, etc. Some academics try to avoid the term 'race' completely; but most recognize it as a social rather than a scientific construct, thus:

> the term race is applied more often to phenotype—the physical characteristics such as colour, more frequently found in particular ethnic groups—than genotype—those distinctions which have some biological underpinning. Socially race has a significance dependent not on science but upon belief. (McEwen, 1991)

Use of the term becomes unavoidable, though, when discussing 'racism'—that is, prejudice against particular groups based on the 'beliefs' referred to by McEwen.

Ethnicity

The concept of ethnicity arguably provides a more meaningful basis for distinguishing between social groups. Even so, the ethnic distinctions which have been made for policy purposes (as discussed later in this chapter) have also been criticized—whether on the grounds that they are divisive *per se* or that they are a diversion from tackling racism or class divisions (Sivanandan, 1985).

Ethnic distinctions between people are *not* made on the basis of presumed biological differences but on the understanding that groups of people may have shared a particular range of experiences over centuries and developed some degree of shared culture related to this which now provides the basis for a common sense of identity. At the same time, others may *assume* that individuals who share these characteristics identify with each other; so they may be categorized as belonging to a particular ethnic category regardless of whether they would choose to describe themselves in this way.

Milton Yinger sums up many of the commonly agreed elements of ethnicity when he suggests that an ethnic group

> exists *in the full sense* when three conditions are present: a segment of a larger society is seen by others to be different in some combination of the following characteristics—language, religion, race and ancestral homeland with its related culture; the members also perceive themselves in that way; and they participate in shared activities built around their (real or mythical) common origin or culture. (Yinger, 1986, emphasis added)

REVIEW QUESTIONS

1 What is the difference between 'race' and ethnicity?

2 Why are the terms controversial?

3 How would you describe your own ethnicity?

BACKGROUND

As the previous section implies, most people could claim some form of ethnic identity if they chose to do so; but, the term 'ethnic minorities' has come to be used in a British context primarily to describe groups associated with particular waves of **immigration** since World War II.

Successive British governments had tried to control immigration from at least the early part of the twentieth century; but the population of countries which were part of the British Empire were *not* thought of as foreigners—they were British subjects. And as these countries began to gain independence in the period following World War II, special measures were taken to hold on to their allegiance, including by giving their citizens full rights of entry into the United Kingdom.

At first many were actively recruited from ex-colonies in the Caribbean to fill labour shortages in Britain in the late 1950s and early 1960s. This 'Caribbean' immigration was followed by a second major wave of 'Asian' immigration from the Indian subcontinent (India, Pakistan and Bangladesh) in the 1960s and 1970s, with further additions of Asians who had settled in countries of East Africa but were now being expelled as a result of racially discriminatory policies pursued by the governments of those states. By now, though, popular demands for immigration control as well as changes in the economic and international context resulted in progressively tighter legislation to keep out new immigrants from the 'New Commonwealth', the main exceptions being spouses and children coming to join those who had already been admitted.

Previous immigrants to Britain had often suffered prejudice and **discrimination**; but, because they were White, they and their children had more options for blending in to the 'host' society, even if this meant sacrificing some of their ethnic identity. The postwar immigrants from the Caribbean and the Indian subcontinent, however, were *visibly* different both from the host population and from each other. That is, in terms of 'phenotype' they were readily thought of as being racially different, even though there were significant ethnic divisions between and within both groups.

Not only did they suffer overt discrimination—facing notices when seeking work or accommodation which proclaimed 'no coloureds'—they suffered physical harassment. Tensions between Caribbean immigrants and the indigenous White population erupted in violence on the streets in Nottingham and London in the late 1950s (for overviews see Katznelson, 1973; Walvin, 1974), and this seems to have triggered a dual response from the government[1] which was to set the pattern for the future (Layton-Henry, 1992). On the one hand, the 1960s saw the introduction of the selective immigration controls referred to earlier but also the first legislation to outlaw discrimination which was also progressively strengthened over time and culminated in the Race Relations Act 1976.

Meanwhile the Caribbean and Asian immigrants who had settled here before controls were introduced continued to be joined by other family members including children they had initially left at home. Over time, they also began to have children born in Britain—some of whom were of 'mixed' ethnic heritage as a result of relations between the Caribbean group in particular and the indigenous White population. The poorest of these groups faced ongoing disadvantages beyond the immigrant generation; and governments increasingly became aware[2] that, although discrimination still played a part in this, other factors at work were more deeply entrenched. It was apparent that special *proactive* measured would be need to prevent this **disadvantage** being perpetuated from one generation to the next, affecting not only immigrants but their descendants born in Britain.

The Race Relations Act 1976 was the cornerstone of government policies for tackling both discrimination *and* disadvantage. However, to ensure that these policies were working, the government would need to be able to:

a) *measure* the extent to which different groups were disadvantaged on key indicators such as employment, housing and education; and

b) *monitor* whether this changed over time.

The national Census which took place every ten years already included a question on where people were born; but this could not provide the information needed to monitor the impact of 'race relations' policies through subsequent generations. So in the 1980s local authorities and major surveys started collecting information on people's ethnicity as such; and an ethnic question was finally introduced into the Census itself in 1991 which divided the population into ten 'ethnic' categories which had been decided on by government statisticians. In the 2001 Census they added new categories; so the population now comprised 16 'ethnic groups'; and a further question was introduced about people's religion. In what was to be the last Census, in 2011, the population was re-divided into 18 'ethnic' categories.

Table 16.1 2001 Census: Population of England and Wales by ethnic category

White: British	87.5	**White** 91.3
White: Irish	1.2	
White: Other White	2.6	
Mixed: White and Black Caribbean	0.5	**Mixed** 1.3
Mixed: White and Black African	0.2	
Mixed: White and Asian	0.4	
Mixed: Other Mixed	0.3	
Asian or Asian British: Indian	2.0	**Asian** 4.4
Asian or Asian British: Pakistani	1.4	
Asian or Asian British: Bangladeshi	0.5	
Asian or Asian British: Other Asian	0.5	
Black or Black British: Black Caribbean	1.1	**Black** 2.2
Black or Black British: Black African	0.9	
Black or Black British: Other Black	0.2	
Chinese or Other Ethnic Group: Chinese	0.4	**Other** 0.9
Chinese or Other Ethnic Group: Other Ethnic Group	0.4	

Source: Census 2001.

Table 16.2 Socio-economic and demographic characteristics

Selected ethnic groups

	% Living in Inner London	% Aged 10 to 15	% of males aged 16-24 unemployed[1]	% aged 16-20 with no educational qualifications	% of dependent children living in single parent households
White British	5.3	19.6	7.2	16	22.1
Mixed White and Black Caribbean	15.1	57.5	14.5	24.6	54.5
Black Caribbean	33.7	20.4	15.8	16.3	59.1
Black African	47.7	30.2	6.9	12.6	44.3
Indian	8.2	22.9	5.2	10.6	10.9
Pakistani	6.1	35.0	10.1	22.6	16.3
Bangladeshi	45.7	38.4	9.2	21.6	15.1

[1] This figure is based on all 16-24 year olds who were 'economically active' so, as well as those in work, it includes students and seeking work.
Source: Census 2001.

At the time of writing, the results of the 2011 Census were not yet available; and in any case the criminal justice statistics cited later in this chapter are pegged to the 2001 population figures, as shown in Table 16.1, which also groups the 16 categories into the five groups to which they are often aggregated in a criminal justice context. Despite the preoccupation of policy makers with visible minorities, by 2001 the largest single ethnic minority was actually the 'White Other' group (at 2.6 per cent) whereas all of the *visible* minorities together accounted for just over 8 per cent of the total.

In a criminological context it is commonly accepted that certain socio-economic and demographic factors are closely correlated with the risk of individuals becoming involved in the sort of crimes which may bring them to the attention of the police. These risks are greater where a higher proportion of the group is young, where young men lack educational qualifications and/or are unemployed. They can also be intensified by factors associated with household composition, as well as the extent to which people live in high crime urban areas. And the more of these factors are present, the more they may reinforce each other. Table 16.2, therefore, provides a sample of relevant Census statistics comparing the main visible minorities with the figure for the White British population.

REVIEW QUESTIONS

1 What do you think is the reason these particular 16 categories formed the basis for a question on ethnicity in the 2001 Census?

2 What alternative or additional categories might have been included?

3 On the basis of Table 16.2, which groups appear, on average, to be most at risk of offending?

Minorities, crime, and the criminal justice system

1950s to 1970s

Caribbean immigration in particular took place in the context of a tradition of policing which is nostalgically recalled in terms of the friendly neighbourhood police officer who often kept order just by 'having a quiet word'. However, the other side of the coin was a lack of scrutiny over the way the police exercised their powers which facilitated instances of oppressive behaviour, the arbitrary application of the law, and various forms of corruption. Even if this type of malpractice was not endemic, in the climate of prejudice at that time and in the absence of any safeguards against discrimination, the new immigrants found themselves disproportionately on the receiving end of heavy-handed policing and malpractice.

By the late 1960s and early 1970s concerns were already being raised about the police treatment of Caribbean immigrants (Rose *et al.*, 1969; Hunte, 1966; Humphrey, 1972). This was despite the fact that a parliamentary inquiry into 'Police-Immigrant Relations' in 1972 concluded that crime among Asians was lower than average and, among 'West Indians' it was no higher than for Whites (House of Commons Select Committee on Race Relations and Immigration, 1972).

However, the original West Indian immigrants had now begun to bring over children they had left behind in the Caribbean and this, coupled with the fact that the first generation of children born in this country was also starting to reach adolescence, meant that unprecedented numbers of young Black people were entering the peak age range for offending by the mid-1970s. When the same Committee held a further inquiry specifically into 'The West Indian Community' five years later, witnesses from the Metropolitan Police Service (MPS) had decided that criminality among this group *was* now higher than average (House of Commons Select Committee on Race Relations and Immigration, 1977). This coincided with a 'moral panic' about the involvement of young Black men in street crime (Hall *et al.*, 1978); and in London in particular this group was targeted by the police using laws which dated back to 1824 and allowed officers to arrest anyone *on suspicion* that they were *about to* commit an offence (Demuth, 1979).

1980s

The emerging stereotype of Black people as offenders was then further reinforced when young Black people were involved in the first civil disturbances in deprived areas of mainland Britain for over half a century, first in the St Paul's area of Bristol in 1980 and then in parts of London (most notably Brixton) as well as other inner city neighbourhoods, including Toxteth (Liverpool) in 1981. There was a further recurrence in 1985 centring largely on Tottenham (London) and Handsworth (Birmingham). All of these disturbances were triggered by incidents involving the police; but when Lord Scarman was asked to report on the causes of the 1981 riots he insisted on widening his brief beyond the immediate police-related issues. At their core, he found, were issues of structural disadvantage as well as discrimination; and, although his report included extensive criticism of the police, he repudiated any notion of systematic discrimination (Scarman, 1981).

The riots of the early 1980s triggered major reforms not only of police training but also the regulation and scrutiny of police conduct, as embodied in the Police and Criminal Evidence Act 1984 (PACE). Among other things, this took responsibility for prosecution away from the police by setting up the Crown Prosecution Service (CPS) and it also set up new structures for local police accountability. Section 1 of PACE also gave police officers the power to stop and, as necessary, search any individual on the basis of 'reasonable suspicion' that they were carrying illegal, stolen or prohibited goods; but they had to make a record of any such searches.

Meanwhile, Asian immigration had continued but family reunion was often long delayed, especially in the case of the poorer (Pakistani and Bangladeshi) groups. So the equivalent cohort of young people in these groups would only start to reach the peak age for offending by the mid-1990s. At the end of the 1970s, therefore, these groups continued to be seen as unproblematic in terms of criminal activity; but they too were the targets of racial attacks just like the West Indians before them. This meant that the government began (belatedly) to recognize the problem of racial harassment in the early 1980s in a context which lent itself to a dual form of stereotyping where 'Asians' were indiscriminately cast as victims and Black people as offenders.

1990s to 2010

There was no repetition of Black-led disturbances after 1985. There *were* 'rural riots', though, at the end of the 1980s (Tuck, 1989) followed by further serious outbreaks of civil disorder on poor estates during the 1990s. The best known of these took place in Meadowell (Tyneside) and Blackbird Leys (Oxford) in 1991; and all of them involved mainly young White people.

Despite the major changes within the police following the Scarman Report and the introduction of PACE, the legacy of mistrust between the service and Black people of West Indian origin persisted. In 1997 a new Labour government was elected with a far more explicit commitment than its predecessor to tackling racism and one of its earliest initiatives in this context was to set up a public inquiry into the MPS investigation of the racist murder of a young Black man, Stephen Lawrence, in 1993, The inquiry's remit was to look at why the MPS had consistently failed to ensure the prosecution of his killers; but, under the chairmanship of Lord Justice Macpherson (Macpherson, 1999), it broadened its terms of reference to look also at 'the central problem ... of the lack of trust which exists between the police and the minority ethnic communities'.

Macpherson's report concluded that both the failure of the investigations into Stephen Lawrence's murder[3] and the wider 'problem' it considered were due to '**institutional racism**'. As evidence, it cited in particular '**disproportionality**' in searches under s. 1 of PACE (see earlier in this chapter)—that is, the over-representation of ethnic minorities in the search figures compared with their presence in the population as shown in the Census. It defined 'institutional racism' as:

> the collective failure of an organisation to provide an appropriate and professional service to people because of their colour, culture or ethnic origin. It can be seen or detected in processes, attitudes and behaviour which amount to discrimination through unwitting prejudice,

ignorance, thoughtlessness, and racist stereotyping which disadvantage minority ethnic people. (Macpherson, 1999)

But, although Macpherson claimed that the criminal justice system overall, as well as other institutions were similarly tainted, the term has continued to be applied especially to the police.

The government accepted all Macpherson's recommendations and set up a steering group, including one of the members of the inquiry team and the mother of the murdered boy to oversee their implementation, premised on the notion that this and other measures would reduce 'disproportionality'. It was already funding a major programme of police race relations training; and was soon to update the 1976 legislation in the form of the Race Relations Amendment Act 2000 which, among other things, removed some previous exemptions for the police.

However, two years after the publication of the Macpherson Report there was a recurrence of rioting; but the disturbances this time were in deprived areas of Northern towns (notably Bradford, Burnley, and Oldham) and they largely involved Asians. More specifically, they involved young people of Pakistani origin. They also differed from the riots of the early 1980s in that they were not commonly triggered by conflict with the police, but in some instances by confrontations with groups of young Whites. Just as the dust was settling on these, and the relevant inquiries had reported on their causes and likely policy implications (Ouseley, 2001; Cantle, 2002) further confusion was created for policy makers and media commentators alike by disturbances in Birmingham in 2003 as a result of conflict between young Asian and Black people, just two years before the London bombings of 2005. Not only did these events increasingly call into question the benign stereotype of the law-abiding 'Asian', a new and far more sinister stereotype was already attaching itself to particular sub-groups of Asians. In the context of concerns about 'Islamic' terrorism in general and the shock of discovering that those responsible for the bombings had been born and raised in Britain, the religion question in the 2001 Census made it easy to identify the ethnic groups most 'at risk' as those of Pakistani and Bangladeshi origin, since the Census identified over 90 per cent of Pakistanis and Bangladeshis as Muslims; and these groups accounted for nearly 70 per cent of the Muslim population of England and Wales.

By 2007, new concerns began to reach the national media about crime among the growing numbers of new immigrants from Eastern Europe. A number of chief constables began to raise concerns about the impact on their crime figures of new immigrants and the issues raised by this (see, for example, *Daily Telegraph* 24 September 2007), while sections of the media had begun persistently to run stories about Polish criminals (see *Guardian* 15 March 2008). However, those from Eastern Europe in particular could not readily be identified in the police ethnic monitoring returns since they would be classified as White. And, in any case, these concerns were overshadowed by a growing preoccupation with questions about whether Britain was witnessing the emergence of youth 'gangs' and the extent to which these were predominantly Black (Young *et al.*, 2007).

2010 on

With the change of government in 2010, there might have been less expectation that 'race' issues would be high on the policy agenda. The generation of ethnic statistics was by now commonplace but the fact that these had shown little change over time (see further later in this chapter) would not have encouraged any government to promise to do better—especially one preoccupied with cutting public expenditure.

However, a number of developments made it impossible for the new government to consign these issues to the back burner. Late in 2010, the Equalities and Human Rights Commission (EHRC) issued a warning that it would consider taking legal action against police forces whose searches it deemed to be unduly 'disproportionate' (EHRC, 2010). Yet, less than a year later, Black people were very disproportionately involved in the riots of August 2011 which (see other chapters) were to have a major impact on public opinion in general and government criminal justice policies in particular. Nonetheless, in January 2012, politicians of all hues responded to the widespread publicity generated by the conviction of two of the original suspects for the murder of Stephen Lawrence by declaring their uncompromising opposition to racism; and the media coverage of these murder convictions also revived a discussion of the extent to which the police service was still infected with 'institutional racism', not least in view of the continuing evidence of 'disproportionality' cited in the following section.

Ethnic statistics in a criminal justice context

The development of ethnic statistics

Some of the earliest studies to highlight problems between minorities and the police had called for statistics to be kept which would provide evidence of police bias (Rose *et al.*, 1969). The MPS itself had begun to keep its own ethnic data from at least the 1970s; and these were used to justify its conclusions that by 1977, West Indians had become more involved in crime (see earlier). They also provided material for occasional statistical bulletins by the Home Office during the 1980s, as well as valuable information for a number of research studies (Demuth, 1979; Stevens and Willis, 1979; Willis, 1983). Nonetheless the Scarman Report into the 1981 riots had commented critically on the absence of hard factual information about Black people, crime, and policing.

National ethnic monitoring *was* introduced by the government after the riots, but only for the prison population. However, as we have seen, by the early 1990s, the practice of recording ethnicity had become well established to the extent of including an ethnic question in the Census. This made demands for ethnic monitoring at the point of entry to the criminal justice system less controversial; and an amendment to the Criminal Justice Act in 1991 was interpreted in these terms—even though the Act makes no reference to statistics but simply requires the relevant minister to publish 'information' to assist those administering criminal justice to avoid discrimination. Starting in 1996, all 43 police forces in England and Wales had to record the ethnicity of anyone they:

- searched
- arrested or
- cautioned.

There was, however, no requirement for the police to collect information about victims of crime with the exception of victims of homicides.

The topics were chosen in part because forces were already required to provide statistics on these items to the Home Office;[4] and the crudeness of the ethnic categories was largely because the police were initially required to classify people simply on the basis of what they *looked* like to the officer involved since the police had successfully argued that it would be invidious to ask individuals to self-classify while they were being searched by the police and self-classification was, in any case, not an option in the case of homicides.

Since then, ethnic monitoring in a criminal justice context has continued to proliferate among agencies other than the police and the prison service, though it remains patchy. More recently monitoring has been based on self-classification using the 2001 Census codes, although the results are usually aggregated to four or five broad categories; and the police—in addition to continuing to use their own visual classification system— were also formally required from 2003 to use self-classification.

Trends, patterns, and politics

The first year's monitoring figures from the police were available to the Macpherson Inquiry (see earlier); so they provided quantitative support for its finding that police searches reflected 'institutional racism'. Less attention was paid to the statistics on other items and none at all to the homicide figures—even though all of these were available and they too were 'disproportionate' to some degree, at least in the case of Black people (see Figure 16.1).

Subsequently, despite the Labour government's commitment to tackling 'disproportionality' and the implementation of the recommendations of the Macpherson Inquiry, the over-representation of Black people increased on all of these key indicators; and Asians also now started to be over-represented—albeit 'disproportionality' reduces significantly in searches if age is controlled for and the most recently available figures showed that Asians were actually under-represented on other measures (Figure 16.2).

Patterns of offending also appear to vary slightly by ethnic group. The police figures in Figure 16.3 cover all ages but omit arrests for some less serious crimes which do not fall into the category of 'notifiable offences'—that is, offences which the police have to report to the Home Office (see also Chapter 19). The figures published in relation to the youth justice system (Figure 16.4) use slightly different categories and cover all young people aged 10–17 who have been convicted of *any* offence, including non-notifiable offence. Both show some similarities, though. White people are more likely to be arrested and convicted of public order-type offences (including criminal damage), burglary, and theft, whereas a higher proportion of Black people are arrested and convicted of robbery. Both Black people and Asians are also more likely than White people to be arrested and convicted of drugs offences; but the youth justice figures also consistently show a higher proportion of Asian young people to have been convicted of motoring offences. This category does not have an equivalent in the arrest figures shown in Figure 16.3; but it is including in the 'Other' offences category which accounts for a higher proportion of Asian arrests.

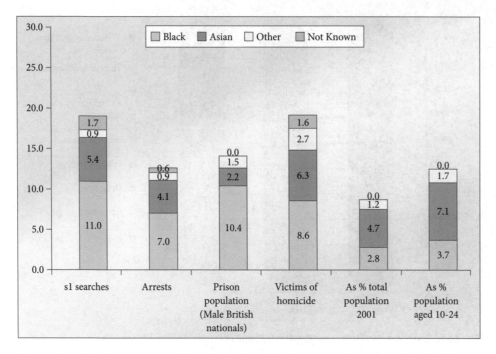

Figure 16.1 Minorities as a proportion of police searches,[5] arrests, prisoners,[6] and homicide victims 1997-8 (compared to their presence in the Census 2001)

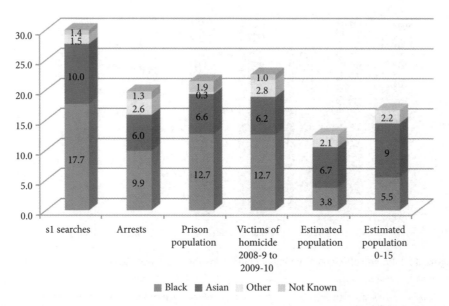

Figure 16.2 Minorities as a proportion of police searches, arrests, prisoners and homicide victims 2009–10 (compared to population estimates for 2009)*

* Both here and in Figure 16.1, the population figures are derived by including the relevant 'mixed' categories into the Black, Asian and Other groups in order to ensure comparability with the criminal justice statistics.
Source: Ministry of Justice 2011, Office for National Statistics 2011a.

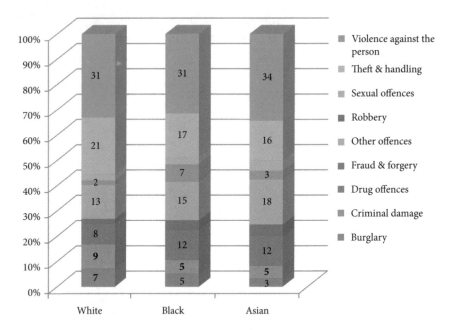

Figure 16.3 Arrests by offence, main ethnic groups 2009–10

Source: Ministry of Justice, 2011.

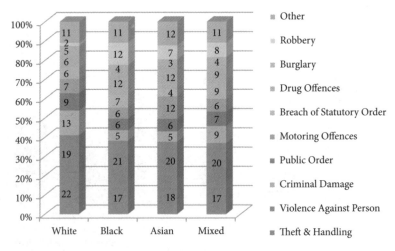

Figure 16.4 Proven offences by young people, main ethnic groups[a] 2009–10

Source: Ministry of Justice, 2011.

[a] The Youth Justice Board publishes figures using a miscellaneous 'Mixed' category which is included in Figure 16.3 since the numbers are slightly larger than the 'Asian' total.

REVIEW QUESTIONS

1 What were the various reasons for introducing ethnic monitoring into the criminal justice system?

2 How do the ethnic categories in the published criminal justice figures relate to the 16 categories in the Census—and do you think aggregating the figures in this way could pose any problems?

3 What might explain the apparent differences between groups in the offences they are caught for?

Interpreting ethnic differences in crime statistics

Interpreting these persistent ethnic differences in the crime statistics poses particular challenges for analysis. Two broad approaches are possible: one is to take the figures at face value; and the other is to take other relevant factors into account before drawing any conclusions about 'ethnic' differences. The first of these is the least satisfactory and involves dangers which hitherto have tended largely to go unrecognized. The second is consistent with the best traditions of intellectual enquiry because it accommodates understandings about the risks of getting involved in crime (and of getting caught) which criminologists have developed internationally over many decades. However, it fails to appreciate the impact of factors which are not specific to any particular group but whose persistent and disproportionate impact on some groups has a collective dimension. Both approaches are now explored in turn, followed by a brief discussion of the group dimension.

Taking the figures at face value

The over-representation of any group in the statistics, if taken at face value, could mean:

(a) that the group is discriminated against at the point of entry into the criminal justice system and then all the way through it to the point of imprisonment; and/or

(b) that the group is more involved in crime than others for reasons which are somehow particular to that group.

The Macpherson Report tended to take the first of these positions in the case of police searches, insisting that the figures must *only* be taken at face value:

> Nobody in the minority ethnic communities believes that the complex arguments which are sometimes used to explain the figures as to stop and search are valid ... [and a]ttempts to justify the disparities through the identification of other factors ... simply exacerbates the climate of distrust. (Macpherson, 1999)

However, the persistence of 'disproportionality' in the available figures, the fact that it is apparent also in the homicide statistics, and the consistent picture of ethnic differences in patterns of crime now make this position seem untenable.

In addition, there is growing evidence of the danger that consistent patterns of over-representation will be used to problematize particular ethnic groups.

Thus, the homicide figures have repeatedly shown that Black victims of homicide are more likely than other groups to be killed by a sharp instrument; and this fact seems to have encouraged the former Prime Minister, Tony Blair, to claim that knife crime was not a general problem but an issue for 'the black community' to resolve (Blair, 2007). The homicide figures for 2007–8 to 2009–10 did indeed show that 53 per cent of Black victims of homicide died as a result of stabbing compared to 34 per cent of White victims of homicide. However, the *number* of White people murdered in this way was more than four times the number of Black people (507 compared to 126).

More routinely the ethnic statistics have repeatedly been used by both the Home Office and the Ministry of Justice since the riots of 2011 to highlight the very significant over-representation of Black people in these events both at the arrest and at the court stage. Thus a Home Office bulletin of October 2011 reported that 40 per cent of those arrested for riot-related offences were White, 39 per cent were Black, and 11 per cent were of 'Mixed' ethnic origins, whereas only 8 per cent were Asian. It then cited Ministry of Justice statistics for those appearing at court for riot-related offences which showed that 'where ethnicity was known' the largest group of defendants were 'from Black or Mixed Black backgrounds', accounting for 46 per cent of the total, followed by White defendants, at 42 per cent (Home Office, 2011).

In fact, ethnicity was not recorded on 13 per cent of defendants appearing before the courts on riot-related charges and this was nearly twice the figure for defendants recorded as Asian. In addition, when the figures were broken down to local authority level, the *total* number of defendants appearing before the courts on riot-related offences at this point was fewer than 100 in most areas. Notwithstanding these limitations and the fact that the Office for National Statistics explicitly cautions that its population estimates for different ethnic groups are unreliable at local authority level (Office for National Statistics, 2011b), the Ministry of Justice further highlighted the extent of Black over-representation in the riots by calculating the number of defendants of different ethnic origins 'per thousand population' in each area. In Wandsworth, for example, on the basis of only 22 Black and 12 White individuals, it estimated that (assuming all of these defendants were convicted) there were 43 Black rioters per thousand population, compared to only one White rioter (Ministry of Justice, 2011).

Taking other factors into account

We have already seen from the Census data in Table 16.2 that different groups vary in terms of some of the known risk factors for involvement in crime; but the statistics are also an important reminder that the very crude categories used in the criminal justice statistics mask many of these differences. Black Africans, for example, have much lower rates of youth unemployment than the Black Caribbean group and the 'mixed' group shares many of the disadvantages of the Black Caribbean group, but its geographic distribution is very different and it is also very much younger. Among the 'Asians' the Indian group is, on average, a very high achieving group in stark contrast to the Pakistanis

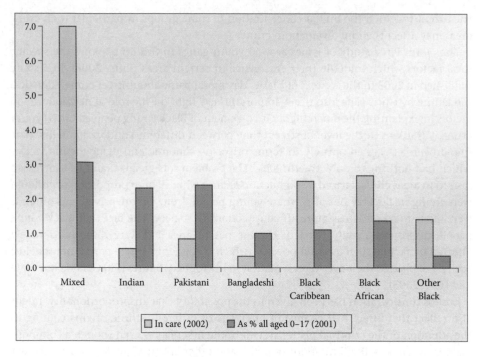

Figure 16.5 Selected minorities as a proportion of children in care compared to their presence in the population aged 0–17

Sources: Department of Health, 2007 and 2001 Census.

and Bangladeshis; yet the difference in their age structure means that these two poorer groups by now outnumber the Indians in the youth population.

Other available statistics further refine the picture which emerges from the Census and these frequently highlight the particular risks for the 'mixed' and Black groups (see Figure 16.5). These groups are, for example, over-represented among young people in care who—as is widely recognized—are especially vulnerable to becoming caught up in the criminal justice system. The situation is reversed, though, in the case of the various Asian groups, even among the poorer Pakistani and Bangladeshi communities.

Two further sets of factors which have been relatively neglected to date but which the research evidence increasingly confirms may be relevant in this context are neighbourhood influences and the chances of offenders of different ethnic origins getting caught.

The American literature has a long tradition of setting crime and criminality in their specific local context which is most closely identified with the Chicago School of the 1920s (see, for example, Park and Burgess, 1925). Ethnographic studies such as Mercer Sullivan's 'Getting Paid' (Sullivan, 1989) show how these local influences may differentially influence patterns of crime among similarly disadvantaged groups of different ethnic origins. While Britain does not have anything like the same levels of residential segregation between ethnic groups, research studies here are also beginning to highlight the extent to which the higher concentration of some groups in particular high crime areas may affect their involvement in crime.

Thus John Pitts' study of issues around youth gangs in Britain explores the specific local factors which underlie their emergence in certain areas (Pitts, 2008). In a study published in 2003 in the context of a latter day moral panic about street crime, statistical modelling by Chris Hale also threw important new light on the role of neighbourhood factors in explaining the much higher involvement of Black young people in this type of crime. Variations in the level of street crime between different London boroughs, Hale found, were explained entirely in terms of socio-economic and demographic factors which had nothing to do with ethnicity. The problem was greatest (and had increased fastest) in areas characterized by population change where a high proportion of children were living in poverty but also where young people from very deprived backgrounds were likely to come across more affluent sections of society. The fact that Black young people disproportionately lived in these types of area *and* were disproportionately affected by factors such as child poverty (which is higher in single parent households) entirely explained their over-representation in the robbery figures (FitzGerald, Stockdale and Hale, 2003).

Far less consideration has been given to the possibility that 'disproportionality' might also reflect the differential chance of offenders of different ethnic origins coming to the attention of the criminal justice system in the first place—even though a common-place in discussing the limitations of police and other criminal justice statistics is that only a minority of the crimes committed may ever come to the attention of the system in the first place. However, the Offending Crime and Justice Survey (OCJS) which the Home Office ran for several years asked respondents whether they had ever committed specific crimes and also whether they had ever come into contact with the criminal justice system. Treating those who said they had never committed any of these crimes as 'non-offenders' the 2003 survey found *no* significant ethnic differences in the extent to which 'non-offenders' had ever been arrested; but, by contrast, Black respondents who admitted to having 'ever' offended were significantly more likely to have been arrested and to have been to court than their White counterparts[7] (Sharp and Budd, 2005).

Importantly, the OCJS shed some light on the possible reasons why Black people (and also those of 'Mixed' origins) who had committed an offence were more likely to be arrested. It identified a number of factors as highly correlated with the likelihood of being arrested. These included the *type* of offence committed—with contact crimes such as robbery more likely to be detected because victims and witnesses can provide descriptions of the offender—and factors such as school exclusion, living in rented accommodation, and associating with people already known to the police. Again, none of these factors is ethnic-specific but they disproportionately affected the OCJS Black sample in particular and to a lesser extent also the 'Mixed' group. (For a fuller discussion, see FitzGerald, 2007.)

The group dimension

An approach which takes other relevant factors into account has far more intellectual legitimacy than basing politically driven conclusions on headline differences between what are, in any case, very crude ethnic categories. However, it runs into a problem which Jefferson hinted at in 1991 when he complained that:

> the currently dominant approach to investigating ethnicity and criminalization ... is a bit like sieving flour with ever finer meshes; eventually there is too little getting through to ... construct a very meaningful account.

That is, dissecting the ethnic differences in the figures according to a list of factors which have nothing to do with ethnicity *except* inasmuch as they disproportionately affect particular ethnic groups risks, obscuring the fact that the resulting experiences may over time contribute to these groups' ongoing sense of a shared identity (as described by Yinger, 1986). It denies the particular configurations in which these factors may cluster around different groups; and it ignores the possibility that the ways in which they interact may have a specific meaning in the light of any group's shared history, especially where this includes memories of conflict with the police.

This collective impact, though, is not simply psychological. For any group, the significant over-representation of its young men in the criminal justice system will inevitably have consequences for its economic prospects and, thereby, on gender and family relations—especially where this situation is perpetuated from one generation to the next.

REVIEW QUESTIONS

1 If you were given a set of figures which showed Black people were significantly over-represented in arrests in a particular police force area compared to their presence in the local population, what information would you want to take into account before deciding whether the force was guilty of widespread discrimination?

2 What criminological theories do you know of which might be relevant to understanding the under- or over-representation of different groups in the criminal justice system?

CONCLUSION

So far this chapter has had nothing to say about the role of discrimination. The findings of the Offending Crime and Justice Survey cited in the previous section have received little publicity, but they were the first to suggest that minorities who have never offended are nowadays no more likely to be picked on by the police than other similar members of the public. In addition, one of the most important studies of ethnic minorities within the criminal justice system was a study of Crown Court sentencing in the West Midlands (Hood, 1992) which took a wide range of relevant factors into account in analysing the reasons for very large differences in the proportion of defendants from ethnic minorities who received custodial sentences. Once these were controlled for, most of the differences disappeared and those which remained were not evenly spread. They mainly affected adult males; and the Crown Court centre from which the majority of the cases were drawn appeared to be completely equitable in its sentencing of defendants, regardless of their ethnic origin. That is, if discrimination *was* occurring, it was confined to a minority of cases in particular areas. Rather than supporting an assumption that *every* decision with regard to a defendant of minority ethnic origin was *de facto* likely to be biased, Hood's findings showed that, once all relevant factors were taken into account, defendants of all ethnic origins were treated equally by the courts in most cases.

Certainly the ethnic monitoring statistics reported in this chapter are far too crude to be of much use (if any) in proving the extent of any discrimination and still less where and how this may occur. For example, the average number of s. 1 searches per constable in a given year is probably less than two per month.[8] Since nearly three-quarters of these are searches of White people and if (following Hood) we assumed that *at least* half of the searches on minorities would be found to be justified, it would be very difficult—if not impossible—to identify any officers who were using their powers in a discriminatory way simply by analysing the statistics.

This is not to say there is room for complacency about discrimination; and safeguards will always be needed. However, it is also worth bearing in mind that officials who are ready to abuse their powers on the basis of prejudice will not do so only in relation to ethnic minorities. In areas where they deal almost exclusively with White people, they might still discriminate, for example, against gypsies, homosexuals or young people whose appearance offends them. So robust *systems* are needed to pick up abuse of *any* sort but the effectiveness of these systems is likely to depend on supervision rather than statistics.

Here again, therefore, we are thrown back on the need to set the experience of ethnic minorities in a wider context. As the previous section argued, it is important to appreciate the particularity of their experience and its implications for the group as a whole; but it is essential here to distinguish between cause and effect. Well-established criminological understandings about the risk factors for involvement in the criminal justice process should be the starting point for appreciating the *reasons* for the over-representation of different groups in the criminal justice system; and these, in turn, may readily be framed in terms of criminological theory.

Criminologists may differ over which theories are most relevant for this purpose; but it cannot seriously be suggested that new theories are needed to understand the particular situation of specific minorities in a peculiarly British context at this precise moment in history. The groups who have most recently been of concern in this context are themselves undergoing constant internal change; and as we have seen, it is likely that the 'Mixed' group and the poorer Asian groups may displace the Black group as the folk devils of the future. It is arguable that these particular groups have been more vulnerable insofar as they are visibly different so a higher proportion may *de facto* be the victims of negative stereotyping and discrimination and this may endure far beyond the immigrant generation. Yet until the riots of 2011 threw the focus back again onto Black people (albeit often now including people of Black 'Mixed' heritage) the spotlight had already started to turn onto the criminal involvement of newer groups of immigrants, some of whom are White (see earlier).

Finally, a failure to contextualize the experiences of those minorities on whom we currently keep statistics in these ways increasingly threatens the interests of the minorities themselves. For we are now witnessing the publication of figures which year after year continue to show the same groups as over-represented among tried and convicted offenders—apparently impervious to all attempts to change this picture; and there is a real danger that this will fuel 'statistical racism'. That is, just as the scientific knowledge of past eras was used to justify racist beliefs in ways which may now appear to us as ludicrous (see Introduction), so the current reliance on ranking groups according to statistical averages could itself—as the former Prime Minister's comments on knife crime demonstrated—lend a cloak of respectability to generalized statements about whole groups.

QUESTIONS FOR DISCUSSION

1 What are the reasons why different governments might want to collect information on offending by different ethnic groups?

2 What is the likely impact on government policy and on public perceptions if, over many years, ethnic statistics appear to show that particular ethnic groups consistently have higher than average levels of offending?

3 What contribution should criminology make to understanding the reasons for apparent ethnic differences in offending and the policy implications of these?

GUIDE TO FURTHER READING

For differing perspectives on these issues:

a) in Britain

Webster C. (2008) *Understanding Race and Crime*. Maidenhead. Open University Press.

Bowling B. and Phillips C. (2002) *Racism, Crime and Justice*. Harlow. Longman.

b) internationally

Tonry M. (ed) (1997) *Ethnicity, Crime and Immigration: Comparative and Cross-national Perspectives*. Chicago. University of Chicago Press.

Marshall I.H. (1997) *Minorities, Migrants and Crime: Diversity and Similarity across Europe and the United States*. London. Sage.

WEB LINKS

http://tandf.co.uk/journals/routledge/01419870.html
'Ethnic and Racial Studies', the main British journal devoted to these issues, can be accessed direct via this link or through subscribing libraries

http://www.justice.gov.uk/
The Ministry of Justice now publishes the 's. 95' statistics ('Statistics on Race and the Criminal Justice System') which were originally published by the Home Office, as well as regular statistical series regarding offenders, including the 'Youth Justice Statistics cited in this chapter. The Ministry of Justice report on those involved in the riots of 2011 can be found at http://www.justice.gov.uk/statistics/criminal-justice/public-disorder-august-11/public-disorder-august-11-editions.

http://www.dh.gov.uk/en/Publicationsandstatistics/Statistics/StatisticalWorkAreas/Statisticalsocialcare/DH_4015858 is the source for the Department of Health figures cited for looked after children.
http://www.dfes.gov.uk/rsgateway/DB/SFR/s000759/CrosstabsforSFR.xls is the Department for Education source for data on school attainment.

See http://www.number-10.gov.uk/output/Page11472.asp
for Tony Blair's speech on Black involvement in knife crime.

REFERENCES

Brown, C. (1984) *Black and White Britain*. London: PSI.

Cantle, T. (2002) *Community Cohesion: A Report of the Independent Review Team*. London: Home Office.

Clegg, M. and Kirwan, S. (2006) *Police Service Strength England and Wales* Home Office Statistical Bulletin 13/06. London: Home Office.

Daily Telegraph (24 September 2007) *Foreigners 'commit fifth of crime in London'*.

Demuth, C. (1979) *'Sus': a Report on the Vagrancy Act 1824*. London: Runnymede Trust.

Equalities and Human Rights Commission (2010) *Stop and think: A critical review of the use of stop and search powers in England and Wales*. London.

FitzGerald, M., Stockdale, J., and Hale, C. (2003) *Young People and Street Crime*. London: Youth Justice Board.

FitzGerald, M. (2007) *Supplementary memorandum submitted by Dr Marian FitzGerald, Specialist Adviser to the Committee* in Young Black People and the Criminal Justice System, Second Report of Session 2006–7: Volume II Oral and Written Evidence. HC 181-II. London: The Stationery Office.

Gould S.J. (1981) *The Mismeasure of Man*. London: W.W. Norton and Company.

Guardian (15 March 2008) 'Polish federation accuses Daily Mail of defamation'.

Hall, S., Crichter, C., Jefferson, T., Clarke, J., and Roberts, B. (1978) *Policing the Crisis*. London: Macmillan.

Home Office (1998) Statistics on Race and the Criminal Justice System: A Home Office publication under section 95 of the Criminal Justice Act 1991. London: Home Office.

Home Office (2011) *An Overview of Recorded Crimes and Arrests Resulting from Disorder Events in August 2011*. London: Home Office.

Hood, R. (1992) *Race and Sentencing*. Oxford: Oxford University Press.

House of Commons Select Committee on Race Relations and Immigration (1972) *Police Immigrant Relations*. London: HMSO.

House of Commons Select Committee on Race Relations and Immigration (1977) *The West Indian Community*. London: HMSO.

House of Commons Select Committee on Race Relations and Immigration (1981) *Racial Disadvantage*. London: HMSO.

Humphrey, D. (1972) *Police Power and Black People*. London: Panther Books.

Hunte, J. (1966) *NiggerHunting in England*. London: West Indian Standing Conference.

Jansson, K. (2006) *Black and Minority Ethnic groups' experiences and perceptions of crime, racially motivated crime and the police: findings from the 2004/05 British Crime Survey*. Home Office Online Report 25/06.

Jefferson, T. (1991) 'Discrimination, Disadvantage and Police Work' in Cashmore, E. and McLaughlin, E. (eds) *Out of Order? Policing and Black People*. London: Routledge.

Jones, A. (1996) *Making Monitoring Work: A Handbook for Racial Equality*. Centre for Research in Ethnic Relations, University of Warwick.

Katznelson, I. (1973) *Black Men, White Cities*. London: Institute of Race Relations/Oxford University Press.

Layton-Henry, Z. (1992) *The Politics of Immigration*. Oxford: Blackwell.

Macpherson, W. (1999) *The Stephen Lawrence Inquiry*. London: The Stationery Office.

McEwen, M. (1991) *Housing, Race and Law; the British Experience*. London: Routledge.

Modood, T., Berthoud, R., Lakey, J., Nazroo, J., Smith, P., Virdee, S., and Beishon, S. (1997) *Ethnic Minorities in Britain: Diversity and Disadvantage; The Fourth National Survey of Ethnic Minorities*. London: PSI.

Office for National Statistics (2011a) *Annual Abstract of Statistics*, Chapter 15. http://www.ons.gov.uk/ons/rel/ctu/annual-abstract-of-statistics/quarter-3-2011/art-quarter-3.html

Office for National Statistics (2011b) *Population Estimates by Ethnic Group: Important Note on Reliability of Estimates for Subnational Areas*. June 2011. London: ONS.

Ouseley, H. (2001) *Community Pride Not Prejudice: Making Diversity Work in Bradford*. Bradford: Bradford Vision.

Park, R. and Burgess, E. (eds) (1925) *The City*. Chicago: Chicago University Press.

Pitts, J. (2008) *Reluctant Gangsters: the Changing Shape of Youth Crime*. Cullompton: Willan Publishing.

Rose, E.J.B., Deakin, N., Abrams, M., Jackson, V., Peston, M., Vanags, A.H., Cohen, B., Gaitskell, J., and Ward, P. (1969) *Colour and Citizenship*. Oxford: Institute of Race Relations/Oxford University Press.

Scarman (1981) *The Brixton Disorders: Report on an Inquiry by the Rt. Hon. Lord Justice Scarman OBE*. London: HMSO.

Sharp, C. and Budd, T. (2005) *Minority ethnic groups and crime: findings from the Offending, Crime and Justice Survey 2003*. Home Office Online Report 33/05.

Shaw, C. (1988) *Latest Estimates of the Ethnic Minority Populations*. Population Trends No 51. Spring 1988. London: Office of Population Censuses and Surveys.

Sivanandan, A. (1985) 'RAT and the degradation of the black struggle', *Race and Class XXVI:4*.

Smith, D. (1974) *The Facts of Racial Disadvantage*. London: PSI.

Stevens, P. and Willis, C. (1979) *Race Crime and Arrests*. Home Office Research Study 58. London: Home Office.

Sullivan, M. (1989) *'Getting Paid': Youth Crime and Work in the Inner City*. Ithaca: Cornell University Press.

Tuck, M. (1989) *Drinking and Disorder: A Study of Non-Metropolitan Violence*. Home Office Research Study 108. London: Home Office.

Walvin, J. (1984) *Passage to Britain*. London: Penguin.

Willis, C. (1983) *The Use, Effectiveness and Impact of Police Stop and Search Powers*. RPUP 15. London: Home Office.

Yinger, M. (1986) 'Intersecting Strands' in Rex, J. and Mason, D. (eds) *Theories of Race and Ethnic Relations*. Cambridge: Cambridge University Press.

Young, K. and Connelly, N. (1981) *Policy and Practice in the Multi-Racial City*. London: PSI.

NOTES

1. The 'New' Commonwealth comprised countries where the majority of citizens were non-White, as opposed to 'Old' Commonwealth countries such as Canada, Australia, and New Zealand, many of whose citizens were descended from people who had emigrated from Britain in the first place.

2. A major study in the mid-1970s was particularly influential in this regard (Smith, 1974) and the issues were again taken up by the House of Commons Home Affairs Committee in its report on 'Racial Disadvantage' in 1981.

3. The second police investigation had, in fact, identified the suspects, but the Crown Prosecution Service decided not to charge them.

4. Following a recommendation in the Macpherson Report, the government eventually required the police from 2005 to start keeping a record each time they stopped someone and asked them to account for their movements, with the additional requirement that they would record the person's ethnicity using self-classification. In 2011, the Coalition government dropped this requirement in the name of reducing police bureaucracy.

5. The police have several different powers under which they can search members of the public. Figures given here are for the most common searches which are conducted under s. 1 of the 1984 Police and Criminal Evidence Act. This requires an officer to have 'reasonable grounds for suspicion' that anyone they search is carrying illegal, prohibited or stolen goods (and, as of 2003, items for committing criminal damage).

6. Figures are given for male prisoners with British nationality only, since women form only a very small proportion of all prisoners and they tend to be sentenced for different types of offence from men. Also, the inclusion of foreign prisoners can seriously distort inter-ethnic comparisons.

7. Although the proportion is also higher for the 'Mixed' group , the difference is not statistically significant (possibly due to small numbers) whereas it is noticeable that 'Asians' who say they have offended are significantly less likely to have come to the attention of the system.

8. In 2006 there were 109, 228 police constables (Clegg and Kirwan, 2006) and 878,153 recorded s. 1 searches (Ministry of Justice, 2007). Even if only half of those constables were on active duty they would average 16 searches per year.

17 Young people and crime

Derek Kirton

INTRODUCTION

There are many reasons for examining the relationship between young people and crime. One of the more obvious is that levels of involvement in criminal activity, whether judged by official statistics or self-report studies, are at their highest in the teenage years. Crime statistics for England and Wales (Ministry of Justice, 2012) show that for males the peak age range for committing the most serious (indictable) offences is 18–20 years closely followed by 15–17. Offending by females is also most frequent in these two age groups, but with a slightly higher rate in the 15–17 years range. A similar pattern emerges from self-report studies which consider a wider range of offences, including minor ones. The 2006 Offending, Crime and Justice Survey found that the peak ages for offending were between 14 and 17 for males and between 12 and 17 for females (Roe and Ashe, 2008). A second reason is that childhood and youth are commonly seen as times when patterns for later life are being set. Effective intervention, or the lack of it, may decide whether young offenders become 'hardened criminals' or upright citizens.

This chapter focuses on analysing both youth crime and responses to it. The latter are concentrated largely on the youth justice system, but may also involve initiatives relating to parenting, schooling, problem drug and alcohol use or social exclusion through promoting education, employment or positive activities. In the main body of the chapter, we will discuss the key principles around which youth justice has evolved and how the balance between them has changed over time. This will be followed by examination of some of the main theories and models that have been put forward to explain youth crime, including patterns linked to social divisions based on class, ethnicity and gender. Attention will also be given to recent 'moral panics' such as young people's use of weapons, gang activity and involvement in the 2011 riots. Finally, a review of contemporary youth justice policy and debate regarding its future direction is provided. First, however, the context will be set with an overview of some key concepts and debates relating to young people and crime.

BACKGROUND

In considering young people's involvement in crime and their experiences of the criminal justice system, it is important to acknowledge that they share many similarities with adult offenders. For example, in both instances there are debates regarding the appropriate balance between punishment, rehabilitation and deterrence and that between the rights and responsibilities (including to victims) of offenders. Similarly, both may be subject to pre court disposals and a range of sentencing options from fines and discharges to custody. Within the field of criminology, the tensions between crime as an act of free will or as a product of other factors (psychological, sociological, biological) apply to young and adult offenders alike. It should be noted here that 'young' has different meanings depending on context. Within the criminal justice system in England and Wales, those aged between ten and 17 are dealt with through a distinct youth justice system with its own courts, custodial institutions, professional personnel and in many cases, sentences. Young adulthood is also marked through separate custodial facilities, with Young Offender Institutions catering for those between the ages of 15 and 21. In research, 'young' has sometimes been taken up to the age of 25 or even 30, in order to explore further the process of 'growing out of crime'.

Despite the similarities, however, there are important differences between the domains of young and 'adult' offenders, differences that in broad terms are reflective of perspectives on childhood and youth as life stages. Crucially, they are seen as periods of evolving understanding and morality, rendering children and young people less responsible than adults for their actions. This is generally embodied within criminal justice systems in four main ways. First, there is a minimum age of criminal responsibility (currently ten in England, Wales and Northern Ireland and effectively 12 in Scotland as this is the minimum age of prosecution), below which the child cannot legally commit a crime. The rationale for this is that they lack the *mens rea* (or 'guilty mind') required. Second, even above the age of criminal responsibility, children and young people tend to be treated differently from adult offenders, through separate courts (or alternatives to courts) and specific sentencing options. A third feature is that of parental responsibility, either directly for their children's behaviour or failure to control their offspring. Finally, the State is usually regarded as having responsibilities, to address the behaviour of young people but also to protect their rights as children and ensure their 'welfare'. However, these seemingly straightforward features of youth justice systems hide great complexity and often fierce controversy. One example of this is that the age of criminal responsibility has varied significantly over time and between countries—ranging in one fairly recent international survey from six to 18 years of age (Hazel, 2008).

As will be seen later in this chapter, understandings of, and responses to, youth crime were transformed during the nineteenth century and much of the twentieth. A growing sense of children's 'innocence' was reflected in their separation from adult offenders and other corrupting influences. Links were increasingly drawn between childhood deprivation and later involvement in crime. This gave rise to what is generally referred to as a welfare model for dealing with youth crime, in which offending is taken to be a symptom of psychological or social deprivation. For proponents of this model, the response rests with providing expert-led treatment to meet the child's needs and so reduce offending. The high spot of the welfare model occurred in the late 1960s but thereafter, its core assumptions were largely rejected and replaced by what became known as the justice model. The latter places the offence itself centrally, regarding it as an act of free will, with the offender to be punished in line with the seriousness of the crime.

The shift from welfare to justice highlighted a crucial aspect of responses to youth crime, namely that intervention can sometimes be seen as counter-productive. This may occur through the effects of labelling young people as criminals (see Chapter 4) but also because any reoffending tends to provoke more severe ('high tariff') sentences. Interventions for minor offences or even 'risk' of offending are often characterized as net-widening, to describe the way they draw young people into the youth justice system, perhaps unnecessarily and with negative consequences, accelerating pathways towards custody and potentially deepening involvement in offending. For young offenders, attempts to avoid the effects of net-widening are underpinned by the notion that they generally 'grow out of crime' and that diversion from the youth justice system is more effective. The strategy of diversion describes efforts to minimize young offenders' involvement with the formal youth justice system, and to seek the 'least restrictive alternative'.

While debates on welfare, justice, diversion and net-widening focus on the perceived effectiveness of particular interventions, some analysts have argued that the youth justice system is driven by other considerations, notably concern with management of the system and its 'value for money'. The concept of corporatism was developed by Pratt (1989). Its main elements are those of centralization, government intervention and cooperation of agencies and professionals working towards common goals. This can also be seen to fit well with the rise of an 'audit culture' focusing on targets and performance measurement, and in turn with the dominance of 'risk management' in the criminal justice system, to which we return later.

The Development of Youth Justice in England and Wales

A specific focus on young offenders is generally traced to the early nineteenth century when organizations emerged to highlight offending by the young as a social problem and campaign for reform (Muncie, 2009). At the heart of their work was a plea to move away from harsh, generally physical punishment towards more subtle means. A growing sense that children and young people could be moulded heightened awareness of the potential for both rehabilitation and corruption.

The rise and fall of the welfare model

During the nineteenth century, there was increasing separation of young and adult offenders through the establishment of juvenile prisons and the Reformatory and Industrial Schools of the 1850s, which emphasized strict discipline and training for modest but respectable trades, but also sought to offer children a more caring environment. Such developments can, in turn, be seen as part of a wider movement to regulate childhood through protective legislation, removal from the streets, compulsory schooling and organized leisure (Hendrick, 1994), accompanied by increasing powers of surveillance and intervention in relation to families (Donzelot, 1980).

In line with ideas of childhood as a period of 'natural innocence', stronger links were drawn between deprivation and involvement or risk of offending. Establishment of juvenile courts and separate custodial institutions (known as 'Borstals') under the Children Act 1908 marked a clearer separation from adult criminal justice, while the Children and Young Persons (CYP) Act 1933 highlighted the need to protect children from bad company, moral danger and neglect and strengthened the legal powers to remove children from their families.

These trends continued after 1945, as offending came to be explained more in psychological and sociological terms. The new orthodoxy that youthful offending had to be understood and addressed in the context of child welfare was enshrined in the CYP Acts of 1963 and 1969, with a raising of the age of criminal responsibility from eight to ten and then to 14 and a significant transfer of responsibility for young offenders from the criminal justice system to local authorities.

In hindsight, the CYP Act 1969 can be seen as the high point of the welfare model. It quickly came under attack from the emerging 'new right' who blamed 'permissiveness' for a rising crime rate (Hall *et al.*, 1978) and portrayed the welfare model as 'soft on crime'. The incoming Conservative government declined to implement the new age of criminal responsibility, leaving it at ten. While criticism from the political right was predictable, the welfare model also came under fire from the left, arguing that whatever the intentions behind the model, its effects were often harsh (Thorpe *et al.*, 1980). For example, children could be taken into care until aged 18, effectively creating indeterminate sentences. Through its various welfare-based interventions, the Act was also seen as net-widening, making those committing relatively minor offences or even adjudged 'at risk' of offending more vulnerable to surveillance and harsher sentencing. These pressures led to the development of the justice model (see earlier) which attempted to shift focus from the backgrounds of offenders to their behaviour (Morris *et al.*, 1980).

Diversion in the 1980s: a quiet revolution

The 1980s present something of a paradox in relation to youth justice, with a Conservative government committed to taking a tough stance on crime presiding over a fall in youth custody of over 80 per cent in the decade from 1981 to 1991 (Smith, 2007). As Pitts (2001) argues, this was not a reflection of any corresponding fall in youth crime, but rather, the government's attempt to reconcile 'law and order' policies with a desire to contain public expenditure. In broad terms, the answer was to be found under the slogan 'punishment in the community', and within the new community programmes, youth justice workers were able to develop a strategy of 'diversion', emphasizing responsibility on the part of offenders, including making reparation to victims or to the wider community (Bottoms *et al.*,1990).

As noted earlier, diversion rested on the notion that as most young people 'grow out of crime' and that interventions are often counter-productive, the 'least restrictive alternative' should always be pursued. Despite high youth unemployment, withdrawal of welfare benefits and numerous inner city disturbances in the 1980s, offending by young people generated few moral panics. It was thus that the 'quiet consensus' (Haines and Drakeford, 1998: 32) developed in support of the diversionary strategy and its principles were enshrined in the Criminal Justice Act 1991. This stressed custody as a last resort and introduced measures to reduce its use, while community sentences were promoted as 'tough alternatives' and the responsibilities of parents for their children were strengthened.

The punitive turn

Repeating in many respects the earlier fate of welfarism in the 1970s, the diversionary philosophy of the Criminal Justice Act 1991 was soon undermined due to mounting opposition and a series of moral panics. Pitts (2001: 11) suggests there was a growing realization both that many young people were not 'growing out of crime' and that some youth crime was 'serious'. Combined with increased awareness of victimization, especially in economically deprived areas, this called into question the relatively 'hands off' approach embodied in the Act. Equally influential, however, was a string of moral panics. Debate on an emerging 'underclass' in Britain (Murray, 1990) was augmented by a series of folk devils, both individual ('rat boy' and 'safari boy') and collective (the 'joyrider', 'bail bandit' and 'persistent young offender') (Hagell and Newburn, 1994). The common thread, however, was of growing lawlessness and dangerous young criminals who had become 'untouchable'. Into this volatile situation came the tragic murder of toddler James Bulger by two boys barely above the age of criminal responsibility. Responding to John Major's call to 'condemn a little more and understand a little less' (*The Mail on Sunday* 21 February 1993), the government introduced a wide-ranging set of 'get tough' measures. The use of cautions was restricted, bail conditions tightened and custody was both extended (including to younger children) and toughened. This punitive turn went hand in hand with what Pitts (2001) has referred to as 'dejuvenilization'; that is, eroding the principle of treating children and young people separately from adults. Electronic tagging was extended to those under 16, and the Crime (Sentences) Act 1997 allowed young offenders to be publicly named.

New Labour—'tough on crime and tough on the causes of crime'?

Tony Blair's famous soundbite indicated that New Labour would attempt to match the Conservatives in terms of 'toughness' but also outflank them with a wider approach to preventing crime. Once in government, New Labour launched an ambitious new programme, with the provisions contained in the Crime and Disorder Act 1998 and subsequent legislation. Key measures included the removal of *doli incapax* (literally 'incapable of evil'), the requirement to establish that those under 14 years of age understood the consequences of their actions; a new Detention and Training Order (DTO), allowing sentences to be split between custody and the community; and a new 'Intensive Supervision and Surveillance Programme' in the community. With the introduction of the youth rehabilitation order in 2009, (intensive) supervision and surveillance became one of the many conditions that could be attached to the order. Others include requirements regarding residence, curfews, exclusions, prescribed and proscribed activities, drug testing and/or treatment, mental health treatment, education and unpaid work.

The New Labour government was also keen to promote the use of restorative approaches within youth justice, with the offender through word, deed or by other means making direct restoration to the victim (or community) for the offence. Restorative justice was enshrined in measures such as the reparation order and the referral order (under the Youth Justice and Criminal Evidence Act 1999). The latter entailed first-time offenders being referred to a Youth Offender Panel (comprising two local community volunteers and one representative from a Youth Offending Team) whose main focus would be to consider how restoration could be made.

While measures to combat poverty and social exclusion and initiatives such as Sure Start were seen as contributing to crime reduction, being 'tough on the causes of crime' focused above all on preventing it through early intervention, including within youth justice. Such intervention, however, entailed controversial extension of legal powers. Drawing on principles of 'zero tolerance', young people could be made the subject of anti-social behaviour orders (ASBOs) or subject to curfews. Another key element in the strategy of early intervention lay in addressing perceived deficiencies of parenting, including the introduction of the parenting order, obliging parents of young offenders to attend classes to improve their skills (Drakeford and McCarthy, 2000).

New Labour's 'tough' stance was reflected in a steady rise in custodial sentences, with figures peaking in 2003 and thereafter remaining fairly stable until a sharp decline from 2008 onwards (Ministry of Justice, 2012). The decline marked a significant policy shift, away from a concern with ensuring 'consequences' by 'bringing offenders to justice' towards reducing the number of 'first time entrants' into the youth justice system. However, it remains too early to judge whether this represents a more enduring reversal of the punitive turn. For example, Bateman (2011) notes that the number of young people being returned to court for breaches of orders remains very high and contributes significantly to the population of those in custody. Reflecting on the period of New Labour government(s), Goldson (2010) has argued persuasively that policy was shaped much less by reason and evidence than the power of 'punitive emotion'. He suggests that policy ran counter to key consistent and powerful messages flowing from research, namely that youth offending is relatively 'normal'; youth crime trends are relatively stable and diversion and minimum intervention are key.

Corporatism and managerialism: an alternative explanation?

Thus far, this historical review has been couched largely in terms of competing principles or philosophies relating to youth crime—welfare and justice, diversion and intervention. However, some writers argue that better explanations can be found by examining the organization and management of youth justice services. 'Corporatism' (described earlier), with its emphases on management, performance and cost-effectiveness, became more prominent during the 1980s and in the 1990s the Audit Commission produced a series of influential reports on youth justice (1996; 1998). These reports highlighted organizational inefficiencies such as delays in taking offenders to court, but also promoted the idea of potential long-term savings from effective early interventions. For its critics (Smith, 2007), corporatism is seen as a repressive force, using State power to increase surveillance and control over those who deliver and receive services. For supporters, however, it offers potential for 'joined up' responses, with agencies working together towards the common goal of reducing offending. This view was readily apparent in the Labour government's establishment of a Youth Justice Board and local Youth Offending Teams, with representation from police, probation, child social care, education and health services. Auditing bodies have remained influential policy commentators, with the National Audit Office (2010) recently highlighting the economic cost of youth crime (which it estimates at between £8.5 and £11 billion annually), and continuing to advocate prevention on grounds of cost-saving and efficacy.

REVIEW QUESTIONS

1 How would you explain the declining influence of 'welfarism' in youth justice?

2 Critically evaluate the record of New Labour governments in dealing with youth crime.

3 Assess the strengths and limitations of corporatist approaches to understanding youth justice.

Understanding Youth Crime

As noted earlier, explanations advanced for youth crime are similar in many ways to those within criminology more generally (see Chapter 4), but are also significantly influenced by perspectives on childhood and youth as life stages, including questions relating to 'growing out of crime'. An interesting recent example has come from neuroscientific evidence suggesting that young people's brains may not mature in respect of decision-making and behavioural control until at least the age of 20 (Walsh, 2011). However, Walsh rightly contends that even if accepted, this evidence can lead policy in very different directions, for example towards diversionary measures or early intervention programmes and even neurobiological treatments for those 'at risk'. It is not our intention here to offer a review of theoretical explanations (for discussion see, for example Muncie, 2009), but rather, to focus on the relationship between explanations and policy and practice in youth justice. Earlier, it was seen how ideas about deprivation influenced the rise of the welfare model and how interactionist accounts of 'labelling' effects and stigma (Becker, 1963) helped to underpin diversion strategies. Similarly, the influences of realist perspectives can be seen from the 1980s onwards. For 'right realism' this meant emphasizing personal responsibility and moral culpability while for 'left realism', a focus on social causation had to be tempered by 'taking crime seriously'. In both instances, a stronger focus on victims supported the growing interest in restorative justice.

Risk factors: the new orthodoxy

In recent times, the dominant paradigm for understanding and addressing youth crime has been provided by the concept of risk factors (Farrington, 1996). During a period of some pessimism regarding youth crime, the risk factor approach appeared to point a way forward, identifying a range of factors associated with youth crime, which might then be targeted for intervention, singly or in combination. Farrington's research was based on a longitudinal study, following a group of 411 working-class boys from the age of eight in 1961 through to 32. Its obvious strength was the potential to track offending careers over many years and to identify factors associated with their progression. Farrington (1996) highlights the following major risk factors:

- low income and poor housing;
- living in 'deteriorated' inner city areas;
- high degree of impulsiveness and hyperactivity;
- low intelligence and low school attainment;
- poor parental supervision and harsh and erratic discipline;
- parental conflict and broken families;

to which might be added:

- the influence of delinquent friends/gang membership;
- use of drugs or alcohol (Smith and Mcvie, 2003).

The risk factors approach has been taken up by the Youth Justice Board and is reflected in risk assessment tools such as ASSET which scores a list of factors to gauge the likelihood of reoffending. For New Labour, while the risk factors noted could readily be linked to wider initiatives in respect of social exclusion and education, arguably the most influential to be taken up was the notion of parenting. Not only were family stability and parental supervision directly important in lowering the risk of offending, but (poor) parents could also act as 'shock absorbers', instilling self-control in their children regardless of material deprivation or social pressures (Smith, 2007). In recent times, what is now referred to as the risk factor prevention paradigm (RFPP) has been further refined by calibrating responses more precisely to risk scores as shown by ASSET. Yet the RFPP has been widely criticized on theoretical and methodological grounds and for its impact on young offenders.

In the theoretical domain, it has been argued that the RFPP lacks social and political context and space for personal agency (Haines and Case, 2008; O'Mahony, 2009). For example, risk factors identifiable from the 1960s and 1970s may be less applicable to today's society, with its different ethnic make-up, family structures, gender relations and lifestyles. Moreover, they cannot be assumed to work in a similar fashion irrespective of social context, including neighbourhood effects (Pitts, 2000). It may also be argued that in practice, the RFPP allows the locus of 'responsibility' to rest firmly with young people and their families. Offending behaviour has been explained in terms of the way young people 'think' and their lack of self-control rather than as a product of the situations in which they find themselves. Such ultimately individualistic (or at most, familial) perspectives have recently been reiterated in research from Wikstrom *et al.* (2012) which emphasized the importance of 'morals' in understanding youthful offending and the Riots Communities and Victims Panel (RCVP) (2012) which reprises the theme of 'character' several times in its analysis of the 2011 riots (see later).

Methodologically, the RFPP has been criticized for its often poorly defined and measured (risk factor) variables, its assumption that research participants can be neatly divided into offenders and non-offenders and as offering an 'atheoretical mishmash of ideas which inevitably fails to provide a meaningful and compelling explanation of the origins of juvenile offending' (O'Mahony, 2009: 108). In this context, qualitative research can be useful for exploring contingencies and the part played by 'life events' and identities in offending careers (Murray, 2009; Bottrell *et al.*, 2010).

In relation to policy and practice, there are concerns that the RFPP may be stigmatizing, labelling those who fall into the risk categories (including those deriving from social disadvantage) as 'potential offenders' and often targeting them for intervention. Evidence from a large longitudinal study has shown both that prediction is extremely difficult and that those drawn into the youth justice system were less likely to desist from offending than those who faced minimal or no intervention (McAra and Mcvie, 2010).

Profiling youth crime: lessons from self-report surveys

In recent years, knowledge of youth crime has been boosted by a series of self-report studies, typically sampling around 5,000 young people of varying ages between ten and 25 or even 30 (see, for example, Flood-Page *et al.*, 2000; Roe and Ashe, 2008). Collectively, these self-report studies provide a useful complement and counterweight to official statistics, bearing in mind that most 'crime' goes undetected. These studies show a fairly consistent pattern over recent years and tend to confirm a number of key facets of youthful offending. One is that it is by no means uncommon, with 22 per cent of respondents in Roe and Ashe's (2008) survey reporting at least one offence in the previous year. A second is that a relatively small number of young people account for a significant proportion of crime. In Wilson *et al.*'s (2006) study, 7 per cent of respondents reported responsibility for 83 per cent of offences. Third, only a minority of offenders are 'caught', with around 10 per cent of self-confessed offenders reporting being arrested during the past year and only 5 per cent being taken to court (Wilson *et al.*, 2006). Another key finding is that the vast majority of those involved in youthful offending do indeed 'grow out of crime'. The surveys confirm the importance of the risk factors cited above, grouping them into domains such as family, schooling, community and individual/personal, but often giving them different weight. This highlights the fact that statistical association does not demonstrate causality, and complex questions remain about how risk factors interact. It should also be noted that self-report studies raise important methodological issues, including sampling, response rates and perhaps above all, reliability, and data from them must be interpreted with caution (Coleman and Moynihan, 1996).

Young people as victims: a neglected story?

When young people and crime hit the headlines it is usually when 'they' (young people) are perceived as a threat to 'us' (respectable, 'adult' society). Young people (aged 10–15) have only recently been included in the Crime Survey for England and Wales (known as the British Crime Survey until 2012) and findings there have confirmed earlier research (Anderson *et al.*, 1994; Hartless *et al.*, 1995) showing that they face higher levels of victimization than adults and are less likely to report incidents to the police (Millard and Flatley, 2010). These higher rates apply to 'visible' crimes, such as theft or violence as well as abuse within the family. Surveys have also shown how widespread 'fear of crime' is by no means restricted to adults (Young NCB, 2010).

Another important finding to emerge is that levels of victimization are higher among those who are involved in offending or excluded from school (Smith and McVie, 2003). The reasons for this link are complex and may include participation in risky activities, and the higher incidences of crime and victimization found in particular areas, or among peer groups (Smith and Ecob, 2007). While offending can lead to victimization both directly (for example, if an initial victim retaliates) or indirectly (for example, becoming a victim whilst placed in custody), it is also the case that many offenders have themselves previously been victims (Day *et al.*, 2008).

REVIEW QUESTIONS

1 Assess the strengths and weaknesses of the 'risk factors prevention paradigm'.

2 How useful are self-report studies in understanding youth crime?

3 Why have young people's experiences as victims of crime received so little attention?

Young people, Crime, and Social Divisions

In discussing youth crime, it is important to remember that the term 'youth' brings together those with widely differing backgrounds and circumstances, not least arising from major social divisions, such as those of class, ethnicity and gender.

Class

There is a long-established pattern of over-representation in official crime statistics of those from working class backgrounds. Debate, however, has often raged as to whether this reflects levels of participation in crime or is generated by discriminatory policing and processes within the criminal justice system (Muncie, 2009). Findings from self-report studies suggest that both factors are present to a degree. The importance of socio-economic deprivation as a risk factor has already been noted and while self-report studies show a rising class gradient from Social Class I to V, this is less steep than that found in recorded crime statistics (Flood-Page et al., 2000; Smith and McVie, 2003). Explaining 'over-representation' is arguably as difficult and controversial as gauging its extent. Conceptualizations of class are varied and have their own complex relationships with factors such as education, unemployment, drug use and neighbourhood. Additionally, they are open to cultural/behavioural and structural interpretations which provide very different explanations for involvement in crime. White and Cunneen (2006) argue that class continues to be important in understanding youth crime, whether in terms of the impact of marginalization in a globalized economy or the contribution of street culture to identities when those rooted in work and consumption are denied.

'Race' and ethnicity

Debate on minority ethnic 'over-representation' has focused particularly on young black people and those of mixed race, whose presence in the youth justice system is roughly twice that in the population (Ministry of Justice, 2012). Findings from self-report studies have produced mixed evidence, with some studies reporting higher levels of offending than among their white peers, while in others rates have been similar or lower (Flood-Page et al., 2000; Armstrong et al., 2005). There is, however, evidence from these surveys that young black people committing offences are more likely to be arrested, whether because of the types of crime involved, use of public space, greater surveillance or discriminatory policing.

Over-representation has also given rise to claims of discrimination within the various stages of the criminal justice system. In a very detailed examination, Feilzer and Hood (2004) concluded that although there was no pervasive discrimination in the youth justice system, there were aspects and processes that had discriminatory effects. These included use of pre-court disposals and unconditional bail, referral to Crown Court, and longer custodial sentences. More recently, May et al.'s (2010) study of policing and subsequent progression through the youth justice system found that black and especially mixed race young people were, in comparable circumstances, more likely to face prosecution, receive community (rather than first tier, for example, referral order or fine) sentences and be remanded in custody (rather than bailed) than white or Asian peers. The cumulative effect of these higher tariffs and higher rates of breach (Bateman, 2010) is clearly discernible in their over-representation in custody, with the proportion of black and minority ethnic young people rising to 36 per cent, more than double their representation in the wider population (Ministry of Justice, 2012). In a recent survey of those in custody, Summerfield (2011) also found a significant and growing population

(16 per cent) of young Muslim men, who were more likely than others to report negative experiences including feelings of safety and relationships with staff.

Gender

Gender inequalities raise a qualitatively different set of issues from those associated with class or ethnicity. Despite recent rises (see later), young women are far less likely than young men to appear in criminal statistics, being responsible for around a fifth of proven offences. Self-report studies, however suggest that the gender gap is much narrower, with young male offenders outnumbering females by ratios between 1.5:1 and 3:1 (Smith and McVie, 2003; Roe and Ashe, 2008). The ratios tend to be a little higher for serious offending, and Smith and McAra (2004) suggest that crimes such as carrying a weapon, housebreaking, robbery, theft from cars, and cruelty to animals are overwhelmingly committed by young men. There are many competing explanations for such differences (see Chapter 15 for fuller discussion) but part of the answer clearly lies with different patterns of socialization, where conformity is highly valued for girls and young women and behaviour more tightly monitored and controlled. Gender stereotypes tend to portray offending as relatively 'normal' for young men, while running counter to the 'nature' of women. Yet, as Brown (2005) argues, these norms may be so taken for granted that the relationship between masculinity and crime is rarely scrutinized.

Stereotyping appears to produce mixed results for young female offenders. On the one hand, beliefs that they are less likely to become persistent or serious offenders may lead to more lenient treatment and sentencing patterns lend some support to this (Table 17.1).

However, young women may also suffer more from the negative aspects of welfarism and when they commit violent crimes, may be 'doubly damned', having transgressed the bounds of femininity as well as the criminal law (Brown, 2005). Fuelled by moral panics relating to binge drinking, 'ladette' behaviour and violence, there has been a sharp rise in the processing and sentencing severity of female transgression, seemingly unrelated to underlying rates of offending (Sharpe and Gelsthorpe, 2009). While this can be seen as a move towards 'gender neutrality', it may also be interpreted as an attempt to re-assert boundaries of femininity. Given evidence that young women tend to 'grow

Table 17.1 Type of disposals for offenders (aged 10–17) by gender

	Boys		Girls	
	N	%	N	%
Pre-court	43,241	36	19,894	57
First tier*	47,333	39	10,013	29
Community sentences	25,654	21	4,564	13
Custody	4,714	4	416	1

Source: Youth Justice Annual workload data 2009–10, London: Youth Justice Board.

out of crime' more quickly than male counterparts, this net-widening may represent a counter-productive exercise in criminalization, exacerbated by a continuing focus on sexuality (Sharpe, 2009).

REVIEW QUESTIONS

1 To what extent does the over-representation of minority ethnic young people in the official crime statistics reflect discriminatory processes?

2 How do gender stereotypes affect responses to youth crime?

3 Is class still important to understanding youth crime? If so, in what ways?

Contemporary Youth Justice and Future Directions

New moral panics? Knife crime, gangs, and young rioters

If in some senses, youth crime has been depoliticized in recent years, this trend has been regularly punctuated with moral panics associated with violence and perceived lawlessness. Knife (and to a lesser extent gun) crime became a prominent issue following a rise in fatal stabbings of young people in the mid-2000s. As Squires (2011) describes, this prompted a wide range of countermeasures including technology-led searching, controls over sales, amnesties, awareness programmes and multi-agency work, but above all, a tougher sentencing regime. Following their peak, the numbers of both knife/firearm convictions and deaths involving weapons for young people fell significantly, but research has suggested that this was not (directly) attributable to the new intervention measures (Ward *et al.*, 2011).

The extent and operation of gangs in the UK has also attracted considerable media and political attention, whilst also sparking significant criminological debate. Goldson (2011a) has argued that gangs are currently at the apogee of concern regarding youth crime, used as a symbol of 'broken Britain' by the political right. While there is a plethora of international literature on gangs, research in the UK has been fairly limited. A key challenge for criminological study and theorizing has been the question of definition— what constitutes a 'gang', gang membership or 'gang-related' behaviour. The 'gang' label has been used across a wide spectrum, from delinquent youth groups to (adult) serious organized crime and estimates of gang membership have varied from 5 to 20 per cent of young people (Goldson, 2011a). Conceptual challenges and scepticism regarding the uses of gang discourse have prompted divergent responses within criminology. Writing in the left realist tradition, Pitts (2008) has argued that gangs do represent a threat to their neighbourhoods and beyond and should be a matter of policy concern. While noting the difficulties of research in what is inevitably a 'secretive' area, Pitts contends that this should not be used to cast doubt on the gang phenomenon itself or its seriousness. Hallsworth (2011) however, without denying the existence of gangs, suggests that their degree of organization and influence is exaggerated. He explains this as a product of the 'gang control industry' (including politicians, moral entrepreneurs, State, private and voluntary agencies, journalists and academics) who have a vested interest in emphasizing the scale and severity of the 'gang problem'. Squires (2011) develops this argument to suggest that anti-gang initiatives may be counter-productive, hardening group cohesion and increasing marginalization. Whatever their differences, Pitts and Hallsworth both emphasize the importance of understanding gangs within broader social and economic contexts and along with other research have highlighted important spatial elements linked to notions and meanings of territoriality (see contributions to Goldson, 2011b).

Recognizing complexity has also been central to discussion of racialization and gendering as they relate to gangs. White (2008) has highlighted the dangers of profiling risk factors linked to ethnically defining youth gangs, while writers such as Young (2011) and Batchelor (2011) have explored some of the gendered assumptions associated with gangs. In particular, they have used qualitative methods to examine stereotypical perceptions on the one hand, of the 'shemale' gangster who is equally embroiled in violence and crime as male peers and on the other, the image of female gang members as exploited, providing a range of services (from hiding weapons to luring rivals) and being sexually available to male gang members. Young's and Batchelor's work goes beyond these images (significantly refuting both stereotypes) to portray the complexity, fluidity and ambivalences of gang associations.

The urban riots which erupted in 2011 also brought young people under the spotlight, with youth involvement foregrounded by politicians (Bateman, 2012). Children and young people aged under 18 were disproportionately represented among those convicted—comprising 26 per cent of offenders compared with 9 per cent of the population—but the majority of offenders were young adults (RCVP, 2012). Analysis of those children charged showed they were markedly more likely than their peers to live in low-income areas, receive free school meals, lack qualifications, have special educational needs and regularly miss school, but a significant minority did not fit this profile and/ or were first time entrants to the youth justice system (RCVP, 2012). This has sparked considerable debate regarding the part played by socio-economic factors as compared with the perceived influences of parenting, schooling and wider cultural forces such as consumerism. Research by the *Guardian* and London School of Economics (Lewis, 2012) has highlighted a wide range of 'motives' for participants but variants of 'injustice' figured significantly among them. Crucially, riot-related offences attracted harsh sentences, with Bateman (2012) reporting that in the first two months following the riots, 31 per cent of 10–17-year-olds convicted received custodial sentences compared with 5 per cent for comparable offences in the previous year.

Youth justice under the Coalition government

The Conservative-Liberal Democrat Coalition elected in 2010 set out its policy framework in an early Green Paper (Ministry of Justice, 2010) that in many ways represented a continuation of later policy under the previous government. Thus, while there remained an emphasis on punishment and payback and a 'tougher' approach to restorative justice and use of parenting orders, the Green Paper also stressed the importance of rehabilitation and for youth justice in particular, the importance of prevention and reducing custody. The value of preventing entry into and progression through the youth justice system was openly acknowledged and to facilitate the former, greater discretion proposed for the police regarding the number and nature of pre-court disposals. Further reduction in custody was to be sought not only by emphasizing its use as a last resort but by proscribing remands in cases where a custodial sentence was unlikely and signalling a shift of financial responsibility for custody towards local authorities. This was intended to incentivize them towards preventive measures and discourage a (perceived) divesting of responsibilities onto the prison service.

Mirroring the 1980s in certain respects, there has been an uneasy amalgam of 'tough' rhetoric and action (not least in response to knife crime, gangs and the riots) with a diversionary turn that has seen sharp declines in the numbers of young people in the youth justice system, including custody. The number of children and young people receiving ASBOs had also fallen sharply (from a peak of 1,581 in 2005 to 501 in 2009) before the Coalition government signalled its intention to replace them. The new proposed measures—the criminal behaviour order and the crime prevention order—are in many ways strikingly similar to the criminal ASBO and the ASBO itself, but the crime prevention order is different in one important respect, namely, that breaching it does not constitute a criminal offence (Home Office, 2010).

If pressure groups and 'think tanks' inevitably convey their own distinctive perspectives on youth crime, it is also possible to glean areas of common ground from recent contributions. Perhaps the most obvious is a rejection of the straightforwardly punitive and a desire to reduce the use of custody for young people. The most widely supported measures appear to be increasing the use of restorative justice and intervention with parents (Farrington-Douglas and Durante, 2009; Youth Justice Working Group, 2012). Both, however, can be seen as marginalizing the broader cultural and structural context for youth crime. Although there is some support for diversionary principles of minimum intervention, there is also considerable advocacy for extending therapeutic and familial-based programmes, especially those that are deemed to have 'proven track records' (Margo, 2008; Chambers *et al.*, 2009). Spectacular claims are often made for their long-term cost-saving potential, but such programmes remain very small-scale and resource intensive relative to the number of young offenders, and reflect bold assumptions about targeting and the wider impact of programmes on crime rates.

Children first?

Arguably the most clearly articulated critical stance on recent youth justice policy has been that from a 'children first' perspective that draws significantly upon discourses of children's rights as set out in the United Nations Convention on the Rights of the Child. Beyond compliance with the Convention, Monaghan *et al.* (2003) set out the following requirements for a child-centred youth justice, which should:

(a) be distinct and separate from the adult criminal justice system;

(b) have children's 'best interests' as its guiding principle;

(c) raise the age of criminal responsibility;

(d) treat offenders as children first, that is, in line with children's legislation;

(e) use secure accommodation only as a last resort and ensure it provides a safe and caring environment.

In policy terms, the two most important elements are support for decriminalization and opposition to custody. Decriminalization is partly a matter of raising the age of criminal responsibility, with 14 typically the preferred age, and the principle has recently received surprising endorsement from the right-wing Centre for Social Justice as part of a wider call for a child-centred youth justice (Youth Justice Working Group, 2012). Decriminalization also entails moving away from the 'adversarial' court towards more welfare-focused settings, such as the Scottish hearings system. Opposition to custody focuses strongly on its failure to protect and meet the needs of vulnerable young people. As noted earlier, young offenders have often experienced troubled and abusive childhoods and studies show that up to a third of male and half of female prisoners have been in public care (Worsley, 2007). Mental health problems are estimated to affect between 46 and 81 per cent of those in custody with significant incidence of (attempted) suicide (Hagell, 2002). Penal reform groups, most notably the Howard League for Penal Reform, have waged a long, and fairly successful, campaign to prevent young offenders being remanded to adult prisons and to establish that the protections of the Children Act 1989 apply to Young Offender Institutions (YOIs). They have also sought to promote the use of local authority secure accommodation over YOIs, on the grounds that it provides better care and education, albeit at greater expense (Audit Commission, 2004).

Some supporters of a 'children first' position also oppose restorative justice measures when they take place within a framework of threats and sanctions and are grafted onto a system based on very different principles (Pitts, 2001). Haines and O'Mahony (2006) argue that pressuring young offenders to apologize and make reparation can be very one-sided in situations where they may be more sinned against than sinners, while for Toor (2009) restorative justice may impose a double penalty on British Asian girls already facing stigmatization within their communities.

REVIEW QUESTIONS

1 To what extent can the Coalition government's approach to youth justice be seen as different from that of its New Labour predecessors?

2 Assess the arguments for and against treating young offenders as 'children first'.

3 Do the proposals of pressure groups and 'think tanks' represent fresh thinking on youth crime?

CONCLUSION

In this chapter we have reviewed key aspects of the relationship between young people and crime, whether as offenders, victims or recipients of youth justice. We have seen enormous change over the past two centuries and important continuities. The latter include enduring questions as to whether young offenders should be treated differently from adults, and if so, in what ways? Responses have been shaped by the need to effectively address (youth) crime while also dealing appropriately with offenders as children and young people. It is important here to remember that 'childhood' and 'youth' are socially constructed terms and that different constructions (for example, as vulnerable or dangerous) may point to divergent approaches, such as those based on welfare and justice principles respectively. Competing perspectives on whether young people 'grow out of crime' may alternatively support diversion or early intervention strategies. Following a long period of growing separation between the respective treatment of young and adult offenders, recent decades have witnessed a reversal of this trend (Pitts, 2001), but there now seems to be at least a modest interest in more 'child-centred' approaches. This, in turn, can be seen as (belated) recognition of the limits of 'get tough' policies and their tendency to amplify moral panics surrounding youth crime, while offering expensive and ineffective policy responses.

The chapter has also considered some of the explanations advanced for youth crime and relevant debates linked both to social divisions based on class, gender and ethnicity and certain contemporary matters of concern such as knife crime and gang activity. (Readers should also consult Chapter 4 for further discussion.) Of particular importance is the tension between positivist approaches (typified by the influential risk factor prevention) and those that attach much greater significance to young people as social actors. A further divergence can be detected between those criminological perspectives that focus relatively narrowly on interactions between young people and the criminal justice system and those that situate explanations of offending in broader social and cultural contexts.

Thinking on youth crime and justice currently appears to be at a crossroads. On the one hand, there has been something of a turn from the punitive towards the preventive, although this may well owe as much to economic concerns as any fundamental paradigmatic shift in understanding youth crime. While some authors (Margo, 2008) have detected a resurgence in public acceptance of welfare-based approaches, any such trend remains fragile and liable to change in response to new moral panics. The concept of prevention itself is also far from straightforward. On the one hand, there are widely differing views on whether prevention is best achieved by relatively 'hands off' policies or by intensive forms of intervention. Similarly, theorists and policy makers alike may differ on whether effective crime prevention is best achieved through the proximal workings of youth justice or the distal impact of wider structural forces. Each of these positions has its own supportive research evidence or interpretations placed on what is 'known' about youth crime and readers are encouraged to delve more deeply into these competing perspectives to evaluate their strengths and limitations. In the broader policy field, it is difficult to predict whether the recent direction of travel towards decarceration and more modestly towards welfare-based approaches will continue and this may well be influenced by the occurrence of particular 'events' as much as any underlying 'balance of forces' among youth justice protagonists.

QUESTIONS FOR DISCUSSION

1 Is the current age of criminal responsibility in the UK too low?

2 What is meant by prevention and how best might it be achieved?

3 Based on this chapter and Chapter 7, to what extent do you consider that the moral panics surrounding youth crime can be blamed on media coverage?

4 Should youth justice be more 'child-centred'?

5 How might a focus on social inequalities contribute to reducing youth crime?

GUIDE TO FURTHER READING

Muncie, J. (2009) *Youth and Crime: A Critical Introduction* (3rd edn) London: Sage.

This book is probably the most useful of the overview texts in the field of youth crime and youth justice. It provides a good historical account of youth crime and locates discussion in a wider context of theorizing about youth and youth culture(s).

Smith, R. (2011) *Doing Justice to Young People: Youth Crime and Social Justice*. Cullompton: Willan Publishing.

This book analyses the workings of the youth justice system and argues for a new approach based on rights, welfare and social justice

Youth Justice

This journal is produced by the National Association for Youth Justice and offers many topical articles on the workings of the youth justice system.

Muncie, J. and Goldson B. (eds) (2006) *Comparative Youth Justice: Critical Issues*. London: Sage.

This collection comprises analyses and commentary on youth justice in 12 countries and a useful concluding chapter discussing broad trends and variations between and within countries.

Goldson, B. (2008) *A Dictionary of Youth Justice*. Cullompton: Willan Publishing.

This work provides introductory coverage in dictionary format of a range of issues—historical, legal, theoretical, policy, practice and research—relating to youth justice in the UK.

WEB LINKS

http://www.justice.gov.uk/about/yjb

The website for the Youth Justice Board (YJB) provides a useful guide to the workings of the youth justice system, including information on sentences, courts, and custody. It also highlights the YJB's publications and research and provides links to relevant legislation and reports.

http://thenayj.org.uk/

The National Association for Youth Justice broadly advocates an approach to youth justice based on the rights of children and young people. It publishes a newsletter and the journal *Youth Justice*.

http://society.guardian.co.uk/youthjustice/

This section within the *Guardian's* Society website provides useful links to other relevant sites and details of recent articles dealing with youth crime and youth justice.

http://www.howardleague.org/

Along with other penal reform groups such as Nacro, the Howard League runs various projects and campaigns linked to youth justice in addition to producing publications and reports.

http://www.barnardos.org.uk

Like other major children's charities, Barnardo's takes a keen interest in youth justice issues. The website provides details of the project work undertaken and of relevant research.

REFERENCES

Anderson, S., Kinsey, R., Loader, I., and Smith, C. (1994) *Cautionary Tales: Young People, Crime and Policing in Edinburgh*. Aldershot: Avebury.

Armstrong, D., Hine, J., Hacking, S., Armaos, R., Jones, R., Klessinger, N., and France, A. (2005) *Children, Risk and Crime: the On Track Youth Lifestyles Surveys*. Home Office Research Study 278. London: Home Office.

Audit Commission (1996) *Misspent Youth: Young People and Crime*. London: Audit Commission.

Audit Commission (1998) *Misspent Youth '98: the Challenge for Youth Justice*. London: Audit Commission.

Audit Commission (2004) *Youth Justice 2004: A Review of the Reformed Youth Justice System*. London: Audit Commission.

Batchelor, S. (2011) 'Beyond dichotomy: towards an explanation of young women's involvement in violent street gangs' in B. Goldson and J. Muncie (eds) *Youth Crime and Justice: Critical Issues*. London: Sage.

Bateman, T. (2010) Youth Justice News, *Youth Justice* 10(2): 186–96.

Bateman, T. (2011) '"We Now Breach More Kids in a Week Than We Used to in a Whole Year": The Punitive Turn, Enforcement and Custody', *Youth Justice* 11(2): 115–33.

Bateman, T. (2012) 'Who Pulled the Plug? Towards an Explanation of the Fall in Child Imprisonment in England and Wales', *Youth Justice* 12(1): 36–52.

Becker, H. (1963) *Outsiders: Studies in the Sociology of Deviance*. New York: Free Press.

Bottoms, A., Brown, P., McWilliams, B., McWilliams, W., and Nellis, M. (1990) *Intermediate Treatment and Juvenile Justice: Key Findings and Implication from a National Survey of Intermediate Treatment Policy and Practice*. London: HMSO.

Bottrell, D., Armstrong, D., and France, A. (2010) 'Young People's Relations to Crime: Pathways across Ecologies', *Youth Justice* 10(1): 56–72.

Brown, S. (2005) *Understanding Youth and Crime: Listening to Youth?* (2nd edn) Buckingham: Open University Press.

Chambers, M., Ullmann, B., and Waller, I. (2009) *Less Crime, Lower Costs: Implementing Effective Early Crime Reduction Programmes in England and Wales*. London: Policy Exchange.

Coleman, C. and Moynihan, J. (1996) *Understanding Crime Data*. Buckingham: Open University Press.

Day, C., Cadman, S., and Hibbert, P. (2008) *A Literature Review into Children Abused and/or Neglected Prior to Custody*. London: Youth Justice Board.

Donzelot, J. (1980) *The Policing of Families*. London: Hutchinson.

Drakeford, M. and McCarthy, K. (2000) 'Parents, responsibility and the new youth justice' in B. Goldson (ed) *The New Youth Justice*. Lyme Regis: Russell House Publishing.

Farrington, D. (1996) *Understanding and Preventing Youth Crime*. York: York Publishing Services.

Farrington-Douglas, J. and Durante, L. (2009) *Towards a Popular, Preventative Youth Justice System*. London: Institute for Public Policy Research.

Feilzer, M. and Hood, R. (2004) *Differences or Discrimination?: Minority Ethnic Young People In The Youth Justice System*. London: Youth Justice Board.

Flood-Page, C., Campbell, S., Harrington, V., and Miller, J. (2000) *Youth Crime: Findings from the 1998/99 Youth Lifestyles Survey*. London: Home Office.

Goldson, B. (2010) 'The sleep of (criminological) reason: Knowledge—policy rupture and New Labour's youth justice legacy', *Criminology and Criminal Justice* 10(2): 155–78.

Goldson, B. (2011a) 'Youth in Crisis?' in B. Goldson (ed) *Youth in Crisis?: Gangs, Territoriality and Violence*. London: Routledge.

Goldson, B. (ed) (2011b) *Youth in Crisis?: Gangs, Territoriality and Violence*. London: Routledge.

Hagell, A. (2002) *The Mental Health Needs of Young Offenders*. London: Mental Health Foundation.

Hagell, A. and Newburn, T. (1994) *Persistent Young Offenders*. London: Policy Studies Institute.

Haines, K. and Drakeford, M. (1998) *Young People and Youth Justice*. Basingstoke: Macmillan.

Haines, K. and O'Mahony, D. (2006) 'Restorative approaches, young people and youth justice' in B. Goldson and J. Muncie (eds) *Youth Crime and Justice: Critical Issues*. London: Sage.

Haines, K. and Case, S. (2008) 'The Rhetoric and Reality of the "Risk Factor Prevention Paradigm" Approach to Preventing and Reducing Youth Offending', *Youth Justice* 8(1): 5–20.

Hall, S., Critcher, C., Jefferson, T., Clarke, J., and Roberts, B. (1978) *Policing the Crisis: Mugging, the State and Law and Order*. London: Macmillan.

Hallsworth, S. (2011) 'Gangland Britain?: realities, fantasies and industry' in B. Goldson (ed) *Youth in Crisis?: Gangs, Territoriality and Violence*. London: Routledge.

Hartless, J, Ditton, J, Nair, G., and Phillips, S. (1995) 'More Sinned Against Than Sinning: a Study of Young Teenagers' Experiences of Crime', *British Journal of Criminology* 35(1): 114–33.

Hazel, N. (2008) *Cross-National Comparison of Youth Justice*. London: Youth Justice Board.

Hendrick, H. (1994) *Child Welfare, England 1872–1989*. London: Routledge.

Home Office (2010) *More Effective Responses to Anti-social Behaviour*. London: Stationery Office.

Lewis, P. (2011) *Reading the Riots: Investigating England's Summer of Disorder*. London: Guardian.

McAra, L. and McVie, S. (2010) 'Youth crime and justice: Key messages from the Edinburgh Study of Youth Transitions and Crime', *Criminology and Criminal Justice* 10(2): 179–209.

Margo, J. (2008) *Make Me a Criminal: Preventing Youth Crime*. London: Institute for Public Policy Research.

May, T., Gyateng, T., and Hough, M. (2010) *Differential Treatment in the Youth Justice System*. London: Equality and Human Rights Commission.

Millard, B. and Flatley, J. (2010) *Experimental Statistics on Victimisation of Children Aged 10 to 15: Findings from the British Crime Survey for the year ending December 2009*. London: Home Office.

Ministry of Justice (2010) *Breaking the Cycle: Effective Punishment, Rehabilitation and Sentencing of Offenders*. London: Stationery Office.

Ministry of Justice (2012) *Criminal Statistics England and Wales 2011*. London: Stationery Office.

Monaghan, G. Hibbert, P., and Moore, S. (2003) *Children in Trouble: Time for Change*. Ilford: Barnardo's.

Morris, A., Giller, H., Geach, H., and Szwed, E. (1980) *Justice for Children*. London: Macmillan.

Muncie, J. (2009) *Youth and Crime: a Critical Introduction* (3rd edn) London: Sage.

Murray, C. (Cathy) (2009) 'Typologies of Young Resisters and Desisters', *Youth Justice* 9(2): 115–29.

Murray, C. (Charles) (1990) *The Emerging British Underclass*. London: Institute of Economic Affairs.

National Audit Office (2010) *The Youth Justice System in England and Wales: Reducing Offending by Young People*. London: The Stationery Office.

O'Mahony, P. (2009) 'The Risk Factors Prevention Paradigm and the Causes of Youth Crime: A Deceptively Useful Analysis?' *Youth Justice* 9(2): 99–114.

Pitts, J. (2000) 'The New Youth Justice and the Politics of Electoral Anxiety' in B. Goldson (ed) *The New Youth Justice*. Lyme Regis: Russell House Publishing.

Pitts, J. (2001) *The New Politics of Youth Crime: Discipline or Solidarity*. Basingstoke: Palgrave.

Pitts, J. (2008) *Reluctant Gangsters: the Changing Face of Youth Crime*. Cullompton: Willan.

Pratt, J. (1989) 'Corporatism: the Third Model of Juvenile Justice', *British Journal of Criminology* 29(3): 236–54.

Riots Communities and Victims Panel (2012) *After the Riots: The Final Report of the Riots Communities and Victims Panel*. London: RCVP.

Roe, S. and Ashe, J. (2008) *Young People and Crime: Findings from the 2006 Offending, Crime and Justice Survey*, Home Office Statistical Bulletin 09/08. London: Home Office.

Sharpe, G. (2012) *Offending Girls: Young Women and Youth Justice*. London: Routledge.

Sharpe, G. and Gelsthorpe, L. (2009) 'Engendering the Agenda: Girls, Young Women and Youth Justice', *Youth Justice* 9(3): 195–208.

Smith, D. and Ecob, R. (2007) 'An Investigation into Casual Links between Victimization and Offending', *British Journal of Sociology* 58(4); 633–59.

Smith, D. and McAra, L. (2004) *Gender and Youth Offending*. Edinburgh Study of Youth Transitions and Crime, Research Digest, No. 2.

Smith, D. and McVie, S. (2003) 'Theory and Method in the Edinburgh Study of Youth Transitions and Crime', *British Journal of Criminology* 43(1): 169–95.

Smith, R. (2007) *Youth Justice: Ideas, Policy, Practice* (2nd edn) Cullompton: Willan.

Squires, P. (2011) 'Young people and "weaponisation"' in B. Goldson (ed) *Youth in Crisis?: Gangs, Territoriality and Violence*. London: Routledge.

Summerfield, A. (2011) *Children and Young People in Custody 2010/11: An Analysis of the Experiences of 15–18 Year-olds in Prison*. London: HM Inspectorate of Prisons/Youth Justice Board.

Thorpe, D., Smith, D., Green, C., and Paley, J. (1980) *Out of Care: the Community Support of Juvenile Offenders*. London: Allen & Unwin.

Toor, S. (2009) 'British Asian Girls, Crime and Youth Justice', *Youth Justice* 9(3): 239–53.

Walsh, C. (2011) 'Youth Justice and Neuroscience: A Dual-Use Dilemma', *British Journal of Criminology* 51(1): 21–39.

Ward, L., Nicholas, S., and Willoughby, M. (2011) *An Assessment of the Tackling Knives and Serious Youth Violence Action Programme (TKAP)—Phase II*. London: Home Office.

White, R. (2008) 'Disputed Definitions and Fluid Identities: The Limitations of Social Profiling In Relation to Ethnic Youth Gangs', *Youth Justice* 8(2): 149–61.

White, R. and Cunneen, C. (2006) 'Social class, youth crime and justice' in B. Goldson and J. Muncie (eds) *Youth Crime and Justice: Critical Issues*. London: Sage.

Wikström, P.-O., Oberwittler, D., Treiber, K., and Hardie, B. (2012) *Breaking Rules: The Social and Situational Dynamics of Young People's Urban Crime.* Oxford: Oxford University Press.

Wilson, D., Sharp, C., and Patterson, A. (2006) *Young People and Crime: Findings from the 2005 Offending, Crime and Justice Survey*, Home Office Statistical Bulletin 17/06. London: Home Office.

Worsley, R. (2007) *Young People in Custody 2004–2006: An Analysis Of Children's Experiences Of Prison*. London: HM Inspectorate of Prisons/Youth Justice Board.

Young NCB (2010) *Children and Young People's Fear of Crime Survey 2010*. London: National Children's Bureau.

Young, T. (2011) 'In search of the "shemale" gangster' in B. Goldson and J. Muncie (eds) *Youth Crime and Justice: Critical Issues*. London: Sage.

Youth Justice Working Group (2012) *Rules of Engagement: Changing the Heart of Youth Justice*. London: Centre for Social Justice.

18 Crime, culture, and everyday life

Jeff Ferrell and Jonathan Ilan

INTRODUCTION

In contemporary society, criminal practices and cultural dynamics intertwine within the experiences of everyday life. Indeed, crime and its control can themselves be thought of as cultural constructs that emerge from the interplay of contested meanings and shared understandings. Many forms of criminality emerge out of criminal and deviant subcultures; for members of these groups, crime may be experienced as part of a mundane daily routine, or equally as a pleasurable thrill, a sought-after emotional state which can support behaviours that spawn further marginalization. For others, crime is seldom directly experienced and yet remains ever present in their everyday lives: in the fabric of their urban landscape and as the spice added to their daily media intake. Indeed, it is the accumulation of countless direct and indirect everyday experiences that constitute both patterns of criminality and the laws, policies and practices which form the architecture of crime control. Cultural criminologists thus seek to understand both micro-social and macro-social aspects of crime, and their interplay: how the great inequalities of late-modern life play out in everyday situations of crime or transgression, and how large-scale legal or political campaigns tap into individualized fears and sensibilities. There is a need to understand how crime, both in everyday life and as represented within the omnipresent media, has the power to produce a repulsed fascination and a seductive edginess which can be harnessed to sell a range of products or policies. In short, cultural criminologists argue that a critical awareness of every-day cultural dynamics is necessary if we are to understand even the most basic dimensions of crime and crime control.

BACKGROUND

Over the past few decades a number of criminologists have attempted to locate issues of crime and crime control within broader cultural dynamics. For such criminologists, 'culture' and 'cultural dynamics' refer to the shared symbolic environment in which people operate—that is, the shared way of life within which everyday objects, practices, and interactions come to have meaning. Crucial to these notions is the early work of American criminologist Howard Becker (1963), who demonstrated that the meaning of human activity is in large part defined by others' responses to it—in the case of crime and deviance, by the labelling of certain activities as criminal or deviant. Moreover, he showed that this labelling is a contested process, undertaken by powerful groups in their attempts to censure the behaviour of the less powerful. Given this, Becker and others (Polsky, 1998 [1967]) argued that criminologists cannot simply rely on conventional definitions of crime and criminality; instead, they must investigate the process of labelling, and go inside marginalized subcultures to explore their distinctive symbolic practices and modes of understanding and resistance.

This line of thinking was pursued during the 1970s, for example, by the British 'Birmingham School' of cultural studies and the radical theorists associated with the 'new criminology' (for example, Taylor *et al.*, 1973). Not only were such theorists interested in the colourful youth subcultures springing up around Britain, and the meanings of such subcultures for their participants; they were particularly attuned to the broader social structures that shaped these subcultures, including the perceptions organized by actors within mainstream social institutions. Stanley Cohen (2002 [1972/1980/1987]) noted how the media cast 'Mods and Rockers' as 'folk devils': symbols of a supposed social collapse and the subject of a 'moral panic' which saw social institutions queue up to condemn and punish young people for minor offences. Similarly, Jock Young (1971) demonstrated how media, political and policing reactions to recreational drug taking contributed both to the deviant identity of users and to their growing criminalization—an ironic and self-defeating process that has in turn underpinned today's 'war on drugs'. Indeed, the work of Hall *et al.* (1978) revealed how public officials and the mass media at times generate public concern over crimes as a way of furthering their own political agendas.

Whilst much of mainstream criminology in the 1980s and 1990s focused on a more limited range of administrative crime control concerns, these earlier theoretical positions formed the basis for the development of a fresh perspective at the close of the twentieth century: cultural criminology. Drawing additionally on symbolic interactionism, an approach that understands social reality to be constructed out of ongoing, meaningful interaction among individuals and groups, cultural criminology proposes:

> the placing of crime and its control in the context of culture; that is, viewing both crime and the agencies of control as cultural products as creative constructs. As such they must be read in terms of the meanings they carry. Furthermore, cultural criminology seeks to highlight how power affects the upwards and downwards constructions of criminological phenomena: rules created, rules broken, a constant interplay of moral entrepreneurship, political innovation and transgression (Hayward and Young, 2012: 113).

Cultural criminology (Ferrell, 1999; Ferrell, Hayward, and Young, 2008; Ferrell and Sanders, 1995; Presdee, 2000; Ferrell *et al.*, 2004; Hayward and Young, 2004, 2012) in addition constitutes a critical discourse particularly attuned to the contemporary conditions of late-modernity: an era of staggering global inequalities, material and ontological insecurity, media saturation, rabid consumerism, cultural fluidity, and social exclusion (see Bauman, 2000; Young, 2007). For some, these conditions spawn motivations to commit emotionally charged or materially advantageous criminal acts. For others, these conditions produce such crushing social and economic exclusion that they are reduced to quotidian acts of law breaking and the continuous avoidance of victimization as part of their everyday struggles for survival. The conditions of late-modernity in turn predispose the precariously included majority to view the marginalized and their behaviour as increasingly threatening (Young, 1999). In this context cultural criminologists are dedicated to speaking truth to power, and to exploring the ways in which vast social inequalities manifest in everyday moments of desperation, rage, fear, desire, humiliation and envy (Presdee, 2000). Cultural criminologists in addition explore everyday styles of dress or comportment, not as aesthetic abstractions, but as the symbolic medium through which illicit subcultures define and display their identities, crime control agents respond to the subculture's public presence, and mass media institutions appropriate and commodify transgression. Investigating also the internal meanings of illicit subcultures, cultural criminologists embrace their own first-hand understanding of criminality, their own sense of criminological *verstehen* (see later in this chapter, and Ferrell, 1997), as they attempt to penetrate the situated logic and emotion of these worlds.

Culture and criminology

As already noted, 'culture' refers to shared symbolic environments and meaningful human activity; put differently, culture denotes the human processes of understanding the world, assigning meaning to it, performing roles within it, and engaging in ritualized patterns of behaviour. In this light, crime can be understood as behaviour which is assigned the meaning of 'being wrong' and which has been judged to be so according to the historically developed cultural artefact that is the criminal law. Culture and cultural processes, both historical and contemporary, are in this way central to our understanding of criminality, crime control, and their perception and execution. Culture, moreover, is extraordinarily complex, a product of the situated (the here and now, local and specific) and the historical and the structural (class, ethnicity, gender, age, race and background). Even with its historical roots, cultural is also dynamic, constantly shifting, and subject to contestation. In the context of street crime, for example, young men deeply embedded in 'street (sub) culture' may see their acts of theft and drug taking as culturally desirable indicators of a tough masculine persona, while at the same time perceiving the actions of the police and youth justice workers as either oppressive or meddlesome, but certainly illegitimate (see further: Ilan, 2010). In short, a group or individual's cultural orientation largely defines the kinds of behaviour they perceive as threatening or valuable, criminal or legitimate.

There is good cause, moreover, to investigate broader cultural dynamics like those of the mass media, which provide the preponderance of the public's information on crime and crime control, and whose consumption animates a significant proportion of everyday life. Cultural criminology maintains that contemporary media do not simply report, with greater or lesser accuracy, on existing crime and crime control issues; instead, the media actively participate in constructing the social reality of these very issues. Media representations of crime and control are not secondary responses to the 'reality' of crime; instead, they are endlessly entangled in a series of mediated loops and spirals whereby each phenomenon reflects and embodies images of the other within everyday life (Ferrell, Hayward, and Young, 2008; Hayward and Presdee, 2010; Manning, 1998). Politicians and moral entrepreneurs utilize the media to deploy evocative crime imagery as they work to consolidate political power or criminalize marginal groups. Policing agencies increasingly coordinate their operations with those of existing media institutions, and develop their own channels of mediated communication and surveillance, in the interest of gaining public support, recruiting new members, and apprehending criminals. Everyday policing operations in turn become fodder for 'reality' television programming, with televised police chases and high-profile sting operations presented in the form of morally-charged entertainment (see Fishman and Cavender, 1998). All the while, commercial films, popular music, and nightly television programming offer a swarm of crime and crime control characterizations, by turns celebrating and condemning the activities of outlaws, police officers, and judges. In the end, this ongoing stream of dramatic imagery accumulates into a vast cultural stockpile, a complex of images, symbols, and meanings by which individuals and groups come to make sense of crime, violence, and crime control within their own lives.

The media, furthermore, allow those occupying criminal or criminalized worlds to participate in this endless process of mediated negotiation, such that their message can penetrate the everyday lives of media consumers as well. Young people who pro-fess membership of London street 'gangs' produce music videos for consumption on YouTube (Ilan, 2012). Outlaw BASE jumpers wear helmet-mounted video cameras to record their own illegal parachuting from bridges and buildings, circulate these videos within the BASE jumping underground, and often sell them to mass media outlets as a way of raising funds for the next illegal jump (Ferrell, Milovanovic, and Lyng, 2001). Within progressive political groups, videographers play an increasingly important role, as they employ video cameras to document police misconduct (and police video surveil-lance) during street protests, and to create their own alternative news footage (see also Greer and McLaughlin, 2010). Both the mass media and the micro media of marginal or criminal groups engage in an endless appropriation and reinvention of each other's images and understandings.

It is possible thus to understand much of what passes us by in everyday life as laden with competing messages and meanings about crime and its control, even if we are sel-dom prompted to pause and take stock of them. Indeed, as 'everyday life' has emerged more forcefully as a subject of study in its own right (see Highmore, 2002), it becomes a useful project to consider what this means for criminology. Cultural criminology has sought to demonstrate that the reality of gross global inequalities can be found in some-thing as small as a prawn sandwich (see O'Brien, 2006) or an iPhone, and that the critical criminological gaze need not only be trained on mass atrocities and large institutions (see Box 18.1). A simple day in the life of any individual can be unpacked in such a way as to reveal the deluge of crime images and crime control dynamics that permeate even the most 'mundane' existence (Ferrell, Hayward, and Young, 2008: Chapter 4). There may, indeed, be little that is actually mundane about everyday life; it may well be the theatre in which the great drama of crime, crime control, and inequality is most effect-ively rehearsed.

Crime and control in everyday life

We often think of criminology as the scholarly investigation of prisons, courtrooms, and violent criminality—yet the first thing most people do when leaving their home is to turn around and lock their door: a security action. Crime and its control are not just the stuff of police pursuits, high-visibility offences and lengthy trials: they are woven into the fabric of everyday life. Walk through many cities and you will notice lampposts and utility boxes coated with a coarse black substance that protects them against graffiti; CCTV cameras abound; gates are locked and signs warn against innumerable illegalities. These are crime control features, and indeed perceptions and understandings of crime, built into the urban environment. Such forms of situational crime prevention (or SCP, see Hough *et al.*, 1980) are designed to reduce the everyday opportunities for crime. Theorizing this approach, the criminologist Marcus Felson (2002) argues that crime should not be seen as an exceptional part of human life, but rather, a 'routine activity' that will occur where there is a motivated offender, criminal opportunity and the lack of a capable guardian. Most crime, he claims, is petty and unremarkable. Yet he and other rational choice theorists (for example, Cornish and Clarke, 1986) do little to examine

---

Box 18.1: The designer trainer

Cultural criminologists maintain that the huge and far reaching effects of global socio-economic inequality are visible even in small items and aspects of everyday life. Take, for example, a designer 'trainer', 'sneaker' or running shoe (depending on your preferred mode of slang—if any). Such a seemingly small item can tell significant stories about the nature of crime and global inequality in late-modernity. Designer trainers, hot fashion commodities and the footwear of choice for many street criminals, are almost always manufactured in the developing world. This was not always the case; once the garment and footwear industries provided a large amount of stable, decently paid employment for those living in urban centres within the developed world. Under neo-liberal economic policies, companies became free to shift their manufacturing base to countries where wages and labour welfare standards are considerably lower. The trainer-related jobs that remain within the developed world fall under two rough categories: first, designers and marketeers—skilled, mobile, middle-class professionals who must maintain the 'cool' and desirability of the trainer; and second, retail workers, insecure, low-paid employees with little possibility for advancement. Where the grandparents of the contemporary street criminal may have found decent employment manufacturing shoes, the socio-economically disadvantaged can now only compete for a job selling them. The economy of the inner-city becomes desiccated and poverty-ridden and certain individuals come to understand street crime as one of the few opportunities to feel a sense of respect for themselves 'at work' (see Bourgouis, 2002; Hall and Winlow, 2008). The proceeds of drug deals and robberies are often then spent on 'fresh' trainers, so that the strict mandates of street cultural style can be met. Moreover, the marketers have been working hard to stoke up a powerful sense of desire in their target market, encouraging them to be more impulsive, to consume by any means necessary without overly reflecting on the consequences (Hayward, 2004). In this way, we can understand that the street crime of the first world urban youth and the wage slavery of workers in the developing world are linked—and that even the biggest issues of crime and control can be understood through considering small and seemingly unrelated objects like trainers.

---

the particular circumstances of this motivated offender; indeed, the potential offender is imagined to be a sort of human calculator, weighing up the benefits of offending versus the risk of failure and punishment. From this theoretical perspective, everyday life is thus a series of opportunities for gain which, when criminal, can be closed off through environmental design or the watchful eye of a guardian. The characteristics of those involved in criminality, their feelings, experiences, and world views, are considered to be of little consequence within an everyday life assumed to be largely homogenous.

Certainly there are some common features of everyday life that have a bearing on criminal opportunity. Consider, for example, the proliferation of small-sized, high-value goods that circulate through everyday life: smart phones, iPods, notebook computers, and the like. These common, everyday devices are relatively easy to steal—but as important, because they are desirable consumer commodities, criminal markets which trade in them can exist (see Felson, 2002). Cultural criminology shares the sense that such issues of consumer culture underpin many criminal behaviours, but apart from this, cultural criminology is generally critical of the position taken by 'routine activity' and 'rational choice' theories of everyday criminality and crime control. According to Hayward (2007, 2012) these perspectives impose a model of rationality on a deeply diverse group of actors without sufficiently recognizing the degree to which 'irrational' factors affect offending; likewise, forms of provisional rationality may flourish in one set of circumstances, but seem nonsensical in others. It is furthermore questionable to assume that the accumulation of material goods constitutes only rational economic activity, when in our contemporary late-modern society, consumer products are often interwoven with strong desires and incendiary emotions.

Indeed, Hayward (2004) and Ferrell (2006) demonstrate how mainstream consumer culture can generate precisely the sorts of 'irrational' emotions that can be found within criminal behaviour: impulsivity, desire, and a demand for immediate pleasure and control, with little thought to potential consequences. Of course, here it becomes necessary once again to include an analysis of socio-economic structures, something rational choice theorists seldom undertake. For those who can afford to spend money gained 'legitimately' on the commodified thrills, pleasures and excitements offered by consumer culture, there may be less impetus to offend; for those who lack those means, criminality may offer the opportunity to attain these well-marketed emotional states (Hall, Winlow, and Ancrum, 2008). Furthermore, the existence of consumer culture itself is part and parcel of the broad social, economic and cultural changes that have taken place over the last number of decades. These have included falling incomes for a large section of the Western population, the erosion of job security, and the fading away of traditional communities and certainties. These factors have contributed to what Jock Young has called an 'exclusive society' (1999) where there has been a move away from attempting to rehabilitate the offender back into society, and toward a system of designing out and holding away the offending 'other'. Fear and insecurity are the emotions underpinning this process, and thus the move towards the increasing use of situational crime prevention (however effective or ineffective) cannot itself be understood as belonging to a purely rational practice or discipline. The everyday 'irrational' emotions of fear and insecurity underpin the increasingly tough crime control policies that exist within many Western societies.

It is important to recognize that everyday life can also be a place of petty acts of criminality. In fact, these can be so ingrained into patterns of work and/or leisure that in the popular imagination they may not register as criminal at all. In his consideration of '**volume crime**', Mike Presdee notes that liberties are routinely taken with regards to aspects of claiming expenses, filing tax returns or, indeed, respecting the laws of copyright (2009). To give a contemporary example, the Internet facilitates the routine, widespread exchange of pirated material: criminal acts abound as music, movies and games are copied and distributed without the permission of the copyright holder. Yet, such actions are often given no more thought than that necessary to drive the muscle of the finger clicking the mouse. Acts such as these are usually mundane acts of petty criminality that often do not generate thrills or indeed emotions of any enduring strength. Likewise, reports around metal theft in the UK and the USA indicate the extent to which the (building) fabric of everyday life can become the object of **quotidian crime** where pipes, roofing, doors, cables and railway materials become valuable scrap in an era of rising impoverishment (see Lipscombe and Bennet, 2012). A range of illegal and quasi-legal forms of recycling, repurposing and improvisation, for example, squatting or scrounging (see Ferrell, 2006), thus become part of the everyday lives of some of the most excluded in contemporary society: from the homeless in the developed world, to the residents of slums in the developing world. Furthermore, the mechanisms of the law may extend to effectively criminalize certain aspects of everyday life which may not have been considered criminal in times past or indeed do not seem criminal to those taking part in them. A prime example of this phenomenon is the Anti-Social Behaviour Agenda that pervades within the UK. Routine acts such as littering, making noise or even 'hanging around' in public spaces can become the subject of Anti-Social Behaviour Orders (ASBOs) where others perceive them to be threatening or, indeed, a nuisance (see further Squires and Stephen, 2005). Where breached, such orders can lead to punitive sanctions and thus individuals, particularly young people, may find their everyday activities censured.

REVIEW QUESTIONS

1 Given the high levels of violence and inequality in contemporary society, how can cultural criminologists justify studying the minutiae of 'everyday life'?

2 To what extent can the physical environment be changed to reduce the likelihood of crime occurring? On what assumptions would such changes be based?

Edgework, emotions, and *verstehen*

So far we have highlighted the degree to which crime can be grounded in various emotional and meaningful collective experiences. In investigating a wide range of criminal activities, from street violence to graffiti writing to fire setting, researchers have found that criminals often embrace the extreme risk and danger that accompanies their criminal activity; rather than shying away from such risk, or seeing it only as an unfortunate consequence of their illicit occupations, they come to enjoy it—to the point that they regularly report being 'addicted' to the dangerous experiences and 'adrenalin rush' of criminality (Katz, 1988; Lyng, 1990; Ferrell, 1996; Hayward, 2004: Chapter 5; Jackson-Jacobs, 2004). Often outsiders misunderstand this enjoyment of extreme risk as embodying an out-of-control, haphazard orientation on the part of wildly violent criminals; others assume that this enjoyment of danger must constitute some sort of nihilistic death wish on the part of those disconnected from conventional morality. In fact, cultural criminological research shows, it is most often neither. Instead of seeking death in these moments of extreme risk, illicit risk takers seem to be seeking a more vivid version of life itself, an experience that transcends the conventions of everyday living. And rather than simply being the by-products of out-of-control individual behaviour, these so-called 'edgework' (Lyng, 1990, 2005) experiences seem clearly to embody the work of criminal subcultures, integrating as they do illicit subcultural skills with moments of meaningful danger. In fact, it is precisely these subcultural skills and attitudes that define the allure of edgework experiences; in such moments the countercultural values of the subcultural are confirmed at the level of existential experience, the value of the subculture's illicit skills now measured, and proven, against the risk of violent failure. After all, a car thief's skills matter most when surreptitiously prying open a car window, a joy rider's most when balancing speed and control to avoid catastrophe or capture.

Jack Katz (1988) has in turn argued that these vivid, seductive experiences of crime's 'foreground' call into question the usual assumption that criminological theories can account for crime by focusing only on 'background' or structural factors such as social class or ethnic inequality. While these background factors certainly remain interwoven with criminal acts, they seem clearly to take on meaning inside the act itself, rather than simply 'causing' it in some exterior or deterministic fashion. The specific dynamics of these edgework experiences also undermine—both conceptually and practically—crime control or crime deterrence models based on aggressive policing strategies. As the catalyst that brings these edgework experiences to life, risk is desired by illicit edgeworkers, who regularly report that the increased possibility of legal apprehension or harassment generally amplifies, rather than diminishes, the seductions of the criminal experience. In another sense, as demonstrated by Eleanor Miller (1991), risk does not solely represent a motivation to offend, but can instead represent a factor that must be negotiated as part of everyday life, subject to the issues of power that stem from class, race and gender. Those seeking to avoid criminal victimization thus involve themselves in processes to *reduce risk*, as much as their levels of power might allow them.

Emotions such as the excitement derived from risky activities, of course, form only part of the complex emotional dynamics intertwined with the criminal experience. Jack Katz also analyses the functions of rage, power and humiliation (1988). Emotions are dynamic, and the route they travel can reveal much about the experience of criminality. Katz argues that the 'righteous killer' purges humiliation through rage and taking action, but may be left with remorse when this emotion burns out. The role of less incendiary emotions such as boredom must also be remembered (see Ferrell, 2004). Indeed, when considering the petty misdemeanours of young people who are 'hanging around' in public space, understanding boredom and the drive to overcome it becomes essential. As Paul Corrigan (1979) demonstrated in his classic study of young people negotiating the monotony of 'doing nothing', 'weird ideas' (outlandish acts of mischief such as smashing bottles and ritualized fighting) become vehicles both to pass the time and as fuel for a conversation culture that fills many other boring hours.

To the extent that moments of edgework and emotion shape the reality of criminality, conventional criminological methods of research must be reconsidered as well. Methods that simply accumulate crime statistics or tabulate survey responses cannot penetrate the subcultural meanings of these vivid foreground experiences; instead, methods are needed that can situate criminologists as close as possible to the immediacy of criminal situations and events. Because of this, cultural criminologists often utilize field research or ethnographic methods that place them, as best as possible, inside the actual lives and experiences of criminals (see, for example, Ferrell and Hamm, 1998). Pushing this methodology further still, these criminologists often pursue the goal of achieving criminological *verstehen*—a deep, emotional understanding of the dangerous experiences that define criminality—as a way of gaining criminological insight unavailable to others (Weber, 1949; Ferrell, 1997). Such a methodology of course challenges conventional notions of research 'objectivity', and of criminology as a 'social science' of crime and crime control; it also raises for criminologists difficult issues of morality and legality. Still, if the meaning of crime is regularly constructed in the immediacy of its experiences and emotions, how else are criminologists to investigate and understand it?

REVIEW QUESTIONS

1 Which types of crime are more likely to be underpinned by edgework? In what ways might crimes which are not motivated by a search for excitement be different to those that are?

2 To what extent should criminologists, morally or legally, be allowed to participate in the situations and emotions of criminality?

Subculture, style, and the criminalization of culture

Much of the illicit behaviour that criminologists study is organized and defined by criminal subcultures. Criminal subcultures provide repositories of skill from which subcultural members learn the techniques essential to successful criminal conduct, whether they be the skills needed for efficient drug use, surreptitious embezzlement, or effective violence. Perhaps more importantly, these subcultures create a collective ethos, a fluid set of values and orientations that define their members' criminal behaviour as appropriate, even honourable; in this way criminal subcultures also function as countercultures, ways of life that to some degree oppose or defy conventional understandings of legality, morality, and achievement. In many cases, these subcultural orientations come to be embodied in the subculture's distinctive style—subtle conventions of dress and comportment, distinctive linguistic codes often incomprehensible to the outsider, and everyday rituals designed to mark the boundaries of subcultural membership. Given this constellation of skills, attitudes, and styles, criminal subcultures operate as much more than proximities of personal association among their members. They become symbolic communities of shared meaning that define for their members the nature of criminality perhaps more than the criminal act itself.

Understood in this way, the powerful pull of criminal subcultures operates in ways that are as much cultural as interpersonal. Dressed in clothes that embody a host of illicit sartorial codes, fluent in the nuances of subcultural argot, wrapped in the defiant assurance of an 'outlaw' identity, a street gang member or dance drug aficionado maintains subcultural membership even when no others are around; the subculture surrounds its members even when they wander from it. At the extreme, this cultural dynamic alerts criminologists to the ways in which criminal subcultures can operate effectively even when their members seldom if ever come face-to-face; from anonymous computer hackers to dispersed human trafficking networks, the cohesion of the subculture transcends the limits of physical location. This dynamic in turn suggests that, for those concerned with controlling criminal subcultures and their dissemination, the task will not be as simple as arresting one member or another.

In the USA and increasingly within the UK, for example, graffiti writers have for many decades operated within conventions of style so carefully constructed that writers could effectively communicate status and meaning by way of 'tags' and murals even when they had never met, and could therefore know and understand one another as members of a shared urban subculture even without direct association. An illicit subculture exists that now stretches from New York City to the city of York and beyond, communicating, solidifying—even recruiting—by means of dislocated subcultural symbolism (see Ferrell, 1998). At the other end of the technological spectrum from rusty trains and spray paint cans, illicit cyber-communities now operate within a welter of fabricated identities and stylized language practices that form powerful, encompassing associations among strangers around the world. In fact, it is just this symbolic construction of the subculture itself, this profound lack of face-to-face interaction that keeps on-line communities of child pornographers or sex workers so impenetrable to outside authorities (Jewkes, 2003; Jenkins, 2001).

Legal authorities themselves increasingly understand these cultural dynamics also, and so turn to these very subcultural symbols and styles in their attempts to prevent or control criminal activity. Watching for the emergence of new linguistic or sartorial styles among marginal groups, instituting surveillance programmes based on subtleties of appearance or comportment, assigning gang status to young people on the basis of their music productions, reading gang graffiti for signs of impending trouble, legal and political authorities contribute their own complex of meanings to these subculture styles and symbols, and so themselves come to participate in this ongoing cultural interplay. In doing so, they raise a host of troubling questions regarding definitions of crime and legitimate measures of crime control—questions that are essentially *cultural* in nature. Is it appropriate for probation officers to violate the probation of a young offender on the basis of their new 'gang' tattoo or alleged choice of 'gang-related' attire (Miller, 1995)? Is 'racial profiling' or 'terrorist profiling' an appropriate response to subtle displays of criminal affiliation or political threat, or a form of institutionalized racism based on unfair stereotypes (Harcourt, 2007)? Is it fair that some British shopping centres prevent young people wearing 'hoodies' from entering (see Hayward and Yar, 2006), or that ASBOs can be issued to groups of young people on the basis that they are *perceived to be* intimidating? Most broadly, in their attempts to respond to the everyday symbolism and style of marginal subcultures, do legal authorities in effect criminalize the lives and activities of those on the margins by defining their styles as *de facto* indicators of criminality?

Such questions around cultural production and the stuff of everyday lifestyles are not without historical precedent. Over the years, the cultural, artistic and aesthetic products of various individuals and groups have been subject to condemnation, censorship, and criminalization. Numerous groups have been ensnared in such legal and cultural difficulties, with political campaigners and moral entrepreneurs (Becker, 1963) over time proclaiming the allegedly deleterious effects of everything from jazz improvisations to punk music, from erotic literature to violent video games. This long historical record confirms the ongoing interplay of crime and cultural process, and the ongoing capacity for the manufacturing of fear and insecurity. It also reveals an interesting, and suspect, form of criminological reasoning. Such campaigns often locate in a particular cultural product—a song or film or style of dress—a simple sort of criminogenic causality, with the product allegedly inducing moral depravity or spawning 'copy-cat' crimes. In contrast, we should endeavour to understand such cultural products within the morass of images, narratives and meanings that constitute the contested cultural script of any particular period. How could it be, for example, that a particular video game could 'cause' violent criminality, when it exists within a daily storm of televised violence, both fictional and real—and when the great majority of the game's users do not subsequently turn to criminality? For criminologists interested in crime, culture, and everyday life, the task is not to isolate cultural products, but to drill down into the complex processes that define the cultural dynamics of crime and control.

REVIEW QUESTIONS

1 What features distinguish criminal subcultures from other social groupings such as sports teams?

2 By displaying illicit styles, do members of criminal subcultures 'invite' legal surveillance and control? Are legal authorities justified in using these styles as indicators of criminality? If so, in what circumstances, and with what limitations?

The commodification of transgression and the carnival of crime

For cultural criminologists, controversies surrounding particular films, video games and music genres are in turn of interest for what they reveal about how images of criminality and transgression are used within mainstream cultural industries as marketing strategies. Increasingly, clothing manufacturers, advertisers, and other members of the corporate economy responsible for many of the products that feature in our everyday lives recognize that the styles of illicit subcultures lend a degree of street legitimacy to fashion, music, and other commodities, especially when these commodities are designed for sale to young people (see Hayward, 2004: 166–73; Snyder, 2009). For McRobbie and Thornton (1995), it is thus inadequate to conceptualize contemporary moral panics as purely negative or one-dimensional constructions. In a world where the youth cultural industries are particularly mindful of the ways in which controversy sells, moral panic can come to operate as political ideology for some and a marketing campaign for others. Here, corporations 'harvest' criminal imagery or moral outrage to lend a transgressive edge to the appeal of their goods.

Losing ground to Japanese motorcycles and on the brink of bankruptcy, Harley-Davidson Motorcycles, for example, reinvented its product line, building the previously illicit, after-market styles of the outlaw biker subculture into the motorcycles produced in the Harley-Davidson factory, and promoting these newly stylized motorcycles through corporate advertising campaigns; as a result, the company was reborn as a viable, profitable, and high-profile icon of leisure consumption (Lyng and Bracey, 1995). Similarly, as Heitor Alvelos (2004) has shown, corporate marketers in the UK and elsewhere have begun to copy the symbolism, style, and placement of street graffiti—to the point that the quasi-legal, street-level graffiti of corporate advertising campaigns is at times indistinguishable from the illegal, street-level images of graffiti writers and other illicit artists (see Snyder, 2009). Entire music genres, themselves part of multi-billion dollar business empires, similarly engage with this dynamic (see Ilan, 2012). Take for example, 'Gangsta Rap' which, to varying degrees of authenticity and accuracy, reflects the violent street worlds of the post-industrial USA (see Kubrin, 2005). This genre, whose main audience is composed of relatively affluent suburban youth, appeals to such a demographic due precisely to its transgressive character and its identification with controversy; depending on the particularities of local youth markets, this identification carries the ability to transform gangsta rap into a readily purchasable form of youthful rebellion. Corporate marketeers, like legal authorities, add yet another layer of cultural meaning to the illicit codes of criminal subcultures—and in doing so, often do more to undermine the subcultural integrity of these codes, and to sanitize their illicit purposes, than the legal authorities themselves.

The ongoing consumption and celebration of transgression in everyday life reflects other historical processes and historical ironies as well. Mike Presdee (2000) argues that contemporary dynamics of everyday cultural transgression can be traced to the traditions of carnival: historically, carefully circumscribed times of the year when the moral and social orders were turned on their heads. In carnival, the dominant concerns of work, discipline, rationality, sobriety and propriety were inverted, with leisure, excess, intoxication, laughter and sensuality celebrated. Carnival thus constituted a remarkable cultural construction: a festive, vulgar, spectacular and participatory event where otherwise illicit pursuits could be celebrated and embraced, if only temporarily. Yet Presdee argues that over time, these carnivals of vulgar excess came to be tamed, commodified, and regulated, thereby losing their power to both confirm and contain transgression. As a result, the shattered remains of carnival now litter our everyday lives. Consider for example the contemporary night time leisure industry. As the skies grow darker, legions of (particularly younger) people leave their unsatisfying work and seek self-realization and identity in an array of licensed bars, pubs, clubs and concert venues. Extreme intoxication, the allure of possible sexual encounters and the ever present potential for violence create a seductive environment for millions of revellers across Great Britain and other late capitalist economies, vastly enriching the alcohol and licensed leisure industries with their consumption. In the post-industrial era, such economic activities are increasingly significant as sources of State and private revenue—and yet, having created such a criminogenic milieu, policymakers are quick to blame the individual 'binge-drinker' for subsequent problems (Hayward and Hobbs, 2007). Indeed, the antics of drunken revellers filmed by ubiquitous CCTV cameras can be processed for further carnivalesque pleasures and economic gain. Millions of viewers tune in to reality TV shows from 'Booze Britain' to 'Night Cops' to take private guilty pleasure at the sight of others' public humiliations. This carnivalesque 'second life' is present throughout everyday (and every night) life, not only for those stumbling from bar to bar, but for those safely home, their televisions or computer screens tuned to 'Booze Britain', police chase compilations, and pornography.

REVIEW QUESTIONS

1 Is it appropriate for criminal or criminalized groups to market and profit from their own websites or videos? In what ways might they differ from crime-related films or television shows produced by mainstream media companies?

2 Should there be limits on the degree to which crime-related images can be used to sell youth cultural products?

CONCLUSION

In the many confluences of crime and culture in everyday life, certain patterns can be seen time and again. Subcultures organized around criminal or marginal behaviour emerge also as communities of shared symbolism and meaning, encoding common experience in counter-cultural values and expectations, inventing rituals that confirm and celebrate legal marginality, and indulging in nuances of alternative language, demeanour, and style. For their part, legal authorities attend to these symbolic displays in their efforts at surveillance and control, often policing the culture of crime as much as crime itself; corporate marketeers work to appropriate such displays, hoping to capture something of their edgy currency; and the mass media utilize such symbolic displays as dramatic markers of crime, drafting from them gross caricatures of criminality to captivate the interest of their ever more anxious audiences. In this way, all the parties to crime and crime control operate within a common if contested cultural milieu, shaping the reality of crime through the medium of symbolism and style.

Cultures of crime and control permeate everyday life in a multitude of ways; broad socio-economic forces, media flows, and staggering global inequalities manifest in daily micro-occurrences, items and interactions. The human landscape is dotted with public displays of criminality, crime control, and victimization. Within this contested cultural vortex, members of criminal subcultures continue to find experiences of intense, situated affirmation, edgework and adrenalin—if only for a moment. Meanwhile, they and others often remain locked in everyday, more mundane struggles for subsistence (whether physical or existential) and safety.

These ongoing cultural constructions of crime and crime control intertwine with other areas of criminological concern as well, many of them considered in this volume. It is of course within this larger context of culture and crime that the importance of critically analysing 'media images of crime' (see Chapter 7) begins to make sense. 'Young people and crime' (see Chapter 17) seem especially to be connected by way of illegal or marginal subcultures, stylized representations of illicit identity, and mediated images of criminality—and for young people and others, the experience of edgework and adrenalin offers one of many powerful links between 'psychology and crime' (see Chapter 6). As already seen, such stylized identities in turn provide opportunities for 'surveillance' on the part of legal authorities (see Chapter 21). In these ways the study of crime, culture and everyday life has become an essential component in the larger practice of criminological inquiry—and yet it has also begun to take shape as a distinctly cultural criminology that today contributes to the pantheon of 'criminological theory' (see Chapter 4).

Perhaps most importantly, the connections between crime and culture in everyday life continue always to evolve; crime and crime control can best be understood not as accomplished cultural facts, but as ongoing cultural processes. For this reason any attempt to document the subtleties of subcultural style or to catalogue the range of mediated crime representations becomes, at the moment of its writing, a cultural history—important in its own right, but already a step behind the emerging trajectory of crime and culture. And for this reason it is essential that students—those who are already becoming the next generation of criminological scholars—become involved in researching and analysing the connections between crime and culture. Existing scholarship, no matter what its merits, can never be enough; it can only offer a foundation from which to build new understandings of crime and culture. This task takes on particular significance when the contemporary politics of crime and culture are considered. The intersection of culture and crime is today emerging as an essential domain of political and moral conflict; it is here that fundamental issues of human identity and social justice are being contested, and here that powerful socio-economic forces manifest in everyday occurrences. Because of this, the critical analysis of crime and culture is no abstract intellectual exercise; it is, at its best, an exercise in engaged citizenship and informed activism.

QUESTIONS FOR DISCUSSION

1 Select a controversial issue having to do with crime or crime control—urban riots, for example, or the prevalence of domestic violence. Using only images culled from the mass media and popular culture, create a visual essay that presents your critical understanding of this issue.

2 Construct a set of guidelines for mass media coverage of everyday crime. Consider not only the fairness and accuracy of particular news reports, but ways to ensure that the cumulative effect of ongoing crime reporting is helpful to the public's understanding of larger crime issues.

3 If the possession and consumption of coffee were to be made illegal, what sort of illicit subculture might evolve among users of coffee? What sorts of subcultural values, styles, rituals, and experiences might emerge? Why?

4 Collect flyers and advertisements for various bars, nightclubs and alcoholic drinks. Reviewing this material, discuss the extent to which the night time economy might be thought of as creating a 'carnival' within and against everyday life.

5 This chapter has discussed the styles, rituals, and practices of criminal subcultures. But what is the subculture of policing? In what ways is this police subculture similar to, or different from, the subcultures formed by criminal or marginalized groups?

GUIDE TO FURTHER READING

Ferrell, J., Hayward, K., and Young, J. (2008) *Cultural Criminology: An Invitation*. London: Sage.
Attempting to develop a relatively comprehensive account of crime, culture, and cultural criminology, this book considers not only topics like media, emotions, and everyday life, but the methods of cultural criminology, and its history and future.

Ferrell, J., Hayward, K., Morrison, W., and Presdee, M. (eds) (2004) *Cultural Criminology Unleashed*. London: GlassHouse Press.
This book expands the theoretical and substantive range of cultural criminology, and includes research into culture and crime across a variety of local, regional, and national settings.

Ferrell, J. and Sanders, C.R. (eds) (1995) *Cultural Criminology*. Boston: Northeastern University Press.
The first book to define the new criminological approach known as 'cultural criminology', this work builds from earlier British and American studies of crime and culture, and includes chapters on mass media, music, subcultures, and style.

Cohen, S. (2002 [1972, 1980, 1987]) *Folk Devils and Moral Panics* (3rd edn) London: Routledge.
Now in its third edition, this book remains a classic study in the intersections of culture and crime. The ongoing vitality and importance of Cohen's 'folk devil' and 'moral panic' concepts are highlighted in a new introduction to this third edition.

Presdee, M. (2000) *Cultural Criminology and the Carnival of Crime*. London: Routledge.
This book utilizes the lens of cultural criminology to examine a wide range of everyday practices—raving, joyriding, and sadomasochism, for example—and finds among them the shattered remains of human carnival.

Hayward, K. (2004) *City Limits: Crime, Consumer Culture and the Urban Experience*. London: GlassHouse Press.
This book offers the reader a series of unique cultural insights into the way that urban space is changing. Expanding the vision of criminology by drawing on cultural studies, social theory, urban studies, architectural

theory and research into urban consumerism practices, Hayward argues that consumption is now central to understanding the crime-city relationship.

Crime, Media, Culture: An International Journal. London: SAGE.

This award-winning criminological journal provides a forum for international research into crime and culture. The journal includes articles on crime and media, and on the cultural dynamics of crime and criminal justice; it also includes photographs, photographic essays, drawings, and poems, relating to crime and culture.

Simon, David, creator (2002–08) *The Wire* (TV Series) USA: HBO.

HBO's realist masterpiece traces crime and security's pervasiveness throughout myriad aspects of everyday life by introducing us to characters that are morally complex and thoroughly human.

Silver, Tony, director (1983) *Style Wars*. New York: Plexifilm.

Produced by Henry Chalfant, this historic documentary traces the evolution of contemporary graffiti within the larger hip hop culture of music and dance.

Redmon, David, director (2005) *Mardi Gras: Made in China*. Boston: Carnivalesque Films.

A cultural criminological documentary that demonstrates how aspects of raucous partying in New Orleans are connected to the tough conditions faced by young workers in China.

WEB LINKS

http://blogs.kent.ac.uk/culturalcriminology/

This site includes key writings, biographies, photographs, films, event listings, and links, with special focus on cultural criminology at the University of Kent.

http://www.indiana.edu/~culturex/

Maintained by Professor Stephanie Kane, this site offers a guide to issues in culture, law, and crime.

http://stopviolence.com/ and http://www.paulsjusticepage.com/

Maintained by Professor Paul Leighton, these two sites offer a variety of resources, essays, images, and links relating to contemporary crime and crime control issues.

REFERENCES

Alvelos, H. (2004) 'The Desert of Imagination in the City of Signs: Cultural Implications of Sponsored Transgression and Branded Graffiti' in J. Ferrell, K.J. Hayward, W. Morrison, and M. Presdee (eds) *Cultural Criminology Unleashed*. London: GlassHouse Press.

Bauman, Z. (2000). *Liquid Modernity*. London: Polity.

Becker, Howard S. (1963) *Outsiders: Studies in the Sociology of Deviance*. New York: Free Press.

Bourgois, P. (2002) *In Search of Respect: Selling Crack in El Barrio* (2nd edn) New York: Cambridge University Press.

Cohen, Stanley (2002 [1972, 1980, 1987]) *Folk Devils and Moral Panics* (3rd edn) London: Routledge.

Cornish, D. and Clarke, R. (1986) *The Reasoning Criminal*. New York: Springer-Verlag.

Corrigan, P. (1979) *Schooling the Smash Street Kids*. London: Macmillan.

Felson, M. (2002) *Crime and Everyday Life* (3rd edn) Thousand Oaks: Sage.

Ferrell, J. (1992) 'Making Sense of Crime', *Social Justice* 19(2): 110–23.

Ferrell, J. (1996) *Crimes of Style: Urban Graffiti and the Politics of Criminality*. Boston: Northeastern University Press.

Ferrell, J. (1997) 'Criminological Verstehen: Inside the Immediacy of Crime', *Justice Quarterly* 14(1): 3–23.

Ferrell, J. (1998) 'Freight Train Graffiti: Subculture, Crime, Dislocation', *Justice Quarterly* 15(4): 587–608.

Ferrell, J. (2002) *Tearing Down the Streets: Adventures in Urban Anarchy*. New York: Palgrave/Macmillan.

Ferrell, J. (2003) 'Speed Kills', *Critical Criminology* 11(3): 185–98.

Ferrell, J. (2004) 'Boredom, Crime, and Criminology', *Theoretical Criminology* 8(3): 287–302.

Ferrell, J. (2006) *Empire of Scrounge: Inside the Urban Underground of Dumpster Diving, Trash Picking, and Street Scavenging*. New York: New York University Press

Ferrell, J. and Hamm, M. (eds) (1998) *Ethnography at the Edge: Crime, Deviance and Field Research*. Boston: Northeastern University Press.

Ferrell, J. and Sanders, C.R. (eds) (1995) *Cultural Criminology*. Boston: Northeastern University Press.

Ferrell, J., Hayward, K., and Young, J. (2008) *Cultural Criminology: An Invitation*. London: SAGE.

Ferrell, J., Hayward, K.J., Morrison, W., and Presdee, M. (eds) (2004) *Cultural Criminology Unleashed*. London: GlassHouse Press.

Ferrell, J., Milovanovic, D., and Lyng, S. (2001) 'Edgework, Media Practices, and the Elongation of Meaning', *Theoretical Criminology* 5(2): 177–202.

Fishman, M. and Cavender, G. (eds) (1998). *Entertaining crime: Television reality programs*. New York: Aldine De Gruyter.

Greer, C. and McLaughlin, E. (2010) 'We Predict a Riot: Public Order Policing, News Coverage and the Rise of the Citizen Journalist', *British Journal of Criminology* 50(6): 1041–59.

Hall S., Winlow, S., and Ancrum, C. (2008) *Criminal Identities and Consumer Culture*. Collumpton: Willan.

Hall, S., Critcher, C., Jefferson, A., Clarke, J., and Roberts, B. (1978) *Policing the Crisis: Mugging, the State, and Law and Order*. London: Macmillan.

Harcourt, B.E. (2007) *Against Prediction: Profiling, Policing, and Punishing in an Actuarial Age*. Chicago: University of Chicago Press.

Hayward, K. and Hobbs, D. (2007) 'Beyond the Binge in "Booze Britain": Market-led liminalisation and the spectacle of binge drinking', *British Journal of Sociology* 58(1): 437–56.

Hayward, K. and Yar, M. (2006) 'The Chav Phenomenon: Consumption, Media and the Construction of a New Underclass', *Crime Media Culture* 2: 9–28.

Hayward, K.J. (2007) 'Situational crime prevention and its discontents: rational choice theory versus the "culture of now"', *Social Policy and Administration* 41(3): 232–50.

Hayward, K.J. and Young, J. (2012) 'Cultural criminology' in M. Maguire, R. Morgan, and R. Reiner (eds) *Oxford Handbook of Criminology* (5th edn) Oxford: Oxford University Press.

Hayward, K.J. (2012) 'A response to Farrell', *Social Policy and Administration* 46(1): 21–34.

Hayward, K.J. (2004) *City Limits: Crime, Consumer Culture and the Urban Expression*. London: GlassHouse.

Hayward, K.J. and Presdee, M. (2010) *Framing Crime: Cultural Criminology and the Image*. London: Routledge.

Hayward, K.J. and Young, J. (2004) 'Cultural criminology: some notes on the script', *Theoretical Criminology* 8(3): 259–85.

Highmore, B. (2002) *Everyday Life and Cultural Theory*. London: Routledge.

Hough, J. M., Clarke, R.V.G. and Mayhew, P. (1980) 'Introduction' in R.V.G. Clarke and P. Mayhew (eds) *Designing Out Crime*. London: HMSO.

Ilan, J. (2010) 'If you don't let us in, we'll get arrested: Class-cultural dynamics in the delivery of, and resistance to, youth justice work', *Youth Justice* 10(1): 25–39.

Ilan, J. (2012) '"The Industry's the New Road": Crime, Commodification and Street Cultural Tropes in UK Urban Music', *Crime Media Culture* 8(1): 39–55.

Jackson-Jacobs, C. (2004) 'Taking a Beating: Narrative Gratifications of Fighting as an Underdog' in J. Ferrell, K.J. Hayward, W. Morrison, and M. Presdee (eds) *Cultural Criminology Unleashed*. London: GlassHouse Press, 231–44.

Jenkins, P. (2001) *Beyond Tolerance: Child Pornography on the Internet*. New York: New York University Press.

Jewkes, Y. (ed.) (2003) *Dot.cons: Crime, Deviance and Identity on the Internet*. Devon, UK: Willan.

Katz, J. (1988) *Seductions of Crime: Moral and Sensual Attractions in Doing Evil*. New York: Basic Books.

Kubrin, C. (2005) 'Gangstas, Thugs and Hustlas: Identity and the Code of the Street in Rap Music', *Social Problems* 52 (3): 360–78.

Lipscombe, S. and Bennett, O. (2012) 'Metal Theft', London: House of Commons Library, available at: http://www.parliament.uk/briefing-papers/SN06150.pdf.

Lyng, S. (1990) 'Edgework: A Social Psychological Analysis of Voluntary Risk Taking', *American Journal of Sociology* 95: 851–86.

Lyng, S. (ed) (2005) *Edgework: The Sociology of Risk-Taking*. New York: Routledge.

Lyng, S. and Bracey, Jr., M.L. (1995) 'Squaring the One Percent: Biker Style and the Selling of Cultural Resistance' in J. Ferrell and C.R. Sanders (eds), Boston: Northeastern University Press, 235–76.

Manning, P. (1998) 'Media Loops' in F. Bailey and D. Hale (eds) *Popular Culture, Crime, and Justice*. Belmont, CA: West/Wadsworth, 25–39.

McRobbie, A. and Thornton, S.L. (1995) 'Rethinking "Moral Panic" for Multi-Mediated Social Worlds', *British Journal of Sociology* 46: 559–74.

Miller, E. (1991) 'Assessing the Risk of Inattention to Class, Race/Ethnicity, and Gender: Comment on Lyng', *American Journal of Sociology* 96 (6): 1530–4.

Miller, J. (1995) 'Struggles Over the Symbolic: Gang Style and the Meanings of Social Control' in J. Ferrell and C.R. Sanders (eds) *Cultural Criminology*. Boston: Northeastern University Press, 213–34.

O'Brien, M. (2006) 'Not Keane on Prawn Sandwiches: criminal impoverishments of consumer culture', paper presented at the Second International Conference on Cultural Criminology, May, London.

Polsky, N. (1998 [1967]) *Hustlers, Beats, and Others*. New York: Lyons Press.

Presdee, M. (2009) '"Volume Crime" and Everyday Life' in C. Hale, K. Hayward, A. Wahidin, and E. Wincup (eds) *Criminology* (2nd edn) Oxford: Oxford University Press.

Presdee, M. (2000) *Cultural Criminology and the Carnival of Crime*. London: Routledge.

Snyder, G. (2009) *Graffiti Lives*. New York: New York University Press.

Squires, P. and Stephen, D. (2005) *Rougher Justice: Anti-social Behaviour and Young People*. Cullompton: Willan.

Taylor, I., Walton, P., and Young, J. (1973) *The New Criminology*. New York: Harper & Row.

Weber, M. (1949) *The Methodology of the Social Sciences*. New York: The Free Press.

Young, J. (1971) 'The Role of the Police as Amplifiers of Deviancy, Negotiators of Reality and Translators of Fantasy' in Stanley Cohen (ed) *Images of Deviance*. Harmondsworth, UK: Penguin, 27–61.

Young, J. (1999) *The Exclusive Society, Social Exclusion, Crime and Difference in Late Modernity*. London: Sage.

Young, J. (2003) 'Merton with Energy, Katz with Structure: The Sociology of Vindictiveness and the Criminology of Transgression', *Theoretical Criminology* 7(3): 389–414.

Young, J. (2007) *The Vertigo of Late Modernity*. London: Sage.

Part IV
RESPONSES TO CRIME

19 The politics of law and order

Marian FitzGerald and Chris Hale

The modern State is expected to provide for the safety and well-being of its citizens, protecting them from both external and internal threats, including becoming victims of crime.

A key theme of many of the chapters in this volume is the fluidity of definitions of 'crime'. These vary across time and place and, as this chapter illustrates, governments themselves may strongly influence trends in crime, not only by passing laws creating new offences but also by defining how crime should be measured officially. Despite these politically determined variations, overall trends and patterns in crime are driven primarily by social and economic developments (see Chapter 14). Although the relationships involved are complex it could be argued nevertheless that it is governments' social and economic policies which are most likely to have long term impact on crime. The influence of criminal justice policies will, at best, be relatively modest. The main role of the criminal justice system (CJS) is to respond effectively to crime when it happens—including ensuring that the way offenders are dealt with reduces the risk of their re-offending. The CJS is also responsible for preventing crime in the short term in the sense of averting specific crimes that are verifiably in planning; but any such intervention to must take full account of its parallel responsibilities for safeguarding human rights and freedoms (see Chapter 20).

The fall in recorded crime in England and Wales following the end of World War II, reinforced utopian assumptions that this was directly related to improvements in social conditions. But even as reverses in the trends began to challenge these assumptions, the political parties maintained the consensus that decision making within the CJS should appear to be 'above politics': while parliament made the laws it should not interfere in how they were applied.

This chapter traces the breakdown in that consensus and the ways in which crime became an increasingly contested arena of political competition. All the main political parties now make claims and counter-claims about trends in crime (see Chapter 3). Each promises to reduce crime and make the public safer in ways which once reflected ideological differences between them. These distinctions have been increasingly blurred since the 1990s such that the current approach of both Labour and the Conservatives has been described as one of **'populist punitiveness'** (Bottoms, 1995). Politicians increasingly depict the CJS itself as key to controlling crime; and many commentators, observing similar trends in other Western countries, have suggested nation-states, conscious of their weakening influence over social and economic developments, have resorted to 'governing through crime' (Simon, 2007).

One evident consequence in England and Wales is that the agencies of the CJS have been affected by the changes in the politics of law and order described later in this chapter. Until relatively recently, though, the focus of successive governments has been the crimes which *directly* affect most people and there has been a perceptible widening of this focus in order to sanction formally even the least serious offences as well as incidents of nuisance behaviour; and the CJS itself has traditionally targeted the more deprived sections of society. However, a series of unrelated scandals within recent years have made it more difficult to overlook the crimes of the powerful, and their significant—but often indirect—impact on the population at large (see Chapter 11).

REVIEW QUESTIONS

1   In what sense might crime be described as 'political'?

2   What are the main influences on trends in crime?

The politics of law and order in the UK since 1945

Trends in crime

Crime in England and Wales changed from being an exceptional experience in the period immediately after World War II to one that has become relatively normal (see Figure 19.1). Yet the trend has not been uniform; rather, building on Hale (1999) and McClintock and Avison (1968) it is possible to identify four distinct periods:

1.   1945–54—recorded crime fluctuates around low level;

2.   1955–72—recorded crime begins to grow steadily;

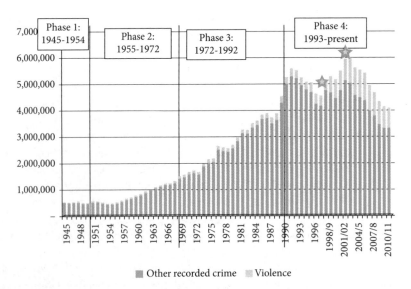

Figure 19.1 Recorded crime in England and Wales 1945 to 2011–12 (major changes to **counting rules** indicated by *).

Source: Home Office Criminal Statistics

CHAPTER 19 THE POLITICS OF LAW AND ORDER

3. 1973–92—recorded crime growth accelerates;

4. 1992–present—levels of recorded crime become more volatile—rising sharply to two peaks (related to major changes to the way crime had previously been recorded—see Chapter 3), each followed by a sharp fall.

This upward trend, followed by a downturn in the early 1990s has been observed in other countries over the same period; and the main factors at work have been identified as long-run economic and social trends, combined with short-term economic fluctuations. These suggest that while **violence** tends to rise in times of affluence but fall during **recessions** whereas **acquisitive crime** shows the opposite pattern (Field, 1990). Loader and Sparks (2007) identify long-term structural changes to the turn of the century at the level of economic, social and cultural relations. Economic trends in particular are considered in more detail in Chapter 14 but factors highlighted by Loader and Sparks are:

(a) the shift from economies predominantly based on manufacturing industry to ones based on the service sector and the rise of consumerism;

(b) changes in family structures and living arrangements (including the suburbanization of cities);

(c) the proliferation of electronic mass media; and

(d) a 'democratization' of everyday life ', including altered relations between men and women, parents and children and, more generally, a marked decline in unthinking adherence towards authority.

The impact of these changes on the recorded crime figures, however, has recently been obscured in two main ways. One was the changes made by the government from 1997 to crime recording requirements, especially those indicated in *Figure 19.1* (see also Chapter 3). However, the other is changes in the types of property crimes which account for most of the recorded crime total (see Figure 19.1). By the turn of the century technological developments, including Internet shopping and the increasing use of credit and debit cards, were rapidly opening up new opportunities of illegitimately parting people from their money and were rarely reported to the **police** (Yar, 2006; Wall, 2007).

Trends in the politics of crime

The changes in the politics of law and order—and in particular the breakdown of the consensus referred to in the Introduction—have not coincided with the trends in crime described above. Downes and Morgan (2002) see them as falling into three phases:[1]

(a) Politics phase 1: 1945–70—political census around support for penal-welfare approach.

(b) Politics phase 2: 1970–92—political division and sharp disagreements between the main political parties.

(c) Politics phase 3: 1992–present—a new consensus based around 'populist punitiveness'.

Each is now examined in turn, though constraints of space mean less coverage is given to the first.

REVIEW QUESTIONS

1 Describe the major trends in recorded crime in England and Wales since 1945.

2 What are the main explanations for these trends?

3 What were the key political phases in the UK following the end of World War II?

Politics phase 1: 1945–70

Crime had grown at around 7 per cent annually between 1930 and 1948; but, with the establishment of the welfare state by the Labour government of 1945 to 1951, crime stabilized. Successive Conservative governments continued to support the welfare state and it became an unquestioned fixture of British political life. Crime was expected to fall as social conditions improved (McClintock and Avison, 1968: 19) and by 1954 it was indeed about 18 per cent lower per head of population than in 1948. However not only was **unemployment** low over this period, some war-time rationing continued and there was little growth in **consumption**.

With the end of rationing, after years of post-war austerity, 1955 saw the start of a consumer boom; and recorded crime started to increase by around 10 per cent each year. Yet, despite the Prime Minister (Harold Macmillan) declaring that Britons had 'never had it so good', the UK's global economic position was already in relative decline and the post-war expansion began to falter. By the time Labour returned to power in 1964 it had effectively abandoned its commitment to full employment; and the policies it pursued from 1967 led to a major rise in industrial unrest. By now, the post-war baby boom had produced a bulge in the demographic group at the peak age for offending and political upheavals around the globe, particularly in 1968, further fuelled moral panics around the behaviour of increasingly rebellious youth.

Nonetheless, in contrast with other policy areas such as economic management, foreign affairs, health or education, the Conservative and the Labour Parties followed an essentially bi-partisan approach to law and order. Both supported policies combining elements of punishment and welfare but left the institutions of the CJS to administer a 'penal-welfare state' (Garland, 2001) which aimed to identify and reform the individual 'delinquent' in the context of a more general aspiration to improve social conditions through the application of scientific knowledge. Thus 'correctionalist' treatment programmes aimed to return offenders 'to the fold of social democratic citizenship' (Loader and Sparks, 2004: 84), and a small group of civil servants and senior CJS practitioners used the findings of research to shape the direction of crime policy, free of influence from politicians or public opinion (Faulkner and Burnett, 2012: 40–1).

There were hints of change in the terms of the political debate over law and order during this period (for more detail, see Downes and Morgan 2002, 2007) but, as yet 'no party manifesto [had] suggested that the level or form of crime was itself attributable to the politics of the party in government' (Downes and Morgan, 1994: 187).

REVIEW QUESTIONS

1 What happened to the relative global economic position of the UK between 1945 and 1970?
2 Why had crime initially fallen and why did it later begin to rise?
3 What were the main features of the 'penal-welfare state'?

Politics phase 2: 1970–92

The 1970s were a period of political instability and industrial unrest. The Conservatives ousted Labour from power in 1970 but lost the general election in February 1974, with no party winning an overall majority. The minority Labour government which took over called a further election in October and secured a majority; but after Labour lost the 1979 general election, the Conservatives were to remain in power for a further 18 years. Between 1970 and 1992, the increase in recorded offences was very large by historical standards. This coincided with varied but recurrent outbreaks of mass disorder against a backdrop of economic decline and insecurity.

By the 1970 election campaign, crime was no longer seen purely in individual terms: it now became symbolic of wider and more deep-seated problems—symptomatic of a threat to the rule of law and order—and the post-war consensus had broken down. Not only did the party manifestos in 1970 devote more space than ever before to crime; for the first time, the Conservatives linked the problem directly to the policies of the Labour government. They also began to identify crime with mass forms of unrest including political protest, industrial disputes and picketing. They claimed the law needed modernizing 'for dealing with public order—peculiar to the age of demonstration and disruption'. Though Labour responded by deploring the 'cynical . . . attempts of our opponents to exploit for Party Political ends the issue of crime and law enforcement', they lost the election.

Once in power, the Conservatives were forced to modify their manifesto commitment to allow wages to find their own level. Trade union resistance, combined with the struggle of Britain's traditional manufacturing industries to survive in the global economy, forced the government to adopt income policies and to intervene to mitigate fluctuations in demand.

Meanwhile **crime rates** had remained fairly constant, so the Conservatives claimed in the first of the general elections of 1974 that they had been successful in fighting crime. Labour remained silent on the issue; and by the second 1974 election, the Conservatives returned to the attack. They explicitly criticized Labour's record on crime and, for the first time, accused Labour of failing to support the 'rule of law' because some Labour MPs had supported the use of mass picketing in the 1973 miners' strike.

Having nevertheless won a parliamentary majority, by 1975 Labour was itself arguing that unemployment was part of the price to be paid for combating inflation. Its intensified efforts to restrict money supply and cut public expenditure following a series of currency crises exacerbated social divisions. The Labour government argued that the conditions imposed by the International Monetary Fund (IMF) when it intervened to shore up the British economy in 1976 demanded sacrifices from everyone; but the flat rate cap it introduced on pay rises for public sector workers inevitably fell hardest on the lowest paid. The resulting widespread strikes in the winter of 1978–79 badly affected the public at large since many strikers were in menial but essential jobs such as refuse disposal and digging graves.

So despite the Conservatives' commitment to the same, unpopular level of economic stringency as Labour, public reaction to 'The Winter of Discontent' undoubtedly helped them to win the 1979 general election. Their campaign successfully exploited the theme of law and order by associating industrial militancy and public protest with a general decline in morality and breakdown of respect for authority. Blaming the latter on a dependency culture fostered by the welfare state the party's new leader, Margaret Thatcher, declared:

> In their muddled but different ways, the vandals on the picket lines and the muggers in our streets have got the same confused message—'we want our demands met or else' and 'get out of the way give us your handbag'. (Thatcher 1979)

The new Conservative government's approach to law and order was based on notions of morality which required individual self-discipline and which regarded social conditions as irrelevant. It was reinforced by the emerging '**nothing works**' strand of criminological thinking (see Chapter 24) which put punishment and retribution rather than rehabilitation at the centre of government policy,[2] along with a shift of focus to crime *prevention*. Despite its emphasis on individual responsibility, the government significantly increased expenditure on the CJS. Between 1979 and 1988 the number of police officers increased by 11 per cent, there was a 12 per cent increase in civilian staff and a 64 per cent increase in real terms in total police expenditure. At the same time the Conservatives implemented a major prison building programme as the prison population increased from around 42,220 in 1979 to 47,200 in 1986–87, 13 per cent above existing capacity (Brake and Hale, 1992).

Soon after returning to office, though, the Conservative government had been faced with the first major, sustained outbreak of public disorder on the British mainland since the 1930s. The civil disturbances of 1980 were triggered by conflict between black people and the police and were followed on a larger scale by similar outbreaks in 1981. It was already apparent that the government's commitments to strong **policing** and tough **sentencing** were having little impact on rising levels of crime. Consequently the government began to look at other ways of proving to the electorate that it could control the problem. Rather than taking an enforcement-based response to the disturbances, more liberal elements within the party persuaded the government to pursue a strategy which included urban regeneration and police reform, culminating in the Police and Criminal Evidence Act 1984 (PACE) (see Chapter 20).

By the 1983 general election, the party's rhetoric on law and order had again changed. Crime, it asserted, could not be controlled solely through strong police powers and tougher sentencing; the responsibility also rested with:

teachers and parents—and television producers too—who influence the moral standards of the next generation. (Conservative Party, 1983)

The government nonetheless made full use of the police and the courts to break union resistance to its economic and social policies (for example, in the 1984 miners' strike). Yet still crime continued to rise, with an increase of just under 20 per cent between 1983 and 1987; and 1985 saw a further recurrence of inner city rioting, this time involving loss of life. From being an electoral asset, law and order by now risked becoming the Conservatives' biggest failure. Pragmatically, the government's rhetoric now shifted again to distance it as far as possible from responsibility for the 1985 riots, with the Home Secretary claiming that they were 'not a cry for help but a cry for loot', while several of his parliamentary colleagues were quick to link the riots to the policies of 'Looney Left' Labour authorities in the areas where many of them occurred (FitzGerald, 1987, 1989). The police's responsibility for ensuring order, though, was played down in favour of renewed emphasis on the role of the 'community' and the 'active citizen'.

The Labour leadership at this time was already trying to re-invent the party by distancing itself from the ideas of its more left wing elements; the work of the Left Realists (see, for example, Lea and Young, 1984) fed into this by highlighting the dangers of continuing to ignore the impact of crime on Labour's traditional supporters. By the 1987 election all the main parties were making explicit commitments to crime prevention, but while Labour stressed the need for a collective approach involving local authorities the Conservatives placed the responsibility on individual householders and voluntary local schemes (such as **Neighbourhood Watch**).

By now, despite the government's punitive rhetoric, the cost of the rising numbers in prison was causing increasing concern. Expenditure on the prison service had risen by 36 per cent in real terms between 1979 and 1989 and—despite Home Office ministers continuing to claim that they would not interfere with the judicial process—in the 1980s they began to argue consistently that prison was *only* to be used for violent and serious offenders. A growing awareness that prison was an expensive way of making bad people worse[3] led to further attempts to persuade courts and the public that, if properly applied, non-custodial community sentences (see Chapter 24) were not soft options. So the Criminal Justice Act 1991 (CJA) reflected the '**Just Deserts**' principle: sentencing decisions should focus on the seriousness of the offence and an offender's previous convictions should not normally be taken into account. The Act outlined a clear hierarchy of sentences, reserving custodial sentences for the most serious offences or, in the case of violent or sexual offences, where they were necessary to protect the public.

By the end of the 1980s, further disturbances—this time in all-white, rural areas—took the government by surprise (see Chapter 16). They were followed in 1990 by rioting associated with its introduction of the poll tax and again in 1991 by riots involving young whites on outer estates in several British cities, triggering media-fuelled anxiety over joyriding and ram raiders. Meanwhile ongoing concerns over football hooliganism which had first become an issue in the 1960s risked seriously tarnishing Britain's image abroad, particularly after it resulted in fatalities at the European Cup Final in Belgium in 1985. Coinciding with the severe economic recession of 1989–92, recorded crime in 1992 was 50 per cent higher than in 1988. After replacing Margaret Thatcher as Prime Minister with John Major in 1990, the Conservatives succeeded in winning the 1992 general election, albeit with a significantly reduced majority.

REVIEW QUESTIONS

1 What links did the Conservative government elected in 1979 make between crime and industrial unrest?

2 What did the Conservative government of the 1980s claim had been the effect of the welfare state?

3 What changes occurred in Conservative policies on law and order, and why?

Politics phase 3: post-1992

The most recent phase in the politics of law and order is distinguished primarily by the development of competition between the two main political parties to persuade the electorate they were tougher on crime than the other. Yet this plays out against a backdrop which echoes earlier phases, starting with a recession, followed by recovery and a sustained growth in consumption but ending with a further deep-seated recession which, in terms of political rhetoric, demanded sacrifices from everyone but which justified cuts in public expenditure which would inevitably fall on the most disadvantaged sections of society. It begins with the Conservatives' last term in office since coming to power in 1979. The Labour government which took over in 1997 then won three successive general elections. However, in the 2010 general election, no party won enough seats to form a majority government. By contrast with 1974, however, the Conservatives did not attempt to rule as minority government but formed a Coalition with the Liberal Democrats and legislated to create fixed-term parliaments to last a full five years.

1992–1997

Following the recession of 1988–92, in September 1992 currency speculation forced sterling out of the European Exchange Rate Mechanism (ERM), and exacerbated internal divisions within a Conservative party which had been in government for 14 years but was starting to see its hold on power slip away. With crime also rising, Faulkner notes a fundamental and dramatic change to the government's political style during 1993 which he ascribes to:

> an urgent need for the Government to re-unite the Party around a suitable populist issue, and crime and law and order were a natural choice. (Faulkner, 2001: 122)

It became almost unthinkable to challenge this approach after 1993 when the abduction and brutal murder of the toddler James Bulger by two ten-year-old boys became:

> a powerful symbol of our collective helplessness, of a malaise that goes beyond a single case, beyond even crime figures. (*Independent on Sunday*, 28 February 1993)

The diversionary impact of the CJA 1991 (see earlier in this chapter) was already becoming clear as the monthly prison population figures fell continuously from a peak of 47,605 in April 2002 to 40,722 by the end of December 2003. However, the liberal thinking behind the Act was overtaken by the Conservatives' new populist strategy which also sought to damage their Labour opponents by labelling them as weak on law and order. The Prime Minister's call to go 'back to basics' signalled a more general return to the punitively authoritarian approach of the 1970s, while the bald assertion in 1993 by the Conservatives' new Home Secretary Michael Howard that 'prison works' was followed by a further increase in the prison population. This also coincided with a fall in crime (see Figure 19.1), although it is arguable that this was strongly correlated with the devaluation which resulted from sterling leaving the ERM, leading to a period of sustained and steady economic growth.

Meanwhile, one indication of the makeover taking place within the Labour party was its efforts to overtake the Conservatives as *the* party of law and order. Although several Labour policy papers between 1993 and 1996 linked crime with social problems, publicly the party focused on criticizing the operation of the criminal justice system under the Conservatives (Downes and Morgan, 1997). In addition, the Opposition began actively tapping in to popular anxieties fuelled by recurrent outbreaks of violent group disorder under the Conservatives. It now widened the scope of its criminal justice policies to include minor, everyday 'incivilities' which were already known to be closely associated with '**fear of crime**' (for an overview see Hale, 1996, also Farrell *et al.*, 2009) and which it re-badged as 'antisocial behaviour'.

The more punitive the government became, the more determinedly the Opposition seemed to track them. It criticized the Just Deserts principles underpinning the CJA 1991 and attacked the operation of the CJS under the Conservatives more generally, citing falling conviction rates and delays in dealing with juvenile offenders. Despite claiming that '*New*' Labour would be 'tough on crime and tough on the causes of crime' (Blair, 1993), the Opposition made no attempt to link the rise in crime to Conservative economic and social policies. Rather, this soundbite seemed calculated to exploit public concerns about rising crime—promising that a New Labour government would be 'tough on crime' *whatever* its causes (Downes and Morgan, 2002: 296).

Howard continued to raise the stakes—for example, by doubling the maximum custodial sentence for 15–17-year-olds, and introducing new custodial sentences for 12–14-year-olds. However, Tony Blair and Jack Straw, as successive shadow Home Secretaries, often appeared to take the lead in a bidding war on toughness. Straw's enthusiasm for New York-style policing (see Chapter 23) with its 'zero tolerance' of low-level nuisance succeeded in generating headlines for the party, for example when he excoriated beggars and car washers at traffic lights (*Guardian*, 5 September 1995).

Labour acknowledged the wider social issues related to crime in papers such as *Tackling the Causes of Crime* (Labour Party, 1996a); but these social issues fell squarely under the '**social exclusion**' agenda which the party was developing in parallel to—and sometimes in tension with—its criminal justice policies (see Young and Matthews, 2003; Hale and FitzGerald, 2007; and Chapter 14). In the run-up to the 1997 election, it reasserted its 'tough' stand on crime with proposals for more secure places for juveniles and lengthy periods of imprisonment for breaching community safety orders, combined with a new programme of measures to crack down on anti-social behaviour.

1997 to 2010

When 'New Labour' came to power in 1997, its administrative style contrasted starkly with that of its predecessors. Far from distancing themselves from events which they could not control, Labour ministers took a '**managerialist**' approach to all public services including the agencies of the CJS. Successive targets, performance indicators and action plans for particular strands of policy were often overseen by new, dedicated units within government departments, while special short-term funding was used to encourage relevant agencies to participate in a succession of government initiatives.[4] By the time Labour had been in power for 11 years it had enacted between 50 and 70 criminal-justice related statutes and created 3,000 to 4,000 new offences (Morgan, 2008). Every institution in the CJS had been affected by its zeal for reform. Other chapters (especially Chapters 17, 20, 23, 24 and 25) variously describe the major structural changes the government made to existing bodies and the new ones it created both at national and local level.

Labour's appetite for reorganization appeared undiminished by its third and final term when, in 2007, it split the Home Office and created a new Ministry of Justice (MoJ). The former retained responsibility for a police service whose size and remit had progressively expanded during Labour's first two terms in office (see Chapter 23). Meanwhile the MoJ inherited a prison population which had already increased to such an extent that—as previously under Conservative governments—ministers were faced with growing tensions between their private concerns about its cost and their continued determination to appear publicly tough on crime. The Labour government maintained its punitive rhetoric throughout all of its three terms in office, distinguishing 'the law abiding public' from the criminal minority. Ignoring the evidence that victims may also be offenders and vice versa (Tonry, 2004: 27), it pledged to reform the CJS in order to 're-balance [it] in favour of the victim' (Home Office, 2002). However, the focus of its criminal justice policies was to change over time.

Labour started its first term with the aim of proving to the public that, in addition to tackling the long neglected problem of anti-social behaviour, it could significantly reduce the overall level of crime. In relation to the former it introduced a wide range of measures, the best known of which was the Anti-Social Behaviour Order (ASBO), and it made clear to police forces that they would be found wanting if they failed to use them. It set apparently ambitious targets for all 43 police forces to reduce domestic burglaries and motor vehicle offences which, at the time, were the main types of 'volume crime', adding a target for reducing robberies in just five areas where this seemed to be a problem. In fact, numbers of domestic burglaries and motor vehicle offences had already started to reduce, largely as a result of improved security measures but also (see earlier) because technological developments were providing new opportunities for property crime.

The main, unexpected development of the government's first term was the riots by young Asians in Northern towns (see Chapter 16). But rather than responding to these events as a 'law and order' issue the government succeeded in treating them as issue of 'social cohesion', creating yet another Home Office unit to manage this newly minted area of policy.

By the end of its first term, the government was frustrated by the lack of public acclaim for the fall in crime. Though domestic burglaries and motor vehicle offences continued to decline, the British Crime Survey (BCS) showed the public obstinately clinging to the belief that crime had risen. Meanwhile, Labour's strategy of highlighting antisocial behaviour appeared to have backfired as perceptions of 'incivilities' (including 'teenagers hanging around on the street') had also increased.

In setting its initial crime reduction targets, the government had failed to anticipate the surge in the ownership of mobile phones. Early in its second term this had resulted in a major rise in the robbery figures, triggering the Street Crime Initiative which was launched and personally led by the Prime Minister over six months in 2002. A detailed inspection report subsequently highlighted the weaknesses in this type of approach, including many of the perverse effects of political pressure to meet arbitrarily set targets; and it raised questions over the sustainability of any gains once political priorities changed and dedicated funding ran out (HMIC, 2003).

However, by its second term the government seems to have decided that official figures which showed that crime was falling were insufficient to 'reassure' the public: the problem was that people lacked confidence in the CJS generally. So the policy focus now widened to 'bridging the justice gap', setting targets for the police to increase the proportion of crimes they recorded which resulted in the offenders being detected and subjected to some form of 'sanction'. The targets were met largely by an increase in cautions and the use of new 'out of court disposals' available to the police such as cannabis warnings and penalty notices for disorder (PNDs) rather than by increasing the numbers of offenders charged and tried by the courts. Nevertheless the prison population had already risen to record levels under Labour (see Chapter 25).

Meanwhile, despite the relative peace achieved in Northern Ireland following the Good Friday agreement during Labour's first term, the issue of terrorism had again resurfaced on the Home Office agenda. This was not only as a result of the 9/11 bombings in the United States in 2001 but of British citizens being the victims (and in some instances the perpetrators) of terrorist acts abroad. The bombings on public transport in Madrid in 2004 had already highlighted the particular vulnerability of countries involved in the 2003 invasion of Iraq and the government's 'Contest' counter-terrorism strategy dated from the same year.

In the run-up to the 2005 general election the government relied on the BCS to claim that, thanks to Labour:

Today, there is less chance of being a victim of crime than for more than 20 years.

The Conservatives, however, found it opportune to cite the police recorded crime figures instead, despite the fact that government changes to the way these were counted meant that trying to read any trends from this source was now 'like reading tea leaves' (Patrick, 2011). In doing so, they chose to highlight the issue of violent crime:

> Crime today is out of control. There is a gun crime every hour. A million violent crimes are committed each year.

Hitherto, violence (with the partial exception of robbery) had not featured explicitly as a priority for the Labour government. As noted earlier, in aiming to show it could significantly reduce crime overall, it had focused on volume crime which comprises property-related offences. In addition to accounting for only a small proportion of all crime (see Figure 19.1), most crimes of violence were recorded as 'less serious violence' against the person. The government had failed to appreciate that what the public fears most are the exceptional but much more serious forms of violence[5] and to recognize that serious violence had steadily been rising since the early 1990s.[6] Concerns about the issue began only belatedly to have a political impact once it started to affect young people, particularly following the shooting of two girls in Birmingham at the start of 2003.

Labour's third term had hardly begun when in July 2005 there were terrorist attacks on public transport in London. In response, it significantly elaborated its 'Contest' strategy; and some of the associated measures (such as the introduction of control orders and proposals to introduce identity cards) created further tensions within a party already deeply divided over the Iraq war. The party was further unsettled, when in 2006, a formal complaint was made that individuals who had made it large secret loans prior to the 2005 general election had subsequently been nominated for peerages. The Metropolitan Police inquiry into the Cash for Honours' affair sustained a high media profile, especially when it targeted associates of the Prime Minister, although it did not result in any prosecutions.

By 2009, however, all the political parties came under attack when the *Daily Telegraph* launched a sustained campaign against abuses of the expenses system used by Members of Parliament (MPs). This resulted in some MPs resigning or being sacked, with many more having to make public apologies and repayments. Several MPs and members of the House of Lords were prosecuted and sentenced to terms of imprisonment.

Meanwhile, the recession and the banking crisis which began in 2008 had imposed serious constraints on government expenditure. Jack Straw who, as Home Secretary in Labour's first term had instigated the ongoing steep rise in the prison population, was made Justice Minister in 2007 and, following a review of prison overcrowding (Carter, 2007) secured Treasury funding to build three new 'Titan' prisons to hold 2,500 inmates each (*Guardian*, 6 December 2007). However, he also began trying to reduce prison numbers, urging magistrates in particular to consider community sentences in preference to custody (Ministry of Justice, 2008). The number of police constables had already begun falling steadily from its 2005 election year peak although the Police Community Support Officers (PCSOs) created by Labour during its second term had increased thirteen fold since 2004 (Bullock and Gunning, 2007). While Labour continued to make claims about falling crime, the public was now more inclined to believe that crime was rising than they had been before the government first took office in 1997 (Nicholas, Kershaw, and Walker, 2007; Mirrlees-Black and Allen, 1998).

The Labour government, rather than trying to distance itself from these concerns in its third term, sought instead to inject new life into its approaches to law and order. An early move on returning to office in 2005 was to raise further the profile of its campaign to tackle anti-social behaviour, re-badging it the 'Respect' agenda. In tandem, the Ministry of Justice launched a succession of measures to reassert the government's commitment to supporting victims of crime (see Chapter 22). Disregarding the lessons of the street crime initiative, in 2008 alone the government launched a Tackling Knife Crime Action Plan, a Tackling Gangs Action Plan and a Youth Crime Action Plan. Having previously largely ignored the issue of violence, Labour now also set a target for reducing violence by 2011 in the context of a further Tackling Violence Action Plan.

However, a target for violence reduction was *not* set for the police or any other agency. In 2008 the government announced that it was abolishing *all* current police targets and replacing them with a single target of improving 'public confidence', to be measured by the BCS. Meanwhile, the Home Office's relentless interference with the police recorded crime figures continued:

> Since 2005, there have been three major updates to the Home Office Counting Rules relating to fraud, violence against the person and non-sanction detections. There have also been 150 minor changes to reflect the introduction of new laws; and there have been 170 clarifications. (HMIC, 2009)

One related, but largely unnoticed, change was that from 2008 the annual **crime statistics** no longer included a 'most serious violence' subcategory. As the recession started to bite, total violence predictably fell—putting the government on track to meet its new 'violence' target.

However, the Conservative Opposition under their new leader, David Cameron, had started to exploit the issue of violence for political ends. They began to weave it into a wider narrative which indicted the government for its failure to heal the 'broken society' which had given rise to the teenage killings which were now regularly reported in the media (Cameron, 2007). The major political clash over law and order in New Labour's third term, though, arose from an unexpected quarter and was a portent of things to come.

The Greater London Council had been abolished by the Conservative government in 1986 but, in restoring a form of London government early in its first term, Labour made two important innovations. It created the post of an elected London Mayor and it remedied the anomaly that there was no London police authority. Unlike the other 41 forces, where police authorities were directly responsible for the 'efficiency and effectiveness' of the service,[7] the Metropolitan Police had hitherto been directly accountable to the Home Secretary. The government also gave the Mayor the power to appoint the Chair and Vice Chair of the Metropolitan Police Authority. However, in the Mayoral election of May 2008 the incumbent Labour Mayor lost to a high-profile Conservative politician, Boris Johnson. In October of that year, despite having no formal power of dismissal, Johnson effectively forced Sir Ian Blair, head of the Metropolitan Police, to resign. The move brought him directly into conflict with the Home Secretary who attacked Johnson on the grounds that 'party politics should be kept out of policing' (*Daily Telegraph*, 3 October 2008).

2010 on

When the general election of 2010 failed to return a majority government, the Conservatives, as the largest party, did not try to govern alone but formed a Coalition with the Liberal Democrats. This necessitated mutual concessions which exacerbated tensions *within* both parties. In particular, more traditional Conservatives were wary of the coalition becoming a pretext for adopting unacceptably liberal policies, including with regard to law and order. In any case

> [t]he government took office at a time of frustration that comparatively little seemed to have been achieved from the legislation and administrative reforms that had consumed so much energy over the previous 20 years, or from the increase in expenditure that had accompanied them—an increase of two thirds since 1997. (Faulkner and Burnett, 2012: 5)

While new Prime Minister David Cameron followed up his rhetoric about 'broken Britain' by heralding the era of 'the Big Society', from the outset the main preoccupations of his Coalition government were economic (see further later in this chapter); and this was to have far-reaching implications for all public services. Notionally, 'the Big Society' would encourage individual citizen volunteering and, in particular, would engage voluntary sector organizations far more extensively in the delivery of local services; but in practice, most were dependent on grant aid from the public sector, so they were among the first casualties of the major cuts in public spending announced by the new government (Downes and Morgan, 2012).

The need for significant financial savings was the bedrock of the Green Paper 'Breaking the Cycle' (Ministry of Justice, 2010a) published by the new Justice Secretary, Ken Clarke (a former Conservative Home Secretary). The Coalition had inherited a prison population, the cost of which was already unaffordable and, with justice policy now independent of the Home Office, Clarke appeared initially to take the lead in setting out the Coalition's approach to crime and punishment. Although some of his proposals—in particular for major restrictions on legal aid—were greeted with concern in many quarters, including the judiciary (Judge's Council, 2011), groups campaigning for more liberal criminal justice policies welcomed many others. In particular, the Green Paper highlighted the problem of re-offending by individuals once they were in the CJS; and, since re-offending was highest among those given short prison sentences,[8] it cogently argued that the only alternative was to make much greater and more effective use of community sentences.

By citing the risk factors associated with offending—including unemployment, homelessness and drug, alcohol and mental health problems—the MoJ also argued that these would need to be addressed if re-offending was to be reduced (Ministry of Justice, 2010b). The Green Paper's specific proposals for reducing re-offending while cutting costs included competitive tendering for work with offenders, to be rewarded on a 'payment by results' basis. But it also contained measures which aimed more directly at reducing the prison population such as abolishing the indeterminate sentences introduced by Labour and—still more controversially—a proposal for further reducing the discount on a custodial sentence if offenders pleaded 'guilty'. Its further emphasis on the right of judges and magistrates to determine sentencing according to the full facts of each individual case may also have anticipated a reduction in the number of custodial sentences.

Effectively the Green Paper challenged the long-held orthodoxy that the CJS itself held the key to cutting crime. Rather, it implied that the responsibilities went much wider and even implied that the operation of the CJS currently *increased* crime, especially among people who were given short prison sentences. The backlash was immediate, led by Clarke's successor as Home Secretary, Michael Howard, who quickly reasserted his 'prison works' *mantra* (*Times*, 14 December 2010). By early June, the Justice Secretary had been forced to abandon his proposals for increasing the discount for guilty pleas; and later that month it was reported that:

> David Cameron has forced Kenneth Clarke to drop more than 60% of his original proposals ... (*Guardian*, 21 June 2011)

Meanwhile, Clarke's counterpart at the Home Office, Theresa May, might have expected larger than average cuts to her budget, given the claim that crime had fallen relentlessly under Labour. So she commissioned the government's Chief Statistician to undertake a review of crime statistics which, in addition to 4.3 million 'notifiable' offences in 2009–10, uncovered 3.5 million reported incidents of anti-social behaviour and 9.5 million 'calls for assistance' to the police, both of which included 'non-notifiable' offences which would *de facto* not be included in the official total (Matheson, 2011). May had already signalled her intention of giving further priority to anti-social behaviour. Labour's flagship ASBO was to be abolished on the grounds that over half of these orders were breached; but by early 2011 the Home Office proposed a raft of further measures to deal with the problem, including two new orders to replace the ASBO and giving citizens right of redress if the police failed to act on reports of anti-social behaviour (Home Office, 2011a).

Within two months of taking office the Coalition published a Green Paper promising major reforms to the police service (Home Office, 2010), including dismantling structures set up relatively recently under Labour and destroying the Tripartite Agreement by abolishing police authorities and replacing them with elected Police and Crime Commissioners (for more detail see Chapters 20 and 23). While the service was to suffer significant cuts in funding, the government was also aware that any reduction in the level of police visibility would be electorally unpopular. However it claimed that by restoring discretion, abolishing targets and reducing police bureaucracy 'frontline' policing would nonetheless be protected. By contrast with the MoJ Green Paper, all of the Home Office proposals seem to have had the active backing of the Prime Minister; and, despite strong opposition, including in the House of Lords, elections for Police and Crime Commissioners took place in November 2012.[9]

Home Office measures to reform the police, though, went much further than the proposals in the Green Paper and included setting up a major review of police pay and conditions (Winsor, 2012). With relations between the Home Office and ACPO already more than usually strained, Winsor's far-reaching proposals put the government even more squarely on a collision course with parts of the police service; and rank-and-file officers staging a large protest march in May 2012. Nonetheless, several forces responded positively to a government-backed scheme to contract out large areas of police business to the private sector (*Guardian*, 13 March 2012).

Though the Coalition initially blamed the need for financial stringency on its pre-decessor's mismanagement of the economy, the ongoing repercussions of global banking failures were soon further compounded by the escalating crisis in the Eurozone;[10] and by 2012 the UK was facing a 'double-dip' recession which was as bad, if not worse, than the one which faced a previous Conservative government between 1988 and 1992. While the police recorded crime figures had been irreparably compromised as a reliable indicator of trends, the BCS showed rises in property crime in each of the first two years of the new government. However, outbreaks of disorder had again started to raise wider concerns about law and order which were compounded by the police's perceived failure to respond effectively.

Following severe criticism of their handling of the anti-capitalist protests of 2009 in which a member of the public died after being struck by a police officer, the Metropolitan Police appear initially to have taken a low-key approach to demonstrations. So they were severely criticized again when a march against the rise in university tuition fees in November 2010 resulted in some protesters breaking into and occupying the Conservative Party's campaign headquarters and attacking a car occupied by the Prince of Wales and his wife. The following March, a massive and largely peaceful demonstra-tion against public expenditure cuts was disrupted by apparently organized episodes of violence against commercial properties in central London and confrontations with the police. Then in August 2011, rioting broke out after members of a specialist police unit tackling Black-on-Black gun crime intercepted and shot dead a Black man in Tottenham. The rioting quickly spread to other parts of London and thence to several cities, resulting in fatalities. The police were widely criticized for failing to prevent the trouble from esca-lating (see, for example, Singh, 2012), with officers in many areas seen to be impotent in the face of arson and large-scale looting.

All the main parties were quick to condemn the rioters and, with the Labour Opposition still trying to look tougher on crime that the Conservatives, the Justice Secretary appeared increasingly marginalized. In the immediate aftermath of the riots, his Labour predeces-sor challenged the Prime Minister as follows:

> [D]oes he not understand that his repetition of what amount to Treasury lines about police numbers and police budgets, and about prison numbers, sounds very complacent? I beg of him to recognise not only the reality that those cuts will lead to fewer police on the streets, but that he must reverse the softer sentencing plans of his Justice Secretary and stop the ludicrous plan that the Justice Secretary has to close prisons when there is patently now an urgent need for more prison places. (Hansard, 11 August 2011, Col 1061)

By March 2012, the prison population stood at 88,000 compared to 85,000 twelve months previously and 61,000 when Labour took office in 1997. Ken Clarke's bid to reverse the trend had failed and he had been forced to make numerous other concessions which ran counter to the spirit of his Green Paper and, in some cases, its letter. By the autumn of that year, he and his team had been ousted from the Ministry of Justice to be replaced by ministers whose hardline approach seemed more in tune with the mood in the Conservative Party following the riots and less likely to result in tensions with their Home Office counterparts.

Yet the moral opprobrium of the political class had already been undermined as the 'crimes of the powerful' began to come under the spotlight as never before (see Chapter 11). Even Ed Miliband, the new Labour leader, 'linked the riots to a wider collapse in social responsibility exemplified by the banking crisis and MPs expenses scandal' (BBC, 12 August 2011).

REVIEW QUESTIONS

1 How did the Labour government's approach to law and order differ from its Conservative predecessors when it came to power in 1997?

2 Why did violent crime fall in Labour's third term?

3 In what ways had the Coalition government come to appear vulnerable in terms of law and order by mid-2012?

CONCLUSION

This chapter began by arguing that crime is in some measure politically defined; the Labour government from 1997 exemplified this by the extent to which it created new offences and redefined what officially counts as crime. The chapter has also shown how crime and its control has assumed increasing political salience in the context of more general insecurity among the electorate about threats to law and order which, in turn, have challenged the ability of governments to provide the protection expected by the public. In the third of our political phases in particular these threats have had an increasingly international dimension which makes it ever more difficult for the government to claim that it can control them. Yet, at the same time, the competition for electoral advantage makes it irresistible for opposition parties to exploit any apparent weakness on the part of government, as necessary by playing on the fears of the public. So while Labour in opposition before 1997 discovered the largely untapped political potential of anti-social behaviour, the Conservatives after 2005 attacked the Labour government on the issue of violence which hitherto they had tended to neglect but which had begun increasingly to worry the public.

Thus Gilling (2007) identifies the phenomenon of 'governing through disorder' in the UK although this is by no means peculiar to Britain. It implies proactive efforts by politicians to heighten public fears, such that:

> public feelings of insecurity seem to have been actually produced or at least amplified by political elites in search of **moral panics** and public enemies. (De Giorgi, 2008)

Many of the same commentators argue that the temptation to resort to this strategy has increased as the role of international capital, combined with increased international mobility and communication have resulted in a loss of control by nation states over the factors which affect the lives of their citizens, such that:

> crime becomes the major arena for what is left of politics. (Christie, 2004: 37)

However, any short-term political gains may be more than offset if politicians then fail to allay the feelings of insecurity they have inflamed; and the risks are further increased when governments are overtaken by events which significantly increase people's fears. This happened to the Conservative government of

1979 and parallels may be drawn in this regard with the Coalition of 2010; but developments both nationally and internationally over the intervening three decades may significantly affect the scope, the style and the political efficacy of their response at a time when the spotlight has now been turned on 'the crimes of the powerful', including politicians and those close to them.

QUESTIONS FOR DISCUSSION

1 When and why did crime become a party political issue?
2 What do you understand by the term 'governing through crime' and what are the associated risks of this strategy?
3 How do the political challenges posed by the riots of the early 1980s compare with and differ from those facing the government following the riots of 2010?

GUIDE TO FURTHER READING

Brake, M. and Hale, C. (1992) *Public Order and Private Lives: The Politics of Law and Order*. London: Routledge.
Covers the impact of Conservative policies through the 1970s and 1980s.

Downes, D. and Morgan, R. (1992, 1997, 2002, 2007 and 2012) in M. Maguire, M. Morgan, and R. Reiner (eds) *The Oxford Handbook of Criminology*. Oxford: Clarendon Press.
Downes and Morgan provide the most comprehensive reviews of the politics of law and order in the period since 1945.

Garland, D. (2001) *The Culture of Control: Crime and Social Order in Contemporary Society*. Oxford: Oxford University Press.
Provide a broad review of all of these issues.

Young, J. and Matthews, R. (2003) 'New Labour Crime Control and Social Exclusion' in J. Young and R. Matthews (eds) *The New Politics of Crime and Punishment*. Cullompton: Willan Publishing (includes chapters covering various aspects of New Labour's Law and order policies).

WEB LINKS

There are no websites dedicated to the politics of law and order. You should check out the websites of the main parties to see how their views and policies are developing.

http://www.conservatives.com/
The website of the Conservative Party.

http://www.labour.org.uk/
The website of the Labour Party.

http://www.libdems.org.uk
The website of the Liberal-Democrat Party.

For helpful information and critiques of current policies the websites of the campaigning groups are useful as follows:

http://www.nacro.org.uk/
The website of NACRO.

http://www.prisonreformtrust.org.uk/
The website of the Prison Reform Trust.

http://www.howardleague.org/
The website of the Howard League for Penal Reform.

REFERENCES

Blair, T. (1993) 'Why Crime is a Socialist Issue', *New Statesman* 29(12), 27–8.

Bottoms, A.E. (1995) 'The Philosophy and Politics of Punishment and Sentencing' in C.M.V. Clarkson and R. Morgan (eds) *The Politics of Sentencing Reform*. Oxford: Clarendon Press.

Brake, M. and Hale, C. (1992) *Public Order and Private Lives: The Politics of Law and Order*. London: Routledge.

Cameron, D. (2007) '*Crime and our broken society*' http://www.conservatives.com/tile.do?def=news.story. page&obj_id=138147&speeches=1

Brain, T. (2010) *A History of Policing in England and Wales from 1974*. Oxford: Oxford University Press.

Bullock, S. and Gunning, N. (2007) *Police Service Strength England and Wales 31 March 2007*. Home Office Research Development and Statistics Directorate Statistical Bulletin 13/07.

Carter, Lord (2007) *Securing the future: Proposals for the efficient and sustainable use of custody in England and Wales*. London. Ministry of Justice.

Chaplin, R., Flatley, J., and Smith, K. (2011) *Crime in England and Wales 2010/11: Findings from the British Crime Survey and police recorded crime (2nd Edition)*. Home Office Statistical Bulletin10/11. London: Home Office.

Christie, N. (2004) *A Suitable Amount of Crime*. London: Routledge.

Conservative Party (1970) *A Better Tomorrow*. London: Conservative Party.

Conservative Party (1983) *Conservative Party Manifesto*. London: Conservative Party Central Office.

De Georgi, A. (2008) 'Book review. Ruth Gilmore, Golden Gulag. Prisons, Surplus, Crisis, and Opposition in Globalizing California'. *Critical Criminology* 16(2), 157–63.

Downes, D. and Morgan, R. (1994) '"Hostages to Fortune"? The Politics of Law and Order in Post War Britain' in M. Maguire, M. Morgan and R. Reiner (eds) *The Oxford Handbook of Criminology* (1st edn) Oxford: Clarendon Press.

Downes, D. and Morgan, R. (1997) 'Dumping the "hostages to fortune"? The politics of law and order in post war Britain' in M. Maguire, M. Morgan and R. Reiner (eds) *The Oxford Handbook of Criminology* (2nd edn) Oxford: Clarendon Press.

Downes, D. and Morgan, R. (2002) 'The skeletons in the cupboard: The politics of law and order at the turn of the Millenium' in M. Maguire, M. Morgan and R. Reiner (eds) *The Oxford Handbook of Criminology* (3rd edn) Oxford: Clarendon Press.

Downes, D. and Morgan, R. (2007) 'No turning back: The politics of law and order into the Millenium' in M. Maguire, M. Morgan and R. Reiner (eds) *The Oxford Handbook of Criminology* (4th edn). Oxford: Clarendon Press.

Farrell, S., Jackson, J., and Gray, E. (2009) *Social Order and the Fear of Crime in Contemporary Times*. Oxford: Oxford University Press.

Faulkner, D. (2001) *Crime, State and Citizen: A Field Full of Folk*. Winchester: Waterside Press.

Faulkner, D. and Burnett, R. (2012) *Where Next for Criminal Justice?* Bristol: The Policy Press.

Field, S. (1990) *Trends in Crime and their Interpretation: a study of recorded Crime in post-war England and Wales*. Home Office Research Study No. 119. London: Home Office.

FitzGerald, M. (1987) *Black People and Party Politics in Britain*. London: The Runnymede Trust.

FitzGerald, M. (1989) 'Race in the 1987 Election Campaign' in M. Crewe and M. Harrop *Political Communications: the General Election Campaign of 1987*. Cambridge: Cambridge University Press.

Garland, D. (2001) *The Culture of Control: Crime and Social Order in Contemporary Society*. Oxford: Oxford University Press.

Gilling, D. (2007) *Crime Reduction and Community Safety: Labour and the Politics of Local Crime Control*. Cullompton: Willan Publishing.

Hale, C. (1996) 'Fear of Crime', *International Review of Victimology* 4, 79–150.

Hale, C. (1999) 'The labour market and post-war crime trends in England and Wales' in P. Carlen and R. Morgan (eds) *Crime Unlimited? Questions for the 21st Century*. Basingstoke: Macmillan.

Hale, C. and FitzGerald, M. (2007) 'Social Exclusion and Crime' in D. Abrams, J. Christian, and D. Gordon (eds) *The Multidisciplinary Handbook of Social Exclusion Research*. Chichester: John Wiley and Sons.

HMIC (2003) *Streets Ahead*. London: Her Majesty's Inspectorate of Constabulary.

HMIC (2009) *Crime Counts: a Review of Data Quality for Offences of the most serious Violence*. London: Her Majesty's Inspectorate of Constabulary.

Home Office (2002) *Justice for All*. Cm. 5563. London: Home Office.

Home Office (2010) *Policing in the 21st century: reconnecting the police with the public*. London: Home Office.

Home Office (2011) *More effective Responses to antisocial Behaviour*. London: Home Office.

Judges' Council of England and Wales (2011) *Response of a sub-committee of the Judges' Council to the Government's Consultation Paper CP12/10*. Available at http://www.judiciary.gov.uk/Resources/JCO/Documents/Consultations/response-judges-council-legal-aid-reform-consultation.pdf

Lea, J. and Young, J. (1984) *What is to be done about Law and Order*. Harmondsworth: Penguin.

Loader, I. and Sparks, R. (2007) 'Contemporary Landscapes of Crime, Order and Control: Governance, Risk and Globalization' in M. Maguire, M. Morgan and R. Reiner (eds) *The Oxford Handbook of Criminology* (4th edn) Oxford: Clarendon Press.

Matheson, J. (2011) *National Statistician's Review of Crime Statistics: England and Wales*. London: Government Statistical Services.

McClintock, F.H. and Avison, N.H. (1968) *Crime in England and Wales*. London: Heinemann.

Martinson, R. (1974) 'What Works? Questions and Answers about Prison Reform', *The Public Interest* 35, 22–54.

Mirrlees-Black, C. and Allen, J. (1998) *Concern about Crime: Findings from the 1998 British Crime Survey. Home Office Research Development and Statistics Directorate. Research Findings 83*. London: Home Office.

Morgan, R. (2008) 'Engaging with honest Polticians', *Criminal Justice Matters* 72, 24–5.

Ministry of Justice (2010a) *Breaking the Cycle: Effective Punishment, Rehabilitation and Sentencing of Offenders*. London: Ministry of Justice.

Ministry of Justice (2010b) *Green Paper Evidence Report*. London: Ministry of Justice.

Nicholas, S., Kershaw, C., and Walker, A. (eds) (2007) *Crime in England and Wales 2006/07*. Home Office Research Development and Statistics Directorate Statistical Bulletin 11/07 London: Home Office.

Patrick, R. (2011) 'Reading Tea Leaves: an Assessment of the Reliability of police recorded Crime Statistics', *The Police Journal* 81(1) 47–68.

Simon, J. (2007) *Governing through Crime: How the War on Crime Transformed American democracy and Created a Culture of Fear*. Oxford: Oxford University Press.

Singh, D. (2012) *After the Riots: the Final Report of the Riots Communities and Victims Panel*. London: The Riots Communities and Victims Panel.

Thatcher, M. (1979) *Speech to Conservative rally, Birmingham*, 19 April http://www.margaretthatcher.org/document/104026

Tonry, M. (2004) *Punishment and Politics: Evidence and Emulation in the making of English Crime control Policy*. Cullompton: Willan Publishing.

Wall, D. (2007) *Cybercrime*. Cambridge: Polity.

Winsor, T. (2012) *Independent Review of Police Officer and Staff Remuneration and Conditions: Final Report*. Cm 8325-I. London: TSO.

Yaar, M. (2006) *Cybercrime and Society*. London: Sage.

Young, J. and Matthews, R. (2003) 'New Labour crime control and social exclusion' in J. Young and R. Matthews (eds) *The New Politics of Crime and Punishment*. Cullompton: Willan.

NOTES

1. See also Faulkner and Burnett, 2012.

2. See Martinson (1974) for a clear statement of this view. Although by 1979 Martinson was to recant his pessimism, the 'nothing works' school of thought undermined confidence in treatment programmes for offenders.

3. For example, in 1989 NACRO (the National Association for the Care and Resettlement of Offenders) published figures showing the annual cost in 1986–87 of keeping an offender in prison was £14,976 compared to £900 for Probation Orders and £520 for Community Service Orders. See Chapter 23 for further discussion of the use of non-custodial sentences.

4. By 2000, the journal *Criminal Justice Matters* was to devote its summer edition (no. 40) to 'managerialism'.

5. In 2001–2 serious violence accounted for only 3 per cent of all recorded offences of violence against the person and for less than 0.5 per cent of total crime. Yet the 2011 annual crime statistics report that:

    > In 2009/10 and 2010/11, 10% of adults were worried about burglary and car crime and 13% of adults were worried about violent crime. (Chaplin, Flatley and Smith, 2011)

6. The police figures are likely to be a more reliable indicator of trends for serious violence than the British Crime Survey, at least until they were affected by the 2002–3 changes to the counting rules. For a sample survey may produce anomalous results in relation to offences which affect only a tiny minority of the population; and the victims of violence also tend disproportionately to be the most difficult demographic group to sample–that is, young men living in high crime inner city areas.

7. Successive governments had changed the composition of Police Authorities, diluting the proportion of councillors (that is, locally elected representatives) and increasingly marginalizing their role (see Chapter 25 and Brain, 2010).

8. The published prison statistics consistently show that over half of all prisoners are serving sentences of six months or less.

9. In London the Metropolitan Police Authority had already been abolished as of January 2012 and responsibility transferred to a new 'Mayor's Office for Policing and Crime'.

10. Britain was not a member of the Eurozone but the crisis had a global impact, with specific implications nonetheless for Britain, as a member of the European Union.

20 The criminal justice system

Steve Uglow

Within Western civil society, issues concerning criminal justice best highlight the coercive nature of the State. Its powers of surveillance and investigation of private lives, its right to detain people against their will and to punish them can interfere with fundamental rights. This demands a bedrock of clear principles laying out why we should make certain sorts of conduct criminal but not others, the limits of State investigation of private life, and the objectives of any punishment. Determining these principles raises questions about how we live with each other, the constraints on individual freedom, the nature of common interests, and the problems of fair treatment. There are no simple answers to these questions and their complexity is reflected in the many dimensions—ethical, political, constitutional, and economic—which affect criminal justice policy making (see Chapter 19).

This chapter examines the adult criminal justice system in England and Wales[1] but also touches briefly on the ways in which the youth justice system differs. We devote significant public resources to the criminal justice system, in 2010–11, in excess of £27 billion annually on **police** forces, **prosecution** and defence lawyers, courts, probation, and prisons (HM Treasury, 2012). Despite this investment, the criminal justice system persistently comes under significant criticism. Perhaps one problem is that 'system' is the wrong, albeit convenient, word. A system implies clear and consistent objectives, transparent demarcation of responsibilities and lines of management, understood procedures and good communication between its different elements. In the case of public services, it may also raise expectations of recognized and effective means of **accountability**, normally ending with ministerial responsibility to Parliament. While these characteristics may broadly apply to our education or health systems, it is difficult to identify any of these characteristics within the criminal justice process in England and Wales.

The reason for this is that the criminal justice 'system' is a collection of autonomous and semi-autonomous agencies, mainly comprising the police, the Crown Prosecution Service (CPS), the Crown and magistrates' courts, and the correctional services. Each has its own objectives, principles, and core responsibilities for different aspects of criminal justice—prosecuting and punishing offenders, reducing crime, maintaining community safety, caring for victims, as well as protecting the rights and interests of the accused. The perspective of the probation officer may be poles apart from that of the prison officer; the police investigator sees the defence solicitor as an opponent; the volunteer supporting the victim seeks to protect the witness, while the barrister[2] may see her as simply a means to winning his case. These tensions may be exacerbated by the fact that the system in England and Wales is adversarial rather than inquisitorial (for a full discussion, see Uglow, 2006: Chapter 6) and the competitive nature of the criminal **trial** itself.

This is the outcome of an institutional history, the consequence of which is that there is no overarching ministry with parliamentary responsibility for the whole structure. Despite two Royal Commissions—in 1981 the Royal Commission on **Criminal Procedure** (RCCP) and in 1993 the Royal Commission on Criminal

Justice (RCCJ)—no reform of the overall structure was attempted. Piecemeal tinkering constantly occurs with little consideration of its wider impact. While the Home Office had overarching responsibility for much of the system until 2007, it was split to create a separate Ministry of Justice without any public review or Parliamentary debate. The Ministry of Justice took over the responsibilities of the Department for Constitutional Affairs (a short-lived successor of the Lord Chancellor's Department) which included constitutional affairs, criminal law, criminal justice and **sentencing** policy, the courts' service and legal aid; but it also took over responsibility for probation, prisons, youth justice, and parole from the Home Office, leaving the latter responsible for the police, security, counter-terrorism, and immigration and border controls. The Attorney General (AG) is responsible for the CPS and the Director of Public Prosecutions as well as the Serious Fraud Office and HM Revenue and Customs (HMRC) Prosecution Office. Since ministerial responsibilities overlap, the Home Secretary and Justice Secretary may advocate different policy approaches to the same issue, but their roles are also limited—for example, ministers are not answerable in Parliament for day-to-day operational matters relating to the police and the courts. Allied to the autonomy of the agencies, this fragmentation invariably affects the extent of mutual cooperation and coherence of policy objectives.

This chapter starts with a short overview of the system as a whole, followed by individual sections on its main components.

BACKGROUND

The main the building bricks of criminal justice policy and of the system itself can be outlined as follows:

- *Substantive criminal laws*—the police and the courts require legal authority to exercise their powers of investigation and trial. These are all based upon the existence of constitutionally defined criminal offences—laws that forbid particular conduct and lay down punishments. All offences are nowadays 'statutory'—that is, they derive from legislation passed by Parliament. Originally the courts themselves were able to create criminal offences; and some offences are still based on 'common law' (that is, court decisions), including murder and manslaughter. Although the courts can no longer create new crimes, their decisions inevitably shape the boundaries of statutory offences.

- *Procedural criminal law*—procedural laws empower and constrain law enforcement agencies. They specify, for example, the powers available for investigation, arrest, detention, pre-trial procedures and the conduct of trials; but they also include safeguards for suspects. Key statutes in relation to investigation and pre-trial issues are the Police and Criminal Evidence Act 1984 (PACE), the Criminal Procedure and Investigations Act 1996 and the **Regulation** of Investigatory Powers Act 2000. The trial procedures—which cover everything from jury selection, through the roles and conduct of prosecuting or defending lawyers, to the taking of **verdicts**—derive variously from the Courts Act 1971, the Magistrates Courts Act 1980, and the Juries Act 1974, although all have been amended piecemeal in recent years, especially by the Courts Act 2003 and the Criminal Justice Act 2003. Procedure is a highly technical area but the rules reflect key ethical principles and are underpinned by the concept of a 'fair' trial, a right reinforced by Article 6 of the European Convention on Human Rights.

- *Law enforcement agencies*—the police service (see Chapter 23) is the main agency responsible for the investigation of criminal offences, but other agencies are also involved in law enforcement, such as HMRC. However, their role is limited to their specific responsibilities for investigating crime, gathering of evidence, interviewing witnesses and suspects, and preparing the case for the prosecuting authorities. Their functions also include such matters as the maintenance of public order, the prevention of crime, and the regulation of traffic. Recognizing that the police alone cannot fulfil some of these wider functions, the Crime and Disorder Act 1988 made them jointly responsible with local authorities for 'community safety'.

- *Prosecution of offenders*—the preparation of a case for trial and the presentation of that case at magistrates' and Crown Courts is predominantly undertaken by the CPS, although agencies such as HMRC may take responsibility for mounting their own prosecutions.

- *Legal representation of offenders*—the criminal justice system also provides for defendants to be assisted by lawyers paid out of public funds. In April 2000, the Legal Services Commission became responsible for the public funding of defence work and established the Criminal Defence Service—which introduced a mixed system by which criminal defence would be organized through, on the one hand, contracted private practitioners and on the other, public salaried employees.

- *Trial and sentencing of the accused*—magistrates' courts and Crown Courts are responsible for making the initial decision of guilty or not guilty as well as for imposing penalties. These range from the financial to community-based sanctions to imprisonment (see Chapter 24 and Chapter 25). These decisions are subject to **appeal**, either on the question of the conviction itself or the appropriateness of the sentence. The initial appeal is normally to the Court of Appeal with the possibility of a further appeal to the Supreme Court.

- *A correctional system*—courts may impose three types of sentence. Magistrates' courts are responsible for fines, the National Probation Service for **community sentences** and the Prison Service Agency for custodial sentences. The enforcement of sentences passed by the Youth Court is in the hands of local Youth Offending Teams, overseen nationally by the Youth Justice Board (see Chapter 17).

- *Policy formulation*— as indicated earlier, this is undertaken by a range of government departments responsible for differing parts of the criminal justice system. The Home Office (police and security), the Ministry of Justice (the court service and prisons), the Attorney General (the prosecution system) all play a role, as do executive agencies such as the Youth Justice Board. In addition, Crime and Disorder Reduction Partnerships created by the 1998 Crime and Disorder Act gave local authorities a role in developing local policies. In 2002, a National Criminal Justice Board was created linked to local criminal justice boards (LCJBs) comprising all of the criminal justice agencies in the 42 criminal justice areas. Funding was withdrawn from LCJBs in 2011, but some continued to work on a self-funding basis.

A criminal justice system is concerned first and foremost with 'crime'. This chapter sidesteps important debates covered elsewhere about what should be defined as a crime and the selective enforcement of the **criminal law** (see in particular Chapter 1 and Chapter 11). Instead it takes 'crime' for granted as acts which are forbidden by law; but even here, mapping the extent of crime throws up problems since the two main sources of official statistics—the police recorded crime figures and the British Crime Survey (BCS)—may not agree and both have their limitations (see Chapter 3).

For the purposes of this chapter, the main point of reference is the police recorded crime figures since the BCS counts criminal acts which may not have been reported, whereas the criminal justice system can only deal with those acts which come to official notice. As noted earlier, other agencies such as HMRC may pursue cases through the system in their own right; but the police nonetheless form *the* main gateway into the criminal justice system.

As Chapter 19 shows, crimes recorded by the police increased dramatically since the 1950s but particularly in the 1980s, peaking in 1992, although changes to the ways in which the police are required to record crime have created confusion over trends since 1998 (see also Chapter 3 and Chapter 23).

Once an offence has been recorded by the police, the legal process that operates is set out in straightforward terms in Figure 20.1.

REVIEW QUESTIONS

1 Identify the major agencies of the criminal justice system and their responsibilities.

2 Outline the steps in the criminal justice process from commission of the offence to prison.

The police

While the police are not only the gateway to the criminal justice system, they are the most visible of all its agencies and have traditionally had a significant influence on the development of criminal justice policy.

The police are widely visible for many reasons—in particular because we regularly see officers patrolling on foot or in cars and because they have a much higher media profile in relation to news coverage of crime than any other criminal justice agency. However, their interaction with the public is by no means confined to making arrests and their legal obligation to investigate crime (for which purpose they may, for example, detain suspects in custody and mount surveillance operations). It also reflects their wider responsibilities referred to earlier and for dealing with public requests for help, the majority of which are not crime related (see also Chapter 3 and Chapter 19). In addition, the police exercise some coercive powers which may *not* result in cases entering the criminal justice system at all. These include searches (the majority of which do not result in an arrest), issuing cautions and, more recently, an extension of powers to impose 'summary justice' by issuing fixed penalty notices or penalty notices for disorder (see Chapter 19).

With regard to the police's role in the development of criminal justice policy, it is arguable that the influence of the Association of Chief Police Officers (ACPO) on national policy has diminished in recent years; and the advent of Police and Crime Commissioners may limit the local influence of senior officers (see Chapter 23). However, the fact that the police have a higher public profile than that of other criminal justice agencies ensures that governments continue to need to take account of their views. Hence ministers regularly attend police annual conferences and the media tend to report on the reception they receive as if this were an important political barometer.

In terms of their routine work, the police's response to the crimes which come to their notice has a significant influence on the business of the criminal justice system overall because of the choices the police make about the resources to allocate to different types of crime, which offences will be investigated and to what extent. For example, white collar crime will receive little police attention compared to residential burglary (see Chapter 11) but resource constraints may mean that many incidents of burglary will only be

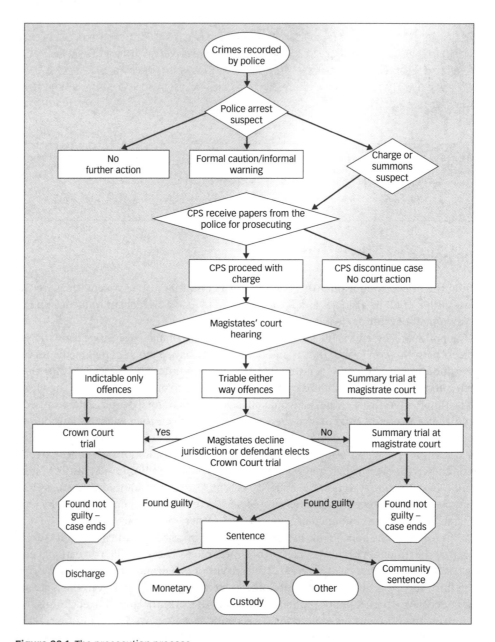

Figure 20.1 The prosecution process

Source: CJS Online 2004; © Crown Copyright.

subject to a telephone investigation. The fact that the police in England and Wales are responsible for investigations, though, means that they are not only key decision makers at this pre-trial stage, their role is very much more powerful than that of their counterparts in other countries such as the Netherlands and France where the key players in the criminal justice process are perceived as the public prosecutors or the judiciary. In part these cross-national differences reflect different legal systems—in particular where the tradition is inquisitorial rather than adversarial (see earlier in this chapter)—but they are also in part the result of the way in which the police are organized.

Unusually for a public service today, the police are not a single national force directly organized under a government department. In the mid-nineteenth century, the modern police force had its origins in the obligation of each local authority to maintain an efficient police force and, despite a number of subsequent mergers, this emphasis on the local nature of **policing** means that there are still 43 separate local forces. These are organized geographically either on the basis of urban conurbations (the Metropolitan force for London or the West Midlands force for Birmingham) or on counties (such as Sussex) or groups of counties (such as the Thames Valley force). These forces are financed by both local and national government, but they are autonomous legal entities which determine their own operational strategies independently of political control and which may have distinctive identities based on their perceived style of policing (Tilley, 2003).

Although Chief Constables are free from political control over operational matters, they are nonetheless subject to significant political influence at a number of levels which may, in turn, have implications for the operational options available to them. This is not simply a question of the resources allocated to each force by central and local government but also the priorities, targets and performance measures to which they were increasingly subjected by central government in recent years (see Chapter 19 and Chapter 23). While the Coalition government formally promised to abolish many of these measures, their introduction of elected Police and Crime Commissioners was nonetheless intended to increase the direct political accountability of the police at force level; but forces would still be expected to follow guidance from, cooperate with and be subject to inspection by a range of national bodies specified by the Home Office and Commissioners themselves were under an obligation to take account of a list of national priorities.

While the police have the responsibility to investigate crime, gather evidence, and initiate action against suspects, as indicated earlier, by no means every crime is investigated and, in those cases which are, it is rare for the police to use their powers of investigation to the full—bearing in mind that these can involve resource-intensive measures such as forensic examination of the crime scene, house-to-house inquiries, tracking down and questioning witnesses, the use of informants, covert surveillance, and the interviewing of suspects. Most crimes recorded by the police are not detected; and some which are do not result from a police investigation so much as resolve themselves—for example, where the suspect is still at the scene or is clearly identified by a witness or when a suspect arrested for one offence admits to committing others.

Even where an offender has been identified, the police may decide to take no further action (for example, if the perpetrator is dead or is currently on trial for another, more serious offence) so the Home Office preferred measure of detection became only those cases which resulted in some form of 'sanction' (see Chapter 19). The 'sanctioned detection rate' included not only cases which would be charged or summonsed to appear in court but those directly sanctioned by the police—whether by a caution, a fixed penalty notice (see earlier) or by issuing the offender with a warning for possessing cannabis. In 2011–12, the rate of 'sanction detections' for notifiable offences recorded by the police (see Chapter 3 for a definition of 'notifiable' offences) was 27 per cent; but only 60 per cent of these were offences sanctioned by means of a charge or summons (Home Office, 2012). Both are liable to be heard at court; but only those charged will be referred by the police to the Crown Prosecution Service who, in turn (see next section) may decide not to pursue some of these to the court stage of the system, thereby compounding what is already a high rate of 'attrition' between the number of offences recorded by the police and the number which reach court.

REVIEW QUESTIONS

1 Why are the police the best known of the criminal justice agencies?

2 What are the main ways indicated in this chapter in which the police in England and Wales may differ from their counterparts in other countries?

3 What is meant by the 'detection rate' and how does this contribute to the process of 'attrition'?

Prosecution

For much of the twentieth century, the police acted not only as investigators but also as prosecutors. Police forces developed prosecuting solicitors' departments which employed barristers to appear in the Crown Court. In magistrates' courts it was often a uniformed police inspector who was the prosecutor. The system was: inefficient, especially in the preparation of cases; unfair because, in principle, investigation and prosecution should be separate processes; and it lacked any executive or democratic accountability (Royal Commission on Criminal Procedure, 1981). In 1985, an independent prosecuting body, the Crown Prosecution Service, was set up, organized on a regional basis—there are 13 CPS areas so that each is co-terminous with a group of police forces. Each has a Chief Crown Prosecutor who is answerable to the national executive director, the Director of Public Prosecutions (DPP), who in turn answers to the Attorney General who is responsible to Parliament.

The CPS is 'the Government Department responsible for prosecuting criminal cases investigated by the police in England and Wales and its main functions are to:

- advise the police on cases for possible prosecution;
- review cases submitted by the police;
- determine any charges in more serious or complex cases;
- prepare cases for court; and
- present cases at court.

While the police retain the primary responsibility for investigations, CPS lawyers increasingly play a role in this field. Under the Criminal Justice Act 2003, the CPS were given more responsibility for determining the charge in cases other than for routine offences or where the police need to make a holding charge. By involving the prosecutor at an earlier stage, after a suspect has been identified but before a charge is preferred, investigators are in a better position to ensure that relevant and sufficient evidence is obtained and that the suspect is charged with the appropriate offence. Nowadays CPS Direct provides out-of-hours charging advice to the police. However, the process of attrition referred to earlier continues at the CPS stage of the criminal justice system in two main ways.

In the first place, each CPS lawyer (or prosecutor) who receives a file from the police is required by the CPS Code to decide whether the case should proceed to court; and some of the cases which are counted as 'sanction detections' because they have been charged by the police will fall at this first hurdle. The two tests which the prosecutor must initially apply (see CPS, 2010) are as follows:

(a) Whether there is sufficient evidence to ensure a realistic prospect of conviction. This is an objective test, namely, whether a court would be more likely than not to convict the defendant of the charge alleged. The prosecutor must consider whether there is admissible, substantial, and reliable evidence to support the accusation.

(b) Whether a prosecution is in the public interest. The prosecutor should then consider whether the public interest requires a prosecution. The Code suggests that there is a presumption in favour of prosecution but its constant refrain is the 'seriousness' of the offence and the prosecutor is enjoined that, broadly speaking, the graver the offence, the more likely it is that the public interest requires prosecution. Factors against prosecution include the trivial nature of the incident and the likelihood of a nominal penalty, any delay in bringing proceedings, and the health and age of the accused.

There is also the possibility of negotiation—discontinuance of all charges is not the only option since the defendant may wish to plead guilty to a lesser charge while maintaining a plea of not guilty to more serious charges. There are often hidden negotiations known as 'plea bargaining'. The CPS can accept such 'deals', but the Code stresses that the overriding consideration in accepting guilty pleas is that the court must not be left in the position where it is unable to pass a sentence consistent with the gravity of the actions. Guilty pleas account for the majority of the cases going through the criminal courts and since these, obviously, consume far fewer resources than contested cases negotiating a plea may risk administrative convenience taking precedence over interests of justice.

In the second place, by no means all of the cases which pass the CPS tests result in a conviction. The CPS may start the process of prosecution but abandon it (for example, in the face of victims or witnesses failing to cooperate) before the case even reaches court; or, often for the same reasons, the CPS may offer no evidence at the court stage so that the accused is immediately discharged by the judge or magistrates. Alternatively, the CPS may present such a weak case that the magistrates throw out the case or the judge directs the jury to acquit. A CPS lawyer will always present the case in magistrates' courts and more occasionally will act as advocate in Crown Court, although the CPS will usually engage a barrister for this purpose.

Legal representation for the defendant

Defendants were not permitted professional assistance to examine witnesses or to speak on their behalf until 1836, but it is now taken for granted that the right to a **fair trial** includes legal representation, not only in court but also in the police station and for other pre-trial procedures. For most defendants, the cost of legal advice and representation would be prohibitive. The legal aid scheme allows for the costs of conducting the defence to be borne by the State and not by the defendant. The scheme gives any suspect in police custody the right to free advice from a lawyer, usually one provided under a 'duty solicitor' scheme organized by local solicitors.[3] Representation in court is means-tested but in a magistrates' court, about half of the defendants will receive free legal aid, rising to about three defendants out of four in the Crown Court. Fee rates for lawyers' representation as well as for provison of such matters as experts' reports were cut in 2011 following a Ministry of Justice consultation in 2010 (Ministry of Justice, 2010).

The management of this provision was reformed in April 2000 when the Legal Services Commission took over the public funding of defence work from the Legal Aid Board[4] and established the Criminal Defence Service (CDS) referred to earlier, comprising both publicly funded and private lawyers. The most radical change was the introduction of salaried public defenders, although the scheme in England and Wales is limited (Bridges, 2007). While such schemes are common in North America and Australia, a review of research (Scottish Office, 1998) found that the average case costs of staff lawyers were cheaper than private lawyers—yet staff lawyers achieved broadly similar or slightly better outcomes for their clients than private lawyers.

Defendants are more likely to be unrepresented in magistrates' courts but proceedings are much less adversarial than in higher courts and both the bench and the clerk will often question the defendant to obtain the information that they need, whether in relation to their plea, to identify mitigating circumstances before sentence, or to work out a suitable payment plan for any fine.[5]

REVIEW QUESTIONS

1 What are the main responsibilities of the CPS?

2 What are the key considerations in deciding whether to prosecute?

3 What are the main ways in which the CPS may contribute to 'attrition'?

The courts

Two systems of courts currently hear and decide criminal cases: minor cases are heard at the magistrates' courts while the Crown Court tries more serious cases. The first are referred to as 'summary' cases and the second are referred to as 'indictable' cases, terms which are explained more fully later in this chapter. Decisions in these courts can be challenged through a number of channels. These structures can be seen in Figures 20.2 and 20.3.

Most criminal cases (95 per cent) are dealt with in the magistrates' courts. Some 1.8 million defendants were proceeded against in magistrates' courts in 2010, whereas approximately 112,000 were dealt with at the Crown Court (Ministry of Justice, 2011).

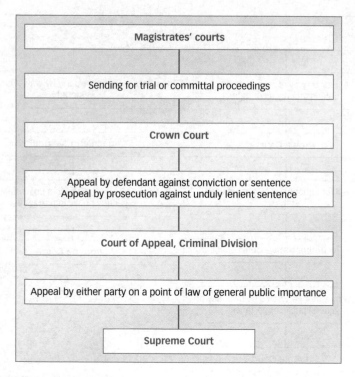

Figure 20.2 Trial on indictment

Magistrates ('justices of the peace' or JPs) are not lawyers but local people who take time from their jobs to serve as unpaid judges. However, in major cities they are often replaced by paid and legally qualified magistrates, known as District Judges. In contrast, the judge in the Crown Court will have been a lawyer of some experience before being appointed to the judiciary. The Crown Court trial takes place in front of a jury, a body of 12 people randomly selected by a Crown Court official from the local electoral register.

As indicated earlier, magistrates' courts and the Crown Court deal with two distinct categories of offence but a third, intermediate category may be tried by either. The three categories are:

(a) *Summary offences:* these are the most minor crimes and are only triable 'summarily' in the magistrates' court. 'Summary' does not refer to the speed or the lack of quality of justice in magistrates' courts (although often dozens of cases may be dealt with in a morning), but to the process of ordering the defendant to attend the court by summons, a written order usually delivered by post.

(b) *Triable either way offences:* these can be tried either in the magistrates' court or in the Crown Court. The most common examples are theft and burglary, but the category also includes indecent assault, arson, and criminal damage. There is no clear conceptual boundary here: theft is triable either way, whereas social security fraud is a summary offence.

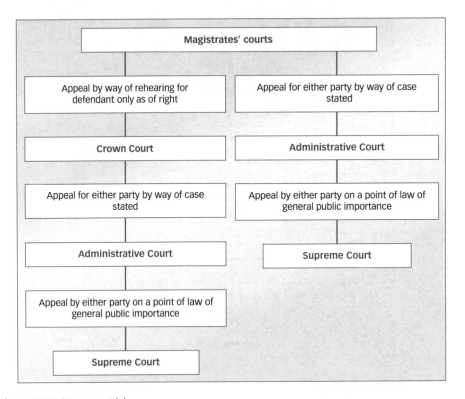

Figure 20.3 Summary trial

(c) *Indictable offences:* these are the most serious crimes, triable only on indictment (discussed later) in a Crown Court in front of a judge and jury. This category includes homicide, serious assault, rape, kidnapping, robbery, conspiracy, and Official Secrets Acts offences.

Where an offence is triable either way, summary trial is only possible if both the accused and the magistrates assent to it. The defendant has the right to insist on jury trial and if the magistrates consider summary trial inappropriate, they, too, can elect for trial on indictment. Most defendants opt for summary trial, not least because of the speed of the proceedings and the ceiling placed on the punishments that magistrates' courts can impose. However where cases are passed to the Crown Court, the eventual sentence in the majority of triable-either-way cases may still be within the magistrates' own sentencing powers.

Where the offence can only be heard on indictment, the magistrates' involvement is limited—there may be a decision on whether to grant bail, but the case is then sent for trial to the Crown Court.

Magistrates and clerks

The JP, along with the jury, may be seen as examples of ordinary citizens having an input into the processes of justice. As of April 2011, there were 26,966 magistrates, 137 district judges and 143 deputy district judges operating in magistrates' courts throughout England & Wales (Ministry of Justice, 2012).

Until the Constitutional Reform Act 2005, magistrates were appointed by the Lord Chancellor acting on the advice of local advisory committees. There are over 100 of these and each is left to devise its own methods of generating applications. Individuals and organizations (including local political parties) can put forward candidates for consideration. Since 2005, the Lord Chief Justice has approved appointments, as the head of the judiciary. The magistrates' bench should 'reflect the community it serves' (Auld, 2001: Chapters 3 and 4), but problems of balance persist, less in terms of **gender** than of age, **race**, and class. It has proved very difficult to appoint sufficient working-class or minority ethnic magistrates. The fact that magistrates are unpaid (although there is a modest allowance for financial loss and subsistence) poses problems for those on low incomes; and compulsory training before they are allowed to adjudicate, as well as continuing refresher courses, means that JPs spend about a week a year on training activities. This is in addition to being required to sit for a minimum of 26 half-day court sittings each year, which in practice averages 40 or more.

Sitting part-time and normally in 'benches' of three, magistrates deal mainly with criminal matters, but also with some civil cases, in the main family matters. In many conurbations, a District Judge (see earlier) often takes the place of the lay magistrates and normally sits alone.

Magistrates in the youth court (which deals with criminal offences by defendants aged 17 or under) are specially selected; and the rules and procedures are different from the adult court, as is its philosophy, which has traditionally been based on the welfare of the child (see later in this chapter, Chapter 17).

The 'clerk to the court' who assists the magistrates in the adult and youth court is a fully trained and paid lawyer. The clerk plays a central role since they are responsible not only for tendering legal advice to the justices, but for the administration of the courthouse: listing cases for hearing; summoning witnesses; handling adjournments; collecting the fines; as well as managing the personnel of the court. Despite their advisory role, clerks must not play any part in making findings of fact, although they may ask questions of the main parties and witnesses, as part of their duty to ensure every case is conducted fairly.

Unlike trial in the Crown Court, an accused does not have to be present for summary trial. Cases can take place in the absence of the accused who may have pleaded guilty by post or simply have failed to turn up. The CPS will normally conduct the prosecution.

The accused may be legally represented, either by a barrister or solicitor—or they may represent themselves, in which case the clerk should assist them in explaining the procedure and perhaps suggesting the sort of questions that may be asked in cross-examination.

Common law trial is adversarial in nature (see earlier), meaning that where there is a 'not guilty' plea, the prosecution and defence will call and examine their own witnesses, who will be subject to cross-examination by the other party's lawyer. Both sides have the opportunity to address the court, although the defence has the right to the last word. The magistrates play no part in calling or examining witnesses but listen to the evidence and reach a verdict at the end of the trial. They sentence most defendants who have pleaded, or been found, guilty, imposing a range of penalties from discharges to fines to community penalties to imprisonment. The maximum penalty will be specified in the statute creating the offence, but until 2003 a magistrates' court could not imprison anyone for more than six months for a single offence[6] or for more than one year in cases involving more than one offence. Where magistrates have tried a case summarily but have decided that their sentencing powers are insufficient, they can commit the defendant to the Crown Court for sentence. The Crown Court also hears appeals against conviction or sentence from the magistrates' courts.

The Crown Court

When an offence is too serious for the magistrates' court, an 'indictment'—that is, a formal document containing the alleged offences—is drawn up for Crown Court trial. The indictment supersedes all other accusations such as the police charge or the information laid before the magistrates. It is to the indictment that the accused pleads guilty or not guilty; and it is the key point of reference for the judge and the jury.

The Crown Court is more formal and traditional in its layout and proceedings than magistrates' courts. It is presided over by a single 'professional' judge—a lawyer of at least ten years' experience, recommended by the Judicial Appointments Commission. There are different categories of judge—the most senior are High Court judges, normally attached to the Queen's Bench Division in London; but the routine work is handled by a circuit judge or recorder (the latter being the part-time equivalent of the former) who between them undertake 95 per cent of the work of the Crown Court.

The jurisdiction of the Crown Court is narrower than that of the magistrates' court—the major work is hearing criminal trials on indictment, both for offences that are indictable only and for those triable 'either way' cases which reach the Crown Court. The wide diversity in the complexity and seriousness of cases is reflected in the division of work between High Court judges and circuit judges.

Guilty pleas are less common in the Crown Court than in the magistrates' courts—65 per cent of those tried in the first quarter of 2012 pleaded guilty to all counts at Crown Court. Thirty-one per cent entered a plea of 'not guilty' to at least one count and 4 per cent did not enter a plea (Ministry of Justice, 2012: 33). The course of a contested trial is very similar to that in a magistrates' court (see earlier) except that, after the closing speeches for the prosecution and defence, the judge addresses the jury. They explain the legal issues that have to be decided, summarize the evidence, and explain what is called 'the burden of proof', namely, that it is the job of the prosecution to present sufficient evidence to satisfy the jurors of the accused's guilt beyond reasonable doubt. After the judge's summing up, the jury retire to consider their verdict.

REVIEW QUESTIONS

1 What is the structure of the criminal courts?

2 Describe the work of the magistrates' courts and the Crown Court.

3 What is the job of the clerk to the magistrates' court?

Sentencing and the correctional system

By contrast with the magistrates' court which may impose a maximum penalty of one year's imprisonment, the maximum penalty which can be imposed by the Crown Court is specified in the statute creating the offence. In general, this will specify a maximum rather than minimum penalty; so sentencers have a certain freedom in what punishment to impose in most cases. A few offences are subject to mandatory sentences—such as life for those convicted of murder—but here judges must specify the minimum term (or 'tariff', see later) to be served before the offender can be considered for release from custody. With these exceptions, the court can choose from the range of penalties from the minimum (an absolute discharge) to the maximum specified for the particular offence (Dickson, 2002). The options include:

- absolute and conditional discharges;
- fines;
- community punishments including community **rehabilitation** orders and community punishment orders (see Chapter 24);
- prison (see Chapter 25).

In addition, the 2003 Act introduced a new sentence which was intended to protect the public by leaving open the term of a custodial sentence such that those responsible for certain serious offences could not be released until it was deemed safe to do so[7] (see Chapter 19).

But a court cannot exercise an unfettered discretion in imposing a sentence—a statutory sentencing framework was originally introduced in 1991 which, despite modifications in subsequent legislation, essentially conceives of sentencing as a two-stage process:

(a) The primary decision is the type of penalty. The fine is the presumptive penalty[8] and the court must be satisfied, if it wishes to move from a fine to a community penalty or from there to custody, that the offence is sufficiently serious to warrant this.

(b) The secondary decision is that of the tariff. Having decided on the type of penalty, the court must decide on the size of the fine, the content of the community sentence, or the length of the prison sentence.

The sentencing court's discretion is also subject to other controls and influences. Defendants have the right to appeal against sentence (discussed later) and this means that the Court of Appeal exercises significant oversight and has regularly issued guideline judgments as to the appropriate level of sentencing for particular offences. For example, in *Billam*[9] the court provided sentencing guidelines for offences of rape, including aggravating and mitigating factors. In addition, the Sentencing Council, which undertakes its own research, produces sentencing guidelines and monitors their effect. The Council's Crown Court Sentencing Survey (Sentencing Council, 2011) suggests that judges infrequently depart from sentencing guidelines. Notwithstanding all of these constraints, concerns continue to be raised regarding disparities in the sentences handed down for apparently similar offences, especially by different magistrates' courts (Roberts, 2011).

Depending on the sentence, its enforcement will rest with the magistrates' court, the National Probation Service and the Prison Service as outlined earlier. For those prisoners serving more than four years, the decision to release them is in the hands of the Parole Board, whose decisions are based on risk assessments. Release is usually 'on licence' for a period, during which the Board can also recall prisoners as necessary.

The organization of the probation and prison services has been subject to considerable change in recent years. As a result of the Carter Report (Carter, 2003) their headquarters were brought together under the National **Offender Management** Service (NOMS)—an executive agency within the Ministry of Justice. The expectation was that integrating the management of offenders whilst in custody or under supervision in the community would improve effectiveness and efficiency, including through forging links and joint strategies 'with complementary services, including health, education, and employment' (Home Office, 2004: 10). NOMS itself, however, has continued to be subject to criticism, not least for serious flaws in its management information system (*The Independent*, 19 January 2010) and, while its two constituent services retain their respective remits for ensuring the community and custodial sentences imposed by the courts are carried out effectively, both have increasingly been open to competition from private and voluntary sector providers in recent years. Under the Coalition government of 2010, the role of the Probation Service in particular seemed set to change from directly supervising offenders serving community sentences to commissioning others to do so.

REVIEW QUESTIONS

1 Describe the range of sentences available to different courts.

2 What are the limits on magistrates' sentencing powers?

3 What controls exist over the courts' discretion in passing sentence?

The Youth Justice System

The origins of the youth justice system are described in Chapter 17, along with the ways in which it has changed, with particular reference to the new national and local arrangements established by the Labour government under its Crime and Disorder Act 1998 (see also Chapter 19). In discussing the criminal justice process as it applies to young people in England and Wales, it is important to emphasize that successive governments have maintained the age of criminal responsibility at ten, which is very much lower than in most other European countries and contrasts starkly for example with Scandinavian countries where it is 15.

When a young person aged between ten and 17 has been arrested and taken to a police station, special provisions under PACE mean that, as well as the right to legal advice, an 'appropriate adult' must be present to advise the young person and ensure that the interview is conducted fairly. Where the young person admits responsibility, as long as the offence is below a specified level of seriousness and, especially, where they have no prior criminal convictions, the police may 'divert' them from the criminal justice system in several ways. On their first offence they may simply be given a reprimand (or verbal warning) by a police officer; or they may receive a 'final warning'. This is a verbal warning given by a police officer for a first or second offence which additionally involves referring the young person to the YOT for an assessment to determine the causes of their offending and engage them in a programme of activities designed to address these. Other forms of diversionary 'pre-court disposal' for young people include, for example, them signing up to an acceptable behaviour contract (ABC).

Where the young person has failed to comply with the conditions of any pre-court disposal or has re-offended (especially if their offending is escalating in seriousness)—they can be taken to the Youth Court. This is within the magistrates' court system but, as noted earlier, Youth Court magistrates are specially selected, the proceedings are separate from adult courts, and there are restrictions on the press and public. Very serious cases involving young people still go to the Crown Court under ss. 90 and 91 of the Powers of Criminal Courts Act 2000, although this practice was criticized by the European Court of Human Rights in *Venables v UK*.[10]

Young people who are not sentenced at first hearing are usually released on bail, and YOTs have bail support and supervision programmes. However, a minority may be remanded in custody. There were 72,011 court disposals of young people aged 10–17 in 2010–11 and in the same year nearly 3,500 were remanded in custody. Seventeen per cent of these were subsequently acquitted of the charges against them while a further third were found guilty but did not receive a custodial sentence (Youth Justice Board, 2012).

The Youth Court has a wide range of sentencing powers. But importantly, where a young person is before court for the first time *and* pleads guilty, the court must normally make a referral order which involves referral to a Youth Offender Panel consisting of two community members working with a YOT member. This has elements of **restorative justice** as the Panel works out a contract with the young person. However, so far there is only a limited role for victims. Successful completion means that the conviction is 'spent' and need not be disclosed, for example, when applying for employment.

As well as discharges and fines, the Criminal Justice and Immigration Act 2008 introduced a new generic community sentence, the youth rehabilitation order, allowing for more flexible interventions which may include curfew orders, electronic monitoring, mental health treatment, drug testing and attendance centre orders among others.

Additional interventions alongside sentences include child safety orders, parenting orders, or drug treatment and testing orders.

The basic custodial sentence for 12- to 17-year-olds is a detention and training order which is a two-part sentence that combines a period of custody and a period of supervision in the community. This can last from four to 24 months. Longer sentences for serious offences are available under ss. 90 and 91 of the Powers of Criminal Courts Act 2000.

The Youth Justice Board is responsible for placing young people subject to a custodial sentence in secure accommodation, of which there are three types. First, there are secure training centres which are purpose-built centres for young offenders up to the age of 17 with a high staff-offender ratio and a high level of education and training.

Secondly, there are secure children's homes which are generally small facilities, run by local authority social services departments, again with a high ratio of staff to young people. Finally there are young offender institutions which can accommodate young people aged from 15 to 21. These have lower staff-offender ratios and tend to be less able to address individual needs.

REVIEW QUESTIONS

1 What mechanisms are available to divert young people from the criminal justice system?

2 What sentences are available to a youth court?

3 Why might there be concerns over remanding young people in custody?

Appeals

The right of appeal is an essential element of any criminal justice system. But the appellate system in England and Wales is complex and has changed over time. Those convicted of an offence have a right of appeal which varies according to the court where they were sentenced; but so, too, does the prosecution and also in some cases the State. Until relatively recently, defendants were protected from 'double jeopardy', meaning that they could not be tried again for the same offence having once been acquitted; but there are now exceptions to this rule.

Defendants convicted by magistrates may appeal either to the Crown Court or to the Divisional Court of the Queen's Bench. The first of these involves the entire case being re-heard by a circuit judge, assisted normally by two JPs, who may uphold or quash the conviction or vary the sentence. The second option (which may also be instigated by the prosecution) is called a 'case stated' appeal which is heard under an ancient jurisdiction whereby the Queen's Bench controls the decisions of inferior judicial bodies. In this instance the case is *not* re-heard since the appeal relates only to whether the magistrates applied the law wrongly.

A defendant convicted in the Crown Court may appeal against conviction or sentence to the Criminal Division of the Court of Appeal under s. 2 of the Criminal Appeals Act 1995. This does not involve re-hearing the case but rests solely on establishing that the conviction was 'unsafe' inasmuch as the judge can be shown to have made a significant procedural error—for example, in explaining the law to the jury or in allowing the introduction of inadmissible evidence. If the appeal succeeds, the conviction may be quashed or the sentence varied or a re-trial may be ordered.

The final court of appeal in criminal matters for England, Wales and Northern Ireland is the Supreme Court where appeals involving a point of law of general public importance will be heard by a panel normally consisting of five senior judges. Few such appeals concern criminal law, although the Human Rights Act 1998 has led to a number of challenges, especially in relation to anti-terrorism legislation.

However, appeals against conviction or sentence are not always resolved by direct application to the court by or on behalf of the defendant. Although the Court of Appeal is meant to ensure that the errors which result in wrongful convictions are rectified, these errors can arise in numerous ways—for example, from police malpractice, from the prosecution withholding evidence, from trial judge bias, or from faulty forensic evidence. A number of cases from the 1970s onwards in which the appeal had been turned down but had to be referred back by the Home Secretary had increasingly raised questions about whether the Court of Appeal alone was inadequate for this task. One of the best known of these cases was that of the Birmingham Six who were convicted of the Birmingham pub bombings in 1974 and had their first appeal against conviction rejected in 1976 (Mullin, 1986). When the case was referred back by the Home Secretary in 1987 the appeals were dismissed again; but the court finally quashed the convictions in 1991 on the basis of evidence that the men's confessions had been obtained by coercion and that expert forensic testimony that they had been handling explosives was flawed. Yet this was essentially the same evidence as was heard by the court in 1987.

Cases like this suggested that an organization was needed which could not only instigate but also supervise further investigation into cases of wrongful conviction. Responsibility was first assigned to a department in the Home Office and this occasionally referred cases to the Court; but its political independence was inevitably called into question and in 1995 an independent Criminal Cases Review Commission was set up for this purpose. From its inception in 1997 it had received just over 15,000 applications by July 2012 and had referred just over 500 to the Court of Appeal, resulting in 461 being heard, with convictions quashed in 325 of these.

Prosecution appeals

English common law had until relatively recently not allowed the prosecution any right to appeal against acquittal or sentence. Limited right of appeal, though, was first introduced under the 'case stated' procedure at common law which allowed magistrates to present a statement of the facts and their decision for the High Court in London to give a binding opinion. This limited mechanism of appeal was extended by the Attorney General's Reference system introduced by the Criminal Justice Act 1972 which allowed the Attorney General to refer to the Court of Appeal any point of law—even in cases where the defendant had been acquitted (though this could not alter the verdict). In 1988, the Attorney General was given a further right of appeal against sentences which in the eyes of the prosecution were 'unduly lenient' and this right of appeal was extended further in 1996 to cover 'tainted acquittals', allowing the prosecution to appeal against acquittals of defendants if they were convicted of intimidating or interfering with a juror or witness in a given case.

Finally, the Criminal Justice Act 2003 followed the recommendations of the 1999 Macpherson Inquiry into the 1993 murder of the black teenager Stephen Lawrence (for which no-one had yet been convicted) by allowing retrial for a number of serious offences where new evidence had come to light.

The European Court of Human Rights

A final port of call for those who feel that they have been mistreated by the criminal justice system is the European Court of Human Rights. The basis of any appeal must be that a signatory State has acted in breach of its obligations under the European Convention on Human Rights (ECHR), such as by denying a person a fair trial, or by infringing a person's right to liberty, privacy, or freedom of expression. If the appeal is upheld, this is embarrassing for the government; and, while it does not overturn a domestic judgment or invalidate government action, it may place the government under moral pressure to amend domestic law to ensure compatibility with the ECHR. The passage of the Human Rights Act 1998 in England and Wales did not make the European Convention part of English law, but it obliged public authorities to act in a manner which was compatible with Convention rights wherever possible[11] including the courts' interpretation of all legislation. Courts thereby had to take account, not merely of the Convention itself, but of the body of **jurisprudence** developed through the decisions of the European Court of Human Rights.

The onus nonetheless remains on the government to amend the law accordingly and there have been numerous examples of the impact of the ECHR on the criminal justice system, including amendments to laws on the admissibility of hearsay, allowing inferences to be drawn from silence or using answers obtained under compulsion as evidence. However the court ruling in 2012 that Britain should give prisoners the right to vote met strong political opposition and, at the time of writing, it seemed unlikely that this would be fully implemented.

REVIEW QUESTIONS

1 Describe the process of appeal from conviction in magistrates' court.

2 To whom do you appeal from conviction in Crown Court and on what grounds?

3 When can the prosecution appeal?

CONCLUSION

As described in this chapter, the criminal justice system in England and Wales is a complex amalgam of different agencies. The key unifying principle to which all should subscribe is that the accused has the right to a fair and just process, from investigation to arrest, to trial and sentencing, through to release from prison. The criminal justice system largely measures up to this yardstick as a result of its history and, in particular, the decisions of courts and judges and Parliament. These have resulted in a number of checks and balances on the power of the State which, when put together, can be seen as ensuring that an accused person has the right to a fair trial: and these safeguards have been reinforced by the passage of the Human Rights Act 1998.

However, its responsibility for criminal justice routinely provides the State with coercive powers: people who are arrested lose their freedom of movement until it is restored by the police or a court; they may be obliged to account for their actions to police officers or to a court; on conviction they may forfeit their money, leisure or liberty depending on the sentence they receive. And the State frequently seeks to expand these powers, as when the Terrorism Act 2001 permitted extensions to detention without trial and the Criminal Justice Act 2003 abandoned the double jeopardy rule. For those who believe in the **rule of law,** the burden must always be on the State to demonstrate the absolute necessity for increasing its coercive powers rather than on individuals to justify their freedom of movement and action.

QUESTIONS FOR DISCUSSION

1 What should be the principal objectives of a criminal justice system?

2 What factors should a court consider in sentencing an offender?

3 Should the prosecution have a right to appeal against conviction and/or sentence?

GUIDE TO FURTHER READING

Ashworth, A. and Redmayne, M. (2010) *The Criminal Process* (4th edn) Oxford: Oxford University Press.

A valuable look at the principles and policies underlying the key decisions in the criminal process.

Davies, M., Croall, H., and Tyrer, J. (2010) *An Introduction to the Criminal Justice System* (4th edn) London: Longmans.

A comprehensive and detailed overview of the criminal justice system.

Home Office *Justice for All* (Cm 5563) (2002). London: Home Office.

The key policy document which formed the basis for the rebalancing of the criminal justice system under New Labour.

McConville, M. and Wilson, G. (2002) *The Handbook of the Criminal Justice Process*. Oxford: Oxford University Press.

Somewhat dated but still important collection of essays from the leading criminal justice scholars.

Padfield, N. (2008) *Text and Materials on the Criminal Justice Process* (4th edn) London: Butterworths.

A useful collection of source material with an accompanying commentary.

Pakes, F. (2010) *Comparative Criminal Justice* (2nd edn) Cullompton: Willan Publishing.

A short introduction to the manner in which different countries approach some of the key stages of the criminal justice system.

Sanders, A. and Young, R. (2010) *Criminal Justice* (4th edn) London: Butterworths.

A critical socio-legal account which concentrates particularly on the process of investigation and enforcement.

WEB LINKS

The following websites contain links to most official criminal justice system webpages:

http://www.homeoffice.gov.uk
Home Office.

http://www.justice.gov.uk/
Ministry of Justice.
More specialist webpages include:

http://www.acpo.police.uk/
Association of Chief Police Officers.

http://www.courtservice.gov.uk
The Court Service.

http://www.ccrc.gov.uk
Criminal Cases Review Commission.

http://www.criminal-courts-review.org.uk/
Criminal Courts Review (the Auld Report).

http://www.legalservices.gov.uk/criminal.asp
Criminal Defence Service.

http://www.cps.gov.uk
Crown Prosecution Service.

http://www.judicialappointments.gov.uk/
Judicial Appointments Commission.

http://www.magistrates-association.org.uk
Magistrates' Association.

http://www.justice.gov.uk/about/noms
National Offender Management Service (archived August 2008).

http://www.paroleboard.gov.uk/
Parole Board.

http://www.homeoffice.gov.uk/police/
Police Service.

http://www.justice.gov.uk/about/hmps
Prison Service.

http://www.justice.gov.uk/about/probation
Probation Service.

http://sentencingcouncil.judiciary.gov.uk/
Sentencing Council.

http://www.victimsupport.com
Victim Support.

http://www.justice.gov.uk/about/yjb/
Youth Justice Board.

REFERENCES

Auld, L.J. (2001) *Review of the Criminal Courts of England and Wales*. London: Lord Chancellor's Department.

Bridges, L., Cape, E., Fenn, P., Mitchell, A., Moorhead, R., and Sherr, A. (2007) *Evaluation of the Public Defender Service*. London: Legal Services Commission.

Carter, P. (2003) *Managing Offenders, Reducing Crime*. London: Home Office.

CPS (2010) *Code for Crown Prosecutors*. London: DPP.

Croall, H., Mooney, G., and Munro, M., (2010) *Criminal Justice in Scotland*. Aldershot: Dartmouth.

Dickson, L. (2002) 'Issues in sentencing' in S. Uglow, *Criminal Justice* (2nd edn) London: Sweet & Maxwell.

HM Treasury (2012) *Public Expenditure Statistical Analyses*. London: Her Majesty's Treasury.

Home Office (1997) *Review of Delay in the Criminal Justice System*. London: Home Office.

Home Office (1997) *No More Excuses*. London: Home Office Cm 3809.

Home Office (2002) *Narrowing the Justice Gap—A Framework Document*. London: Home Office.

Home Office (2004) *Reducing Crime—Changing Lives*. London: Home Office.

Home Office (2011) *Crime in England and Wales 2010/2011* (Home Office Statistical Bulletin 10/11). London: Home Office.

Home Office (2012) *Crimes Detected in England and Wales 2011/12* (Home Office Statistical Bulletin 08/12). London: Home Office.

McBarnet, D. (1981) *Conviction*. London: Macmillan.

Ministry of Justice (2010) *Proposals for the Reform of Legal Aid*. London: HMSO.

Ministry of Justice (2012) *Judicial and Court Statistics 2011*. London: HMSO.

Mullin, C. (1986) *Error of Judgement*. London: Chatto and Windus.

Roberts, J.V. (2011) 'Sentencing Guidelines and Judicial Discretion: Evolution of the Duty of the Courts to Comply in England and Wales', *British Journal of Criminology*, 51, 6: 997–1013.

Royal Commission on Criminal Procedure (1981) *Report* Cmnd 8092. London: HMSO.

Royal Commission on Criminal Justice (1993) *Report* Cmnd 2263. London: HMSO.

Scottish Office (1998) *A Literature Review of Public Defender or Staff Lawyer Schemes*. Legal Studies Research Findings 19. Edinburgh: Scottish Office.

Simmons, J., Legg, C., and Hosking, R. (2003) *National Crime Recording Standard: an analysis of the impact on recorded crime*. Home Office Online Report 31/03. http://www.homeoffice.gov.uk/rds/pdfs2/rdsolr3103.pdf.

Solomon, E., Eades, C., Garside, R., and Rutherford, M. (2007) *Ten Years of Criminal Justice Under Labour: An Independent Audit*. London: Centre for Crime and Justice Studies.

Tilley, N. (2003) 'Community policing, problem-oriented policing and intelligence-led policing' in T. Newburn (ed) *Handbook of Policing*. Cullompton: Willan.

Uglow, S. (2006) *Criminal Justice*. London: Sweet and Maxwell.

Youth Justice Board (2012) *Youth Justice Statistics 2010/11*. London: Ministry of Justice.

NOTES

1. An account of the Scottish system can be found in Croall *et al*. (2010) or on the Scottish Executive website at http://www.scotland.gov.uk/Topics/Justice/. Information on the system in Northern Ireland can be found at http://www.nidirect.gov.uk/justice.

2. There are two categories of lawyer in England and Wales: the solicitor is the general practitioner, available to the public for legal advice and limited representation; the barrister is the consultant and advocate (only available through a solicitor) who will provide specialist advice and represent clients in court.

3. This is provided for by ss. 58 and 60 of the Police and Criminal Evidence Act 1984 (PACE).

4. Access to Justice Act 1999.

5. This was once described in provincial courts as 'benevolent paternalism' (McBarnet, 1981).

6. The extension to 12 months in 2003 had never been used at the time of writing; the first Justice Secretary under the Coalition government of 2010 was unsuccessful in trying to return the limit to six months.

7. At the time of writing the future of IPPs (indeterminate sentences for public protection) was under review.

8. There are other financial penalties such as compensation orders. Confiscation of assets is also possible under the provisions of the Proceeds of Crime Act 2002.

9. [1986] 8 Crim App Rep (S) 48.

10. (2000) 30 EHRR 121; [2000] 2 All ER 102.

11. If it is not possible to interpret the law in this way, the High Court, Court of Appeal or Supreme Court may make a 'declaration of incompatibility'.

21 Surveillance and security in a risk society

Richard Jones

INTRODUCTION

This chapter discusses the topics of security, risk and surveillance. The aims of this chapter are: to introduce and discuss what is meant by these terms within criminology; to introduce key relevant theories; to summarize criminological research in these areas; and to identify some new security and surveillance technologies and discuss their implications, concerns and debates surrounding their use.

BACKGROUND

The topics of security, risk and surveillance raise a number of important issues, concerns and questions. In relation to security, the key question seems to be the degree to which society is prepared to relinquish various rights, liberties and freedoms in the name of increased security—or conversely to prioritize the former at the potential cost of the latter. Similarly, surveillance practices seem to stand in conflict with privacy; increasing one may be to the detriment of the other. If this is the case, then deciding which to prioritize thus becomes a matter of social and political values. However, some writers have challenged this opposition, seeing the relationship as less straightforward and more complex (see, for example, Goold and Lazarus, 2007). Loader and Walker (2007) have interestingly argued that we should conceive of 'security' as less a set of practices to be 'balanced', and more as a 'public good', as underpinning and intimately connected to social solidarity and social relationships. Elsewhere, in relation to surveillance, various writers have questioned what is meant by 'privacy' and hence how it might be protected. Nissenbaum (2010) argues that rather than think of certain information as intrinsically 'private', surveillance is problematic insofar as it violates what she terms 'contextual integrity', the social norms governing the acceptability of the flow of information. If this is correct, the problem with surveillance is less its 'intrusiveness' *per se*, and more the question as to how the data obtained are used and who gets to see this data. A narrow way of facilitating surveillance while respecting privacy—and thus of reconciling competing values—may be to employ 'privacy enhancing technologies' (PETs). For example, it is possible to design ID card systems to answer legitimate questions ('is the person over the age of 18?') without disclosing the person's age or date of birth.

A second kind of concern regarding security and surveillance relates to the symbolic messages that practices send, or worse, their negative effects and social consequences. For example, surveillance seems inherently 'suspicious' of people, potentially undermining social trust, and in the extreme case, may have a 'chilling effect' in which citizens refrain from the kind of open dialogue characteristic of healthy and vibrant societies; similarly, some security practices have a 'dehumanizing' quality. A third concern relates to cost, or to social and economic priorities more generally; are surveillance or security systems the best use of our scarce resources? A fourth and related issue is about the effectiveness of measures, for which clear evidence is not always available. Fifthly, Schneier (2006: 38) has drawn attention to how some practices can be viewed as what he terms 'security theatre', by which he means measures designed to reassure the public without actually making them any safer. Lastly, there is the problem of 'function creep', the phenomenon in which a measure is introduced for one purpose, but which subsequently ends up being used for another (perhaps more insidious) one.

Various surveillance and security technologies and practices are in use today, and one of the important questions to ask is how criminology has made sense of these developments. One of the ways this can be done is by situating these developments within wider concepts and debates around the nature of contemporary society. Among these is the notion that we live today in the 'risk society' (Beck, 1992), or that responses to crime today can only be understood within the wider context of 'the insecurity that characterizes Western societies in the 21st century' (Ericson, 2007: 3). Indeed, the concept of 'risk' has become influential in recent years, and seems closely related to those of security and surveillance: security appears to be a response to threats or risks; while surveillance is typically directed toward possible risks with a view to anticipating or following their occurrence. A distinction is often drawn between the 'likelihood' of a particular risk occurring, and the 'magnitude' of the harm done should it occur. A second important distinction can be drawn between perceived risk as opposed to actual risk (the statistical likelihood of occurrence). This draws attention to the psychological dimension of risk perception. Today, a discourse and set of practices related to the identification of risks permeates organizations and social policy, involving activities such as 'risk assessment' audits, and strategies to try to ensure that possible disruptions are anticipated and contingency plans drawn up (as for example in 'business continuity management'). For key organizations and for 'critical national infrastructure', the concept of 'resilience' draws attention to two ways of anticipating major disruptions or attacks: the 'target hardening' of vital facilities; and recovery plans to help get up-and-running again as quickly as possible afterwards. The 'management' of risk appears rational (in the Weberian sense), but from a cultural perspective we can enquire why some things are constructed as more risky than others (see Douglas and Wildavsky, 1982). More generally still, the British sociologist Anthony Giddens (1990: Chapter III) argues that our 'late modern' societies both generate certain historically specific risks, and have devised particular technological and rational strategies to address these, generate trust, and stabilize social relations.

Despite Giddens' analytically neutral characterization of 'late modernity', apart from a few exceptions (see Bottoms and Wiles, 1996) within criminology the term has tended to be used in a more critical or even 'dystopian' way. Zygmunt Bauman's (2000) variant of the concept of 'late modernity', namely 'liquid modernity', emphasizes the social disintegration, precariousness and short-termism brought about by the inexorable pace of contemporary social change. Jock Young's (1999) analysis of late modernity is similarly critical, pointing out the various reactionary social processes of 'social exclusion' used to defend privileged vested interests, giving rise to distinctive patterning of social space and skewed social geography. In a more Foucauldian vein, Feeley and Simon (1992) suggest that criminal justice today has been informed by a 'new penology', with a new 'language of probability and risk' replacing both criminological positivism and retributivism (1992: 450). The penal system, they argue, assigns 'risk profiles' to offenders, who are then sorted into similar groups, and dealt with accordingly—with prison used to incapacitate the highest risk offenders and surveillance used for those posing a lower risk (1992: 459). As they note, this apparently simple innovation in fact represents a significant shift away from traditional ways of understanding criminals and criminality. Discussing this and other sociological accounts of the rise of risk discourses and practices, O'Malley (2004: Chapter 7) argues that while 'risk' has indeed become an influential 'technique for governing crime', it has not in fact wholly replaced other paradigms such as retributivism—witness the parallel emergence of 'penal populism', for example—though Simon (1998) argues that while in many respects the new penology and penal populism are quite different and merely coexist, in respect of recent sex offender legislation the two 'are being merged' into a position advocating use of the prison to incapacitate high-risk offenders in order to protect the public. More recently, Aas (2011) has argued that practices of distinction, inclusion and exclusion play out at international border controls as globalization processes generate their own contradictions. Within the American political arena, Simon (2007) has argued that the (genuine) fears of citizens regarding increasing crime rates (especially for violent crime) from the 1970s onwards has become highly politicized and indeed part of a wider political process of what he provocatively describes as 'governing through crime'.

David Garland's (2001) characterization of our contemporary 'culture of control' also invokes the concept of late modernity, using it as the backdrop against which the historical shift from the 1970s onwards towards such a culture plays out. Garland argues that there has been a move away from the penal welfarism that was dominant in the early twentieth century, towards a cluster of policies, practices and ideas (including criminological ones) that fit with the realities of relatively high crime rates, the limited ability of government to reduce reoffending, and a sceptical and anxious public now accustomed to (and demanding of) localized self-protection. Among other approaches, academic criminology today features two opposing 'frameworks' both of which have appeal to the authorities in different ways, and which Garland (2001: 137) nicely terms a 'criminology of the other' and a 'criminology of the self'—a psychoanalytically-tinged opposition reflecting wider public sentiment about crime that is at once fearful of and vengeful toward the most abhorrent crimes and their perpetrators, and at the same time wearily resigned to the ambient risks of 'everyday' crimes such as theft and vandalism. While conceived before the 9/11 terror attacks of 2001 and the ensuing repressive measures instituted in the name of a 'war on terror', Garland's model anticipates these developments well. His account offers a nuanced historical and sociological interpretation of the rise of certain kinds of crime control and criminal justice practices, arguing that they emerge as a response to wider social changes, and in the context of political and institutional adaptations to the problem of crime. Part of the new configuration of control is to be found in the private sector, with private security expanding dramatically. Security is now something to be 'consumed' (Goold, Loader and Thumala, 2010)—though ironically the security industry itself appears insecure as to its social position and aware of the limits to its legitimacy (Thumala, Goold and Loader, 2011). Today the security industry can be found expanding in the online world too, selling products and services such as anti-virus software to address 'virtual insecurity' which Yar (2009: 199–200) sees as 'part of the broader reconfiguration of crime control and policing' in neo-liberal societies today.

Security

Theories of physical and spatial security

Territoriality and 'defensible space'

One of the ways in which we might speak of 'security' is in relation to places, and in particular to the places where people live, work and play. 'Security' here might refer to specific security measures (for example, door code systems or CCTV systems), but it could also refer to the sense of security people have, and whether they feel secure or insecure in those places. Seeking to explain why certain residential housing blocks in

America in the 1960s had become the sites of high levels of crime, the American archi-
tect Oscar Newman (1972) considered the problem and, drawing from his architectural
training, suggested reasons why the physical design of residential tower blocks and their
surrounding areas may inadvertently have made it harder for people to interact with
each other, or worse, even facilitated various forms of criminal and anti-social behaviour. For Newman, the failure of public housing, and the communal fears and insecurities it unwittingly generated, were explicable in terms of the relationship between the
residential area and the people who lived there. The architecture of some new housing
had inadvertently introduced physical qualities that interfered with residents' abilities to
engage with their surroundings. Newman argued that residents in general typically liked
to interact with others in their environs, and would as a result gain symbolic attachment
to these places, to the extent that they would often 'defend' their spaces, challenging
outsiders and quickly invoking the authorities (such as security guards or the police) if
they saw anything untoward happening. Shorn of this connection and involvement,
the public spaces outside people's flats were left undefended, and residents were left to
retreat indoors to their homes, their last line of security—thus perpetuating the problem
in the process. The solution, then, in Newman's view, was to reintroduce architecture
featuring what he termed 'defensible space', space that would encourage pro-social participation and which would encourage local residents somehow to 'guard' or exercise
'natural surveillance' over their local environment. The 'optics' of the public spaces
were thus of crucial importance: designing clear lines of sight would allow residents to
exercise guardianship over places and each other; whereas narrow, dimly lit, angular
concrete stairwells meant that criminality could take place unchecked. Newman's book
is detailed and visionary, and helped inspire a similar British study (Coleman, 1985),
as well as inform the approach known as Crime Prevention Through Environmental
Design (CPTED) (see Crowe, 2000; Atlas, 2008). However, in the UK there was a political
dimension to the reception of Coleman's book, with her attack on State-planned housing
and support for owner-occupancy and the private housing market finding favour with
Thatcherism and the political right, even if ironically her prescriptive 'corrective measures' appear an attempt to further refine social planning rather than reject it.

Still, the idea that places that are 'guarded' are likely to have lower rates of offending
than otherwise is an enduring one. A criminological theory that explicitly incorporates
the concept of the 'guardian' into its account of offending is Cohen and Felson's (1979)
'Routine Activities Theory'.[1] Famously, this theory argues that for crime to occur, it must
feature three essential 'ingredients': a suitable target, a likely offender, and the absence of
a 'capable guardian'. In fact, the authors' original aim was not to develop a new theory of
offending as such, but rather, to answer a different (but no less huge) question, namely,
why crime rates had risen so dramatically in the US after the 1950s. Their answer was
stunning in its simplicity and far-reaching in its implications: people's lifestyles (their
day-to-day, 'routine' activities) had changed—in many ways for the better, and yet in
ways that at the same time introduced numerous new criminal opportunities. For example, social norms had changed and more women had entered the workplace—but this
meant that more homes were left unattended during the daytime which in turn meant
that burglaries were less likely to be interrupted. Social change (including changing social
norms, employment practices, and leisure activities) accounted for the rise in criminal

opportunities, and hence of crime. Identifying the three basic 'ingredients' required in the 'chemistry' of crime is said thus to help understand the basic mechanism behind all crime. Moreover, this approach has clear policy implications, since crime would be prevented by removing any one of its essential ingredients. It has also been suggested that there are points of connection between the theory of defensible space and routine activities theory—for example, the degree to which residents act as capable guardians and defend their spaces may depend in part on their routine activities (Reynald and Elffers, 2009: 40).

Situational crime prevention

Another criminological theory relating to security is 'situational crime prevention' (SCP), an approach pioneered in the 1980s by Ronald V. Clarke (1983) and colleagues, and developed by numerous researchers since. Like routine activities theory, instead of focusing on individual criminals it focuses on the circumstances and situations in which crime takes place. If crime requires the co-presence of a likely offender, a suitable target and the absence of a guardian, what specific measures might disrupt these? Situational crime prevention answers this question by suggesting key strategies of disruption, famously articulated in the first three principles of situational crime prevention: increase the effort (required by the offender to commit the crime); reduce the reward (so that even if reached, it has less value to the offender); and increase the risk (to the offender of being detected while offending). According to situational crime prevention, with careful thought these principles can be implemented in a specific situation where crime is repeatedly occurring or may occur. Situational crime prevention is known for its advocacy of 'target hardening'—increasing the effort required to commit crime, typically by physical measures such as adding bolts, bars or barriers. Over the years, however, situational crime prevention has added a fourth and then later a fifth principle to its core, namely, remove the excuses, and reduce the provocations (Cornish and Clarke, 2003)— principles that appear more 'social psychological' in the mechanisms they employ. Accounts of many 'successful case studies' have been published (see, for example, Clarke, 1997); and situational crime prevention has also sought to extend its applicability to other fields—for example, in preventing cybercrime (Newman and Clarke, 2003), and in combatting terrorism (Clarke and Newman, 2006). SCP is extremely practice-oriented; and in recent years, Ronald Clarke and many of his colleagues have advocated and developed what they term 'crime science', which they see as standing in distinction to 'criminology' (see Knepper, 2009; Clarke, 2004). As Ken Pease and others have argued, effective situational crime prevention is likely to require a future-oriented analysis, not just a responsive one. Moreover, as Paul Ekblom (1999) has pointed out, SCP theory may need developing, in order to recognize the dynamic 'arms race' or 'evolutionary struggle' quality to the measure/counter-measure cycle sometimes encountered (for example, in relation to attempts to prevent digital media piracy).

SCP has a penchant for typologies and acronyms, especially used as mnemonics, which it employs quite deliberately with practical applications in mind, figuring, correctly, that its insights are more likely to be applied if they can be remembered. These can be quite useful: for example, Clarke (1999) suggests that certain items are particularly sought after by thieves, and that this is attributable to the items having certain qualities, namely, that they are 'CRAVED' (concealable, removable, available, valuable, enjoyable and disposable). Recognizing these qualities may then usefully be a first step to successful crime prevention. Although SCP has been accused of 'over-simplifying' crime prevention strategies (see Ekblom, 2011: Chapter 4), one of its interesting aspects nevertheless is its attempt to identify some of the particular features, mechanisms and sequential processes of crime commission. Felson and Boba (2010), for example, draw attention to the role of markets for stolen goods in understanding the process of theft.

Criticisms of situational crime prevention and crime science can be divided into the following kinds. The first set of objections relate to effectiveness over time, problems associated with scaling up or replicating successful interventions, and the problem of adaptation by offenders. A second kind of objection is levelled by critical and cultural criminologists who view opportunity theory as failing to account for 'expressive crimes'; or failing adequately to capture the emotional essence of offending (see Hayward, 2007). The response from opportunity theory advocates is that their approach can help reduce crime and is of wide practical social benefit (see Farrell, 2010). A third, and related though different, objection is that opportunity theory turns the crime problem from a societal problem into one for individual people and places to deal with, shunting the 'responsibility' for (and cost of implementing) crime reduction away from governments and directly onto citizens. This, though, seems less a theoretical failing of situational crime prevention as such and more a political matter of resource allocation.

Surveillance

Theories of surveillance

Foucault, 'discipline' and surveillance

One of the most influential theories of surveillance derives from Michel Foucault's (1926–84) work on 'discipline', set out in closest detail in his book *Discipline and Punish*. The original title of the book on its publication in France in 1975 was *Surveiller et Punir*. On its translation into English, the publishers discussed with Foucault what English title to give the book; he thought 'discipline' a better word to use than 'surveillance', perhaps because the latter usually has a more detached meaning in English, generally implying only the watching rather than the correcting of behaviour, and thus fails to capture the interactive quality of 'corrections' that Foucault's book sets out to describe. Nevertheless, surveillance, optics, observation, and knowledge, are all central themes of Foucault's book, and the book has made a distinctive contribution to a certain type of critical sociological criminology, particularly in the areas of (critical) theoretical criminology, the sociology of punishment and the study of social control.

At the same time, it is important to realize that Foucault was not a criminologist, that his book is not intended as a criminological text as such, and that his interest ultimately is in the study of the Western 'subject' (perceiving person) in modern societies. It makes a certain sense to think, at least in the first instance, of the criminological topic of *Discipline and Punish* as one Foucault happened by chance to use as the case study for his book; he could have written the same book, he once noted, instead about the school, factory, hospital or army barracks.

Discipline and Punish (Foucault, 1979) famously opens with brief descriptions of two, very different, forms of punishment from French history: the brutal execution of Damiens the regicide in 1757, and a prison timetable from about 1838. The public execution is gory and brutal, taking place in public before a large crowd, and today seems quite barbaric to us. The prison timetable, in contrast, appears infinitely more civilized and modern and, in its specifications of when and where prisoners should be doing things at different times of the day, in its form strikes us as familiar today, even if its content is now somewhat old-fashioned. Foucault notes that these two very different types of punishment are separated by a period of only about 80 years. How, he asks, did the change from one to the other come about? His answer rejects the obvious liberal explanation that the change is attributable to French society becoming more civilized and humane. Instead, and controversially, he suggests that modern prisons evolved not because they are *kinder* ways of punishing but because they are more *efficient* ways of punishing; to use Foucault's terminology, modern prisons are based on a more efficient 'technology of power'.

A technology of power, Foucault writes, is a particular, historically specific way by which humans exercise power over one another. A technology of power is comprised both of *knowledges* and of *practices*. Different technologies of power are dominant during different phases of history. Foucault's model of history is reminiscent of Rusche and Kirkheimer's (1968), in that it characterizes history as being composed of a succession of phases (each phase lasting for decades or centuries). During each phase, social organization follows certain patterns. But social life changes dramatically at certain points, as one phase gives way to another. (As such, Foucault rejects the conventional liberal understanding of history as a process of continual and gradual change.)

According to Foucault, technologies of power are be found within all areas of social life, including health and medicine, education, the military, and factories. *Discipline and Punish* is concerned specifically with the role that three, historically successive, technologies of power play within the spheres of punishment and of social control: monarchical power, juridical power, and disciplinary power. Monarchical punishment is the spectacular, brutal, public form of punishment being carried out in the execution of Damiens. It is a display of the monarch's absolute power, and typically involves some sort of visible marking or disfiguring of the offender's body; but it is also, says Foucault, an unstable, hard-to-control, form of punishment; its use of brute force and heady emotions can backfire, and the impassioned crowd might even turn on the executioner and the State. Juridical punishment is the punishment of classical criminology ('let the punishment fit the crime') from the late eighteenth century. Punishment is to be proportionate, with length of time spent in prison intended to reflect the gravity of the offence committed. It is not particularly concerned with the offender as such, who is simply readmitted as a full citizen once the prison sentence has been served.

According to Foucault, disciplinary punishment began towards the beginning of the nineteenth century, after 'discipline' (an older set of techniques that had been used in places such as monasteries for several centuries) took root in the newly formed modern prisons, and began guiding penal practices and knowledge. Discipline is based on supervision, training, correction of unwanted behaviour, and the continual examination and testing of each individual person. (The illustrations in the middle of the book *Discipline and Punish* are helpful in quickly grasping what Foucault had in mind.) Rather than seek to crush offenders (an aim of monarchical punishment), or merely incarcerate them for a time but do little more (as juridical punishment had done), disciplinary punishment seeks to rehabilitate. Discipline utilizes measures of time and space to bring order to the social world. Groups of soldiers can be taught to march in step in orderly rows and columns, the sick can each be assigned one hospital bed, schoolchildren a desk each, and prisoners their own cell. By individualizing each person in this way, 'abnormal' or 'incorrect' behaviour becomes easier for a supervisor to identify, study and address. Foucault argues that this is what surveillance is; a system by which a small number of supervisors can efficiently exercise dominance and control over individuals and groups by constituting them in a certain way. The aim is to 'normalize' each person, by identifying and dealing with any abnormal behaviour, however small. Once this has been done, the individual can successfully and safely be handed over to a different, less intensive part of the surveillance apparatus. But remember that it is a very specific form of dominance, in that its aim is not violent repression, but rather, the detailed study of each individual's behaviour, record, and history, with a view to reforming and rehabilitating them, at least in part. Foucault notes that 'experts' have an important role to play here (particularly in the more problematic cases) because of their role in generating and applying specific knowledge within each field, but that equally important are the specific practices facilitated by each institution's architecture. Foucault sees Jeremy Bentham's 'Panopticon' prison design as an illustration of the relationship between knowledge and architecture within institutions, as well as epitomizing disciplinary surveillance in particular. The circular prison design, featuring a central guard's tower from which a guard can see into every single prison cell while themselves remaining hidden, separates out the prisoners (one to each cell), thus helping control order in the prison, but also generates knowledge and practices relating to the prisoners through facilitating study of them as individuals.

Foucault claims that the social scientific study of people, and in particular academic disciplines such as psychology and criminology (which he collectively terms 'the disciplines') emerged at this time, alongside the birth of the modern prison. Yet the maximum security prison is not the only place within the criminal justice and crime control system in which discipline and surveillance (in Foucault's sense) are to be found. Disciplinary punishment, Foucault claims in his 'dispersal of discipline' thesis, underpins not only all other, less secure prisons, but also probation work, diversion schemes, half-way houses, and outreach work—a network of sorts that he terms the 'carceral archipelago'. Moreover, disciplinary surveillance penetrates deep into the social body, with various professions exercising implicit watching-and-judging powers through their specialized forms of surveillance: the teacher-judge, the lawyer-judge, the police officer-judge. Further still, this judging (surveillance and normalization) is exercised to some extent by us all. In this way, disciplinary *punishment* and disciplinary *social control* are 'genetically' related to one another, as it were, with discipline (active surveillance) being their shared characteristic.

As David Garland (1990) has noted, Foucault's account of discipline and surveillance practices constitutes an original and thought-provoking reinterpretation not only of punishment in modern society, but also of the connections between punishment and social control. As Garland has also noted, there are various problems with Foucault's account. Garland (1985) has shown that in England, at least, modern rehabilitative punishment actually appears to have begun almost a century later than Foucault suggests. Moreover, Foucault's 'power perspective' (his insistence that social relations and historical change must be understood principally in terms of power and domination), and his related 'antihumanist' approach, are highly questionable as analytic frameworks (see Garland, 1990: Chapter 7). They also beg certain questions: Is power really as one-sided as Foucault portrays? Is resistance to power possible? Are people really primarily motivated by (and is history really explicable in terms of) power alone? To some extent, Foucault addresses these and other criticisms in interviews and essays after *Discipline and Punish* was published (see for example, Gordon, 1980), though in other respects they remain fundamental questions regarding his whole approach during the early to mid-1970s.

Although Foucault (1979) was clearly very interested in the topic of surveillance, and indeed built this whole book around a particular, unique interpretation of this term, he was only partly concerned with alerting his readership to the 'Big Brother' nature of the State, and instead more concerned with trying to say something about the individualizing practices of surveillance—about the *formation* of the modern disciplined individual, rather than the *repression* of the individual. Foucault was very interested in the history of the Western 'subject' (crudely, our conscious, subjective experience as a person), about how this particular subject formation came about, about knowledge-production, and relations between knowledge formations and power formations (note however that Foucault does not say that 'knowledge is power') (see Dreyfus and Rabinow, 1982). Nevertheless, Foucault's work continues to be influential within the study of surveillance today, perhaps because of his critical and ominous account of the insidious, ubiquitous social-controlling functions of surveillance, and perhaps because of the apparent applicability of his discussion of the Panopticon to electronic surveillance technologies: 'the electronic Panopticon' (see Lyon, 1993, 1994).

Theories of surveillance 'after Foucault'

In the early 1990s, Feeley and Simon (1992) claimed that a new guiding logic was emerging within punishment, which they termed 'The New Penology'. They suggested that this new logic was a historical successor to disciplinary punishment, or at least that it stood in sharp contrast to it. The characteristics of the new penology were said to involve an interest in aggregates rather than individuals; use of actuarial analysis; and an appeal to incapacitation rather than rehabilitation as a sentencing rationale. In a subsequent essay, Feeley and Simon (1994) broadened the 'new penology' argument and argued that similar practices could be seen emerging across various different parts of criminal justice and crime control systems; they termed this 'actuarial justice'. The relevance of their work to the study of surveillance lies in their identification of a crime control approach that utilizes a form of surveillance seemingly rather different to the involved, individualizing approach modelled by Foucault. In a discussion of screening techniques used in airport security checks of passengers, Feeley and Simon (1994: 177) argue that such screening may now be based on identifying typical offender risk factors, and utilizing this information in risk identification systems. By using basic information such as a passenger's age, nationality, transit origin and destination, and so on, a risk instrument can quickly derive an initial risk 'score' for each passenger. 'High risk' passengers scoring above a certain predefined level can be questioned or investigated further. Such systems do not claim the predictions they generate are correct; rather, the aim is to help allocate the scarce resources of airline security (equipment, personnel and their time) in focusing on potentially higher risk individuals. The key point for us here is that this represents a move away from Foucauldian surveillance practices and towards a new, 'post-disciplinary' form of surveillance (a historical shift which seems to have been hinted at, at least, by Feeley and Simon (1992) in the title of their original article).

In an article inspired by Foucault's Panopticon, but with a novel twist, Thomas Mathiesen (1997) points out that while the Panopticon enabled the few to see the many, today the mass media enables the many to see the few—which he suggests is part of a system of social control and which he dubs the 'Synopticon'. Further 'post-disciplinary' perspectives can be found in two separate essays by French post-structuralist writers Jean Baudrillard (1929–2007) and Gilles Deleuze (1925–95). In a short, critical book entitled *Forget Foucault*, Baudrillard (1987) claims that Foucault's work in *Discipline and Punish* gives too much credence to the concept of power, and indeed that Foucault's book was itself part of a fading era; as such, Baudrillard seems to reject Foucault's power perspective, including the concept of 'technologies of power'. Baudrillard (1983, 1993) argues instead that contemporary Western societies are societies of 'simulation' (of surface, image, appearance, digitization, and perfect replicability, an era in which the electronic or genetic 'copy' is indistinguishable from the 'original'). From this perspective, the imagery produced by CCTV cameras, for example, should not be theorized in terms of attempts to 'know' the truth about the person under surveillance, but instead as part of society's safety-inspired desire to achieve an exact yet sterile reflection of itself. Although Baudrillard considered himself as standing in stark opposition to Foucault, others see certain linkages between their work. Bogard (1996) has argued that Foucault's work on surveillance can be combined with Baudrillard's work on simulation, suggesting that electronic forms of surveillance today may involve elements both of Foucauldian surveillance and of Baudrillard's simulation in their (digital) representation of the person under surveillance. With the emergence of electronic forms of surveillance producing electronic representations of the person or thing under surveillance, we also enter an era in which those representations can be electronically recorded, analysed and replayed. For Bogard, the possibilities that various electronic surveillance systems offer in terms of their enabling surveillance to begin to escape from the ties of the here-and-now, are one aspect of the wider emergence not just of an information society but of 'the conversion of persons and social relations into the universal ether of information, which is their simulation' (1996: 69).

Deleuze, too, has contributed (albeit briefly) to post-disciplinary perspectives in an essay suggesting that Foucault's third type of 'technology of power' (disciplinary power) may presently be being replaced by a fourth, which he terms 'control'. Deleuze's (1995) essay is more than a little opaque, but he seems to be suggesting that contemporary capitalism, with its electronic communications, dynamic consumer economy, geographic mobility, and fluid organizational techniques, gives rise to a cultural form in which disciplinary institutions become superseded by flow-control systems (see Jones, 2000; Haggerty and Ericson, 2000; see also Lyon, 2003). Deleuze might point to electronic tagging of offenders (particularly involving satellite tracking) as an example of this form of control; rather than being detained in a prison, today's society is able to punish and control even while permitting certain mobility. Tracking tags and electronic access cards can permit/disallow or warn against entry to a particular zone or place, including at particular times or on particular days. In this way, offender tracking tags could aim to 'modulate' a given offender's daily routine, rather than simply restricting it or subjecting it to traditional surveillance supervision.

Haggerty and Ericson develop some further themes drawn from Deleuze and Guattari in their notion of the 'surveillant assemblage' (2000). Haggerty and Ericson note that much analysis of surveillance focuses on specific technologies or practices, but that one emerging aspect of contemporary surveillance practices is their combination 'into a larger whole' (2000: 610). Instead of trying to claim that this is part of a single Orwellian design, Haggerty and Ericson invoke Deleuze and Guattari's notion of the 'assemblage', which refers to how several discrete objects or systems come together and interact. The notion of the 'surveillant assemblage' seems well placed today to capture the likely integration that digital surveillance and the Internet will afford, linking separately created and discrete systems. Moreover, they suggest that with the combination this way of sufficient surveillant data about a person's various activities, one could even go so far as to speak of the combined profile as a sort of 'data double' of the individual—a challenging and troubling notion, however remote it remains from reality today (2000: 606).

One of the leading figures in the field of surveillance studies today is David Lyon, who has argued that the most important characteristic of surveillance on which to focus is the use to which the data acquired are put, and specifically data's role in what he terms 'social sorting'. According to Lyon, the 'drive of contemporary surveillance' is to classify and record data, in order better to 'plan, predict and prevent' (2003: 13). Searchable databases play a key role, informing the management of populations, by sorting and classifying data about individuals. Access to social opportunity is now policed at virtual 'gates and barriers', which effectively 'sort' people. For Lyon (2007: 16) the significance of such practices lie in their use by government and others for social sorting and hence ultimately for social governance.

REVIEW QUESTIONS

1 Whose responsibility is it to control and act as the guardian of public spaces?

2 What are the strengths and weaknesses of situational crime prevention?

3 What does Foucault mean by 'discipline' and 'surveillance'? For Foucault, what is the relationship between punishment and social control?

4 What are 'post-disciplinary' theories of surveillance, and why might there be a need for such theories today?

Contemporary security and surveillance technologies

Having considered some leading theories on the topics of physical security and surveillance, this section will discuss different practical security and surveillance technologies and approaches, drawing attention to their various roles but also the ways they overlap.

Surveillance cameras

Perhaps one of the best-known forms of surveillance today is CCTV camera surveillance. (CCTV is an abbreviation of 'closed-circuit television', meaning a system in which only certain people can view the camera images, as opposed to those television cameras designed to capture images for public broadcast. Today, 'CCTV' perhaps refers to any fixed, remote camera used for surveillance or monitoring purposes.) In the UK, CCTV camera usage expanded dramatically during the 1990s, partly as a result of Home Office backing of CCTV city street schemes. The number of CCTV cameras also increased over this same time period in shopping centres, on roads and highways, within private premises (homes, offices, shops) and in institutions such as prisons. Their increase in popularity over this time is probably due to the technology becoming more affordable, a belief that CCTV cameras would somehow reduce crime, and a wider shift toward usage of situational crime prevention measures generally on the part of individuals and organizations (see Garland, 2001).

CCTV is often also thought of as being a form of situational crime prevention (SCP), following Clarke's (1995) classic classification of situational crime prevention techniques. In this and the following examples we therefore see how particular technologies and approaches can be understood as having both surveillance and security roles and objectives. Clarke identifies 'increasing the risk of detection' as one of the three main ways in which SCP can work. During the 1990s it was often presumed that the deployment of CCTV cameras in a place or area would 'deter' offenders from offending because of the offender's perception of the greatly increased risk of getting caught. Much of the research into CCTV during this time were evaluations of schemes (whether in a city centre, or certain shops or institutions), trying to establish whether schemes did indeed have such an effect; whether they were having no effect; whether they were instead merely 'displacing' criminal activity to other areas nearby lacking CCTV; or whether they were not only working but were also 'diffusing' benefits to other areas nearby lacking CCTV (Brown, 1995; Tilley, 1993; Ditton and Short, 1999). Research findings are mixed, but seem to suggest that in many cases CCTV schemes do not seem nearly as effective at crime reduction as their early proponents had hoped. In a review of research on the effectiveness of the crime preventive effects of CCTV surveillance cameras, Welsh and Farrington found that studies 'showed that CCTV had a small but significant desirable effect on crime, has been most effective in reducing crime in car parks, has been most effective when targeted at vehicle crime ... and has been more effective in reducing crime in the U.K. than in North America'. They note too that greater public support 'for the use of CCTV cameras in public settings to prevent crime' has been found in the UK than has been found in North America (Welsh and Farrington, 2007: 204–5).

Additionally, during the commission of an offence, CCTV surveillance cameras may prove useful in coordinating police or security staff deployment. Another possible use of CCTV surveillance is in generating video evidence for use in court. However, other researchers have pointed out that in practice, CCTV may be used to target certain people or categories of person who are not necessarily offenders, such as the homeless or groups of young males, but who are perceived as (potentially) disorderly by CCTV operators and security staff. Monitoring of surveillance imagery can also be automated. Norris *et al.* (1998) explore how CCTV can be combined with other technologies, namely, through computerized image recognition of CCTV footage, which they term 'algorithmic surveillance'. Among the possible applications of such technology are facial recognition systems, automated number (that is, car licence) plate recognition (ANPR) systems, and systems designed to identify unattended and hence potentially dangerous baggage at places such as airports and train stations.

Newburn and Hayman (2002) studied the effects of the introduction of CCTV in the custody suite in a police station in London. Their study shows how the roles the CCTV system performed were not always as had been anticipated, and that to understand CCTV's use and effects one needs to understand the social dynamics of the police custody suite itself. Studying specific implementations of CCTV can also challenge the assumption that they have a particular 'function', or that their introduction automatically heralds the departure from established practices. Goold (2004: 212), for instance, studied policing practices in six towns in the South of England, and found that these 'did not change significantly as a result of the introduction of CCTV'. Smith (2007) has shown how CCTV operators manage the emotional strains of their jobs through creative construction of narrative to accompany the events they witness on screen. Camera surveillance today seems set to continue to proliferate around the world, finding ever-new uses, taking on new cultural symbolism, and raising questions concerning its social acceptability and legal regulation (Doyle *et al.*, 2011).

Several aspects of the development of surveillance cameras seem likely to shape their usage over the coming decade. Camera miniaturization, mobility, concealment and ubiquity, will increase the likelihood of cameras being used to record many different activities. This is likely to have social and political ramifications as areas and activities previously hidden from public view or otherwise unrecorded become more visible (see also Goffman's (1990) distinction between 'back stage' and 'front stage' activities). Such recordings may be made by law enforcement personnel (by hand-held or police helmet-mounted cameras); but another possibility is that they are made by members of the public recording the authorities such as the police themselves—a practice that has been dubbed 'souveillance' (Mann *et al.*, 2003; see also Greer and McLaughlin, 2010). Another (and related) aspect seems likely to be the connection of miniature video cameras to mobile communications devices, which becomes increasingly feasible as the connection speed of mobile data networks increases. The significance of this latter development is that it will allow real-time transmission of video from mobile cameras.

Electronic monitoring of convicted offenders

Research into the possibility of 'electronically tagging' convicted offenders can be dated back to the early 1960s. In 1964, four Harvard University academics published an article on 'behavioural electronics', one of whom by 1970 had developed a prototype electronic system for tracking a person's movements within a city (Schwitzgebel *et al.*, 1964; Schwitzgebel, 1970). Bulky, cumbersome, and impractical, their device was essentially experimental. By 1982, however, the advent of the silicon chip permitted smaller electronic devices to be developed, and in the US a New Mexico judge is said to have pioneered the introduction of the electronic monitoring of convicted offenders as a feasible sentencing option for the courts (Nellis, 2005). The first time a person in England was electronically tagged in a criminal justice context was in 1989, when a man was granted bail on condition that he 'voluntarily agreed' to have a device attached to him (Lilly and Himan, 1993: 1). Electronic tagging of offenders was promoted by the then Conservative government in the UK during the late 1980s and early 1990s, though tagging schemes were opposed on moral and ethical grounds by various groups. The Labour government elected in 1997 sought to expand rather than contract such schemes, and opposition on political or ethical grounds to the electronic tagging of offenders, though still sometimes voiced, is presently much less pronounced. In recent years in England and Wales the number of offenders commencing an electronically monitored curfew order has increased to around 80,000 in total and (after the US) runs one of the largest such schemes in the world.

In formal terms, the 'tagging' of offenders with electronic 'tags' is not a punishment in and of itself, but rather, a means by which compliance with a specific other penalty can be monitored. In England and Wales in the 1980s and 1990s, the most common application of the electronic monitoring of offenders was in relation to a home detention curfew order. The 'first generation' of electronic tags do not have any capability of 'tracking' an individual tagged offender's movements. Rather, the tag knows only whether the offender is in their home or not, and hence whether they are in compliance with their home curfew order (which may be between 7 p.m. and 7 a.m., for example). The tag is attached to the offender after sentencing, usually in the form of a small plastic anklet in which the transmitter is encased, and a base unit is installed in the offender's home and connected to a dedicated telephone line. If the offender breaches their curfew order the base unit automatically dials a monitoring centre, which can then alert a member of their staff (or potentially a probation or police officer) and request they investigate the breach. Electronic monitoring is now used in many countries to monitor offender compliance with court orders, and in England and Wales is also used on a scheme allowing for the conditional early release of certain prisoners, subject to home detention curfew. Research on the first generation of tags by Hucklesby (2008) suggests that some offenders were helped in reducing their offending by reducing their ties with 'anti-social capital' (for example, certain friends or places) and helping build 'pro-social capital' such as family bonds. However, other offenders experienced 'negative impacts', for example in terms of employment. In a discussion as to why an electronically monitored offender would comply with a curfew order, Nellis (2006) has proposed a useful typology, drawing attention not merely to the consequences of breach (which could include imprisonment) but also the offender's sense of continually being 'under surveillance'.

Recent years have witnessed the emergence of a 'second generation' of electronic tags, which look set gradually to supersede and replace the first generation tags. These newer 'tracking' tags use GPS technology to enable the tag to identify its wearer's exact geographical location, and so can be used to monitor compliance not only with home curfew orders, but also with attendance or exclusion orders, for example (see Nellis, 2010). Advocates of such tags argue that a possible benefit of their implementation could be that they could provide additional geographical evidence linking the tagged offender with any subsequent offences (or indeed exonerating them of these offences), and that they might provide further reassurance to the public while contributing to a reduction in reliance on custodial sentences. Critics argue that, as with the earlier tags, tagging by itself does nothing meaningful by way of addressing an offender's offending behaviour; and that the continual, detailed geographical monitoring of a person's movements (even those of a convicted offender), is a worrying development within liberal democratic societies. Burrell and Gable (2008), however, champion the possible future rehabilitative potential of the use of electronic monitoring devices in helping to modify offenders' behaviours. A 'third generation' of electronic tags featuring alcohol and/or drug sensors is already being used in the US. It remains to be seen whether these can play a helpful role in reducing substance abuse or whether these tags represent a further expansion of electronic social control.

Access control and biometric security

While certain aspects of the above situational crime prevention approaches involve the use of surveillance (for example, 'natural surveillance' or 'increasing the risks of detection') other aspects, such as 'target hardening' or 'increasing the effort' more generally can be viewed as security practices. Computer and security expert Bruce Schneier (2006: 182–3) has argued that in both computer and real-world security system design it is important to distinguish between identification ('who are you?'), authentication ('prove it'), and authorization ('here is what you are allowed to do'). Allowing access to places and systems is important because, 'With a very few exceptions, all security barriers need to be penetrated—under authorized circumstances by trusted people' (2006: 181). Access can be controlled by using 'swipe cards' or PIN numbers, for example. Another way of controlling access is by using biometrics (see Lyon, 2001: Chapter 5; van der Ploeg, 2003; Franko Aas, 2006). Biometric sensors can be used in conjunction with a smart card in order to authenticate a person (in place of a PIN code, for example); or can be compared with data stored on a remote computer database in order to identify individuals. Such sensors work by obtaining various measurements of biological features unique to each individual, such as iris pattern, fingerprint or handprint, and comparing this data to previously recorded data of the same type. A common application for biometric devices is as part of access control systems, such as for airport check-in, at immigration desks, office entry systems, or in order to log on to a computing device. However, as with any such access control information, the information about who has passed through the access control could be used for surveillance purposes, either of a generalized kind (aggregate information) or for conducting surveillance of a specific individual. The difference between biometric access control systems and other types (such as using passwords, identity documents, or electronic cards) is that it is much harder for an individual to use a false identity. A separate type of technology that measures aspects of a person's body is the drug or alcohol test. Whereas biometrics measures bodily characteristics that remain the same over time, drug and alcohol tests can be used as a form of surveillance of a person's recent use of intoxicating substances. Alcohol 'breathalysers' have been used for several decades in countries around the world, principally in the area of motoring, though they appear increasingly to be used in other areas of transportation, such as to ensure that airline pilots are not intoxicated prior to flight.

'Dataveillance'

The neologism 'dataveillance' was suggested by one forward-looking writer to describe the surveillance of electronic data, an important area given our increasing reliance on the Internet and digital communications for all aspects of social life (Clarke, 1988). Internet 'surveillance' can take many forms, but arguably can be reduced to one of three main types. The first type involves gathering information about a specific user. The second type, on the other hand, involves gathering aggregate data about a group of Internet users (for example, all visitors to a particular website). Surveillance of the first kind (a specific user's Internet usage) might be carried out, for example, by an employer who suspects an employee of improper Internet usage, or of betraying commercial secrets to a rival company. Internet surveillance of an individual might also be carried out by the police (for example, investigating an individual suspected of downloading or trading in computer images of child pornography), or indeed by State intelligence agencies seeking to gather information on a specific individual or group's communications, activities or associates. Monitoring of groups of people's usage of the Internet, on the other hand, might be conducted by a website administrator, an Internet Service Provider (ISP) interested in patterns of usage by their customers, or by a computer security chief tracking the changing methods used by the many hackers trying to hack into their organization's network. Powerful computers and huge data storage devices enable a third type of surveillance, which can be termed 'mass surveillance'. A technique known as 'deep packet inspection', for example, can be used by governments or ISPs to scan the content of all data passing within their countries' or their companies' Internet networks (see, for example, Mueller *et al.*, 2012). In many countries laws have been introduced requiring ISPs, web-based service providers (for example, search engines or email service providers), and mobile phone operator companies, for example, to retain summaries of all of their users' Internet use and communications for a certain period of time (for example, 12 months) in order to help law enforcement agencies investigate specific past crimes and terrorist activities. These sets of 'big data' could potentially be used for 'data mining' or 'data combining' purposes. Concerns with such practices include that they involve conducting 'surveillance' on large numbers of entirely innocent individuals. On the other hand, in practice, most people's data may be stored for a period of time but never actually seen by humans.

Surveillance of individual Internet users might be carried out a company or institution simply by examining log files routinely generated by network servers, which record which user logged on from which computer, at what time, and for how long; by examining server or router logs which may reveal which websites an individual visited; or email servers to establish what emails a user has sent, when, to whom, and what information these contained (Casey, 2004). In addition, considerable information may be obtained by examining the hard disk drive of a specific computer or, alternatively, by capturing a copy of network traffic as it passes through a network. Additional means of tracking an individual user's computing activities include keystroke monitors; spyware installed on the computer; and remote screen-view software, enabling remote viewing of an individual's computer screen in real time. Most computer activities leave an electronic 'trace' of some sort, on a hard disk or on a network server, or both, and network activity is usually traceable back to specific network addresses and ultimately back to specific computers. However, as with all forms of surveillance, the more knowledgeable the person (potentially) under surveillance is about the surveillance practices likely to be used against them, the more strategies they can employ to try to evade surveillance.

REVIEW QUESTIONS

1 What are some of the surveillance technologies in use today? How does each work, and what information do they gather?

2 Why and how might people resist surveillance systems? Under what circumstances, or in what forms, do you think people are likely to find surveillance more acceptable?

CONCLUSION

This chapter began by introducing the topics of security, risk and surveillance. It then discussed some key approaches, theories, and research studies. Finally, it explored several contemporary practical technologies used for the purposes of surveillance, crime control and/or security.

Today, we are faced with a plethora of existing and emerging technologies, reopening existing debates or raising new fears and challenges. While the fields of crime prevention, surveillance, risk, and security are in many respects separate from one another, there are also various points of convergence between them. These include a focus on themes such as the controlling of access to places and systems; watching over places (whether using cameras, other technologies, or through 'natural surveillance' by locals); the defence of spaces and the exercise of territoriality and control; and the problem of dealing with flows of people accessing and moving through places. Many of these themes can be found in relation both to the real world and to virtual environments—and indeed to our emerging 'hybrid' and indivisible use of the two in parallel. Many of the more critical theories discussed in this chapter focus on the security, surveillance and crime prevention measures themselves, identifying common patterns and themes, ways to interpret specific practices within wider critical theories, and drawing attention to the various social and political concerns that arise in the exercise of these measures. The most general of the critical theories 'zoom out' further still, and ask why it is that SCP, private security, securitization, and surveillance systems, for example, come to proliferate at this particular historical point in time, and why these rather than other possible approaches dominate the policy agenda. Garland's (2001: 199–200) explanation is that they have 'social roots' in 'social organization and political culture', and specifically that they are compatible with the neo-liberal market forces that have taken hold as the State has retreated in the face of its own ineffectiveness. As Garland (2001: Chapter 4) also notes, this is within the context of the profound changes in everyday life in the post-war period brought about by car ownership, increased geographic mobility, changing family patterns, electronic mass media, and democratization processes. As persuasive as this explanation is, we can add in both narrower and wider factors. More narrowly, we can note simply that surveillance and security technologies are now far more affordable than they once were, helping drive their uptake; and more prosaically still, note that to some extent at least these technologies and practices have a degree of effectiveness, however imperfect these may be.

Finally, and adopting a wider perspective of the kind proposed by Giddens or Bauman, it is possible to see the situation in terms of the broader social and economic transformations underway today. These range from globalization processes to newly experienced localities, from 'traditional' community to social media, and the reworking of economic and social relationships that these bring about. From this perspective, the appeal of security and surveillance may lie in social awareness of the risks and insecurities of our time, and represent the attempt to use the same sorts of social and technological processes that have transformed our societies also to provide us with safety and security. Whether this will deliver the vibrant and safe locales so yearned for only time will tell.

QUESTIONS FOR DISCUSSION

1 What is Michel Foucault's contribution to the study of surveillance?

2 What are some different kinds of surveillance that could be carried out, what sort of information do these technologies gather, and how useful is this information likely to be in practice in controlling crime or conferring security?

3 What particular issues and concerns are raised today by practices of 'dataveillance'?

4 How should society balance surveillance and privacy concerns?

5 Why might someone try to resist surveillance, and how might they try to do this?

6 Does a world of security mean that our public spaces will increasingly feature 'airport-style' security?

7 Are we moving toward a 'surveillance society' or a 'security State', and does it matter?

GUIDE TO FURTHER READING

Felson, M. and Boba, R. (2010), *Crime and Everyday Life* (4th edn) Thousand Oaks, CA: Sage Publications, Inc.
An introductory book explaining and advocating (situational) crime prevention through opportunity reduction.

Foucault, M. (1979) *Discipline and Punish: The Birth of the Prison*. London: Penguin.
While primarily concerned with punishment, and not always an easy read, this book nevertheless remains an essential part of the repertoire for anyone interested in surveillance. See especially centre illustrative plates, 3–8, Parts 3.2, 3.3 and 4.3.

Lyon, D. (2007) *Surveillance Studies: An Overview.* Cambridge: Polity Press.
An excellent introduction and overview of contemporary surveillance theories, technologies, and issues.

WEB LINKS

http://www.sscqueens.org

The Surveillance Studies Centre. Run by David Lyon and colleagues at the sociology department of the Queen's University, Canada.

http://www.surveillance-and-society.org

Surveillance and Society. Online surveillance studies journal.

http://www.liberty-human-rights.org.uk

Liberty. Website of a leading UK civil liberties pressure group. Includes information on their privacy concerns regarding various surveillance policies and technologies.

http://www.wired.com

Wired. US-based magazine containing a wide range of news stories and features on the latest technological developments, including cultural, governmental, and privacy issues.

http://www.homeoffice.gov.uk

Home Office. Website of the UK ministry responsible for dealing with crime, policing, criminal justice, counter-terrorism, and immigration.

REFERENCES

Aas, K.F. (2011) '"Crimmigrant" bodies and bona fide travellers: Surveillance, citizenship and global governance', *Theoretical Criminology*, Vol. 15(3): 331–46.

Atlas, R. (2008) *21st Century Security and CPTED* Boca Raton, FL: Auerback Publications.

Baudrillard, J. (1983) *Simulations [aka 'Simulacra and Simulations']* New York: Semiotext(e).

Baudrillard, J. (1987) *Forget Foucault* New York: Semiotext(e).

Baudrillard, J. (1993) *Symbolic Exchange and Death* London: Sage.

Bauman, Z. (2000) *Liquid Modernity* Cambridge: Polity Press.

Beck, U. (1992) *Risk Society: Towards a New Modernity* London: Sage.

Black, M. and Smith, R.G. (2003) 'Electronic Monitoring in the Criminal Justice System', *Trends and Issues in Crime and Criminal Justice* No. 254. Canberra: Australian Institute of Criminology.

Bogard, W. (1996) *The Simulation of Surveillance: Hypercontrol in Telematic Societies* Cambridge: Cambridge University Press.

Bottoms, A. and Wiles, P. (1996) 'Crime prevention and late modernity' in T. Bennett (ed) *Crime Prevention*: The Cropwood Papers. Cambridge: Cropwood.

Bottoms, A.E. (2001) 'Compliance and community penalties' in A.E. Bottoms, L. Gelsthorpe and S. Rex (eds) *Community Penalties: Change and Challenges* Cullompton: Willan.

Brown, B. (1995) *CCTV in Town Centres: Three case studies (Crime Detection and Prevention Series: Paper 68)* London: Home Office, Police Department.

Burrell, W. and Gable, R. (2008) 'From B.F. Skinner to Spiderman and Martha Stewart: The Past, Present and Future of Electronic Monitoring of Offenders', *Journal of Offender Rehabilitation*, Vol. 46 (3 & 4): 101–18.

Casey, E. (2004) *Digital Evidence and Computer Crime* (2nd edn) London: Academic Press.

Clarke, R.A. (1988), 'Information Technology and Dataveillance', *Communications of the ACM*, May 1988, Vol. 31, No. 5, 498–512.

Clarke, R.V. (1983), 'Situational Crime Prevention: Its Theoretical Basis and Practical Scope', *Crime and Justice*, Vol. 4: 225–56.

Clarke, R.V. (1995) 'Situational crime prevention' in M. Tonry and D. Farrington (eds), *Building a Safer Society: Crime and Justice: A Review of Research*, Vol. 19. Chicago: University of Chicago Press.

Clarke, R.V. (1999) *Hot products: understanding, anticipating and reducing demand for stolen goods*, Police Research Series Paper 112. London: Home Office, Policing and Reducing Crime Unit.

Clarke, R.V. (ed) (1997) *Situational Crime Prevention: Successful Case Studies* (2nd edn) Guilderland, NY: Harrow and Heston.

Clarke, R.V. (2004) 'Technology, Criminology and Crime Science', *European Journal on Criminal Policy and Research*, Vol. 10: 55–63.

Cohen, L. and Felson, M. (1979), 'Social Change and Crime Rate Trends: A Routine Activity Approach', *American Sociological Review*, Vol. 44 (August): 588–608.

Clarke, R.V. and Newman, G. (2006) *Outsmarting the Terrorists* Westport, CT: Praeger Security International.

Cohen, S. (1985) *Visions of Social Control: Crime, Punishment and Classification* Cambridge: Polity.

Cohen, S. and Scull, A. (eds) (1983) *Social Control and the State* Oxford: Martin Robertson.

Cornish, D. and Clarke, R.V. (2003) 'Opportunities, Precipitators and Criminal Decisions: A Reply to Wortley's Critique of Situational Crime Prevention' in M. Smith and D. Cornish (eds), *Theory for Practice in Situational Crime Prevention* Cullompton: Willan Publishing.

Crowe, T. (2000) *Crime Prevention Through Environmental Design* (2nd edn) Stoneham, MA: Butterworth-Heinemann.

Deleuze, G. (1995) 'Postscript on control societies' in *Negotiations: 1972–1990* New York: Columbia University Press.

Ditton, J. and Short, E. (1999) 'Yes, it works—no, it doesn't: Comparing the effects of open-street CCTV in two adjacent town centres', *Crime Prevention Studies*, Vol. 10: 201–23.

Douglas, M. and Wildavsky, A. (1982) *Risk and Culture: An essay on the selection of technical and environmental dangers* Berkeley: University of California Press.

Doyle, A., Lippert, R., and Lyon, D. (2011) *Eyes Everywhere: The Global Growth of Camera Surveillance* London: Routledge.

Dreyfus, H. and Rabinow, P. (1982) *Michel Foucault: Beyond Structuralism and Hermeneutics* Hemel Hempstead: Harvester Wheatsheaf.

Ekblom, P. (1999) 'Can we make crime prevention adaptive by learning from other evolutionary struggles?', *Studies on Crime and Crime Prevention*, 8/1: 27–51.

Ekblom, P. (2011) *Crime Prevention, Security and Community Safety Using the 5Is Framework* Basingstoke: Palgrave Macmillan.

Ericson, R. (2007) *Crime in an Insecure World* Cambridge: Polity Press.

Farrell, G. (2010) 'Situational Crime Prevention and its Discontents: Rational Choice and Harm Reduction versus 'Cultural Criminology', *Social Policy & Administration*, Vol. 44(1): 40–66.

Feeley, M. and Simon, J. (1992) 'The New Penology: Notes on the Emerging Strategy of Corrections and its Implications', *Criminology*, Vol. 30 (4): 449–74.

Feeley, M. and Simon, J. (1994) 'Actuarial justice: the emerging new criminal law' in D. Nelken (ed) *The Futures of Criminology* London: Sage.

Felson, M. and Boba, R. (2010) *Crime and Everyday Life* (4th edn) Thousand Oaks, CA: Sage Publications, Inc.

Foucault, M. (1979) *Discipline and Punish: The Birth of the Prison* London: Penguin.

Franko Aas, K. (2006) 'The body does not lie: Identity, risk and trust in technoculture', *Crime, Media, Culture*, Vol. 2(2): 143–58.

Franko Aas, K. (2007) 'Analysing a world in motion: Global flows meet "criminology of the other"', *Theoretical Criminology*, Vol. 11(2): 283–303.

Garland, D. (1985) *Punishment and Welfare: A History of Penal Strategies* Aldershot: Gower.

Garland, D. (1990) *Punishment and Modern Society: A Study in Social Theory* Oxford: Clarendon.

Garland, D. (2001) *The Culture of Control: Crime and Social Order in Contemporary Society* Oxford: Oxford University Press.

Giddens, A. (1990) *The Consequences of Modernity* Cambridge: Polity Press.

Giddens, A. (1991) *Modernity and Self-Identity* Cambridge: Polity Press.

Goffman, E. (1990) *The Presentation of Self in Everyday Life* London: Penguin.

Goold, B. (2004) *CCTV and Policing*. Oxford: Oxford University Press.

Goold, B., Loader, I., and Thumala, A. (2010) 'Consuming security?: Tools for a sociology of security consumption', *Theoretical Criminology*, Vol. 14(1): 3–30.

Gordon, C. (ed) (1980) *Power/Knowledge: Selected Interviews and Other Writings* Hemel Hempstead: Harvester Wheatsheaf.

Greer, C. and McLaughlin, E. (2010) 'We Predict a Riot?: Public Order Policing, New Media Environments and the Rise of the Citizen Journalist', *British Journal of Criminology*, Vol. 50 (6): 1041–59.

Haggerty, K. and Ericson, R.V. (2000) 'The surveillant assemblage', *British Journal of Sociology*, 51 (4): 605–22.

Haggerty, K. and Ericson, R.V. (eds) (2006) *The New Politics of Surveillance and Visibility* Toronto: University of Toronto Press.

Hayward, K. (2007) 'Situational Crime Prevention and its Discontents: Rational Choice Theory versus the "Culture of Now"', *Social Policy & Administration*, Vol. 41(3): 232–50.

Home Office (2001) *Electronic monitoring of released prisoners: an evaluation of the Home Detention Curfew scheme: Home Office Research Studies 222* London: Home Office.

Jones, R. (2000) 'Digital Rule: Punishment, Control and Technology', *Punishment and Society*, 2 (1): 5–22.

Knepper, P. (2009) 'How Situational Crime Prevention Contributes to Social Welfare', *Liverpool Law Review*, Vol. 30: 57–75.

Lilly, J.R. and Himan, J. (eds) (1993) *The Electronic Monitoring of Offenders: Symposium Papers, Second Series* Leicester: De Montfort University Law School Monographs.

Lyon, D. (2003) 'Surveillance as social sorting: Computer codes and mobile bodies' in D. Lyon (ed) *Surveillance as Social Sorting: Privacy, Risk and Digital Discrimination* London: Routledge.

Lyon, D. (1993) 'An Electronic Panopticon? A Sociological Critique of Surveillance Theory', *Sociological Review*, 41 (4): 653.

Lyon, D. (1994) *The Electronic Eye: The Rise of Surveillance Society* Cambridge: Polity.

Lyon, D. (2001) *Surveillance Society: Monitoring Everyday Life* Buckingham: Open University Press.

Lyon, D. (2003) *Surveillance after September 11* Cambridge: Polity Press.

Lyon, D. (ed) (2006) *Theorizing Surveillance: The panopticon and beyond* Cullompton: Willan Publishing.

Lyon, D. (2007) *Surveillance Studies: An Overview* Cambridge: Polity Press.

Mann, S. *et al.* (2003) 'Souveillance', *Surveillance & Society*, Vol. 1(3): 331–55

Mathiesen, T. (1997) 'The Viewer Society: Michel Foucault's "Panopticon" Revisited', *Theoretical Criminology*, Vol. 1(2): 215–34.

Monmonier, M. (2002) *Spying with Maps: Surveillance technologies and the future of privacy* Chicago: Chicago University Press.

Mueller, M., Kuehn, A., and Santoso, S.M. (2012) 'Policing the Network: Using DPI for Copyright Enforcement', *Surveillance & Security*, Vol. 9(4): 348–64.

Nellis, M. (2005) 'Out of this World: The Advent of the Satellite Tracking of Offenders in England and Wales', *The Howard Journal*, Vol. 44(2): 125–50.

Nellis, M. (2006), 'Surveillance, Rehabilitation, and Electronic Monitoring: Getting the Issues Clear', *Criminology and Public Policy*, Vol. 5(1): 103–8.

Nellis, M. (2010) 'Eternal Vigilance Inc.: The Satellite Tracking of Offenders in "Real Time"', *Journal of Technology in Human Services*, Vol. 28 (1&2): 23–43.

Newburn, T. and Hayman, S. (2002) *Policing, Surveillance and Social Control* Cullompton: Willan Publishing.

Newman, G., Clarke, R.V., and Shoham, S.G. (eds) (1997) *Rational Choice and Situational Crime Prevention: Theoretical Foundations* Aldershot: Dartmouth (Ashgate) Publishing.

Newman, G. and Clarke, R.V. (2003) *Superhighway Robbery: Preventing e-commerce crime* Cullompton: Willan Publishing.

Newman, O. (1972) *Defensible Space: People and Design in the Violent City* New York: Macmillan.

Norris, C., Moran, J., and Armstrong, G. (1998) 'Algorithmic surveillance—The future of automated visual surveillance' in C. Norris, J. Moran, and G. Armstrong (eds) *Surveillance, Closed Circuit Television and Social Control* Aldershot: Ashgate.

O'Malley, P. (2004) *Risk, Uncertainty and Government* London: The GlassHouse Press (Cavendish Publishing).

Reynald, D.M. and Elffers, H. (2009) 'The Future of Newman's Defensible Space Theory: Linking Defensible Space and the Routine Activities of Place', *European Journal of Criminology*, Vol. 6(1): 25–46.

Schneier, B. (2006) *Beyond Fear* United States: Springer.

Schwitzgebel, R.K. (1970) 'Behavioral Electronics Could Empty the World's Prisons', *The Futurist*, April 1970: 59–60.

Schwitzgebel, R.K. *et al.* (1964) 'A Program of Research in Behavioral Electronics', *Behavioral Electronics*, 9: 233–8.

Shute, S. (2007) *Satellite Tracking of Offenders: A Study of the Pilots in England and Wales* (Research Summary 4). London: Ministry of Justice.

Simon, J. (1988) 'The Ideological Effects of Actuarial Practice', *Law and Society Review*, 22: 772–800.

Simon, J. (1998) 'Managing the Monstrous: Sex Offenders and the New Penology', *Psychology, Public Policy, and Law* Vol. 4: 452–67.

Simon, J. (2007) *Governing Through Crime* New York: Oxford University Press, Inc.

Smith, G. (2007), 'Exploring Relations between Watchers and Watched in Control(led) Systems: Strategies and Tactics', *Surveillance & Society*, Vol. 4(4): 280–313.

Thumala, A., Goold, B., and Loader, I. (2011) 'A tainted trade?: Moral ambivalence and legitimation work in the private security industry', *The British Journal of Sociology*, Vol. 62(2): 283–303.

Tilley, N. (1993) *Understanding Car Parks, Crime and CCTV: Evaluation Lesson from Safer Cities (Crime Prevention Unit: Paper 42)* London: Home Office.

Van der Ploeg, I. (2003) 'Biometrics and the body as information' in D. Lyon (ed) *Surveillance as Social Sorting* London: Routledge.

Welsh, B. and Farrington, D. (2007) 'Closed-Circuit Television Surveillance' in *Preventing Crime: What Works for Children Offenders, Victims and Places*, New York: Springer.

Yar, M. (2007) 'Computer crime control as industry: Virtual insecurity and the market for private policing' in K.F. Aas, H.O. Gundhus, and H.M. Lomell (eds) *Technologies of Insecurity* Abingdon: Routledge-Cavendish.

Young, J. (1999) *The Exclusive Society* London: Sage.

Zureik, E. and Salter, M. (eds) (2005) *Global Surveillance and Policing: Borders, Security, Identity* Cullompton: Willan Publishing.

NOTE

1. Sometimes known as 'Routine Activity Theory', in the singular.

22 Victims

Pamela Davies

INTRODUCTION

This chapter explores the parameters of the study of the **crime victim** and the history and scope of the academic sub discipline within criminology known as **victimology**. The chapter encompasses: theory; research; policy and practice issues as related to the study of victims of crime and understanding victimization in societies. The chapter highlights a selection of topical issues and debates for students to think about throughout their reading of this chapter which should be done through a victim lens. Gendered vulnerabilities and risks to **victimization** will be foregrounded in the illustrations offered though questions posed are designed so that the reader can focus on class-race-age-gender-spatial dimensions to victimization and the reader is encouraged to do so.

A number of key terms in the study of victimization are highlighted throughout the chapter. The main body of the chapter is divided into four sections. These are: **victimological perspectives**, researching victims of crime, the extent and nature of, and risks to criminal victimization and the fourth section is victims, public policy and practice. Though there are separate headings for each of these, they interconnect. The development of each victimological perspective noted in section one means that measuring crime and victimization and generating information on the nature and extent of victimization and risks to being victimized and policy issues are not mutually exclusive. Before exploring different aspects of the study of the victim under the four headings identified, the context for an examination of 'victims' is outlined.

BACKGROUND

The first academic and systematic studies of victims of crime are a comparatively recent development. Positivist victimology, sometimes referred to as administrative or conservative victimology, can be traced back to the work of Mendelsohn and Von Hentig in the late 1940s. These authors attempted to understand the relationships between victims and offenders, and the victimization process itself. Typologies of victimization (see Walklate for a succinct discussion of typologies 2007a: 145–9) emerged from their work. This early work was to prove hugely influential, indeed Von Hentig (1948) and Mendelsohn (1956) are portrayed in much of the literature as the founders of the discipline of victimology. They paved the way for Wolfgang (1958), Amir (1971), Hindelang, Gottfredson and Garafalo (1978) for example, to build upon these ways of differentiating between the victim and the non-victim, understanding the dynamics of victimization and the dimensions of risk to victimization. We will return to positivist victimology in the next section.

Alongside the academic study of the crime victim, and amidst the social and political changes in the 1970s in particular, there was growing pressure for change from a victim movement and from feminist influences. The former—the increasingly vocal victims movement—has helped to bring the concerns of victims further towards the centre of debates about crime and criminal justice and this has often manifested itself in debates about victims' rights and victims' needs. The feminist movement has

Table 22.1 Fifty years of victim legislation/services in the UK

Date	Legislation/Service
1964	Criminal Injuries Compensation Board set up to administer the Criminal Injuries Compensation Scheme (CICS) for victims of violent crime
1972	First UK Women's Aid refuge set up - Chiswick, London
1974	First Victim Support project set up - Bristol
1975	Community Service Orders introduced
1976	First UK Rape Crisis Centre opened - London
1982	Roger Graef's film on Thames Valley Police - treatment of women reporting rape first shown on TV First British Crime Survey
1986	Childline introduced The Islington Crime Survey - first local victimization survey
1987	First Home Office funding for Victim Support
1989	Victim Support launched the first victim/witness in court project
1990	First Victim's Charter
1991	The Home Office fund Victim Supports' Crown Court Witness Service
1995	Victim Support UK publishes The Rights of Victims of Crime Criminal Injuries Compensation Act - set out statutory tariff of injuries
1996	Victim's Charter, revised edition, 'One Stop Shops' and 'Victim Statements' to be piloted National network of Victim Support's Victim/Witness Support schemes in Crown Courts
1999	Home Office funding to establish the Witness Service in Magistrates' Courts
2000	Criminal and Court Services Act – imposes duties on Probation Service to inform victims about serious and violent and sexual offenders
2001	Victim Personal Statements (VPS) introduced
2002	Victim's Charter (third edition)
2003	Victim Support provides a Witness Service in all criminal courts
2004	Domestic Violence, Crime and Victims Act
2006	Code of Practice for Victims of Crime
2011	Victims' Services Alliance formed

had an academic and policy impact. The 'policy turn' has been fuelled by more systematic and varied approaches to researching victimization, all of which has produced keener knowledge about the nature, extent, risks and patterns to crime and victimization in society. Table 22.1 illustrates some key victim-related landmarks over the last 50 years or so.

The study of the victim of crime is concerned with theoretical debates about victimization in society, research inquiries about the nature and extent of victimization, and issues that are related to policy and practice. The study of crime victims and the discipline of victimology has the potential to contribute towards a more informed understanding and appreciation of topical issues across the globe today, such as prejudice and hate (see International Review of Victimology, 2012: 18), tolerance and justice. What is it that a victim perspective can contribute to the key debates around crime, offending and justice in societies? How can responses to these problems and types of victimizations be guided by sound research informed theorising, policy and practice developments? What does a victim-oriented approach have to offer? What observations and issues would a victimologist focus on in relation to the following crime controversies and news stories?

- The phone hacking scandal surrounding News International and the Leveson Inquiry (2012) relating to wrongdoing by newspapers and media standards.
- Convictions for rape and the way rape complaints are handled by police and other authorities.
- Internet and web-based risks—for example, staying safe from identity theft or online dating and relationship scams.
- Child abduction and abuse/child protection.
- War, atrocity and conflict.
- The worst environmental disaster in US history—the 2010 Gulf of Mexico Oil Spill.
- Compensation.
- Killing in the name of family honour.

REVIEW QUESTIONS

1 What are the parameters of the study of the crime victim?

2 What are the key milestones in the history of the development of the study of the crime victim?

3 What is the contemporary relevance and applied nature of the study of victimization in society?

Victimological perspectives

This section will examine the three main theoretical perspectives that feature in victimology:

- positivist victimology
- radical victimology
- critical victimology

Positivist victimology

Postivist victimology has already been referred to in the context of the first studies of victims of crime and early work on understanding the dynamics of victimization. Much of that work was speculative rather than empirically grounded (Davies *et al.*, 2007) though some relied upon the officially recorded criminal statistics provided by central and local government. Scholars working in this vein focused attention towards what they variously term **victim precipitation**, victim proneness, victim culpability, victim provocation, all of which are connected to a victim's lifestyle and the notion of **victim blaming**. They were interested in the extent to which victims of crime contributed to crime and to their own victimization. Thus Von Hentig (1948) focused upon the role of the victim in the perpetration and thus creation of a criminal event. He worked with the concept of victim proneness and the belief that some people are much more prone to victimization than others, identifying 13 psychological and sociological classes of victim. Mendelsohn focused upon the responsibility of the victim for a criminal event occurring. He produced a six-fold typology amounting to a continuum of victim culpability. A victim could be identified as completely innocent through to being culpable of an offence where a victim starts out as a perpetrator and during the course of an incident ends as the victim. Hindelang and colleagues (1978) were particularly interested in exploring the likelihood of violent victimization in relation to people's routine patterns of behaviour, their daily activities and exposure to risks of victimization. Each of these concepts—victim culpability, precipitation and lifestyle are used to try to explain the process of victimization. This work focused upon the visible—that is, victims of conventional crimes such as interpersonal crimes of violence and street crime. This approach established a particular construction of a crime victim—an '**ideal victim**' (Christie, 1984).

Positivist victimology has ensured the development and refinement of quantitative measures of victimization and it has influenced responses to victimization. The legacy of positivism remains controversial for several reasons. As a result of the lack of empirical work and flaws concerning the over-reliance on officially recorded crime data, these early victimologists were unaware of the 'true levels' of crime or victimization. By focusing on individual risk factors and relying on quantitative research, much victimization remained hidden. Largely as a result of its focus upon conventional crimes, the 'private sphere' has remained until recently a neglected site for victimological research and intervention, as have the victims of the State and its agencies, as well as corporate excesses. Finally, its denial of any political and/or structural analyses has meant a complacent view of the victim where risks to higher levels of victimization are concealed including heightened risks to the poor and women in respect of certain types of victimization. Similarly, the nuances of risks are downplayed by overlooking the ethnic and age dimensions to victimization experiences. In effect, positivist approaches have produced a **hierarchy of victimization**, a pecking order representing the differential status of particular types and categories of crime victim. Ideal victims (some child murder victims) are at the top of the hierarchy, and non-deserving victims (habitually violent youths injured in a drunken fight) near the bottom. This hierarchy is most visible in media constructions of criminal victimization where graphic coverage is often given for example, to elderly females as victims of violent crime and blame attributed to youthful males. Such coverage persists despite consistent evidence that those most likely to be the victim of violent crime are young males with risky routine activities such as drinking in public places.

Radical victimology

Radical victimology does not have as lengthy an intellectual heritage as positivist victimology, having developed in response to the partiality of the positivist perspective. The emergence of radical victimology particularly in the 1970s and 1980s can be associated with on the one hand the feminist movement, new left ideals and the protest and counter cultures and on the other developments such as the victimization survey and the theoretical contributions of new left thinkers. There are two variations around the theme of radical victimology. The first, associated with the work of those working in the US, and in the UK radical left realism associated collectively with the work of Jones, Maclean, Matthews and Young (Davies *et al.*, 2003).

In response to the positivist agenda, radical victimology has been concerned with combining analysis of the State and its actions with the lived experiences of victims of crime (Young, 1986). This perspective is concerned with facing up to the reality of crime from a social democratic standpoint. As Young (1986: 23) argues, 'a radical victimology notes two key elements of criminal victimization. Firstly that crime is focused both geographically and socially on the most vulnerable sections of the community. Secondly, that the impact of victimization is a product of risk rates and vulnerability'. Moreover, as Young continues, a radical victimology must not 'deny the impact of crimes of the powerful or indeed the social problems created by capitalism' (Young, 1986: 23).

The second wave of feminism and the political climate in the US and later in the UK fuelled radical and left unrest and activism. Scholarly work of this ilk in the 1970s and 1980s reflected criminologically this changing political mood. This work challenged and critiqued conventional and traditional definitions of the crime problem and positivistic victimology. It also offered an alternative focus for the crime problem focusing upon the role of the State and also upon women's roles and experiences in public and private and in some cases a strong policy agenda for placing previously marginalized victims more firmly centre stage. This critique together with political activities, developed many of the initiatives which were specifically aimed at providing a response to women's unmet needs. For example, the formation of Women's Aid and Refuge provisions for female victims of domestic abuse, rape crisis interventions and later rape suites, all of which helped put women victims at least, firmly onto the victimological agenda.

Radical feminism was particularly concerned with policy change and challenged the concept of the victim in relation to women, preferring the term **'survivor'**. They also challenged the visible picture of victimization focusing attention on those victimizations that are rendered invisible such as violence, rape and assaults that take place in the home—the 'dark figure' of crime. In consequence radical criminologists have engaged in locally orientated political struggles, drawn attention to State excesses, acknowledged the experiences of victims of crime in many socially deprived neighbourhoods and behind closed doors where domestic violence was revealed as a gendered crime with men as perpetrators and women as victims. Thus those from a radical perspective have worked alongside the voluntary, feminist and left wing movements as much as they have the State.

In terms of alternative research agendas, feminist-inspired approaches have tended to favour appreciative studies. These surveys are less concerned with seeking precision in estimates of victimization in the community and more with the qualitative descriptions of the experience of crime from the victim's point of view. They have also sought to examine victims' experiences of being processed within the criminal justice system, for example by the police and by courts. Whilst feminist research has often featured appreciative qualitative approaches, local cross-sectional sample surveys exemplify research associated with radical left realist criminology. Surveys are done of the population of a particular area or district. Individuals are asked if they have been the victim of crime within a specified period of time and also whether they reported such crimes to the police. Sometimes they are asked about their experiences of, and relationships with the police in that particular area. Left realist surveys pay attention to the experiences of vulnerable groups within a particular locality. There is the opportunity for such cross-sectional surveys to be repeated, as with the first and the second Islington Crime Surveys, thereby facilitating some comparison over time (see, for example, Jones, McClean and Young, 1986; Crawford, Jones, Woodhouse and Young, 1990).

Radical victimology's wish to contextualize victimization within a broader socio-economic and political framework, its ability to refocus the victimological telescope towards the actions of the State and its agents and agencies, its aim to take victimization seriously and its engagement with local policy makers, have contributed to the developing victimological enterprise. Nevertheless, as with the positivist perspective it set out to supplant, radical victimology has also attracted criticism. First, it has in parts mirrored much of the positivist work it set out to replace. Second, despite its focus upon State power it has provided a simplified understanding of the law and State; and third, it has offered a limited research agenda (Davies *et al.*, 2007). The next section will examine the role of critical victimology.

Critical victimology

Critical victimology is a perspective which endeavours to address the problematic aspects of both positivist and radical criminology. For Walklate, it is a perspective which incorporates the interests of radical victimology and also those of feminism in seeking what constitutes the real. She has long argued for a victimology that takes seriously the need for a development of an empirically based, rational and objective science which gets beyond the 'mere appearance' of things (Mawby and Walklate, 1994; Walklate, 1989; 2004; 2007a and b). In her critique of positivist and radical victimologies, Walklate articulates her own framework for a critical social scientific analysis of victimization and together with Mawby (1994: 177–86), they noted that the key issues to be addressed were three intrinsically linked concepts or debates that centred around rights, citizenship and the State:

- The needs/rights debate and the emotive and political questions of whether or not victims of crime have needs or rights. The proposed way forward was a justice-based, approach to the question of victims' rights irrespective of need yet incorporating public opinion.

- The question of citizenship is relevant for understanding responses to victims of crime. Whilst the concept of citizenship is problematic and the interrelationship of the struggle for citizenship with the role of the State is complex, all of these questions about citizenship are variously and differently connected to various victimological perspectives. A critical perspective would take account of the limitations inherent in other approaches and suggests it may be necessary to construct policy on the basis of both individual and collective concerns.

- The question of the State. Here the economic, political and ideological dimensions to the role of the State are seen as crucial to the development of a critical victimology.

The state of theoretical victimology is ripe for re-assessment, not least due to the significant contributions that feminist thought and more recently masculinities theorizing has to offer. Walklate has continued to contribute to debates about rights, citizenship and the State and has observed how, if at all, victimology has responded to these key concepts. In 2003, she posed the provocative question: 'Can there be a feminist victimology?' In 2007, she examined men and their relationship to victimization. At this point she challenged a long-held presumption that to be male is to be a non-victim and she showed how men are perpetually constrained by hegemonic masculinity. What is needed is a perspective that sees victimization structurally taking into account multiple identities around class-ethnicity-age-gender-sexual orientation. Is the research agenda in victimology up to the task of challenging established interpretations of who can be vulnerable, fearful and at risk? For example, can women be victimizers and can men be victims? (Davies, 2007, 2011). The research agenda to victimology, which has been touched upon in this section is a more central focus of the next.

REVIEW QUESTIONS

1 Is there a 'natural' victim? Explain your answer with reference to positivist, radical and critical victim perspectives.

2 Are class-race-age-gender sufficiently accounted for in perspectives on victimization?

3 Explain some of the key concepts that contribute to the false dichotomies in the study of the crime victim.

Researching victims of crime

Of central importance in the development of victimological perspectives has been researching victims of crime. How crime and victimization are measured, how much victimization there is, what varieties of victimization exist, who and what is victimized are highly important questions if criminal victimization and other types of harm and injustice are to be tackled effectively. While the early pioneering work of Von Hentig was speculative rather than empirically grounded, others have relied upon officially recorded statistical information and victimization surveys. Feminist approaches as already noted, as well as others throughout the 1980s to the noughties (Genn, 1988; Walklate, 1989;

Bowling, 1998; Jefferson, 1996; Pain *et al.*, 2002) have argued for a more qualitative methodology for researching victims of crime. However, since the early 1970s, the direct questioning of the victim of crime through crime surveys has been central to the victimological enterprise. Crime surveys are carried out on a sample of the population. Victim surveys collect data on the occurrence of criminal acts irrespective of whether such acts have been reported to the police and, thereby, gain some measure of the extent of the 'dark figure' of unreported crime (Bottomley and Pease, 1986).

In part, victim surveys developed as a result of recognized deficiencies in official crime statistics as valid measures of the extent of crime in society. For example, crimes recorded by the police rely to a great extent on members of the public reporting such crimes. There are several reasons for the public not reporting crime and the belief that officially recorded criminal statistics indicate more about the organizational processes involved in the collation and collection of data/statistics than about levels of crime and victimization has had an enormous impact upon engaging criminologists and victimologists in alternative and competing strategies of collecting data about crime and experiences of victimization.

A further impetus to the development of victim surveys came from direct concerns for the victim within criminology and also within criminal justice policy. With the growth in interest in the victims of crime during the late 1970s in the US and the 1980s in Britain, coupled with the enormous impact of feminist research and methodologies, new information was derived from the crime survey. Since then, crime surveys have become a popular research tool. In a variety of ways, surveys of victims of crime have been concerned with differing dimensions of victimization. These include crime level measurement and reasons for non- or under-reporting; the correlates of victimization; the risk of victimization; the fear of crime and its relationship to the probability of victimization; the experience of crime from the viewpoint of victims; the relationships between crime and victimization; the impact of victimization and the treatment of victims in the criminal justice system. Four important questions on the patterns of victimization, risks and effects are:

1. The **level** of victimization. How many victimizations occur each year? What is the rate of criminal victimization? Is it increasing or decreasing over time?

2. The **correlates** of victimization. Who are the typical victims of crime? Do victim characteristics vary by crime and type? How is victimization distributed across time and space?

3. The **dynamics** of victimization. What is the nature of the relationship between victims and their offenders? Do victims contribute to their own victimizations? Do victims resist during victimization occurrences and with what results?

4. The **consequences** of criminal victimization. How often do victims report their victimizations to the police? What is the nature and extent of the injury suffered by victims of crime?

Different types of victim surveys include local cross-sectional sample surveys, appreciative surveys, national trend sample surveys, cross-national surveys such as the International Crime Survey and police 'consumer' or satisfaction surveys. Appreciative surveys and studies have already been referred to in association with feminist-inspired perspectives in victimology. From the contrasting perspective of administrative/positivist criminology, victim data has been collected via national trend studies, typified in the United Kingdom by the British Crime Survey (BCS) sponsored by the Home Office.

The BCS has been published in England and Wales since 1982 (Hough and Mayhew, 1983) and annually since 2001, on each occasion measuring crime and victimization in the previous year. The BCS measures crime experienced by people living in private households. The survey asks people aged 16 and over living about their experiences of crime in the last 12 months. These experiences are used to estimate levels of crime in England and Wales. In January 2009 the scope of the Survey was extended to ask 10- to 15-year-olds about their victimization experiences and views on crime-related topics. In the 2010–11 BCS, around 51,000 people were interviewed, that is, around 47,000 adults aged 16 or over in the main survey and a further 4,000 interviews conducted with children aged 10 to 15.

A series of bulletins presents crime statistics from the BCS and police recorded crime. The bulletin for 2010–11 is the tenth report in an annual series combining crimes recorded by the police and interviews from the BCS for the financial year 2010–11. Some key findings are reported upon in the next section—the extent and nature of, and risks to criminal victimization. Each source—police data and the BCS—has different strengths and weaknesses but together they provide a more comprehensive picture of crime than could be obtained from either series alone, that is, they are complementary. For the crime types and population groups it covers, the BCS provides a reliable measure of trends in crime. Unlike police data, the BCS is unaffected by methodology changes or levels of reporting to the police. The BCS therefore offers a better indication of trends in crime over time and, for the crime types it covers, the BCS gives a truer reflection of crime because it includes crimes which are not reported to the police. Police figures provide a good measure in trends of reported crimes and can be used for local crime pattern analysis.

The weakness of the BCS is that it does not capture sufficiently the extent of sensitive crimes, especially sexual crimes and domestic violence. Many crimes such as fraud or shoplifting cannot be adequately covered using household surveys. Fraud is not well measured by either recorded crime or the main BCS count. In addition to not covering fraud especially effectively, the BCS does not cover homicide and drug offences. Furthermore, despite efforts to include children in the BCS some difficult issues remain with regard to classifying criminal incidents and because of methodological differences between the child and adult survey, direct comparisons cannot be made between the child and adult victimization data. Both are weak in terms of providing estimates of 'victimless' crimes, in not addressing crimes such as mass pollution affecting large populations, in being unable to explore the victimization of 'hard to reach groups' (Pain *et al.*, 2002) and in not providing measures of crimes, for example fraud, of which individuals are not aware (Jupp, 1989; Walklate, 1989).

Two national surveys of commercial victimization have also been carried out by the Home Office. The first was in 1994 and the second was in 2002. A scoping exercise for a new survey of businesses has been carried out (Home Office, 2010b). The intention of a third survey is to update the data provided by these previous surveys and have more regular surveys of commercial and industrial victimization to supplement measures of victimization of households and individuals provided by the British Crime Survey. Victimization surveys have played an important role in criminology and in policy making. They especially provide better estimates of the extent of crime than that provided by official statistics and they also give insights into victims' experiences of crime and of the criminal justice system.

REVIEW QUESTIONS

1 What are the main criticisms of victim survey research?

2 Are surveys appropriate for finding out about how children are victimized?

3 What ethical issues are raised when researching sensitive topics and vulnerable populations?

The extent and nature of, and risks to, criminal victimization

In this section what we do and do not know about who and what is victimized, and who and what is at risk is explored. From a combination of police recorded crime and BCS data a wealth of information is available on general trends, absolute and estimated levels of crime. Key points about crime tend to be systematically and widely reported as in the example in Figure 22.1, whereas, *victim*-related data on household and individual victimization rates, violent and sexual crime, fraud offences, statistics on the victimization of children is less visible, accessible, systematic and reliable.

However, successive sweeps of the BCS have identified the risk of victimization is often related closely to geographical area and the risk of personal victimization is closely correlated with variables such as social class (Croall, 2007a and b) as well as age, sex, race and patterns of routine activity, such as going out in the evening and alcohol consumption or weapon use and alcohol intoxication (Brennan *et al.*, 2010; Zedner, 2002). What emerges is a complex picture of actual and perceived risks to victimization often related to particular variables such as ethnicity, age, gender and residence.

Information about *Crime in England and Wales 2010/11* (Home Office 2011)

Key Points:

Overall there were an estimated 9.6 million crimes as measured by the BCS in 2010/11.

9.5 million crimes were measured in 2009/10 – the previous year's survey.

Overall BCS crime remained at the lowest level since the survey started in 1981.

The above compares with 4.2 million crimes recorded by the police in 2010/11, the lowest level since the major change to counting rules in 2002.

Figure 22.1 Crime in England and Wales 2010–11

Findings from the 2008–09 BCS suggest the risk of adults being a victim of crime were higher for those from a Mixed background (35 per cent of people within this group were victims) than from other ethnic groups; and greater for those from an Asian (26 per cent) than from a White ethnic background (23 per cent) (Home Office, 2010a). The risk of personal victimization is established as being closely correlated with variables such as age, sex and race, as is the impact of crime (Dixon *et al.*, 2006). Partly, the higher risk rates of black and minority ethnic households to crime is the result of the fact that they are more likely to be over-represented in social demographic groups associated with higher risks of victimization. As Zedner (2002) points out, members of minority ethnic communities are more likely to live in younger households of lower socio-economic status and generally to reside in social disadvantaged communities. However, as Fitzgerald and Hale (1996) note, this is not to suggest that ethnicity plays no part in their victimization.

Young people are still primarily constructed as offenders; their victimization and fear are rarely mentioned and addressed in crime prevention policy, indeed 'in popular and policy discourse such issues are often treated with cynicism, disdain or vehement denial' (Brown, 1998: 116–17). For Muncie (2004) young people are victims of crime, victims of familial violence and neglect, victims of institutional violence, are overly controlled and recipients of high levels of regulation and surveillance. Offending and victimization are unevenly distributed between young people, with certain groups experiencing higher levels of both. Some, though by no means all, of this victimization takes place between young people. Therefore particular groups of young people, often those who have been labelled 'hard-to-reach' or 'excluded' are key to issues around crime, victimization and youth.

The elderly are often identified in much media and political discourse as a group of people who are more socially and economically vulnerable to victimization and who lack the physical or psychological strength to resist it. While older people often do have different risk rates of victimization compared to younger people, the relationship between older people and crime victimization is complex. For Pain (2004: 73):

> the structures of class, gender, race and ability are the key determinants of how older people experience old age. It is these which underpin where older people live, their socio-economic status and their risk of victimization, whether from property crime, harassment in the community or abuse by carers within domestic spheres.

Analysis of the various associations between older people and victimization unpacks the popular stereotype that the elderly are a homogenous, vulnerable social group especially susceptible to victimization and least able to resist the threat of crime.

We have sketched out how and why particular groups such as young ethnic minorities may be more at risk of crime victimization than others. Equally clear from the research literature is that the burden of crime does not fall equally on all geographical areas. Three types of areas can be identified as suffering from the highest incidence of crime. These are: mixed inner metropolitan or multi-racial areas with a mixture of poor, private rented housing and owner occupation, non-family areas with a mixture of affluent housing and private rented housing in multi-occupation and the poorest local authority estates, located either in inner city or overspill areas (Evans and Fraser, 2004). In the main these areas are low status, urban areas of low quality housing with above average concentrations of children, teenagers and young adults and with a preponderance of single-adult households. These commonalities suggest that neighbourhoods themselves can be seen as victims of crime.

The risks just outlined are evidenced from survey research. Combined with these patterns of victimization, qualitative data reveals an even more uneven distribution of victimization, share of its impact and details about gendered risks. At the start of this chapter you were asked to think about convictions for rape and the way rape complaints are handled by police and other authorities. What do we know about gender and rape? We know that:

- Rape is an exception to the more general pattern of victimization, which is usually higher for males than females.
- Rape is a highly gendered crime and type of victimization.
- Rape primarily affects women.
- The majority of women's assailants with respect to interpersonal violence are men and men who are known to the raped woman.
- Age combined with sex renders some women more at risk to sexual violence.
- Gender and age structure women's fear of sexual violence with women being particularly fearful of violence from men.
- Women, fear, perceive and deal with risk and experiences via different day-to-day coping strategies and support networks.

We know this from a triangulated mix of research methodologies and from qualitative and quantitative data (Davies, 2011). These increasingly sophisticated and detailed knowledges are derived from information on victimization and research inquiries informed by positivist, radical, feminist and critical inspired approaches to the study of the victims of crime.

REVIEW QUESTIONS

1 Do the combined data from police recorded crime and the BCS provide an accurate representation of the nature and extent of victimization in society?

2 What evidence is there that the economic and physical costs of crime fall disproportionally on the disadvantaged and the poorest sections of society?

3 What are the advantages and disadvantages of using qualitative research methods to research the lived experiences of young people/women as victims of crime?

Victims, public policy, and practice

Several have argued that the criminal justice system has largely overlooked the victim of crime and given little attention to any rights or needs that they may have (Doak, 2008; Goodey, 2005; Hall, 2009; Rock, 2004; Spalek, 2006; Victim Support, 1995, 2010; Williams, 2009). Given the functional importance of victims of crime to the operation of the criminal justice process in England and Wales, it is interesting to note that by 1945 there was no real sense in which victims of crime had a voice in the political or policy arenas. It was during the post-war period, and the construction of the welfare state that mechanisms were introduced allowing for the introduction of criminal injuries compensation and over the last five decades numerous developments relating to victims policy and practice have taken place. In international jurisdictions, too, the official victim movement has gathered pace over the last 50 years (Mawby, 2004). A range of supportive provisions and victim assistance schemes can now be identified in most social systems across the world, all of which will have differing relationships to their respective criminal justice systems. Some victim services are at arm's length or fully independent of the government and criminal justice system, some are provided under statute, others by voluntary groups and charities. Many have had a positive impact, especially in terms of changing the status of the victim.

In England and Wales, there has been a proliferation of different victimagogic activities (see Table 22.1). The impetus for putting the victim 'centre stage' gained particular momentum in the 1990s after the publication of the ambitiously sub-titled *Victims' Charter: A Statement of the Rights of Victims of Crime* (Home Office, 1990). Certainly in recent years, better support and assistance for victims of crime has featured on the official policy-making agenda and improving service delivery and the experiences of victims and witnesses is a key priority for the UK Ministry of Justice. Much support comes in the form of practical advice and help. Other support includes information about compensation and insurance. Developments have resulted in a mix of onus for provision and delivery of help and assistance with boundaries becoming blurred between public-private-voluntary and statutory domains. The question of entitlement or right to support remains controversial. Commentators have questioned the politicization of some service provision (Phipps, 1988) and the extent to which support and assistance have been introduced as efficiency measures and for value for money (National Audit Office, 2002). Are changes in the interests of the victim first and foremost, that is, victim-focused/oriented, or in the interests of the smooth running of the criminal justice system, that is, system-focused? The victim of crime has a major interest in the effectiveness of the criminal justice system. Is the crime victim a disenfranchised party of sentencing policy? (Victim Support, 2010).

In terms of analysing policy initiatives and developments, a number of key themes emerge. The changing relationship between victims of crime and the operation of the State, its agencies and related charitable and voluntary sectors is a dominant theme. Victims' representation or lack of representation in criminal justice policy and practice and the neglect of the victim of crime is another. Some have explored how State responses can result in further or **secondary victimization** (see Davies *et al.*, 2003). Others have explored the roles of both the State and the voluntary sector in the development and delivery of victim support, representation and compensation, and several have drawn cross-national comparisons. As noted earlier, Mawby focuses upon service development and delivery in England and Wales, the Netherlands, the United States and Germany as well as two post-communist societies in Eastern Europe (Mawby, 2004). Several commentators highlight recent developments, especially in the UK over the last decade, in the provision of mediation and restorative justice programmes (Wright, 2004) many of which have borrowed from ideas and traditions practised elsewhere in the world, most notably New Zealand. Such analyses signify the relevance of, and need for, comparative analysis of support services offered to, and policies affecting, victims of crime in an increasingly global world.

At the beginning of this chapter both the terms 'crime' and 'victim' were flagged as problematic. Victims of crime who appear in the public arena usually do so because they have made contact with the police. These individuals are a selective category only and form a small minority of the total number of crime victims. They are the most visible victims, men, women and children who have come to official notice. Their experiences are officially known about. They may qualify for assistance and support, especially if the criminal justice system requires them to help achieve justice. This highly selective group of victims have had a changing role in criminal justice and incrementally their status has been moved towards centre stage. This specific group of victims, however, risk suffering further by way of secondary victimization.

Secondary victimization

For some victim-witnesses who engage with the criminal justice process there may be unintended consequences which may incur further harm. There is a delicate balance between doing justice/achieving victimization, of promoting harmony/incurring harm and sometimes the victim/witness is left feeling further victimized.

In terms of secondary victimization, let us again focus on the example of rape. In the UK, the adversarial system assumes innocence on the part of the accused and attempts to establish guilt. In terms of police interviewing of rape victims, Roger Graef's pioneering 'fly on the wall' *Police* film in 1982 of Thames Valley Police treatment of women reporting rape was to force a change in police practice, so poor was their treatment of women accusing men of rape. Whilst the adversarial system might appear to encourage this form of re-victimization in the form of hostile police interrogations and similar approaches from defence solicitors and barristers and members of the judiciary whose questioning, cross-examinations and judgments assume the woman is an 'alleged victim', this does not excuse the treatment some women have been subjected to by the various institutions and personnel of the criminal justice system. Thus the reality of the rape victim's experience in court is that she has often been forced to relive her ordeal in the witness box—almost as if to prove her innocence in the crime (see, for example, *R v Allen* 1982, 'Ipswich Rape Case') or, as in a case in 1989 the judge has suggested that she precipitated or caused her rape. Following immediate survival of the ordeal of rape and other forms of sexual victimization women and girls must cope with the longer-term aftermath and this includes psychological damage and the suffering of stigmatization or ostracization (Human Rights Watch, 2004). (See also the Police and Crown Prosecution Service handling of sexual abuse (Barrett, 2013).)

This final section subjects public policy and practice to a critical discussion. How and why 'victim' is a problematic concept is considered in the context of compensation. In the discussion that follows a number of taken for granted victimological concepts such as victimization and crime victim are problematized and a number of key concepts such as victim precipitation, culpability, provocation, ideal victim are shown to connect to particular ways of constructing the crime victim and understanding victimization.

Compensating victims of violent crime—the case of England, Scotland and Wales and the Criminal Injuries Compensation Scheme (CICS)

The CICS in the UK originated in the 1960s and has since developed into a statutory, tariff-based scheme for victims of unlawful violence. Despite this scheme being one of the most generous in the world (Brienen and Hoegen, 2000), there are several contentious issues related to this form of State compensation. Fundamental features of the scheme's 'rules' and 'eligibility' criteria, which are explored further later, focus on the blameless and innocent victims of violent crime (Criminal Injuries Compensation Authority (CICA), 2011). Such victims are headlined in the online publicity and documents related to the scheme (see http://www.justice.gov.uk/about/criminal-injuries-compensation-authority). This inherent positivist approach as to who can be a victim of crime is now explored.

When is a victim not a victim?

According to the rules and eligibility criteria of the CICS there are victims who deserve (but do not have a right to) compensation and there are others who can be discriminated against and can be denied their application for a variety of reasons. Some of these reasons are related to keeping down the cost of the scheme, some appear to punish or re-victimize those who have failed to help in the criminal justice process and there are other 'disentitling conditions' (Goodey, 2005).

The CICS notes:

We may also refuse or reduce an award because of:

- your behaviour before, during or after the incident in which you were injured
- your criminal record
- your failure to co-operate with the police or with us
- your delay in informing the police or other organisation or person of the incident

Figures 22.2 and 22.3 summarize the assumptions that are implicit within the CICS in effect illustrating when a victim is not a victim.

Victims of non-violent crimes are excluded; those with greater financial resources as well as those with very little economic power continue to be subjected to penalty point

---

Not a (CICS deserving) victim if: undeserving, blameworthy, culpable, partially responsible, contributed to the attack/injury, participated in the violence, attracted, incited, precipitated the injury/assault/attack, engaged in provocative behaviour, was the author of own misfortune, brought the suffering on own head, fraudulent, the criminal is likely to gain from any payment, in collusion with the offender, no violence was involved, behaviour before, during or after the criminal event disqualifies you, involved in excessive risk taking, failed to co-operate with the authorities, refused to make a statement, refused to go to court, refused or failed to report the incident without delay, refused or failed to co-operate with the police, refused to go on an identity parade, the injuries were received abroad, do not qualify for the minimum award, have previous (unspent) criminal convictions, suffered from a minor assault, suffered from the effects of a non-violent crime, don't know of the existence of the CICS.

Figure 22.2 When a victim is not a victim

> Are a (CICS) victim if: blameless, innocent, not at fault, are a worthy victim (i.e. are an ideal victim), suffer physical and mental pain and injury due to criminal injury (a physical attack, an assault, wounding or sexual attack, arson, death of a close relative) but are none of the above in *Figure 22.2*

Figure 22.3 Real victims

deductions. Those whose injuries do not meet the lower threshold of compensation are excluded entirely from the scheme.

This shows explicit and implicit value judgements about 'undeserving' and 'real' victims and the CICS emphasis on moral desert as opposed to moral complicity (Rock, 2004). Positivist approaches to responding to victims of crime seem set to continue according to recent proposals which suggest that crime victim payouts will be cut so that thousands hurt in violent assaults and those with permanent burns scars will no longer merit compensation (Doyle, 2012).

Eligibility criteria and entitlement conditions attached to criminal injuries compensation payments are in alignment with the 'domain assumptions' of victimology—deep-seated, taken for granted beliefs that originated in the work of the founders of the discipline in the 1940s and 1950s (see Walklate, 2007a and b). As discussed earlier, Von Hentig (1948) and Mendelsohn (1956) were concerned with identifying and differentiating victim characteristics and non-victim characteristics and with identifying victim traits in their attempt to understand the victim-offender relationship. Notions of victim proneness, victim precipitation, victim-blaming and victim provocation, victim culpability and lifestyle as compared and contrasted with the ideal victim are deeply embedded in the dominant ways of thinking about victimhood and the study of victims more generally. Such assumptions fit very comfortably alongside the domain assumptions that are at the heart of positivist *criminology*. For feminist commentators in particular, the legacy of such domain assumptions, with their stereotypical implications about women and men as variously deserving/undeserving victims and their inherent sexism, is particularly problematic.

REVIEW QUESTIONS

Looking through a class/race/age/gendered lens, how appropriate are:

- police responses to victimization?
- criminal justice responses to victimization?
- Victim Support responses to victimization?

Again looking through a class/race/age/gendered lens, how do:

- rich/poor victims experience the criminal justice system?
- ethnic minorities victims experience the criminal justice system?
- young/older victims experience the criminal justice system?
- men/women victims experience the criminal justice system?

CONCLUSION

This chapter has outlined the history, scope and parameters of the study of the crime victim. It has done so with reference to the key victimological perspectives evident in understanding victim issues and the key ways of researching crime victims and wider social harms. The chapter has also explored the extent and nature of victimization in society as evidenced from different approaches to researching vulnerabilities and risks to various types of victimization in an increasingly fearful cultural climate. Victim surveys in particular provide an enormous amount of information about crime and its impact. However, surveys tend to under-represent the subjective and differential impact of crime on different victim groups and individuals. This structural distribution of victimization has increasingly been evidenced in the work of radical and critical scholars. Questions surrounding the definition of crime and therefore criminal victimization are also brought to the fore in these perspectives. In terms of victims, public policy and practice, the changing relationship between victims of crime, the State and other sectors and agencies has been highlighted as significantly impacting upon victims' satisfaction with responses to their victimization. This chapter dwells on the concept of secondary victimization to highlight some of the ways in which responses to victimization can do more harm than good. Comparative and international research is instructive with regard to policy and practice developments too, showing supportive provisions are not always emerging as responsive to victims' needs. Changing relationships between crime victims and support providers are likely to continue to be of great import in increasing victims' satisfactory experiences of support following victimization. Victims' representation and treatment in criminal justice policy and practice will no doubt continue also to be a key feature of victim support and scholarly interest. Academic research, assisted by the insights and pressure of a growing victims' movement, has helped to change our understanding of victimization and has increased our understanding of victims' needs. Though the victim of crime has been afforded greater centrality in debates about crime, and there has been progress too in terms of the criminal justice system changing to reflect our increased understanding of victims' needs, this has not always meant greater sensitivity on the part of politicians or criminal justice practitioners (Williams, 2009).

Throughout the chapter readers have been encouraged to think about how victimologists would approach current debates that connect to crime, justice and human rights. You have been encouraged to consider the social world through a victim-oriented lens and perspective. The chapter has problematized the concept of 'victim' and clearly victimhood remains a contested and socially constructed concept. Some definitions of the crime victim are restrictive and result in exclusivity with many experiences of injustice and prejudice, unfairness, hate and hardship obscured. A range of crimes, social harms and injustices often take place yet are hidden from public view. As a corollary, they are often under-reported and/or under-regulated/controlled and investigated, they are certainly often neglected in much mainstream victimological inquiries and research. Yet such crimes still impact substantially on the lives of their victims and communities in which they occur and impact heavily on the work of criminal justice agencies, the State and other regulatory bodies. They are crimes or harms that often impact substantially in terms of cost and resources, and the breadth of their impact can be far reaching over time and space. Green and environmental crime are examples, cybercrime another, as are human rights abuses carried out by agencies of the State. The range of invisible crimes and harms occur across and throughout different strata and cultures: from the level of the body to the home, to the street and further to the environment, the corporate suite and to the State. Examples include crimes committed by employees against organizations; crimes perpetrated by organizations against their employees; fraudulent behaviour including the mis-selling of pensions, the selling of infected food products, the installation of unsafe utility products and the production and selling of counterfeit goods; pollution, health (and safety) and cultural sector crimes, all of which expand the nature, extent and impact of victimization across the globe.

Crime and victimization are social constructions and this means that the boundaries and scope of the discipline of victimology—what should and should not be included within the study of the crime victim—is contested. This chapter illustrates there is a need to continue to be innovative in both methodology and theoretical exploration of the connections between power, politics and practice which help construct knowledge of any particular act or event. It is necessary also to develop explicit yet informed critiques and evaluation of much current victim policy and practice in comparative and international contexts. A victim-oriented and focused agenda that can include these debates and concerns will contribute greatly to the study and knowledge of criminology and victimology in the future.

QUESTIONS FOR DISCUSSION

1 Whose interests, apart from those of the victims themselves, are served by legislation and policies which purport to meet the needs of victims of crime?

2 Why were services for victims of crime so slow to emerge, and why have policy initiatives and legislation in this area become so much more common in recent years?

3 Why are some groups of victims seen as more 'deserving' as victims than others and why are some victims seen as more 'worthy' victims than others? Which groups and what victims does this particularly apply to?

4 What are the pros and cons of the term 'victim'?

5 Can a restorative approach to justice increase victims' confidence in the criminal justice system?

GUIDE TO FURTHER READING

Bottoms, A.E. and Roberts, J.V. (2010) *Hearing the victim: adversarial justice, crime victims and the state*. Cullompton: Willan.
Brings together leading authorities in the field to review the role of the victim in the criminal justice system.

Davies, P. (2011) *Gender, Crime and Victimization*. London: Sage.
Explores gender patterns to offending and victimization and how these patterns are variously established and represented, researched, explained and responded to by policy makers and criminal justice agencies.

Davies, P., Francis, P., and Greer, C. (2007) (eds) *Victims, Crime and Society*. London: Sage.
Organized around the intersecting social divisions of class, race, age and gender, this book addresses the defining issues relating to victimization.

Rock, P.E. (2010) *Victims, policy-making and criminological theory: selected essays*. Farnham: Ashgate.
Brings together work by leading authorities in contemporary criminological theory.

Victim Support (2010) *Victims' justice? What victims and witnesses really want from sentencing*. London: Victim Support.

A report containing evidence and recommendations that outlines how victims and witnesses have been historically marginalized in sentencing practices with serious consequences.

Walklate, S. (2007) (ed) *Handbook on Victims and Victimology*. Cullompton: Willan.

This handbook offers 18 thought-provoking chapters from a wide range of respected authors. It is a very accessible, comprehensive and useful handbook.

International Review of Victimology. London: Sage.

This journal covers traditional areas of victimological research, such as the victim-offender relationship, victimization surveys, victim compensation, the victim in the criminal justice system, reparation and restitution by offenders, crime prevention for victims and restorative justice, together with broader theoretical issues such as definitions of victimization and the philosophy of victimology.

WEB LINKS

http://www.justice.gov.uk/about/criminal-injuries-compensation-authority

The Criminal Injuries Compensation Authority (CICA) is the government body responsible for administering the Criminal Injuries Compensation Scheme (CICS) in England and Wales, and Scotland. It is part of the Ministry of Justice. This site details the services offered to the victims of violent crime.

http://www.victimsupport.org/

Victim Support is an independent charity offering emotional support, practical help and information—for example, on police and court procedures, compensation and insurance—if you have been a victim of and/or witness to any crime or have been affected by a crime committed against someone you know and regardless of whether or not the crime has been reported or when it happened.

http://www.worldsocietyofvictimology.org/

World Society of Victimology is a not-for-profit, non-governmental organization whose purpose is to advance victimological research and practices around the world; to encourage interdisciplinary and comparative work and research in this field, and to advance cooperation between international, national, regional and local agencies and other groups who are concerned with the problems of victims.

http://www.justice.gov.uk/victim-witness-audience

This government website provides information about criminal injuries compensation. It also offers practitioner guidance for those who work with victims and witnesses including guidance for police about interviewing vulnerable and/or intimidated witnesses.

http://www.restorativejustice.org

This is a comprehensive resource on restorative justice with information on everything from police use of restorative justice to restorative justice and peace commissions.

REFERENCES

Amir, M. (1971) *Patterns of Forcible Rape*. Chicago: University of Chicago Press.

Barrett, D. (2013) 'Police argue over who told abuse victim: "don't get help"', The Sunday Telegraph, 10 February, p. 9.

Bottomley, K. and Pease, K. (1986) *Crime and Punishment: Interpreting the data*. Milton Keynes: Open University Press.

Bowling, B. (1998) *Violent Racism: victimisation, policing and social context*. Oxford: Clarendon Press.

Brennan, I.R., Moore, S.C., and Shepherd, J.P. (2010) 'Risk Factors for Violent Victimisation and Injury from Six Years of the British Crime Survey', *International Review of Victimology* 17:2: 209–29.

Brienen, M.E.I. and Hoegen, E.H. (2000) *Victims of Crime in 22 European Criminal Justice Systems*. Nijmegen, the Netherlands: University of Tilburg.

Brown, S. (1998) *Understanding youth and crime: listening to youth?* Buckingham: Open University Press.

Christie, N. (1984) 'The Ideal Victim' in E. Fattah (ed) *From Crime Policy to Victim Policy*. London: Macmillan.

Crawford, A., Jones, T., Woodhouse, T., and Young, J. (1990) *Second Islington Crime Survey*. London: Centre for Criminology, Middlesex Polytechnic.

Criminal Injuries Compensation Authority (2011) *Annual Report & Accounts 2009-10*. London: CICA.

Croall, H. (2007a) 'Social Class, Social Exclusion, Victims and Crime' in P. Davies, P. Francis, and C. Greer (eds) *Victims, Crime and Society*. London: Sage.

Croall, H. (2007b) 'Victims of White-Collar and Corporate Crime' in P. Davies, P. Francis, and C. Greer (eds) *Victims, Crime and Society*. London: Sage.

Davies, P. (2007) *Chapter 17*: 'Lessons from the gender agenda' in S. Walklate (ed) *Handbook on Victims and Victimology*. Cullompton: Willan.

Davies, P. (2011) *Gender, Crime and Victimisation*. London: Sage.

Davies, P., Francis, P., and Jupp, V. (2003) *Victimisation: Theory Research and Policy*. Basingstoke: Macmillan Palgrave.

Davies, P., Francis, P., and Greer, C. (2007) (eds) *Victims, Crime and Society*. London: Sage.

Dixon, M., Reed, H., Rogers, B., and Stone, L. (2006) *Crime Share: The Unequal Impact of Crime*. London: Institute for Public Policy Research.

Doak, J. (2008) *Victims' Rights, Human Rights and Criminal Justice. Reconceiving the role of third parties*. Oxford: Hart Publishing.

Doyle, J. (2012) http://www.dailymail.co.uk/news/article-2094083/Crime-victim-payouts-axed-Thousands-hurt-violent-assaults-longer-merit-compensation.html#ixzz1nrTSdlUf

Evans, K. and Fraser, P. (2004) 'Communities and Victimisation' in P. Davies, P. Francis, and V. Jupp (eds) *Victimisation: Theory, Research and Practice*. Basingstoke: Palgrave/Macmillan.

Fitzgerald, M. and Hale, C. (1996) *Ethnic Minorities, Victimisation and Racial Harassment: Findings from the 1988 and 1992 British Crime Surveys*. Home Office Research Study 154. London: Home Office.

Genn, H. (1988) 'Multiple victimization' in M. Maguire and J. Pointing (eds) *Victims of Crime: A New Deal?* Milton Keynes: Open University Press, 90–100.

Goodey, J. (2005) *Victims and Victimology: Research, Policy and Practice*. London: Longman.

Hall, M. (2009) *Victims of Crime: Policy and practice in criminal justice*. Cullompton: Willan.

Hindelang, M.J., Gottfredson, M.R., and Garofalo, J. (1978) *Victims of Personal Crime: An Empirical Foundation for a Theory of Personal Victimisation*. Cambridge, Mass.: Ballinger.

Home Office (1990) *The Victims Charter: A Statement of Rights for Victims of Crime*. London: Home Office.

Home Office (2010a) *British Crime Survey 2008-2009*. Home Office Research, Development and Statistics Directorate.

Home Office (2010b) *Business Crime Scoping Exercise*. Home Office Research Report 33.

Home Office 2011 Crime in England and Wales 2010/11 accessed at http://www.homeoffice.gov.uk/publications/science-research-statistics/research-statistics/crime-research/hosb1011/ on 26 February 2012.

Hough, M. and Mayhew, P. (1983) *The British Crime Survey*. Home Office Research Study No 76 London: HMSO.

Human Rights Watch (2004) *The Aftermath of Rape and Other Forms of Sexual Violence*. New York: Human Rights Watch.

Jefferson, T. (1996) 'From "little fairy boy" to "complete destroyer": subjectivity and transformation in the biography of Mike Tyson' in M. Mac an Ghiall (ed) *Understanding Masculinities*. Buckingham: Open University Press.

Jones, T., MacLean, B. and Young, J. (1986) *The Islington Crime Survey*. Aldershot: Gower.

Jupp, V.R. (1989) *Methods of Criminological Research*. London: Unwin Hyman.

Mawby, R.I. (2004) 'The Provision of Victim Support and Assistance Programmes: A cross-national perspective' in P. Davies, P. Francis, and V. Jupp (eds) *Victimisation: Theory, Research and Practice*. Basingstoke: Palgrave/Macmillan.

Mawby, R.I. and Walklate, S. (1994) *Critical victimology: international perspectives*. London: Sage.

Mendelsohn, B. (1956) 'Une nouvelle branche de la science bio-psycho-sociale: la victimologie', *Revue Internationale de Criminologie et de Police Technique*, 95–109.

Muncie, J. (2004) *Youth and Crime* (2nd edn) London: Sage.

National Audit Office (2002) *Helping Victims and Witnesses: the work of Victim Support*. London: The Stationery Office.

Pain, R. (2004) 'Old Age and Victimisation' in P. Davies, P. Francis, and V. Jupp (eds) *Victimisation: Theory, Research and Practice*. Basingstoke: Palgrave/Macmillan.

Pain, R., Francis, P., Fuller, I., O'Brien, K., and Williams, S. (2002) *'Hard-to-Reach' Young People and Community Safety: A Model for Participatory Research and Consultation*. Police Research Series Paper 152. London: Home Office.

Phipps, A. (1988) 'Ideologies, political parties and victims of crime', in M. Maguire and J. Pointing (eds) *Victims of Crime: A New Deal?* Milton Keynes: Open University Press.

Rock, P. (2004) *Constructing Victims' Rights. The Home Office, New Labour, and Victims*. Oxford: Oxford University Press.

Spalek, B. (2006) *Crime Victims: Theory, Policy and Practice*. Basingstoke: Palgrave/Macmillan.

Victim Support (1995) *The Rights of Victims of Crime*. London: Victim Support.

Victim Support (2010) *Victims' justice? What victims and witnesses really want from sentencing*. London: Victim Support.

von Hentig, H. (1948) *The Criminal and his Victim: studies in the socio-biology of crime*. New Haven: Yale University Press.

Walklate, S. (1989) *Victimology: the victim and the criminal justice process*. London: Unwin Hyman.

Walklate, S. (2003) 'Can there be a Feminist Victimology?' in P. Davies, P. Francis, and V. Jupp (eds) *Victimisation: Theory, Research and Policy*. London: Palgrave/Macmillan.

Walklate, S. (2004) *Gender, Crime and Criminal Justice*. Cullompton: Willan.

Walklate, S. (2007a) 'Men, Victims and Crime' in P. Davies, P. Francis, and C. Greer (eds) *Victims, Crime and Society*. London: Sage.

Walklate, S. (2007b) *Imagining the Victim of Crime*. Maidenhead: Open University Press.

Williams, B. (2009) 'Victims' in K. Hayward, A. Wahidin, and E. Wincup (eds) *Criminology*. Oxford: Oxford University Press.

Wolfgang, M.E. (1958) *Patterns in Criminal Homicide*. Philadelphia, Pa: University of Pennsylvania Press.

Wright, M. (2004) 'Preventing Harm, Promoting Harmony' in P. Davies, P. Francis, and V. Jupp (eds) *Victimisation Theory, Research and Policy*. Basingstoke: Palgrave/Macmillan.

Young, J. (1986) 'The failure of criminology: The need for a radical realism' in R. Matthews and J. Young (eds) *Confronting Crime*. London: Sage.

Zedner, L. (2002) 'Victims' in M. Maguire, R. Morgan, and R. Reiner (eds) *The Oxford Handbook of Criminology* (3rd edn) Oxford: Oxford University Press.

23 Policing

Trevor Jones

INTRODUCTION

The study of policing is now a major sub-field within criminology, with policing research undertaken by universities, national and local government, market research agencies, think tanks and pressure groups, as well as the police themselves (Newburn and Reiner, 2012). This chapter provides an overview of some key themes within this major body of work. It begins by discussing the definition of 'policing', and its growth as a focus of political concern and criminological enquiry, before outlining in brief the organization and structure of policing in England and Wales. The third section examines what the police actually do in practice and provides an overview of some contrasting models of policing. The next section explores several key debates within the policing literature. The primary focus is upon policing in England and Wales,[1] although the similar themes are visible across most Western industrial democracies.

BACKGROUND

Criminological studies of policing have been criticized for their traditional 'State centric' focus upon the specialist State agency—'the police'—tasked with law enforcement, crime investigation, public reassurance and peace-keeping (Shearing, 2006). It is argued that this approach erroneously implies a conceptual conflation of 'policing' with 'what the police do', suggests that in empirical terms public constabularies are the most important providers of policing services in contemporary societies, and further implies that policing *should* be provided primarily by State institutions.

As Shearing and others have demonstrated, the law enforcement, investigation, peacekeeping and other activities undertaken by State *police* institutions are a subset of a broader range of *policing* functions authorized and undertaken by a variety of State, commercial, voluntary and community bodies. All of these are themselves subsets of the wider system of social controls. This raises the challenge of providing working definitions of policing that are sufficiently specific to capture the distinctive features of policing within the broader mesh of formal and informal social controls, but at the same time general enough to include the range of activities undertaken by, or on behalf of, non-State bodies. One such definition denoted policing as 'organized forms of order maintenance, peacekeeping, rule or law enforcement, crime investigation and prevention … undertaken by individuals or organizations where such activities are viewed by them and/or others as a … key defining part of their purpose' (Jones and Newburn, 1998: 18–19).

The State-oriented focus of policing research has been challenged over the past two decades by a body of work that shows how 'policing' activities are regularly undertaken by a range of public, commercial and voluntary agencies (Johnston, 2000; Crawford *et al.*, 2005). Regulation, order maintenance, and law enforcement activities are increasingly 'pluralized' in contemporary societies and the public police are one among many policing bodies (Jones and Newburn, 2006). This changed policing landscape includes a burgeoning commercial security sector (Wakefield, 2003), new forms of public sector policing provision such as local authority patrol forces and municipal police forces (Crawford, 2008), the creation of new patrolling ranks—such as 'Police Community Support Officers' (PCSOs)—within public police organizations (Johnston, 2006), the development of informal policing forms such as vigilantism (Sharp and Wilson, 2002), and the emergence of transnational policing forms above the nation-state (Goldsmith and Sheptycki, 2007).

The literature on plural policing, as well as challenging dominant empirical understandings of *what policing is*, has stimulated normative debates about *how policing should be* (Jones, 2012). On the one hand, there are concerns about the standard of service provided by non-State policing forms, and about the perceived lack of public accountability of private policing agents. On one view, private policing exacerbates social polarization and aggravates feelings of insecurity (Zedner, 2009). Against this, some authors have argued that non-State forms of security provision and governance provide an important opportunity to develop more equitable and effective forms of security provision in local communities (Johnston and Shearing, 2003; Shearing, 2006). On this view, governmental authorities should seek to facilitate the participation of disadvantaged groups in security markets, and help communities to develop their own locally-designed forms of private governance (Wood, 2006).

Although non-State policing forms play an increasingly important role within policing generally, it is important not to underplay the continuing importance of State-organized arrangements (Reiner, 2010). Some commentators have argued that State policing should be viewed as something more than 'one node among many' (Crawford, 2008), and a number of authors have provided compelling arguments in favour of retaining a conception of policing as a social good, and one which should be promoted and organized—if not always directly delivered—by democratically accountable collective political institutions (Loader and Walker, 2007). Thus, whilst acknowledging the important contributions of recent research on pluralization, the remainder of this chapter will focus mostly upon State-organized policing arrangements.

Prior to the 1960s, the police and policing were rather invisible within criminology (Reiner, 1997). To the extent that policing was considered by academics, this was in rather straightforward terms as the agency providing institutional responses to the more sociologically interesting concept of crime. From the late 1960s onwards, however, this approach was challenged by the emergence of 'labelling' perspectives that analysed crime and deviance as the product of complex interactions between individuals and the social audience (Becker, 1963; Lemert 1964). In order to fully comprehend the problem of crime and its construction, criminologists needed a detailed knowledge and understanding of police interactions with members of the public, the factors that shape police attitudes and behaviour, and the ways in which organizational policies are formed and translated (or not) into practice (Reiner, 1997). Subsequent developments in critical criminology also placed policing centre stage to analyses of crime and deviance, this time as a key weapon deployed by the capitalist state to control the working classes, demonize marginal groups, and maintain the existing system of class relations (Hall *et al.*, 1978).

In addition to these developments in academic thinking, social and political developments contributed more generally to a growing awareness of—and critical discussion about—policing and the police (Newburn, 2008). These themes are discussed in more detail in Chapter 19, but they include the sustained increases in recorded crime rates from the 1950s to the mid-1990s, sporadic outbreaks of serious urban disorder in the big English cities, the contentious involvement of the police in dealing with major industrial disputes such as the 1984–85 miners' strike, and the increasing politicization of law and order (Downes and Morgan, 2012). All these developments have contributed to much more critical scrutiny of policing, and a decline in levels of public confidence in the police from the high levels of police legitimacy in the 1950s (Reiner, 2010). Nevertheless, it is clear that the police institution retains a significant, perhaps unique, cultural and symbolic significance in England and Wales (Loader and Mulcahy, 2003). Public demands for increased levels of policing remain as strident as ever, typified by the frequent call for 'more bobbies on the beat'. Representations of the police remain a central part of our popular culture, with crime and policing stories providing a core part of both news reporting and popular fiction on film and television (Reiner, 2008; 2010; Leishman and Mason, 2003). Despite the increasing tide of criticism and scrutiny over recent decades, we retain a peculiar attachment to, and fascination with, the police.

The structure of policing in England and Wales

A distinctive feature of policing in England and Wales, compared to the national police forces that exist in a number of continental European countries, is the continued attachment to local organization. As we will discuss later, there have been considerable concerns in recent years about the centralization of control over policing amounting to a *de facto* nationalization of policing (Reiner, 2010). However, the current structure remains organized primarily around sub-national policing units. There are 41 'provincial' police forces outside of London, some covering a single county and others cover two or more county areas. In addition, there are two police forces covering London (the Metropolitan Police and the City of London Police). Police forces vary in terms of size, ranging from the largest force, the Metropolitan Police, with over 30,000 officers, to the smallest provincial force (Warwickshire) with about 1,000 officers. In the quarter century until 2006 there were very substantial increases in police staffing such that the total number of police officers in England and Wales reached a record high of over 143,000 in 2006, supplemented by 83,000 civilian support staff, 6,700 PCSOs and 13,000 volunteer 'Special Constables' (Clegg and Kirwan, 2006). Public expenditure cuts by the current Coalition government will mean that substantial falls in total police staffing are likely to continue over the coming years. The typical structure of a police force involves a headquarters (encompassing the strategic management of the force plus managerial and support departments) plus a number of local territorial units delivering operational policing in particular geographical areas of the force. These territorial policing units are called 'Basic Command Units' (BCUs). Each police force is headed by a Chief Constable, with a Deputy Chief Constable and one or more Assistant Chief Constables, who make up the Chief Officer Team (COT)—the senior strategic management body for the police force. Each BCU has a senior officer in charge—usually a Chief Superintendent—who will report to the Chief Constable for policing matters in his or her area. There is significant variation in the size of BCUs, ranging from under 100 to over 1,000 police officers, covering populations from 4,000 to 300,000 residents, but the general trend is towards larger units (Loveday, 2006). A number of national policing agencies have been established during recent decades, including the Serious Organised Crime Agency (SOCA), which became operational in 2006. This merged the previously existing National Crime Squad,

National Criminal Intelligence Service, the drugs trafficking investigation and intelligence sections of HM Revenue and Customs, the Immigration Service responsibilities for organized immigration crime, and various other national policing functions. Under the reform programme of the current government, SOCA is being subsumed under a National Crime Agency.

What do the police do?

Policing functions

The American sociologist, Egon Bittner, highlighted two core defining characteristics of the (public) police (Bittner, 1980). The first concerned the very broad functional mandate of the police that makes them an omnibus or 'catch all' public service. The second key feature highlighted by Bittner was the distinctive legal capacity that the police bring to this broad mandate—their access to the legitimate use of force.

Despite this broad and flexible functional mandate, there is little doubt that 'crime-fighting' is central to the occupational self-image of many police officers, as well as the wider representations of policing in media and public debate. However, the strong conclusion of research on what police officers actually do is that crime-related activities only take up a minority of the everyday work of most police officers (Punch, 1979; PA Consulting Group, 2001). The police are called upon to preserve tranquillity, ease the flow of traffic, serve as a clearing house for reports of a variety of community problems, assist in civil emergencies, and help people find their way. However, this view has been challenged in a number of ways in recent years. Reiner (2010) argued that changes in the organization of police forces have expanded the number of law-enforcement specialists, and increased the involvement of uniformed officers in the investigation of routine crime. The primary focus of government reforms since the early 1990s has been upon improving police performance. The emphasis on demonstrable improvements in performance indicators (such as 'sanction detections') has possibly focused more on crime-related aspects of policing by virtue of their being more amenable to statistical measurement. Thus, while the view of the police as primarily 'crime-fighters' remains a gross simplification of the realities of everyday police work, dealing with crime remains not only symbolically important to policing, but a key part of how police effectiveness is perceived and measured.

Nevertheless, most research on what police officers actually do in practice still supports the view that the primary police task is peace-keeping or 'order maintenance'. The majority of daily police activity involves settling of disputes without recourse to their formal legal powers (Reiner, 2010). Officers will not invoke the law in every situation where a crime has been committed, but in circumstances where they believe that a crime has been committed *and* they deem it appropriate to apply their legal powers. Decisions to enforce the law are often made in pursuit of this broader objective of 'peace-keeping'. This was recognized by Lord Scarman in his 1981 report on the Brixton riots, when he argued that in situations where law enforcement may conflict with maintaining the public peace, it is the latter that must take priority (Scarman, 1981). These order maintenance activities come in many different forms, most frequently involving mediation by officers in relatively minor disputes or providing a visible police patrol presence at public events such as football matches or demonstrations. However, they can also include major 'paramilitary-style' interventions of organized force to deal with serious outbreaks of public disorder (Waddington, D., 2007; Waddington, P.A.J. and Wright, 2008).

Models of policing

We consider briefly here two contrasting models of delivering policing functions outlined earlier, 'community policing' and 'zero tolerance policing' (ZTP).

Community policing

Most police forces in contemporary democracies claim to support 'community policing'. However, what precisely this means in terms of practical policing strategies and tactics is less easy to pin down. In general terms, community policing suggests that policing should be undertaken in partnership with the public; that citizens are co-producers of policing, and the control of crime and disorder is not just the responsibility of the police (Tilley, 2008). This implies a broad social role for the police and that they should not be seen simply as enforcers of the law, but as delivering a range of order maintenance and social service functions as well. Another key theme within discussions of community policing is that policing strategies should be proactive. The police should not simply respond to calls from the public or reports of crime, but should attempt to identify and address the complex problems that underpin problems of crime and disorder. Community policing also implies organizational reforms of the traditional militaristic police hierarchy, with core responsibilities devolved to front line officers, multi-functional units attached to particular localities, and organizational emphasis on team work and problem-solving (Newburn and Reiner, 2012). During the past decade, a significant development in England and Wales has been the creation of neighbourhood policing teams based on 'wards' (sub-units of smaller areas covered by local government). The aim was to provide citizens with access to local policing services through a named point of contact, an opportunity to exert influence over local policing priorities, facilitate the effective development and implementation of joint action to reduce crime and disorder with key partners and the public, and to provide clear accountability and feedback to local people about what is being done in their area. By the end of 2008, all local areas had a local team consisting of police officers and PCSOs, sometimes also including a mix of Special Constables, local authority wardens, volunteers and partners.

Whilst community policing approaches have been enormously influential in contemporary policing systems, research has produced mixed findings about the effectiveness of such approaches. Part of the problem lies in the lack of clarity about what exactly is involved. Even where clear policy prescriptions can be identified, research has uncovered significant problems of planning and implementation (Newburn and Reiner, 2012).

Nevertheless, many of the policing initiatives listed here have—either on their own or in combination—formed a central part of community policing policies introduced periodically in England and Wales since the 1970s.

Zero tolerance policing

'Zero tolerance policing' (ZTP) is associated with a vigorous enforcement-oriented policing approach that focuses upon minor offences and 'disorder' as much as upon more serious crimes. During the 1990s, there was considerable attention paid by the British media to developments in the policing of New York City where there had been very significant drops in crime. This became associated, at least in popular consciousness, with a 'zero tolerance' approach to policing (Jones and Newburn, 2007). Concern about growing levels of street crime led UK politicians from both main parties to gaze across the Atlantic for inspiration and call for the introduction of police strategies similar to those adopted in New York City under the then mayor Rudolph Giuliani and his police chief, William Bratton (Harcourt, 2002). The policing strategies associated with zero tolerance have been variously described as 'Quality of Life', 'Order Maintenance' or 'Broken Windows' policing. This last term derives from the famous *Atlantic Monthly* article by US academics James Q. Wilson and George Kelling (Wilson and Kelling, 1982).

The article focused upon the relationship between 'disorders' (graffiti, public drunkenness, prostitution, vandalism, begging, etc.) and the growth of more serious crime. The paper argued that serious crimes and neighbourhood disorder are linked in a 'kind of developmental sequence'. Neighbourhood disorder signals that nobody cares. Disorders and incivilities, left unchallenged, result in reduced use of public spaces by residents, and also signal to potential law-breakers that community controls and surveillance are weak. This analysis suggested that the police should deal firmly with disorderly behaviour and 'minor' crimes in local areas in order to have an impact on serious crime. ZTP (and related approaches) are associated with a number of concrete policing practices introduced in New York City by Commissioner Bratton. These included a vastly increased uniformed presence on the streets, a vigorous law-enforcement response to minor crime and disorder, the use of civil remedies against those perceived to be involved in criminal activities, enhanced accountability of local police managers for crime and disorder in their areas, and aggressive action against street crimes (Jones and Newburn, 2007). These policing practices became associated with massive drops in recorded crime in New York, although there has been vigorous (at times, bitter) debate about the relative contribution of policing practices and other factors (Harcourt, 2001). Concerns have also been raised about the potential impact of aggressive enforcement-oriented policing approaches upon police-community relations in general, and upon the incidence of police brutality and aggression in particular (Greene, 1999).

Both the terminology and the concrete policing practices associated with ZTP as developed in New York have been resisted by senior police officers in the UK, and experiments with 'New York' style policing have been rather limited (Jones and Newburn, 2007). However, the broader ideas associated with 'Broken Windows' have been enormously influential over wider government policy on crime and anti-social behaviour. New Labour's adoption of such approaches is evidenced by the title and the contents of the Crime and Disorder Act 1998, the more recent Anti-Social Behaviour Act 2003, and the architecture of government anti-social behaviour policy more generally (Burney, 2005).

REVIEW QUESTIONS

1 What kinds of things do police officers actually spend most of their time doing?

2 What are the key elements of community policing and how might they be implemented?

3 What does zero tolerance policing (ZTP) mean in practice and what are its associated benefits and disadvantages?

Key debates in contemporary policing

This section focuses upon a selected number of key contemporary debates about policing. Space restrictions mean that inevitably a number of important issues cannot be covered, but for a more comprehensive overview the reader is referred to the general texts on policing recommended in the further reading suggestions at the end of this chapter.

Police occupational cultures

It is a distinctive feature of policing that scope for discretion increases for officers the further they are down the police hierarchy (Manning, 1977). Policing activities are 'low visibility' and much policing involves interactions with individuals of low social power that take place away from the gaze of supervisors or the general public. In addition, it is not possible to legislate in advance for the wide range of possible situations that police officers may face, and thus professional discretion is a necessary part of doing policing. A key question for police researchers has concerned the degree to which informal working cultures shape the ways in which officers use their discretion.

Occupational police cultures can be defined as beliefs, norms, working practices and informal rules that help police officers to make sense of their world (Reiner, 2010). The early observational studies of policing—mainly focused on uniformed patrol officers—suggested there was a relatively stable set of dimensions that appeared to characterize 'cop culture' in a range of different societies. Skolnik (1966) highlighted how common tensions associated with policing in liberal societies appeared to foster a common set of cultural responses. Police officers face the problem of constant pressure for results, combined with the difficult position of being symbols of social authority in a way which sets them apart from their fellow citizens. Skolnik argued that these structural problems tend to generate a series of traits within a shared police sub-culture, and highlighted in particular suspicion, social isolation/group solidarity, and conservatism. More recent studies have added other elements to the standard 'list' of features that are said to characterize 'cop culture'. These include the sense of mission, cynicism/pragmatism, machismo and racial prejudice (Reiner, 2010). Although notions of cop culture have tended to be used in pejorative terms, it is important to understand the relationship between these features and the structural context of policing. In addition, they need not always be viewed as *necessarily* negative in themselves. For example, police officers are trained and socialized to suspect that things are not always as they seem. Whilst this is arguably an important skill for effective police work, it can also lead to the unfair stereotyping of particular groups or individuals. Group solidarity can be linked to the vital interdependence between police officers, who often face potentially dangerous situations in which they are outnumbered by hostile members of the public. The need to rely upon colleagues to back each other up in difficult situations helps to foster a strong sense of in-group loyalty. However, this strong group identification brings with it the danger of negatively stereotyping 'outsiders', and also a marked tendency to close ranks in the face of investigations of police malpractice. Though racial prejudice and machismo can never be regarded as positive, it is also important to understand the complex dynamics via which these traits also arise and are perpetuated in the police organisation. Crucially, they are linked to the experience of 'doing policing' in societies characterized by structural inequalities of race and gender. They are also connected to the practical realities of new recruits 'learning on the job' in the company of more experienced officers (Jones, 1998).

An important question is how far can these cultural tendencies be explained with reference to the individual dispositions that police recruits bring to the job. Most research on this matter suggests that occupational police subcultures are better understood as a collective cultural adaption to the everyday realities of policework, rather than being the product of individual personality traits (Newburn and Reiner, 2012). Thus, whilst reforming the police organization in order to eliminate the negative aspects of police culture has been seen as a prerequisite for better policing, this is a far more difficult task than simply weeding out individual officers with inappropriate attitudes. For example, once we accept occupational culture as a complex collective phenomenon, we can begin to understand the limitations on traditional approaches to changing the culture. Interventions such as better recruitment practices or improved 'cultural awareness' training tend to individualize problems such as prejudice, and not allow for the fact that much policing is learned on the streets.

More recent work has questioned the continued utility of traditional notions of occupational police culture given the changed policing landscape since the classic studies of cop culture during the 1960s. In particular, such work has criticized the tendency to discuss cop culture as though it is a universal and homogenous phenomenon (Cockcroft, 2012; Westmarland, 2008). Indeed, it may be more accurate to talk about 'police cultures', given the noted differences within police forces. For example, there appear to be significant contrasts in occupational cultures between different functional specialisms, officers of different ranks, and urban and rural force areas. Furthermore, although the standard 'checklist' of cultural traits associated with cop culture is still rehearsed faithfully in most undergraduate courses on policing, we should remember that it is now three decades or more since the 'classic' studies of cop culture. It would be reasonable to expect at least some changes in the nature of cultural responses to the structural pressures of policework reflecting developments in wider society and the emergence of a new generation of police officers. There is no doubt that the composition of the police service has changed quite significantly during the past few decades, with greater numbers of women and ethnic minority officers, working alongside civilian staff who now constitute over a third of the total police workforce.

However, recent empirical work by Loftus (2009, 2010) has suggested that traditional notions of cop culture are still relevant. She observes that a number of the cultural characteristics first highlighted in the cop culture studies of the 1960s appeared to be alive and well in a provincial English police force towards the end of the first decade of the millennium. Loftus explains the durability of such cultural traits with reference to the continued relevance of the tensions of the police role in liberal democratic societies first highlighted by Skolnik. As she argues: 'The timeless qualities of police culture endure because the basic pressures associated with the police role have not been removed and because social transformations have exacerbated, rather than reduced, the basic definitions of inequality' (Loftus, 2010: 17).

Whilst 'cop culture' is still a useful concept, we should beware of assuming a straightforward connection between cultural traits and patterns of behaviour. Waddington (1999) argues that 'canteen culture' is primarily an oral phenomenon that involves the telling of 'war stories' away from the front-line of policing. Many of these verbal accounts of policing as told by one officer to another bear little relation to the more mundane reality of police work. For Waddington, this demonstrates that the oral culture fulfils a number of functions for the officers who participate within it. It helps bolster occupational self-esteem, and provides mutual reassurance that they are doing a dangerous and valuable job. It provides a gloss that enables officers to cope—practically and emotionally—with the often depressing, difficult and messy situations with which they are faced (Reiner, 2010). Finally, although elements of this oral culture are undoubtedly unpalatable, it cannot be related to practical police behaviour in a straightforward causal way. Individual officers are not helpless in the face of an all-pervasive culture, but actively interpret and react to it (Waddington, 1999). We therefore need to understand better the ways in which some officers resist and rework the occupational cultures in which they find themselves.

Policing a diverse society

During recent decades, Britain, along with most Western industrial societies, has experienced increasing social and cultural diversity. For example, social differences along lines of religion, age, gender, region, nationality, ethnicity, sexuality, and lifestyles are becoming more important as a source of individual and group identity. At the same time, social and economic inequality has increased substantially over the past 20 years (Dorling, 2011). An important challenge for contemporary policing is to balance and respond to conflicting demands from an increasingly diverse society.

However, a central finding of much policing research is that the adversarial aspects of policing have always been experienced disproportionately by those at the lower end of the social hierarchy (Reiner, 2010). The unemployed, the poor, people living in inner-city areas, immigrants and ethnic minorities consistently find themselves more likely to be on the end of police powers (see also Chapter 9 (dealing with race issues) and 16 (discussing violent crime)). We will focus here on the arena of race relations, although it should be noted that similar arguments have applied to the policing experiences of other social groups. In particular, concerns have been raised about the experiences of women and LGB (lesbian, gay and bisexual) people both as police officers, and also as receivers of policing services (Heidensohn, 2008; Johnson, 2010). In addition, as society has become more diverse during the latter half of the twentieth century, police relations with a range of other minority groups have come under scrutiny (Jones and Newburn, 2001).

The subject of crime, ethnicity and policing remains highly controversial and explanations have too often been reduced to those entirely related to police racism, or alternatively, to alleged higher offending rates among minority ethnic groups. Recent work has provided a more sophisticated understanding of the different forms of racial discrimination that operate within the police organization and in wider society (Phillips and Bowling, 2012). It has also highlighted the important impact of wider structural patterns of disadvantage that disproportionately place some ethnic minority communities in the geographical places and social groups that are more likely to be on the end of adversarial policing. The research also continues to demonstrate that, despite over 20 years of official attention to the issue, it is clear that relationships between the police and minority ethnic communities remain problematic in a number of respects (Bowling et al., 2008; Phillips and Bowling, 2012). First, considering the dimension of suspects/offenders, it is clear that ethnic minority people (and especially black people) are substantially over-represented in police stop and arrest statistics. Recent data at the national level shows very stark differences, with black people about eight times as likely as whites (on average) to be stopped by the police, and about five times as likely overall to be arrested (Ministry of Justice, 2012). Second, there is strong evidence that ethnic minorities remain 'under-protected' as well as 'over-policed'. Particular concerns have been raised about levels of racist harassment and violence (Bowling, 1998). The police service has come under strong criticism for failure to deal effectively with such crimes, although it is accepted that significant improvements have been made in recent years. Despite over two decades of official attention, ethnic minorities remain markedly under-represented among police officers (Ministry of Justice, 2012).

There are a number of possible explanations for these different experiences of policing. Direct discrimination may be a contributory factor, although studies in the past decade or so have found little clear evidence of overt racism by police officers (Fitzgerald et al., 2002; Foster et al., 2005). More recent official attention has been applied to the concept of 'institutional discrimination' highlighted in the MacPherson Report into the racist murder of the black teenager Stephen Lawrence. MacPherson defined institutional racism as unwitting and unintentional discrimination that is built into organizational policies and practices, with the (sometimes unintended) effect of disadvantaging members of particular ethnic groups. This clearly moves us towards a more sophisticated notion of discrimination, one in which discriminatory practices arise out of the everyday functioning of an organization rather than being equated simply with examples of individual racial discrimination. However, the concept as outlined by MacPherson has itself come under criticism for its lack of specificity, and its failure to identify the particular policies (and the organizational dynamics that underpin them) that lead to discriminatory outcomes (McLaughlin and Murji, 1999; Lea, 2000; Fitzgerald, 2001).

On the other hand, there is evidence that factors other than police discrimination (direct and institutional) contribute at a more fundamental level to problematic relationships. For example, although definitive conclusions cannot be drawn, there is some evidence that there are disproportionately high numbers of some ethnic minority groups involved in crime and disorder (Home Affairs Committee, 2007). This should not be a contentious finding given what is known about wider patterns of racial disadvantage, and associations with offending of socio-economic problems such as unemployment and poverty (Jarjoura *et al.*, 2002; see also Chapter 16). As mentioned earlier, these wider structural features often work to place ethnic minorities at greater risk of police attention, in a very practical sense. For example, a number of factors, including higher levels of unemployment and more school exclusions among young black people, mean that they are disproportionately 'available' in public places for police stops (Waddington *et al.*, 2004). It is increasingly recognized that socio-economic disadvantage contributes both to higher offending and greater targeting by the police. This, in turn, helps generate further mutual hostility between the police and some ethnic minority groups, which fosters resentment on the part of the community and prejudice within the police organization. In turn, these processes help to reinforce and exacerbate the wider patterns of ethnic disadvantage. As Reiner (2010) has stated, 'the police are reproducers rather than creators of social injustice, although their prejudices may amplify it'. Without a more general reduction in socio-economic inequality and racial disadvantage, changes in policing policy can only bring about rather limited improvements.

Police effectiveness and performance

It is arguable that during the past two decades, the issue of police performance and effectiveness has been *the* central political concern about policing in England and Wales. Despite the evidence of decreasing crime victimization since the mid-1990s, a central part of New Labour's police reform programme between 1997 and 2010 was to improve effectiveness via increasingly forensic performance management by central government. This approach dates back to the early 1980s, when the then Conservative government's 'Financial Management Initiative' (designed to promote economy, efficiency and effectiveness in public services) was extended to the police service. Following this time, the Audit Commission became increasingly influential, promoting 'value for money' within police forces. The Police and Magistrates Courts Act 1994 introduced a range of reforms, including the introduction of a 'purchaser-provider' split between police authority and force, the development of national policing objectives and key performance indicators, the introduction of costed local 'business plans' for policing, the appointment of independent members to police authorities to make them more 'businesslike', the encouragement of charging for some police services and the promotion of sponsorship, and the devolution of some budgetary controls to the local level (Jones, 2008). There were particular concerns about police performance in the arena of crime investigation and control. The Audit Commission promoted a more 'proactive' strategy in contrast to more traditional case-based methods of detective work. This includes a more calculative and risk-oriented approach towards crime investigation, including crime management, case screening, the increasing use of surveillance technologies, and more systematic quantitative methods of crime analysis (Johnston, 2000). These developments were promoted across all police forces in England and Wales with the development of the National Intelligence Model (NIM), which provides a 'business model' for the organization of police crime control activities (Maguire, 2008).

Two of the most significant developments introduced by New Labour were the stringent national planning framework established by the Police Reform Act 2002 (including the publication of a detailed National Policing Plan) and the emergence of the Police Standards Unit—a Home Office Unit with a brief to promote improvements in 'under-performing' police force areas—in the same year. Following this, New Labour set up the National Policing Improvement Agency (NPIA), a powerful national body with a remit for promoting improvement performance in local police force areas. These specific developments were accompanied by an ever more strident rhetoric on the part of government ministers expressing frustration at levels of police performance and the need for more radical reform.

The election of the Coalition government in 2010 marked an end to the approach of managing police performance via nationally-set performance targets. In a striking reversal of the approach of the previous two decades, detailed nationally-set performance indicators were abolished in 2011. Whilst it is clear that the Coalition government strongly opposes centrally-set performance targets, other aspects of their reform package demonstrate that it is not so much the measurement of performance that concerns them, but rather, where the locus of control for such measurement and targets lies. A further set of changes has concerned the public availability of crime statistics and crime maps. The Coalition gave new emphasis to the use of local 'crime maps', first introduced under the previous Labour government, in order to help citizens hold the police to account for their performance. In some ways, then, it could be argued that the issue of police effectiveness has become even more prominent than ever, given the over-arching government priority of tackling the budget deficit. The October 2010 Comprehensive Spending Review (CSR) set out a 20 per cent cut in the central government police funding grant for all 43 forces in England and Wales by 2014/15 (in real terms). It was argued that restrictions in police expenditure should not mean a reduction in the quality of 'frontline policing' in that forces would need to seek ways of improving efficiency, and using their staffing resources in more innovative ways. The Coalition has also stated its intention to bring about a radical reform of the pay and working conditions of police officers in order to improve efficiency. In October 2010, the Home Secretary commissioned a formal review—chaired by the former Railways Regulator Tom Winsor—of the remuneration and conditions of services for police officers and staff in England and Wales. The review was asked to make recommendations about using pay and conditions of service to maximize officer and staff deployment to frontline roles, to establish remuneration and conditions of service that are fair to both the taxpayer and police officers and staff, and to introduce to the police service modern management practices in line with those in other parts of the public and private sectors (Home Affairs Committee, 2011).

Police governance and accountability

A key strand of the current Coalition government's package of police reforms involves plans to introduce, from November 2012, directly elected Police and Crime Commissioners (PCCs) in each of the 41 provincial police forces in England and Wales (Jones *et al.*, 2012). This aims to reverse a long-standing centralization of control over police governance that has characterized policing policy-making for decades (Jones, 2008).

The Police Act 1964 divided responsibility for the framing and monitoring of police policy between a 'tripartite structure' comprising chief constables, the Home Office, and local government (in the form of police authorities). It is clear that the local element of this structure became increasingly weakened over the latter part of the twentieth century. This was related to a variety of factors. For example, the Home Office has taken a much more proactive role in promoting central government priorities and has exerted greater control over the training and promotion of senior police officers (Reiner, 2010). Local police authorities have traditionally been weak in terms of legal powers, and rather reluctant to use the few powers that they do have (Jones, 2008). The autonomy of local forces has been constrained by the emergence of national level policing institutions during the late 1990s, including the National Criminal Intelligence Service (NCIS) and the National Crime Squad (NCS) (Johnston, 2000), both of which were later incorporated under SOCA (see earlier), which is itself now being subsumed under a National Crime Agency (NCA). In addition, the senior officers' professional association—the Association of Chief Police Officers (ACPO)—emerged as a significant policy-making and lobbying body at the national level (Savage *et al.*, 2000). Whilst centralization of police governance has been in process for many decades, there is no doubt that the embrace of a rigorous 'performance model' by successive governments from the 1990s onwards contributed significantly to the erosion of local democratic controls. A key development in this regard was the introduction of the National Policing Plan (and attendant matrix of detailed performance targets) that was introduced by the then Labour government under the Police Reform Act 2002. This centrally driven performance management framework remained in place for much of the first decade of the millennium.

The Coalition government that took office in May 2010 set out explicitly to reverse the long-term centralization of police governance. The Police Reform and Social Responsibility Act 2011 included provisions for the abolition of local police authorities and the election of Police and Crime Commissioners (PCCs) in each provincial force area for a four-year term. The first elections of PCCs took place in November 2012. In London, the Metropolitan Police Authority (MPA) has now been replaced with a Mayor's Office for Policing and Crime. The PCC responsibilities include securing the maintenance of the police force, ensuring that it is efficient and effective, as well as holding the Chief Constable to account for the exercise of a range of duties. The PCC is also responsible for appointing and dismissing the Chief and for agreeing the appointments of deputy and assistant chief constables, and for the publication of Police and Crime Plans which would which will set out the strategic policing objectives for the area.

Crucially, the Chief Constable will now be appointed by the PCC and, under specific circumstances, the PCC may suspend the Chief Constable from duty and may call upon them to resign or retire. The local authorities in each force area will be required to establish a Police and Crime Panel (PCP), consisting of between ten and 20 members. This will include councillors from the local authorities covered by the police force area, and also some independent members. The PCP will have a duty to review, scrutinize and make reports on the activities of the PCC. In doing so, it may hold public meetings at which it may require the attendance of the PCC and any staff employed by the PCC. It may also request written reports from the PCC. However, it does appear that if push comes to shove, the PCP will have little actual power compared to that of the PCC. Following the first PCC elections in November 2012, it is as yet unclear how the balance between national interests and local concerns will be play out under the new arrangements.

The position in London is somewhat different from the rest of the country. As the capital already has an elected Mayor it will not need to elect a Police and Crime Commissioner. Nor did it need to wait until late 2012 before beginning to make new arrangements for police governance. In January 2012, London Mayor Boris Johnson appointed the deputy mayor Kit Malthouse as head of the Mayor's Office for Policing and Crime (MOPC). Malthouse thus became responsible publicly for the performance of the police in the capital, for setting the strategic direction of the Metropolitan Police and for allocating its resources. Interestingly, of course, and unlike PCCs outside of London, Malthouse was not directly elected to this position. As other areas will do subsequently, a PCP will be established. This panel, though working alongside the MOPC, will enable a degree of independent oversight of the MOPC and will therefore be one means by which the London Assembly can hold the Mayor to account in his 'PCC' role.

Police accountability can also be considered in terms of the accountability and control of police officers as they go about their day-to-day activities. There have been significant developments regarding the regulation of police behaviour in particular cases. Two of the most significant involve the regulation and control of police powers in dealing with suspects in criminal investigations, and the development of effective complaints mechanisms for the police. Although space prevents a detailed discussion, the Police and Criminal Evidence Act 1984 (PACE) introduced a number of regulations over the powers held by the police over suspects in custody. These included things such as the introduction of a custody officer to monitor visits to suspects detained in police cells, time limits for how long a person can be held without charge, the right to legal representation, and tape recording of interviews. Although a number of criticisms have been raised regarding the impact of PACE (Sanders and Young, 2008), the balance of research does suggest that there has been a significant effect on police behaviour within the police station, and possibly on wider detective culture (Maguire, 2002). Whatever the ongoing problems about controlling police discretion via the imposition of rules, it seems fair to say that the police are certainly more accountable than they were 30 years ago for their use of powers in particular investigations.

Turning to the areas of police complaints mechanisms, until just over a decade ago a major criticism of the arrangements has focussed around the independence (or rather the perceived lack of it) of the complaints process from the police organization. Ultimately, police officers have investigated serious complaints against other officers, although there was an independent element in the supervision of such investigations in the form of the Police Complaints Authority (PCA) (Maguire and Corbett, 1991).

The Police Reform Act 2002 established the Independent Police Complaints Commission (IPCC), staffed entirely by non-police officers and with a greater remit and more powers than the old PCA.

REVIEW QUESTIONS

1 What is 'cop culture' and where does it come from?

2 How and why do some ethnic minority groups experience difficult relationships with the police?

3 What are the advantages and dangers of increasing local elected control over policing policy?

CONCLUSION

This chapter has presented an overview of some of the key themes surrounding police and policing in contemporary England and Wales. It has demonstrated how the study of the policing emerged from a position of relative invisibility during the 1960s, to the forefront of debate in the latter years of the twentieth century. For much of the past 40 years, this renewed academic and political interest in policing has focused on the State institution known as 'the police'. Recent years, however, have seen a growing focus upon the idea of pluralization of policing. This has led some to question the relevance of a continued focus on public constabularies. However, although there have been some highly significant developments within the policing systems of the UK (such as the growth of commercial security), it still seems that for the foreseeable future at least, State-organized policing arrangements will remain central to domestic security provision. Thus, it remains of vital importance for criminologists to understand public police forces, their structure and organization, what they do, how they do it, and what key debates have arisen in relation to them. Such debates include the issue of the nature, sources and dimensions of police occupational cultures, and how they might relate to problematic behaviour by police officers. Also important is the challenge of providing equitable policing services to an increasingly diverse society in which a range of groups make contrasting demands upon the police. Governmental concerns with police performance and effectiveness remain at the forefront of public policy debate, although the Coalition government has broken with the orthodoxy of recent administrations in its view that enhanced local control (rather than national performance targets) is the best way forward. Finally, there is the challenge of how best to make the police accountable to the publics they serve. The introduction of elected PCCs marks the most radical change in police governance in over a century, and may mark an end to decades of centralization of control over policing in England and Wales. Although the policing landscape has undoubtedly become considerably more complex in recent decades, these areas of debate—and others connected with the police and policing—are likely to remain hot topics of discussion for the foreseeable future amongst students, academics and the police themselves.

QUESTIONS FOR DISCUSSION

During the coming week, explore 'factual' and/or ' fictional' representations of the police and policing. For 'factual' images, focus upon news reports or documentaries (on television/radio and/or newspapers) involving the police and policing. For fictional images, watch at least two police-related dramas or films. Take notes and then reflect upon the following questions in relation to what you have watched and/or read.

1 What images of the police and policing are presented? Are they broadly positive, negative, or neither?

2 What aspects of police work are highlighted? Do these representations focus upon law enforcement, peacekeeping/order maintenance, emergency response, service functions, or other aspects of policing?

3 What are the underlying representations of the nature of crime and criminality? Is crime presented primarily as a result of individual wickedness/pathology or as more related to social problems?

4 What kinds of factors might help to shape these representations of policing and of crime?

5 What impact do you think these representations have upon people's views about policing and the police?

GUIDE TO FURTHER READING

Newburn, T. and Reiner, R. (2012) 'Policing and the Police' in M. Maguire, R. Morgan, and R. Reiner (eds) *The Oxford Handbook of Criminology* (5th edn) Oxford: Oxford University Press.

This chapter provides an up-to-date and detailed review of the key themes of recent British (and other) policing research and a helpful guide for further reading in the field.

Rogers, C., Lewis, R., John, T., and Read, T. (2011) *Police Work: Principles and Practice*. Cullompton: Willan.

This book provides a highly readable and up-to-date account of contemporary police work, and focuses on three key areas of policing: community, investigation and intelligence. It includes a wide range of questions and exercises to help readers apply their knowledge to different situations and scenarios.

Newburn, T. (ed) (2008) *Handbook of Policing*. Cullompton: Willan.

This handbook, now in its second edition, provides an authoritative and comprehensive overview of British policing, and draws on the expertise of both academics and senior police practitioners.

Reiner, R. (2010) *The Politics of the Police*. Oxford: Oxford University Press.

This is the fourth edition of a widely praised book that provides a detailed review of the history, politics and sociology of the police in England and Wales. This edition remains a key text for students, and is now comprehensively updated with a wealth of research data published during the past decade.

WEB LINKS

http://www.homeoffice.gov.uk/hmic/hmic.htm

Her Majesty's Inspectorate of Constabulary (HMIC) has a statutory responsibility to promote the efficiency and effectiveness of police forces in England and Wales via a programme of regular force inspections and reports. It has become increasingly influential in recent years in promoting the Home Office agenda on performance improvement, as well as producing influential thematic reports on such matters as race relations and equal opportunities. This website includes a range of useful information and statistics on policing in England and Wales, and also provides online access to HMIC reports.

http://www.homeoffice.gov.uk/police/

The Home Office is the central government department with responsibility for policing in England and Wales, and this website allows access to a wide range of relevant material for students interested in research and current policy developments on policing. In particular, students can access online a large body of Home Office research studies on policing.

http://www.police.uk

This is a police service website with important details and contact addresses for all the police forces (and related organizations) in the United Kingdom. This includes a range of relevant service-related information about current issues of concern, and allows access to details for local crime maps and data.

REFERENCES

Becker, H. (1963) *Outsiders: Studies in the Sociology of Deviance.* New York: Free Press.

Bittner, E. (1980) *The Functions of the Police in Modern Society.* Cambridge, MA: Olgeschlager, Gunn and Hain.

Bowling, B. (1998) *Violent Racism.* Oxford: Clarendon Press.

Bowling, B., Parmar, A., and Phillips, C. (2008) 'Policing Ethnic Minorities' in T. Newburn (ed) *Handbook of Policing* (2nd edn) Cullompton: Willan.

Clegg, M. and Kirwan, S. (2006) *Police Service Strength, England and Wales, 31st March 2006,* Home Office Statistical Bulletin 13/06. London: Home Office.

Cockcroft, T. (2012) *Police Culture: Themes and Concepts.* London: Routledge.

Crawford, A., Lister, S., Blackburn, S., and Burnett, J. (2005) *Plural Policing: The Mixed Economy of Visible Patrols in England and Wales.* Bristol: The Policy Press.

Crawford, A. (2008) 'Plural Policing in the UK: Policing Beyond the Police' in T. Newburn (ed) *Handbook of Policing.* Cullompton: Willan.

Donnelly, D. and Scott, K. (2008) 'Policing in Scotland' in T. Newburn (ed) *Handbook of Policing* (2nd edn) Cullompton: Willan.

Dorling, D. (2011) *Injustice: Why social inequality persists.* Bristol: The Policy Press.

Downes, D. and Morgan, R. (2012) 'Overtaking on the Left? The Politics of Law and Order in the "Big Society"' in M. Maguire, R. Morgan, and R. Reiner (eds) *The Oxford Handbook of Criminology* (5th edn) Oxford: Oxford University Press.

Fitzgerald, M. (2001) 'Ethnic Minorities and Community Safety' in R. Matthews and J. Pitts (eds) *Crime, Disorder and Community Safety: A New Agenda.* London: Routledge.

Fitzgerald, M., Hough, M., Joseph, I., and Qureshi, T. (2002) *Policing for London.* Cullompton: Willan.

Foster, J., Newburn, T., and Souhami, A. (2005) *Assessing the impact of the Stephen Lawrence Inquiry,* Home Office Research Study 294, London: Home Office.

Harcourt, B. (2001) *Illusion of Order: The False Promise of Broken Windows Policing.* Cambridge, MA: Harvard University Press.

Heidensohn, F. (2008) 'Gender and Policing' in T. Newburn (ed) *The Handbook of Policing* (2nd edn) Cullompton: Willan.

Home Affairs Committee (2007) *Young black people and the criminal justice system* (Second Report). London: HMSO.

Home Affairs Committee (2011) *New Landscape of Policing* (14th Report). London: HMSO.

Home Office (2010) *Policing in the 21st Century: Reconnecting the Police and the People.* London: Home Office.

Home Office (2011) *Police and Crime Commissioners Update No. 2 September 2011.* London: Home Office.

Jarjoura, G., Triplett, R., and Brinker, G. (2002) 'Growing up poor: Examining the link between persistent childhood poverty and delinquency', *Journal of Quantitative Criminology* 18(2): 159–87.

Johnson, P. (2010) 'The Enforcement of Morality: Law, Sexuality and Policing in New South Wales', *Australian and New Zealand Journal of Criminology* 43(3): 399–422.

Johnston, L. (2000) *Policing Britain: Risk, Security. and Governance.* London: Longman.

Johnston, L. (2006) 'Diversifying Police Recruitment? The Deployment of Police Community Support Officers in London', *Howard Journal of Criminal Justice* 45(4): 388–402.

Johnston, L. and Shearing, C. (2003) *Governing Security: Explorations in Policing and Justice.* London: Routledge.

Jones, T. (1998) 'Police and Race Relations' in R. Chadwick (ed) *The Encyclopedia of Applied Ethics.* San Diego, CA: Academic Press.

Jones, T. (2008) 'The Accountability of Policing' in T. Newburn (ed) *Handbook of Policing* (2nd edn) Cullompton: Willan.

Jones, T. (2012) 'Governing Security: Pluralization, Privatization and Paradigm Shifts in Crime Control and Policing' in M. Maguire, R. Morgan, and R. Reiner (eds) *The Oxford Handbook of Criminology* (5th edn) Oxford: Oxford University Press.

Jones, T. and Newburn, T. (1998) *Private Security and Public Policing.* Oxford: Clarendon Press.

Jones, T. and Newburn, T. (2001) *Widening Access: Improving relations with 'hard to reach groups'.* London: Home Office.

Jones, T. and Newburn, T. (eds) (2006) *Plural Policing: A Comparative Perspective.* London: Routledge.

Jones, T. and Newburn, T. (2007) *Policy Transfer and Criminal Justice.* Buckingham: Open University Press.

Jones, T., Newburn, T., and Smith, D.J. (2012) 'Democracy and Police and Crime Commissioners' in T. Newburn and J. Peay (eds) *Policing: Politics, Culture and Control.* Oxford: Hart Publishing.

Lea, J. (2000) 'The Macpherson Report and the Question of Institutional Racism', *Howard Journal of Criminal Justice* 39(3): 219–33.

Leishman, F. and Mason, P. (2003) *Policing and the Media: Facts, Fictions and Factions.* Cullompton: Willan.

Lemert, E. (1964) 'Social structure, social control and deviation' in M. Clinard (ed) *Anomie and Deviant Behaviour.* New York: Free Press.

Loader, I. and Mulcahy, A. (2003) *Policing and the Condition of England: Memory, Politics and Culture.* Oxford: Oxford University Press.

Loader, I. and Walker, N. (2007) *Civilizing Security.* Cambridge: Cambridge University Press.

Loftus, B. (2009) *Police Culture in a Changing World.* Oxford: Clarendon Press.

Loftus, B. (2010) 'Police Occupational Culture: Classic Themes, Altered Times', *Policing and Society* 20(1): 1–20.

Loveday, B. (2006) *Size isn't everything: Restructuring policing in England & Wales.* London: Policy Exchange.

McLaughlin, E. and Murji, K. (1999) 'After the Stephen Lawrence Inquiry', *Critical Social Policy* 19(3): 371–85.

Maguire, M. (2002) 'Regulating the Police Station: The Case of the Police and Criminal Evidence Act 1984' in M. McConville and G. Wilson (eds) *The Handbook of the Criminal Justice Process.* Oxford: Oxford University Press.

Maguire, M. (2008) 'Criminal Investigation and Crime Control' in T. Newburn (ed) *Handbook of Policing* (2nd edn) Cullompton: Willan.

Maguire, M. (2012) 'Criminal Statistics and the Construction of Crime' in M. Maguire, R. Morgan, and R. Reiner (eds) *The Oxford Handbook of Criminology* (5th edn) Oxford: Oxford University Press.

Manning, P. (1977) *Police Work.* Cambridge, MA: MIT Press.

Ministry of Justice (2012) *Statistics on Race and the Criminal Justice System 2010-11.* London: Ministry of Justice.

Mulcahy, A. (2008) 'The Police Service of Northern Ireland' in T. Newburn (ed) *Handbook of Policing* (2nd edn) Cullompton: Willan.

MVA and Miller, J. (2000) *Profiling Populations Available for Stops and Searches* (Police Research Series Paper 131). London: Home Office.

Newburn, T. (2008) 'Introduction: Understanding Policing' in T. Newburn (ed) *Handbook of Policing* (2nd edn) Cullompton: Willan.

Newburn, T. and Reiner, R. (2012) 'Policing and the Police' in M. Maguire, R. Morgan, and R. Reiner (eds) *The Oxford Handbook of Criminology* (5th edn) Oxford: Oxford University Press.

PA Consulting Group (2001) *Diary of a Police Officer* (Police Research Paper 149). London: Home Office.

Phillips, C. and Bowling, B. (2012) 'Ethnicities, Racism, Crime and Criminal Justice' in M. Maguire, R. Morgan, and R. Reiner (eds) *The Oxford Handbook of Criminology* (5th edn) Oxford: Oxford University Press.

Punch, M. (1979) 'The Secret Social Service' in S. Holdaway (ed) *The British Police.* London: Edward Arnold.

Reiner, R. (1997) 'Policing and the Police' in M. Maguire, R. Morgan, and R. Reiner (eds) *The Oxford Handbook of Criminology* (2nd edn) Oxford: Oxford University Press.

Reiner, R. (2008) 'Policing and the Media' in T. Newburn (ed) *Handbook of Policing* (2nd edn) Cullompton: Willan.

Reiner, R. (2010) *The Politics of the Police* (4th edn) Oxford: Oxford University Press.

Savage, S., Charman, S., and Cope, S. (2000) 'The Policy-Making Context: Who Shapes Policing Policy?' in F. Leishman *et al.* (eds) *Core Issues in Policing.* Harlow: Longman.

Scarman, Lord. (1981) *The Brixton Disorders 10-12 April 1981: Report of an Inquiry by Lord Scarman.* London: HMSO.

Sharp, D. and Wilson, D. (2002) '"Household Security": Private policing and vigilantism in Doncaster', *Howard Journal of Criminal Justice* 39(2): 113–31.

Shearing, C. (2000) 'A "New Beginning" for Policing', *Journal of Law and Society* 27(3): 386–93.

Skolnik, J. (1966) *Justice Without Trial: Law Enforcement in a Democratic Society.* New York: Wiley.

Waddington, D. (2007) *Public Order Policing: Theory and Practice.* Cullompton: Willan.

Waddington, P.A.J. (1999) 'Police (Canteen) Sub-Culture: An Appreciation', *British Journal of Criminology* 39(2): 286–308.

Waddington, P.A.J. and Wright, M. (2008) 'Police Use of Force, Firearms and Riot Control' in T. Newburn (ed) *Handbook of Policing* (2nd edn) Cullompton: Willan.

Waddington, P.A.J., Stenson, K., and Don, D. (2004) 'In proportion: Race and police stop and search', *British Journal of Criminology* 44(6): 889–914.

Wakefield, A. (2003) *Selling Security: The Private Policing of Public Space.* Cullompton: Willan.

Walker, N. (2000) *Policing in a Changing Constitutional Order.* London: Sweet and Maxwell.

Westmarland, L. (2008) 'Police Cultures' in T. Newburn (2008) *Handbook of Policing* (2nd edn) Cullompton: Willan.

Zedner, L. (2009) *Security.* London: Routledge.

NOTE

1. For more information about the policing arrangements in Scotland and Northern Ireland, the reader is referred to Donnelly and Scott (2008), and Mulcahy (2008), respectively.

24

Community sentences and offender management for adults

Anne Worrall and Rob Canton

INTRODUCTION

When the topic of punishment is discussed, many people think first about imprisonment. Yet the vast majority of people who are sentenced for crimes are not sent to prison but punished in the community (see Figure 24.1). This chapter explores and explains the history, philosophies, current practices and policy debates surrounding those sanctions which are, though misleadingly, frequently referred to as 'alternatives to prison'. It will be argued that community sentences should not be viewed merely as 'alternatives' to prison but understood as representing a different sphere of penal regulation which is based on enabling and requiring offenders to take responsibility for changing their own lives and behaviour without the physical constraints of imprisonment. Discussion begins with a brief introduction to the terminology and key concepts of community sentences. There will then follow a more detailed description of the range of sentences available to courts, the relevant legislation and the extent to which these sentences are used. A brief history of the Probation Service—the agency responsible for most community sentences—will follow, concluding with the creation of the National Offender Management Service and the setting up of probation trusts. The chapter then proceeds to an analysis of the main issues and problems presented by offender management, including an exploration of the impact of the 'What Works' agenda, which dominated developments in this area during the late 1990s and into the early part of the twenty-first century. It ends by considering probation in other countries. The concluding section of the chapter will summarize the relevant key facts, concepts and debates.

BACKGROUND

There is no single generic term for punishment that does not involve imprisonment. The most commonly used terms are 'alternatives to custody' or 'non-custodial sentences', but 'community punishment', 'community corrections', 'community penalties', 'community sentences' and, in Europe, 'community sanctions and measures' are now widely recognized terms, though 'community' in this context means little more than 'not in prison'. The term 'community' is difficult to define because it has different meanings in different contexts. It conjures up images of neighbourliness, mutual aid and a positive sense of belonging, while, at the same time, blurring the boundaries of responsibility between the State and the individual. In relation to crime, it is not clear whether 'the community' is tolerant, resourceful and healing or intolerant, fearful and punitive (Worrall and Hoy, 2005) nor whether the community has responsibilities towards offenders and ex-offenders. The extent to which the 'community' is involved in community sentences in practice is generally very limited and the implication that such sentences enhance social inclusion, rather than exacerbate social exclusion, is also debatable (see Chapter 14). The phrase 'punishment in the community' entered penal vocabulary in a government discussion paper in 1988 (Home Office, 1988) and was an attempt to dislodge prison from its central position in penal thinking. It became integrated into legislation in the Criminal Justice Act 1991, which was the overarching legal framework for sentencing until the Criminal Justice Act 2003 introduced the term 'community order'.

Non-custodial sentences can be classified in three ways: self-regulatory, financial and supervisory (Worrall and Hoy, 2005). Self-regulatory penalties involve some form of public admonition or reprimand which is assumed to be sufficiently shaming of itself to deter the offender from further law-breaking. Financial penalties are of two kinds: fines serve as a form of retribution and deterrence (see Chapter 4) and are paid to the criminal justice system; compensation is paid (through the courts) to the victim of a crime and is intended to provide reparation. Supervisory sentences are imposed when courts believe that the offender should be punished in another way or is unable to stop committing crimes without support or surveillance. They may contain one or more of three elements: (a) rehabilitation (through education, therapeutic programmes, counselling and welfare advice); (b) reparation (through unpaid work for the community); and (c) incapacitation (through curfews and electronic monitoring).

Some community sentences have long histories, while others have been introduced more recently. For example, the origins of probation (the main form of supervision) can be traced back to the late nineteenth century, whereas community service (now unpaid work) was introduced in the 1970s and electronic monitoring in the 1980s. Expansion in the use of supervisory sentences since the 1970s has been due to the desire of governments to be seen to be finding less expensive, but equally demanding, alternatives to imprisonment. This has been termed the 'decarceration' debate and resulted from a loss of confidence in the 1950s and 1960s in the 'rehabilitative ideal' (based on the discredited therapeutic possibilities of institutions such as prisons and psychiatric hospitals). In reality, such expansion has been an accompaniment, rather than an alternative, to a rising prison population (Scull, 1984; Cohen, 1985, see later in this chapter).

It could be argued that community sentences might have several advantages over imprisonment. They allow offenders to retain family ties and employment while also giving them the opportunity to repair the damage they have done to the community and resolve the personal and social problems which may have led to their offending. They enable offenders to avoid the stigma of imprisonment and the risk of becoming embedded in a criminal culture through constant association with other prisoners. Community sentences are also less costly to administer than imprisonment (Centre for Crime and Justice Studies, 2010). Despite these apparent advantages, penal debates and policies have tended to focus mainly on prisons, with community punishment relatively neglected or valued solely for its perceived contribution to reducing levels of imprisonment. Attempts to raise the profile and increase the use of community sentences have encountered a number of difficulties.

First, and of most significance, is the public and media perception that community punishment is a poor substitute for the 'real punishment' of prison. Viewed as 'soft options', community sentences are often represented in debate as weak and undemanding 'let offs', which do not command public confidence. There is, therefore, a constant search among advocates of community sentences to include more—and more demanding—conditions in an attempt to represent community sentences as 'credible' punishment. Second is the hazard of 'net-widening', a term which entered criminal justice vocabulary in the 1960s in the wake of labelling theory (see Chapter 4). With the proliferation of alternatives to custody comes the danger that instead of keeping people out of prison, community sentences will simply draw more and more people into the 'net' of the criminal justice system (Cohen, 1985), thus increasing the likelihood that they will eventually end up in prison (see later). Thirdly, community sentences require people to *do* something and this creates the possibility that they may fail to comply. Since it is not possible to default on imprisonment in this way, prison can seem like an attractive option in responding to non-compliance. Courts accordingly have (and quite often exercise) the right to send to prison any offender who fails to pay a fine or who breaches the conditions of a supervisory order. In this way, community sentencing always functions 'in the shadow' of imprisonment. A fourth problem arises from the increased political emphasis since the early/mid-1990s on public protection. While curfews and electronic monitoring can be used to regulate people's movements, the physical restraints of imprisonment are felt to provide a level of protection that community sentences could never achieve. In short, if punishment and public protection are regarded as the priorities in sentencing, prison seems uniquely suitable and community sentences are always likely to struggle to demonstrate their credibility.

Types of community sentences and sentencing trends

Just as there is no agreement on a collective name for penalties that do not involve imprisonment, there is also dispute about whether or not the term 'community sentences' should include sentences that do not involve some form of supervision by the Probation Service (see later in this chapter). For the purposes of this chapter and in order to provide a comprehensive introduction to the full range of non-custodial sentences, we will use the term in its broadest sense.

Self-regulatory sentences are those which do not impose any immediate sanction on an offender. They assume that the very fact of being detected, arrested and, in some cases, taken to court, will discourage further offending, without need of further penalty. Formal police cautions, reprimands and warnings are used very widely for juvenile offenders (see Chapter 17), especially those committing first or minor offences. They are also available for adults but are used less frequently, accounting for some 22 per cent of all known offenders in 2011 (Ministry of Justice, 2012a). For adults, the most common self-regulatory sentence is known as a 'conditional discharge'. This involves a court appearance but the offender is put 'on trust' for a period of time. If they re-offend during that period, they are liable to be resentenced for the original offence, as well as for the new one. Over the past decade, the use of the conditional discharge has declined from 7.2 per cent of all sentences to 6.6 per cent (Ministry of Justice, 2012a). Other self-regulatory sentences are available for special situations but are used less frequently. For example, it is possible for a court to 'bind over' people 'to keep the peace' for a specified length of time. Financial penalties remain the most commonly imposed sentences in the courts of England and Wales although their use has declined from 70 per cent of all sentences in 2001 to 65 per cent in 2011 (Ministry of Justice, 2012a), possibly in part due to the increase in police-administered, out-of-court, on-the-spot fines. The two main types of financial penalty are fines and compensation. Advocates of the fine argue that it is a very flexible sentence which can take account of the offender's ability to pay as well as the seriousness of the offence. Thus, it combines elements of retribution (reflecting the seriousness of a crime), deterrence (convincing the offender that crime, literally, 'does not pay') and reparation (paying society and/or compensating the victim for harm done). However, many people are either unable or unwilling to pay fines and are then sent to prison 'in default'. In an attempt to resolve this problem, in the early 1990s, courts experimented with 'unit fines' which involved a specific formula whereby the amount of the fine was determined not only by the seriousness of their offence but also by the offender's disposable income (Home Office, 1990). This system received an (unfairly) bad press (Cavadino, Crow and Dignan, 1999) and the experiment was quickly discontinued. Fewer offenders now go to prison for 'fine default' than in the past but, because they usually spend only a few days there, they are under-represented in prison population statistics (Ministry of Justice, 2012b). Aware of this problem, courts have become more cautious about imposing fines, especially on unemployed offenders and also on women, who often do not have an independent source of income and are responsible for the care of children (Hedderman and Gelsthorpe, 1997). The core problem is that the amount of the fine must look like an adequate response to the seriousness of the crime, but must be realistically payable by offenders, most of whom have limited means. Compensation to a victim can be ordered as a separate sentence or as an adjunct to any other sentence. It is also possible for courts to confiscate the proceeds from serious offences.

Supervisory sentences come in many forms. Under the Criminal Justice Act 2003, implemented in 2005, all formerly separate orders were subsumed under the generic term 'community sentence'. A community order is made up of one or more of the following requirements: supervision (formerly known as a probation order); unpaid work (formerly known as community service); activities; programmes; prohibited activities; curfew (with or without electronic monitoring); exclusion; residence; mental health treatment; drug rehabilitation; alcohol treatment; and attendance centre (for those under age 25). Traditionally, supervisory sentences have aimed to reform or rehabilitate offenders through advice, counselling, treatment and constructive activity. Unpaid work also contains strong elements of reparation to the community. Increasingly, however, the term 'supervision' is accompanied by the terms 'intensive' and/or 'monitoring', reflecting a change of ethos towards the principle of 'incapacitation' in the name of public protection. Restricting offenders' liberty, checking on their whereabouts and gathering ever more information (or 'intelligence') about them, are routine features of contemporary supervision which, especially for those assessed as likely to commit offences resulting in serious harm, typically involves the police and the probation service working closely together in multi-agency public protection arrangements (MAPPA). The use of electronic monitoring to ensure compliance with curfew requirements is but an extreme example of current trends towards 'incapacitation in the community'.

Figure 24.1 shows the comparative proportionate sentencing trends in prison (including suspended sentences), supervisory sentences, fines and conditional discharges over the past decade. As will be discussed, there is little evidence that the increased use of community sentences has reduced the use of imprisonment and some evidence that they have been used as alternatives to fines and conditional discharges.

Supervision

The probation order has a long history dating back to 1907 in England and Wales. Its traditional purpose was to offer advice, assistance and friendship to offenders, in the belief that they could thus be reformed or rehabilitated. More emphasis is now placed on restricting offenders' liberty, protecting the public and preventing re-offending. Offenders are selected for probation through a process of assessment by a probation officer who advises

Year	2001	2002	2003	2004	2005	2006	2007	2008	2009	2010	2011
Immediate custody and suspended sentence	8	8	8	7	7	8	10	10	10	11	11
Community sentences	12	13	14	13	14	14	14	14	14	14	14
Fines	71	69	68	70	70	68	67	66	66	67	65
Conditional discharges	7	7	7	7	6	6	7	7	6	6	7

Figure 24.1 Rate (%) of selected sentencing outcomes for adult offenders in England and Wales

Source: Table Q5.4, Ministry of Justice (2012a).

the court in a pre-sentence report. Supervision, which can be between six months and three years in length, requires the offender to maintain contact with their supervising officer and to tell their supervisor about changes in their circumstances. Failure to comply with these conditions constitutes a breach of the order and the offender can be resentenced, and, as we have seen, this may lead to imprisonment.

Supervision may also be combined with other requirements, so that an offender must live at an approved residence (which can include probation hostels, now known as Approved Premises), undergo psychiatric treatment or attend treatment programmes or other activities. Since effective practice often calls for the intervention of a number of different organizations and disciplines, the work of the probation service has come to be understood as *offender management*. Rather than seeking to provide all services personally, the offender manager undertakes assessment, makes referral to other specialist agencies as appropriate, coordinates their work and ensures that the sentence plan is put into effect.

Unpaid work

Community service was introduced in England and Wales in 1973 and requires offenders to undertake unpaid work in the community for between 60 and 300 hours. It was introduced because of concern about the rising prison population and the apparent ineffectiveness of probation orders to reduce re-offending. It has a chameleon-like ability to adapt its aims and objectives to almost every traditional justification of punishment—retribution (visible hard work), reparation (unpaid work for the community), deterrence (working for no reward), and rehabilitation (learning skills and/or achieving something of worth). This has made it very popular with sentencers, who see it as having the flexibility of a fine but without its disadvantages. It has been described as a fine on time. Offenders typically work in groups on projects involving land restoration, painting, decorating and woodwork, or on individual placements with charity shops, voluntary organizations and so on. Unpaid work is now represented as *community payback*—a perhaps intentionally ambiguous term that has both retributive and repara-tive connotations—and members of the public have been invited to identify suitable tasks. Offenders are normally required to wear high visibility jackets to mark their status so that the consequences of crime and the realities of the punishment are more apparent. Although unpaid work has been supervised by the probation service since its beginning, it is likely that the voluntary and commercial sectors will become increasingly involved as the recommendations of the Carter Review and the Offender Management Act 2007 are put into effect (see later). In 2011, a tendering exercise took place to deliver unpaid work and proposals were put forward by private companies, sometimes in joint bids with the public sector probation trusts.

Curfew requirement with electronic monitoring

Electronic monitoring was introduced experimentally in England and Wales in the 1980s for a number of reasons. It was seen as a way to reduce prison overcrowding and costs and was used in its early pilot schemes for offenders awaiting trial or sentence who might otherwise have been held in custody (Nellis, 2004). It was seen as a sophisticated way to subject offenders to some of the restrictions of prison without inflicting the damage of removing them from their home environment. The Probation Service regarded the innovation with suspicion and sometimes explicitly opposed it, leaving the way open for an opportunity, welcomed by the government, to promote private sector involvement in punishment in the community as well as running prisons.

Offenders are fitted with a special anklet which is connected electronically to a tele-phone which is, in turn, connected to a call centre, which monitors the offender's whereabouts. Offenders have individualized schedules requiring them to be at home between certain hours. There are now two distinct ways in which electronic monitor-ing is used: first, courts can include curfew requirements with electronic monitoring in a community sentence; second, prisoners may be released several weeks before the end of their sentence, on condition that they are monitored. Both measures have been avail-able nationally since 1999 and electronic monitoring has been incorporated increasingly into a number of community sentences, especially intensive ones, in order to provide a stronger element of surveillance (Hucklesby, 2008).

Although most of the early technological problems relating to 'tagging' have now been overcome, there remain other matters of concern. Some people argue that it is an infringe-ment of civil liberties and encourages 'net-widening' (resulting in minor offenders being 'tagged' who would not have gone to prison anyway). Others point to the visible stigma of the tag (or, alternatively, the danger that it becomes a 'badge of honour' for some young offenders). Yet others have suggested that confining certain offenders to their homes may place a strain on other members of their family. The tag can only tell the monitoring system that the offender is not at home: it cannot help to locate people. There have therefore been experimental schemes to monitor the whereabouts of offenders through *satellite tracking* although this is not widely used in UK (Shute, 2007). If tracking were to become more com-mon, there would appear to be considerable potential for more reliable community incapaci-tation, but at the same time difficult questions about human rights would certainly arise.

Drug rehabilitation requirements

Drug Treatment and Testing Orders were introduced with the Crime and Disorder Act 1998 and drug rehabilitation is included as a requirement of a community order. These orders constitute a government response to the increasing number of offenders who appear to commit crimes to finance their drug addictions and are aimed at those who are willing to cooperate with treatment, supervision and urine testing. They have been criticized for over-simplifying the link between drug use and crime. There is also an argument that, since drug users must be motivated to reduce or abstain, treatment under compulsion is unlikely to be effective, although Hough and Mitchell showed that 'coerced treatment is no less effective than treatment on a voluntary basis' (2003: 42), recognizing that many substance users are ambivalent about their usage. As with other penal innovations, drug treatment orders have also been criticized for being used for 'petty' offenders (net-widening), for not taking sufficient account of the needs of women and minority ethnic offenders, and for not providing sufficient social support to ensure that rehabilitation is sustained (Rumgay, 2004). An interesting feature of drug rehabilitation orders is that they involve continuing oversight by the court, who will see the offender regularly to monitor progress. Since there have been some positive experiences here, this may foreshadow greater involvement by courts in the management of an order in other circumstances as well.

Suspended sentences

Finally, suspended sentences of imprisonment now commonly involve an element of supervision. Legally, a suspended sentence is a term of imprisonment and should only be imposed when the offence is so serious that no other sentence can be justified. This sentence had fallen into disuse after the 1991 Act, but the Criminal Justice Act 2003 gave courts the power to impose the same range of requirements when imposing a suspended sentence as are available for a community order, so that the positive advantages of supervision may be combined with the specific threat of imprisonment for a further offence. There is little evidence, however, that the new suspended sentences are being used instead of short custodial sentences and indeed, some signs of widening the net by drawing in numbers of people who might have been dealt with by a community order or less (Mair and Mills, 2009; Mair, 2011). One reason why this was a particular worry was that breach of the suspended sentence ought (in law) to lead to an immediate custodial sentence, although in practice this does not always occur.

REVIEW QUESTION

1 What different types of community penalties are there?

2 What principles of sentencing underpin these different sentences?

3 What have been the main features of trends in community sentencing over the past decade?

The National Probation Service and National Offender Management Service (NOMS)

In this section we briefly trace the history of the Probation Service (for more detail, see Canton, 2011; Mair and Burke, 2012). There is a broad consensus that the earliest recognizable 'probation officers' were the 'police court missionaries' who worked in London courts in the last quarter of the nineteenth century. Their job, which was religiously motivated, was to rescue and befriend drunken offenders, setting them on the path to redemption. Secular probation officers have been a presence in all criminal courts since the Probation of Offenders Act 1907, and from the 1930s, they were trained as social workers, influenced by 'welfare' and 'medical' models of delinquency (Chui and Nellis, 2003). From the 1970s, however, such models became discredited and probation officers became increasingly influenced by 'non-treatment paradigms' (Bottoms and McWilliams, 1979) and increasingly exercised about securing the correct balance between 'care' and 'control' in their work with offenders. By the end of the twentieth century, probation officers had to accept that their role was to 'confront, control and monitor' and not merely to 'advise, assist and befriend' (Worrall and Hoy, 2005). Organizationally, until 2001, each of over 50 area Probation Services was managed locally, although most of the Service's funding came from central government. Each Probation Service had its own Chief Probation Officer and, like the police, there was no centralized organization or spokesperson for the Service. The Home Office did not significantly direct the running of local services until 1984 when it produced a Statement of National Objectives and Priorities (SNOP). The content of SNOP was not particularly contentious, but the fact that it had been produced at all certainly was and it proved to be the start of a debate lasting almost two decades on the management of the Probation Service. By the 1990s, a *National Standards* document was promulgated, stipulating how supervision had to be undertaken and, by the middle of the decade, training for probation officers (which had previously constituted a specialism within social work training courses) had been separated completely from social work. By the end of that decade, the government was mooting the abolition of the name 'Probation' altogether and considering the merger of probation and prisons into one correctional service (Home Office, 1998; Raynor, 2007). This caused much protest and the eventual compromise was the creation in 2001 of a centralized National Probation Service with a Director. The number of areas was reduced from 54 to 42 and, as we have already seen, the names of the main court orders were changed. These changes both reflected and confirmed a major change of ethos for the Probation Service which now affirmed its objectives as 'enforcement, rehabilitation and public protection' (National Probation Service, 2001). This has had considerable implications for work with offenders:

- *Enforcement* meant ensuring that offenders met the requirements of their orders. Returning an offender to court for non-compliance with an order (known as 'breaching'), which had been seen in the past as an admission of failure by the probation officer, was now viewed as essential to maintaining the credibility of orders and an act of strength (Hedderman, 2003; Hedderman and Hough, 2004).

- *Rehabilitation* was to shift away from focusing on the welfare of the offender (with some ill-defined hope that this would lead in some way to reform) towards the reduction of re-offending measured through reduced reconviction rates.

- *Public protection* was to be achieved through robust assessment and management of risk. The level of risk became the single most important criterion in determining the amount and type of subsequent intervention. Every offender who goes to prison or is placed on a community order is subject to an assessment of their risk of re-offending and of causing serious harm. There are various methods of calculating risk but the most widely used is a computerized system called the Offender Assessment System (OASys) (Burnett, Baker and Roberts, 2007; Kemshall and Wood, 2007). Under the National Offender Management Model, work with offenders is now divided into four 'tiers', depending on levels of risk and dangerousness. Tier 1 offenders are to be punished; tier 2 offenders are to be punished and helped; tier 3 offenders punished, helped and changed; tier 4 offenders punished, helped, changed and controlled (NOMS, 2006).

There have been further radical changes in the governance of probation. In 2003, the Carter Review (Carter, 2003) and subsequent government response (Home Office, 2004a) proposed a new National Offender Management Service (NOMS) which would finally bring together the Prison and Probation Services (from June 2004) to provide 'end-to-end management of all offenders, whether they are serving sentences in prison, the community or both' (Home Office, 2004b). Carter had envisaged that the services typically provided by probation areas might be provided by others—independent, 'voluntary' organizations and even by the private and commercial sector. It was argued that competition between providers would raise standards generally. The Offender Management Act 2007 therefore empowered the Secretary of State (the Minister of Justice) to commission services directly, with the clear implication that they may be commissioned from other providers. In 2010, the 42 probation areas of England and Wales were reconstituted as 35 Probation Trusts, who would both provide probation services and would also themselves commission services from others. In January 2013, developments were given a further impetus in a government proposal to commission much more work from the voluntary and commercial sectors. A great deal of work that has until now been undertaken by probation staff in the public sector is likely to be provided in future by other sectors who will be 'paid by results' (as measured by reconviction rates). The government believes that market competition will raise standards generally and that many less risky offenders should be supervised by independent agencies. Critics object that the proposals represent a triumph of ideological conviction over the evidence of past experiences, that the public sector trusts are already working effectively with other providers and that the distinction between more and less risky offenders erroneously assumes that risk is static.

REVIEW QUESTION

1 In what ways has the Probation Service changed since its early days in the late nineteenth century?

2 What are the priorities of the National Offender Management Service (NOMS)?

3 What might be the advantages and drawbacks of involving the private sector in the work of offender management?

Ways of understanding the politics of punishment in the community

In this section we consider different ways of explaining and understanding (or theorizing about) the development of community penalties.

A conventional account argues that penal reform has been uneven but progressive and that alternatives to custody represent the enlightened values of an ever more civilized society. Most histories see probation as rejection of the excesses of punishment within the humanitarian considerations of Victorian and Edwardian penal reformers. Raynor and Vanstone (2002), however, provide a more critical summary, emphasizing the dimension of 'moral training': reformers came to believe that crime was a social disease to be cured through 'specific practices of normalization, classification, categorization and discrimination between criminal types' (Garland, 1985: 32). Social control could now be achieved 'through attention to the material, social and psychological welfare of criminals' (Worrall and Hoy, 2005: 4) rather than by sending them to prison. Throughout the twentieth century a range of non-custodial penalties developed, adding increasing numbers of conditions and restrictions on offenders' freedom, while stopping short of imprisonment. As we have seen, courts are now able to require offenders to reside in certain places, to receive psychiatric or drug treatment, to attend therapeutic programmes, to perform unpaid work or to observe curfews that are monitored electronically. The aim of all these requirements is to prevent offenders from re-offending without resorting to prison. In this way, it is argued, the public is more likely to be protected in the longer term because imprisonment protects the public for only a short while and, by cutting offenders' social ties and fuelling their resentment, may make them more likely to re-offend (Maruna, 2000; Farrall, 2002).

But the rehabilitative ideal came increasingly under attack in the 1960s and 1970s for both ideological and pragmatic reasons. Ideologically, attempts at offender rehabilitation were regarded as, on the one hand, intrusive and an infringement of civil liberties and, on the other hand, as a 'soft option'—an indulgence of middle-class liberals out of touch with the 'real' world of crime victimization. Pragmatically, it seemed that rehabilitation just did not 'work' and, in some cases, made matters worse (Worrall and Hoy, 2005: 24). At the same time, imprisonment was increasingly seen as both unsuccessful and expensive. In an attempt to manage a swelling prison population, while responding to a popular demand for stern punishment, the government urged *punishment in the community*: punishment was fitting and proper, but did not have to take place in prison. The implications of this political position for probation have been profound. Probation has had to describe its work and present its worth in the terms of a debate set by punitive priorities, to show itself as tough and prison-like. Its success in this respect, not surprisingly, has been limited. This account, then, understands community sentencing not as benevolent progress, but as a pragmatic strategy to deal with a large prison population.

Yet a more radical critique questions the assumed relationship between prison and community sentences: rather than cutting into the prison population, 'alternatives' commonly take the place of other alternatives—or are imposed on offenders who might at other times been given a lesser penalty. Cohen (1985) argued that the relationship between prison and its supposed alternatives is more symbiotic than competitive:

they work together to extend and disperse social control. One well-known hazard of non-custodial sanctions is their net widening potential (Cohen, 1985): they may divert some offenders from custody, but draw in many more who might otherwise have been dealt with in less intrusive and cheaper ways—notably by financial penalties. It is indeed difficult to point to contemporary examples of 'alternatives' leading directly to a reduction in a prison population. Between 1998 and 2008 the number of people receiving a custodial sentence increased by 2 per cent but during the same period the number of community sentences also increased and was nearly one-third higher in 2009 (when the prison population was about 83,000) than in 1999 (when the prison population was 64,770) (Ministry of Justice, 2011).

Community sentences can even perversely serve to increase the numbers of prisoners. There may be a 'recoil' effect (Bottoms, 1987) whereby people sentenced to an 'alternative' come back to court, are regarded as having failed on their last chance and deserving of imprisonment. Again, the attempt to make community sanctions more demanding while simultaneously ensuring more rigorous enforcement is also likely to lead to more breach action—and perhaps to custodial sentences as a result.

The aspiration to reduce the prison population by providing community 'alternatives' has brought substantial disappointment. While sanctions introduced as direct alternatives sometimes achieve some initial success in diverting people from terms of imprisonment, over time they go 'down tariff', widening the net to include people who had before been sentenced to other community sanctions or to financial penalties. This has brought onto probation caseloads offenders who not only do not need such levels of intervention, but for whom there is no evidence that such interventions will be effective. This increase in workload dilutes probation's potential to work effectively with those who most need and might benefit from its interventions (Morgan and Smith, 2003). Community programmes, far from reducing the restrictions on criminals who might otherwise have been sent to prison, create a new clientele of criminals who are controlled or disciplined by other mechanisms. Once caught in the 'net' of social control, the penetration of disciplinary intervention is ever deeper, reaching every aspect of an offender's life.

REVIEW QUESTION

1 How might we explain the historical development of community penalties?

2 Why have community orders failed to reduce the prison population?

3 Should community orders be made 'tougher'? How?

Diversity and punishment in the community

There has been a long-standing concern about equality and diversity with regard to community punishment, involving complex questions about how unfairness is to be identified and redressed. Gelsthorpe (2007) notes that there have been accusations of *too much* disparity between black and white offenders (an unfair exaggeration of difference) and *not enough* differentiation between men and women (an unfair denial of difference). While this section attends particularly to race and gender, there are other dimensions of difference that need careful attention (Canton, 2011: Chapter 3).

Traditionally, the probation order was the sentence 'of choice' for women. They were considered ideally suited to being 'advised, assisted and befriended' (to adapt the words of the original Probation of Offenders Act 1907), in need of help rather than punishment. But the influence of feminist perspectives on criminal justice (further informed by theories of labelling and deviancy amplification—see Chapter 4) led many probation officers to be concerned that too many women were being placed on probation and, more significantly, too early in their criminal careers. The good intentions of probation officers in recommending supervisory sentences for women appeared to result in 'net-widening' and ultimately accelerated a woman's journey to custody. There was an assumption that diverting women from probation would automatically reduce the numbers in prison. As Eaton (1986) and Worrall (1990) demonstrated, probation officers' court reports constructed women within the ideological constraints of the family and inadvertently reinforced sentencers' stereotyped views on 'good' and 'bad' women. This emerging gender awareness among probation officers resulted in a concerted effort to write non- or anti-discriminatory reports striving to avoid collusion with such stereotyping.

The effort was partially successful: fewer women were placed on probation for minor offences, and for a while in the early 1990s, there was some cause for optimism. The Criminal Justice Act 1991, based on the principle of 'just deserts', *should* have resulted in a fairer deal for women criminals. If sentencing was to depend predominantly on the seriousness of the current offence, the implication *should* have been that fewer women would go to prison for relatively minor offences, however frequently committed. But as the overall prison population rose (see Chapter 25), the numbers of women being sent to prison sharply increased, rising steadily from 1,500 in 1992 to 4,300 in 2002 (remaining around that figure ever since and constituting about 5 per cent of the total prison population)—even though this cannot be explained by the seriousness or frequency of their offending (Gelsthorpe and Morris, 2002). The traditional probation order came to be seen as inadequate punishment for women who were typically no longer regarded as in need of 'help' and courts made increasing use of community sentences that were regarded as more punitive—community service orders and orders combining probation and community service.

In the early days of community service (now unpaid work), there was a marked gender difference with disproportionately fewer women receiving these orders (McIvor, 2004; Worrall and Hoy, 2005: 120). Courts have always viewed it as not quite an appropriate sentence for women and the practicalities have always been an obstacle—mainly the absence of childcare facilities (Howard League, 1999). The numbers are now more nearly proportionate, but there remain differences in the age profile of men and women undertaking unpaid work, their criminal histories and in the likelihood of successful completion of the order (McIvor, 2007). There is debate about what constitutes appropriate unpaid work for women. Should they be encouraged to broaden their horizons and do 'male' work or should they stick to what they know in order to get through the hours? Such problems are well known and by no means irresolvable. What is required is a change from the attitude that regards unpaid work as predominantly a punishment for 'fit, young men' (Worrall and Hoy, 2005: 133). Better childcare arrangements, more female supervisors and consideration for the kind of working environments most suit-able for women would also result in greater use. Whatever the perceived disadvantages to women of doing unpaid work, they cannot possibly outweigh the disadvantages of imprisoning those same women. More generally, despite a commitment to challenging unfair discrimination over many years—and some undoubted progress—community provision for women offenders remains uneven and often inadequate (Gelsthorpe, Sharp and Roberts 2007; Worrall and Gelsthorpe, 2009).

The use of community sentences for black and minority ethnic (BME) offenders has also been controversial (Durrance and Williams, 2003). It is well-established that BME offenders are over-represented in prison in relation to their distribution in the gen-eral population—26 per cent of the prison population was from a BME group in 2010 (Ministry of Justice, 2012b). What is less clear is whether or not this over-representation is due to discrimination (either direct or indirect) within society and/or the criminal jus-tice system (see Chapter 16) and what contribution, if any, the Probation Service makes to that discrimination. The proportion of BME offenders on community sentences remains stable at around 15 per cent but the proportion on post-prison release supervision has risen to 22 per cent, due to an increase in Asian and 'mixed other' prisoners (Ministry of Justice, 2011). Research literature is inconclusive (Powis and Walmsley, 2002; Phillips and Bowling, 2007) but there is widespread concern that community sentences are not meet-ing the needs of BME offenders. This may be because the theoretical underpinnings of contemporary rehabilitative programmes (see later) fail to take sufficient account of the particular experiences of poverty, racism and exclusion of many black and Asian offend-ers. Projects which seek to combine the cognitive behavioural methods with approaches that emphasize issues of identity and empowerment may be the most promising (Lewis *et al.*, 2006; Gelsthorpe and McIvor, 2007).

REVIEW QUESTION

1 What issues arise when considering the appropriateness of community sentences for different demographic groups?

2 How might the use of community sentences discriminate against BME offenders?

3 Do you think that women's offending is more likely to be linked with their welfare needs? If so, is supervision (probation) the best response?

Soft options? Community sentences and populist punitiveness

The policy of 'bifurcation' (separating out the 'minor' from the 'dangerous' criminals) has been a feature of the politicization of crime in the past two decades and has allowed successive governments to sustain a paradoxical rhetoric of supporting alternatives to prison while arguing that there are many 'dangerous' criminals for whom alternatives are simply not 'suitable' (Bottoms, 2007). Since criminal 'dangerousness' is very much 'in the eye of the beholder', this line of official rhetoric has stimulated 'populist punitive-ness', resulting in the chronic under-use and under-resourcing of alternatives to custody. Raynor and Vanstone (2002) argue that 'crime-related issues [are] defined by political elites as problems of insufficient punishment or as being "soft" on criminals' (2002: 69). By playing on understandable public concerns about crime, supporting biased media coverage and fuelling moral panics, it is argued that politicians use crime-related issues to manipulate public opinion. Within this discourse, the only acceptable kind of community sentence is a 'tough' one, the implication being that most community sentences are far from 'tough'—even though prison, for all its pains and hardships, makes few demands, while taking responsibility for one's own behaviour in the context of a community penalty can be truly challenging. The dialogue between probation officers and governments (for a detailed account of one such dialogue, see Worrall and Hoy, 2005) has been centred on the so-called 'strengthening' of community sentences by imposing increasingly unrealistic 'conditions'. Carlen (1989) has referred to this process as being one which disregards 'sentencing feasibility'. Practitioners often refer to it as 'setting an offender up to fail'.

Attempts have been made to show that community sentences are tough, by emphasizing punitive components and by increasing the intensity of supervision, coupled with greater monitoring or surveillance. Building on the perceived achievements of multi-agency public protection arrangements established mainly to manage the risks of known sex offenders, the police and probation have worked in partnership in prolific (or persistent) offender projects in England and Wales, which represent an extension of the theoretical underpinnings, policy objectives and multi-agency practices of previous intensive supervision schemes. Combining penal philosophies of deterrence, incapacitation and rehabilitation, they seek to provide a mix of frequent contact, access to treatment (particularly drugs treatment) and community facilities, and constant monitoring. They also seek to demonstrate cost-effectiveness and increased public safety. Further extension of these principles to groups of less serious, but prolific, offenders—including those who have been released after short sentences of imprisonment—have led to schemes known as *integrated offender management* (see Canton, 2011: Chapter 10).

The major departure from previous projects, however, is that such schemes do not merely rely on offenders to reduce their own rates of re-offending. This was always the weakest link in the chain and the one which consistently undermined claims of success. Instead, it is now accepted that prompt re-arrest (resulting from increased intelligence and monitoring) is also a measure of success. There is, however, a serious flaw in this logic. The possibility that a project could claim success entirely on the basis of numbers of arrests and breaches of orders does seem to be somewhat at odds with the spirit of the exercise. Nevertheless, the political expectation is that those who do not respond promptly to the 'carrot' of rehabilitative efforts should experience the 'stick' of enforcement (Farrall, Mawby and Worrall, 2007).

REVIEW QUESTION

1 What is meant by the term 'populist punitiveness' in relation to community sentences?

2 In what ways have community sentences been 'strengthened' in response to calls for greater public protection?

3 If more offenders subject to intensive supervision are arrested for their offending or for a breach of requirements, is this a success in detection/enforcement—or a failure of the scheme?

Community sentences and the 'What Works?' agenda

The nature of probation intervention has changed radically in the past two decades. Personal counselling, based on psychotherapeutic approaches, has been replaced by cognitive behavioural programmes, based on social learning theory (McGuire, 2001). Rather than attempting to change the whole personality or circumstances of an offender, cognitive behavioural programmes focus on specific unacceptable behaviours and seek to modify these by correcting distortions in the way offenders think about their crimes. Offenders are required to accept full responsibility for their actions (instead of blaming the victim or their circumstances), empathize with the victim of their offences and expand their repertoire of responses to those situations which have previously triggered a criminal response. Programmes may focus on generic cognitive skills or cover a range of specific problem behaviours such as anger management, drink-impaired driving and sex offending.

These programmes collectively formed the 'What Works?' agenda—an explicit rejoinder to the claim that *nothing works* (that no intervention can be shown to be more effective than any other). The 'discovery' of cognitive behavioural programmes (initially in North America) gave rise to a series of conferences entitled 'What Works?' (McGuire, 1995). The phrase caught the imagination of politicians and professionals and came to dominate probation intervention in the English-speaking world. Evaluation research gives cause for cautious optimism in respect of the effectiveness of such programmes in reducing re-offending (Stanley, 2009) although critics have argued that enthusiasm for the cognitive behavioural approach should not result in the neglect of other provision such as basic literacy skills and social skills. Nor should the wider social problems that may lead people into crime be overlooked (Mair, 2004; Raynor, 2007). The recognition that rehabilitation depends not only on changes in offenders' thinking and attitudes, but on fair access to opportunities has been supported by findings from desistance research (McNeill and Weaver, 2010). Desistance—stopping offending and continuing to lead a law-abiding life—depends upon the individuals coming to see themselves no longer as an offender but as a different kind of person, ceasing to regard crime an option for excitement or as a likely response to difficulties. The 'good lives' (Ward and Maruna, 2007) in which this becomes possible depend upon not only a changed self-identity, but on relationships and on opportunities (including employment and accommodation) which allow people to develop ways of living in which offending comes to have no place. These insights point to the limits of what criminal justice and the penal system can achieve on their own and to the need for probation to work in partnership with other agencies of civil society, including health, education, housing and employment services. This in turn has implications for how probation should be organized and managed.

REVIEW QUESTION

1 What are the main components of contemporary rehabilitative interventions with offenders?

2 What criticisms have been made of the 'What Works?' agenda?

3 If desistance depends 'on relationships and on opportunities (including employment and accommodation) which allow people to develop ways of living in which offending comes to have no place', what is the role of probation in supporting these processes?

Community sentences and probation in other countries

Some of the challenges and limitations of community sentences are not peculiar to England and Wales. Probation agencies are the main provider of community punishments in many other countries. There are several differences between nations in the use of community sentences, the purposes and tasks of probation agencies, their organization and management, the education and training of the workforce (Canton, 2011). At the same time, while the political context of development has been different, some of the experiences of England and Wales have been shared by other countries. Common challenges include:

- Gaining the confidence of the public, politicians and judiciary, especially where probation is new or emerging.

- Improving the quality of service to victims. Probation agencies are acknowledging the legitimate concerns about victims, although they may reject punishment as the best way of vindicating a victim's experience.

- Trying to make sure that tougher community sanctions and enforcement do not lead to more imprisonment.

- Responding to popular punitiveness (Snacken, 2010). Although the origins of punitive attitudes towards offenders are many and complex, they probably include anxiety about risk and uncertainty. Crime, notoriously, can become a focus for all kinds of other concerns, including economic hardship and social change. Perceived threat and insecurity commonly lead to fear and intolerance which may manifest themselves in calls for tougher sentencing. In this context, it becomes difficult for probation to affirm its value and effectiveness without becoming embroiled in the volatile politics of crime and punishment.

- 'Exporting' specific techniques and methods—notably the insights of the 'What Works' research and methods of assessing risk (Canton, 2009; *Probation Journal Special Issue* 2011). Yet, as in England and Wales, it is hard to find evidence from any country that the prison population can be reduced by providing 'alternatives'.

CONCLUSION

In this chapter we have explored the range of punishments which do not involve incarceration that are available to courts. The aim of the chapter has been to demonstrate that, despite the overwhelming focus of the media, penal policy and academic literature on prison and imprisonment, the vast majority of convicted offenders are punished in ways that require them to self-regulate, pay money or cooperate with some form of supervision or monitoring of their behaviour within their own communities. We have identified a number of advantages to dealing with offenders in this way. Apart from the high cost of imprisonment, allowing offenders to remain in conditions of freedom enables them to retain family, social and employment ties, all of which may reduce the likelihood of re-offending. It also avoids the stigma of imprisonment, which is a major contributor to persistent offending, not least by blocking opportunities to desistance.

The chapter has provided an overview of the historical and political development of community penalties, suggesting a number of different ways of theorizing (or explaining) that development. It has traced the main features of the Probation Service over the past century and the changes which have taken it from its religious origins, through to a secular social work profession and its culmination in the twenty-first century as a law enforcement agency concerned primarily with public protection.

However, we have also discussed a number of issues and problems related to community penalties. These include the 'image' of community sentences as being 'soft options' and poor substitutes for imprisonment. The recent history of community penalties has been characterized by the need to respond to populist punitiveness by making such sentences 'tougher'. This has involved a proliferation of additional requirements, combinations of orders, increased intensity of contact and close collaboration with the police and prison services as well as voluntary and private organisations working in the community. Ultimately, it has involved the Probation Service in accepting physical restrictions on an offender's liberty such as electronic monitoring, mandatory drug treatment and even prompt rearrest and incarceration, as being measures of success, rather than measures which undermine the fundamental values of the Service.

The chapter has also explored the issue of diversity and the potential for discrimination in the implementation of community penalties. The particular needs of women offenders and those from minority ethnic groups have been highlighted. Finally, some of the ideas that are central to the 'What Works' agenda for offender rehabilitation have been introduced, as well as more recent research that shows that changes in thinking and behaviour will not be sufficient without fair opportunities for offenders to access services and resources in support of desistance.

QUESTIONS FOR DISCUSSION

1 What are the advantages and disadvantages of dealing with offenders in the community rather than sending them to prison?

2 To what extent do community sentences meet the requirements of punishment for retribution, deterrence, incapacitation, rehabilitation, and/or reparation?

3 Which of the existing community sentences are most suitable for women and why?

4 What are the central principles of the 'What Works' agenda and what are its implications for the treatment of offenders?

5 How, if at all, should community sentences contribute to the reduction of the prison population?

GUIDE TO FURTHER READING

Although research into community sentences remains overshadowed by research into prisons, there now exists an interesting and accessible body of literature in this area.

Canton. R. (2011) *Probation: Working with Offenders*. Abingdon: Routledge.
An up-to-date text that covers all aspects of the work of probation.

Canton, R. and Hancock, D. (2007) *Dictionary of Probation and Offender Management*. Cullompton: Willan Publishing.

An excellent reference book for clarifying all those policy and practice issues that other texts never explain in quite enough detail.

Gelsthorpe, L. and Morgan, R. (2007) *Handbook of Probation*. Cullompton: Willan Publishing.

An edited collection of research-based chapters about probation and offender management.

Mair, G. and Burke, L. (2012) *Redemption, Rehabilitation and Risk Management: a History of Probation*. Abingdon: Routledge.

An engaging and challenging history of the Probation Service.

Robinson, A. (2011) *Foundations for Offender Management*. Bristol: The Policy Press.

A useful handbook for those interested in working in offender management.

WEB LINKS

http://www.justice.gov.uk/about/noms/

The NOMS website includes links to a range of information, research and statistics relating to offender management (prisons and probation).

http://www.homeoffice.gov.uk/

The Home Office website continues to provide a wealth of information and statistics about crime and criminal justice policy, practice and research. It also provides links to many other relevant websites.

http://www.crimeandjustice.org.uk/

The Centre for Crime and Justice Studies offers many invaluable publications, statistics and reports, both about crime and punishment in general and specifically about community punishment (for example, the Community Sentences Digest).

http://www.cep-probation.org/

The website of CEP, the European Probation Organisation, has many useful resources and offers an international perspective on several of the topics considered in this chapter.

http://www.clinks.org/

Clinks supports the voluntary and community sector in working with offenders in England and Wales and gives a good idea of the sector's provision and potential.

REFERENCES

Bottoms, A. and McWilliams, W. (1979) 'A Non-treatment Paradigm for Probation Practice', *British Journal of Social Work* 9, 2: 159–202.

Bottoms, A. (1987) 'Limiting prison use: experiences in England and Wales', *Howard Journal* 26: 177–202.

Bottoms, A. (2007) 'Bifurcation' in R. Canton and D. Hancock (eds) *Dictionary of probation and offender management*. Cullompton: Willan Publishing.

Burnett, R., Baker, K., and Roberts, C. (2007) 'Assessment, supervision and intervention: fundamental practice in probation' in L. Gelsthorpe and R. Morgan (eds) *Handbook of Probation*. Cullompton: Willan Publishing.

Canton, R. (2009) 'Taking probation abroad', *European Probation Journal* 1 (1): 66–78.

Canton. R. (2011) *Probation: Working with Offenders*. Abingdon: Routledge.

Carlen, P. (1989) 'Crime, inequality and sentencing' in P. Carlen and D. Cook (eds) *Paying for Crime*. Milton Keynes: Open University Press.

Carter, P. (2003) *Managing Offenders, Changing Lives*. London: Home Office.

Cavadino, M., Crow, I., and Dignan, J. (1999) *Criminal Justice 2000: Strategies for a New Century*. Winchester: Waterside Press.

Centre for Crime and Justice Studies (2010) *Prison and probation expenditure, 1999–2009* available online at http://www.crimeandjustice.org.uk/opus1793/Prison_and_probation_expenditure_1999-2009.pdf.

Chui, W.H. and Nellis, M. (eds) (2003) *Moving Probation Forward: Evidence, Arguments and Practice*. Harlow: Pearson Longman.

Cohen, S. (1985) *Visions of Social Control*. Cambridge: Polity Press.

Durrance, P. and Williams, P. (2003) 'Broadening the agenda around what works for black and Asian offenders', *Probation Journal* 50, 3: 211–24.

Eaton, M. (1986) *Justice for Women?* Milton Keynes: Open University Press.

Farrall, S. (2002) *Rethinking what Works with Offenders: Probation, Social Context and Desistance from Crime*. Cullompton: Willan Publishing.

Farrall. S., Mawby, R.C., and Worrall, A. (2007) 'Prolific/ persistent offenders and desistance' in L. Gelsthorpe and R. Morgan (eds) *Handbook of Probation*. Cullompton: Willan Publishing.

Gelsthorpe, L. (2007) 'Dealing with Diversity' in Gill McIvor and Peter Raynor (eds) *Developments in Social Work with Offenders, Research Highlights in Social Work 48*. London: Jessica Kingsley.

Gelsthorpe, L. and McIvor, G. (2007) 'Difference and diversity in probation' in L. Gelsthorpe and R. Morgan (eds) *Handbook of Probation*. Cullompton: Willan Publishing.

Gelsthorpe, L. and Morris, A. (2002) 'Women's imprisonment in England and Wales: A penal paradox', *Criminal Justice* 2 (3): 277–301.

Gelsthorpe, L., Sharp, G., and Roberts, J. (2007) *Provision for women offenders in the community*. London: Fawcett Society, available online at http://www.swdc.org.uk/silo/files/provision-for-women-offenders-in-the-community-july-2007-final-report.pdf.

Garland, D. (1985) *Punishment and Welfare: A History of Penal Strategies*. Aldershot: Gower.

Hedderman, C. (2003) 'Enforcing supervision and encouraging compliance' in W.H. Chui and M. Nellis (eds) (2003) *Moving Probation Forward: Evidence, Arguments and Practice*. Harlow: Pearson Longman.

Hedderman, C. and Gelsthorpe, L. (1997) *Understanding the Sentencing of Women* Home Office Research Study 170. London: HMSO.

Hedderman, C. and Hough, M. (2004) 'Getting tough or being effective: what matters?' in G. Mair (ed) *What Matters in Probation*. Cullompton: Willan Publishing.

Home Office (1988) *Punishment, Custody and the Community*, Cm 424. London: HMSO.

Home Office (1990) *Crime, Justice and Protecting the Public*, Cm 965. London: HMSO.

Home Office (1998) *Joining Forces to Protect the Public: Prisons-Probation—A Consultation Document*. London: Home Office.

Home Office (2004a) *Reducing Crime, Changing Lives*. London: Home Office (also available at http://www.homeoffice.gov.uk).

Home Office (2004b) *Reducing Crime, Changing Lives* (press release 5/2004). London: Home Office.

Hough, M. and Mitchell, D. (2003) 'Drug-dependent offenders and Justice for All', in M. Tonry (ed.), *Confronting Crime: Crime Control Policy under New Labour*. Cullompton: Willan.

Howard League (1999) *Do women paint fences too? Women's experience of community service*. London: Howard League for Penal Reform.

Hucklesby, A. (2008) 'Vehicles of desistance? The impact of electronically monitored curfew orders', *Criminology and Criminal Justice*, 8 (1): 51–71.

Lewis, S., Raynor, P., Smith, D., and Wardak, A. (eds) (2006) *Race and Probation*. Cullompton: Willan Publishing.

McGuire, J. (ed) (1995) *What Works: Reducing Reoffending*. Chichester: John Wiley.

McGuire, J. (2001) *Cognitive-Behavioural Approaches—An introduction to theory and research*. London: Home Office.

McIvor, G. (2004) 'Service with a smile? Women and community punishment' in G. McIvor (ed) *Women who Offend, Research highlights in Social Work 44*. London: Jessica Kingsley.

McIvor, G. (2007) 'Paying Back: Unpaid Work by Offenders' in Gill McIvor and Peter Raynor (eds) *Developments in Social Work with Offenders, Research Highlights in Social Work 48*. London: Jessica Kingsley.

McNeill, F. and Weaver, B. (2010) *Changing Lives? Desistance Research and Offender Management*, available online at http://www.sccjr.ac.uk/pubs/Changing-Lives-Desistance-Research-and-Offender-Management/ 255.

Mair, G. (ed) (2004) *What Matters in Probation*. Cullompton: Willan.

Mair, G. (2011) 'The Community Order in England and Wales: Policy and Practice', *Probation Journal* 58 (3): 215–232.

Mair, G. and Mills, H. (2009) *The Community Order and the Suspended Sentence Order three years on: The views and experiences of probation officers and offenders*. London: Centre for Crime and Justice Studies, available at http://www.crimeandjustice.org.uk/publications.html.

Maruna, S. (2000) *Making Good: How Ex-Convicts Reform and Rebuild their Lives*. Washington DC: American Psychological Association.

Ministry of Justice (2011) *Statistics on Race and the Criminal Justice System 2010*. London: National Statistics (see website noted earlier).

Ministry of Justice (2012a) *Criminal Statistics 2011 England and Wales*. London: National Statistics (see website noted earlier).

Ministry of Justice (2012b) *Offender Management Caseload Statistics 2010*. London: National Statistics (see website noted earlier).

Morgan, R. and Smith, A. (2003) 'The Criminal Justice Bill 2002: the future role and workload of the National Probation Service', *British Journal of Community Justice* 2 (2): 7–23.

NOMS (National Offender Management Service) (2006) *The NOMS Offender Management Model*. London: NOMS.

National Probation Service (2001) *A New Choreography: An Integrated Strategy for the National Probation service for England and Wales—Strategic Framework 2001–2004*. London: Home Office.

Nellis, M. (2004) 'Electronic monitoring and the community supervision of offenders' in A. Bottoms, S. Rex, and G. Robinson (eds) *Alternatives to Prison: Options for an insecure society*. Cullompton: Willan.

Phillips, C. and Bowling, B. (2007) 'Ethnicities, Racism, Crime and Criminal Justice' in B. Mike Powis and R. Walmsley (2002) *Programmes for black and Asian offenders on probation: lessons for developing practice*. Home Office Research Study 250. London: Home Office.

Probation Journal (2011) *Special Issue—Mapping Probation: International perspectives* 58 (4):311–405.

Raynor, P. (2007) 'Community penalties: probation, "what works" and offender management' in M. Maguire, R. Morgan and R. Reiner (eds) *The Oxford Handbook of Criminology*. Oxford: Oxford University Press, 1061–99.

Raynor, P. and Vanstone, M. (2002) *Understanding Community Penalties*. Buckingham: Open University Press.

Rumgay, J. (2004) 'Dealing with substance-misusing offenders in the community' in A. Bottoms, S. Rex, and G. Robinson (eds) *Alternatives to Prison: Options for an insecure society*. Cullompton: Willan

Scull, A. (1984) *Decarceration: Community Treatment and the Deviant*. Cambridge: Polity Press.

Shute, S. (2007) *Satellite Tracking Of Offenders: A Study Of The Pilots In England And Wales* Ministry of Justice Research Summary 4.

Snacken, S. (2010) 'Resisting punitiveness in Europe?', *Theoretical Criminology* 14 (3): 273–92.

Stanley, S. (2009) 'What works in 2009: Progress or stagnation?', *Probation Journal* 56 (2): 153–74.

Ward, T. and Maruna, S. (2007) *Rehabilitation*. London: Routledge.

Worrall, A. (1990) *Offending Women: Female Lawbreakers and the Criminal Justice System*. London: Routledge.

Worrall, A. and Hoy, C. (2005) *Punishment in the Community: Managing Offenders, Making Choices* (2nd edn) Cullompton: Willan.

Worrall, A. and Gelsthorpe, L. (2009) 'What Works with Women Offenders: the past 30 years', *Probation Journal* 56 (4): 329–45.

25

Prisons

Roger Matthews

INTRODUCTION

Imprisonment has been the dominant form of punishment in western societies for the last 200 years. In that period, however, the role, scale and functions of imprisonment has changed considerably. Since its inception the modern prison has been the focus of debate and controversy. From the initial construction of the modern prison at the beginning of the nineteenth century, through to the perceived 'crisis' of imprisonment at the end of the twentieth century, the prison has been subject to critical examination. The recent growth in the size of the prison population in England and Wales, together with the adoption of a policy of mass incarceration over the last 20 years in the US with an estimated three million people incarcerated in State, Federal and local prisons, has raised issues about the use and costs of imprisonment (Elsner, 2006; Jacobson, 2005). In this chapter we will explore the contours of these changes and attempt to understand something about the processes involved. Taking a historical perspective the aim will be to outline some of the more significant developments in incarceration over the last two centuries and focusing particularly on the role and impact of imprisonment, changes in its scale and purpose, as well as an examination of who goes to prison and the relation between prison and the wider community. In the course of examining these issues a number of key themes will be discussed, while providing an introduction to the terminology and some of the central concepts that have become associated with this topic.

BACKGROUND

The word 'prison' is a generic term applied to a range of institutions that hold captives. The word 'prison' also tends to have a different meaning in American and British contexts and while Americans commonly use terms such as 'correctional facilities' and 'jails' to describe different types of custodial institutions the British tend to use mainly the generic term 'prison' (McConville, 1995). It is also necessary to distinguish between different types of prisons. In America, the term prison is reserved for State and Federal segregative institutions for offenders sentenced to imprisonment for more than one year. The term 'jail' is normally used for those institutions that hold prisoners who are sentenced to less than one year. In the UK prisons the Prison Service allocates prisoners according to an assessment of their security risk. There are four main categories of prisoners ranging from A to D. Category A prisoners are those deemed to be highly dangerous. Category B prisoners are those for whom the very highest conditions of security are not necessary but for whom escape must be made very difficult. Category C prisoners are those that cannot be trusted in open conditions but are felt to have a low probability of trying to escape. Category D prisoners are those that can be trusted in open conditions. There are also remand prisons or 'local prisons' as they are sometimes called, that hold those awaiting trial or sentence. These are designated as category B prisons. There are also dispersal prisons which are top security prisons holding Category A

prisoners in the UK and 'Supermax' prisons in the US, which as the name suggests, are designed to provide maximum security and tend to involve the restricted mobility of inmates. Young offenders between
the ages of 15 and 21 are held in Young Offender Institutions. Women are held in all-female prisons, or in
separate all-female wings within male prisons.

The birth of the modern prison

We can identify the birth of the modern prison with some precision. In the UK the
modern prison was introduced in 1842 with the construction of Pentonville prison in
London. Pentonville prison, which still stands on its original site, became the model for the
construction of many local prisons in the decades that followed and attracted worldwide
attention. This modern prison was a different kind of institution from forms of confinement
and 'prisons' such as Newgate that had been in operation in the eighteenth century that
functioned mainly as sites of containment and as places of detention for those awaiting trial
or paying off their debts. The new generation of prisons that were built in the course of the
nineteenth century in both Europe and America were distinguished according to Michel
Foucault (1977) from previous forms of confinement by three essential characteristics—the
focus on labour **discipline**, the introduction of new forms of spatial design and control,
and thirdly the use of more finely calibrated time-based punishments.

In prisons such as Newgate, in the eighteenth century, it was difficult to distinguish
the prisoners from the visitors except that the former were often chained in irons. The
jail appeared as a kind of lodging house with some inhabitants living in ease and others
in squalor. Some prisoners gambled while others stood drinking at the prison tap. These
were privately run establishments and jailers made a living from selling beer and providing other services to those who could afford them. Debtors, who made up a significant
percentage of the detainees tended to live in separate quarters—sometimes with their
families. Evangelical campaigners such as John Howard, Elizabeth Fry and philanthro-
pists like Jonas Hanway campaigned against the conditions, abuses, lack of discipline
and poor hygiene in these institutions and argued for the creation of a well-ordered
prison that was quiet and functional (McGowan, 1995). These and other like minded
reformers were instrumental in campaigning for the introduction of the modern 'well-
ordered' prison in the nineteenth century (Rothman, 1971).

The new model prisons like Pentonville that were introduced in the nineteenth century
were designed as 'total institutions'. Erving Goffman (1968) identifies **'total institutions'**
as those in which the inmates are largely cut off from their families, their work and their
communities. In relation to prisons this meant the exclusion of the public and casual visitors. In these quiet and orderly institutions convicts were required to wear uniforms and
masks and conversation and pleasure was strictly outlawed. The main focus of these modern prisons was labour discipline. As Jeremy Bentham suggested one of the main purposes
of the Victorian prison was 'to grind rogues honest'. Through the application of labour,
prisons it was claimed, would instil discipline and the habits of industry. Through a mixture of hard work and reflection on their transgressions prisoners would, it was believed,
come to see the error of their ways and become law abiding and productive workers. While

male prisoners were mostly sentenced to 'hard labour', which involved industrial labour women prisoners typically spent their days cleaning and mending (Zedner, 1991).

The aim of making prisons productive and self-financing through the manufacture of goods was however undermined by the fact that most prisoners had poor work skills and little motivation. It was also the case that trade unions objected to what they saw as unfair competition from unpaid prisoners. Consequently, restrictions were placed on the goods that could be manufactured in prison and increasingly through the nineteenth century the emphasis on productive labour gave way to the introduction of unproductive forms of labour involving the use of the tread wheel and the crank.

Changes in the design and the use of space within the modern prison were also significant. Prison cells were to be of a uniform size and prisons were constructed along new lines with a series of wings radiating from a central point. The aim of this design was to maximize the control and surveillance of prisoners with the least amount of staff. The epitome of the use of surveillance to control the activities of prisoners was the **panoptical** design (Foucault, 1977). Although this design maximized the surveillance of prisoners by employing a central vantage point from which all prisoners could be observed—without the observer being seen by the prisoners—this model was in fact only employed in a limited number of prisons such as Stateville in America and a few **panopticon**-inspired prisons in the Netherlands and Spain (Jacobs, 1977). Although the radial design predominated for most of the nineteenth century, the use of specialist designs and the ongoing debates about the best type of design reflected a growing preoccupation with spatial control as a way of maintaining order in prisons (Evans, 1982).

Time represents the third important dimension of the modern prison. The prison became a punishment of measured time. The attractiveness of imprisonment as a form of punishment was the ability to link the period of time served to the perceived seriousness of the crime committed. Previous systems of detention appeared arbitrary and unfair. Linking the use of imprisonment to a certain number of months or years of confinement gave the prison an objectivity and solidity not found in previous forms of punishment. The ultimate attractiveness of time-based punishments is that they have social and universal quality and operate independently of each individual and which embodies an element of formal equality before the law.

Thus the modern prison was distinguished from previous forms of punishment by its construction around the three elements of labour discipline, spatial design and control and the use of a time-based punishment (Matthews, 2009). Although the nature of these three elements was to change over time they remained the key distinguishing features of the modern prison. Indeed it was these three elements that contributed as Michel Foucault (1977) argued to the 'naturalness' and acceptability of the prison.

REVIEW QUESTIONS

1 Outline and discuss the roles played by labour discipline in the modern prison.

2 Discuss the significance of the panopticism in relation to the design of the modern prison.

3 What are the main characteristics and effects of 'total institutions'?

The demise and re-expansion of the prison

Imprisonment became the dominant form of punishment in the nineteenth century. The number of people incarcerated grew during the century and a number of new prisons were built. However, towards the end of the century prisons increasingly became the object of critical scrutiny. As a social experiment in reforming offenders the prison became widely viewed as failing while the costs of incarceration were increasing. The problem of making a profit from the production of goods became more pronounced as the century went on and overcrowding, corruption and cruelty became more evident. Confinement in small cells was increasingly seen as being detrimental to the health and well-being of prisoners and reports of brutality by prison staff were widespread. There were growing concerns about security and control as a result of reports of repeated escapes and riots. The Gladstone Committee in 1895 pronounced that the prison was a failing institution and that as a consequence of the evidence that it gathered on the operation of the prison system 'a sweeping indictment had been laid against the whole prison administration' (Ignatieff, 1978).

Prison, it appeared, had little apparent effect on criminal behaviour and the growth of recidivism and violent crime were seen to indicate the failure of prisons to reform offenders or to act as a general deterrent. The numbers of people in prison peaked on both sides of the Atlantic. As Rusche and Kirchheimer (2005) pointed out, changing economic conditions during the age of imperialism, together with changing working practices affected the significance of labour discipline in prison. At the same time there was a reorientation of sentencing policy away from strict proportionality and it became increasingly orientated towards the **rehabilitation** of offenders. These changes came to redefine the role of imprisonment. At this point in time there was shift to a Fordist mode of production with its emphasis on the reproduction of labour power rather than solely on labour discipline and this involved a growing focus on the socialization of the young, the development of the modern 'cornflake' family and introduction of compulsory education (Melossi, 1979).

The growth of the welfare state at the beginning of the twentieth century signalled a significant change in the nature of social control. The aim was to develop more inclusive forms of regulation tied to providing support to individuals and their families principally through the expansion of social work, which as Jacques Donzelot (1979) pointed out, became the agency that was able to link problematic individuals to the family, the school and the court. The growing emphasis on trying to address problems in the community represented a shift in the form of regulation and a consequent expansion of *inclusive* forms of social control (Cohen, 1985). The prison, with its emphasis on exclusion, became less prominent and its use more restricted, and it increasingly came to operate as back up sanction to what David Garland (1981) has referred to as the 'welfare sanction'. Thus for most of the twentieth century the dominant forms of social control oscillated between exclusion associated with imprisonment, on one side, and the more inclusive strategies linked to the operation of the welfare sanction, on the other.

In England the number of people imprisoned fell from just under 33,000 in 1880 to around 14,000 by 1931. Other European counties experienced equally dramatic levels of decrease (see Rusche and Kirchheimer, 2005: Chapter 1X). The average daily population of women imprisoned in England decreased from 1,249 in 1860 to 302 in 1890 (Zedner, 1991). Women were sent in increasing numbers to newly established reformatories designed to train and re-socialize them into domesticity (Rafter, 1983). Similarly, juveniles were also increasingly redirected towards reformatories or given probation as an alternative to custody. On the basis of these trends across Europe Rusche and Kirchheimer concluded in 1939, when they wrote their classic text 'Punishment and Social Structure', that the decline of the prison would continue towards the end of the century and that the fine would become more widely used. For them the prison was essentially a nineteenth-century institution that was becoming increasingly anachronistic. However, it has become apparent in the post-war period that Rusche and Kirchheimer's predictions have not materialized. On the contrary, the scale of imprisonment has increased in many European countries and the increase in the number of people incarcerated has been particularly pronounced in the US.

The question that arises is why this re-expansion of the prison occurred. American penologists have suggested that the increase in the use of incarceration during the 1980s and 1990s was largely the result of the 'war on drugs' that provided the justification for the deployment of harsher policies towards certain types of drug user. Michael Tonry (1995), for example, has argued that it was the focus on crack cocaine, that was the drug of choice amongst poor African Americans living in the inner cities of America, that fuelled the dramatic expansion in the use of imprisonment, and also resulted in the growing racial disproportionality amongst the prison population. However, the increase in the scale of imprisonment in England and Wales and other European countries cannot be explained as a function of the 'war against drugs'. Although the numbers of people incarcerated for drug-related offences has increased in recent years, this increase only accounts fort a small proportion of the total increase in the number of people imprisoned. An alternative explanation for the growth in the use of imprisonment is the perceived increase in punitiveness. It is argued that both politicians and the public have become increasingly punitive in recent years and that this punitiveness has been translated into longer prison sentences and the more widespread use of imprisonment (Pratt, 2007). However, the evidence that has been presented to explain this apparent surge in punitiveness is less than convincing and it would seem that the explanation for the growth of imprisonment over the last two decades lies elsewhere (Matthews, 2005; Meyer and O'Malley, 2005).

REVIEW QUESTIONS

1 In what sense was the nineteenth-century prison a failure?

2 What factors have caused the increase in the prison population over the last two decades?

3 To what extent has the 'war on drugs' contributed to the expansion of the prison population in recent years?

Who goes to prison?

One in 16 of the general population in England and Wales, it is estimated, will spend some time in prison in the course of their lives (Harvey and Pease, 1987). In the US it is one in 20 (Bonczar and Beck, 1997). These general figures, however, mask significant differences in the sections of the population who make up the prison population since this population is not drawn evenly from across the whole of society. We can examine the composition of the prison population by a number of different criteria—age, gender, race, offence types and social class.

It is important to note the difference between prison population and prison admissions—what is sometimes referred to as *stock* and *flow*. The size and nature of the prison population at any time is a function of the number of people sentenced to imprisonment and the length of time they actually serve. Thus it is possible that there could be a decrease in the number of people sent to prison in a period but that if the period of time

Table 25.1 Characteristics of the prison population

Characteristic	General population	Prison population
Ran away from home as a child	11%	47% of male sentenced prisoners and 50% of female sentenced prisoners
Taken into care as a child	2%	27%
Regularly truanted from school	3%	30%
Excluded from school	2%	49% of male and 33% of female sentenced prisoners
No qualifications	15%	52% of men and 71% of women
Numeracy at or below Level 1 (the level expected of an 11-year-old)	23%	65%
Reading ability at or below Level 1	21–23%	48%
Unemployed before imprisonment	5%	67%
Homeless	0.9%	32%
Suffer from two or more mental disorders	5% of men and 2% of women	72% of male sentenced prisoners and 70% of female sentenced prisoners
Psychotic disorder	0.5% of men and 0.6% of women	7% of male sentenced prisoners and 14% of female sentenced prisoners
Drug use in the previous year	13% of men 8% of women	66% of male sentenced prisoners and 55% of female sentenced prisoners
Hazardous drinking	38% of men and 15% of women	63% of male sentenced prisoners and 39% of female sentenced prisoners

(*Source*: Social Exclusion Unit Report 'Reducing re-offending by ex-prisoners', July 2002)

served increases significantly the average daily prison population could rise. Similarly, changes in the lengths of sentences issued to different categories of offenders will affect the composition of the prison population.

The custodial population custody tends to mainly be made up of those between 18 and 40 years of age, although there has been a 'greying' of the prison population in England and Wales in recent years with an increase in the number sentenced to long terms of imprisonment (Wahidin and Aday, 2011). Males make up the vast majority of the prison population in England and Wales and women comprise just under 6 per cent, although it should be noted that the number of women in prison in England and Wales has increased by 85 per cent over the past 15 years (Ministry of Justice, 2012). In June 2011 one in four of those in prison were drawn from minority ethnic groups. It is estimated that the incarceration for those defined as 'black' is seven times that of whites, while approximately one in eight of the prison population are foreign nationals (Prison Reform Trust, 2012). The number of juveniles in custody is a frequent point of reference. A survey carried out by the United Nations in 2002 found that that the rate of juvenile/youth custody per 100,000 of the population revealed that the rate was 38.40 per 100,000 in the US and 18.26 per 100,000 in England and Wales. According to these statistics England and Wales currently incarcerate young people at a higher rate than any other country in Europe (Muncie, 2005).

The background of those in prison typically involves a history of marginalization, deprivation and poor achievement. Those in prison tend to have low educational levels, few skills and poor work histories. Nearly half of all prisoners have been excluded from school. One third of them did not have permanent accommodation prior to imprisonment (Social Exclusion Unit, 2002). A survey carried out by Nick Davies in 2004 found that over 70 per cent of prisoners suffer from two or more mental health disorders. See Table 25.1.

If we look at the composition of the prison population by offence type it is apparent there have been significant changes over the last decade or so. For male prisoners there has

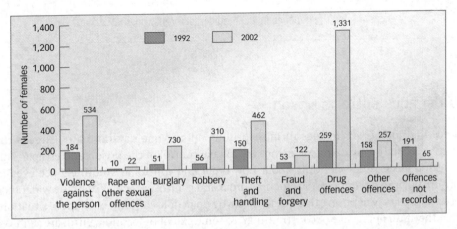

Figure 25.1 Male prison population under an immediate sentence 1992 and 2002

Source: Home Office, 2003.

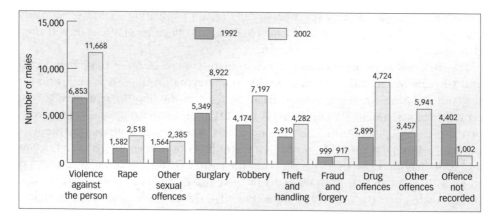

Figure 25.2 Female prison population under an immediate sentence 1992 and 2002

Source: Home Office, 2003.

been a significant increase in the number imprisoned for violence, burglary, robbery and drug offences between 1992 and 2002 (Councell, 2003). There has also been an increase in the number of women imprisoned for violence-related offences, but the most dramatic change has been the number imprisoned for drug-related offences (see Figures 25.1 and 25.2). A further significant change is an increase in the number of people serving life sentences. The proportion of the sentenced population serving life sentences increased from 9 per cent in 1995 to 19 per cent in 2011 (Ministry of Justice, 2012).

REVIEW QUESTIONS

1 Most of those who are physically excluded in prisons are already socially and economically excluded. Discuss.

2 How can we account for the racial disproportionality of the prison population?

3 In what ways is women's experience of incarceration different from that of men?

Order and control in prison

Since the number of inmates in most prisons on any one day normally exceeds the number of staff, why do prisoners not try to take control of the prison and escape? This question raises issues, not only about how order and control are routinely achieved in prison, but also has implications for how order and control are achieved in the wider society. Another way of posing this question is why do people conform or adapt to situations that they find oppressive or constraining? To some extent order and control are achieved in prison through the mobilization of its three basic elements–labour, space and time. Despite the problems of engaging in profitable forms of production in prison, most prisons engage inmates in some form of labour even if it is only working in the prison grounds, in the kitchen or cleaning up. It is seen as important to keep prisoners occupied as much as possible, and the aim of instilling some form of work discipline in prisoners remains an objective of prison authorities. Prisoners are also controlled through spatial segregation and by the organized distribution of bodies so that forms of congregation are limited. High walls and continuous surveillance also make escape difficult. For those who try to escape solitary confinement has been used historically as a form of punishment. Order in prison is also achieved through the use of a strict timetable that structures the prisoner's day and is used to establish routines and orchestrate activities. For those who misbehave adding time onto the existing sentence has been a widely used sanction.

Apart from these basic organizing themes there are a number of other ways in which order and discipline is maintained in prison. Some penologists have emphasized the role of subcultures within prison that serve to establish normative codes amongst inmates which establish a set of informal rules or an 'inmate code' which sets out how inmates should behave towards each other and the prison authorities (Clemmer, 1940). From this perspective it is argued that it is not so much that order is imposed, but negotiated, and that rather than the custodians being omnipotent, achieving order is a continuous process of negotiation and struggle (Sykes, 1958). In some prisons it has been suggested that the inmates exercise considerable control in relation to each other (Edgar *et al.*, 2003). American research has drawn attention to the role of gangs in prison and the considerable degree of control that they exercise (Elsner, 2006).

Order and discipline is routinely achieved through the use of incentives and disincentives. Virtually all prison regimes employ some version of a 'stick and carrot' approach which includes a loss of privileges, on one hand, to being given more attractive forms of work, increased number of visits and other 'perks', on the other. Of particular significance in relation to good behaviour is the issue of parole and early release. To the extent that early release is based on assessment of 'good behaviour' prisoners have a major incentive to demonstrate compliance. Apart from the traditional range of incentives and disincentives the prisons department deal with problems of order in prisons by identifying 'troublemakers' in certain prisons on the basis of risk assessments and transfer them to other prisons.

Violence, however, is an endemic feature of prisons and it tends to take a number of forms—interpersonal violence between inmates or between inmates and staff and collective violence in the form of riots and disturbances. Research on prisons in England and Wales carried out in the 1990s revealed that remand centres and Young Offender Institutions had the largest number of assaults on inmates and reports of fighting. Serious violence is significantly higher in men's than in women's prisons (Bottoms, 1999). King and McDermott's (1995) study of five prisons in England and Wales which employed self-completion questionnaires reported that 12.5 per cent of their sample said that they had been assaulted at some time while in their current prisons; 6.8 per cent of respondents claimed to have been sexually attacked and 33 per cent said that they had been threatened with violence. Although the authors note that much prison violence is not reported they conclude from the research that inmates behave differently in different prison settings and that different prison regimes, systems of management, variations in design and the like, can all have an impact on the level and frequency of violence in prison.

In response to reports of violence and abuse there are mechanisms in place in the prison system for expressing grievances and exercising accountability. Every prison in England and Wales is served by a Board of Visitors and body of lay volunteers. Boards of Visitors were involved in disciplinary hearings until 1992 when they were relieved of this duty as it was held that it was incompatible their role as inspecting prisons and hearing prisoners' grievances. Prisoners are now expected to refer complaints to unit managers or their duty governor and they still have the option to refer complaints to the prisons ombudsman or their MP. These is also a prison inspectorate that makes announced and unannounced visits to prisons and has provided some of the most critical accounts of the conditions and management of prisons in recent years (Home Office, 2007).

The key indicators of breakdown of order in prisons are riots and disturbances. The distinction between riots and disturbances is that riots involve collective actions that aim to take control of the whole or part of the prison while disturbances tend to involve more localized and short-lived disruptions. There is no consensus on the causes of riots but the Woolf Report (1991) is seen as providing an authoritative analysis of the conditions and processes that led up to the riots at Strangeways prison in Manchester in 1990. Lord Woolf argued that if riots were to be avoided there needed to be a proper balance between 'security, control and justice' within prisons, although the report placed the primary emphasis on control and made it clear that the delivery of 'justice' was dependent on the maintenance of an adequate level of security (Sim, 1994a). What was clear from the Woolf Report, however, is that there is no single cause of riots, whether it is poor conditions or a 'toxic mix' of prisoners. Riots, as Rod Morgan (1997) has argued, tend to be the outcome of what he refers to as a 'disorder amplification spiral' in which poor conditions are linked to a growing sense of injustice and the polarization of relations between staff and inmates. When this process is set in motion any one of a number of 'triggers' can turn anger and frustration into a riot.

Another outcome of this process of the breakdown of control is the intensification of a sense of anomie and insecurity amongst prisoners, which allows stronger prisoners to exercise greater control over weaker and more vulnerable prisoners. This scenario is seen as producing the conditions for an increase in the suicides in prison, particularly when those being victimized are isolated (Leibling, 1992). In 2004 the number of suicides in prison in England and Wales was 95, 13 of which were women and five were under 21 years of age. This is the highest number of suicides recorded in one year.

REVIEW QUESTIONS

1 Outline and discuss the main mechanisms for securing order and control in prisons.

2 The prison system lacks accountability and transparency. Discuss.

3 What are the main causes of prison riots?

Does prison work?

The question 'does prison work?' is deceptively difficult to answer. While on one side there are conservative criminologists like Charles Murray (1997) and John Dilulio (1987) in the US and conservative politicians like Michael Howard in the UK who claim unequivocally that prison works to reduce crime, there is a wide body of liberal opinion that flatly denies that this is the case. The truth is somewhere in between and a closer examination of the issue reveals that there are a number of dimensions to this question and consequently a range of possible answers. Thus while some commentators might argue that prisons work to deter potential offenders and thereby reduce crime, they might simultaneously deny that prisons work to reform or rehabilitate offenders.

If by the phrase 'prison works' we mean that it acts as an instrument for simply punishing offenders then we might concede the truth of the statement. However, this immediately raises the question of whether it works any better than other forms of punishment. In terms of general deterrence and the effectiveness of sanction of imprisonment to deter prospective offenders from committing crime is extremely difficult to determine with any precision. The extent to which people think about the possible punishments for crimes they might commit is difficult to determine and whether they think about the possibility of imprisonment is even less certain (Wilson, 1983).

In terms of rehabilitation we have seen the development of an impressive array of programmes in prisons in recent years to address what the authorities describe as the 'criminogenic needs' of offenders. Under the slogan of 'Making Prisons Work' the government has introduced a number of programmes designed to address drug use and violence amongst prisoners as well as develop education and training programmes. However well-intentioned these programmes might be, critics of incarceration have argued that the nature of imprisonment militates against rehabilitation and that prisons tend to debilitate rather than rehabilitate offenders (Goffman, 1986; Mathieson, 1990).

In the same way the claim associated with Robert Martinson's (1974) review of rehabilitation programmes that 'nothing works' has served to undermine rehabilitation as a rationale for imprisonment (Bottoms and Preston, 1980). Although Martinson and others have qualified and criticized this conclusion and pointed out that the research results indicate that some programmes work for some people under some conditions, the general belief that rehabilitation programmes are of limited value has persisted (Pawson and Tilley, 1997; Martinson, 1979; Palmer, 1975). The dismissal of the ideal of rehabilitation has, however, been challenged by some penologists. Indeed, it has been argued that rehabilitation is the only justification for imprisonment that obligates the State to care for offenders' needs and welfare (Cullen and Gilbert, 1982). It is also the case that the widespread critiques of rehabilitation in the 1970s and 1980s led to a greater emphasis on incapacitation and the warehousing of prisoners.

One of the major obstacles to properly evaluating the effects of rehabilitation programmes as well as the effects of specific deterrence is that they are predominantly assessed in relation to recidivism. Recidivism, however, is a difficult and unreliable measure (Maltz, 1984). This is primarily because the concept of recidivism is conceived as involving at four different processes—reoffending, rearrest, and reconviction and prison re-entry. It is, however, possible that individuals might reoffend without being rearrested or reconvicted. Thus the level of recidivism can change depending on which of the four elements are taken as the point of reference. At the same time, offenders may commit less serious crimes less often after leaving prison, but they can still count as recidivists and seen as examples of the 'failure' of incarceration.

A more complex and difficult question to answer in relation to the claim that prison works is whether a five-year sentence, for example, works better than a two-year sentence. Some critics have argued that there is a diminishing effect in extending the length of sentences beyond a certain period of time because individuals' personal time horizons do not allow them to adequately conceptualize the meaning of time beyond a certain number of years in the future (Cohen and Taylor, 1972). An equally perplexing question is whether a short period of imprisonment is likely to have any impact on rehabilitation or a greater effect on specific deterrence than a fine or a non-custodial sentence.

An equally difficult question is whether the increased use of imprisonment in both Britain and America has reduced crime levels as some observers claim. Certainly, there is a correlation between the increased use of imprisonment and the decline in both counties in recent years. But are these changes causally linked? Other countries have reported a decrease in crime while prison numbers have remained stable or declined, while in others both crime rates and imprisonment rates have increased simultaneously (Jacobson, 2005). These variations demonstrate at the very least that any suggestion that a drop in crime rates is likely to result from the increased use of prison needs to be treated with extreme caution. We also know that the level of crime in any period is influenced by a range of social and economic factors that operate independently of imprisonment and other forms of punishment. The available evidence suggests that while the increased use of imprisonment may convey a significant message about 'getting tough' on crime that the impact of imprisonment on what are generally considered to be the most serious crimes—murder, violence, rape and sexual offences—appears to be limited. If a deterrent effect is in operation it is more likely to be effective in relation to the prospective offenders' assessment of their likelihood of being caught, rather than the nature and severity of the available sanctions (Currie, 1998).

One variant on the claim that prison works is the claim that 'prison pays'. That is, some criminologists argue that there are significant financial savings to be made by removing offenders from the community and locking them up (Dilulio and Piehl, 1991; Wilson and Abraham, 1992). Those that have argued that 'prison pays' have examined the number and cost of crimes committed by offenders in the period before incarceration and then tried to work out the amount saved by removing the offender from the community. This cost is then compared to the cost of incarceration, and where the cost of crimes that have been predicted to have been committed is less than the cost of imprisoning offenders it is argued that 'prison pays'. There are problems in this analysis in relation to which costs are taken into account and how they are calculated. In particular, the costs of the 'collateral damage' associated with incarceration, which disrupts families, neighbourhoods and communities sustaining cycles of disadvantage are not normally taken into account (Mauer and Chesney-Lind, 2002). It is also the case that the experience of imprisonment can further marginalize individuals and adversely affect their opportunities on the job market. Indeed, in the words of one government report published during the Thatcher years 'prison can be an expensive way of making bad people worse' (Home Office, 1988). Moreover, a significant proportion of offenders enter prison at or near the peak of their offending and the assumption that they would have carried on offending at the same rate year on year may not be justified. Also, offending patterns change with age and as those in prison grow older it is likely that their level of offending would predictably decline.

The arguments that 'prison works' or 'prison pays' are generally weakened by the fact that most of the advocates assume that the option is between sending people to prison or doing nothing. But doing nothing is never in practice an option. There are alternative means available to prevent and respond to crime and the critical question is whether the enormous sums of money spent on prisons could be more usefully is employed in other ways.

REVIEW QUESTIONS

1 To what extent can it be claimed that 'prison works'?

2 The real costs of imprisonment do not arise in relation to the containment of prisoners but from the 'collateral damage' inflicted upon families and communities. Discuss.

3 How useful is recidivism as a measure of the effectiveness of imprisonment?

The crisis of imprisonment

The term' crisis' has become increasingly associated with imprisonment in recent years. But what exactly does it mean to say that the prison is in a state of 'crisis'? Is the term crisis a synonym for 'problems' or tensions' in the prison system or does it signify something deeper and more serious? It is clear in newspaper reports and academic publications that different commentators provide different examples of what they consider constitutes the 'crisis' and it is not clear whether these different points of reference are different aspects of the same crisis or whether they represent different forms of crisis (King and McDermott, 1989).

In their book, *British Prisons* (1979), Mike Fitzgerald and Joe Sim argue that there are in fact a series of 'crises' that have become associated with imprisonment and that these involve a crisis of visibility, authority, conditions, containment and legitimacy. The crisis of visibility refers to the limited public access and information regarding the prison system. The segregated nature of imprisonment and restrictions on entry mean that the day-to-day activities that go on in prison are largely shielded from public view. This, it is argued, provides the conditions for abuse, maltreatment and other excesses within prisons. It was not until the late 1980s that television cameras were allowed to film in prisons and different agencies were allowed regular access to certain prisons. Consequently, in previous periods prisoners resorted to rooftop protests in order to make themselves visible and to bring attention to their grievances.

The crisis of authority involves the perceived undermining of the traditional forms of authority and discipline exercised in prisons, particularly as they have become more accessible and accountable. Prison staff complain that changes in prison rules and working practices have undermined their authority in prisons and made it harder to maintain order. The declining support for the rehabilitative ideal during the 1970s and 1980s brought into question the professional ideology of prison staff and the shift towards incapacitation and the warehousing of prisoners which intensified the problems of maintaining order in prisons. In 2007 prison officers went on strike over pay and conditions and prison overcrowding was cited as one of the factors that increased pressures on prison staff (Campbell, 2007).

The crisis of conditions refers to the poor and in some cases the deteriorating conditions in a number of prisons. Many of the remand prisons in England and Wales, for example, were built in the Victorian era and are in a poor state of repair. In these prisons and elsewhere in the prison system the level of overcrowding has become a major point of concern as prison populations increase. In 2010–11 an average of 20,211 prisoners were held in overcrowded accommodation, accounting for 24 per cent of the prison population (Prison Reform Trust, 2012). Overcrowding has the effect of not only making the physical conditions in prison worse, but it also affects the time out of cells, recreational activities and other forms of association amongst prisoners. It also puts increasing pressure on staff–inmate relations. Worsening conditions can also lead to crisis of containment since these processes directly and indirectly affect control and security in prisons. As prison conditions worsen and overcrowding increases the possibility of disturbances in prison increases, as does the likelihood of escape. One response to the overcrowding in certain prisons has been to move prisoners around the country to prisons where there are vacant beds. This process, however, causes disruption and difficulties for prisoners and their families who have to travel further to visit them.

These various 'crises' have been well documented in the criminological literature, but Fitzgerald and Sim (1979) argue that the 'crisis' facing the prison system goes far beyond the *internal* problems facing the prison system. For Fitzgerald and Sim, resolving the specific crises of visibility, authority, containment and conditions would—even if it were possible—not entirely solve the crisis of imprisonment because there is, they argue, 'no evidence to suggest that if we had a hygienic, clean, antiseptic, single occupant cells throughout the penal system, there would be no crisis' (1979: 19). Instead, they suggest there is an underlying crisis, which 'reveals the essential bankruptcy of penal policy' and which 'transcends the prisons walls' (1979: 24). This involves what they refer to as the 'crisis of legitimacy' involving external processes and wider dimensions of politics and power. The prison, the authors argue, suffers from two fundamental flaws. First, they claim that prison simply does not work and that the high levels of recidivism are testimony to its failure. Secondly, that 'imprisonment is consistently invoked against the marginal working classes' and it is part of 'a class based legal system' which singles out particular offenders for punishment. The implications of this 'crisis of legitimacy' are that there is no real justification for the continued use of imprisonment and that prisons should be abolished (Sim, 1994b).

Paul Cavadino and James Dignan (2002) have taken up the issue of the prison crisis and like Fitzgerald and Sim make a distinction between internal and external nature of the 'crisis', distinguishing between what they see as a material crisis which they describe as a 'crisis of penological resources', on one side, and an ideological crisis, or a 'crisis of legitimacy', on the other. However, they see the 'crisis of legitimacy' in a very different way from Fitzgerald and Sim. For Cavadino and Dignan the crisis of legitimacy centres around the sense of injustice amongst inmates. Thus rather than focus on the way in which the prison is linked to wider political processes, Cavadino and Dignan tend to locate the legitimacy crisis within the penal sphere itself and it is seen, on one hand, as the culmination 'of all the individual crises' within the penal system, while they also claim that it operates on a distinctly different 'ideological' plane. From what they describe as a radical pluralist position, the 'crisis' can be overcome by increasing resources and by addressing instances of injustice. It is not clear, however, from their account if these two options are exclusive, or for that matter, how they relate to each other.

A similar approach to the penal crisis is adopted by Richard Sparks and Anthony Bottoms (1995) who focus in particular on the issue of legitimacy. For them prisons lose their legitimacy when the rules and procedures are not followed or when staff do not operate professionally. In line with the approach advocated by Lord Woolf (1991) in his review of the Strangeways riots, Bottoms and Sparks suggest that improved systems of justice within prisons will improve security and control within prisons. Thus, there remains a tension and uncertainty in the criminological literature over the precise meaning of the 'crisis of imprisonment'. Articles in the media that frequently refer to the prisons 'crisis' tend to focus on the conditions in prison or overcrowding. Criminologists, however, like Cavadino and Dignan and Bottoms and Sparks tend to see the 'crisis' on two levels—one a crisis of conditions and the other a crisis of legitimacy. For them legitimacy is mainly seen in procedural terms, while for Fitzgerald and Sim the 'crisis of legitimacy' goes far beyond the penal sphere and is bound up with wider political and economic changes that increasingly call into question the role of imprisonment and its class-based nature (Reiman, 2004). It has, however, been claimed that the growth in prison population over the last decade or so indicates that there is little sign of a crisis of imprisonment if by crisis we mean the imminent breakdown and demise of imprisonment (Morgan, 1997). However, there may be no contradiction between the expansion of the prison and its growing legitimacy deficit.

REVIEW QUESTIONS

1 The prison system suffers not from one 'crisis' but a series of 'crises'. Discuss.

2 The major problem facing the prison system is one of legitimation. Discuss.

3 What evidence is there that prisons are in a deepening crisis?

The future of imprisonment

Predicting the future is always a precarious business. However, in recognizing that the prison system is facing a series of 'crises' it is important to think about the development of an appropriate response. Francis Cullen and John Wright (1996) have suggested that there are, in essence, two ways forward for penal reform. One involves the adoption of what they call the 'punishment paradigm', which is associated with conservative criminologists like Charles Murray and John Dilulio. The other option they refer to as the 'progressive paradigm', which is associated with a more liberal approach. The punishment paradigm claims that crime can be effectively reduced through the increased use of imprisonment but that the use of imprisonment needs to be rationalized in order to reduce costs. Consequently, the preferred option for some conservative criminologists is to contract the running of prisons to private operators, or alternatively to build high-tech prisons that rely on new forms of design and surveillance that are able to operate with a reduced number of staff (Beyens and Snacken, 1996; Harding, 1997). Staff costs account for some 80 per cent of the running costs of the prison and therefore any attempt to significantly reduce overall costs will necessarily involve reducing the number of staff or alternatively reducing the amount that they are paid. Another way of reducing costs is to limit the number of training and rehabilitation programmes offered in prison and to keep prisoners locked up in their cells for a greater percentage of their time. Consequently, within this approach there is a tendency towards penal austerity and the warehousing of prisoners.

The more liberal 'progressive paradigm' as outlined by Cullen and Wright (1996) takes a different approach. It claims that the punishment paradigm has persistently failed to reduce crime and claims that the large financial investments that have been made in prisons has brought only marginal and diminishing returns (Currie, 1998). Liberal critics point to public opinion surveys that suggest that the general public do not support an increase in the use of imprisonment. They also argue that prisons should be used *as* punishment rather than *for* punishment. The penalty of imprisonment is the deprivation of liberty for a specified period of time. In that time the aim should be to address the needs of offenders and develop rehabilitative programmes, rather than prisons serving as 'schools of crime', which only serve to release dangerous and disillusioned offenders back into neighbourhoods that already have more than their fair share of problems. Rehabilitation, it is argued, offers a humane and effective way to reduce crime and improve the lives of certain groups of offenders.

In the meantime the various 'crises' confronting the prison have motivated policy makers, activists and practitioners alike to develop strategies to reduce reliance on imprisonment. Over the past two or three decades a number of measures have been developed to achieve this objective. The measures adopted include the development of alternatives to custody, introducing new sentencing policies and guidelines, extending the use of early release from prison. In brief, any strategy designed to reduce the number of people in prison must divert people away from prison or reduce the period of time they spend in prison. The first element of this strategy is seen to be dependent on changing the nature of sentencing and increasing the availability of non-custodial sanctions. Changing sentencing policies is, however, a complex business. Deciding when prison is appropriate, the duration of a prison sentence and where alternative sanctions should be used raises complex moral and legal concerns (Hudson, 2003).

The discussions about the role of rehabilitation has also been affected by the development of what Jonathon Simon and Malcolm Feeley (1992) have referred to as 'The New Penology'. These authors argue that the 'old' penal strategies that were directed at the reform or rehabilitation of the individual are being increasingly replaced by a 'New Penology' that is based on risk analysis and is more concerned with the management of the underclass rather than its reform. In this actuarial approach the authors claim that the role of imprisonment is changing and that its rationale is gravitating towards incapacitation rather than rehabilitation.

Finally, it was suggested above that the modern prison was constructed in relation to three central element – labour discipline, time and space. At the beginning of the nineteenth century developing a mode of punishment around these elements seemed obvious and 'natural'. However, it has been argued that the preoccupation with labour discipline is less evident in the contemporary prison system and that there are changes in the significance of time and space in the 'information society' in which the notion of confinement as mode of punishment appears less appropriate. Consequently, there is a general shift towards what Giles Deleuze (1995) has called the 'control society' in which social control becomes continuous and comprehensive relying increasingly on monitoring and surveillance. As the 'control society' develops, he suggests, future generations will look back with nostalgia at the notion of punishing people by confining them to limited spaces for a designated period of time.

QUESTIONS FOR DISCUSSION

1 What could be done to reduce the size of the prison population?
2 To what extent is it reasonable to suggest that the 'old penology' is being superseded by the 'new penology'?
3 Is there a case for defending the continued use of rehabilitation programmes in prison?
4 The privatization of prisons will make them more cost-effective. Discuss.
5 The prison is becoming an anachronistic institution and will soon disappear. Discuss.

GUIDE TO FURTHER READING

Matthews, R. (2002) *Imprisonment*. Aldershot, Ashgate.
This book contains approximately 20 classic articles on imprisonment.

Jewkes Y. and Johnstone H. (2006) *Prison Readings: A Critical Introduction Prisons and Imprsonment*. Collumpton: Willan.
This is another useful collection of articles on different aspects of imprisonment.

Carlen, P. (2002) *Women and Punishment: The Struggle for Justice*. Collumpton: Willan.
This is a collection of articles focusing particularly on the relationship between women and punishment.

Mauer, M. (1999) *Race to Incarcerate*. New York: The New Press.
This book examines the relationship between crime control and the use of imprisonment and in particular the significance of class and race in relation to the increased use of imprisonment.

Ramsbotham, D. (2003) *Prisongate: The Shocking State of Britain's Prisons and the need for Visionary Change*. London: The Free Press.
This book is written by a former prison inspector and provides a unique insight into the state of the prison system and the politics of penal reform.

Crow, I. (2001) *The Treatment and Rehabilitation of Offenders*. London: Sage.
This book examines the concepts of treatment and rehabilitation in prisons and discusses the role of different agencies in developing types of intervention.

WEB LINKS

http://www.justice.gov.uk

This site covers the work and activities of the recently established Ministry of Justice. It contains a useful link to the National Offender Management Service (NOMS) which provides details of NOMS role in reducing reoffending and its publications.

http://www.howardleague.org

This site contains details of the work of the Howard League in relation to penal reform, news of developments in the penal system as well as listing a number of publications.

http://www.prisonreformtrust.org.uk

In a similar way to the Howard League the Prison Reform Trust website contains information on their current activities as well as listing a number of publications on different aspects of the penal system and prison reform.

http://dojni.gov.uk

This site provides information on the operation of the prison system in Northern Ireland as well as providing some useful links to other organizations involved with the issues relating to imprisonment.

http://www.ppo.gov.uk

This site provides details of the work of the Prisons and Probation Ombudsman, who deals mainly with complaints from prisoners and those subject to probation supervision. It also contains a reasonably comprehensive listing of organizations that deal with different aspects of imprisonment and lists their respective websites.

REFERENCES

Beyens, K. and Snacken S. (1996) 'Prison Privatization: An International Perspective' in R. Matthews and P. Francis (eds) *Prisons 2000*. London: Macmillan.

Bonczar, T. and Beck, A. (1997) *Lifetime Likelihood of Going to State or Federal Prison*. Bureau of Justice Statistics. US Department of Justice.

Bottoms, A. (1999) 'Interpersonal Violence and Social Order in Prisons' in M. Tonry and J. Petersilia (eds) *Prisons*. Chicago: University of Chicago Press.

Bottoms, A. and Preston, R. (1980) *The Coming Penal Crisis*. Edinburgh: Scottish Academic Press.

Campbell, D. (2007) 'Simmering Anger That Finally Boiled Over', *The Guardian*, 30 August.

Cavadino, P. and Dignan, J. (2002) *The Penal System: An Introduction*. London: Sage.

Clemmer, D. (1940) *The Prison Community*. New York: Holt, Rinehart and Winston.

Cohen, S. (1985) *Visions of Social Control*. Cambridge: Polity Press.

Cohen, S. and Taylor, L. (1972) *Psychological Survival*. Harmondsworth: Penguin.

Councell, R. (2003) *The Prison Population in 2002: A Statistical Review*. Findings 228. London: HMSO.

Cullen, F. and Gilbert, K. (1982) *Reaffirming Rehabilitation*. Cincinnati: Anderson Publishing.

Cullen, F. and Wright J. (1996) 'The Future of Corrections' in B. Maguire and P. Radosh (eds) *The Past, Present and Future of American Criminal Justice*. New York: General Hall.

Currie, E. (1998) *Crime and Punishment in America*. New York: Metropolitan Books.

Deleuze, G. (1995) *Negotiations*. New York: Columbia University Press.

Dilulio, J. (1987) *Governing Prisons*. New York: Free Press.

Dilulio, J. and Piehl, A. (1991) 'Does Prison Pay?' *Brookings Review*, Fall. Part 4: 29–35.

Donzelot, J. (1979) *The Policing of Families*. London: Hutchinson.

Edgar, K., O'Donnell, I., and Martin, C. (2003) *Prison Violence: The Dynamics of Conflict, Fear and Power*. Collumpton: Willan.

Elsner, A. (2006) *Gates of Injustice*. New York: Pearson Education.

Evans, R. (1982) *The Fabrication of Virtue: English Prison Architecture 1750–1840*. Cambridge: Cambridge University Press.

Fitzgerald, M. and Sim, J. (1979) *British Prisons*. Oxford: Blackwell.

Foucault, M. (1977) *Discipline and Punish: The Birth of the Prison*. London: Allen Lane.

Garland, D. (1981) 'The Birth of the Welfare Sanction', *British Journal of Law and Society* Vol. 8: 29–45.

Goffman, A. (1968) *Asylums*. Harmondsworth: Pelican.

Harding, R. (1997) *Private Prisons and Public Accountability*. Buckingham: Open University Press.

Harvey, L. and Pease, K. (1987) 'Prevalence of Imprisonment in England and Wales', *British Journal of Criminology*. Vol. 27: 65–9.

Home Office (1988) *Punishment, Custody and the Community*. Cmnd. 424. London: HMSO.

Home Office (2007) *HM Inspectorate Annual Report 2005–06*. London: HMSO.

Hudson, B. (2003) *Justice in the Risk Society*. London: Sage.

Ignatieff, M. (1978) *A Just Measure of Pain: The Penitentiary in the Industrial Revolution 1750–1850*. London: Macmillan.

Jacobs, J. (1977) *Stateville: The Penitentiary in Mass Society*.Chicago: University of Chicago Press.

Jacobson, M. (2005) *Downsizing Prisons*. New York: New York University Press.

King, R. and McDermott, K. (1989) 'British Prisons 1970-1987: The Ever-Deepening Crisis', *British Journal of Criminology* Vol. 29 No. 2: 107–28.

King, R. and McDermott, K. (1995) *The State of Our Prisons*. Oxford: Clarendon Press.

Leibling, A. (1992) *Suicides in Prison*. London: Routledge.

Maltz, M. (1984) *Recidivism*. Orlando: Academic Press.

Martinson, R. (1974) 'What Works? Questions and Answers About Prison Reform', *Public Interest* 35: 22–54.

Martinson, R. (1979) 'Symposium on Sentencing', *Hofra Law Review* Vol. 7 No. 2: 243–58.

Matthews, R. (2005) 'The Myth of Punitiveness', *Theoretical Criminology* Vol. 9 No. 2: 175–201.

Matthews, R. (2009) *Doing Time: An Introduction to the Sociology of Imprisonment* (2nd edn) London: Palgrave.

Mathieson, T. (1990) *Prison on Trial*. London: Sage.

Mauer, M. and Chesney-Lind, M. (2002) *Invisible Punishment: The Collateral Consequences of Mass Imprisonment*. New York: The New Press.

McConville, S. (1995) 'The Victorian Prison: England 1865-1965' in N. Morris and D. Rothman (eds) *The Oxford History of the Prison*. New York: Oxford University Press.

Melossi, D. (1979) 'Institutions of Social Control and Capitalist Organisation of Work' in Ministry of Justice (2012) *Population and Capacity Briefing 22nd June*. London: Ministry of Justice.

Morgan, R. (1997) 'The Aims of Imprisonment Revisited' in A. Liebling and T. Ward (eds) *Deaths in Custody: International Perspectives*. London: Whiting and Birch.

Murray, C. (1997) *Does Prison Work?* London: Institute of Economic Affairs.

Muncie, J. (2005) 'The Globalisation of Crime Control—The Case of Youth and Juvenile Justice: Neo-Liberalism, Policy Convergence and International Conventions', *Theoretical Criminology* Vol. 9 No. 1: 35–64.

Palmer, T. (1975) 'Martinson Revisited', *Journal of Research in Crime and Delinquency* Vol. 12: 133–92.

Pawson, R. and Tilley, N. (1997) *Realistic Evaluation*. London: Sage.

Pratt, J. (2007) *Penal Populism*. London: Routledge.

Prison Reform Trust (2012) *Prison Fact File. Bromley Briefings*. London: PRT.

Rafter, N. (1983) 'Prisons For Women 1870-1980' in M. Tonry and N. Morris (eds) *Crime and Justice: An Annual Review of Research*, Vol. 5. Chicago: University of Chicago Press.

Reiman, J. (2004) *The Rich Get Richer and the Poor Get Prison* (7th edn) Boston: Pearson.

Rothman, D. (1971) *The Discovery of the Asylum Social Order and Disorder in the New Republic*. Boston: Little, Brown and Co.

Rusche, G. and Kirchheimer, O. (2005) *Punishment and Social Structure*. New Brunswick: Transaction.

Sim, J. (1994a) 'Reforming the Penal Wasteland? A Critical Review of the Woolf Report' in E. Player and M. Jenkins (eds) *Prisons After Woolf: Reform Through Riot*. London: Routledge.

Sim, J. (1994b) 'The Abolitionist Approach: A British Perspective' in A. Duff *et al.* (eds) *Penal Theory and Practice*. Manchester: Manchester University Press.

Social Exclusion Unit (2002) *Reducing Re-Offending by Ex-Offenders*. London: ODPM.

Sparks, R. and Bottoms, A. (1995) 'Legitimacy and Order in Prisons', *British Journal of Sociology* Vol. 46 No. 1: 45–62.

Sykes, G. (1958) *Society of Captives*. Princeton, NJ: Princeton University Press.

Tonry, M. (1995) *Malign Neglect: Race Crime and Punishment in America*. New York: Oxford University Press.

Wahidin, A. and Aday, R. (2011) 'Later Life and Imprisonment' in C. Phillipson (ed) *Handbook of Social Gerontology*. London: Sage.

Wilson, J. (1983) *Thinking About Crime*. New York: Basic Books.

Wilson J. and Abraham, A. (1992) 'Does Crime Pay?', *Justice Quarterly*. Vol. 9 No. 3; 359–77.

Woolf, Lord (1991) *Prison Disturbances April 1990*. London: HMSO.

Zedner, L. (1991) *Women, Crime and Custody in Victorian England*. Oxford: Clarendon.

Abolitionism A political and criminological perspective that advocates the radical transformation/replacement of modern punishment forms with a more reflexive and multifaceted approach capable of better understanding dominant ideological constructions of crime.

Accountability The ways in which organizations and individuals are rendered answerable for their policies and day-to-day activities, exerted by internal and external mechanisms.

Acquisitive crime A term used to categorize economically motivated crimes such as burglary and theft.

Actuarial justice A term coined by Malcolm Feeley and Jonathan Simon to try to characterize a possible emerging aspect of criminal law and criminal justice. The term derives from 'actuary', meaning a statistician who works for an insurance company to calculate risks, premiums and pay-outs. Actuarial justice thus suggests a form of justice based on calculation of risks, and the statistical use of past data to predict the likelihood of future events.

Administrative criminology A form of practical policy-relevant criminology that focuses almost exclusively on the nature of the criminal event and the particular setting in which it occurs. Under this perspective, the offender is considered only as a 'rational actor' who makes calculated decisions about the costs and benefits of criminal action. Administrative criminologists seek to reduce the opportunities for crime, thus making the costs/risks of crime outweigh the potential benefits.

Aetiological crisis The majority of post-war criminology was predicated on the basis that poor social conditions caused crime. Consequently, if a meaningful reduction in crime was to occur, then governments needed to implement a series of social democratic policies specifically aimed at reducing unemployment and raising general living standards. Despite substantial improvements in the Western world in these and other areas during the years 1950–70, recorded crime soared to unprecedented levels. This refutation of the then major thinking in the social sciences has been described by Jock Young as the 'aetiological crisis'.

Aetiology The philosophy of causation; the study of causes.

Appeal The initial decisions made by magistrates' or Crown Courts can be challenged by a convicted defendant (or in some cases by the prosecution). This is known as an 'appeal' and can be either on the question of the correctness of the conviction itself or the appropriateness of the sentence. The appeal will be to a higher court—this will normally be to the Crown Court from the magistrates' or to the Court of Appeal from the Crown Court.

Atavism The recurrence of certain primitive characteristics that were present in an ancestor but have not occurred in intermediate generations.

Behaviourism A psychological approach (first promoted by J.B. Watson in 1913) that stresses that the only proper subject matter for scientific study in psychology is directly observable behaviour.

Bifurcation A dual-edged approach to the problem of offending which allows governments to reserve custody for the most serious offenders and to use community penalties for not-so-serious offenders. In practice, it often involves a more punitive approach across the whole range of punishments.

Binge drinking Refers to the consumption of large amounts of alcohol in a single drinking session.

Business (or economic) cycle The ups and downs often seen simultaneously in most parts of a country's economy. They tend to repeat at fairly regular time intervals. This involves shifts over time between periods of relatively rapid growth of output (recovery and prosperity), alternating with periods of recession or relatively slow economic growth.

Civilizing process A concept associated particularly with Norbert Elias that refers to a long-term tendency in European societies from the Middle Ages to the present towards increased pacification of society arising from social interdependencies and State centralization. This 'civilizing process' involved, increasingly mannered social interactions, self-control, and therefore a reduction in interpersonal violence.

Cognition A somewhat inexact, indeterminate term that encompasses concepts such as memory, imagery, intelligence and reasoning. Often described as 'a synonym for thinking'.

Community notification Allows communities to know when a sexual offender who may pose a risk has moved into their midst. This policy is not pursued in the UK, but is in the USA where it is sometimes known as 'Megan's Law'. The policy is premised on the idea that information on the offender known to the professionals and practitioners working with the offender should not be held only by those professionals and practitioners and that with such 'notification' the community will be better able to protect itself.

Community penalties In its broadest sense, this term refers to any sentence that does not involve imprisonment and therefore includes cautions, discharges and fines as well as sentences involving supervision or monitoring. In its narrower sense, the term refers to community orders.

Conscious mind Being aware (cognizant) of one's actions and emotions. Actions undertaken by the conscious mind are intentional.

Consent In terms of sexual activity is the freely given consent of two or more people to the activities in question; the consent should be informed and not given under duress. Informed consent may be invalidated by the person's age (for example, children), intellectual disability (for example, a person with learning difficulties), the effects of drugs, or alcohol, and by other factors.

Consumer expenditure (or in shorthand, consumption) The money from income, savings, or from borrowing spent on the purchase of currently produced goods and services. Consumption tends to increase as income increases, but not by as much.

Corporate crime Those illegal acts or omissions, punishable by the State under administrative, civil or criminal law which are the result of deliberate decision making or culpable negligence within a legitimate formal organization. These acts or omisions are based in legitimate, formal, business organizations, made in accordance with the normative goals, standard operating procedures, and/or cultural norms of the organization, and are intended to benefit the corporation itself.

Corporation Used here to denote all companies registered under the UK Companies Acts, from the smallest limited liability company to the largest multinational.

Corporatism A word used to describe an approach to criminal justice based on centralization, government intervention and cooperation of agencies and professionals working towards common goals. Typically, it has also been associated with the use of targets, and prescribed ways of working.

Crime count The number of offences occurring within a given referent of time and space, for example, the number of burglary offences in England and Wales per year.

Crime flux A concept that defines the crime rate as a product of the prevalence of victims in the population, and the frequency with which they are victimized.

Crime frequency How the counts of criminal offences are distributed amongst a population, for example, how many people are victims, and how frequently they are victimized.

Crime markets A market that deals specifically with the acquisition, distribution and consumption of illegal goods and services.

Crime rate The measure that gives an index of crime occurring in a particular jurisdiction for a specific time period.

Crime statistics The accounts that the State compiles of the actions of its agencies concerning those acts which the law proscribes.

Crime victim Both the terms 'crime' and 'victim' are problematic. The label 'victim' is contingent, complex and dynamic. It has been argued that it suggests 'victim' is an identity and a social artefact or construction. The term 'victim' is usually associated with crime but also relates to someone suffering some kind of misfortune.

Crime victimization surveys Large-scale sample surveys of general populations whose purpose is to estimate, describe and explain the distribution of crime victimization and victims.

Crimes of the powerful A broad-ranging term, and the title of a classic text (Pearce, 1976), denoting crimes by States, companies and powerful individuals—its key effect is to seek to turn the criminological gaze up and away from the relatively powerless or marginalized.

Criminal law This is the regulation of conduct by the creation of criminal offences—laws, made by Parliament, that forbid particular conduct and lay down punishments. Nowadays the courts no longer create new offences, although their decisions shape the boundaries of offences.

Criminological psychology A sub-discipline existing broadly at the interface between psychology and criminology that seeks to apply psychology to help explain criminal behaviour.

Criminological *verstehen* Sympathetic or affective understanding regarding the situated experiences and emotions of criminals, crime control agents and crime victims.

Crisis of masculinity A disputed term that is used to suggest that traditional expectations of the masculine role have changed in the wake of economic flexibilization, de-industrialization, the increasing power and status of women, cultural changes within the family and wider society that are experienced by some (especially working-class) men as profound confusion as to their role and identity.

Cultural criminology A distinct theoretical, methodological and interventionist approach to the study of crime that places criminality and its control in the context of culture; that is, it views crime and the agencies and institutions of crime control as cultural products—as creative constructs. As such they must be read in terms of the meanings they carry. With its focus on situated meaning, identity, space, style, and media culture, along with its commitment to understand and account for the ongoing transformations and fluctuations associated with hypercapitalism, cultural criminology is an attempt to create a 'post' or 'late' modern theory of crime.

Culture The symbolic environment created by social groups; the meaningful way of life shared by group members.

Cybercrime Criminal activities which take place in 'virtual' space using networked technologies. They cut across national boundaries, which has implications for law enforcement and punishment.

Dangerousness An individual's actions or behaviour pattern considered dangerous to the safety of that individual or other people—a person may be so disposed by individual characteristics or by pre-disposing circumstances in their immediate environment—the behaviour is usually associated with elements of unpredictability.

***De minimis* trap** Derived from *de minimis non curat lex* ('the law does not concern itself with trifles'). A common characteristic of many cybercrimes is that they lead to low-impact, bulk victimizations that cause large aggregated losses which are spread globally, but *individually* the crimes may not warrant investigation by the police or prosecution by the Crown Prosecution Service.

Decarceration Refers to policies and practices that aim to reduce the numbers of offenders in prison by providing alternative measures for dealing with them in the community. Theoretically, the debate about decarceration was at its height in the 1960s and 1970s and included reduction in the use of other institutions, most notably psychiatric hospitals. With the dramatic increase in the prison population in the 1990s, the term and the debate has largely fallen into disuse.

Defence representation A key element of a fair trial is that of 'equality of arms'—that the prosecution and defence are allowed the same facilities to put their case. An individual defendant will never have the same resources as the State

but the State must provide for adequate representation of offenders, whether in the police station or in court. The criminal justice system also provides for defendants to be assisted by lawyers, paid out of public funds.

Deterrence The idea that crime can be reduced if people fear the punishment they may receive if they offend.

Discipline A term used by Michel Foucault to describe a method by which some people can efficiently control others, and which he claims is at the heart of modern public institutions such as the prison, school and hospital. Discipline is the analysis and 'correction' of others' behaviour, especially in relation to time and space, and is a key part of his understanding of how surveillance operates and what it is trying to achieve.

Discrimination The unfavourable treatment based on a person's colour, age, sexuality, gender or ethnicity.

Distal control In cyber cases that involve more serious transgressions, where the criminal law of a jurisdiction has been clearly breached, *distal* mechanisms of control may be more appropriate. These can include the application of the terrestrial law via offline police intervention, or a similar cognate body (for example, Trading Standards).

Diversion strategy Describes efforts to minimize young offenders' involvement with the formal youth justice system, steering them away from the more punitive sentences such as custody, and where possible keeping them out of the system entirely.

Domestic violence An incident or pattern of incidents of controlling, coercive or threatening behaviour, violence or abuse among those who are or have been intimate partners or family members regardless of gender or sexuality. This includes (but is not limited to) psychological, physical, sexual, financial and emotional abuse.

Edgework The momentary integration of subcultural practices with experiences of extreme risk and excitement.

Empathy The ability to identify mentally with another person and thus understand how others feel.

Empirical research Research based upon the analysis of data rather than solely conceptual analysis.

Enforcement (Within the corporate sphere) the oversight of compliance with regulations designed to control business activity, typically this term covers ongoing enforcement in terms of inspection but also other forms of business-agency interaction, including the issuing of advice and educative programmes; it also covers formal enforcement tools which may be used in the light of violations, which can range from verbal or written advice or warnings through to criminal prosecution.

Environmental criminology A form of criminology that focuses on the complex relationships that exist between crime, space and environment.

Ethnicity The problem that arises from using the biological concept of 'race' to describe social phenomena has led some theorists to reject the term 'race' in favour of 'ethnicity'. Like the terms 'race' and 'racism', 'ethnicity' has no universally agreed definition. The term ethnicity characterizes social groups based upon a shared identity rooted in geographical, cultural, historical factors and migratory patterns.

Ethnography The study of groups of people in their natural setting, typically involving the researcher being present for extended periods of time in order to collect data systematically about their daily activities and the meanings they attach to them.

Evaluation research A form of research, which prioritizes solving practical problems over the generation of new theoretical knowledge. Typically it involves the collection and analysis of data to reach conclusions about the effectiveness of policy and practice.

Experiments An approach to social research which involves emulating the approach of the natural scientists by collecting data from an 'experimental' and a 'comparison' group to test a hypothesis.

'Fair trial' and criminal procedure Procedural laws govern the actions of law enforcement agencies. In the pre-trial process, such laws provide legal powers for the police enabling them to arrest and detain suspects. The rules also ensure that suspects are treated with due respect. Equally important are trial procedures—the idea of a 'fair trial' is enshrined in many human rights conventions and this idea governs such matters as the way in which defendants can defend themselves from accusations, the roles of the judge, as well as of the prosecuting or defending lawyers, the presentation of evidence, the questioning of witnesses and the taking of verdicts.

Fear of crime General term that suffers from lack of clarity in its definition. Generally taken to refer to concern, worry or anxiety about crime but there is research evidence that it may be a conduit for broader concerns about change and uncertainty. At the start of the twenty-first century the focus for the police has broadened to encompass a reassurance

agenda as politicians struggle with falling recorded crime levels and rising levels of public anxiety.

Focus groups A data collection method which takes advantages of the dynamic interaction of groups to collect largely qualitative data.

Folk devil As constructed by the mass media and public officials, a public identity that comes to embody a larger sense of threat and social insecurity.

Functionalism A structuralist perspective, which argues that, although crime and deviance are problematic, they also serve a social function by contributing to the smooth running of the social system as a whole.

Gender A socially constructed phenomenon that refers to differences ascribed by society relating to expectations about appropriate social and cultural roles.

Generalizabilty The extent to which research findings can be applied beyond the sample being studied; for example, to other groups or to different locations.

Governance This is often used as a general term to denote governing strategies originating from inside and outside the State, though in this volume is used more straightforwardly to refer to the constitutional and institutional arrangements for framing and monitoring the policies of the police.

Governmentality A term invented by Michel Foucault to describe certain specific techniques developed over the centuries by governments and the State, so as to exercise power over populations as a whole. It complements 'discipline', which refers to the operation of power at the level of public institutions.

Gross Domestic Product (GDP) The total value of all goods and services produced within a country during a specified period (most commonly per year).

Hate crime Also called 'bias crimes'. Most broadly these are crimes motivated or accompanied by animus towards the victims' membership of a social category, which has typically included characteristics of race, ethnicity, nationality, religion, gender, sexuality, disability and physical appearance. Hate crime statutes vary considerably between jurisdictions in terms of what is included and how 'hate motivation' is understood. The definition set out in the UK Macpherson Report ('A racist incident is any incident which is perceived to be racist by the victim or any other person') is the broadest of all definitions.

Hegemonic masculinity This refers to a culturally normative ideal of male behaviour. It claims that there is a hierarchy of masculine behaviour but that most societies encourage men to embody a dominant (hegemonic) version. This is a cultural ideal of heterosexuality, assertion and competitiveness that involves domination over other men and the subordination of women. However, this is not a fixed trait but is always performed and enacted drawing upon cultural resources that define masculinity and femininity—so gender is not given (for example by one's biological or psychological nature) but is an active performance that will differ in different contexts.

Hegemony The dominance of one particular ideology, resulting in the empowerment of particular values, beliefs and practices over others and frequently resulting in the naturalization of those values, beliefs and practices throughout the social body.

Hierarchy of victimization A pecking or status order of victim worthiness where different types and categories of crime victim achieve different rankings. Ideal victims are at the top of the hierarchy, offending victims at the bottom.

History from below A form of historical narrative developed and popularized in the 1960s. This form of history focuses on the study and analysis of the lives of 'ordinary' individuals within society as well as individuals and regions that were not previously considered historically important. This has given rise to the important developments in such fields as women's history, black history, and gay and lesbian history.

Home Office Counting Rules Official instructions that set out how, and in what ways, incidents are to be recorded and counted as offences.

Hybrid cybercrimes 'traditional' or legislated crimes for which network technology has created entirely new global opportunities. They are distinguished from ordinary crimes (where technology assists traditional crimes) by the fact that they are committed across networks. The removal of the Internet means that the behaviour will continue by other means, but not on such a global scale. They include hacking and fraud across networks and the global distribution of illegal content.

Hypothesis A theoretical assertion about the relationship between two or more variables which can be tested.

Ideal victim Denotes the major attributes belonging to a model crime victim. It is a contentious term suggesting an 'innocent' victim where the victim has played no part in their own victimization and fits the stereotyped view of a victim. Such victims need to be vulnerable, innocent, incapable of fighting back against an assailant, previously unacquainted with the offender, with no offending history of their own.

Incapacitation Punishment which calculates the risk of future crimes and uses a custodial setting to remove the offender from society to protect the public from further harm.

Institutionalized racism The term 'institutionalized racism' was first introduced in 1968 by Carmichael and Hamilton in their seminal text, *Black Power: The Politics of Liberation in America*. Common to most definitions of institutionalized racism is the collective failure of an organization to provide an appropriate service to people because of their colour, culture, or ethnic origin.

Interviews A data collection method based upon the posing of a series of questions, usually face-to-face but sometimes using more indirect approaches (for example, telephone).

Intimate (domestic) violence Predominantly (but not exclusively) violence against women and children within the family, which can take many forms including physical assault, rape and sexual violence, psychological or emotional violence, torture, financial abuse including dowry-related violence, and control of movement and of social contacts.

Jurisprudence The science or philosophy of law.

Justice model One that places the offence at the centre, regarding it as an act of will. Consequently, punishment should reflect the seriousness of the crime.

Labelling theory A criminological perspective that locates the meaning of human activity not in the activity itself, but in others' reactions to it.

Late modernity A period in the historical development of capitalism characterized by individualization, globalization, personal insecurity, hyperconsumption and the decline of large-scale collective initiatives such as the welfare state.

Legal psychology A sub-discipline of psychology specifically concerned with the application of psychological knowledge and research to the process of law.

Managerialism The use of a more corporatist strategy to deal with crime. The 'managerial' approach aims not necessarily to deliver 'welfare' or 'justice', but to find the most efficient and effective way of managing a visible crime problem.

Media Any technological form of communication or expression designed to impart meaning (for example, television, newspapers, Internet, radio).

Method triangulation The practice of using more than one research method when conducting empirical research.

Moral entrepreneur A powerful person or group seeking to impose a moral agenda by creating a new category of crime and crime control.

Moral panic As generated by the mass media and public authorities, the public's belief that a particular crime or criminal is symptomatic of larger moral failures and social harms.

National Crime Recording Standard A protocol to standardize crime recording practices amongst police forces, effective since April 2002.

Neighbourhood Watch Voluntary organizations that are devoted to preventing crime and disorder in local neighbourhoods. Members are not expected to intervene in possible criminal incidents but to be the eyes and ears of the police by being alert to unusual activity. Grew rapidly in numbers during the 1980s as part of the Conservative government's emphasis on active citizenship.

Netwidening A term used to identify the counter-intuitive problem posed by the proliferation of 'alternatives' to prison. There is a risk that innovative non-custodial sentences might be used by sentencers for offenders who would previously have received *less* severe sentences rather than *more* severe sentences. If this happens, it means that *more*, rather than *fewer* offenders are likely to end up in prison. In this way, the *net* of criminal justice intervention is thrown *wider*.

Night-time economy Used to describe bars, pubs, nightclubs and fast-food outlets, often clustered in town and city centres.

Normalization thesis Particularly associated with the work of Howard Parker and his colleagues who argue that recreational drug use has become a central component of contemporary youth culture.

Nothing works The notion that became popular in the 1970s and 1980s that nothing could be done to reduce re-offending. It fitted well with the anti-welfarist views of the time, which have now been replaced by the more nuanced view that some interventions work for some offenders in some situations.

Observation A research method which involves watching, and sometimes participating in, social activities.

Offender management A term used to describe the process of working with offenders at different stages of the criminal justice process with the aspiration of preventing reoffending.

The nature and extent of 'management' is determined by the level of risk and harm the offender is judged to pose to the public.

Organizational culture Culture has been defined as 'the way we do things around here', and while organizations themselves tend to have their distinct cultures, these often take distinct forms within different parts of an organization.

Organizational structure Refers to the lines of authority, decision-making, accountability, management systems and the relationships between constituent parts of an organization.

Panopticon The term used by Jeremy Bentham in 1791 to describe his idea of an 'inspection house' to be used for surveillance purposes in public institutions such as prisons, asylums and workhouses.

Patriarchy Refers to a system of social structure and practices in which men dominate.

Phenomenology A method of philosophical investigation that seeks to describe and understand experienced phenomena. Although phenomenological methodologies are deliberately complex and opaque, one could say that the 'goal' of phenomenology is to challenge and question the foundational knowledge claims.

Phrenology Phrenology is the study of the structure of the skull to determine a person's character and mental capacity. It is associated with the work of the Austrian physician Franz Joseph Gall (1758–1828). Gall was one of the first to consider the brain as the home of all mental activities.

Physiognomy Physiognomy is the interpretation of outward appearance, especially the features of the face, to discover a person's predominant temper and character.

Police The specialist State agency tasked with law enforcement and order maintenance.

Policing Organized and purposive forms of social control and regulation, involving surveillance and the threat of sanctions for discovered rule-breaking.

Positivism Positivism is a form of empiricism that was established by the sociologist Auguste Comte in the nineteenth century. Rejecting metaphysical or theological explanations, it attempted to emulate the methods of natural science. Thus only scientific or empirical investigation and observation will enable a true understanding of social structures and institutions.

Post-disciplinary Refers to theories of surveillance and/or punishment that derive from, and accept in part, Foucault's theory of technologies of power and of discipline, but which argue that the disciplinary historical phase is in the process of being superseded by a new technology of power.

Problem drug use Problem drug use involves dependency, regular excessive use or use which creates serious health risks (for example, injecting) and it is usually associated with the use of Class A drugs.

Proportionality A philosophical ideal stating that punishment should be proportionate to the criminal act.

Prosecution and trial In its technical sense, 'prosecution' means bringing an offender in front of a properly constituted tribunal (the magistrates' or Crown Court) in order to test the validity of a formal accusation made against the defendant. The obligation is on the State as prosecutor to satisfy the tribunal that the accusation is true beyond reasonable doubt. The preparation of a case for trial and the presentation of that case is predominantly undertaken by the Crown Prosecution Service, although other agencies such as Customs and Excise and Inland Revenue may take responsibility for mounting their own prosecutions.

Proximal control Low-level cyber deviance, such as harassment within virtual worlds may be best dealt with via *proximal* control mechanisms. These include social and technological controls within online environments. Various theories that have been tested within online environments, such as Control Theory, suggesting social/informal controls are most effective at regulating the behaviour of online community users.

Psychometrics The measurement (typically via questionnaires or inventories) of psychological characteristics such as intelligence, personality and creativity.

Punitive populism (or variants on it such as populist punitiveness, penal populism) The pursuit of a set of penal policies to win votes rather than to reduce crime rates or to promote justice. Central to this strategy is the support of imprisonment and, generally, the advocacy of tough measures to deal with offenders.

Qualitative data Textual, visual or audio data which are not amenable to measurement, provide an insight into social phenomena (for example, crime, sentencing, victimization) and convey, for example, subjective interpretations of meaning.

Quantitative data Numerical data which measure social phenomena (for example, crime or victimization), typically through some form of counting and subsequent statistical manipulation.

Quantitative history Quantitative history involves the use of empirical, statistical historical data (such as census returns, crop yields, tax records) in the study of historical topics. It is often associated with the emergence of social history, which borrowed methodologies from the social sciences.

Questionnaires A standardized research instrument used to collect data from respondents about a particular topic.

Quotidian crime Everyday acts of petty law breaking, which are often ignored by the media and popular imagination due to their focus on more sensational events.

Race The terms race and ethnicity have been used interchangeably but are not synonymous. Current notions of race are centred exclusively on visible (usually skin colour) distinctions among populations, although its historical origins and usage were broader and included religious and linguistic groups (such as Jews or the Irish) who were considered to be 'races'.

Racism Many authors define racism as a 'doctrine, dogma, ideology, or set of beliefs'. All definitions of racism have a set of common themes—typically the belief that certain groups are innately, biologically, socially, morally superior to other groups, based upon an assumption held about them.

Racist violence Any incident, including threats, harassment, emotional and physical harm, which is perceived to be racist by the victim, or any other person.

Rational choice theory of crime A classical model of human choice that assumes that offenders rationally calculate the costs and benefits of committing a crime. The rational choice theory is the leading perspective behind the majority of contemporary situational crime prevention initiatives.

Rational economic (wo)man An ideal type economists use to derive theories about human behaviour. The assumption is that, faced with choices and given their preferences, individuals will always act in such a way as to optimize their economic well-being. They weigh up the costs and benefits of different actions and choose the one that will leave them the best off.

Recession (economic recession) Defined formally by economists as occurring when the amount of goods and services produced by a country's economy falls in two successive quarters. A sustained recession, such as that in the 1930s, is often referred to as a depression. A recession will lead to fewer jobs and higher levels of unemployment.

Recreational drug use Characteristically centred on the use of cannabis and 'dance drugs' (for example, ecstasy), recreational drug use may be frequent but does not involve excessive use, dependency or serious risks to health.

Recidivism Refers to the process by which prisoners who leave prison are reconvicted within a certain period of time, normally two years.

Reflexive A heightened degree of self-understanding and reflection about one's theorizing or particular standpoint/position; from the Latin term *Reflectere*, meaning 'to turn back on oneself'.

Regulation The determination of bodies of law and the establishment of some agency, often a State agency but increasingly alongside a range of other actors, for enforcing and overseeing compliance with such laws. The typical interest of criminologists has been not with the determination of regulatory policy but with the nature and effects of regulatory enforcement.

Rehabilitation The belief that it is possible to tackle the factors that cause offenders to commit crimes and so reduce or prevent re-offending. The focus is usually on individual factors such as employability, problem substance use, and anger management.

Relativism The perspective that knowledge is relative and contingent rather than absolute and determined.

Resettlement Refers to a long tradition of work which aims to reintegrate imprisoned offenders back into the community.

Restoration In the History of England the term 'Restoration' has a specific meaning in as much as it is used to describe the process whereby Charles II regained the English throne after the Parliamentarian rule in the wake of the English Civil War. More commonly, though, the Restoration period refers to the subsequent years of Charles II's reign (1660–85).

Restorative justice An approach to criminal justice which aims to restore victims, offenders and the wider community as far as possible to the position they were in before the offence was committed, by involving them in the decision-making process and attempting to reconcile their conflicts through informal (but structured) discussion. Mechanisms for implementing RJ include victim–offender mediation; direct or indirect reparation; family group conferences; changes to sentencing arrangements which involve wider community representation; and community involvement in supervising offenders using circles of support and accountability.

Retribution/Just desert Punishment that seeks to express social disapproval and concern but which is proportionate to the harm caused by the crime.

Revisionist history Historical revisionism is the re-examination and reviewing of the stories told as history with an eye to updating them with more recently discovered, more unbiased or more accurate information. Broadly, it is the approach that history as it has been traditionally told may not be entirely accurate and may be subject to review. Revisionist history challenges orthodox and traditional approaches to an historical problem. A revisionist history of crime offers new perspectives to the orthodox (often called *Whig*) version that many historians accept.

Risk assessment The activity of collating information on an individual, their immediate circumstances and social environment with a view to assessing the likelihood of particular behaviour patterns occurring in the future. This may divide into clinical collection and assessment, and actuarial assessment; the latter implying a statistical analysis based on particular categories of people. In the case of sexual offenders this is an increasingly formalized and coordinated activity sometimes using risk assessment 'instruments'.

Risk factors Increasingly used to refer to individual or social factors which increase the probability of involvement in crime.

Risk management The activity of using a risk assessment to manage the future risk an individual may pose. In the case of sexual offending this is an increasingly formalized and coordinated activity involving various forms of containment and incapacitation to achieve public protection (for example, supervision, registration, routine surveillance, longer custodial or hospital detention).

'Rule of law' The idea of the 'rule of law' is that individuals and the State should regulate their conduct according to the law. Laws must be created in a constitutionally proper fashion to be effective, normally through legislation passed by Parliament but such statutory offences can be contrasted with 'common law' offences which are based on the decisions of courts. Law enforcement agencies such as the police, the prosecution, the courts or prisons can only exercise their powers (such as those of investigation, trial or detention) where they have legal authority to do so.

Secondary victimization Has two meanings. One refers to those who are indirectly harmed for example, the friends and family of murder or rape victims. The other meaning is akin to being re-victimized. This victimization occurs in the process of criminal justice whereby victim-witnesses suffer insensitive treatment—often inadvertently—by the criminal justice system (or by friends and acquaintances).

Self-regulation Self-regulation refers to the expectation that most people are capable of complying with the law most of the time, not because of the fear of punishment but because they have internalized the values and norms of society and consider that it is in their own interests, and the interests of those that matter to them, to comply. If they occasionally break the law then it is assumed that this will produce a sufficient feeling of guilt and shame for them to *regulate* their behaviour without either restrictions or assistance from other people. The ultimate aim of criminal justice policy, therefore, is to produce *self-regulating* citizens who require minimal outside intervention to be law-abiding.

Sex Refers to biological criteria for classifying persons as male or female.

Sex Offender Register Refers to an administrative policy whereby convicted sex offenders must notify the holders of the register (the police in the UK) of any change in their circumstances including address, travel abroad, etc. The sex offender register is designed to help police identify the whereabouts of such offenders in a given community in the interests of better public protection; it is not a form of punishment of the offender.

Sexism Refers to oppressive attitudes and behaviours directed towards either sex.

Sexual offending The majority of sexual offending consists of sexual activity between two or more people that takes place with one person not consenting to that activity; a minority of sexual offending is behaviour that has been criminalized regardless of the presence of consent, for example, teacher-pupil relations where there is considered to be a 'breach of trust', or incestuous relations between siblings.

Situational crime prevention An approach to crime prevention involving the management, design or implementation of the immediate environment in which crimes occur in order to reduce opportunities for crime.

Social control A term used in various different ways in criminology. In the context of surveillance, its most frequent use is to claim (following Marxist theories of class conflict and domination) that the essential 'function' of surveillance is to help the State gather information on individuals or groups it perceives as representing a threat to its (class-based) interests, and/or to prevent such threats from arising in the first place.

Social exclusion A term used to describe people or areas suffering from a combination of problems such as unemployment, poor skills, low incomes, poor housing, high crime environments, bad health and family breakdown. It is distinguished from financial poverty and focused rather on constricted access to civil, political and social rights and opportunities.

Social harm Referring to an economic, physical or psychological harm inflicted upon people or peoples by a legitimate organization, this term has in recent years specifically been used to refocus criminological attention upon State and corporate decisions and actions which affect detrimentally a variety of groups of people but which are either not in fact violations of any law or, if they may in principle may be illegal, are not in fact processed as such.

Social interactionism A theoretical approach that stresses the interactions between individuals as 'symbolic and linguistic exchanges'. Within this rubric, crime is understood as a product of social interaction.

State-corporate crime Described as those 'illegal or socially injurious actions that occur when one or more institutions of political governance pursue a goal in direct co-operation with one or more institutions of economic production and distribution'. Thus, State-corporate crimes are produced at the 'intersection' of business and government, either initiated or facilitated by States.

Style A symbolic medium for the display of collective identity and affiliation; style often serves also as the medium for others' attempts at surveillance and control.

Subculture The distinctive symbolic environment of a criminal group, often embodying language, rituals and symbols that, when considered in relation to the study of crime and deviance, run counter to the legal constraints and conventional understandings proffered by mainstream society.

Survivor This term, as opposed to that of victim, acknowledges victims' agency, and active resistance. This label challenges the notion of victim passivity, and in particular it is often used by feminists in connection with women's resistance to their apparent structural powerlessness and potential victimization.

Tautology/Tautological (In theoretical terms) something that relies upon circular reasoning.

Thatcherism A label given to a set of political values associated with Margaret Thatcher, the Conservative Prime Minister of the UK from 1979 until 1990. Economically committed to allowing markets to operate freely and opposed to supporting firms or industries that performed badly, its policies involved privatizing nationalized industries, reducing State expenditure particularly on welfare. Its advocates believed the welfare state was to blame for the growth in a 'dependency culture' where people relied on State handouts rather than working and providing for themselves and their families.

Time series data Refers to data collected from a particular geographical unit—town, region or country—at fixed intervals—daily, weekly, monthly, quarterly, annually—for example, annual recorded crime in England for each year from 1950 to 2003. Time series analysis refers to statistical techniques that examine how the measurement varies over time. In contrast, cross-section data is collected for a particular time period across different geographic units, for example, recorded crime in each local authority in the UK in 2004.

Total institution An organization which controls all aspects of people's daily lives. Primarily associated with the work of sociologist Erving Goffman, who saw the total institution as a social microcosm which was controlled by an hegemony with clear hierarchies and sets of rules. Examples include prisons, schools, mental institutions and workhouses.

Traditional crime Those acts upon which criminal justice agencies—and criminologists—have typically focused their energies, such as interpersonal violence, theft, burglary, the use and distribution of illegal substances, public order offences, and so on; also frequently referred to as 'street' crime or 'conventional' crime.

Transnational organized crime A relatively recent term that is applied to activities carried out by crime groups across jurisdictions, either by the same group or in collaboration with others. It is intended to reflect the globalizing tendency of organized crime.

True cybercrimes These cybercrimes are solely the product of the Internet; they are high-end cybercrimes that depend completely on technology. The removal of the Internet means they cannot be committed. They include spamming, phishing (identity theft) and pharming (hijacking browsers) and variations of online intellectual property piracy.

Unconscious mind The part of the mind that is inaccessible to the conscious mind but which still affects behaviour and emotions.

Unemployment The state of being available and able to work but unable to find a paid job. In practice, difficult to identify and measure. For example, government rules as to the meaning of 'available for work' or eligibility for benefit can change, altering the numbers counted as unemployed without the material position of any particular individual altering.

Validity The extent to which the conclusions reached are credible and plausible.

Verdicts and sentencing At the end of a trial, the magistrates (or the jury in a Crown Court) will bring in a verdict—this derives from the Latin for a 'true statement'. This verdict will be guilty or not guilty. After a verdict of guilty, the court will proceed to sentence. A sentence is a court order which specifies the penalty (from fines to community-based sanctions to imprisonment) to be imposed and which gives legal authority to agencies such as probation or the prison service to enforce that penalty.

Victim blaming An emotively charged term closely associated with the phrase victim-precipitation. Victim blaming can result from attempts to understand how people become victims of crime. Early writers about victims created a tradition of victim blaming by putting the victims of particular types of crime into a variety of categories, partly according to how blameworthy they appeared to be. They focused on the individual victim's conduct and the victim's relationship with the offender.

Victim impact statements A mechanism for allowing victims of crime to give a written statement of the impact of the offence upon them, materially and emotionally, so that courts and other criminal justice agencies can take this information into account. An apparently straightforward and sensible innovation which has been controversial and largely ineffective in practice.

Victim perspectives Different ways of viewing the victim of crime. Sometimes called theoretical perspectives, these approaches differ as to how they approach the study of the victim of crime including who counts as a victim, how research is conducted and how policies might be developed. The main three are: positivist, radical and critical perspectives.

Victim precipitation/provocation Closely associated with the concept of victim culpability (the extent to which the victim can be held to be responsible for what has happened to them) and victim proneness (the notion that there are some people, by virtue of their structural characteristics, who are much more likely to be victims of crime than other people), this concept draws attention to what it was that the victim did that resulted in their victimization.

Victimology A sub-discipline of criminology that is concerned with the study of victims of crime and other social harms. It is also concerned with exploring the causes, nature, extent and impact of victimization in society and the dynamics of relationships between victims, offenders and the spacial and social structural environments in which they occur.

Victimization The processes associated with the impact of crime.

Violence Behaviour that intentionally threatens or does physical harm, and involves the infliction of emotional, psychological, sexual, physical and material damage.

Volume crime A term used to describe the petty crimes which dominate crime statistics.

Welfare model One in which offending is taken to be a symptom of psychological or social deprivation. The response rests with providing expert-led treatment in order to meet the individuals' needs and so reduce offending.

Welfare state Any part of the State which takes the responsibility for providing basic services to its population. Through systems of social security it guarantees to meet people's basic needs for housing, health, education and income.

'What works' In its narrowest sense, 'What works' refers to a movement that emerged in the 1980s and 1990s in North America and spread worldwide. Its aim has been to revive interest in offender rehabilitation through the promotion of programmes for offenders, based on cognitive behavioural psychology and supported by scientific evidence of success in reducing rates of re-offending. The term is intended to counteract the claim that 'nothing works' in offender rehabilitation. In its broader sense, the term has come to refer to a very wide-ranging and controversial political and ideological agenda that emphasizes individual responsibility for offending and minimizes the role of social determinants.

Whig history A term used to describe the views of some eighteenth- and nineteenth-century British historians that British history was a march of progress whose inevitable outcome was the constitutional monarchy. It takes its name from the British Whigs, advocates of the power of Parliament, who opposed the Tories, supporters of the power of the King and the aristocracy. Whig history is criticized for its overemphasis of the roles played by key political figures and for downplaying the historical importance of the struggles between different classes and groups.

White-collar crime A heterogeneous group of offences committed by people of relatively high status or enjoying relatively high levels of trust, and made possible by their legitimate employment; such crimes typically include fraud, embezzlement, tax violations and other accounting offences, and various forms of workplace theft in which the organization or its customers are the victims.

INDEX